D0780299

3 0600 00443 5302

Discourse Semantics

The chief habit of thought antagonistic to a regard for special context is, beyond dispute I suppose, that due to the attempt to make Logic Formal, or (worse) symbolic. Whatever value these developments of Logic undoubtedly have is bought at a cost which deserves to be reckoned rather than ignored. But ... there is hardly a suspicion in the minds of formal logicians that they have any cost to pay.

A. Sidgwick (*Mind* 1895: 282)

Discourse Semantics

PIETER A.M. SEUREN

With an appendix by A. Weijters

Basil Blackwell

Basil Blackwell Ltd
108 Cowley Road, Oxford OX4 1JF, UK

Basil Blackwell Inc.
432 Park Avenue South, Suite 1505,
New York, NY 10016, USA

British Library Cataloguing in Publication Data

Seuren, Pieter A. M.
   Discourse semantics.
   1. Semantics
   I. Title
   412 P325

   ISBN 0-631-13594-4

Library of Congress Cataloging in Publication Data

Seuren, Pieter A. M.
   Discourse semantics.

   Bibliography: p.
   Includes index.
   1. Semantics. 2. Semantics (Philosophy) 3. Generative grammar.
   I. Title.
   P325.S42 1985 415 84-20463
   ISBN 0-631-13594-4

Typeset by Unicus Graphics Ltd, Horsham, Sussex
Printed in Great Britain by T.J. Press Ltd, Padstow, Cornwall

Contents

Contents

Preface

This book is intended for those readers who feel that the study of language should have as its primary aim an insight into the cognitive machinery which enables humans to use it the way they do. In the eyes of many, the study of language amounts to the construction of a logical language and a system of semantic interpretation in the sense of mathematical model-theory. They will find that this book does not confirm them in their beliefs.

Readers will not find this book easy to read, and I can assure them that it has not been easy to write either, mainly because of the radical departure from the many notions and theories held in the mainstream of current philosophical and linguistic thought. The ways paved by twentieth-century philosophy, formal semantics and, to some extent, also linguistics, proved to be unusable and to lead to wrong destinations, with the inevitable consequence that much of the going has been through rough country. Yet, and perhaps also because of this, writing the book has had its great fascination, and it is hoped that some of the fascination will be felt by those who read it.

It is a pleasure to express my gratitude towards the many people who have, over the years, encouraged me and given me the strength to continue. Thanks are due also to those colleagues and students, mostly in Nijmegen and in Edinburgh, who by their keen criticism and often stubborn resistance to my ideas forced me to look again and better. As regards them, the least I hope is that they will detect some substance and power in the work presented.

No special grant funds have been relied on during or for the writing of the book, with the exception of the second half of chapter 4 which deals with anaphora. This part of the book reflects work done in the context of the project "Descriptive Language", and in particular the subproject "Anaphora", which ran from 1978 until 1982, and was sponsored by the Netherlands Organization for Pure Research ZWO (The Hague), in association with the Max-Planck-Institut für Psycholinguistik at Nijmegen.

P.A.M.S.

List of Abbreviations

AP	Assignment Procedure	PPI	Positive Polarity Item
CA	controlling antecedent	PR	Predicate Raising
CFPS	context-free phrase structure	PSE	Principle of Substitutivity
CR	Conjunction Reduction		and Existential Entailment
D	domain	RR	restoration rules
DD	definite description	S	Sentence
DIV	dative intransitive verb	SA	Semantic Analysis
DPC	Discourse Precede Condition	SD	set-denoting
DS	Deep Structure	ShS	Shallow Structure
FVP	Finite Verb Phrase	SOC	Scope Ordering Constraint
GS	Generative Semantics	SOIV	Subject–Object–Indirect
INC	(Object) Incorporation		Object–Verb
IT	*it*-insertion	SOV	Subject–Object–Verb
NP	Noun Phrase	SR	Subject Raising/Semantic
NPI	Negative Polarity Item		Representation
NPSC	NP-Subject Constraint	SS	Surface Structure
NR	Negative Raising	SSD	Secondary Subject Deletion
PET	Principle of the Excluded	SVO	Subject–Verb–Object
	Third	TAC	True Alternatives Condition
PL	Predicate Lowering	V	Verb/verification domain
PNCC	Precede-and-not-Command	VC	Verbal Complex
	Condition	VP	Verb Phrase
PP	Prepositional Phrase	VSO	Verb–Subject–Object
PPC	Presuppositional Propositional		
	Calculus		

Prologue

This book is in large part a report on extensive forays into unknown territory, the territory of discourse-dependent linguistic interpretation. In so far as it treads on more familiar ground, it does so because a base camp and supply stations are needed. The forays have been extensive, but clearly not extensive enough to provide the material for a surveyor's map. Yet some main features of the land, and here and there even a close-up picture of details, have emerged.

The reasons for leaving better known areas and venturing more widely abroad lie in a deeply felt dissatisfaction with some central features of dominant present-day thought about meaning and grammar. One important unsatisfactory feature is the obvious lack of a natural and organic link between theories of meaning and theories of grammar. This is a serious defect in present-day linguistics-cum-semantics, and it seems to be largely the result of an alarming lack of sensitivity with regard to the great natural richness of language. What is all too often found is a single-minded passion for either sweeping grammatical generalizations (meant to be universal), or well-ironed formal semantic systems. Complete formalization as well as all-embracing generality are, of course, ideals to be pursued, but one wonders what the point is of developing highly detailed formal systems or of formulating 'universal' principles if there is insufficient factual support, too much counter-evidence, and hardly any unexpected confirmation. In semantics one all too often has the impression that natural language is treated as a playground for builders of formal systems to try out various new formalisms. The facts of language come in useful as handicaps to make the game more interesting. But the handicaps must not be too heavy, or the game is spoiled. This attitude is particularly obvious in works that are linguistic in name but are produced by logicians whose primary interest lies in the mathematical properties of their systems, and not in the nature of language. Since my primary interest is the unravelling of the nature of human natural language, I am inevitably unhappy with the massive amount of work produced these days in this 'formalist' vein, especially since this work is usually presented as aiming at an increased insight into the facts and the nature of language – whereas it is, in reality, aimed at an improved insight into the mathematical properties of some formal system.

I am, of course, overstating the point a little (although there is more than a grain of truth to what has been said). There are many who share this feeling of dissatisfaction to some degree, and they have produced a certain body of literature aiming at improving precisely this situation. Yet, in this literature there still is quite a strong allegiance to the systems developed by those who are more sensitive to logical and mathematical beauty than to the beauty of linguistic reality. It is my conviction that a more radical departure from established systems is called for.

The formalists may, and will, defend themselves by saying that it is good methodology to start by setting up formal systems which may be too idealized to begin with, but which can be made more realistic by building in more and more linguistic 'handicaps'. In the end, they will say, some formal system will be felt to capture linguistic reality in so many crucial respects that it can be looked upon as a serious candidate in the competition for the empirical prize. But then the inevitable answer will be that this is good methodology only if no previous overall problem analysis shows that the approach in question stands little chance. And here the formalists lose.

What is needed is some general problem analysis, providing a global view of the problem area and a general strategy to be applied in getting the better of it. However, what is found all too often is a more or less arbitrarily delimited "fragment of the language", whose chances at extrapolation are unknown, and a largely *ad hoc* formal apparatus aimed at some empirically ill-defined account. This state of affairs is highly unsatisfactory, especially since it carries the risk of a massive misdirection of precious energies. It must be feared that large sections of now fashionable work will turn out to miss the point of linguistic reality.

Extensive portions of this book can be regarded as problem analyses of the kind just mentioned. In particular the sections on psychological reality (1.4; 3.1), the section against surface semantics (2.1), the section on three-valuedness (3.2.4), on the discourse-semantic aspects of presupposition (3.3), and the section on background knowledge (3.4) show the characteristic of a general survey of the kind of problems and complications that will be encountered by any theory of grammar and meaning. At the same time, directions are pointed out, partly new and partly rooted in existing work (in particular "generative semantics"), for research with maximum chance of success.

The general 'philosophy' underlying the whole of this work is, first, that language is a product of nature, with all the apparent irregularities and unexpected complications that products of nature tend to bring along. This work, in other words, is clearly part of the tradition in language studies that started with the ancient anomalists, who were opposed to the analogists where the search for a system took precedence over concern with the complex facts. The ancient opposition is as alive now as ever, and the modern analogists are, at the moment, on the winning side. There is a widespread tendency, in theoretical linguistics as well as in formal semantics, to jump to conclusions of a very general nature although the 'database' is flimsy. It is my feeling that the recent developments in universalist linguistics, where the enormous amount of surface variety in the languages of the world is investigated systematically, are of great help in stemming this tide of premature system building. It is, in a way, an indictment of modern linguistics that the theorists (including the formal semanticists) and the universalists have so little to say to each other. There should, of course, be a lively interaction between theory and data survey, but, for reasons probably to do mainly with entrenchment of positions taken, that interaction is much less lively than it could be.

Although this book is clearly not a contribution to universalist linguistics, it is data-oriented in a different, much more fastidious way. The concern with observational detail which is apparent in many parts in this book does not spring from anything like a collector's passion but from the conviction that it will not be possible to understand natural language unless very careful attention is paid to even minute details when they are relevant, and that no description can claim success unless it covers all the relevant facts.

It is inevitable, in this approach, that there is a tension between full formalization or worldwide generalization on the one hand and the investigation of facts on the other. A well-defined formal system or a valid universal generalization for whatever area of linguistic reality is being investigated remains the ultimate goal, but it can be attained only after painstaking and alert collecting of not always so readily available facts. In the context of linguistic theorizing this has been denied. According to Lightfoot (1982: 84-5), "Instead of listing and describing more phenomena, we should try first to give some account for readily available data. As we improve our accounts, we shall need to seek out certain kinds of less readily available facts relevant to the refinements." Whoever follows this principle presupposes a non-existing link between ready availability of facts on the one hand, and essentially correct theories on the other. The latter need at most "refinements" which are then based on more remotely accessible facts. Such a correlation is, of course, illusory, and a methodology based on it is dangerous in that it will give rise to schools of thought where a reluctance is cultivated with regard to the whole-hearted acceptance of disturbing facts. Such facts will be called "obscure", "remote" or "marginal", and their relevance will be further slighted by usually false statements to the effect that their occurrence is limited to some dialectal or substandard form of a language, or to geographically remote languages of small speech communities – as though it would matter if that were true (cp. Lightfoot 1982: 84).

It is often wise to hold back a little before presenting a fully formalized account or a theoretically crucial generalization on all of human language. The facts are always more complex than one thinks they are. This attitude is reflected in the present book: the exposé is often 'gradual' in that formalization is not achieved straight away, but prepared through analyses, arguments and observations. The general picture is evoked first, and the formalization follows, if at all. It is to be expected that there are many loose ends and fraying seams left. This is a result of the methodology followed and the complexity of the subject matter. It will not do to say that counter-examples are irrelevant as long as no alternative theory of comparable (presumed) coverage is presented, or that disturbing facts are left out of account because "they are not in the fragment". The view is taken here that unformalized or partially formalized work which does justice to the facts is of greater value than fully formalized work that is in conflict with them, and, analogously, that a less rarified and generalized view of language that gives a better picture of the complexities of linguistic reality is to be valued a great deal more highly than premature and inadequate generalizations.

A second element in the 'philosophy' behind the present work is the idea of *underground calculus* in the human mind and its extensions to sense organs and motor command systems. What is meant by this is that cognitive and behavioural processes involve massive amounts of computing in a multitude of more or less autonomous compartments. This view, which has been described as modern functionalism in psychology, is based on a materialist theory of the mind, together with a weak form of reductionism whereby the object of investigation, the mind, is considered to be material in so far as any implementation is of necessity material, but its functional and organizational principles are considered 'autonomous', i.e. describable within some more or less clearly delimited framework of a special science. The mind is thus a gigantic (and as yet almost totally opaque) information processing plant with some compartments built for general purposes and others especially made for highly specific tasks. It appears that much of the processing takes place 'underground', i.e. beyond the grasp of any general purpose function that may be held responsible for what is called "awareness" and which records all its inputs and outputs in the great memory store called "knowledge". In fact, there may well be a correlation between the specificity of the cognitive function involved and its distance from awareness and the possibility of introspection. The view is taken here that virtually all of gram-matical processing is 'underground' in this sense, and that, likewise, virtually all of semantic processing, in particular in so far as it involves discourse structures, is also way beyond any accessibility to awareness and hence any conscious interference. Only lexical knowledge is "declarative", in current terminology, at least to the extent that speakers are in a position to comment upon lexical meanings.

This computing view of the mind and its extensions to external organs is illustrated vividly by phonological and morphological rule systems as they have been developed in linguistics over the past twenty or so years. One only has to take a cursory look at such rule systems (provided they are of sufficient quality) to be impressed by their richness and complexity together with their great precision (and, often, their beauty). There is no escaping from the conclusion that such rule systems, if adequate, *must* correspond to what actually takes place during the production and perception of speech. This says nothing about the precise place in the human organism where the calculus is implemented, although in some cases an approximate answer can easily be given. Phonetic realization rules, for example, will be located in the peripheral part of the neurological system where motor commands are signalled to the speech organs. (The analytic procedures in perception are probably geared to the motor system.) But where exactly the rules are located that account for grammatical and semantic processing is a question we must leave aside. Such questions will have to be broached in a theory of rule implementation, and such a theory is well beyond both the scope of this book and the competence of its author.

The (underground) calculus point of view brings along a criterion of adequacy, in that the rule systems developed are constrained by considerations of what is usually called "psychological plausibility". This criterion is not as stringent as it might have been, mainly because too little is known about the conditions that must be fulfilled for any system carrying out calculus by rule to qualify as staying within the limits of psychological plausibility. A few general conditions are obvious. Thus, the rule system must be practically implementable and thus not involve, say, functions with infinite domains. (It is for this reason that calculi developed within the framework of classical possible world semantics are unfit to qualify as psychologically plausible in any possible sense.) But the constraints derived from psychological plausibility are, for the most part, based on and drawn from experimental results. These, however, are too often multiply interpretable to be of great practical use in specific instances of analysis and description. Psychological plausibility as a criterion of adequacy is felt less as a practical constraint than as a commitment with respect to serious theorizing in psychology: whatever theory is developed in grammar or semantics must be at least compatible with psychological theory, and preferably a natural part of it.

In certain sections of the linguistic literature, great store has been set recently by the criterion of learnability: if it can be shown that a particular rule system is *per se* not learnable, then it is ruled out as a psychologically plausible system. Why this criterion has been given such a prominent place in the literature concerned, as opposed to other thinkable and equally valid criteria for psychological plausibility, is not clear. What is clear, however, is that this criterion has virtually no empirical impact. If it could indeed be shown for a given rule system that it is or is not learnable, then, clearly, this criterion would be of great value. But the means required for decisions of this kind are simply not available, the reason being that no clear demarcation can be drawn between what portions of a proposed rule system must be learnt and what portions can be assumed to be 'prewired' into the system as a consequence of genetic make-up. It is, moreover, totally unknown on independent grounds what powers of specialized hypothesis formation human learners have at their disposal for the various specialized learning tasks, such as the acquisition of a linguistic system, which they perform. If a link is to be forged between the study of linguistic (and semantic) rule systems on the one hand and learning theory on the other, then the implications go the other way: it is more realistic to suggest that learning theory should be constrained by what is found in the way of successful rule systems than the other way round. If a rule system is really crucially successful (such as the rule system of Predicate Raising for Dutch and German; see chapter 2), then this has consequences for learning theory which must incorporate hypotheses about genetically fixed learning equipment that are sufficiently rich to account for the acquisition of such rule systems. As a consequence, no use is made in this book of any form of learnability criterion.

This book is called *Discourse Semantics*, but it might just as well have been given the title *The Proposition*, since it is entirely organized around the concept of proposition as defined in section 1.2: a proposition is an ordered pair consisting, first, of the Semantic Analysis of a given sentence A, and, second, of a given discourse D in which A is uttered. The proposition then defines the increment brought about in D by the uttering of A. This idea is so central that it has dictated the overall structure of the book. After the first chapter, which is largely introductory, there is the lengthy chapter 2 which is devoted to the status and structure of Semantic Analyses and their relation to Surface Structures. It thus deals with the first element of the ordered pair defining a proposition. Chapters 3, 4, and 5 deal with the discourse structures and processes involved. Here, presupposition is the central notion, discussed and elaborated in chapter 3. Chapters 4 and 5 deal with the actual construction of discourse domains (with truth-domains and intensional subdomains), and with the mechanism of denotation, i.e. the assignment of particular discourse addresses to definite terms, including pronouns. The last chapter considers the proposition in its capacity as truth-value bearer. It deals with questions of truth and reference as properties of the propositional component of an uttered sentence, as well as of the discourse domains generated by successive utterances.

Here and there, mainly to illustrate the descriptive and explanatory power of the theory, an in-depth analysis is presented. To the extent that such detailed excursions prove successful they support the general and basic principles of the approach adopted. This applies in particular to the sections 2.1.6–2.1.8, and 2.4.5, where Predicate Raising phenomena are analysed in a few languages, especially Dutch, to the point of completeness. The point of this analysis is to show that a particular non-trivial syntactic construction, which has resisted adequate treatment in any of the existing alternative theories of grammar, falls into place naturally and effortlessly in the theory of grammar presented here (and based directly on work done in the tradition of "generative semantics" of the late 1960s and early 1970s). This point is important in the light of a particular and conspicuous body of linguistic literature produced over roughly the past fifteen years, where it has become customary to neglect the facts and debunk the notion of a complete and adequate description, while a fanciful array of ever-changing and invariably inadequate generalities about syntactic rules and structures is presented as the indubitable truth. Analogously to what was said above in connection with the learnability criterion, we can take it to be sounder policy to let any theory of universal properties of rules of grammar be constrained by whatever is available in the way of really successful descriptions, than to let descriptive efforts be hampered by preconceived and ill-founded alleged universals.

An area which is particularly fascinating but has remained relatively opaque and riddled with questions and unclarities is the interface of lexical truth-conditions and grammatical analysis, or, as it is generally known, the area of prelexical analysis. Its fascination consists in the intriguing similarities between known syntactic constructions and what can be hypothesized in the way of syntactic structure built into the lexical semantic description of certain classes of lexical items. But the problems are manifold, as will become clear on reading the text. Fledgling attempts are made in this book to come to some form of reasonable account of the phenomena concerned. If anywhere, it is painfully obvious here that the theory and the analyses are badly lacking in precision and completeness. Yet a few new ideas are developed in this respect (sections 2.3.1 and 2.5), which may prove of use to further research. This area is no doubt potentially very fruitful, even though we are only beginning to understand some of the connections – and that only in a highly incomplete fashion. A total dodging of the issue, as has become customary in almost all approaches since the days of prelexical analysis in "generative semantics", is, of course, not the right answer.

The theory of presupposition as presented in chapter 3 is the result of some fifteen years of work in this area. During this period it became clear with every increasing certainty that presupposition is not only a highly complex but also a very fundamental phenomenon in semantic structures and processes. A three-valued logical notion of presupposition was first developed out of the traditional Frege–Strawson notion. But as the ideas about the importance of discourse factors were shaping up, it became necessary to reinterpret the logical notion and to regard the logical system underlying presuppositional entailments as part of a psychologically real system of constructing (truth-conditional) discourse domains. Presupposition is finally defined as a semantic property of sentences requiring that presuppositional entailments be represented in preceding discourse for the proposition formed with that sentence to be interpretable. In this connection, the notion of *prejection* is developed: any sentence whose representation is required in preceding discourse is a prejection (section 3.3). Prejections which are also entailed are presuppositions, but prejections which are not entailed because their presence is not required in the truth-domain (as with presuppositions) but simply in any (sub)domain of the preceding discourse, are 'suggested' or 'invited' inferences ('implicatures', if one wishes) as long as certain acceptability conditions are fulfilled. Prejections are always presuppositions, either of the main clause or of some embedded clause. If the (embedded) clause is entailed, the prejection is a presupposition of the whole sentence.

Apart from the prejection aspect, a great deal of attention is devoted to two further questions. First, it is argued in great detail, and on the basis of numerous linguistic observations, that natural language has two truth-conditionally distinct negations and that its logical properties are best described with the help of a three-valued presuppositional calculus. The outlines of this calculus are presented in the text of chapter 3, but the appendix by Weijters provides a systematic survey of the logic and of the hierarchy of n-valued logics of which the trivalent calculus used here is the three-valued representative, just as classical bivalent logic is the two-valued representative. Secondly, the origin of presuppositions (as indeed of all psychologically real entailments, i.e. inferences) is sought in the conditions associated with each predicate for the truth of any proposition formed with it. In this respect the theory presented here differs from virtually all studies in the presuppositional field, which tend to look on presuppositions as somehow brought about by otherwise mysterious "inducers". In our theory, presuppositions are an integral part of the logic as well as of the machinery of discourse semantics.

What has contributed greatly to the joy of writing this book is the fact that, here and there, unexpected by-products could be seen to develop. Thus, in section 3.3, where the semantic notion of presupposition is discussed and where it is shown that presupposition is essentially a discourse phenomenon, a general criterion could be formulated for acceptable additions to a discourse D: a sentence A is acceptably added to D if the addition of A results either in a restriction of the possible situations (verification domains) in which D is true, or in greater informativeness about the verification domain at hand. Any addition to D must thus be *informative* for it to be acceptable. In section 4.1, where the basic principles are discussed of the construction of D's through accumulated increments, it is shown that there are additions creating discourse structures which are such that if further material is added to them, they become more informative (i.e. restrictive with regard to possible verification domains, or containing new information with regard to V). There are, however, also additions, such as negative sentences (whose addition results in an 'embargo' on any further development of D in the sense that if the negated proposition is added falsity will ensue) which create discourse structures where further addition of material has the opposite effect: further addition of material to these structures results in a widening of the possible situations in which D is true, or fails to add new information about V anyway. For example, addition of *The girl was happy* to any given appropriate D restricts the set of possible verification domains (Vs) to those where the corresponding fact obtains, and further addition of material to this sentence, such as *and beautiful*, has the effect of further restricting the set of Vs: the new sentence is more informative than the old one. Likewise, the addition of the negative sentence, instead of the positive one, i.e. of *The girl was not happy*, again restricts the set of Vs. But if I now add further material, such as *and beautiful*, this further addition has the inverse effect of widening the set of Vs in which the domain D as a whole is true: now the longer sentence is less informative. This fact in itself would have little importance were it not that there seems to be a correlation between those domain positions where further addition of material has a V-relaxing effect on the one hand, and the possibility of occurrence of, if not the whole class, certainly a substantial subclass of Negative Polarity Items (NPIs). This is exciting for those who, like the present author, have been on the lookout for years for a rationale behind the behaviour of NPIs (and who find Ladusaw (1979) unsatisfactory in the presence of too numerous counter-examples). Yet, exciting though this may seem, there was neither time nor space to elaborate this thought, so that only hints, and hopefully suggestive ones, could be given.

Another such promising looking by-product, this time in section 4.2.4 (which likewise had to be left for what it was), concerns the generic character of existentials like *a shopkeeper* in conditional structures of the type *If a shopkeeper deceives his customers, he will soon go bankrupt*. The generic character of the subject of the *if*-clause appears to be an automatic by-product of the description of existential quantification plus the description of *if*-clauses. The latter place an 'embargo' on domain building to the effect that, for structures of the form "if *A* then *B*", *A* may be added only if *B* is added too. In cases like the one just given, the discourse semantics of *if* thus says that the new address set up as a result of the existential (i.e. the discourse semantics of existential quantification) must always be enriched with the material "will soon go bankrupt", and that this goes for *any* such address to be set up.

The main yield, however, of the theory consists in an explanatory account of presuppositional and intensional phenomena. This account is based on the introduction of intensional subdomains under the truth-domain D^0. These subdomains are either set up or denoted or otherwise exploited by sentential terms under a predicate which is intensional with respect to that term. Subdomains are universes of incrementation in their own right, but they are linked up with D^0 and with other subdomains in all sorts of ways. Two links are systematically present, however: unless explicitly specified otherwise, addresses from D^0 percolate into lower domains, and prejections made into lower domains automatically climb up into higher domains, till they reach D^0, unless they are rejected by a higher domain. In chapter 5 different classes of intensional verbs are distinguished, and different scales of intensionality are set up, each with subdomains of varying depth. In this way an impression is given of the complexities of intensionality phenomena in natural language, and of a machinery of domains and subdomains which would explain the phenomena observed in this respect. It would seem that this approach achieves a far better fit with regard to observable facts of language than what is found in current formal semantic literature.

The same machinery of domains and subdomains is shown to account for the so-called projection phenomena of presupposition. The projection problem of presuppositions is based on the observation that presuppositions of embedded non-entailed clauses are sometimes preserved as full presuppositions of the superordinate sentence, sometimes only as suggestions or 'invited inferences' of varying strength, and are also sometimes lost altogether so that not even a suggestion of their truth remains. The problem is to explain why this should be so. Van der Sandt (1982) found that the projection behaviour of presuppositions can be seen to be a consequence of general acceptability conditions for discourse incrementations. This idea is taken over in this book, and it is shown that a taxonomy of acceptability conditions for complex sentences can be avoided, and the theory can accordingly be simplified, by the assumption of a domain and subdomain machinery, actually implemented in the brain and at work as an integral part during the production and comprehension of utterances of sentences. The problem is then no longer one of logic (which is taken to be epiphenomenal with regard to the machinery), but of cognitive psychology.

A particularly upsetting problem is discussed and solved in terms of domain semantics. The problem is called here the problem of the gatecrash falsifier, and it is posed by sentences such as *Either Ben has no dog, or (he has one and) it is black*, or *If Ben has a dog it is black*. The problem is, taking the disjunction first, that the truth of one disjunct suffices for the truth of the whole sentence. Now suppose Ben has two dogs, one black and one white, then *Ben has a dog and it is black* is true, just as *Ben has a dog and it is white* is true. Yet in this situation the disjunction quoted above is false, due to the existence of a white dog owned by Ben. This white dog, which should have nothing to do with the whole sentence, is the gatecrash falsifier. And analogously for the conditional sentence: whether it is analysed in the classical way or in our way (section 4.1.5), it should not be falsified by the gatecrash white dog falsifier. Yet it is. It is shown in chapter 6 that this problem is to do with questions of specific versus non-specific reference, and that it is a sort of little gremlin in the logical works of language.

It will be appreciated that a precise formulation of the conditions for constructing discourse domains which retain truth-conditional purity is a non-trivial goal to attain, and that it requires a level of observational refinement not usually achieved in the formal semantics literature. If it is true, as is some-times said, that any theoretical development that leads to an increase in observational techniques and refinement is to be regarded as a positive development, we may feel encouraged, since we notice, time and again, that the task of formulating rules and principles for the construction of truth-conditionally reliable mental discourse domains leads directly to the making of observations which are not found in the established literature but are nevertheless real and directly relevant. It will also be appreciated that the complexities of natural language are such that it must be considered unwise to jump to conclusions of a general nature, no matter whether they relate to constraints on formal semantic calculi or to alleged universal properties of grammars of natural languages. On the contrary, we must accustom ourselves to the idea that the machinery of language, including its connections with other parts of human cognition, is a functional assemblage whose dimensions and rationale are only partially understood. Accordingly, we must be prepared for all kinds of unexpected complications and special provisions which, from a purely mathematical point of view, are not only uninteresting but in fact pointless. Semantics, in other words, being a part of cognitive psychology, is a variety of *applied* mathematics, and certainly not of pure mathematics, or logic. This being so, one should keep up a holy respect for linguistic facts (even when they are highly special and possibly rather subtle), and indulge in generalizing theory only when one feels that the relevant facts have been looked at with sufficient care and detachment. The present study will no doubt fall short of these high standards, but it shows at least an open-mindedness with respect to the complexities of natural language which more 'orthodox' approaches (in that sense of 'orthodoxy' where it is related with what is currently regarded as accepted theory) are not seen to cultivate at all.

1

Discourse and interpretation

1.1 Introduction

The central question that will occupy us in the pages to follow is the empirical question of how humans understand and interpret utterances. This includes the question of what is involved in the ability to talk or write about things, real or imaginary, in this world through the use of sounds or writing symbols – the problem of reference in other words. This problem, or rather, complex of problems, has a history that goes back to the early stages of Greek philosophy, but it is only recently, through the combined efforts of philosophers, especially logicians, of linguists and of psychologists, that questions of meaning and reference have come to be looked at and treated in an empirical vein. The roots of semantics, in others words, are in philosophy. It is important to realize that this is so, mainly because present-day formal semantics betrays its origins in many ways. There is a positive as well as a negative side to this. On the positive side we count, first, the awareness that a theory of meaning and reference has the form of a calculus where truth-conditions play a central role, and, moreover, the actual development of truth-conditional calculi derived from mathematical model-theory. It is fair to say that there would have been no semantics of natural language, had it not been for mathematical model-theory. Yet, there is a negative side as well: there are many (mainly linguists and psychologists) who feel that existing formal semantic calculi do insufficient justice to the insight that all semantic processing is cognitive processing. They also feel that, at least until quite recently, too cavalier an attitude was displayed with regard to what we must assume is going on in language.

This criticism is not entirely unjustified. The great builders of formal semantic systems were philosophers, not linguists or psychologists. They were interested in calculi, and not or hardly in the nitty-gritty details of language or in the reconstruction of mental machinery. But they were also largely unaffected by the vicissitudes of structuralism and behaviourism that had left such deep marks in psychology and linguistics. In fact, this gave the philosophers a head start, since for them there was no need to suffer from the terrible semantic inhibitions caused by behaviourism in psychology and linguistics. Behaviourism had no quarrel with mathematical model-theory, but it vetoed any notion of a mental calculus. And by the time this behaviourist veto had been nullified in the human sciences, formal semantics was well on its way in philosophy.

It wasn't until some fifteen years ago that philosophers, linguists and psychologists sought each other's company in the area of semantics. Steinberg and Jakobovits's interdisciplinary reader *Semantics* (1971) bears clear testimony to this development. The first contacts were difficult. Methodologically, the philosophers were instrumentalists, the formal calculi being the centre of their interest. But the linguists and the psychologists were (and are) realists: the psychologists had never been anything but realists, and the linguists had just regained realism after a period of uncertainty and strife on this issue. In these circumstances it was unfortunate that many of the highly abstract formal semantic functions, such as those from possible worlds to extensions of expressions, cannot be regarded as cognitively computable in any realistic sense. It was felt, with some justice, that a formal semantics constrained by considerations of psychological plausibility would be a great deal more appealing.

There were other difficulties as well. Thus many linguists were confused by what they perceived to be a conspicuous lack of descriptive accuracy in the analyses provided by the formal semanticists. And it is undeniably true that the linguists had some reason for bewilderment. In those days, many formal semanticists were indeed unaware of the incredibly subtle and intricate complexities of human language: they tended to underestimate the difficulty of the task of describing a language, or language in general for that matter. Formal semantics had come to fruition in an area of analytical philosophy where empiricist foundations and formal calculi were paramount (a latter-day version of ancient analogism). There was also, of course, the so-called "ordinary language philosophy", cultivated at Oxford in the 25 years following the Second World War, and originating from Wittgenstein's teachings at Cambridge. But, influential though this form of analytical philosophy was in general philosophy, it had virtually no impact on the more formally and mathematically orientated developments that generated formal semantics. Ordinary language philosophy was distinctly non-formal, and concentrated instead on cultivating observational refinement. When an attempt was made at casting the fruits of observation into a formal mould, such as Strawson's attempt at a formal account of presupposition, it was met with outright antagonism by the formalists. Yet the linguists felt much more at ease with the ordinary language philosophers than with the formalists (as is witnessed by the fact that the notion of presupposition caught on in linguistics much more easily and quickly than the notion of a model-theoretic calculus). Linguists and ordinary language philosophers could easily agree that language is a product of nature (including the natural processes of social convention), and that an adequate understanding of the system of language can only be achieved by painstaking observation and hypothesizing – in other words, a latter-day version of ancient anomalism. Formal semanticists, on the other hand, were inclined to view semantics of natural language as a kind of applied mathematical model-theory. The available apparatus was applied to language, if need be with certain adaptations to improve the fit. But if the fit was still less than perfect, natural language could be blamed for being "imprecise", "vague", "ambiguous" or what have you. It may be oversimplifying a little, but there is more than a grain of truth to saying that in those days language was considered an object for formal semantics only to the extent that it happened to fit the formal system. The remainder was relegated to a secondary discipline of 'pragmatics', which was not subject to the standards of rigour and precision applying to formal semantics.

Needless to say, this situation has changed a great deal since the 1970s. Quite a number of leading semanticists and linguists have been able to build bridges, with the result that realism as a methodological premiss is now gaining ground on instrumentalism, and that the apparent vagaries of language are taken much more seriously than before, and are no longer more or less automatically relegated to the doubtful realm of 'pragmatics'. In principle, one may say, the formal semanticists and the linguists are now much closer together. And there are signs that the psychologists will also be drawn into the picture, so that the triad of disciplines represented in Steinberg and Jakobovits's Reader of 1971 seems to be moving towards a real symbiosis.

As a result, however, of what has been happening in this respect over the past few years, most of what looked like established doctrine five years ago is now under renewed scrutiny, in semantics as well as in linguistics. Possible worlds no longer take the pride of place in semantic theory: many feel that much of the 'work' done by possible worlds in semantic theory should be taken over by other, more realistic explanatory devices. And the relatively rigid paradigm, or couple of paradigms, of grammatical analysis in linguistics have dissolved into a state of near anarchy where anything goes, or at least anything is considered worth re-examining.

One striking factor in this relatively unstable situation is the increasing prominence of the role of discourse and context of use in semantic explanations. In the philosophical tradition it was sentences in isolation that were considered for semantic analysis, not sentences as used in a particular context or discourse. Russell's picture of language, for example, was fairly simple: a language is a set of sentences, and each sentence always has one of two truth-values, true or false – *tertium non datur*. If a sentence looks like being contextually bound, it must be re-analysed in such a way that it no longer is.

A language thus becomes a set of eternal sentences. Quine continued this Russellian programme of "elimination of particulars". The results of this programme, together with the model-theoretic machinery of possible worlds to account for intensionality phenomena, still form the core of formal semantics. Subtheories have been developed to account for deictics, demonstratives, indexicals and other forms of restricted reference, but they tend to have the character of additions to the central core. They can be cut off and a purely 'eternalist' semantics will remain.

Yet at the same time, this central core of formal semantic theory suffers from some very central and fundamental problems. There is no need to elaborate these problems here, since they are widely known. The *problem of the false synonymy* of all logical truths (true in all possible worlds), and of all contradictions (true in no possible world) has not so far been eliminated in formal semantics. It becomes particularly painful in *the problem of propositional attitudes*, due to the identification of what a person believes, hopes, regrets, knows, etc. with a set of possible worlds. This identification has the unfortunate consequence that if a person believes etc. one logical truth, he believes etc. them all. And likewise for contradictions.

These two related problems do not arise from the inherent complications of the object of research, natural language. On the contrary, they arise from a central artefact introduced by the theory – possible worlds. If we can rid ourselves of possible worlds, these problems vanish. Here we come to the main contention of this book: possible worlds should be done away with in semantics; their role should be taken over by a theory of mental machinery accounting for everything, and a great deal more, that possible worlds were meant to account for. As a corollary it follows that the long-cherished Principle of the Excluded Third (PET), while useful for logical systems applied within strict limits of reference and subject-matter, cannot be maintained for natural language. Most sentences of natural language, when used out of context or in an inappropriate context, will be without a truth-value, even though they are both well-formed and perfectly meaningful. Thus the good and meaningful English sentence *The quick brown fox jumps over the lazy dog*, used here and now, is devoid of a truth-value. For it to have a truth-value the fox and the dog referred to, as well as the time of action, must be specified. No amount of analysis can alter this fact. It will, furthermore, be argued (ch. 3) that if a sentence has a truth-value, it has a choice of three, not two truth-values. Natural languages are thus considered to be partially valued trivalent systems.

The mental machinery in question is conceived as a cognitive store containing the accumulated contributions made by successive utterances in the course of a coherent discourse. The store contains substores (subdomains) containing the information provided in the course of a discourse on what some specified person or persons are said to believe, hope, regret, know, etc., or on what is said to be possible, necessary, probable, regrettable, or characterized by whatever intensional sentential predicate. The machinery of stores and substores, or *domains* and *subdomains*, as we shall call them henceforth, is thus used to account for the intensionality phenomena in language. It is also used as an intermediary structure between referring expressions in utterances of sentences on the one hand, and the actual objects of reference on the other. Discourse domains must, furthermore, be thought of as having open access to available stores of background knowledge and to available knowledge immediately derivable from the context of use. This latter form of knowledge will in principle account for references to ostensibly, deictically, or indexically specified reference objects, as well as for references to objects identified by their order of introduction in the discourse (*the former, the latter*). It is the main purpose of this book to provide a specific analysis of the procedures and structures involved in discourse-bound semantic processing. The main claim is that a discourse theory of semantics, without any appeal to "possible worlds", makes for a substantially better fit between the theory and the observed linguistic facts, and must therefore be deemed to be empirically superior to existing standard forms of formal semantics (and concomitant grammatical analyses).

The notion of discourse as a factor in semantic processing has become more and more prominent over the past 10 years. Long lists of references could be cited (including some of my own, going back to 1972). There is a rapidly growing body of literature in psychology and psycholinguistics describing and analysing aspects of discourse-dependent semantic processing. In linguistics, intonation studies tend to place heavy emphasis on the role of preceding discourse for sentence intonation patterns, usually in connection with a distinction between 'topic' and 'comment', or a distinction between 'given' and 'new'. The role of discourse is beginning to be explored in studies on definite noun phrases, in particular sentence-external anaphoric pronouns. What has been lacking, however, is an explicit account of how discourse domains are built up, how they are structured, and what their precise role is in the semantic processing of uttered sentences in discourse. The central theme of this book is a formal elaboration of precisely these points.[1]

What is offered here is nothing more than an outline theory, with some bits filled in but other bits still obviously lacking. This is, it seems, inevitable, since it can hardly be expected that a comprehensive and to a large extent

---

[1] A few formal accounts of discourse incrementation have been presented recently in artificial intelligence (AI) and in formal semantics. These will not be discussed here, mainly because they either aim at a formal treatment of specific semantico-grammatical problems, or, as in AI, concentrate less on descriptive adequacy from a linguistic point of view than on complete computer programs suitable for limited demonstrations of language-like processes in a restricted situational setting. In either case, the possibilities of extrapolation are unclear. These works, moreover, are themselves in initial stages of development, which makes critical comparisons here premature.

new theory of semantics will have satisfactory answers to all problems right away. Yet the more initiated reader will notice that many of the stubborn problems that have made themselves known in currently standard forms of formal semantics, and a few more, are approached here in an original manner, and sometimes even solved.

This applies to some extent to problems connected with traditional distinctions between elements in the sentence that are 'given' and those that are 'new': in general what has been stored in the discourse domain is 'given', whereas what is added with the uttering of a new sentence is 'new'. The related pair of 'topic' and 'comment' can only partially be made explicit. If topic is what the discourse is concentrating on at any given moment, then the element or elements in the sentence denoting that topic must of necessity belong to the domain of the given, but need not, of course, be identical with that domain. What mechanism can be taken to select a topic and to make expressions denoting it 'salient' is a question not answered or even mooted in this work. Instead, the notion of 'topic', and its complement 'comment', will be used but not explained.

Phenomena of vagueness, much discussed though they are, will in principle be ignored. What goes under the name of "vagueness" in the literature covers various distinct classes of cases, such as gradable predicates (adjectives) involving a comparison class (*Harry is tall* ⟨for a Scandinavian/pygmy/ballet dancer/. . .⟩), or lack of specificity (*Harry hurt himself*: his arm? if so, which arm? his leg? if so, which leg?, his head? . . .). The class of cases most properly called "vague", however, are those where a predicate is "only dubiously applicable to marginal objects" (Quine 1960: 129). The ancient Sorites paradox is based on such cases: when do grains of sand trickling down from a container begin to form a heap? Gradable adjectives and colour terms are often cited in this connection, whereby it is standardly observed that some interpretations are fixed collocationally ("flat beer", "flat tire", "red wine", "red herring") and others contextually (if two tires are presented, the one with standard pressure and the other half deflated, then the expression *the flat tire* will select the half deflated one; but if one is half deflated and the other is entirely flat, then that expression will pick the latter, not the former). In general, I agree with Hausser (1983) that it is sensible to assume that semantic processing is a yes/no system ('digital'), though often applied to a world containing gradients ('analogous'). The specific complications which arise out of such a situation are left untouched in this book.

The important area of speech act semantics will, likewise, remain outside the scope of the present study. The fact that formal semantics fails, in general, to provide a satisfactory theory of speech acts (or the performative aspect of utterances) must be both noticed and deplored. The exclusive concern, in accepted standard formal semantics, with truth-conditions may well have been a natural obstacle to a further development of formal semantic theory in the direction of speech act theory. But be that as it may, this problem area cannot be developed here: any attempt in this direction would not be feasible within the boundaries of time and space to which this study is confined. All we can do is note that a further elaboration of the theory presented here encompassing performative aspects of utterances would seem natural: instead of the straightforward function of incrementation to a given discourse domain, as will be developed in the pages to come, a variety of incrementation functions will have to be defined, each corresponding to a specific class of speech acts. Moreover, specific "fulfilment-conditions" will have to be defined for each kind of speech act: an order is fulfilled by it being carried out; a wish by it being fulfilled; a question by it being answered; a request by it being granted; and an assertion by it being true. We must, however, for the time being leave such thoughts to mature.

Another aspect which is quite clearly neglected in this study is the role of speaker shift in semantics. Discourse domains are clearly not the private privilege of single individuals. On the contrary, it is a central fact in semantics that speakers try to make hearers privy to their thoughts, and it is a central contention in this book that the cognitive machinery of discourse domains is highly instrumental in making this come about. It is also undeniably true that there is a general economy principle at work, in the sense that speakers tend to gear the amount of explicit, verbally conveyed information to what they can reasonably expect their interlocutors to know already (see section 3.4 for a further elaboration of this point). We must, however, make a start somewhere, and it seems sensible, for the time being at least, to concentrate on the notion of discourse domains as they are constructed on the basis of incoming linguistic material consisting exclusively of assertions. That is, we place ourselves in the position of a listener interpreting a monologue of coherent assertions: no speech acts other than assertions, no speaker shifts ('turn-taking'), and no topic shifts. Only occasionally will there be references to other speech acts, other speakers, and other topics. But no systematic analysis of the roles of these factors in 'live' communication will be offered.

There may be some significance in this limitation. There is a widespread implicit intuition or feeling, sanctioned by history, that the least marked, 'fundamental' (in an ill-defined sense), or 'prototype' form of sentence is the assertive form. Why this feeling should be common is not clear, but it may just be that it is possible to develop the theory of discourse semantics to a large extent, including the fundamental machinery of domain construction, on the basis of a monologue of coherent assertions alone. It is, in any case, of interest to see how far one gets without invoking the interaction of other factors. It would not seem too wild a guess that it may well be, in particular, the truth-conditional aspects of discourse semantics that are analysable and describable on the basis of just monologues of coherent assertions, offered to listeners.

It does not seem sensible, however, to labour this point too much. For it is not sensible to try and conceive of semantics as limited to merely truth-conditional aspects of meaning. Although it is recognized that truth-conditions form a central and essential part of semantics, there is a great deal about semantics which is not truth-conditional. Speech acts, as is well known, are not truth-conditionally definable. Yet there seems no good reason for excluding them from semantic theory. The same goes for other aspects of meaning, such as what commonly goes under the name of "implicature". The concept of implicature is not well-defined in the literature which deals with these matters, but it is, in a general sense, meant to apply to cases where a particular sentence *A* suggests, more or less strongly, another sentence *B*. That is, *A* neither asserts nor entails *B*, yet there is a suggestion that *B* is the case. The term, as well as an attempt at classification, stem from Grice (1968; 1975; 1978), and Grice's idea was that such phenomena should be seen in the light of some implicit 'contract', a set of 'maxims' tacitly agreed upon, between participants in linguistic interaction. In general, Grice put forward the theory that the formalities of semantics could be left undisturbed, and to the extent that the facts of language turn out not to fit these formalities, an appeal should be made to the maxims of linguistic interaction. A combination of formal semantics and a discipline of verbal interaction, 'pragmatics', should thus be able to provide the empirical 'fit' that formal semantics was found to be unable to achieve.

This pragmatics, however, has turned out to be quite a bit too flexible. In fact, it became the favourite receptable of unexplained facts. And it could fulfil this role because, as though by conspiracy, there was a general willingness to allow pragmatics to be practised as a 'soft' discipline which was not subject to the same standards of rigour and stringency as formal semantics. (Parallel to this Gricean pragmatics, there developed a quite different form of pragmatics within formal semantics, after Montague's example, which was inspired by Morris (1946). This pragmatics is, as would be expected, fully formalized, and deals chiefly with questions of quantification over and reference within restricted domains. The relation between this formal pragmatics and the 'soft' pragmatics flowing from Gricean sources, however, has never been properly specified.)

Although one may feel unhappy with the lack of formal rigour in 'soft' pragmatics, it should be recognized that the 'contract' or 'maxims' mentioned above cannot be denied reality. It is true, of course, that participants in linguistic interaction are caught in a complex network of reasonable expectations about the position of the other participants, along a number of different parameters. And it would be foolhardy to deny that this network of expectations tends to play a role in the understanding and interpretation of utterances. Yet, this does not mean that existing standard formal semantics plus the pragmatics of interaction should together suffice for an adequate empirical account of what makes humans understand each other the way they do. The reason why this cannot be accepted is that the dilemma is false: it is not a question of trade-off between formal semantics and interactional pragmatics, since the role of discourse domains must be taken into account as well. The situation is, in fact, quite complex, since it is not even a question of a trade-off among existing formal semantics, interactional pragmatics and discourse theory (as is very often implicitly assumed in the literature). The situation is more complex than that, because formal semantics, in all its rigour and mathematical beauty, is not untouchable, because discourse theory is still an unknown entity, because pragmatics is ill defined and, finally, because the neurological structures involved may harbour explanations.

It could hardly be my intention to settle this issue in this book. But I do put forward the idea that the kind of formalized discourse theory presented here will take account not only of the clearly truth-conditional aspects of meaning but also of a considerable number of phenomena that tend to be classified as 'pragmatic' in some unsatisfactory sense. Thus, for example, there is a certain class of 'implicatures', all reducible to weakened pre-suppositions (see ch. 3, where they will be called "mere prejections"), which are covered by our semantic theory. An example is the following:

(1) Bob may have used his radio scanner.

This sentence strongly suggests that the Bob in question has a radio scanner. This is, obviously, not asserted, but neither is it entailed, as appears from the fact that one can say, without that entailment:

(2) Bob may have a radio scanner, and he may have used it.

Yet, on hearing (1) one is inclined to assume that Bob has a radio scanner. The question of *why* one is that way inclined is usually answered by an appeal to pragmatics: implicatures are 'pragmatic'. Our theory, however, will provide a formal account of at least this kind of 'implicature'. And our theory is not pragmatic but semantic.

In general, we shall draw the following boundary line between semantic and pragmatic phenomena. Whenever a feature or aspect in the interpretation of a sentence co-varies with non-linguistic knowledge, i.e. knowledge of the world, of general principles of rational behaviour, or the like, we shall treat it as being of pragmatic nature. On the other hand, aspects of understanding processes of utterances which co-vary with what is clearly linguistic knowledge will be treated as semantic. This distinction is not hard and fast, however. In many intermediate cases we will let the theory decide. Take, for example, the well-known example of a person sitting at a breakfast table and asking:

(3) Can you pass me the butter?

The fact that this is, and should be, taken as a request and not as a question is almost universally attributed to pragmatic principles of rational behaviour at a breakfast table. And it is clearly very difficult to argue against that position. Yet there do seem to be linguistic differences involved as well. Instead of asking (3), our character could have said (4), but not (5):

(4) Can you pass me some butter?
(5) Can you pass me any butter?

It is simply not known why (4) can be a request but not (5).
Or take the following two sentences:

(6) Each of the 25 rooms in the hotel has a shower.
(7) Each of the 25 students in the class has a supervisor.

Sentence (6) will be deemed falsified if it turns out that there are only five showers available, even though for each room it is indicated which shower should be used. But (7) is not falsified if there are five supervisors, each taking five students. Is this a direct result of our world-knowledge, *in casu* our knowledge about hotels and about student–supervisor relations? If so, it should be a question of pragmatics. Yet we have the clear intuition that truth-conditions are involved: a sentence like *This room has a shower* is false if the occupants of that room have to go out into the corridor and use a common shower. But *This student has a supervisor* is not false if the student has to share his supervisor with other students. Can such differences be built into the lexical meaning of *have*? Does this mean that truth-conditions are not always linguistically defined, but may occasionally be dependent on para- meters of world-knowledge? Questions such as these are discussed in section 3.4. In general, we shall feel free to let our semantic theory apply to classes of phenomena which are commonly considered pragmatic. Presuppositions and mere prejections (weakened presuppositions), in particular, will receive a great deal of attention.

Certain specific areas of semantic analysis and description will be left out of account. Verbal tenses and aspects, notably, will not be dealt with, mainly because this is a more or less clearly delimited topic, an adequate treatment of which requires a study of considerable bulk and substance – while on the other hand nothing in the theory presented here seems to be threatened by what can be reasonably expected from a study of tenses and aspects. The same goes for questions of number (singular, plural). Quantification phenomena will be touched upon, and a general schema for their treatment will be expounded. But no attempt will be made at a full treatment, for roughly the same reasons as are given for tenses, aspects and number. There are, moreover, many aspects of lexical meaning involved in the analysis of individual quantifiers. A comparison of English quantifiers with those in other languages quickly reveals that, besides the obviously universal aspects involved, there are also many language-specific features. It is not our purpose here to go into such questions. (It must be noted, moreover, that no formal semantic theory has so far provided a full analysis of the quantifier system in English or any other language.)

Definite, non-quantified terms, on the other hand, are of central concern. Unlike some of the existing formal approaches, our theory makes a systematic distinction between definite terms, which are considered non-quantified, and quantified terms. Definite pronouns, proper names and definite descriptions are considered definite terms and are given analyses and treatments in terms of one single category. Quantified terms are processed in terms of a completely different category. It is often claimed, after Montague, that definite terms and quantified terms should be treated on a par, since they occupy the same positions in the surface sentence and can be given a unified treatment (see, e.g., Barwise and Cooper 1981). Against this it should be observed that formal possibility is a necessary but not a sufficient requirement for a particular treatment; empirical support is equally necessary, and the two together hardly come close to being sufficient. The empirical support for a unified treatment of definite terms and quantified terms is doubtful, to say the least. For one thing, quantified terms show scope differences and scope restrictions which definite terms lack. The claim that all possible scope permutations represent different possible readings is clearly false. Often one reading is dominant and the other 'hard to get', or 'recessive', as in:

(8) Nobody here knows two languages.

where the dominant reading is "there is nobody here who is bilingual", and the recessive reading "there are two languages that nobody here knows". Its passive, however, still has, or may have, the two readings, but they have swapped places:

(9) Two languages are known by nobody here.

Sometimes, what could be a recessive reading simply does not exist, as in:

(10) a. I have never bought a racing horse.
    b. John and every woman in the village want to get married.
    c. I don't believe the story that some journalists are aware of the dangers involved in this kind of reporting.
    d. I want to see if someone is at home.

In (8), (9) and (10a), the semantic analysis follows the left-to-right order of the quantifier representatives in the surface sentence, at least for the dominant readings.[2] In (10b) *every woman* cannot take scope over the whole

---

[2] This principle was, of course, discovered by a variety of generative grammarians in the late sixties, who found that semantic readings tend to reflect scope hierarchies in surface left-to-right orderings. They also found, however, that the correspondence was not perfect, and no satisfactory answer was discovered. Note, in this connection, that newspaper headlines always follow the left-to-right principle for quantifiers and other operators: they have no recessive readings. See 2.4.3 for further discussion.

remainder of the sentence; as a consequence it cannot mean that for every woman in the village John and that woman want to get married to each other. Its only possible reading is the one in which John as well as every woman in the village want to get married. This is explained in principle by the theory that quantifying into a co-ordinate structure is ruled out, just as any movement into or out of a co-ordinate structure is ruled out, by the Co-ordinate Structure Constraint (Ross 1967). Likewise, as is demonstrated by (10c), quantifying into a complex noun phrase is ruled out, a consequence of the Complex Noun Phrase Constraint (Ross 1967).[3] (10d) shows that quantifying into an embedded question is ruled out. It can hardly be a coincidence that, as is well known, movement out of complex NPs or embedded questions is generally blocked or subject to heavy constraints (cp. WH-movement). This makes it hard to deny that some rule of quantifier movement (Quantifier Lowering) is involved – as was proposed in generative semantics – whose application is constrained by the universal principles constraining all rules of grammar. In such a theory, however, there is no question of definite terms and quantified terms being treated on a par.

Further observations reinforce this conclusion. Thus, pronominal reference is more limited for quantified terms than for definite terms, as appears from:

(11) a. John didn't leave – because he was tired.
   b. John didn't leave because he was tired; he left because he was bored.
(12) a. Nobody left – because he was tired.
   b. Nobody left because he was tired; those who left did so because they were bored.

The (b)-sentences allow for an anaphoric relation between the pronoun *he* and the subject of the main clause. In the (a)-sentences, however, there is a difference: *he* in (11a) allows for an anaphoric relation with *John*, but *he* in (12a) cannot be found by *nobody*; it must relate to an external antecedent. Definite terms and quantified terms are thus seen to differ in their semantic behaviour. Many more examples of different behaviour can be cited. For example, the negation operator tends to precede a quantified term when this term is in the scope of the negation, even when the quantified term occurs right at the beginning of the sentence:

---

[3] Note that a sentence like:

I don't believe that some journalists are aware of the dangers involved in this kind of reporting.

can be used to convey that there are some journalists who, in the speaker's opinion, are not aware of the dangers involved in the kind of reporting alluded to. In fact, I heard this sentence being used by a man involved in a public scandal as he was interviewed by a radio reporter, and it was clear that this is what he meant.

(13) a. All members present supported the proposal.

    b. Not all members present supported the proposal.

(14) a. Many smokers chew gum.

    b. Not many smokers chew gum.

Needless to say, this position is ruled out with ordinary definite terms in first position.[4]

Particularly strong evidence comes from Dutch and German. In these languages sentence negation and other sentential operators systematically land in different places in the sentences forming their scope, in particular when there is a direct object or a nominal predicate nominal with a copula verb, according to whether these NPs are definite terms or quantified terms. The German sentence *Er trank den Wein* ("he drank the wine"), for example, has the negation *Er trank den Wein nicht*. But the sentence *Er trank viel Wein* ("he drank much wine") has the sentence negation *Er trank nicht viel Wein*. Moreover, the fact that there is also an internal negation for the latter sentence: *Er trank viel Wein nicht* ("there was a lot of wine which he did not drink"), a possibility which *Er trank den Wein* lacks, shows that it makes a great deal of sense to assign to *Er trank viel Wein* a structure which makes it possible to insert a negation in two distinct positions corresponding with distinct truth-conditions. (Admittedly, *Er trank nicht den Wein* is a well-formed sentence in German, but it is not the negation of *Er trank den Wein*, but of *Er trank den WEIN*, with heavy contrastive accent on *WEIN*. It means, accordingly, "it isn't the wine which he drank".)

Careful observation reveals massive evidence for a systematic distinction between definite and quantified terms. Thus, to pick just one example, in English there is no subject-auxiliary inversion with *not only* in front position when it modifies a definite subject term: *Not only William sent his greetings*. But there is such inversion when the subject is a quantified term: *Not only did two friends of mine send their greetings*; *Not only did all of my friends send their greetings*. Such observations can be multiplied at will (see, e.g., Hawkins 1978: 228-65).

In general, it seems that a single unified treatment for definite and quantified terms, though in principle preferable from a methodological point of

---

[4] It is not ruled out when the definite term is under contrastive accent and followed by *but* –, as in:

(i) Not John but Harry voted against the proposal.

In certain other languages, such as German or Dutch, it is not required that a *but*-phrase should follow immediately; it may come at the end or be left out altogether:

(ii) Nicht die Studenten werden die Resolution befürworten (sondern die Professoren).

    (Not the students (but the professors) will support the resolution.)

view, is too risky in view of the facts. A theoretical investment in a distinction between definite and quantified terms seems likely to pay off. The question, often asked in this connection, of why surface structures should have certain NP-positions as favourite targets for both definite and quantified terms (or, in other words, why we don't speak in predicate calculus language if that is what the semantic analysis amounts to), seems to be answered, in principle, by the consideration that language, for good functional reasons, minimizes occurrences of bound variables in surface structures. They seem, in fact, limited to cases where the variable occurs in a separate clause, as in (12b). Moreover, the most striking difference between semantic analyses expressed as tree structures in something like predicate calculus on the one hand, and surface structures of sentences on the other, is that the former typically show many sentential embeddings and few different lexical categories (the trees are 'deep' and 'narrow'), whereas the latter have many different lexical categories and relatively few sentential embeddings (they are 'flat' and 'wide'). There is thus a general reduction in tree structure and an increase in surface categoriality. It is not difficult to see, in a global manner, that a reduction of tree structure and a general 'flattening' of the tree which then houses more different surface categories is highly functional for linear acoustic or visual transmission. Trees, after all, are not perceptible.

This leads us to the question of grammar. Up to the writings of Richard Montague in the 1960s, the whole tradition of Western philosophical grammar has taken it for granted that surface structures of sentences are unfit for direct semantic interpretation. Since at least Plato, it has been commonly accepted that every sentence should be associated with an abstract structure representing its semantic analysis.[5] The correspondence rules between the semantic analyses and the surface structures form the grammar for the language in question. Our work is a direct continuation of this tradition. Montague, however, proposed that surface structures should be regarded as directly interpretable, without the intervention of abstract representations differing structurally from the surface structure. His perspective was that if natural language is to be taken seriously and not glossed over lightly by means of qualifications like "vague", "ambiguous", "imprecise" and what not, then it had better be a formal language interpretable in ways analogous to what semantic interpretation amounts to in mathematical model-theory. This perspective is reinforced by the consideration that it is sound methodology to refuse all abstract entities as long as no convincing case has been made for

---

[5] As far as I know, this idea originated with the school of Heraclitus: the philosopher Cratylus, in the dialogue of that name by Plato, was a Heraclitean. Heraclitus' sayings include "Nature likes to hide herself" and "Invisible harmony is stronger than visible harmony". His followers applied this profound insight to language, as well as to other matters of human interest.

them – a consideration which is based on the general scientific principle of economy in hypotheses, Ockham's razor in other words.

The question of whether surface structures are or are not directly interpretable amounts in principle to the question of whether surface structures are or are not compositional in some well-defined sense. In chapter 2 it will be argued that surface structures are not compositional, so that indeed abstract semantic representations are required, as well as a grammar relating these and their corresponding surface structures. Montague's dilemma was a false one: it is quite possible to take natural language seriously without assuming that it is a formal language in the sense of mathematical model-theory. There is nothing to prevent there being further horns to the dilemma, such as the possibility that the language of abstract semantic representations is compositional and the language of surface structures a transformed derivative, whose justification lies, probably, in functional principles of rapid acoustic transmission. Semantic analyses have, in a sense, too much structure and too little in the way of lexically and categorially distinct terminal elements to reflect that structure. Their trees are too deep and too steep. Surface structures, on the other hand, with their relatively flat trees and a greater variety of surface categories (adverbs, prepositions, adjectives, etc.), have more differentiated and better ordered terminal elements to pack the message into a serially presented acoustic string. It will be argued in chapter 2 that surface structures are transforms of underlying semantic representations, and that this theoretical investment is both necessary and profitable. An outline theory of grammar will be presented there, although a fuller elaboration must wait till some (not too distant) future date. The grammatical theory presented is a form of what used to be called "generative semantics" or "semantic syntax" in the late sixties and early seventies.

1.2 The notion of discourse domain

In standard formal semantics logic fulfils a double role. Logic serves to provide a formal specification of entailments given a set of propositions, and it provides the prototype of semantic interpretation according to the principles of the recently developed mathematical model-theory. In our theory logic fulfils only the first, not the second, role. Mathematical model-theory is considered to be of no direct use to the semantics of natural language. Instead of defining sentences (propositions) by assigning them truth-values for any given possible world, we shall define propositions in relation to discourse domains and incremented discourse domains.

More or less for the sake of convenience we shall adopt the by now traditional view that each uttered sentence contains two main structural parts, its speech act operator and the 'proposition'. This view may well prove wrong, in the end, but we have nothing to replace it with.[6] The 'proposition' is standardly taken to be defined truth-conditionally: a specification of the conditions under which it is to be taken as true is at the same time a specification of its meaning. While this view cannot be denied a certain profundity, it again has its limitations, which, again, we will not try to exploit or explore: we shall accept this truth-conditional view of propositional meaning, or at least we shall not attack it. What we do attack, however, is the idea that a truth-conditional specification of a proposition is at the same time its semantic specification, or, more clearly, we will put forward the idea that *semantics*, as a theory of linguistic comprehension, must primarily define a proposition in terms of what it does with respect to any given discourse domain.

We mean to say that the meaning of a proposition is to be characterized primarily in terms of the structural changes a proposition brings about when it is added as an assertion to a given discourse domain of assertions made by one and the same speaker. The increment value of an asserted proposition to a coherent set of asserted propositions in a single speaker's monologue is thus taken to be both a central defining and a central explanatory factor for an adequate theory of linguistic comprehension. This is not to say that the truth-conditional view of propositions is incorrect or is to be abandoned, since the resulting discourse domains are themselves, if not defined, certainly constrained by specific truth-conditions, and correctness of truth-conditions remains, as before, an adequacy requirement for the theory. But the claim is that the *explanatory* element resides only partially in a specification of the truth-conditions, and to a large extent in a specification of what a proposition does to its discourse domain when added as an assertion. It is this claim which underlies our decision to explore only discourse domains consisting of assertions uttered by a single speaker. Other discourse domains are, of course, real and important, but they seem not, or less, relevant to a theory of propositional semantics. That they will turn out to be of crucial importance for a theory of speech acts, seems beyond doubt.

The truth-conditional part of semantics as a theory of linguistic comprehension is, in our view, limited to the lexicon. Whereas the structural properties of a proposition (or its linguistic representation) relate directly to the way the proposition is to be incremented to any given domain, the lexical

---

[6] This distinction is no doubt too simplistic. It is known, for example, that non-restrictive relative clauses contain their own speech act operator:

(i) So you found your brother, who was working in the library wasn't he?

Epithetic pronouns also seem to carry a separate speech act operator:

(ii) Did you see the boss? Yeah, the pig gave me the sack.

Here the analysis is probably something like "he gave me the sack, and I hereby call him a pig". There are, moreover, the pragmatic complications discussed above.

items used in the proposition all carry a semantic definition which has as a central element a set of truth-conditional predicate conditions ('meaning postulates'), specifying the conditions to be fulfilled by any n-tuple of term denotations for the predicate to be truthfully applicable. It will become clear below that the traditional logical constants *and*, *or*, *if*...*then* and *not* are also treated as predicates, taking propositional structures as arguments. One reason for doing this is that we are thus able to maintain a uniform truth-definition for sentences as well as a uniform distinction between the truth-conditional part and the discourse-incrementation part of semantics. It moreover helps to set off the mathematical properties of logical calculus from the psychologically real ones (section 3.1).

At this stage of the exposé it is perhaps useful to explain formally what we mean by a proposition. Formally we define a proposition as follows. Each sentence in a language is taken to have associated with it a semantic representation. We assume that this semantic representation consists of two main constituents, one accounting for the speech act quality of the sentence, and the other for the truth-conditional aspects. Only the latter will play a part in our definitions. The variable R will be used to range over semantic analyses of sentences without the speech act constituents. A proposition is an ordered pair of some R_i and some given discourse domain D_j, $\langle R_i, D_j \rangle$. Each proposition defines an incremented discourse domain D_j^{+i}, under the general increment function i defined for the language in question (and, obviously, highly constrained by universal linguistic principles). The increment function i is thus a set of ordered pairs consisting of propositions and incremented domains:

$$i: \left\{ \begin{array}{l} \langle\langle R_1, D_1 \rangle, D_1^{+1}\rangle, \langle\langle R_1, D_2 \rangle, D_2^{+1}\rangle \ldots \\ \quad\vdots \\ \langle\langle R_i, D_j \rangle, D_j^{+i}\rangle, \langle\langle R_i, D_k \rangle, D_k^{+i}\rangle \\ \quad\vdots \end{array} \right\}$$

If each propositional representation R_i is regarded as a function from given domains D_j to incremented domains D_j^{+i}, then i can be regarded as the totality of all functions R_i in the language. It is to be noted that each R_i is a partial function, since each R_i can only take a proper subset of the set of all possible discourse domains as its function domain. R_i is undefined for the remaining discourse domains. This must be so since no sentence of any language can be added intelligibly to any arbitrary given domain structure: if the given domain structure contains, for example, the negation of the sentence to which R_i corresponds, then R_i cannot be added. Moreover, all R_is which contain a definite term require that the domain D_j to which they are added either contains a previous specification ('address') for the definite term to be provided with what we shall call a denotation, or allows for an insertion *post hoc* of such a specification. It will become abundantly clear below that not all D_js fulfil this condition for any given R_i.

The meaning of a sentence, in so far as its structural propositional part is concerned, now consists in the specification of its associated function R_i, i.e. in the systematic modification, or increment, which it brings about whenever it is added to an appropriate given discourse domain D_j. But for some marginal cases of sentences without any definite terms and universally quantified over time, it is not sentences in isolation which have a truth-value, but propositions, i.e. pairs of propositional representations R_i and given domain structures D_j. This is in accordance with an ancient tradition which says that it is only sentences in context which can be deemed true or false. There can be little doubt that this tradition is correct. We shall see in a moment that our theory has room for a second intuitively correct notion of truth-value bearer: apart from individual propositions, we can now also say that discourse domains or partial discourse domains can have a truth-value. This corresponds to the intuitive notion that a story is true or partially true, or false or partially false.

A discourse domain D is considered to be defined by at least (a) a finite number of distinct *addresses* d_i, (b) *superaddresses* sd_i, and (c) *instructions*. An address d_i is an information store regarding intended individuals in any bit of the world D might be applied to. The store is built up by what every new asserted sentence in the discourse says about the intended individual referred to by d_i. A superaddress sd_i is like an individual address d_i except for the fact that its stored information is applicable not to individuals in the world but to sets of individuals, of finite or infinite cardinality. (Very little will be said about superaddresses in this study, mainly because it does not contain a semantic theory of plurality.) Instructions are stored separately from the information stored under the (super)addresses. They constrain further developments of D. They result from certain technical predicates in the semantic language, such as the minimal negation ($\sim$) or the disjunctive predicate ($\vee$). As will be shown in chapter 4 in greater detail, the minimal negation prevents its argument proposition from being added to D on pain of falsity of the new increment i. The radical negation does the same, but on stronger grounds: addition to D of its argument proposition will not only result in the simple falsity of i on factual grounds; it says that the falsity of i is necessary because of some falsity earlier on in D, which must therefore be revised *post hoc*. (The distinction between minimal and radical negation, and corresponding falsities, will be elaborated in chapter 3.) A disjunction of the form $A \vee B$ constrains the further development of D in the sense that truth is guaranteed if, on the addition of true $\sim A$, B is added, and on the addition of true $\sim B$, A is added. Chapter 4 contains a detailed discussion of these matters.

The addresses, or discourse denotations, are mapping targets for definite terms in sentences, and at the same time, if the discourse is about real things, they stand in some defined relationship with the things the discourse is about. (This relationship may be straightforward, as when we speak of individuals, but it may also be complex and even require special computation, as when we speak of "the average Englishman's height".) The information stored with each address consists of predicates assigned to the address in question. It is posited as a general principle that new addresses are introduced by an existential quantifier. Thus, an utterance of the sentence *There was a man called "John"* will result in the establishment in D of a new address:

$$(15) \quad \boxed{d_i}$$
$$\text{man}(x)$$
$$\text{"John"}(x)$$

Let another existential statement *There was a chimney* introduce the address:

$$(16) \quad \boxed{d_j}$$
$$\text{chimney}(x)$$

Let the third sentence uttered in this clumsy discourse be *John swept the chimney*, then the increment of that in D will be the addition under d_i of "sweep(x, d_j)", and under d_j of "sweep(d_i, x)":

$$(15) \text{ a.} \quad \boxed{d_i}$$
$$\text{man}(x)$$
$$\text{"John"}(x)$$
$$\overline{\quad\quad\quad}$$
$$\text{sweep}(x, d_j)$$

$$(16) \text{ a.} \quad \boxed{d_j}$$
$$\text{chimney}(x)$$
$$\overline{\quad\quad\quad}$$
$$\text{sweep}(d_i, x)$$

The horizontal line represents the operation of *closure of an address*. Closure of an address is brought about by the first use of a definite term mapping onto that address. Both *John* and *the chimney* are definite terms; they occur in the third uttered sentence in the discourse, and they thus close the address which they denote. The closure operation has a truth-conditional significance. An open address is verified by *any* entity answering the description stored in the address, as long as the entity is in the bit of the world selected for verification, the verification domain V. An open address does not refer, but is true or false in a given V. Closed addresses, besides having a truth-value if a V is defined for them, also refer. If the object of reference is fixed by the simple fact that V contains only one specimen answering the description of the address as it was before closure, we have *specific reference*: from the moment of closure onwards the address stands in a relation of rigid reference, for the duration of the discourse, to the object in question. This is the classical, let us say Fregean, case of reference. It is also possible, however, for a closed address to refer non-specifically. This typically occurs when V contains more than one object of the desired description. The relation of reference is then postponed till the moment where the predicates stored under the address in question suffice to select a unique individual, as in:

(17) There is a house in our village. It was built over 300 years ago by a retired admiral of the king's navy.

The little discourse (17) must, of course, be processed semantically in such a way that no inconsistency arises with, e.g.:

(18) There is a house in our village. It was built last year by a retired businessman.

said by the same speaker in the same discourse. Some philosophers have thought that an inconsistency will arise when (17) and (18) are treated as consisting each of two separate assertions both asserted to be true. (17) would then be of the structure "*A* and *B*", and (18) of the structure "*A* and *C*", where *B* and *C* are contraries, and thus inconsistent. Their proposal was that (17) and (18) should be considered to contain only one assertion, of the logical form "There is a house in our village which was built over 300 years ago by a retired admiral of the king's navy", and "There is a house in our village which was built last year by a retired businessman", respectively. Now, they say, there is no inconsistency left. We shall show in chapter 4 that this 'solution' is not tenable, and that any threat of contradiction is dispelled by the distinction between specific and non-specific reference.

The principle that new addresses are introduced by existentially quantified sentences is naïve and obviously false empirically if taken to imply that these sentences must always be explicitly uttered and be part of the overt discourse. It is a common observation that in actual discourses definite terms are very often used without any explicit previous existential introduction. In such cases we save the principle by stipulating that the existential sentence, and its increment, are supplied *post hoc*. Such *post hoc* or *backward suppletion* is automatic: if the definite term in question has no address to denote in D, then the address is created. This process is, however, constrained by a few factors. First, backward suppletion must be licensed by available knowledge (a condition not formalizable without a given and accessible store of knowledge available). Thus, if the discourse is about a room, and the next sentence is about its steering wheel, then, under normal conditions, backward suppletion is blocked since no knowledge is available about steering wheels of rooms. The blocking means that the discourse remains uninterpretable. Semantic interpretation is thus seen to be crucially dependent on 'pragmatic' factors of available knowledge. This conclusion is reinforced if we consider that the knowledge required need not be 'background' knowledge, but may as well be immediate knowledge derived from the context and situation of speech. Such knowledge typically provides the basis for backward suppletion of addresses for deictic definite terms.

Then, the discourse must not already contain the negation of the address to be supplied. We keep up the idealization that discourses must remain free of contradiction, on pain of being uninterpretable. (Since we are talking about psychological matters, and not, or not primarily, about logical matters, it may well be that some contradiction remains unnoticed during the discourse. Interpretation will then go on blissfully, until the contradiction is spotted.)

Backward suppletion is, of course, frequently employed as a stylistic device at the beginning of stories:

> (19) The room was empty, but for a dirty carpet, some torn curtains, and a big, open trunk.

Semantic interpretation of (19) requires the inference that, if (19) is true, there was a room. This inference is formalized in our theory by the postulation of an occurrence of *post hoc* suppletion. Notice that the expression *the room* in (19) is likely to refer non-specifically, since the normal inference is that if there is one room, there will be other rooms as well in the same V.

The postulation of *post hoc* suppletion of missing addresses has a number of theoretical advantages. First, it makes for a unified treatment of discourse processing and reference, since all definite terms can now be treated as denoting addresses available in D. But there are other advantages as well. Thus, an analogous procedure can now be invoked for missing facts, as in the often observed cases of factive verbs without preceding explicit statements of the facts in question. A notice may read, for example:

> (20) We regret that dogs are not allowed in the College.

The presupposed fact that dogs are not allowed can now be taken to be supplied *post hoc*, which is, of course, what actually happens during interpretation. And quite generally, the procedure of *post hoc* suppletion can be used to supply missing presuppositions in the discourse. It will become clear in chapter 3 how useful this procedure is, in particular for the interpretation of metaphors.

Behind these phenomena of backward suppletion there is a general, highly functional, principle dictating that, even if not all interpretability conditions are fulfilled, listeners must try every rule in the book to make sense of an utterance. There is a *presumption of good sense*, and backward suppletion is a standard means for putting good sense into utterances that would otherwise lack it. This principle is at work again in cases such as the following:

> (21) Yesterday, a Swiss banker was arrested at Heathrow Airport. The 53-year-old bachelor declared that he had come to Britain to kidnap the queen.

The first sentence establishes two addresses, one for the unfortunate Swiss banker, and one, *post hoc*, for Heathrow Airport. Semantic theory must now explain why and how the expression *the 53-year-old bachelor* denotes ('lands at') the address established for the banker, even though the lexical material does not match. Existing theories of semantics have not devoted much attention to this class of problems, problems of reference maintenance that is. The psychological literature has been better on this score (see, e.g., Marslen-Wilson, Levy and Tyler 1982; Garrod and Sanford 1982). It seems clear that the principle of presumption of good sense presses for an address for the description in question, in order that uninterpretability be avoided. But then it seems that there is also an *economy principle* at work, which ensures that no new address will be set up *post hoc* as long as one of the existing addresses will do. In this case, the banker address has strong cognitive backing to fit the description of the 53-year-old bachelor. Moreover, the noun phrase *the 53-year-old bachelor* stands in an ideal position to be an anaphor to the expression *a Swiss banker* in the previous sentence. A combination of these (and possibly other) factors is likely to be responsible for the indubitable fact that we understand the subject of the second sentence as being coreferential with that of the first. Precisely how background knowledge interacts with discourse domains so as to fill in gaps in the latter by recourse to default procedures and values, is a question which cannot be answered in this context. But this inability has no bearing on the theory: as long as no argument demonstrates the impossibility in principle of modelling the interaction between discourse domains and available knowledge, the theory can proceed and leave open the question of the auxiliary routines required.

The central idea is as follows. Taking, for ease of exposition, the listener's point of view, we say that when he listens to a coherent monologue of assertions he first analyses each new assertion in terms of its semantic representation, then maps the semantic representation on to the discourse domain D. The mapping function has been dubbed "*i*" (incrementation). The

procedure followed by *i* depends on the predicate of the clause to be incremented, starting from the highest clause. Ordinary extensional predicates
are the simplest. Their terms (which must be definite, since if they are not,
they are quantified and the quantifier is then the predicate) either find or set
up *post hoc* their discourse addresses, and the predicate is added, in the
appropriate form, to the addresses in question – as has been demonstrated in
examples (15) and (16). Intensional predicates taking definite terms only (not
embedded Ss) allow for the addresses denoted by the terms with respect to
which they are intensional to be located in intensional subdomains (as in:
Harry is looking for the unicorn). Intensional subdomains are created by
some predicates which take as one of their arguments not a definite term but
an embedded S (clausal structure), such as *believe*, or *possible*.

Some predicates are 'technical' in that they prescribe a specific structural
change in D or certain constraints regarding the incrementation of an
embedded clause. The 'technical' predicates include the quantifiers, the
logical operators, the tense operators.

Discourse domains may be associated with a verification domain V. If
they are, they have a truth-value with respect to V, and the addresses are all
connected with ('refer to') either individuals or classes of individuals in V, or
to values of functions computable over individuals or classes of individuals
in V.

Due to what appears to be the whims of history, the question of how a
discourse domain is associated with a verification domain (how speaker and
listener come to agree on the time and space parameters within which their
discourse is meant to apply) has received far less attention than the question
of how definite terms are associated with a reference object (the question of
reference). Yet the two questions are interdependent and of equal importance.
We will, in general, not be concerned with these questions, however. We will
take it for granted that discourse domains sometimes have a verification
domain associated with them and that addresses (and any definite term
denoting them) sometimes refer to reference objects in the verification
domain. Reference relations and truth-values are marginal to our enterprise
because, in the theory to be developed, the central factors responsible for the
ways in which we interpret utterances of sentences lie in the construction of
discourse domains, and not in their possible relations to the actual world.

Throughout, however, we must take care that our theory of discourse
domains predicts truth-values that are intuitively correct in cases where a
discourse domain is linked up with a verification domain. Correctness of
truth-values is thus a constraining factor for the theory. This is why the
distinction between specific and non-specific reference is crucial. We may
dismiss questions of origin of verification domain and origin of reference as
long as they can be considered as having straightforward and uniform
solutions. But when there is a danger of incorrect predictions on account of

certain apparent linguistic features, it is crucial to the theory that those aspects of truth-value assignment and reference object assignment that are at issue should be made explicit. This is why logic and the question of truth-values is so prominent in chapter 3, and why the question of specific and non-specific reference, dealt with in detail in chapter 6, is given so much space. It must be shown that Geach's (1969) argument against treating sentences like:

(22) Alex has a horse and it limps.

as being the type "A and B" is a sophism, and that all apparent problems are solved by a theory of discourse domains plus a distinction between specific and non-specific reference.

The minimal truth-value bearing elements in a discourse domain are the predicate assignments after closure under the addresses that have been set up, or the addresses before closure, or the constraints regarding future incrementations. These minimal truth-value bearing elements coincide with what we have termed *propositions*. (Note that the conjunction predicate *and*, which, as we shall see in section 3.3, has no other incremental consequence than that its dependent propositions are incremented, in the order in which they appear in the sentence, does not stand over one incrementation unit but over two separate such units (if *and* is used in a binary way), each incremented separately and in the order of occurrence.)

The theory of grammar and semantics developed in this book has one further conspicuous characteristic: for all propositions of natural languages the truth-definition is simple and uniform. A proposition $P^n(t_1, \ldots, t_n)$ is true just in case the n-tuple of term extensions $\langle \rho(t_1), \ldots, \rho(t_n) \rangle$ is a member of the extension set $\sigma(P^n)$ of the predicate P^n (where ρ designates the function assigning extensions to terms, and σ designates the function assigning extensions to predicates). The requirement of uniformity of truth-definition functions as a constraint upon semantic analyses and increment functions associated with predicates.

These matters, and others as well, will be discussed more fully in the following chapters. There it will also be shown that it is wise to reckon with three truth-values for natural language propositions as well as for discourse domains, and that the phenomenon of presupposition, often observed but never satisfactorily accounted for in semantic theory, is directly connected with the discourse-dependent character of truth-values for propositions.

1.3 Analogism and anomalism: questions of linguistic formalization

At this point some general historical and notional perspective may well be of use. The perspective to be developed is given by the various ways in which, in the course of history, the idea of a *formal description* of language has been implemented or rejected. The real fascination of science has always been the detection of a *formal system*, preferably a complete formal system, according to which events take place and structures are formed. (By "formal system" we mean a set of production rules for strings of symbols, and an interpretation under which the strings produced are all true. A formal system S is considered complete with respect to an interpretation I if all strings in the vocabulary of S that are true for the domain of I are in fact produced by the rules.) The search for such formal systems is beyond doubt one of the most outstanding features of our Western civilization. No wonder, therefore, that this civilization is characterized by an extremely powerful tradition of investigations into the nature and the properties of formal systems *per se*, the tradition, that is, of mathematics and logic. Step by step, through the ages, nature has had to yield one secret after another. More and more parts of nature have proved to be 'formal' in that they turned out to be predictable in terms of a mathematical or logical system. Whether the whole of nature must be considered, in principle, to be within the grasp of scientific formalization, or whether, perhaps, there will always and necessarily remain areas of randomness escaping formal treatment, is a philosophical question of some standing and of direct relevance to the perspective we are about to develop. Its relevance is mainly methodological: if one is to maximize the grasp (and the applications) of science, then it is essential to try and capture as much of reality as seems at all possible in terms of some formal system. This means that one should think more than twice before one gives up and declares this or that complex of phenomena out of bounds to science. Time and again it has turned out that where, prima facie, indeterminate chaos seemed to reign, there was after all perfect order. All that is needed is the key to the mystery. As long as this is not found it may be inevitable for the time being, and sensible for tactical reasons, to let the matter rest. But it is unwise to surrender unconditionally.

Human language is, of course, a prime target for attempts at formalization, since it is fairly obvious that linguistic behaviour is not entirely random. And, predictably, the question of how much system there is in language, and how much randomness, has dominated linguistic investigations ever since the days of Plato and Aristotle. This question, in fact, seems to have played a more prominent role in linguistics than in most other disciplines, due to what may be called the *formal elusiveness of language*, together with the extreme generality and flexibility of the notion of formal system. What is language? What is a language? Where is it to be found? If we consider a language, then what to do with the dialectal, sociolectal, interactional and idiolectal variations found within it? What is it anyway for a language to be internally variable? What do we want to predict when we try to formulate a formal linguistic system? Surely, it would be unrealistic to try to predict completely when any person is going to say what. Nor would it be very sensible to try to predict what any speaker of a language will say given some preconceived meaning or intention. For a long time it seemed unrealistic to attempt predictions regarding the dialectal, sociolectal or interactional variants a speaker would use in his speech. Labov and others, however, have shown that there is a high degree of statistical predictability if parameters of regional origin, socio-economic status, and kind of verbal interaction are taken into account and combined with long-term and short-term attitudinal parameters.[7] In general, language has proved of such tremendous complexity, tied up with so many sneaky parameters of infinitely varying meanings, contexts and situations, and cognitive backings – not to mention the parameters of regional origin, socio-economic status and category of interaction, as well as those of attitude and ambition, and heaven knows what else – that it took a relatively long while before the angles were found from which language proved empirically accessible and attempts at formalization were beginning to prove fruitful.

A notable example of successful formalization in linguistics is provided by historical phonology. It started around the middle of the nineteenth century as part of the monumental edifice of historical and comparative philology, and it has proved remarkably successful in predicting changes in word forms, within defined geographical and temporal boundaries, and given certain (unformalized) assumptions about identity of words within these boundaries. Theories of changes in word meanings, on the other hand, have been, by and large, unsuccessful: historical word semantics has remained stuck in somewhat untidy taxonomies (Stern 1932). Yet, although historical phonology is as alive now as a hundred years ago, and the web of predictions is forever closing in on the facts, one cannot escape from the feeling that it is somehow marginal to what we conceive as the central reality of language.

Much more central is the area of grammar and meaning. Here we see a variety of attempts at formalization, often from very different angles and perspectives. It is interesting to note that the crucial developments in this respect date either from the very beginning of linguistic studies, i.e. the first few centuries after Plato and Aristotle, or from the last 50 or so years. Due to consistent failure of the initial attempts, it became accepted practice, round the first century AD, to be content with less than full formalization. If the original urge flared up again, as in the late Middle Ages, it soon died down for lack of empirical grip and formal apparatus. Only quite recently, with the combined development of structural linguistics (Bloomfield 1933; Harris 1951) and a vastly expanded theory of formal systems and calculi, did the old idea of formalization of language begin to look more realistic. In fact, considerable successes were booked and linguistics found its place among the

---

[7] See, e.g., Labov 1966, 1972; DeCamp 1971. For a critical discussion and a proposed model for the description of internal variability, see Seuren 1982.

empirical formal sciences. Linguistic studies in the preceding centuries were characterized by tentative and to a large extent implicit statements of regularities, speculative hints or even systems aiming at statements of correspondence between logical or metaphysical analyses on the one hand and linguistic categories and structures on the other. Linguistics, in short, used to be more philosophy than science. The transition came in the twentieth century.

At the very beginning, however, optimism was still rife, at least among the adherents of one school of thought, who were followers of Aristotle. They envisaged a formalization where sentences generated by rule are interpreted on the Aristotelian system of logic and of epistemic categories, together with meaning descriptions of lexical items. The interpretation thus consisted in statements about the logical and categorial (in the Aristotelian sense) properties of sentences, with the lexical variables filled in by lexically interpreted words. For the purpose of this discussion it is the use made of (Aristotelian) logic that interests us most.

Needless to say, the attempt failed, by and large. The programme was far too ambitious for those days. But the attempt was extremely interesting for a variety of reasons. One of these is particularly relevant here: we see that an existing prestigious formal system, Aristotelian logic, is used as a core element in the interpretation of a formal system of grammar. We now know that there are forceful reasons for establishing close links between logical and semantic analyses, but in those days this must have been a step of almost irresponsible daring, given the lack of prima-facie evidence supporting the idea.

The objections, which were immediately obvious, were countered by a defence strategy: language, they said, may not be quite the way we wish it to be, but it really *should* be that way. And, they said, it once really was that way, when mythical ancient mankind first settled, by sensible convention, on what language to use. This primordial language was perfect and pure (and would, of course, fit the Arisotelian interpretation). However, through ages of neglect and moral decline, due to the wickedness of the human race, language degenerated into what it is nowadays – but a faint reflection of the ideal language. The main idea was that language was, in principle, regular and formalizable in terms of an Aristotelian interpretation, given in advance. To the extent that language proved not to fit the theory, an escape route was indicated via the degeneration theory of the human race. The defenders of this programme called themselves *analogists*, after the Greek word *analogía* ("regularity").

The Aristotelian optimists were soon challenged by more Platonistically orientated philosophers of language, in particular the Stoics, who proclaimed the impossibility of the analogist programme. They rejected the analogists' escape route. For them, language was not the result of some mythical ancient convention but a product of nature. And like the rest of nature, it has its own laws or lack of laws. Whatever laws there are must be detected by careful scrutiny. Where there is randomness or, worse, chaos, laws will prove impossible to find. Clearly, the entire approach of the analogists seemed to them illegitimate in that it involved the imposition of a ready-made a-priori system upon the whimsical facts of language while refractory facts had to be ignored or reasoned away. These philosophers of language called themselves *anomalists*, after the Greek word *anōmalía* ("irregularity").

It would take us too far afield to go into all the historical details of the analogy–anomaly dispute. The interested reader is referred to the standard works on the issue,[8] although it must be noted that in present-day scholarship, as well as in the original texts, there is not always perfect clarity about the issues involved. The dispute in question was part of a complex network of philosophical and linguistic issues that were moot in those centuries, and many of the authors whose texts are extant today represent positions which are built up of elements of both schools of thought. It is thus largely a question of careful study and reconstruction to find out what the issues were and in what terms they were discussed. (A typical case in point is the Latin grammarian Varro (first century BC) whose writings on logic and language are one of the most powerful sources of insight into and knowledge of ancient philosophy of language, but whose theoretical position is evaluated quite differently by various modern authors.[9]) Our purpose here is simply to consider the ancient dispute from the point of view of formalization of linguistic phenomena, expecting thereby to shed some light not only on the ancient controversy as such but also on certain aspects in contemporary approaches to language and meaning. It seems to me that much of the interest of the controversy lies in the question of formalization of linguistic phenomena and the attitudes that tend to appear, in antiquity as well as in our days, when linguistic phenomena are to be captured in a formal system. It should be noted, in this context, that virtually all modern general introductory textbooks of linguistics or of the history of linguistics, in so far as they mention the ancient analogy–anomaly controversy, represent the issue as a somewhat strange and in any case fruitless episode in a very alien culture.[10] Yet, in the light of contemporary developments in the study of language, the ancient controversy appears highly relevant. In fact, what we witness today is in many respects a repetition of the ancient events, albeit that our formal instruments are considerably better than those which were available then.

[8] See, e.g., *The Oxford Classical Dictionary*, under 'Analogy', 'Etymology'; Norden 1898, 184 ff.; Steinthal 1890/1961, I. 357 ff.; II. 127 ff.; Barwick 1957.

[9] Steinthal 1890/1961, I. 358, e.g., classifies him as an analogist. But Barwick (1957, 34, 39) considers him essentially a Stoic anomalist.

[10] See, e.g., Bloomfield 1933, 4, which is wrong about the historical facts; Robins 1967, 18 ff.; Lyons 1968, 10–14; Hovdhaugen 1982, 82–3. A clear exception is Steinthal (see note 8), whose exposé is particularly insightful when viewed against the background of nineteenth-century scholarship and linguistics.

Thus we see the powerful school of the Stoics combine an ordinary language approach ("communis consuetudo") with a profound analysis of the nature of linguistic signs (a 'semiotics') and important work in logic. Their theory of the natural origin of language kept them from forcing language into a straightjacket of some preconceived theory. As Steinthal says (1890/1961, I. 359-60): "The Stoics investigated the relation, the parallelism, between linguistic expressions and thought with great care and much acumen, and they concluded finally that language is not built analogously with thought, but in some 'anomalous' way: the principle of language is not *analogy* but *anomaly*." Language is 'natural' in much the same way as human beings are: they combine reason (*ratio*, logic) with habit (*consuetudo*), which need not be logical.[11]

The position held by their opponents, the analogists, was probably less interesting as regards the general questions of the nature of language. But they had the advantage of great formal rigour and systematicity. Where the anomalists often had brilliant ideas, the analogists would take them up and elaborate them systematically. Yet they had a strong tendency, in their formal zeal, to deny obvious linguistic facts or to condemn them as improper. They leaned heavily on the great writers of the past, in particular on Homer, who they claimed were closer to the ideal language of primordial mankind, and whose language was seen as a measure of regularity.

As appears clearly from the work of Varro, a compromise was needed, together with the admission that there is no complete isomorphism between either language and logic, or between language and thought, or language and the world. Such a compromise being beyond their formal grasp, grammarians and philosophers of language fell back, by some form of common consent, on a less ambitious programme involving mainly morphological taxonomies. It became accepted practice to admit that morphological elements simply do not reflect absolute semantic regularities. Past tense suffixes are regularly used to express irreality, besides temporal past. Genitives are notorious for their multiplicity of meanings. An accusative may express in some constructions what is expressed through a preposition in others. Thus the foundations were laid for what is now known as the lore of traditional grammar.

From now on linguistic studies were characterized by the acceptance of less rigorous standards of formal description than the more successful sciences. The ideal of precision was henceforth pursued on a level of taxonomic stock-taking, rather than formal and explanatory description. A great deal of room was thus left for 'philosophy of language', next to straightforward grammatical taxonomy, as is borne out by medieval developments

---

[11] Cp. Steinthal 1890/1961, II.136. The point is relevant also to the question of surface semantics versus SA-semantics, discussed in chapter 2. The Stoics were clearly on the side of SA-semantics.

in this respect, where Speculative Grammar flourished alongside the study of actual grammatical details.

Meanwhile, the old anomalists had scored one important point. It became universally accepted that if there is any hope of understanding how language expresses thought, then each sentence must have associated with it some abstract 'underlying' form. Since surface structures are 'anomalous', there must be an 'analogous' form for each sentence which can *explain* our ways of understanding. (The idea of an abstract underlying form for sentences originated in the general philosophy of nature developed by Heraclitus of Miletus, and reached the Stoa through the writings of Plato.) The problem was, however, that although the notion of an abstract underlying meaning representation is perfectly coherent, rules must be formulated to link up the abstract and the overt structures. And such rules were yet far beyond the technical grasp of the investigators involved. The actual notion of such rules was well known: Varro and other authors speak repeatedly of the processes of *adiectio, detractio, immutatio, transmutatio*,[12] i.e. the basic transformational operations. But they clearly lacked the means and powers required for setting up rule systems in terms of these basic operations. The study of abstract sentence representations thus remained confined to philosophy and did not, or hardly, effect 'scientific' grammar.

This situation did not change until the twentieth century. After a period of intensive theoretical developments, both in Europe and America, a breakthrough occurred around the middle of the century, as mathematics and logic were achieving results as never before in the history of mankind and the theory of formal systems, in particular, was being vastly expanded and implemented in computing machinery. The breakthrough occurred on various fronts. Some of the new ideas of mathematics and formal systems were applied to and introduced into the existing discipline of structural linguistics. This happened in particular, and with striking success, in the school of Z. S. Harris, a student of Bloomfield's, in Philadelphia. (Similar attempts were undertaken by L. Hjelmslev in Denmark, but they were clearly less successful.) The results of this grafting process became known as *transformational grammar*, the general idea of which is as follows.

Let the production rules of the formal system generate strings of symbols whose interpretation is given by the set of sentences of a given natural language.[13] That is, the production rules ('grammar') define the set of all and only the well-formed sentences of the language L. Each generated string is a theorem whose interpretation is given by its correspondence, in certain well-defined ways, with a sentence of L. The system is meant to be complete in the sense that *every* well-formed sentence of L must be captured by a

[12] See, e.g., Barwick 1957, 31.
[13] Cp. Harris 1951, 369–72.

theorem of the system. There is no distinction, in this approach, between well-formed formulas and theorems of the system: all well-formed formulas are theorems.

A limited number of area surveys (problem analyses) soon showed, in the early 1950s, that it would be a good idea to let the production rules operate in two stages, so that a distinction is made between *strict production rules* and *transformations*. By 1960 it was clear that the highest yield could be had by restricting the former to a type known as 'context-free phrase structure rules' (CFPS rules) and interpreting their output as a hypothetical construct called *deep structures*, and by letting the transformations convert these into surface structures, which were interpreted as uniquely specifying sentences of the natural language L. By 1970 it was clear that the current notion of transformation was not sufficiently restricted for generative transformational descriptions to have a minimum of arbitrariness and be maximally motivated. A frantic rush then developed, in certain quarters, for restrictions on transformations, while other linguists preferred to let this issue rest for the moment while they widened their perspective and looked for broader dimensions.

Yet even without a satisfactory theory of restrictions on transformations the two-tiered approach of transformational grammar as it was practised in the 1960s proved highly successful compared with earlier attempts at formalized grammatical description. Many syntactic constructions of, in particular (but not exclusively), English were described in depth (e.g., Klima's analysis of negation in English, 1964). It was a common experience, in those days, to find predictions confirmed by unexpected new observations. There was, generally, an enormous increase in the quantity and quality of syntactic observations. In short, this period in the study of grammar bore the hallmark of power and success.

A notable feature, however, of this early approach was that 'meaning' remained totally outside the formal treatment. This was, in fact, a result of preceding decades of behaviourism in psychology and linguistics, which gave rise to the idea that it was somehow unscientific to operate with mental concepts, in particular 'meaning'. (Both Bloomfield and Harris were staunch behaviourists.) However, as behaviourism waned, it became again socially acceptable to speak of meaning in an academic context, and soon a book was published (Katz and Postal 1964) advocating the integration of meaning in the formal theory of grammar.

They proposed that the formal rule system of transformational grammar should be extended with a third kind of rule, *projection rules* (P-rules), transforming deep structures into so-called 'semantic representations' (SRs). The grammar would thus have a dual output, a set of surface structures (SSs), and a set of semantic representations. More precisely, to each deep structure (DS) there would correspond an SS and an SR, as a result of the rules. An SS, as before, would be interpreted as the surface form of one particular sentence S of L, and the corresponding SR as something that would have to correspond to the meaning of S. It must be said that the notions of projection rule and of SR remained more than a little hazy in this work, so that it can hardly be claimed that the semantic study of language was much furthered. Its main force, however, lay in the constraint it imposed on the transformations or T-rules: if this system was to work at all, the meaning of each sentence S should be readable from its DS as well as from its SS, and the T-rules should not have any semantic effect – they should be *meaning-invariant*. This constraint was not formal but purely intuitive since the reading of meanings from DSs or SSs was as intuitive after 1964 as it had been before. Yet it was operational enough to be used, and it triggered off a dramatic move towards a more and more abstract notion of what a DS should actually look like. The pre-1964 DSs had looked pretty 'surfacy', but now it became clear that they had to be a great deal more remote and abstract than that.

One simple and well-known example may illustrate this. In early forms of transformational grammar it had been current practice to define passive sentences as transforms of active underlying deep structures. The transformation PASSIVE turned the object (more precisely: the first noun phrase after the verb) of the active DS into the subject of the passive SS, and the original subject into an optional *by*-phrase. The verb was augmented with the auxiliary *be* followed by the past participle of the original active verb:

(23) $_{DS}$[the farmer killed the duckling] ⇒ $_{SS}$[the duckling was killed by the farmer]

If, however, the transformation PASSIVE is to be meaning-invariant, this will not do. There are many cases where a passive formed according to the above procedure shows considerable semantic differences from the active representative of the DS in question. These cases include sentences where the subject is said to move some part of his body:

(24) He shook his head ≠ His head was shaken by him.

Verbs of perception or emotion often induce changes of meaning:

(25) I heard something ≠ Something was heard by me.
(26) She loves opera ≠ Opera is loved by her.

And many more problems could be mentioned. (In fact, many serious linguists hold today that PASSIVE is not a syntactic transformation at all but that passive sentences have a passive DS; whatever regularity there is in the relation between active and passive sentences should be accounted for in a theory of the lexicon.) One particular class of cases, however, showed that DSs had to be a great deal more 'abstract' (i.e. closer to representations in terms of predicate calculus), no matter whether one adopts a transformational rule PASSIVE or a lexical account of passive sentences. These cases are to do with the scope of logical operators such as quantifiers or negation. Take the example:

(27) Nobody here knows two languages.

According to the 'old' theory, its passive should be:

(28) Two languages are known by nobody here.

Yet it is intuitively clear that (27) and (28) differ semantically. (27) can only mean that none of those present is bilingual, whereas (28) has a preferred reading "there are two languages which nobody here knows", and a less preferred reading which is equal to that of (27).

It seemed that this difference might be accounted for by casting DSs in a form which is highly reminiscent of predicate calculus. We thus distinguish between:

(29) $\neg \exists x$: person present $\exists 2y$: languages [x knows y]
(30) $\exists 2y$: languages $\neg \exists x$: person present [x knows y]

The bracketed part may be called the 'nucleus',[14] and whatever is involved in PASSIVE must be limited to the nucleus. Then, if something like (29) or (30) is taken to be a DS, restrictions must be formulated for T-rules to the effect that (30) cannot be transformed into (27) but both (29) and (30) can be transformed into (28).[15]

After 1965 quite a few linguists discovered that if T-rules are to be meaning-invariant DSs will have to look more and more like predicate calculus structures (just as, towards the end of Orwell's *Animal Farm*, the pigs begin to look more and more like humans). Although this dazzled some, especially at the beginning,[16] two facts stood out quite clearly. First, the 1964-SRs and the P-rules envisaged by Katz and Postal were superfluous provided the T-rules are kept meaning-invariant: whatever can be demanded of a SR can be achieved by a DS; hence, separate SRs (and P-rules) can be dispensed with. And, secondly, the operational constraint of semantic invariance of the T-rules was highly advantageous in that it seemed to improve quite notably the quality of syntactic descriptions and analyses (in so far as they were not affected by the luxurious negligence which, unfortunately, spoiled some work in this area, as we shall see in a moment). The Katz–Postal theory of 1964 thus proved to be more a contribution to the theory of syntax than to the theory of meaning.

---

[14] See Seuren 1969.

[15] What such restrictions would have to come to will be discussed in chapter 2.

[16] Cp. Ross's famous anecdote about the "turtles all the way down" in the *Fragestellung* of his masterpiece (1967).

The method of transformational syntactic analysis under the constraint of meaning invariance of the T-rules became known as *generative semantics* (GS), or *semantic syntax*, and was highly popular between, roughly, 1967 and 1975. It then went into a sudden decline, due to a variety of factors. First, the whole field of transformational grammar laboured under the lack of plausible constraints for DS-hypotheses and T-rules. In GS this led to the publication of a number of irresponsible descriptive proposals involving all too baroque DSs and wild transformational treatments which discredited GS as a whole (cp. Newmeyer 1980; but see also McCawley's reply, 1980). Meanwhile, its critics behaved analogously: they proposed a series of wild 'universal' constraints, thus behaving irresponsibly on that score. A general confusion arose, and sociological, rather than academic, processes took over, reducing GS, for the time being at least, to relative obscurity. It is important to note, however, that the GS tradition has produced some of the most successful syntactic analyses ever carried out, a feat never accomplished by its critics.

The eclipse of GS in the early and mid-seventies is a curious phenomenon. Normally speaking, one would say, aberrations or irresponsible theorizing within a paradigm should be pointed out for what they are and accordingly criticized. But the mere fact that such work is produced cannot be an indictment of the paradigm itself unless it is shown that there is nothing of worth to be found within it. But this, very clearly, was not the case with GS. On the contrary, some of the work done within this paradigm was extremely inspiring and of very high quality. For example, the ideas developed on Quantifier Lowering, on prelexical analysis (with the highly motivated rule of Predicate Raising), on deletion phenomena, and quite a few other grammatical processes, have never been refuted or shown to be fruitless. On the contrary, it happens regularly that ideas and rule systems that were born in the GS camp are taken over by its critics lock, stock and barrel, and incorporated into a different paradigm under different names, invariably without attribution. (An example which attracted some attention for this reason is May 1977.)

What happened, however, was that the whole paradigm was rejected (to use the mildest possible expression) under the influence of a handful of vociferous rivals. A ban ensued on quoting GS literature, no matter how relevant it might have been. Criticisms were left unanswered. In short, anything to do with GS was declared untouchable. In other words, defamation campaigns took the place of serious argument. It must be observed, as a matter of historical detail (painful though it is) that personality clashes and deep-seated personal grudges, as well as professional envy, played an important part in this unhappy and undesirable development.

An often used so-called argument in this quasi-debate was that GS was 'unconstrained': the transformational formalism was not seen to be subject to a universal charter of formal possibilities. In a way, this was true (with the consequence that, in fact, certain wild analyses were presented). But it was equally true of whatever other theory or paradigm was proposed. Those (concentrated at MIT) who went in for a frantic rush for universal constraints were themselves hardly constrained by any consideration for the facts of language. And, moreover, why should one not try to learn from really successful descriptions and see what formal properties they have in common, so that an inductive process of finding and formulating the constraints required can be made to come about? No such attempt was made, however. GS was simply declared anathema.

Another 'criticism' often heard (see, e.g., Newmeyer 1980: 167–8) was that GS was overconcerned with facts of language and underconcerned with theory. The latter, of course, is a caricature of GS. But the former simply demonstrates the lack of concern for facts which characterized the critics of GS. "Idealization" was the catchword: not all facts are relevant, only some are; one must "idealize". Well, of course one must idealize, but idealization cannot be an excuse for simply disregarding facts that are as significant as other facts, idealized or not, which are taken into account. In reality, the typical GS-attitude towards facts is a great deal less complexed than what one finds with its critics (cp. Lightfoot's pronouncements quoted in the prologue). And, anyway, as long as no reasoned account is presented of what a-priori knowledge (or otherwise privileged insight) justifies the selection of constraints or of facts that should play a role in linguistic theorizing, no one can claim the prerogative of dictating where the lines are to be drawn.

Another, more pertinent, factor contributing to an impasse in GS-work consisted in the fact that it lacked any real semantics. The most it had been able to achieve, in its more sober manifestations, was a formal theory specifying SRs (i.e. the erstwhile DSs), and their transformations into well-formed surface structures of sentences. This, in effect, should not be underestimated, for is this not precisely what the ancient grammarians and philosophers of language had sought and failed to achieve? Yet, the question of meaning was still unsolved: no explicit account was available to generative semantics of what it is for a sentence S to mean M. M could be cast in terms of some SR of S, but that SR still had to be 'read' and understood intuitively. GS was caught in a *circle of synonymy* between surface structures and their semantic representations. We now say, simply, that GS lacked a proper semantics.

A fascinating circumstance with all this was that the SRs found to be most workable bore a striking resemblance to the formulas of well-known classical predicate and propositional calculus. Yet there was no more than a resemblance. There was not complete identity. For one thing, there seem to be categories in language that do not play a role in classical logic. But, perhaps more importantly, there seem to be differences in meaning between the elements that carry and define logical structure in classical predicate and propositional calculus. In particular, the interpretations for the classical truth-functional operators (*not, and, or, if... then*) classically adopted in logic differ considerably from those given to them naturally by native speakers of a language. This point is well known, and will be discussed and illustrated repeatedly in later chapters – whereby it will become clear that the differences are both more profound and more systematic than is customarily assumed.

What was to be done? Should a new language of predicate and propositional calculus be invented for linguistic meanings, or could perhaps the old *language* be kept and would a modified *interpretation* suffice for the purpose? The point, however, was not so much that the answers to these questions were unknown. The point was, rather, that these questions were beyond the powers of those who were engaged in GS-work and GS-foundations in the early seventies. Their knowledge of logic and model-theory was at best elementary, and it was insufficient for the questions at hand.

Here they lost out on *formal semantics*, the powerful movement started by Richard Montague after 1965. The roots of this movement are entirely in mathematics and logic: formal semantics is a direct continuation of the lines set by Frege, Russell, Tarski, Carnap, Kripke and others. Model-theoretic systems had been developed generating not only logically well-defined strings but also truth-values for any given well-formed string paired with some pre-defined model. The pairing consists in assigning extensions to the constants (predicates, proper names) in the strings of the logical language. Strictly speaking we have, in saying this, mixed up the formal system and its interpretation. The interpretation consists in regarding the formulae of the logical language as the (assertive) sentences of some natural language L, the models as possible states of affairs ('possible worlds', according to most), and the binary output of the truth-function from formulae and models as truth-values. This theory provided, for the first time in the long and distinguished history of logic, a formal method for defining what had hitherto been the intuitive 'reading' of logical formulae (or the associated sentences). It was Montague who conceived the idea that model-theoretic semantic treatments as had been developed in logic since Tarski should be applied to natural language sentences. In Montague's view natural languages are logically well defined, the logical definition being provided by assigning a structure to the sentences of L and letting a calculus operate on these structures, yielding a truth-value for each sentence given a model.

From a linguistic point of view, Montague's analyses were woefully inadequate. But they contained the first formal semantics ever to be proposed for natural language, and for that reason his work attracted considerable attention. At this point it is interesting to note the parallel with the analogism–anomalism contrast in antiquity. Here again, the facts of language were forced into a mould which was not their own, and again the fit was bad.

It was bad in essentially two ways. First, the resulting truth-values often fail to correspond to strong natural intuitions (and these are the ultimate empirical base of it all). For example, a sentence like *All the king's men are valiant* comes out as true when there is no king and thus no king's men; but naïve native speakers definitely feel otherwise. Or a sentence like *Nobody here speaks two languages* is considered true (in one reading) in cases where there are a number of bilingual people, but there happen to be two languages unknown to all. Native speakers feel that this reading does not exist. Secondly, the analyses are often *ad hoc* and run counter to statable linguistic regularities, or they generalize where regularities fail to be found. (Such cases are less simple to demonstrate in this rapid survey, since a demonstration would involve making out cases for or against certain grammatical generalizations, and that cannot be done here.) Some of these problems could be screened off by stipulating that only a 'fragment' of the language was being described. But it remained unclear how descriptions offered for such 'fragments' could be extrapolated to encompass the whole language. Another escape was found in an appeal to presumed principles and phenomena of actual human interaction, a non-formal variety of pragmatics.

The linguists protested, like latter-day anomalists, but their protest was feeble in that they had no alternative to offer. Some linguists and formal semanticists came together, aiming at the achievement of empirically improved results by introducing modifications into the original system. And this process is at present in full swing: a constant battle between facts and formalisms on essentially Montagovian principles.

The view taken in this book is that the blends that are being manufactured these days are still far too analogistic. They are all based on a number of apparently unshakeable premises. One is that definite noun phrases, with the exception of proper names, are to be treated as quantified phrases, whereas such an analysis is neither logically necessary nor descriptively useful. It is backed up by a tradition originating in Russell (1905), and by the consideration that it maximizes the uses made of familiar predicate calculus and minimizes the nasty problem of reference. But these are considerations of convenience which will hardly convince those who look for what must be considered the closest approximation possible (given available means and knowledge) to the system really at work in language. Another such premiss is that a constituent analysis of surface structures of sentences of some natural language (possibly combined with a specification of the order in which the rules generating the structures are applied) suffices to provide the formal material required for a calculus of truth-values given some model. This premiss is known as the *compositionality thesis for surface structures*.

It is argued in this book that a much more radical departure from established formal semantics is needed for an adequate formal semantics of natural language. The inadequacies of model-theoretic formal semantics are too general and too profound for the modifications proposed in recent literature to be workable. There are so many untenable but firmly held premises that a radical change in perspective is called for, and not a series of refinements and corrections of the existing theory.

The compositionality thesis, in particular, is denied here. Surface structures must be *transformed* into structures that are essentially of a predicate calculus type and are logically well defined. Surface structures are thus considered 'logically well defined' only in combination with a grammar, i.e. a set of transformational rules relating them to semantic representations. The T-rules result in thorough changes in constituent structure between SRs and surface structures. A constituent-by-constituent truth-function for surface structures is considered intrinsically impossible, and we thus revive the short-lived tradition of generative semantics discussed a few pages earlier. Chapter 2 contains an exposé of the main reasons for this position.

Furthermore, as will be argued in chapter 3, definite noun phrases are better not considered quantified but should be treated on a par with proper names. That is, less use is to be made of predicate calculus and a greater role is to be reserved for reference or, if you like, the assignment of extensions to terms of the language. Moreover, the predicate calculus language of the SRs is non-classical in that it contains two truth-functionally distinct negations and three truth-values, thus taking account of presuppositional phenomena. Then, the idea of a calculus directly yielding truth-values for sentential structures given some model is given up. It is replaced by an indirect procedure whereby sentential (semantic) structures are first mapped onto a cognitive structure (discourse domain), and only then considered for truth or (minimal or radical) falsity. Possible worlds no longer play any role at all in this theory. Their *raison d'être* was the account they provided of intensional phenomena. This role is now taken over by discourse domains, with their subdomains, so that all we need now is the real world to define extensions of definite terms and predicates.

There is thus a world of difference between the method and underlying philosophy of standard formal semantics, and those of the present theory. For us, natural language is a product of nature, an object of wonder, a "storehouse of unimaginable complexities and surprises, to be discerned by looking very closely" (Travis 1981: 1). It is not a product of ingenuity, "something we could have cooked up ourselves ... had this not, in effect, already been done (perhaps none too well)" (ibid.).

This does not mean that we expect language not to be describable in terms of a formal system. On the contrary, we advocate and insist on formal rigour in grammatical and semantic theories. But we wish to capture, if possible, the whole of language from these points of view, and not just those parts that happen to fit, more or less, some preconceived analytical apparatus, relegating refractory phenomena to marginal disciplines where standards of rigour need not be imposed with equal force.

There is, unfortunately, a persistent belief among mathematicians and practitioners of disciplines that rely heavily on mathematics that the only real formal rigour in this world is to be found in this cluster of sciences. As regards the other, especially the human, sciences there is a prevailing (but usually implicit) feeling that formal rigour is not, or only partially, attainable. Yet there is no ground for such a feeling or idea. We may regard the structures and processes studied in the human sciences as implementations of higher-level autonomous 'programmes', reducible in matter, but not in their formal organization, to cells, molecules, atoms, etc. In this perspective there is no reason at all to assume that as the level of operation gets 'higher', the degree of rigorousness goes down. Such an idea is entirely without foundation. It amounts to the view that formal systems do not allow for interpretations in terms of elements whose definition is not provided by the natural sciences but by sciences studying higher order causalities. In fact, to say that an array of facts is 'indeterminate' to some extent, is to say that to that extent it escapes causality. There is no ground for postulating a correlation between indeterminacy and 'high' level of operation. Such ideas are truly pernicious: they give rise to an a-priori defeatism in any search for systematicity and they create facile escape routes if by any chance some system is found not to do its job properly.

Our methodological position in this regard is as follows. We assume, as a general principle, that the whole of natural language, with all its manifold different aspects and ramifications, is describable and explainable in terms of a set of interconnected formal systems. At the same time we accept as a fact of life that language and language use are so intimately linked up with myriads of contingencies, mainly of a social and a historical nature, that it is entirely unrealistic to expect completeness of formal descriptions in all the different aspects of linguistic reality. In some areas, such as syntax, morphology, phonology and discourse semantics, we may hope to be more successful than in others. But in, for example, lexical semantics we should a-priori expect little more than partial formalizations enabling us to make *retrodictions* rather than *predictions*.

We say that a theory is retrodictive when it is not or only partially able to make predictions but, instead, can state systematically which principles are or have been at work once a phenomenon has been observed. Retrodictive theories are explanatory, only less so than predictive theories. In general, science is thrown back on retrodiction when the phenomena under scrutiny are subject to multiply variable factors whose full registration is impracticable due to physical limitations. Typical examples of retrodictive sciences are medicine, meteorology and lexicology. Meteorology, of course, tries very hard to be predictive, but its success in this regard must be judged to be moderate. In medicine one often finds that the occurrence of a disease in a patient cannot be predicted but, once it has manifested itself, can be attributed with certainty to known pre-existing factors.

In lexicology the situation is not much different. It is a well-known fact (though formal semanticists have not been very enthusiastic about accounting for it theoretically) that lexical items allow for systematically varying uses. Polysemy, metonymy and metaphor are widely known but theoretically opaque phenomena. Sometimes, as has been observed in traditional grammar and traditional lexicology, the variation in use corresponds with a distinction known from the grammar of the language. Thus, a lexical verb is often used transitively and intransitively (*look, taste*). Adjectives are often both active-intransitive and causative, like English *sad*, which is conventionalized for active-intransitive use, as in *a sad man*, as well as for causative use, as in *a sad story*. Usually, however, there is no predicting which items will show these distinctions and which will not. *Nervous*, for example cannot be used causatively: **a nervous story* cannot mean "a story which makes one nervous". Or the verb *hear* cannot, in modern English, occur intransitively. The use of *hear well/ill* in the sense of "have a good/bad reputation" is now obsolete. Moreover, lexical items, verbs in particular, act as triggers for certain rules of grammar, especially rules to do with complementation. In most of these and similar cases, the best we can realistically hope for is retrodiction, in the sense that we can point at certain known and recurrent regularities in the lexicon without being able to specify 'beforehand' which individual items will have which specific properties. But when an item is seen to have certain properties, we wish to be able to fit these properties into a universal system of possible options.

Lexicology is, of course, not the only area in linguistics where it is wise to be content, for the time being, with retrodiction. The study of linguistic diversity is another such area. It is unrealistic to hope for complete and precise predictions with regard to the ways in which languages differ and the ways in which dialectal, sociolectal and interactional varieties within one linguistic community manifest themselves. Here again, we are best advised to be content with theories that take stock of the options that exist, of the ways in which languages and language varieties *may* differ, without expecting to be able to predict which options will be realized.

What counts here is that to be resigned to a retrodictive theory is entirely different from assuming that the facts under scrutiny escape formalization because of some inherent 'indeterminacy' or vagueness. If we are ready to accept restrictions on the scope of formalized scientific theories, it is because we realize that our powers of scientific insight are severely limited, and not because we are prepared to make an attempt at formalization only to the extent that some mathematical framework happens to be available.

1.4 Psychological reality[17]

Another general point of methodology, related to the notion of an interpreted formal system, is the question of psychological reality. Given our explicit concern with the problem of actual interpretation of uttered sentences (whether in production or in comprehension), there is no escape from the question of the psychological reality of the theory proposed. Nor is there any wish to escape from this question, since there is greater explanatory power to a theory that claims to approximate real structures and processes underlying the phenomena than to an identical theory not making such a claim. The difference consists, one might say, in assigning an interpretation not only to the theorems (or, more generally, the output strings) of the formal system, but also to the calculus itself. When the calculus is left deliberately un-interpreted we have an instrumentalist theory, otherwise a realist theory. Since it is possible to assign an interpretation to parts or to certain aspects of the calculus only, there are degrees of realism ranging from almost null to full realism.

The issue is of particular relevance since there is a distinct tendency in formal semantics to disclaim any psychological reality of the calculi proposed. When the question is posed, one often finds that an instrumentalist answer is given: no reality is claimed. Sometimes, however, there is a willingness to 'admit' that mental reality is involved, but there it stops: there is a steadfast refusal to go beyond the statement that the formal calculus does anything other than *characterize the powers of the organism* in certain respects. It is not supposed to say anything about the actual works of the organism, which remains a black box. This position often goes by the name of *epiphenomenal* interpretation, since it intends a description of a set of output properties of the system, not of the system itself. It is also a *minimal realist* position, which may be the best we can achieve in certain cases. But it is unsatisfactory as a principled basis for interpretations of theories, since there is no principled reason why a formal theory or calculus should only *characterize an output* and not be an approximation of the apparatus or organism causally generating the output. If the theory or calculus makes precise and complete predictions about the output of the organism, it generates the output, in a technical sense of "generate", and it thus simulates the organism, which also generates its output, albeit in a physical and causal sense. This being so, it is hard to deny that a calculus which is 'plausibly' interpreted in terms of the actual apparatus carries a great deal more interest, in a general intellectual sense, than a calculus whose interpretation is purely

[17] In writing this section I have had the benefit of discussions with Tony Sanford and Simon Garrod, of Glasgow University.

instrumentalist or at most epiphenomenal. For instrumentalist or minimally realist theories (or interpretations) provide no causal explanations for the phenomena under analysis. Causality is typically imputed by imposing a non-minimal interpretation on a calculus, an interpretation in terms of the actual mechanism. And causality seems to be the cornerstone of explanation.

A wayward view on this matter is voiced in Fodor (1983: 45-6):

> Now about language: Just as patterns of visual energy arriving at the retina are correlated, in a complicated but regular way, with certain properties of distal layouts, so too are the patterns of auditory energy that excite the tympanic membrane in speech exchanges. With, of course, this vital difference: What underwrites the correlation between visual stimulations and distal layouts are (roughly) the laws of light reflectance. Whereas, what underwrites the correlation between token-utterances and distal layouts is (roughly) a convention of truth-telling. In the root case, the convention is that we say of x that it is F only if x is F. Because that convention holds, it is possible to infer from what one hears said to the way that the world is.
>
> Of course, in neither the linguistic nor the perceptual case is the information so provided infallible. The world often isn't the way it looks to be or the way that people say it is. But, equally of course, input systems don't have to deliver apodictic truths in order to deliver quite useful information. And, anyhow, *the operation of the input systems should not be identified with the fixation of belief*. What we *believe* depends on the evaluation of how things look, or are said to be, *in light of background information* about (inter alia) how good the seeing is or how trustworthy the source. Fixation of belief is *just* the sort of thing I have in mind as a typical *central* process.

A footnote added at the end of the first paragraph quoted makes it clear that the term *convention* is meant in some sort of Gricean way:

> Strictly speaking, I suppose, a convention must be something one can adhere to if one chooses; so perhaps the principle at issue is not 'Say only what is true' but rather 'Say only what you believe'. General adherence to the latter injunction will license inferences from utterances to how the world is, given the assumption (which is, anyhow, in all sorts of ways epistemologically indispensable) that much of what people believe is true.

This is a very strange attempt at providing formal semantics with psychological reality. Real-world states of affairs are taken as somehow, not causally but by "convention", provoking linguistic utterances. It sounds as though Fodor casts the old behaviourist doctrine in a Gricean mould in order to give a psychological account of formal semantics. Let us first point to the obvious:

what underwrites the correlation between token-utterances and "distal layouts" is (precisely) the laws of propagation and impingement of sound. The "distal layouts" in the auditory case are nothing but the organisms or mechanisms through or with which the sounds in question are produced. The leap from this to "how the world is" in so far as it is reflected in a true proposition is of Pindaric proportions, and it is not made any less mysterious by the appeal to "convention". Moreover, the twofold assumption that "much of what people believe is true" and that there is a convention of only saying what you believe, really is too feeble a basis for a theory of linguistic understanding. But more centrally, let us see what is needed for such an account to work. What is needed includes at least some way of determining what the reference value is of x (in the "root case"), as well as some specification of what it is to "say of x that it is F" - whereby we shall charitably gloss over all kinds of speech act problems. The point is that as soon as we have what is needed to make Fodor's account work we no longer need Fodor's account. For if we have a theory (an account) of reference and a specification of predication, we have a (propositional) semantics, and if the accounts are in psychological terms, we have a psychological theory of (propositional) meaning. It is then no longer to the point to hold "the world" responsible for semantic processing. Nor, of course, is it desirable, for "how the world is" is neither here nor there for propositional understanding (other than by way of background knowledge, but that is not at issue here).

Our realism is not mediated by "convention" but aims at imputing causality to mental structures. This causal, realist view has the advantage that if a calculus is pinned down, by interpretation, on entities or processes of some definable or recognizable ontological status, then this calculus must at least be compatible with any other calculus whose interpretation involves all or some of the same entities, under the same formula of interpretation. This *compatibility requirement* provides an external quality test for realist theories, over and above the standard quality tests of empirical fit and correct predictions under maximal simplicity. Instrumentalist theories lack this extra test.

But quite apart from all debates about instrumentalism versus realism in scientific theories, there is the simple and inescapable fact that we have declared ourselves to be primarily interested in finding out as much as we can about the brain mechanisms underlying the semantic processing of linguistic utterances. Given that explicit goal we can hardly deny reality claims to the theories developed.

This, however, is not all there is to this question. To say that an interpretation is claimed for the calculus, over and above the theorems, is to say something but not very much. If certain entities or processes of a definable or recognizable ontological status are declared the interpretation objects of the theory (calculus), we still face the question *in what way* the various elements of the calculus are to be regarded as related with these objects. What is needed is a *specific formula of interpretation*. The most direct formula provides a hardware interpretation in terms of the actual apparatus, as defined in neurology. But less direct formulae may lead to interpretations of a more schematic, or 'software', nature. Such interpretations will reveal (if the theory is correct) elements of the system implemented in the apparatus, while remaining non-committal on points of physical implementation. A theory which is subjected to a physically more remote interpretation may still be of considerable explanatory interest, even though it fails to specify physical detail. Such a theory is explanatory to the extent that it reveals part of the system at work, at any level of systematicity. But it is necessary to be clear on the issue of the formula under which a theory is to be considered psychologically real, for the compatibility requirement to be usable as a testing criterion for the theory. (It is, incidentally, important to note that this issue of formula of interpretation is quite distinct from the issue of reductionism and the 'level' of operation of a theory, discussed at the end of the preceding section.)

In our case, we must be prepared to live with the idea that, if any interpretation is envisaged, it will have to be restricted to software terms one way or another. But here, again, we are in deep waters. For there are many different levels of 'software', ranging from machine-specific to machine-independent programmes. When we speak of psychological realism we imply a software interpretation, yet we remain non-specific with regard to the degree of closeness to the physical structures involved. Cognitive psychology tends to operate in this twilight area of 'close' and 'remote' interpretations. Often it is impossible to specify to what extent physical closeness can be claimed, given the lack of independent tests of 'reality'. In psycholinguistics, in particular, this difficulty is painfully present: it often proves impossible to specify in anything like a reliable way under what formula given *linguistic* analyses and descriptions are to be considered psychologically real. In short, the old black box is not very forthcoming in showing its true colours.

A great many sophisticated tests have been reported on in the literature, purporting to show the psychological reality or unreality of proposed linguistic descriptions. But the results are often not conclusive because what has been measured in the psycholinguistic experiment may relate to a level of operation distinct from the level at which the linguistic description might perhaps be considered valid. Or it may be that what is described on paper as serial processing is, in actual fact, implemented as parallel processing. There is increasing evidence (Hinton and Anderson 1981) that the brain makes far wider use of parallel processing procedures than had been assumed. This does not make serial descriptions worthless, since there are ways of systematically 'translating' serial procedures into parallel ones provided both are well defined. It is also entirely thinkable that the psychological processes that would be involved if the linguistic description were correct are so deeply embedded as routine procedures, inaccessible to any form of awareness or willed intervention by the speaker or listener, that, for example, reaction time differences are no longer practically measurable (cp. Seuren 1978). Reaction time experiments risk being futile when they are based on hardware expectations that fail to be realistic. One must, in short, be careful and avoid undeserved discrediting of theories whose level or manner of psychological reality is not clear.[18]

It should be noted, furthermore, that the distinction between 'hardware' and 'software' is a fluid one, especially since we are dealing with organic matter. It may well be that what starts out as 'software' acquired by learning gradually turns into 'hardware' as the acquired knowledge or ability turns into a routine skill. In general, there are still many more questions in this respect than reliable answers. It is not even known how many questions there are. Some questions are known. Thus, as has been said, there are questions regarding interpretative differences according to *degrees of physical closeness*, or questions to do with a distinction between *routine procedures* which are not open to awareness or willed intervention and are not recorded in accessible memory, and *declarative procedures* which are open to intro-spection and intervention and whose operations are recorded in memory. There are questions relating to *serial or parallel processing*. In particular, it may be necessary to specify, at some level of physical specificity, whether the organism waits for the *whole input to be available* before it starts working on it, or whether it starts operating as soon as the input begins to be registered, i.e. *'from left to right'*, or in a *'shadowing'* fashion. Or it may become necessary to specify *'chunkwise'* processing strategies adopted by the organism. There are questions involving a distinction between *'hard-wired'*, or, in a different jargon, *'innate'*, aspects of the organism on the one hand, and *'programmed'* or *'learned'* aspects on the other. A specified formula of interpretation will have to make it clear whether or to what extent a given rule system is to be interpreted as part of the innate or of the acquired (learned) elements in the organism. And it is quite certain that many more such questions still lie undiscovered and will have to be answered some day.

It remains, of course, always possible to fall back on the position some-times taken in current formal semantics and commented on at the outset of

---

[18] Seuren (1978) presents the view that a grammar is a mapping system between perceptual (auditory or visual) structures and semantic analyses, and, in particular, that there is a qualitative difference between the perceptual structures and semantic analyses on the one hand and the rules and processes of grammar on the other. The latter are screened off from willed intervention, are automatic, rapid, not open to introspection or awareness, and are typically routine procedures. The former, however, are objects of manipulation and calculus in a central processing compartment, whose operations are all recorded in memory and where 'conscious' thought takes place. It is interesting to see that this view is now (in principle) formulated at length in Fodor's (1983) "modu-larity" view of the mind.

this section. We may wish to deny psychological reality to some bit of description and claim no more than that it characterizes the output of the system in certain ways. In such cases we intend to describe, as has been said, an *epiphenomenon* of the system, rather than the system itself. As long as epiphenomenal interpretations are considered to be one (minimal) variety of realist interpretation and are not looked upon as in any sense epistemically necessary, they will be useful in various stages of research and theory building. Thus we will see below, in chapter 2, that the rules proposed for the characterizations of semantic analyses are probably best interpreted as being epiphenomenal: it would seem rather absurd to claim that the actual generation of semantic analyses in real communication or linguistic processing should take place according to those formation rules. It is much more plausible that the actual generative system is intimately linked up with a network of cognitive and verbal functions, the nature of which is still largely a mystery. Here, the best we can do is try to characterize what we hypothesize to be the output used for semantic processing.

There is one important corollary of practical methodology here. Whenever we feel that a rule system or a bit of formal theory does nothing more than characterize output and should therefore be interpreted epiphenomenally, it should receive no more than passing attention as a theory and (to the extent that this is appropriate) be treated and regarded more as a heuristic for gathering data. This is so because such a theory has little or no explanatory value given its failure to link up with the physical apparatus that is to be held causally responsible for the data. Its value lies precisely in what it claims to do, the characterization of the output, which is either identical with the data or somehow connected with it through procedures of interpretation. From this point of view, the enormous amount of effort that has gone into current formal semantics seems wildly out of proportion with the explanatory benefit that can possibly be reaped. There is no doubt that current formal semantics is highly implausible from a psychological point of view. And those formal semanticists who care to consider the important and valid question of the causal factors involved in the appearance of semantic phenomena (and are thus prepared to take a minimal realist position), do well to keep their realist position minimal. But as soon as one realizes how much effort goes into the construction of calculi and how little attention is given to proper observations, one inevitably begins to fear that there is a massive problem of misdirection of energies.

As regards the theory presented in this book, in most cases we will have to remain uncommitted with respect to interpretative distinctions. Only in isolated cases will we be able to be specific in some limited respect. Thus, we can say without qualms that the formation rules for semantic analyses are to be interpreted epiphenomenally. The same can be said of the logic developed in chapter 3 and in the appendix. Its psychological interpretation can only be epiphenomenal, in the sense that the entailments are 'read' from the discourse model structures built up by successive utterances, as well as from the structures found in the lexicon and in background knowledge. This point of view will be further elaborated in chapter 3.[19] The anaphora algorithm, on the other hand, as presented in section 4.2.5, as well as the whole theory of discourse incrementation, aim at describing physical reality, albeit from a safe distance. These functions are to be taken as 'hard-wired' or 'innate' (though we will certainly not speak of 'ideas' in this context). Wherever we claim that some principle of grammar is universal, we claim that it is part of the innate 'wiring' system with which humans are genetically endowed. We can say that the vast majority of grammatical rules are to be interpreted as routine procedures and that, for most speakers, precious few rules of grammar are declarative. We can say, on the other hand, that many aspects of lexical knowledge are declarative (though a great deal of routine must be assumed there too). The declarative character of much of lexical knowledge appears from the fact that speakers are, on the whole, quite capable of discussing fine points of lexical meaning purely on the basis of their practical command of the language in question. Furthermore, enough is known nowadays for us to feel justified in claiming that parsing procedures, i.e. procedures reducing acoustic (or written) input to semantic analyses, and perhaps also planning procedures involved in production, proceed chunkwise, cutting up the input (or preparing the output) in certain ways to do with structural properties of the full surface structure or proposition.

As regards parsing procedures, the well-known phenomena of 'garden path' parsing failures indicate that processing is in full swing and anticipations are made well before the input is complete. Cases in point are sentences like:

(31) a. The horse raced past the barn fell.
   b. The man looking at the picture frames spies who are dangerous.
   c. The old man places the young people on the committee regard as least important.[20]

We note, furthermore, that the parsing problems connected with such sentences are usually[21] to do with the problem of determining the dominating verbal complex (main verb plus auxiliaries) of the sentence or clause in

---

[19] It is not uninteresting to note that the ontological question of the reality of mathematical and logical entities and facts might be answered by saying that they are epiphenomenal upon the world – in a philosophy that accepts the world as being real. Mathematical and logical reality would thus consist in *necessary epiphenomenality* of any possible world. Mathematics and logic are, in this perspective, essential ingredients of an exact metaphysics.

[20] I owe this last example to Bob Leiser, Ph.D.-student in the Psychology Department of Glasgow University.

[21] Han Reichgelt points out to me that there are garden path sentences whose solution does not depend on spotting the verb:

(i) The doctor told the woman that he was having trouble with to leave the surgery.
(ii) The doctor told the woman that he was having trouble with her husband.

question. This point will prove of some interest in section 2.1.8 of the following chapter.

In general, however, it must be admitted that we cannot claim specificity for interpretation formulae to anything like a sufficient degree. Very often, probably even in most cases, we will have to admit to ignorance on this score, a weakness which we share with all existing theories of grammar and meaning. The best we can do is say that we are committed to a *maximization of the realist position*. Even though it will, in practice, often be impossible to provide a fully specified formula of interpretation for the theory or the analyses presented, the general methodological principle is upheld that a theory gains in explanatory potential to the extent that its interpretation gets closer to physical reality (taking into account the developmental stages of the organism). This might seem a declaration of intent rather than a principle whose value is directly convertible into cash. Yet, if it is a declaration of intent, one should keep in mind that its potential cash value may become palpable any moment, and that, moreover, it creates heavy commitments right now. One such commitment is negative, in that it makes us rule out any theory which appears incompatible with data provided by other disciplines under any formula of interpretation. A positive commitment is that there must be at least one level of interpretation at which the theory proposed is interpretable as being true. Thus our position in this respect, ill defined as it may be, makes us steer away from approaches that lead to theories and analyses which stand little chance of an interpretation in terms of psychological reality under any formula. In particular, it makes us wary of all too abstract notions and theories, such as are found in possible world formal semantics, and it makes us feel more at home with theories formulated as descriptions of processes, since what is presented as a process in the theory may, if we are lucky, turn out to correspond, under some formula of interpretation, to a real process in the material object or set of objects which we are investigating.

The commitment to a maximization of the realist position entails, generally, that we accept constraints imposed upon the theory as a result of the realist interpretation. Thus, the realist, non-epiphenomenal interpretation of grammatical rules automatically subjects them to the criterion of parsability. A transformational grammar defining mappings from semantic analyses to surface structures, but not vice versa, can hardly claim reality in any interesting sense, since it only simulates half of the reality involved: it simulates the production side but it neglects the reception side. We accept, in principle, constraints entailed by the neurological structures and processes of the brain, though it must be admitted that hardly any serious constraints have come to light so far from that angle. We are willing to accept constraints entailed by serious experiments and theories regarding processing schemas or strategies in the brain. Ideally, we would even hope that facts of neural implementation could provide explanations for phenomena observed in semantic or grammatical systems other than limitations of or errors in performance. To take a simple example, it is well known that if a verb takes a sentential subject as well as a sentential object (*That you run a temperature means that you have an infection.*) then the subject clause is always factive. This is an interesting fact, but we haven't the remotest idea why this should be so. Or take the *litotes*-phenomenon, the fact that *not* with a gradable adjective tends to be interpreted not literally but in a bipolar way: *not many* is interpreted as *few*, *not very nice* as *rather awful* – an equally interesting and equally unexplained fact. It cannot be excluded that these or other enigmatic facts will be explained some day as more or less fortuitous consequences of the neural structures underlying semantic and grammatical processing. Obviously, this is mere speculation, but it is nevertheless worth pointing out that 'pragmatics' is not the only refuge for unexplained facts. A situation analysis of linguistic communication reveals a few more possible retreats providing temporary safety. And in this case the retreat may even prove to be a proper home, safer than the shady inn of pragmatics.

2

Grammar and lexicon

2.1 Against surface semantics

2.1.1 Introduction

There is no semantics without grammar. The reason for this is that any theory of linguistic meaning requires structural analyses of the units of linguistic communication, the uttered sentences. And uttered sentences do not carry their structure with them in any physically recognizable form. It is therefore necessary to assign a structure to uttered sentences, and such assignments are the product of grammatical theorizing. In the realist position, this theorizing is aimed at simulating, at some level of abstraction, what the comprehending and producing organisms do. This much is uncontroversial: even staunch formal semanticists will accept that if a realist position is taken, the assignment of structure is meant to simulate the organisms, although they themselves may be wary of such a position. In any case, they fully accept the principle that a grammar is needed to assign structure to uttered sentences. And they also agree with another universally accepted principle which says that structure assignment need not apply to each and every individual *token* utterance, but proceeds according to sentence-*types*: a grammar deals with sentence-types, not with uttered sentence-tokens.

But here the general agreement stops. The traditional view, which goes back to at least Plato and has recently been taken up again by the theory of semantic syntax (or 'generative semantics'), is that structure assignment to sentence types is not enough and that semantic theory requires a grammar which, besides assigning structure, also provides mappings between the 'surface' sentence type with its structure and postulated semantic analyses. These semantic analyses (SA) are meant to be explicit, unambiguous, and semantically 'transparent' in a way to be made explicit by semantic theory. Against this traditional view, modern formal semantics has developed in a climate where the assumption of a separate level of SA is considered un-warranted and therefore unjustified. Standard present-day semantic theory holds that assignment of structure to surface sentences is sufficient for a semantic calculus to operate upon. Let us speak of the principle of *surface semantics*, as against *SA-semantics*.

This chapter is devoted to a vindication of SA-semantics and a debunking of surface semantics. Ideally, it should be demonstrated for each existing variety of surface semantics that it fails on account of factual incorrectness and, moreover, that it will never attain a satisfactory level of descriptive correctness without giving up the principle of surface semantics. But although this would be the proper course, it will not be followed here, the main reason being that varieties of surface semantics have become so numerous that such a demonstration would fill a sizeable volume and require years of work. And even then it will probably not be possible to show for each variety that it cannot attain descriptive adequacy in principle. And suppose even that hurdle is taken, who will then come up with a clinching argument that no new varieties can be thought up that get around all the problems which floored the old ones? It is simply not possible to argue that no new formal means can be developed, as a matter of principle, that will make surface semantics viable. Even mathematicians have not so far gauged the depths of possible formal calculi. We will, therefore, not embark upon such a hopeless procedure, but rather resort to a more practical method. This will consist in pointing out, in a general and perhaps slightly rhetorical way, a number of immediate problems confronting any form of surface semantics, and proceeding subsequently to the proposal of a theory of grammar, semantic syntax, which carries convincing safeguards against problems arising from surface semantics. The connoisseur will often notice that this or that one among the problems raised has found a treatment in this or that surface semantics theory. Yet he will also notice that no single form of surface semantics can cope with all the problems. The strength of the argument in favour of SA-semantics will then lie mainly in the descriptive successes of both the grammar and the semantics developed within this general framework, as well as in the relative parsimony of the formal analytical means required.

It must be said at the outset, however, that from an abstract, general methodological point of view surface semantics is to be preferred: if a semantic calculus of sufficient descriptive adequacy and convincing simplicity and explanatory force can be developed without the postulation of a separate level of semantic analyses for sentences and the concomitant apparatus of transformational mapping rules, then this calculus is to be preferred to other calculi that might achieve the same but with the extra assumptions and apparatus. The reason is simple: science has flourished under Ockham's razor which has systematically cut away all superfluous assumptions. However, if it appears that a given set of assumptions is too poor for a theory to cope with the facts, then it must be enriched, and the 'investment' must be such that it yields ample 'gains' in terms of theoretical coverage. As a general methodological principle this is, of course, not controversial. The controversy is about the question of whether in this particular case the set of assumptions associated with surface semantics is or is not too poor. It is my estimation that it is too poor, and must therefore be enriched – just as traditional philosophy of language has always said. In this respect there is a remarkable parallel with psychological theory over the past seventy years. Behaviourism had the great methodological advantage of working with minimal assumptions about the physical properties of the organism said to house the 'mind', but some 25 years ago it became apparent that those assumptions were too poor in so many ways that a radical change in paradigm was called for. Since then we have witnessed the rebirth of cognitive science.

Our theory of grammar is characterized by the contention that surface structures are unfit for semantic treatment, and that a grammar must define mappings between these and postulated semantic analyses. It furthermore contends that these mappings cannot leave intact all the lexical items occurring in surface sentences. The lexicon, far from being the simple store of meaningful building blocks for sentences, is a dynamic, highly structured and extremely rich quarry whose creative possibilities are open to exploration by its users, and whose intricate principles are of the highest explanatory value in linguistic theory. We shall see that the theory of generative semantics as it flourished until ten years ago was on the right track in this respect, and we shall reopen this track with the help of new and forceful analyses. At the same time we shall see that considerations of simple grammatical descriptive adequacy inevitably lead us to syntactic analyses and descriptions taking as deep structures expressions in a semantic language that bears more than a trivial resemblance to predicate calculus. And our overall impression will be one of a beautiful but infinitely complex system which sometimes allows us to understand it but more often only shows us glimpses that whet the appetite. Language will prove not to be the innocent and well-ordered playground it has been made out to be by naïve formalists. On the contrary, its complexities are only matched by nature, precisely because that is what language is part of.

It should be clear that our argument against surface semantics is independent of any particular semantic theory to which one gives preference. Existing standard formal semantics is based on calculi that yield truth-values for sentences given certain independently defined states of affairs. The semantics proposed in this book envisages calculi that yield mental structures that are constrained, among other things, by truth-conditional definability. And other general frames of semantic theory may be thought up. But what is said here is that no matter what semantic theory one adopts, under the most general possible requirements for any semantic theory of whatever orientation, surface semantics will not do.

Yet our argument is not independent of whatever grammatical theory one adopts. There has been, over the past 50 years, a proliferation of conceptions of grammatical structure, developed not only by professional linguists but also by psychologists, information theorists, logicians and others. In this respect I shall conform, in main outline, to what constitutes the mainstream of linguistic thought. This is based on the notion of 'constituent structure analysis' as it was introduced into linguistics by Bloomfield, first in his *An Introduction to the Study of Language* in 1914 (where he apparently took the notion from Wundt), and subsequently in his extremely influential *Language* in 1933. This notion of structural analysis was new, and it has proved extraordinarily productive and fruitful in linguistic theory. It led to Harris's formulation (1951, 372-3) of the principle of formation rules:

> The work of analysis leads right up to the statements which enable anyone to synthesize or predict utterances in the language. These statements form a deductive system with axiomatically defined initial elements and with theorems concerning the relations among them. The final theorems would indicate the structure of the utterances of the language in terms of the preceding parts of the system.

And it became an essential ingredient in the theory of transformational grammar which followed from Harris's work. I do not wish to say that the Bloomfieldian notion of 'tree structure' is perfect and complete. On the contrary, it lacks certain features which are felt to be indispensable for adequate grammatical analysis and description. Bloomfield himself distinguished between structures with a head and those without a head, but he gave no indication of how this distinction could be expressed in trees. (Recent theory has introduced a system of node labelling to express the difference.) Then, semantic functions such as 'subject', 'object' are not, or inadequately, expressed in Bloomfieldian tree structures, though they are highly relevant in grammar. And, finally, the theory of constituent structure analysis has never come forth with a satisfactory reply to the problem of discontinuous constituents. If we take the sentence *I called him up*, then what is the correct surface structure, (1a) or (1b)?

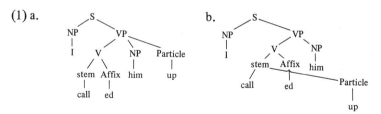

There is a widespread consensus that (1a), and not (1b), should be taken as the correct structural analysis at surface level. But although this consensus is based on the feeling that discontinuous constituents must be avoided, there is no solid argument in the literature to support this feeling, other than the consideration that formation rules do not easily cope with discontinuous constituents. On the other hand, if discontinuous constituents are allowed in and (1b) is reconsidered as a candidate, surface semantics can make the point that with (1b) we can do semantic business, since it expresses in its constituent structure the fact that the past tense affix *-ed* should be treated as attached to the verbal stem *call up*, and not just to the stem *call* with the particle *up* left high and dry, as in (1a). I shall remain uncommitted on the issue of discontinuous constituents in surface structure. In the structures that function as semantic analyses there will not be any discontinuous constituents, all discontinuity being accounted for by the grammar. In the following, discontinuity arguments will be called in only if there are independent reasons for regarding structures containing discontinuous constituents as undesirable.

The argument against surface semantics is directed, in the context of present-day linguistics, against virtually all forms of formal semantics, and also against those theories of grammar that espouse a so-called 'rule-to-rule' semantics (categorial grammar). It does not have as its target those theories which involve some notion of 'logical form', related to Surface Structure by means of a rule system. In these (mainly MIT-based) theories a different terminology is adopted from that used here, mainly because they are part of a paradigm where it is customary to accept that, apart from the rules mapping SA and Surface Structure onto each other, there is also something like an 'autonomous grammar', whose rules are taken to have an independent explanatory function. But although, clearly, the view is taken here that those theories are fundamentally misguided in many respects, they are not open to criticism on account of the argument against surface semantics.

2.1.2 *The compositionality principle*

The question of surface semantics is inextricably bound up with the question of the so-called *compositionality principle* of surface structures. This principle, usually ascribed to Frege (but perhaps incorrectly so; cp. Janssen 1983, ch. 1), is presented in a variety of different forms, but its most general formulation is that a linguistic expression is compositional just in case it is structured in such a way that a calculus can be defined enabling one to determine the meaning of the whole structure as a function of the semantic definitions of the structural parts, *without the intervention of other linguistic structures*. This last condition must be added because, if the calculus makes for other linguistic structures to be put between the original structure and the purely semantic calculus, the damnable SAs have surreptitiously been reintroduced. That is, surface semantics is defined by the claim that surface structures of sentences are compositional in some precise sense. It would be a mistake to think that this claim is directly testable in any empirical sense. The compositionality claim is nothing but a neat formulation of the position of surface semantics. It depends on the notion of 'structure', which is theory-dependent: in one theory, assigning one type of structure, a linguistic expression may prove compositional, whereas in another theory which assigns different structures the same expression is non-compositional.

There have been proposals, in recent linguistic literature, to adorn surface structure trees with various kinds of elements that have no physical counterpart in any realization of the sentences in question. Such 'null-elements' or 'zero-anaphors' have the effect of making the structures thus adorned more amenable to semantic calculus and therefore more compositional. Thus, in a sentence of the type *Harry wants to go*, the surface structure is said to contain an empty element 'e' between *wants* and *to go*. This element will then do the honours for the missing subject of the verb phrase *to go*, and will thus remove an obstacle to surface semantics. Although these proposals were not put forward in the context of surface semantics, they pander to a general trend, found in much linguistic and formal semantic literature of the past ten years, and leading to an overall reduction of the role and value of deep structure hypotheses. Such surface structure assignments, however, can be regarded as a disguise for theories that postulate underlying structures. They are notational variants, which are subject to the constraint that underlying structures can differ from surface structures only in that the former may contain *extra* semantic elements which the latter lack, there being no structural differences other than that. If such a theory were tenable it would be of great interest. Yet, the cases discussed below will make it abundantly clear that this constraint is unrelated to reality. As a consequence, we need not be disturbed by any quibbles about whether or not null elements are part of surface structure, because even if they are, surface semantics will not work.

Clearly, any argument about the compositionality of surface structures (or any linguistic structures, for that matter) depends in part on the formal calculatory means employed or envisaged. The point is of particular relevance here since lambda-calculus has undercut many possible arguments against surface semantics. Lambda-calculus is an elegant and powerful formal method of providing translations for semantic functions in structure trees in such a way that the calculus can carry on with the help of variables even though the values for the variables cannot be given until some later stage in the computation. It will be shown that even with lambda-calculus, however, surface semantics still remains unable to cope with a great many refractory cases. Of course, there is no predicting that no other formal means will ever be invented to get rid of the troublesome cases which remain, but one can hardly derive an argument from such unsubstantiated hopes.

It must be observed, in this context, that lambda-calculus is not to be confused with grammatical deep structure or with paraphrases that sound like lambda-formulae (cp. the warning by Dowty et al. 1981: 110) Lambda-calculus is a method for translating nodes in (surface) trees. It is useful because (a) it is richer in expressive power than classical propositional structures, and (b) because it can 'hold up' constituents till higher up in the tree. Yet all it provides is translations, not underlying structures. There are proposals (e.g. Szabolcsi 1981; Sag 1986; Gazdar 1979: 124-5), often in connection with contrastive accent, to the effect that a special lambda-analysis should account for some grammatical and/or semantic feature (e.g. the contrastive accent). Thus, if:

(2) Mary wrote the letter.

is analysed as "λx (wrote(x, the letter)) (Mary)" (or "Mary is one who wrote the letter"),

(3) Mary wrote the LETTER (not the envelope).

would be assigned a more complex lambda-analysis, such as:

(4) λx (λy(wrote(x, y)) (the letter)) (Mary)

or, more or less, "Mary is such that the letter is something she wrote". However, whereas the analysis of (2) may be justified on grounds of the NP-VP tree structure, there is no tree structure justifying (4) for (3). Nor can the lambda-analysis account for whatever semantic difference there is between (2) and (3), since no matter how complex a lambda-formula may be, it is always equivalent with its conversion. Thus (4) and the analysis of (2) are both equivalent with "wrote(Mary, the letter)". Even though one may concur with the English paraphrases of the lambda-formulae, and perhaps wish to consider them relevant for deep structure purposes, they cannot fulfil that function in surface semantics. Otherwise lambda-calculus is used to introduce by stealth what is professed to be disallowed: underlying structures that help semantic interpretation. Such uses of lambda-calculus reinforce our case against surface semantics rather than weaken it.

2.1.3 The categorial and translation argument

Given these preliminary remarks and provisos, what then are the cases which make the prospects of surface semantics look pale and unappealing? Let us first consider the *categorial argument*, which is, admittedly, more rhetorical than stringent. It rests on cases where languages differ in their selection of word classes for otherwise identical meanings. Take, for example, the case of non-predicative adjectives which are not by themselves semantic predicates, such as:

(5) a. the *alleged* murderer = the one who is alleged to be the murderer
   b. the *former* president = the one who once was president
   c. the *late* Mrs Reid   = Mrs Reid, who died some time ago
   d. an *early* riser   = one who rises early
   e. a *hard* worker   = one who works hard
   f. a *good* teacher   = one who teaches well
   g. a *strong* supporter   = one who supports strongly
   h. a *near* miss   = a miss, but near
   i. a *near* hit   = almost a hit

Intuitively, it seems that a semantic analysis and description of such noun phrases is best done in terms of some equivalent paraphrase formulated in semantically more regular terms, something like the paraphrases given in (5). Technically, we can do this by positing transformational rules relating the paraphrase (in some suitably abstract form) to the surface form containing the adjective. But this means that we operate with a semantic analysis. If we do not want to do that (as in Beesley 1982), then, supposing the formal means are available, the category of adjectives in English will have to be treated as semantically heterogeneous. This in itself need not disturb us, since in a non-surface semantics the heterogeneity is accounted for in the grammar, whereas surface semantics will have the semantics do the explaining. And there is no a priori that semantics should not handle this or other heterogeneities. The facts, heterogeneous as they are, must be accounted for somewhere in the description, not necessarily in either the grammar or the semantics.

The crunch comes, however, when we consider that languages differ considerably in their possibilities of using non-predicative adjectives. It is normal Latin, for example, to speak of *paterna domus*, or *materna oratio*, for "the father's house" and "the mother's speech", respectively, or of *stella matutina* for "the morning star", or of *cena hodierna* for "today's evening meal". Italian might also be called in for expressions such as *acqua piovana* for "rain-water" and the like. Now we might apply surface semantics to all such expressions, and we might even be successful, in a formal sense, in doing so. But then there will be no common level at which the English and the Latin or Italian expressions are identical, and hence the most readily available basis for any explanation of their semantic identity, despite the surface dissimilarity, is lost. Or, in different words, if we want to explain how and why it is possible for humans to *translate* from one language into another (a perfectly rational aim within the context of the human sciences), a deep structural level at which very different surface structures in the respective languages turn out to be identical must be considered a great help.

Identity, or near-identity, of truth-conditions is insufficient for an explanation of translation capabilities, since there is probably no, and certainly no psychologically plausible, computational route from a bunch of truth-conditions (i.e. a definition of a set of possible worlds) to a sentence structure. A deep structural level of semantic analysis underlying surface structures is not sufficient for a translation theory, since (good) translation heavily leans on context, but it cannot be missed. Nor can a context (or discourse) model be missed in a translation theory (and since our semantics has both, it looks as though our semantics is a better basis for translation theory than existing formal semantics based on surface structures alone).

The categorial argument is thus bound up with the *translation argument*: they reinforce each other. In general terms, the categorial argument says that both grammatical and semantic descriptions are helped and simplified by the assumption of no more than a handful of primitive semantic categories which are semantically homogeneous and figure in underlying semantic analyses (deep structures), whereby the grammar contains the rules and principles that are to be held responsible for the omnipresent semantic (and syntactic) heterogeneity of surface categories. The translation argument says that the assumption of a separate level of deep syntactic structure which also acts as a semantic analysis for sentences is indispensable for translation theory, since a specification of semantic identity in terms of either truth-conditions or discourse models is insufficient. Truth-conditions are insufficient given the computational hurdles on any route from them to sentences. Discourse models are insufficient given the fact that sentences are translatable in isolation (but for lexical and presuppositional incongruities). There is thus ample justification for a level of description on the interface between semantics and syntax, at which the similarity or identity underlying translation procedures can be made explicit.

It may be objected that discourse semantics in particular takes away the force of the translation argument, because in discourse semantics it is the discourse domain that can act as the desired universal cognitive level at which sentences from different languages differing widely in grammatical structure can be seen to have the same meaning. Since the discourse domain is supposedly language-independent, there is no need left for a universal or almost universal level of representation called "Semantic Analysis". Sentences in isolation are translatable, it could be said, by virtue of the fact that they create their own miniscule discourse domain, from where and into where translations can take place. Taken in the abstract, this counterargument has some force (which is the reason why the translation argument is more rhetorical than some of the arguments that follow). Yet, consider what would be needed, for example, if surface structures were to be generated directly from discourse representations, that is, without the intervention of intermediate levels of linguistic representation. Suppose the French sentence *Jean a fait voir la lettre à Pierre* (literally: "Jean has made see the letter to Pierre", i.e. "Jean made Pierre see the letter") is to be distilled directly from a domain where it is specified under the address d_1 for Jean that Jean caused fact *e*, represented in a subdomain D^1, and under the address d_2 for Pierre that d_1 caused *e* as in D^1, and under D^1 that d_2, i.e. Pierre, saw d_3, the address for the letter. Now the two predicates *faire* ("cause") and *voir* ("see") must be put together under one V-node; what is normally the subject must become dative for *voir*, and no subordinate clause is allowed into the surface structure despite the fact that a subdomain is involved. It is probably technically feasible to achieve all this, but it will be at the cost of missing out on a massive amount of relevant grammatical generalizations, which are easily captured if, first, 'stock is taken' of the relevant portions of the domain, then, the stocktaking is laid down in the form of a linguistic structure, which is, finally, transformed into a well-formed surface structure (in this case via the rule of Predicate Raising – see section 2.4.5 below). It seems sensible first to 'put down on paper', so to speak – where the 'paper' stands for the cognitive working space reserved for grammar – what the discourse domain contains in the way of semantic information, and then to let the grammar do its work.

The example just discussed of surface adjectives which embody diverse semantic functions is a case of what may be called *categorial syncretism*. Another well-known class of clear examples of categorial syncretism is provided by adverbs in the various languages of the world. The semantic heterogeneity of adverbs is proverbial. Yet the theoretical significance of this fact has not so far been properly appreciated. Let us first look at some examples. Compared with most other languages, English makes a relatively liberal use of adverbs. It is good English, for example, to say:

(6) a. She is *arguably* more suitable for the job than her husband.
   b. The man was *allegedly* hanged.
   c. She is *reputedly* very clever.
   d. He *cleverly* spoke very stupidly.

In hardly any other languages do the italicized adverbs in these sentences find a structurally similar translation. Occasionally English lacks an adverb where other languages have one. Thus, e.g., French *volontiers*, German *gerne*, Dutch *gaarne*, and equivalents in many other languages, are only sometimes, and then only clumsily, rendered in English as *gladly*. Normally English uses not an adverb but a verbal construction with expressions like *be happy*, *like*, *love* or *be keen*. The strategy of using verbs where many other languages use adverbs is typical for, e.g., French:

(7) a. Il *vient de* sortir. (Lit.: he *comes from* leaving; i.e. he has *just* left)
   b. Il a *failli* tomber. (Lit.: he *has failed* to fall; i.e. he *almost* fell)
   c. Il a *fini par* réussir. (Lit.: he *has finished by* succeeding; i.e. he *finally* succeeded)

Languages with serial verb constructions, such as most Caribbean Creoles and many West African languages, typically use verbs for what in European languages tend to be adverbs. Thus, Sranan, the main Creole language of Surinam, has:

(8) Dowwatra ben e dropu *fadon*.

which means literally "dew water was dripping so that it fell down" (*fadon* is a verb which means, and is historically derived from, "fall down"). It is, however, properly translated as "dew drops were dripping down".

It is remarkable to see how central the role is of verbs in this cross-linguistic play with categories. Serial verbs, for example, not only correspond with 'European' adverbs, but also with 'European' prepositions, particles and morphemes. Thus Sranan has:

(9) a. A ben kan luku *go* na liba. (Lit.: he could see *go* to the river; i.e. he could see *towards* the river)
b. A e go tyari switi-mofo *gi* mi. (Lit.: he is going to carry sweet-mouths *give* me; i.e. he is going to bring sweets *for* me)
c. A begi *taki* suma sa kiri a fowru, en sa kisi a kondre. (Lit.: he begged *say* who will kill the bird, he will get the country; i.e. he begged and *said that* he who would kill the bird would get the country)
d. Mi no taygi yu *taki* ala sma musu puru en yas? (Lit.: did I not tell you *say* all people must take off their coats? i.e. did I not tell you *that* everybody must take off his coat?)
e. Eifeltoren he *pasá*. (Lit.: the Eiffel Tower is high *exceed*; i.e. the Eiffel Tower is high*er*)
f. A moro betre *pasá* yu. (Lit.: he is better *exceed* you; i.e. he is better *than* you)[1]

Moreover, a very common feature of verb serialization is that through time certain semantically transparent serial verb constructions 'jell' into semantically opaque, lexically fixed expressions of some derived surface category such as adverb, preposition, particle. Thus, serial use of the Sranan verb *gi* ("give") led to what is now clearly the preposition "for" or "to"; serial verb translations no longer do.

It would be easy to go on for pages and pages, showing examples of category switches from one language to another, or of categorial reanalysis through time. And it would be abundantly clear that the pivotal category in this game of giving and taking is the verb. We shall express this by putting

[1] But for (9f), all Sranan examples are documented. (8) and (9a) are from a story by Trefossa, printed in Voorhoeve and Lichtveld 1975: 208, 210; (9b)–(9d) are from Herskovits and Herskovits 1936: 188, 270, 288; (9e) is from a poem by Trefossa (Voorhoeve and Lichtveld 1975: 204).

forward the hypothesis that all lexical items (other than the complex open items – see section 2.3.1 below) are verbs when used at the structural level of semantic analysis. In order to distinguish these 'deep' verbs from surface structure verbs, we shall speak of "predicates" when referring to the former, and keep the label "verb" for surface verbs only.

What interests us in this context is that it is worth while to look for a level of structural description which is both semantically explicit and transparent, and related to surface structure by means of grammatical rules of relative regularity and simplicity. Such a descriptive level will be either identical or at least non-trivially similar across different languages, and will thus embody a prime linguistic universal. It will moreover be definable in terms of very few semantically homogeneous categories, which allow for category change in surface structure.

2.1.4 Its *and* theres

But let us leave the combined categorial and translation argument behind, and pass on to the *argument of its and theres* in English. Consider the examples:

(10) a. It is impossible to run that fast.
b. *It is impossible to rain with such a clear sky.
c. It is impossible for it to rain with such a clear sky.
(11) a. It is possible for lots of people to be wanting access.
b. *It is possible to be lots of people wanting access.
c. It is possible for there to be lots of people wanting access.

It seems that English allows for more or less 'empty' words to occur in positions and under category labels that are usually reserved for constituents carrying a full semantic load. This applies in particular to the words *it* and *there*. Both are treated as noun phrases (NP), though they do not have much of a meaning themselves. Sentence (10a) has no overt constituent that could serve as a subject to the infinitival verb *run*. (As has been said, it is no use supplying a 'zero' element in surface structure to make up for the deficiency, since that would amount to no more than a notation masking the assumption of an underlying structure.) Now one could propose that there is no need for any subject to the verb phrase *run that fast*, since verb phrases can be defined semantically in their own right as functions from denotations (including empty denotations) to truth-values. But then it cannot be explained why (10b) is unacceptable in English. Staying within the terms of surface semantics, we can then say that there is indeed an implicit generic subject hidden in (10a), and that this missing subject is provided by the translation of *impossible* as a lambda-calculus formula in the vein of "λx[for all persons p [not[possible[p do x]]]]", where the variable x ranges over verb phrases that are functions from denotations to truth-values. This will get (10b) right, since *rain with such a clear sky* is not a verb phrase of the kind required. But then sentence (10c) becomes problematic: the word *impossible* in this sentence cannot be given the same translation as was offered for *impossible* in (10a) and (10b). It will then be necessary to have two items *impossible* in the lexicon, one for (10a) and (10b), and one for (10c). This, however, must be judged to be a most undesirable ploy: such a lexical duplicate would be a prototypical *ad-hoc*ism.

SA-semantics easily steers clear of obstacles of this nature. It stipulates that given an underlying form containing the structure type "impossible for X to Y", the *for*-phrase is deletable only if X is a generic subject. Since *rain* is prevented by its lexical properties from taking such a subject, this deletion is ruled out for cases like (10b) and (10c). It is likewise ruled out for cases like (11b) and (11c), no matter whether *there* is considered a semantically 'original' subject or the result of a transformational rule.

Its and *theres* cause further trouble for surface semantics in English constructions characterized by what goes by the name of Subject-to-Object Raising:

(12) a. I reckon him to be a swindler.
 b. I knew it to be raining.
 c. That kept there from being a riot.

The standard transformational account is that these are derived from underlying structures where what parades as the object of the surface sentences is the subject of the embedded clause:

(13) a. I reckon ₛ[he is a swindler]
 b. I knew ₛ[it be raining]
 c. That kept from ₛ[there be a riot]

A rule of Subject-to-Object Raising is then assumed (not only for English but for many other languages as well) by virtue of which the lower subject is raised to the status of higher object. (The classical study on this rule for English is, of course, Postal 1974.)

There have been misguided proposals to the effect that no such rule exists and that the sentences (12a) and (12b) should be analysed on surface structure level as, respectively:

(14) a. I reckon ₛ[him to be a swindler]
 b. I knew ₛ[it to be raining]

That this is untenable appears in many different ways (see, again, Postal 1974). For example, such an analysis is not applicable to (12c), unless discontinuous constituents are let in, but the authors of this proposal clearly reject that possibility. Constituent structure problems abound for this proposal anyway:

(15) a. I figured him out to be a swindler.
     b. I had expected him for a long time to get over his problems.
     c. I wanted her terribly much to come back.

Without the assumption of discontinuous constituents there is no way of letting the *him*s or the *her* be the surface subject of these sentences. But a solution in terms of discontinuous constituents is not viable here. In (15a), for example, we see that *him* cannot be placed after *out*. Yet a non-pronominal NP does occur in that position, at least optionally:

(16) I figured out that man to be a swindler.

We clearly have here the general phenomenon in English which makes it obligatory for pronominal objects to stand next to the verb when the verb stem contains a particle (*ring up, put out, turn in*, etc.), but only optional for full NPs. The rule in question applies typically to objects, not to other kinds of nominal constituents that might find themselves in that position. Thus, we have (17a) but not (17b):

(17) a.   He didn't turn up last night.
     b.   *He didn't turn last night up.

Therefore, if we wish to let this rule apply to cases like (15a) and (16) we must interpret the NPs *him* and *that man*, respectively, as *objects* of the surface structure, and not as, possibly discontinuous, subjects of the lower clause. More arguments could easily be advanced to show that the discontinuous constituent solution for these cases is a non-starter. So let us be sensible and stick to the traditional account which assigns the following (rough) surface structures to the sentences of (12):

(18) a.

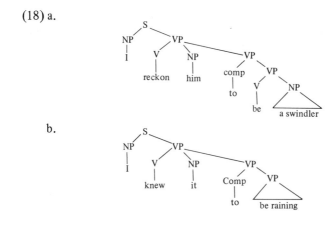

   b.

c.

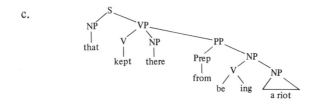

A surface semantics will now have to operate on such structures. If all cases were as simple as (12a) or (18a), the obstacles would probably not be insurmountable. We could define the predicate *reckon* as denoting a relation of three terms: subject, object and verb phrase, whereby the latter is translated as a lambda-function taking the object as argument. This, however, does not work for (18b), nor does it apply (with suitably adapted category labels) to (18c). For the argument to the lambda-function must be a denoting phrase, otherwise there simply is no argument. And *it* and *there* in the respective sentences cannot be used as denoting phrases.[2]

The traditional account is clearly superior. We formulate a rule of Subject-to-Object Raising, governed by the main verb of the higher clause, which turns the lower subject into the higher object. For (12c/18c) we stipulate in the lexicon that *keep from* (just like, e.g., *prevent*) requires a surface object.

2.1.5 The constituency argument

The strongest type of argument against surface semantics, however, is derived from surface constituent structure: the *constituency argument*. If one starts to look around a little, the material for constituency type arguments is well-nigh ubiquitous. Negation is an ever fruitful source:

(19) a. I don't think Jim has arrived yet.
  b. Not until four o'clock did he post the letter.
  c. I didn't do it because I liked it (but because it was my duty).
  d. Il ne viendra certainement pas. (French: "he will certainly not come")
  e. Ça ne doit pas être gai. (French: "that mustn't/can't be very nice")
  f. He's never been no good, not **never**.

---

[2] Note, for example, that the constructions that are typical for denoting NPs are not possible for impersonal *it* and *there*. Specific questions, clefting and pseudoclefting are excluded:

  (i)   *What is raining is it.
  (ii) *What is raining?
  (iii) *It is it that is raining.
  (iv) *It is there that was a riot.
  (v)   *What was a riot was there.

In (19a) the negation must be construed with *yet*, if an adequate account of the meaning of the sentence is to be given. However, the negation is not in construction with *yet*, not by a long shot: the negation is in the main clause, but *yet* stands at the end of the subordinate clause. It is far from clear how surface semantics will make this sentence mean (roughly) the same as "I think Jim hasn't arrived yet". SA-semantics, of course, applies Negative Raising (cp. Seuren 1974), which lifts the negation from the lower clause into the higher clause under the licence of the verb *think*.

(19b) is problematic for surface semantics since, despite the structural bond between *not* and *until* (a bond similar to what is found in sentence initial *not all, not many*), the semantic specification of the sentence requires that *not* be construed with the clause "he Past-post the letter". Let *until* be specified roughly as follows: *until x* means "for all moments of time leading up to x and not after x", then clearly (19b) cannot be analysed as something like "not for all moments of time leading up to four o'clock and not after four o'clock did he post the letter". On the contrary, the structural bond must be undone, and the sentence must read something like "for all moments of time leading up to four o'clock and not after four o'clock it was not the case that he posted the letter". It is not clear how the semantic specification can be grafted onto the syntactic structure in anything like a motivated way other than by the assumption of an underlying structure.[3]

(19c) requires construal of the negation with the *because*-clause. Its construction, however, is with the main clause. It is difficult to see how surface semantics can avoid the incorrect entailment that the "I" did, in fact, not do "it". The entailment should be, of course, that the "I" did do "it".

(19d) would require wildly discontinuous constituents if the right analysis were to be forced out of a structure assigned to the string of words given. It would take a structure like:

(20)

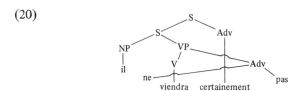

since *certainement* ("certainly") is a sentence adverb taking scope over the (discontinuous) negation *ne . . . pas*. A discontinuity enthusiast might perhaps speak out in favour of (20), but he will then be up against the problem that, for example, the negative particle *ne* is, in French grammar, structurally

---

[3] The case of *until* made punctual by the negation is treated at length in Seuren 1974. The solution proposed there is, in principle, that *until* is analysed as a Negative Raising predicate, so that *until . . . not* is transformed into *not . . . until*.

bound up with the verb form (*viendra*), and not with its better half *pas*. Any theory which insists on surface strucural unity between *ne* and its negative partners, as in *ne ... rien* ("nothing"), *ne ... jamais* ("never"), *ne ... personne* ("nobody"), *ne ... plus* ("no more"), *ne ... plus rien* ("nothing more"), *ne ... aucun* ("not any"), etc., will be up against structures like:

(21) a. Rien ne va plus. ("nothing more goes")
   b. Personne ne faisait plus aucune chose. ("nobody did anything any more")

One would have to be more than enthusiastic for discontinuous constituents to support the idea that in these sentences *ne* is a sister constituent to both *rien* and *plus* for (21a), or to *personne, plus*, and *aucune* for (21b). The answer is clearly that in all these cases *ne* is structurally connected with the verb, and not with its partner or partners in negation. Again, it seems sensible to conclude that surface semantics places constraints on the theory of language which are too hard to follow. We need more breathing space, and this is afforded by the assumption of a separate level of semantic analysis.

Another clear case is provided by (19e). Its verb *doit* is the present tense indicative third person singular of the verb *devoir* which means "must". The sentence means "it is necessary that that is not very nice", or equivalently "it is not possible that that is very nice". The positions of *ne* and *pas* make it unambiguously clear that they are constructed with *doit* and not with the infinitive *être* ("be"). For if the negation were in construction with the infinitive verb *être*, the sentence would have been *Ça doit ne pas être gai*, as in *Tu pourrais aussi ne pas partir* ("you could also not leave"). Any surface semantic theory would thus be forced to assign to (19e) the meaning "it is not necessary that that is very nice", but that is definitely not what the sentence means. Just like the English (slightly dialectal) sentence *That mustn't be very nice*, the French sentence really means "that *can't* be very nice", despite the occurrence of the verb of necessity (*must, devoir*), and not the verb of possibility (*can, pouvoir*). The French sentence (19e), however, makes for a clearer demonstration of the point than the English sentence, because in the French sentence there simply can be no doubt that the negation goes with *doit*, whereas in the English sentence one could still (up to a point) maintain that the negation does not go with *must* but with *be very nice*.

Surface semantics thus faces a very serious problem here, since this French sentence does not mean what its surface structure says. In Seuren (1974) it is argued that in many (perhaps all) languages the modal verb of necessity is a Negative Raising verb, and that in those cases where it does have the effect of lifting the negation of a lower clause up to stand over its own clause, it tends to change lexically into its modal counterpart of possibility, but that occasionally, i.e. in some languages or dialects, and then in some cases, this lexical switch is not put into effect so that the modality of necessity is kept although the negation has hopped over the modal verb. In any case, surface semantics is too straight a corset for an adequate semantics to come about. We cannot operate satisfactorily without a licence for underlying semantic analysis.

(19f), finally, is an instance of Negation Copying, found in a great many dialects of English and in a great many languages other than English in various different forms. Negation Copying, as far as English dialects go, is the phenomenon that a sentence negation is repeated further down in the clause in all positions licensing the occurrence of *any* or words of its class, such as *ever* or *the slightest*. In standard English, (19e) would be more properly formulated as:

(22) He's never been any good, not ever.

There are even dialects where Negation Copying penetrates into relative clauses, as is shown by Labov's sentences taken from Black New York English, such as (1972b: 812):

(23) Ain't nobody know about no club. ("there isn't anybody who knows about any club")

It would, of course, be ludicrous to take the surface structures of sentences such as (19f) or (23) and compute their truth-value relative to some model on the basis of the number of negations occurring in them. (19f), by virtue of its 'literal' structure, would then come to mean "he has always been some good, some time", and (23) if taken 'literally', would then come to mean "everybody knows about some club". It is embarrassingly clear that surface semantics is a noble but unrealistic enterprise. There are too many sentences which do not mean what their surface structures say they should mean.

The constituency argument also links up with the translation argument. Take the following two sentences, with identical meaning, taken from English and Dutch, respectively:

(24) a. I haven't seen him in weeks.
     b. Ik heb hem in geen weken gezien.

The English sentence might be read as something like "for a number of weeks it has not been the case that I saw him". If due precaution is taken, this might perhaps be extracted from the surface structure. The Dutch sentence however reads literally "I have him in no weeks seen", and could thus only be rendered as "for no number of weeks has it been the case that I saw him". Unless, of course, what is taken as semantic input is not the surface structure but an adequate underlying semantic analysis.

Or take the following synonymous sentences in English, Dutch, German and French:

(25) a. He should have eaten. [Nec + Past] — [have + inf] — [eat + pp]
    b. Hij had moeten eten [have + Past] — [Nec + inf] — [eat + inf]
    c. Er hätte essen sollen. [have + subj + Past] — [eat + inf]
                                 — [Nec + inf]
    d. Il aurait dû manger. [have + Fut + Past] — [Nec + pp] — [eat + inf]

("Nec" stands for "verb of necessity"; "inf" for "infinitive"; "pp" for "past participle"; "subj" for "subjunctive"; "Fut" for "Future tense".) One sees immediately that the amount of variation in the combinations of *Nec, have*, and *eat* with *Past, inf*, and *pp* (to say nothing of *subj* and *Fut*) is quite perplexing. How on earth a semantic calculus could possibly extract the one common meaning of these sentences from these very different structures without the help of a linguistic specification of the form "at that past time it was mandatory (but not true) that he ate", while attaching standard meanings to all the morphemes involved and avoiding *ad hoc* leaps, is a problem of such magnitude that one would much prefer not to have to face it. And it does not have to be faced, since the apparent jugglings with morphemes are in each case part of a well-ordered system of transformational mappings between semantic analyses and surface structures, describable in the grammars of the respective languages. There is no objection to calling those grammars a part of the semantics of the languages in question, but then it cannot be surface semantics, not even with lambda-calculus.

2.1.6 Predicate Raising

There was a great deal of wisdom in old Heraclitus' sayings "Nature likes to hide herself" and "Invisible harmony is stronger than visible harmony". The true semantic nature of a sentence is very often disguised by the appearance of a surface structure which lies about its meaning, or hides it meaning beyond recognition – unless there is a key for decoding the scramble. But decoding the scramble leads to another message, this time intelligible and in canonical form.

This is precisely what we find in the Dutch and German so-called 'verb clusterings' at the end of sentences or clauses. This construction has a certain theoretical significance in that it has so far proved a fatal obstacle to all theories of grammar, not only those constrained by surface semantics but also all kinds of grammatical theories kept within constraints to do with notions of 'autonomous syntax' or the like – except the theory of grammar proposed and developed in circles of what used to be called 'generative semantics' and is called here 'semantic syntax'. Despite early publications

(Seuren 1972a; Evers 1975), it took some time for it to become widely known that this construction is a crucial test for theories. Given its importance, and given the extreme simplicity of its description in terms of semantically canonical underlying structures and the transformational rule of *Predicate Raising*, which, moreover, makes the resulting surface structures eminently parsable, a separate section (2.4.5) will be devoted to its analysis and description. Here we shall limit ourselves to some telling examples. There are some **40** odd verbs in Dutch which take embedded clauses in some argument position and either impose or license the rule of Predicate Raising by which the main verb of the lower clause is lifted up to form one single verbal constituent with the Predicate Raising verb (PR-verb) itself. The lower verb is attached either to the right (as in Dutch), or to the left (as in German) of the higher verb. The S-node of the subordinate clause is dissolved (as a consequence of a general principle, as we shall see below (2.3.2)), and all its dependent constituents are re-attached to the higher S. German and Dutch are virtually identical in this respect, except that, as has been said, Dutch takes right-attachment and German takes left-attachment. Since Dutch is my native language, I feel more confident in making assertions about Dutch than about German. I shall, therefore, give examples from Dutch only.

The following sentence is normal and good Dutch:

(26) Ik heb het hem zich   leren laten uitleggen.
     I have it him himself teach let   explain
     ("I have taught him to let it be explained to him")

According to most current analyses, it surface structure is as follows (we shall refrain from commenting on the alternative surface structures that have been proposed):

(27)

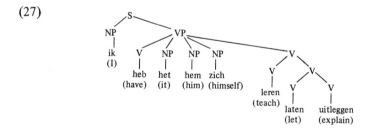

When placed in the position of a subordinate clause, the finite verb *heb* is at the top of the verbal complex at the far right. (I defend the view that the whole verbal complex, at the end of the cycle, stands in second position, as in all proper SVO languages, and that the rule of Verb Final moves the non-finite part of the verb cluster to the far right in main clauses, and the entire verbal complex in subordinate clauses.) The structure is then:

(28) a. ... dat ik het hem zich heb leren laten uitleggen.

b.

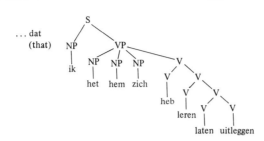

Since the structure of Dutch (and German) subordinate clauses is both more simple and more telling in this respect, I shall work only with subordinate clauses.

We note that any adequate semantic analysis of (28) must specify that the following relations hold between the various verbs and the nominal arguments:

(29) ik PrPf-leren hem$_i$ [hij$_i$ laten [$\emptyset$ uitleggen hem$_i$ het]]
      (I PrPf-teach him$_i$ [he$_i$ let [$\emptyset$ explain him$_i$ it]])

The symbol "PrPf" stands for the tense *present perfect*, expressed by the auxiliary verb *hebben* (*have*). Note that in the most deeply embedded clause "$\emptyset$ uitleggen hem het" the indirect object *hem* precedes the direct object *het*. This is the rule in Dutch, as it is in English, provided the indirect object is not reinforced with a preposition. Yet, in the surface structure of (28), as in (26), this order is reversed. This is due to a late rule of clitic pronoun reshuffling, whereby the semantically 'weakest' *het* (*it*) comes to stand closest to the verb. Thus one has in Dutch:

(30) a. Ik gaf Jan het boek. ("I gave Jan the book")
     b. Ik gaf het hem. ("I gave it him")

This phenomenon of clitic reshuffling in itself is a nasty obstacle to surface semantics, but we shall not concentrate on that here.

The verb *leren* is marked lexically as inducing the rule of Secondary Subject Deletion (SSD), whereby it is required by the formation rules that this lower subject is anaphorically related to the indirect object of *leren*, and as licensing the rule of Predicate Raising. That is, SSD is obligatory but PR is optional. If PR does not apply, the lower infinitive gets the (meaningless) particle *te* preceding it. In (31) PR has not applied on the *leren*-cycle (but it has on the *laten*-cycle, owing to the fact that PR is obligatory for *laten*). We thus get the following structure for (31):

(31) a. ... dat ik hem geleerd heb het zich te laten uitleggen.

b.

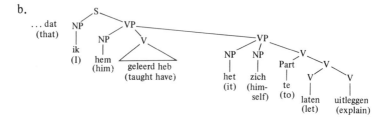

We want our theory to provide (31) with the same semantic description as (28), and, moreover, to predict that (31b) is as good a surface structure as (28b) – and likewise for the main clauses (26) and:

(32) Ik heb hem geleerd het zich te laten uitleggen.

This can be done by assuming the semantic analysis (neglecting tense):

(33)

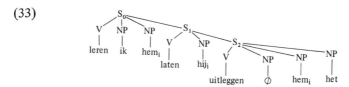

to underlie all sentences considered. We stipulate, furthermore, that *laten* takes obligatory PR but *leren* takes optional PR (besides obligatory SSD). All the rules mentioned so far (except Verb Final and the rule of clitic pronoun reshuffling) are cyclic, i.e. they are induced or licensed by the verb on each S-cycle and the S-cycles are run through from bottom to top. PR takes the verb of the lower clause and attaches it to the verb of the clause in question (i.e. the verb triggering the rule). The attachment is done by creating a copy of the categorial node V above the existing V-node, and attaching the lower structure $_V[-]$ to the right or the left of the existing $_V[-]$. In this case, attachment is to the right (This technique of attachment is typical in grammar. We shall call it *adoption*.) As an automatic consequence of PR the lower S-node is wiped out and the remaining constituents are re-attached to the higher S. Of course, much of what is put forward here needs further explanation and, above all, further motivation. This will be given in section 2.3.1, when the general principles of the grammar are expounded. At this stage we must be content with a mere demonstration in the service of our argument against surface semantics.

Applying these rules and principles, we see that nothing is to be done on the S_2-cycle. On the S_1-cycle we must apply PR:

(34)

                    S_1
              V   NP NP NP NP
          V   V hij_i ∅ hem_i het
          laten uitleggen

At this stage the object pronoun *hem* is reflexivized due to the fact that it is co-referential with the subject *hij*. It is thus changed into *zich*. (As we shall see in section 4.2.2, there is the condition that there isn't any 'old' subject intervening between the new subject and the reflexive pronoun, but we will not go into these complications here.)

On the S_0-cycle, with the main verb *leren*, PR is optional. If we apply PR, the resulting structure is (always taking into account SSD):

(35)

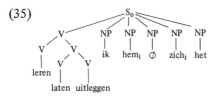

Further apparatus, to be explained below, then lifts the subject *ik* out of this structure and transforms (35) into a structure of the familiar NP–VP type. This marks the end of the application of the cyclic rules. Postcyclic rules now carry out some rearranging and trimming. The clitic *het* is placed closest to the verbal cluster so that it occupies the leftmost position of the NP-series. The node "$\emptyset$" is deleted (i.e. the unspecified subject of *uitleggen* is not expressed phonologically). And the verbal cluster is moved to the far right by the rule of Verb Final. If we take due account of tense processing, the final result is the tree structure given in (28b) above for the subordinate clause version, and in (27) for the main clause version.

If, on the other hand, we do not apply PR on the S_0-cycle, i.e. on the *leren*-cycle, then the result is (always observing SSD):

(36)

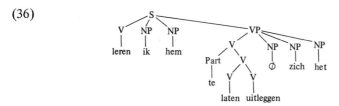

Tense processing changes this into:

(37)

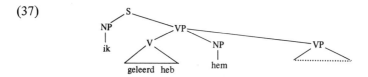

(Note that there is a general principle changing an S-node into a VP-node whenever the subject of the S is removed by some rule.) Now Verb Final moves the V-clusters to the far right, without, however, crossing any S-

Grammar and lexicon

boundaries or VP-boundaries (and, of course, *het* is moved leftwards and "∅" is deleted). This gives (31b) for the subordinate clause version. The main clause version comes about as a result of Verb Final moving only the non-finite part of the main verb of the main clause, i.e. *geleerd*, to the far right of S before the lower VP.

This is, in outline and without the necessary circumstantial evidence supporting the treatment as a whole in general linguistic terms, the account most naturally provided within the framework of semantic syntax. (The missing general support, as well as a more detailed treatment, will be provided below.) The point here is that surface semantics has not, so far, succeeded in providing a satisfactory account of this type of construction. Nor is it likely to do so. Consider, e.g., the subordinate clauses:

(38) a. ... dat ik het hem zich heb leren laten permitteren.

b. ... dat ik geleerd heb het hem zich te laten permitteren.

both meaning "... that I have learned to let him permit it to himself". The Dutch verb *leren* is ambiguous between the causative meaning "teach" and the non-causative "learn". In both meanings it induces SSD, albeit that for the meaning "learn" anaphora is required from the lower subject to the higher subject, not to the higher indirect object. Likewise, in both meanings it licenses PR, while the particle *te* is obligatory when PR is not applied. The surface structure of (38a) is identical to that of (28). Yet, the predicate-argument relations are different:

(39) ik PrPf-leren [ik laten [hij$_i$ permitteren hem$_i$ het]]

(I PrPf-learn [I let [he$_i$ permit him$_i$ it]])

If forced, (38a) could also mean "... that I have taught him to let it be permitted to him", but this reading is far-fetched for pragmatic reasons, just as the reading "I have learned to let him explain it to himself" is awkward and improbable for (26).

It is easy, of course, to derive (38a) from the semantically correct and transparent underlying form (again, disregarding tense):

(40)

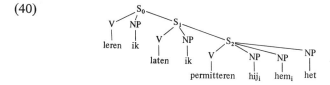

Hem is reflexivized to *zich*. Then, PR on the S_1-cycle gives:

(41)

Morphology changes *hij* into *hem*, since it is no longer clause-subject. Further PR on the S_0-cycle results in:

(42)

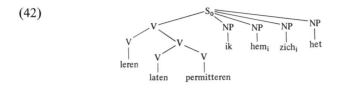

Tense processing and post-cyclic treatment now result in precisely the surface structure (28b) for the subordinate clause version, or (27) for the main clause version – except, of course, that *permitteren* replaces *uitleggen*.

If, however, PR is not applied on the highest cycle, only SSD applies, with the result that S_1 changes into VP:

(43)

A comparison with (36) shows that the nominal argument *hem* is now not an argument of S, as it is there, but of the VP (i.e. the original S_1). This corresponds with the fact that in (31a) and (32) the pronoun *hem* occurs before the past participle *geleerd*, but in (38b) and its main clause version

(44) Ik heb geleerd het hem zich te laten permitteren.

it occurs within the lower VP. Predictably, these sentences, i.e. all cases where PR has *not* applied on the *leren*-cycle, are thus *not* ambiguous the way (26), (28a), (38a) or

(45) Ik heb het hem zich leren laten permitteren.

are – although one reading is always 'far-fetched'. This absence of ambiguity is caused by the fact that non-application of PR on the S_0-cycle ensures that the nominal argument *hem*, whose position and function crucially distinguish the two readings, stays with its clause (of VP) and is not amalgamated into a series of NPs by the rule of PR.

It will become clear below that this grammatical analysis is neither far-fetched nor *ad hoc*, but that it is, in fact, entirely natural and exceptionally successful, as grammatical analyses go. In fact, the PR-description of Dutch and German verbal clusters gets the facts crucially right in all respects in which it has so far been tested. Moreover, the difference between German and Dutch can be accounted for by the simple variation between, respectively, left adoption and right adoption.[4] On the basis of the success of this analysis it is reasonable to claim that a theory which unscrambles surface structures to semantically regular underlying structures holds very strong cards indeed. The more so since no adequate alternative has so far been presented, neither in terms of alternative transformational rules nor in terms of surface semantics.

2.1.7 Steedman's categorial analysis[5]

The only serious challenge to the Predicate Raising analysis of the 'Dutch construction', and indeed the most serious and sustained attempt at a consistent surface semantics, is found in various papers by Steedman (in particular 1983a; 1983b). Steedman's analysis is cast in terms of a variety of categorial grammar. It must be seen in the context of recent claims made by Gazdar and others that the apparatus of phrase structure grammars is sufficiently rich to serve as a general mathematical model for the syntactic description of natural languages. The claim is powerful since not only does it allow for surface semantics, it also keeps the syntax of natural languages within the bounds of well-known mathematical systems. It moreover has the psycholinguistic merit that phrase structure grammars not only generate sentences but also provide directly for parsing methods. In other words, languages generated by such grammars are not just canonical sets but are, in addition, solvable, i.e. there is a finite decision procedure to determine whether a given string of symbols is or is not a string of the language. As long, however, as some construction in some language resists treatment in these terms it remains doubtful whether natural language is of that mathematical type.

Steedman's categorial grammar is easiest to grasp if taken as a partial parser. The rules required for parsing overgenerate strings, so that they must

---

[4] There is also a difference between German and Dutch in the occurrence of past participles. The rule in German seems to be that a past participle is used for a PR-verb under a perfect tense only if the verb in question takes PR *optionally*. Thus, the infinitive occurs with *lassen* ("left"), which has obligatory PR:

    (i) Ich habe es ihn sagen lassen.   ("I have let him say it")
       I   have it him say   let (inf.)

But when, e.g., *lehren* ("teach"), which takes optional PR, is placed under a perfect tense, the past participle is required:

    (ii) Ich habe es ihn sagen gelehrt.   ("I have taught him to say it")
        I   have it him say   taught

Dutch has infinitives in all cases where PR has applied.

[5] I am indebted to Mark Steedman for his willingness to be a most helpful correspondent on the matters discussed in the following section. Our correspondence has helped to clear up a number of potential misunderstandings as well as actual mistakes on my part.

be further constrained if they are to form a generative grammar. This constraining is done, in principle, by the addition of a number of feature specifications limiting the applicability of rules of certain types. In our discussion we shall concentrate on the parsing rules only, that being sufficient for our purpose. The problem of overgeneration will be mentioned only in so far as the parsing rules apply to ungrammatical strings.

Given a sentence, each word is assigned a category based on its lexical specification. Some of these category assignments are subsequently modified on account of the structural position of the word in the sentence or of its morphological characteristics. These modifications affect the subject, the finite verb, and infinitivals. The subject is changed from NP to a function from finite verb phrases (FVP) into sentences (S). The finite verb form is changed from its lexical specification to a function from the remaining elements of VP to an FVP. Infinitives are changed from functions to S into functions to Sinf. The examples below will illustrate this.

Some categories are primitive, others are complex. For our purposes we can take as primitive the categories S and NP. A complex category is a function of the form X/Y, where Y is the input and X the resulting value. Such a function is commonly read as "it takes a Y to form an X". Whether the Y is to be found on the immediate right or the immediate left is specified by "combination rules" which are either given separately or derived from feature-governed conventions. If a category X/Y is forward combining, then, if it is followed by an instance of category Y, the two may be combined into a binary constituent labelled "X" for the sentence under analysis. If the category X/Y is backward combining it must be preceded by a Yf or a subtree labelled "X" to come about. Complex categories may be used again to build further complex categories (X/Y)/Z or X/(Y/Z), etc. (The brackets can be overruled by the parser, but without the semantics being affected.)

This much is fairly common. Steedman does, however, introduce a couple of formal innovations which enable him to 'bridge' discontinuous constituents under certain conditions and also to assign to preposed constituents their correct semantic function, or one of the possible correct semantic functions. The first new device is called Partial Combination, and it works as follows. If a forward combining category X/Y is followed by a category Y/Z which is not preceded or followed by a category Z, then a subtree labelled "X" may be set up in spite of the missing Z, but the new X now 'inherits' the requirement that a Z must be found later to set up a real X. That is, the newly set up subtree will carry the labelling "X/Z". The inherited category Z may be passed on again if the next combination involving X/Z has not eliminated Z. Steedman furthermore stipulates that primitive as well as complex categories may be inherited and that the bracketing structure of the complex categories is irrelevant. An example is the following, where "Sinf", as has been said, is the modification of the lexical S, where the subject is

S/FVP, and the finite verb form *will* is labelled as "FVP/(Sinf/NP)", i.e. a function from infinitival verb phrases (Sinf/NP) to finite verb phrases (FVP):

(46)

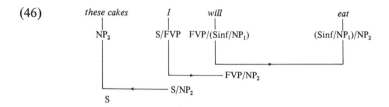

The NP-subscripts are entirely for convenience. They play no role in the parsing. In the semantics they are relevant only for the correct function assignment of embedded subjectless clauses. Thus the missing subject in clauses embedded under *promise* is (an anaphoric correlate of) the higher subject, but with, e.g., *persuade* of the higher indirect object. The former is, accordingly, specified as $S/NP_1/NP_2/(Sinf/NP_1)$, whereas the latter is $S/NP_1/NP_2/(Sinf/NP_2)$. The arrows remind the reader of the direction of the combination in question.

Partial Combination 'bridges' the discontinuous *these cakes...eat* and assigns the correct function to *these cakes*: this NP eliminates the NP inherited from *eat* as object. It is essential for a correct parsing that inherited categories find the right 'heirs', i.e. those which are indeed understood by speakers to fulfil the function assigned to them by the algorithm. The point is of crucial importance since the semantics that goes with the parsing assigns a semantic value to each node in the tree. If, in an extensional model, constituents are eliminated incorrectly the semantics will assign incorrect extensions to nodes and incorrect truth-values will be assigned.

That this danger is real for Dutch sentences is quickly shown. (47a) is the main clause version of the subordinate clause (47b), where, as always, the verb is final:

(47) a. Marie gaf haar zoon geld. ("Marie gave her son money")
   b. ...dat Marie haar zoon geld gaf. ("...that Marie gave her son money")

Assuming, as seems correct, that in lexical specifications of ditransitive verbs the indirect object precedes the direct object, NP_2 is the indirect object and NP_3 is the direct object in the following specification of the verb *geven* ("give"):

geven: $S/NP_1/NP_2/NP_3$

In the sentences of (47) the finite verb form *gaf* ("gave") will receive a modified specification of the form "FVP/NP₂/NP₃". The parsings of (47a) and (47b) now look as follows (the bracketing of complex nodes is ignored):

(47) a′.

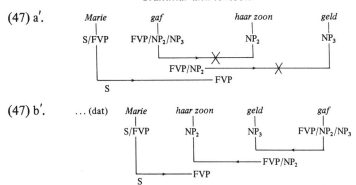

(47) b′.

The parsing in (47b′) is semantically correct: NP_3 eliminates the object-slot in *gaf* and NP_2 eliminates the indirect-object-slot. (47a′), however, is incorrect since it will read as "Marie gave her son to the money".

Topicalizing by fronting in main clauses also goes wrong in some cases. Sentence (48), which may mean "it was her son that I saw Mary give money to", comes out semantically with the son giving money to Marie. (Note that Dutch has a rule inverting subject and finite verb whenever a constituent is fronted.)

(48)

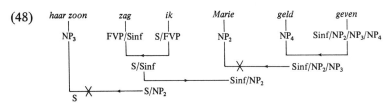

Further problems arise with clitic pronouns. Dutch is like English in that clitic pronouns are drawn towards the verb – the weaker the clitic the closer it stands to the verb. In Dutch this means that in main clauses the weakest clitics stand closest to the finite verb form; in subordinate clauses they follow immediately upon the subject:

(49) a. Ik gaf het haar. ("I gave it her")
    b. ... dat ik het haar gaf. ("... that I gave it her")

Now take the following subordinate clause, meaning "... that I made him drink it":

(50)

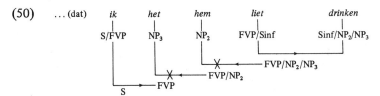

Clearly, (50) reads as "I made it drink him". Similar phenomena occur with certain intransitive verbs which take dative objects, like *overkomen* ("happen to"), *passen* ("fit"), *staan* ("go with", said of clothes), *bevallen* ("please"), *mankeren* ("ail"). These verbs have the peculiarity that the indirect object is allowed to behave positionally as the subject, though the morphology remains orthodox.[6] This leads to complications in many theories,[7] including Steedman's analysis. Take, e.g.:

(51) a. Ik laat Karel een ongeluk overkomen. ("I cause an accident to happen to Karel")

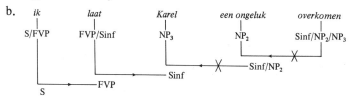

b.

As is seen, this reads as "I cause Karel to happen to an accident", which is not a reading this sentence can have. Note, furthermore, that the following direct question

(52) a. Moet Karel een ongeluk overkomen? ("Must an accident happen to Karel?")

---

[6] In some substandard varieties of Dutch some of these verbs have undergone the complete reanalysis, so that the original indirect object is now subject. E.g., where standard Dutch has optionally:

(i) Marie passen die schoenen niet. ("Those shoes don't fit Marie")

one often finds the substandard:

(ii) Marie past die schoenen niet. ("Marie doesn't fit those shoes").

The same phenomenon, of course, has occurred in the English verb *like*: *I like it* used to be *Me likes it*.

[7] This problem is also mentioned in Koster (1978: 157 ff.). Koster observes that these verbs take the auxiliary *zijn* ("be"), not *hebben* ("have"), for the perfect tenses (p. 159), and that clitic pronouns functioning as indirect object also tend to occupy the position of subject, in particular in passive subordinate clauses:

Ik geloof dat hem het boek verkocht werd. ("I believe that the book was sold him")

Koster's reasoning now is (p. 161) that, since passive perfect tenses also take the auxiliary *zijn*, in sentences containing verbs that take *zijn* as perfect tense auxiliary the surface subject is really an underlying direct object. Sentence (i) in note 6, for example, would then really be a transitive sentence, with *die schoenen* as direct object. Unfortunately, however, it simply is not the case that the dative intransitive verbs in question all take the perfect auxiliary *zijn*. *Passen* ("fit"), *staan* ("go with", "become", of clothes), *mankeren* ("ail"), e.g., take *hebben* without any doubt. Moreover, it is not clear what should be meant by "really" in Koster's analysis. The answer seems to be that in the cases at hand there is an incipient reanalysis of the indirect object as subject.

does not even properly parse in the system as developed so far:

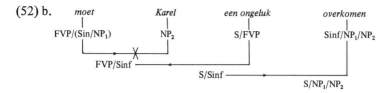

(52) b.

In this parsing, which is the only possible one, *Karel* (indirect object) eliminates the subject-NP. Moreover, the final result is not S, as it should be.

It is thus clear that in this phase of development (represented, e.g., in Steedman 1983a) the system is still highly defective. However, much of the foregoing being recognized by Steedman, he introduces a further device in Steedman 1983b, intended to get around these obstacles. The device consists in assigning all NPs except the subject the category $v/(v/NP)$, where v is a variable category ranging over verbal categories S, FVP, $Sinf(/NP_1/\ldots/NP_n)$, and v/X, but not NP or PP. The value of v in each case is determined by optimal parsability. The following combination rules are allowed:

(53) a. $v/(v/Y) + X/Y \Rightarrow X$ (where X is verbal, and v = X; forward)[8]
    b. $X/Y + v/(v/Z) \Rightarrow X/(Y/Z)$ (where Y is verbal, and v = Y; forward)
    c. $v/(v/X) + v/(v/Y) \Rightarrow v/((v/X)/Y)$ (where v = v/X; forward)

The effect of this device is surprising. For example, (47a) and (47b) are now parsable as follows:

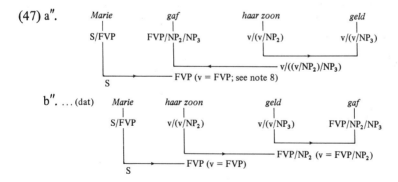

(47) a″.

b″. … (dat)

Now there are no incorrect function assignments. Note, however, that these are not the only possible parsings, and that in (47a) incorrect function

---

[8] Although it is not specified as such by Steedman, rule (53a) must also be allowed in its backward version: $X/Y + v/(v/Y) \Rightarrow X$, since without the backward version (47a″) would not be possible, and (47a) would not be parsable in any semantically correct way.

assignment can be avoided only if *haar zoon* and *geld* are combined into one constituent. These points will be returned to below.

(48) and (52) are now also scot-free:

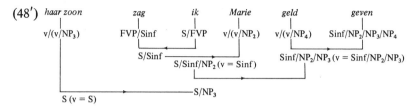

Note that the parsing as given above in (48) remains possible. This will then correspond to a reading where the son gave money to Marie. (52) now parses as follows:

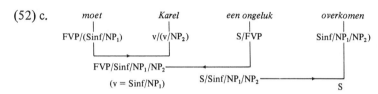

No other parsing is possible. In general, all preposings, including those in relative clauses, are now solved in the sense that correct function assignments are or can be made. No solution is provided, however, for cases like (50) and (51) above. That is, when, contrary to the lexical specification of ditransitive verbs or intransitive verbs with an indirect object, the order of constituents is changed, either by a clitic rule or, as in (51) or (52), by a rule assigning the indirect object the position of subject, then difficulties arise. Although (52) gets through without problems, (50) and (51) do not. The only way of getting the semantics right for these two is:

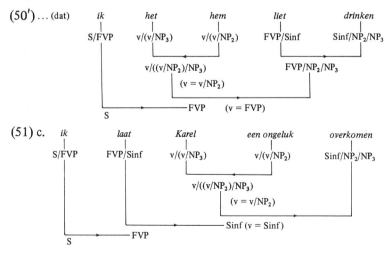

However, in order to get these parsings we had to apply the inverse variance of rule (53c):

(53) d. $v/(v/X) + v/(v/Y) \Rightarrow v/((v/Y)/X)$ (where $v = v/Y$; backward)

But this rule is not allowed in the system as defined by Steedman. And it is easy to see why: if (53d) were an allowable rule, the system would overparse so grossly that it would lose virtually all its value. For example, it would then no longer make any difference whether an indirect object precedes or follows the direct object, so that *Harry gave his son the dogs* would parse optionally as representing the meaning of *Harry gave his son to the dogs.*

A little experimenting with this new notation for NPs shows that Steedman's system gets correct function assignments in virtually all cases, in particular for preposings. This fact makes it a highly interesting, if not the most interesting, challenger to SA-semantics. It is important, therefore, that its defects be spelled out. One problem with Steedman's analysis is its excess power, both in the generation and in the parsing of sentences. Its over-generating property appears from the fact that it parses without any special problems strings which are not well formed, such as:

(54) a. *... dat it Jan probeer de koeien te leren melken.
("... that I try to teach Jan to milk the cows")

b. *De deur te helpen verven zag ik Julia proberen Harry.
("*To help paint the door I saw Julian try Harry")

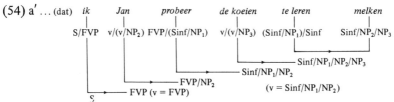

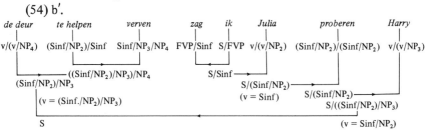

The reason for the ungrammaticality of (54a) is that both *proberen* ("try") and *leren* ("teach") take optional Predicate Raising, so that the following four variants are allowed:

(55) a. ... dat ik Jan de koeien probeer te leren melken. (PR throughout)
b. ... dat ik probeer Jan de koeien te leren melken. (PR on *leren*-cycle only)

    c. ... dat ik Jan probeer te leren de koeien te melken. (PR on *proberen*-cycle only)

    d. ... dat ik probeer Jan te leren de koeien te melken. (No PR at all)

(54a), however, is simply not generated by the rules of our syntax. (54b) is ungrammatical since [*de deur te helpen verven*] is not a constituent in the correct analysis, and only constituents can be preposed. Note that [*Harry de deur te helpen verven*] is a constituent and can, therefore, be preposed (with an optional dummy *doen* ("do")):

(56) Harry de deur te helpen verven zag ik Julia proberen (te doen).

      ("To help Harry paint the door I saw Julia try (to do)")

Steedman's system also overparses, in that it assigns structures, and semantic interpretations, to sentences even though these structures and interpretations are not allowed. Thus, even with the "v/(v/NP)" notation for NPs, Steedman's parser still allows for the incorrect parsing of (47a'), provided the backward version of rule (53a) is allowed in (see note 8: without it, (47a) is not correctly parsable in any case):

(47) a'''.

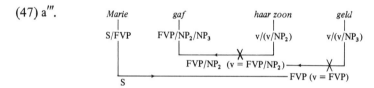

Likewise, the two regular parsings for (51a) assign incorrect functions. (51d) runs parallel to (51b), and (51e) is a further parsing made possible by the "v/(v/NP)" notation:

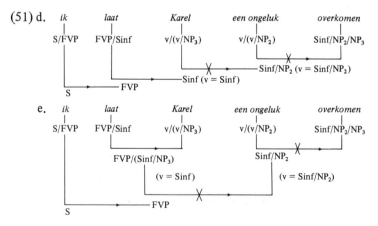

In both cases, the parsing goes through without a hitch; only the subscripts assigned to the NPs fail to match, indicating incorrect function assignments.

A similar incorrect parsing occurs when, for example, the NP *de koeien* in (55c) above is relativized:

(57) a. (de koeien) die ik Jan probeer te leren te melken.
("(the cows) that I try to teach Jan to milk")

This clause is not ambiguous owing to the second occurrence of *te*. As can be gathered from (55a)–(55d), the infinitive after *leren* gets the particle *te* only if PR has not applied on the *leren*-cycle. Given that (55a)–(55d) are the only possible forms, it follows that (57a) can correspond only to (55c). Notice the difference with, e.g.,

(57) b. (de koeien) die ik Jan **probeer te leren melken.**

which can only correspond with (55a). Since, however, the nominal arguments in (55a) are consecutive, (57b) may also correspond to:

(58) a. ... dat ik de koeien Jan probeer te leren melken.
("... that I try to teach the cows to milk John")

The same meaning expressed in the form of (55c) leads to:

(58) b. ... dat ik de koeien probeer te leren Jan te melken.

But extraction of *de koeien* does not yield (57a). Hence, (57b) is ambiguous in a way that (57a) is not. This point is crucial since Steedman's parser does not recognize the differences resulting from application or non-application of PR, and hence can give no account of the difference between (57a) and (57b). In fact, it assigns to both the two analyses that are legitimate for (57b). (57c) illustrates the incorrect parsing of (57a):

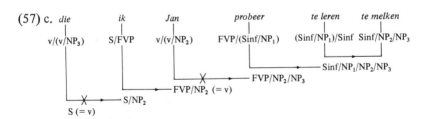

A further problem with Steedman's parser resides in the surface structures which it assigns. For one thing, the parser does not, in many cases, assign one unique surface structure but allows for more than one semantically equivalent structure, as was illustrated in (51d) and (51e) above. Steedman's comment is that this is of no consequence as long as the semantics is correct. Moreover, he says, some of the structures assigned come in handy for the grammatical definition of such processes as conjunction, including Gapping and Right Node Raising. This may be so (although conjunction in Dutch has so far resisted any theory), but conjunction phenomena are not the only criterion by which to judge constituenthood. In fact, the classically accepted necessary and sufficient condition for constituenthood in at least one surface structure is the possibility of preposing: if a part of a sentence can be preposed (with concomitant inversion of finite verb and subject) in main clauses, then that part is a constituent in at least one possible surface structure. And vice versa, if a part of a sentence cannot be preposed, then there is no surface structure in which that part is a constituent. If we now look at (47a″) above, we see that *haar zoon* and *geld* must form one constituent if the parser is to assign correct functions to the NPs. However, that constituent, required by the parser, must be spurious since it cannot be preposed. Separately, the NPs can be preposed:

(59) a. *Haar zoon geld gaf Marie. ("Her son money Marie gave")
   b. Haar zoon gaf Marie geld. ("Her son Marie gave money to")
   c. Geld gaf Marie haar zoon. ("Money Marie gave to her son")

It follows that the constituent created by Steedman's parser for *haar zoon* and *geld* is structurally incorrect. Steedman contends (private communication) that the constituent set up by his parser is needed for Right Node Raising, as in:

(60) a. [Jan leende en Marie gaf] de leraar een boek.
   ("Jan lent and Marie gave the teacher a book")

Against this it must be observed that no argument exists which shows that the identical material on the right must be one constituent. In other words, (60) may well have the surface structure:

(60) b.

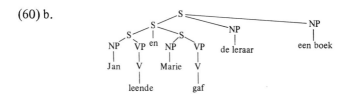

This can arguably be considered to be the result of a rule of Conjunction Reduction operating on (60c) and leaving it intact but for the material which is identical in S_1 and S_2; this material is then re-attached to the right, in the proper order:

(60) c.

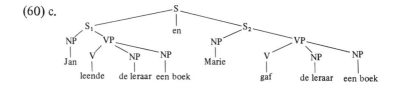

In any case, the Right Node Raising argument cannot be valid in Steedman's analysis, since the following is a well-formed sentence in Dutch:

(61) [Karel moet en Piet kan] een ongeluk overkomen.
("An accident must happen to Karel and may happen to Piet")

If the Right Node Raising argument were correct, then *een ongeluk over-komen* must be one constituent. However, as has been shown, there is only one possible parsing for (52a), i.e. (52c), and no such constituent is found there.

We must conclude, therefore, that there is something amiss with the strong parsing power of Steedman's system: it occasionally assigns grammatically incorrect structures.

Further obstacles consist in the phenomena that are associated with clitic pronouns in Dutch, as well as with the treatment of indirect objects of certain intransitive verbs, as has been shown above, in (50') and (51c).

Other problems might be mentioned, such as the behaviour of reflexives. Dutch reflexives are notoriously hard to treat. It may be that they can be treated in terms of Steedman's analysis, but to the extent that they are understood it seems that they receive the most straightforward explanatory account in terms of a grammar relating SAs to surface structures. We have seen that the reflexive pronoun *zich* in (26), (28), (31) and (32) above is explained by the fact that it takes a subject (clause-mate) antecedent at some stage in the transformational derivation; at that stage the 'deep' pronoun *hem* is morphologically marked for reflexivity. (But see section 4.2.2 for further comment.)

All in all, Steedman's analysis remains intriguing, even though it is bound to provoke doubts. Given the achievements of surface semantics in the past, it is hardly possible to predict whether further refinements or novel devices might circumvent the obstacles that can be pointed out. It is, therefore, fruitless to speculate on that score now. What is less fruitless is to try and see if Steedman's system cannot be made use of, with a few alterations. In the following section an attempt is made to reconcile Steedman's parser with the grammatical treatment proposed here for the Dutch construction.

2.1.8 Parsing from Surface Structure to Semantic Analysis

It seems that all difficulties arising with Steedman's parser can be eliminated when reordering rules are allowed before and during the parsing. Moreover, n-ary branching must be allowed, and the actual parsing procedure must be well ordered. The reorderings mean that any semantics directly attached to the parsing is no longer surface semantics. In fact, the structures resulting from this revised parsing procedure are not surface structures, but so-called *shallow structures*. In generative terms, shallow structures are structures of sentences such as they are at the end of the cycle and before the post-cyclic rules have operated. We shall see that the shallow structures yielded by the new parser are precisely the shallow structures generated by the generative rules proposed, and that ungrammatical surface strings are refused by the parser. The semantic contribution made by the new parser is that correct function assignments are made. The shallow structures plus the correct function assignments then suffice for the reconstruction of the correct SAs. In all this, the novel "v/(v/NP)" notation is no longer needed, so that the apparatus is simplified on that score.

First (A), categories are assigned in much the same way as is done by Steedman. Subjects are S/FVP; finite verbs are FVP/X; infinitivals are re-dubbed Sinf/X. There is, however, one important difference. Verbs which take more than one argument are represented lexically not as (S/NP)/NP or ((S/NP)/NP)/NP, as Steedman wants it, but as S/NP + NP or S/NP + NP + NP. "X/Y + Z" is to be read as a function from ordered pairs of constituents ⟨a, b⟩, where a is of category Y and b is of category Z, to representatives of category X. Likewise for three arguments. The resulting subtree is ternary (or quaternary) branching:

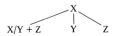

The new parser allows for the overall constraint that *all combination is forward*. As regards the inheritance of surplus material, the following general principle applies: *all elimination is maximal*; *remainders are inherited*. Thus the following combinations are among those allowed:

X/Y + Z	— Y − Z	⇒ X
X/Y + Z	— Z	⇒ X/Y
X/Y + Z	— Y − Z/W	⇒ X/W
X/Y + Z	— Z/W	⇒ X/Y + W
X/Y + Z/W	— Z/W + V	⇒ X/Y + V
X/Y + Z/W	— Z/W/V	⇒ X/Y + V
X/Y/Z	— Y/Z + W	⇒ X/W

However, X/Y + Z followed by Y not followed by Z or Z/W does not parse.

Then follow a few movement parsing rules. They are the inverse of the generative (postcyclic) movement rules needed for Dutch. The first rule spots clitic pronouns and optionally moves clitics within NP sequences. The second rule optionally inverts the positions of subject and indirect object if the verb is a dative intransitive verb (DIV) of the type *overkomen, passen, staan* (i.e. "happen", "fit", "go with" (of clothes), respectively). The third rule moves S/FVP (i.e. the subject) to just left of FVP/X (i.e. the finite verb form) if

S/FVP follows FVP/X. We can thus formulate the following three rules, applied in this order:

B: (a) Optionally move clitics within NP sequences.
   (b) Optionally swap S/FVP and NP$_1$ if verb is a DIV.
   (c) If S/FVP follows FVP/X, move S/FVP to just left of FVP/X.

At this stage we can define the notion of *antesite*: the antesite is the position on the far left, just before S/FVP. If the antesite is filled with lexical material, some preposing has taken place. Any material in the antesite of a sentence must be one constituent which only combines as a whole with other constituents.

From here on we can go to stage C, the actual parsing procedure. Before we can specify this procedure we must define the notion of *cluster*. Given a sequence of verbal forms $V_1, \ldots, V_n$, we have a cluster just in case all V_i take Predicate Raising (PR) with regard to V_{i+1} ($1 \leqslant i < n$). If some V_i takes optional PR, then either V_i is taken as taking PR with regard to V_{i+1}, or else $V_{i+1}, \ldots, V_n$ is a cluster (provided all Vs in $V_{i+1}, \ldots, V_{n-1}$ take PR), and $V_1, \ldots, V_i$ is tested again for clusterhood. Furthermore, we must define the instruction *cluster*: the instruction "cluster" applies to verbal sequences and prescribes cyclical combination from the right:

$$[V_1[\ldots [V_{n-3}[V_{n-2}[V_{n-1} - V_n]]]\ldots]]$$

The instruction "cluster" automatically applies to all clusters. Otherwise it applies as specified.

The parsing procedure C is applied first to any material in the antesite that lends itself to parsing. (Antesite material is parsable when the preposed constituent is complex and contains a verbal form, as in (56) above.) Then C applies cyclically from the right. It runs as follows (VC stands for "verbal complex", i.e. cluster or single verb)

C: (1) Establish *clusters*.
   (2) for rightmost VC in line, *move left*:
      (a) If VC is FVP/X (X may be null), move left to just after S/FVP.
      (b) If the next V to the left takes PR, then move left to just after V, and cluster.
      (c) If there is no V to the left, or if the next V to the left does not take PR, then move left over at most $n-1$ arguments if VC is specified for n arguments. Do not cluster.
   (3) *Combine* from VC to its arguments. Use antesite if required.
   (4) Go to C2.

The expression "use antesite" in C3 is to be understood as follows. If in the process of parsing there is a node $X/Y_1 + Y_2 + \ldots + Y_n$ followed by the right number and kinds of nodes Y_1 to Y_n except that some Y_i is missing, we have a *gap*. In such a case the procedure C checks if the missing constituent Y_i is to be found in the antesite. If it is, Y_i is moved to the gap and fills it. The parsing proceeds.

This machinery suffices for the parsing of Dutch main and subordinate clauses provided they do not contain participles, separated verbal particles (as in *Jan eet de appel op*, i.e. "Jan eats the apple up"; the verb *opeten* ("eat up") has *op* as separable verbal particle), or adverbials. A few examples will illustrate this.

(62) a. Harry wil de deur verven. ("Harry wants to paint the door")

b. A: category assignment

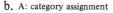

B: movement rules do not apply.

C: parsing

(1) no change

(63) a. Harry zal de deur willen verven. ("Harry will want to paint the door")

b.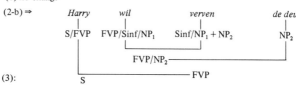

(64) a. Harry besluit de deur te verven. ("Harry decides to paint the door")

b.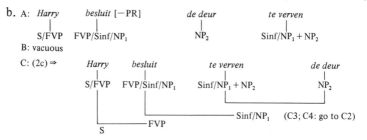

(65) a. Harry liet ik de deur verven. ("Harry I made paint the door")

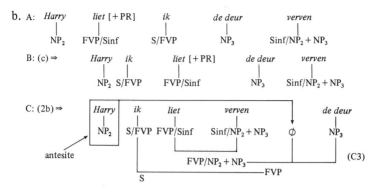

(66) a. ... dat ik Marie geld gaf. ("... that I gave Marie money")

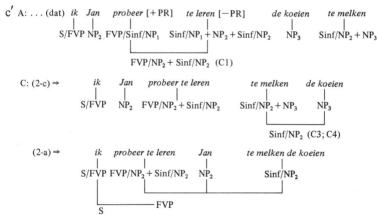

(55) c. ... dat ik Jan probeer te leren de koeien te melken.
("... that I try to teach Jan to milk the cows")

Note that the ungrammatical (54a) is refused:

(54) a. *... dat ik Jan probeer de koeien te leren melken.

The parsing can be tried in two ways, since *proberen* ("try") takes optional
PR. (So does *leren*, but the absence of *te* after *leren* shows that *leren* has in

any case taken PR here. Note that if (54a) reads ... *de koeien te leren te melken*, the parser still rejects it.) We shall first try the parsing with PR:

(54) a′.

A: ... (dat)   ik   Jan   probeer [+PR]   de koeien   te leren [+PR]   melken
            S/FVP   NP₂   FVP/Sinf/NP₁   NP₃   Sinf/NP₁ + NP₂ + Sinf/NP₂   Sinf/NP₂ + NP₃

Sinf/NP₁ + NP₂ + NP₃   (C1)

C: (2-b) ⇒   ik   Jan   probeer   te leren melken   de koeien
          S/FVP | NP₂ | FVP/Sinf/NP₁   Sinf/NP₁ + NP₂ + NP₃   NP₃

FVP/NP₂ + NP₃
FVP/NP₂   (C3)

Here the parsing stops since there is no further VC-cycle to turn to (C4 cannot apply), and the structure as it stands does not allow for any further parsing. If backward combination were allowed the parsing could go on successfully, but this parser only allows forward combination. We now try again, without PR on *proberen*:

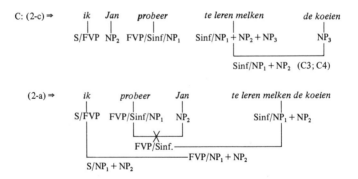

C: (2-c) ⇒   ik   Jan   probeer   te leren melken   de koeien
          S/FVP   NP₂   FVP/Sinf/NP₁   Sinf/NP₁ + NP₂ + NP₃   NP₃

Sinf/NP₁ + NP₂   (C3; C4)

(2-a) ⇒   ik   probeer   Jan   te leren melken de koeien
        S/FVP   FVP/Sinf/NP₁   NP₂   Sinf/NP₁ + NP₂

FVP/Sinf.
FVP/NP₁ + NP₂
S/NP₁ + NP₂

Here the parsing goes on, though at the cost of an incorrect function assignment. But it ends unsuccessfully since the final node is not S. The reader will find out for himself that (55a) and (55d) parse without a hitch.

Finally, it will now be shown that (54b) is rejected by the parser, whereas (56) passes without problems:

(54) b. *De deur te helpen verven zag ik Julia proberen Harry.
(56)   Harry de deur te helpen verven zag ik Julia proberen (te doen).

Let us try (54b) first:

(54) b".

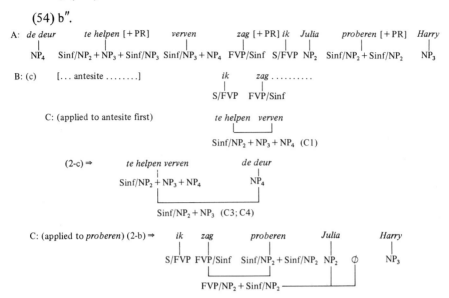

A: de deur   te helpen [+PR]   verven   zag [+PR] ik Julia   proberen [+PR]   Harry

NP₄   Sinf/NP₂ + NP₃ + Sinf/NP₃ Sinf/NP₃ + NP₄ FVP/Sinf S/FVP NP₂ Sinf/NP₂ + Sinf/NP₂   NP₃

B: (c)   [... antesite ....]   ik   zag ....
S/FVP   FVP/Sinf

C: (applied to antesite first)   te helpen   verven

Sinf/NP₂ + NP₃ + NP₄ (C1)

(2-c) ⇒   te helpen verven   de deur
Sinf/NP₂ + NP₃ + NP₄   NP₄

Sinf/NP₂ + NP₃ (C3; C4)

C: (applied to proberen) (2-b) ⇒   ik   zag   proberen   Julia   Harry
S/FVP FVP/Sinf Sinf/NP₂ + Sinf/NP₂ NP₂   ∅   NP₃

FVP/NP₂ + Sinf/NP₂

At this point there is a gap between *Julia* and *Harry*. The antesite can provide only Sinf/NP₂ + NP₃. This does not satisfy the conditions of [*zag – proberen*]: what is needed is Sinf/NP₂. Moreover, the constituent *Harry* remains high and dry. The parsing would go through if after insertion of the antesite in the gap the antesite constituent were allowed to combine with *Harry*, yielding Sinf/NP₂. However, this is not allowed since the application of C to the antesite has been brought to an end.

It is now immediately clear that (56) provides no problems. After application of C2-c and C3, the antesite has the following structure:

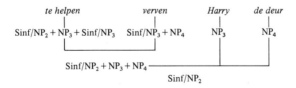

te helpen   verven   Harry   de deur
Sinf/NP₂ + NP₃ + Sinf/NP₃   Sinf/NP₃ + NP₄   NP₃   NP₄

Sinf/NP₂ + NP₃ + NP₄

Sinf/NP₂

Without *te doen*, the remainder of the sentence, with C2 applied to *proberen*, parses exactly like the preceding sentence, however without *Harry* at the end. Now the antesite foots the bill: the gap requires a Sinf/NP₂, which is precisely what the antesite offers. With the addition of the empty pro-form *te doen* (which seems to be preferred by many speakers in cases such as this), the analysis does not change essentially. C will apply first to *te doen*. If *proberen* takes PR, then the cluster [*proberen te doen*] arises through C1:

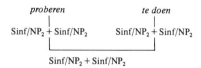

From here on the parsing proceeds as before. If *proberen* does not take PR (which is optional in this case), then C makes *te doen* combine without clustering with *proberen*. Then there is a Sinf/NP₂-gap after *te doen*, duly filled by the antesite. The resulting constituent is labelled Sinf/NP₂ again. After this, *proberen* moves to *zag* and clusters with it to form FVP/NP₂ + Sinf/NP₂. This combines successfully with *Julia* and the final Sinf/NP₂-constituent just formed, yielding FVP. Now *ik* combines with this FVP yielding S.

So far, the revised parsing procedure has taken us up to shallow structure level. We want, however, to push through to the level of Semantic Analyses. This is now relatively simple. We first need *restoration rules* (RR). They undo the effect of the labelling modifications needed for the parser till now:

RR-1 $FVP/X \rightarrow S/NP_1 + X$ (where X may be null)
       $S/FVP \rightarrow NP_1$; go to RR-2.
RR-2 $S/NP_i (+NP_j) + Sinf/NP_\alpha \rightarrow S/NP_i (+NP_j) + S'(\alpha)$ (where "$S'(\alpha)$" stands for the instruction that an anaphoric correlate of NP_i or NP_j is the subject of S'); go to RR-3.
RR-3 $Sinf \rightarrow S$; go to RR-2 if RR-2 is applicable; otherwise CLOSE.

The category specifications directly dominating lexical verbs will now match exactly the predicate-argument structure specified for these verbs in the lexicon. This enables the parser to make a *Predicate–Arguments* inventory (PA-inventory) for all the verbs involved and thus to build a Semantic Analysis. As was pointed out at the beginning of section 2.1.7, missing subjects in subjectless embedded clauses are supplied on the basis of subscripts: the missing subject of the embedded clause is an anaphoric correlate of either the subject or the indirect object of the higher clause. It is the function of RR-2 to ensure suppletion of the correct subject in those cases. At stage A, the parser modifies an embedded S (or Sinf) into Sinf/NP_α whenever the higher verb takes Secondary Subject Deletion (SSD).

The PA-inventory is set up as follows. Take the lexical element E directly dominated by FVP/X before RR-1 applied. Set up E as the main verb. Assign to E the arguments as required by its lexical specification. NP₁ is the subject-term. The remaining arguments, if any, are assigned according to their history of elimination in the shallow structure tree. Anaphoric correlates are represented by the subscript of the antecedent NP.

Having set up a PA-inventory for a sentence S, we can simplify the node-labellings in the shallow structure tree. NP-labels are not changed. But any non-lexical node (i.e. any node not directly dominating lexical material) labelled "S/NP$_i$" can be rewritten as "VP", and all other nodes labelled "S/X" (X must not be null) are rewritten as "V". We can also now build a Semantic Analysis for S in the form of a syntactic labelled tree, with the labels S, V and NP. Let us consider a few examples.

The shallow structure analysis of (62) as given above will look as follows after the restoration rules.

(62) c.

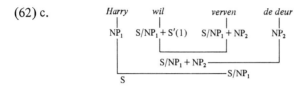

The PA-inventory is:

$_S$[willen(Harry$_1$, $_{S'}$[verven(1, de deur)])]

The shallow structure tree with simplified node labellings (and turned upside down to do justice to notational tradition) is:

(62) d.

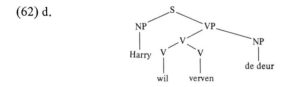

The SA-tree is:

(62) e.

It will be shown in section 2.3.1 below that a simple set of cyclic transformational rules, including PR, maps (62e) – extended with the appropriate tense operators – onto the shallow structure (62d). Postcyclic rules subsequently map (62d) on to the surface structure corresponding to (62a).

The further parsing of (63) proceeds as follows. The restored shallow structure is:

(63) c.

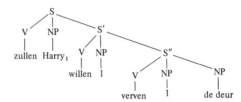

with the PA-inventory: $_S$[zullen(Harry$_1$, $_{S'}$[willen(1, $_{S''}$[verven(1, de deur)])])], and the SA-tree:

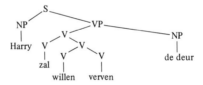

The simplified shallow structure, which results from the cyclic rules of the grammar applied to the SA-tree, is:

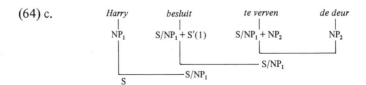

Note that in the PA-inventory the object-S of *zullen* must be the S that has *willen* as predicate. This follows from the fact that $S'(1)$ of *zal* in (63c) is the restoration of Sinf/NP$_1$ in (63b), and this Sinf/NP$_1$ is eliminated there by *willen*. Likewise, the object-S of *willen* must be the S of *verven*, since $S''(1)$ of *willen* is the restoration of Sinf/NP$_1$ in (63b), which is eliminated by *verven*.

The restored shallow structure of (64) is:

(64) c.

       Harry   *besluit*   *te verven*   *de deur*

        NP$_1$ S/NP$_1$ + S$'$(1)   S/NP$_1$ + NP$_2$ NP$_2$

                                  —————— S/NP$_1$

                   ——————— S/NP$_1$
               S

with the PA-inventory: $_S$[besluiten(Harry$_1$, $_{S'}$[verven(1, de deur)])], and the SA-tree:

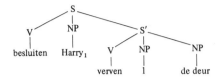

and the simplified shallow structure:

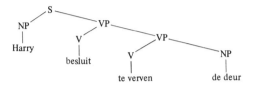

Notice that the shallow structure of (64) differs from that of (62), although their surface strings are entirely analogous (but for the particle *te*, which is not essential here):

(62) a. Harry wil de deur verven.

(64) a. Harry besluit de deur te verven.

The difference is brought about by the fact that *willen* takes obligatory PR, besides SSD, whereas *besluiten* does not take PR but only SSD. The different rule properties of these verbs are manifest in cases of infinitival embedding. Thus, the future tense of (62a) is (63a), but of (64a) it is (64a'), with the shallow structure (64a"). (64a''') is ungrammatical:

(63) a. Harry zal de deur willen verven.

(64) a'. Harry zal besluiten de deur te verven.

a".

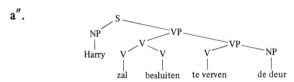

(a''') *Harry zal de deur **besluiten te verven**.

The difference is manifest also in perfect tenses, as in (67a)–(67e). PR-verbs have no past participle when followed by an embedded and clustered infinitive. Instead they use the infinitive. However, verbs which take no PR have an ordinary past participle (*besloten*):

(67) a. Harry heeft de deur willen verven. ("Harry has wanted to paint the door")

b. *Harry heeft gewild de deur verven. (id.)

c. Harry heeft besloten de deur te verven. ("Harry has decided to paint the door")

d. *Harry heeft de deur besluiten te verven. (id.)

e. *Harry heeft de deur besloten te verven. (id.)

As has been observed, some verbs take optional PR. They include *proberen* ("try"), *leren* ("teach", "learn") and *helpen* ("help"). *Proberen* always gives its following infinitive the particle *te*; *leren* and *helpen* only when they do not take PR. *Helpen*, moreover, has different meanings according to whether PR is applied or not. Thus we have, without any semantic difference, the pairs:

(68) a. Harry heeft de deur proberen te verven. ⎫ ("Harry has tried to
     b. Harry heeft geprobeerd de deur te verven. ⎭ paint the door")

(69) a. Harry heeft de deur leren verven. ⎫ ("Harry has learned to
     b. Harry heeft geleerd de deur te verven. ⎭ paint the door")

where *geprobeerd* and *geleerd* are past participles of the respective verbs. But, although (70a) and (70b) are both well formed, they differ in meaning. (70a) is ambiguous in a way in which (70b) is not:

(70) a. Ik heb hem helpen failliet gaan. ((i) "I have been instrumental in
     making him go bankrupt"
     (ii) "I have helped him to go
     bankrupt")

   b. Ik heb hem geholpen failliet te gaan. ("I have helped him to go
     bankrupt" - where *geholpen* is
     the past participle of *helpen*).

The semantic difference between the two verbs *helpen* is expressible in the lexicon by specifying that if *helpen* takes PR it is specified either as $S/NP + S$, or as $S/NP_1 + NP_2 + S(2)$. If it does not take PR, its only specification is $S/NP_1 + NP_2 + S(2)$.[9]

We shall conclude with two final examples, (65) and (55c). The restored shallow structure of (65) is:

(65) c.

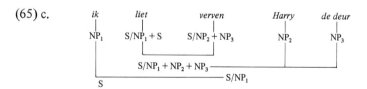

[9] As a consequence of the lexical specification of *helpen* [+ PR], a sentence like (i) is fully grammatical and meaningful, whereas (ii) is absurd:

(i) Dat heeft het helpen regenen. ("That has been instrumental in making it rain")

(ii) !Dat heeft het geholpen te regenen. ("That has helped it to rain")

with the PA-inventory: ₛ[laten(ik, ₛ[verven(Harry, de deur)])] and the SA-tree:

The simplified shallow structure is:

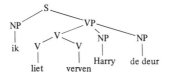

For (55c) the restored shallow structure is:

(55) c″.
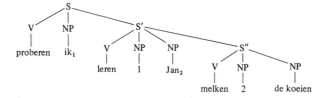

with the PA-inventory: ₛ[proberen(ik₁, ₛ′[leren(1, Jan₂, ₛ″[melken(2, de koeien)])])] and the corresponding SA-tree:

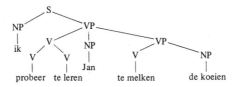

The simplified shallow structure is:

The reader will have no difficulty in applying this procedure to (55a), (55b), (55c) and other sentences. It will be appreciated that the parsing procedure sketched here is far from complete for the whole set of Dutch sentences (and subordinate clauses). Yet the kind of constructions analysed here will inevitably form a core part of any grammar of Dutch. The purpose of the foregoing exposé has been primarily to show the advantages of not letting the semantics operate on surface structures (strings) alone. Instead, it is highly profitable to interpose a grammar establishing Semantic Analyses for any given well-formed surface string. The actual semantic calculus can then proceed from there.

It must be noted, in this connection, that the term "semantics" does not have the same meaning here as in more or less standard model-theoretic approaches. There the term refers to a calculus establishing extensions for constituents and sentences in possible worlds. Here it refers to a calculus establishing increments in a cognitive discourse domain. Given this difference, our purpose is served best by not taking the shallow structures as input to the semantics (as might still be proposed by the model-theorists), but rather the Semantic Analyses. Why this is so will become clear in later chapters. Meanwhile it needs to be stressed that it is still the case that the Dutch construction of PR-taking verbs and resulting infinitival clusters resists any grammatical analysis, generative or parsing, which does not take transformations into account and thus does not operate with different levels of structural representation. Moreover, the PR-account as sketched here and elaborated in greater detail below, still boasts of being the only account available which gets the facts crucially right.

2.2 Formation rules for Semantic Analysis

For a precise definition of the rules of grammar it is necessary that the well-formedness conditions for Semantic Analyses be properly given. This is what the following section aims at doing. The well-formedness conditions in question will be presented in the form of the well-known rewrite rules whose application generates tree structures. These rules consist of one single symbol on the left-hand side of an arrow, the arrow just mentioned, and a string of one or more symbols on the right-hand side of the arrow. On application, the left-hand side symbol is interpreted as a tree node, and the right-hand side string as the node or nodes directly dominated by the first symbol. An application of a rewrite rule thus generates a section of a tree.

The rules in question must not be looked upon as direct reflections of anything actually presented in the brain. As was pointed out in section 1.4, such rules are prime examples of descriptive devices whose interpretation can be no more than *epiphenomenal*. That is, they define the output or input conditions for some bit or bits of machinery in the brain, whose actual structure is a different matter. The description does nothing more than formulate conditions for any realistic hypothesis about the actual system embodied in the bit of mental machinery in question. In the case at hand, the machinery is at least twofold: Semantic Analyses being an intermediate level of representation there is always an input and an output, either in production or in comprehension. The actual machinery involved, at either end, must be understood if anything like an explanation is to come forth. It is prudent, however, to attempt an adequate formulation of the epiphenomenal conditions first, before the actual systems involved are made objects of investigation. In this book more strongly realistic hypotheses will be set up for certain parts of the complex machinery, in particular for the grammar (which relates SAs to surface strings), and for the cognitive discourse domains (which receive input increments from SAs in comprehension). We will, however, leave entirely undiscussed whatever cognitive mechanism or set of procedures must be held responsible for the generation of thoughts as they crystallize in SAs in the production of utterances. This particular faculty of the brain or mind is considered to be still too far out of reach.

Although the *rules* are thus denied any plausible interpretation in terms of psychological reality, the *structures* generated by them (in the mathematical sense of "generate") are certainly expected to correspond to structures that occur in the brain during the comprehension or the production of the sentences in question. Moreover, these structures are expected to be 'universal' to a very high degree. That is, they are in any case not strictly language-specific, as grammars are. On the other hand, they are not universal in the sense that they are entirely independent of the specific language in which they are to be expressed or in which they are understood. First, it is quite likely that the verb-first order of our structures is not universal, and that most languages which have the verb as final element in sentences also have underlying verb-last order. Then, there seem to be more or less language-specific ways of 'organizing' thoughts into SAs and hence into sentences. Thus, some languages have a preference for co-ordination where other languages prefer subordination. Or it may happen that, owing to certain features of grammar, a particular thought is not expressible via an otherwise perfectly well-formed SA. Thus, for example, the grammar of Standard English does not allow for a natural surface expression of the thought corresponding to "This is the man such that I do not know who killed him", given the impossibility in English to extract constituents from an embedded question:

(71) a. *This is the man that I don't know who killed.

In Latin, however, this constraint is relaxed, so that we have the perfectly grammatical:

(71) b. Hic est vir quem qui necaverit nescio.

Another example is the thought corresponding to "I shall make Henry speak to him", which, though unproblematic for English, requires special phrasing in French. One would expect (72a) to be grammatical in French, but, for reasons still largely opaque, it is not. On the other hand, (72b) is fully grammatical but it requires a different (though semantically equivalent) Semantic Analysis:[10]

(72) a. *Je lui ferai parler Henry. (lit.: I to him will make speak Henry)
  b. Je ferai en sorte que Henry lui parle. (lit.: I will make so that Henry to him speak)

The question of the degree of universality of 'deep' structures has often been mentioned in the literature on transformational grammar, especially in its earlier phases of development, but it has never been answered satisfactorily. Nor can it be answered here. What is needed for a satisfactory solution is subtle and detailed, and crucially correct, descriptions of a large number of very different languages, all descriptions being cast in similar or at least comparable theoretical terms. However, despite the fact that the number of professional linguists is larger now than ever before in history, this information is not available. We must, therefore, be content with an imprecise, but open-minded, answer to the question of the universality of Semantic Analyses.

A salient feature of the SAs that figure in our theory is the dramatic widening of the category of predicates. In fact, the category is so wide, for the syntax of SA, that one can safely maintain that the whole lexicon of SA consists of predicates only. Not only surface verbs and adjectives are represented as SA-predicates, but also sentence adverbs (such as *perhaps, fortunately*), subordinating and co-ordinating conjunctions, and quantifiers. Nouns are analysed as predicates destined to be used in NP-positions. Tenses and modalities are likewise SA-predicates. The predicates in the SA-lexicon are all marked with respect to the surface category that must or may represent them. Thus, the SA-predicate *love* is marked for being a verb in surface structure, but *dog* is marked for being a surface noun, and *lovely* for being a surface adjective.

Syntactic descriptions for predicate calculus formulae traditionally and invariably specify atomic formulae first, and then define recursive methods for the construction of complex formulae by means of logical connectives and quantifiers. Separate truth-definitions are then given for the atomic formulae and for the truth-functional operators and the quantifiers. In our analysis the truth-conditional (and other) logical propositional connectives, including negation, as well as the quantifiers, are all treated as SA-predicates. The propositional connectives take one or two propositions as their argu-

[10] For a discussion of (71) and (72), cp. Seuren 1973b.

ments, as the case may be. The quantifiers take two arguments, the first being a set denotation, the second either a set denotation or a definite term. We shall see in a moment how this works. The advantages, as will become clear, are manifold: a greatly simplified syntax for SAs, a greatly simplified cyclic grammar, a greatly simplified semantics, a greatly simplified truth-definition. As for the latter, one single truth-definition will now do for all sentences, including the most complex ones: truth results just in case the n-tuple of the reference values of the terms is a member of the extension set of the predicate. We shall have occasion frequently, in later chapters, to come back to this point, and it will be seen that this simple uniformity in truth-definition for all cases provides us with a supplementary criterion by which to judge the tenability and quality of analyses. In this chapter, however, we shall limit ourselves to the syntactic aspects of complex constructions. The logical and semantic aspects will be looked at later.[11]

SA-structures, then, can be considered as constrained by the following formation rules of well-formedness conditions:

SA formation rules

$$\text{(i) } S \rightarrow \begin{cases} V^1 + \begin{Bmatrix} NP_s \\ S_s \end{Bmatrix} \\ V^2 + \begin{Bmatrix} NP_s \\ S_s \end{Bmatrix} + \begin{Bmatrix} NP_o \\ S_o \end{Bmatrix} \\ V^3 + \begin{Bmatrix} NP_s \\ S_s \end{Bmatrix} + NP_i + \begin{Bmatrix} NP_o \\ S_o \end{Bmatrix} \end{cases}$$

$$\text{(ii) } NP_{s,o} \rightarrow \begin{cases} p \\ x: + S_x^{**} \\ {}^{\wedge}x + S_x^{**} \\ S \end{cases}$$

$$\text{(iii) } NP_i \rightarrow \begin{Bmatrix} p \\ x: + S_x^{**} \end{Bmatrix}$$

The subscript "s" stands for "subject"; "o" for "object"; "i" for "indirect object"; "p" stands for "pronoun". The assumption is made that predicates never take more than *three* arguments. (In fact, the assumption is that predicates never take more than *two* arguments; whenever a surface verb is ditransitive, its prelexical analysis will show it up to be composed out of more primitive predicates; the combination through PR creates the excess argument; see McCawley 1968, and below.) "S_x" stands for "S with at least one (possibly embedded) argument x". "S^{**}" stands for any number of successive Ss. "$x: +S_x$" is to be read as "the x such that $_S[\ldots x \ldots]$". This is the analysis of definite NPs. Thus, *the rose* is analysed as "x: (rose(x))", i.e.

---

[11] The idea of analysing the linguistic counterparts of the traditional logical elements as predicates is, of course, not new. To my knowledge, it was first presented by McCawley; see, e.g., McCawley 1972.

"the x such that x is a rose". Subsequent Ss after the first regularly end up as relative clauses or as adjectives in Surface Structure. The operator "x:" will be called the definite description operator, or *DD-operator*. Terms under a DD-operator denote a discourse address or a set of discourse addresses. If no appropriate discourse address can be found or set up, the sentence in question is uninterpretable in the given discourse. (Sentences which are uninterpretable in any discourse at all are ungrammatical.) Only if a term t under a DD-operator denotes a discourse address can it refer. If it refers, i.e. if the discourse in question is related to a verification domain in the world, it refers either to an actually existing entity or set of entities, or to an intensional entity or a set of those. These and related matters will be discussed at length in the chapters to follow.

The set-denoting operator (*SD-operator*) "^x" has no direct counterpart in the discourse domain under construction: its discourse value is determined by the mechanics of the predicate under which it occurs. It does have a truth-conditional definition, however: "^x(rose(x))" has as its extension the set of all roses in the real world. (The notation will be enriched, and the notions refined, in chapter 5 below.) Set denotations are used in the grammatical and semantic analyses of quantified NPs, as will be demonstrated below.

The *x* which is required or allowed under a DD-operator is *ruled* by that operator, and the DD-operator is called the *ruler* of the variable. The *x* required or allowed under an SD-operator is *bound* by it. The notion of binding is identical to that used in classical predicate calculus, and it is of prime importance, amongst other things, in the interpretation of bound variable pronouns (see section 4.2.3 below). Variable ruling is a very different notion, as will become clear below, in section 4.2.

Bound or ruled variables do not usually show up in Surface Structure. In simple cases they merge into the quantified or definite noun. But when the term in question contains further material this is packed into a relative clause (*the/a/every rose that I admired*). Only when the lexical material under a term t contains another term t' with a relative clause containing the ruled or bound variable, i.e. in indirect relative clauses, does the variable show up as a full pronoun: *the/a rose that I gave to the/a girl who liked it*.

All NPs can be rewritten as a single symbol p, represented in Surface Structure as a denoting pronoun (i.e. non-reflexive and not quantifier-bound) with an antecedent NP outside the term or term complex of which p is a part. That is, p is not a ruled variable. (For questions concerning anaphora and classes of pronouns, see section 4.2 below.)

Ss under the DD-operator usually contain one-term predicates (V^1), resulting in NPs containing a single noun: *dog, man, sun*. There are, however, also 'transitive' nouns, such as *name, centre, picture, set*. These have in common that they cannot be well defined unless it is specified what they are a name, centre, picture, or set of. Accordingly, 'abstract' two-term predicates

(V^2) are invented for such nouns, serving as predicates in Ss under the DD-operator in SAs:

x: (name(x, NP))
x: (be the middle of(x, NP))
x: (depict(x, NP))
x: (collect(x, NP))

It does not really matter much what form is given to such abstract predicates, provided their semantic specification (satisfaction conditions) corresponds with that of their surface counterpart, and provided the lexicon specifies what surface noun they will be represented by in surface strings. The object-NP of such nouns will always be characterized by the preposition *of* in surface structure. When there is a relation of recognizability between a *noun*, transitive or not, and an existing surface *verb*, and the verb is considered 'primary' with regard to the noun, then the latter is often said to be a *nominalization* of the verb. Some nominalizations may even be ditransitive, such as *gift*, derived from the ditransitive verb *give*.

Adjectives are also sometimes transitive, or at least they allow for two arguments. Gradable adjectives are a case in point: they often allow for a definite measure phrase to be added: *20 feet long*, *six years old*. These call for abstract predicates of the type *measure*, *weigh*, *cost*, as in:

(73) a. This measures five feet.
b. This weights five tons.
c. This costs five dollars.

In these cases the second argument (one hesitates to call it "object") precedes the adjective in surface structure. With the adjective *worth*, as in *This is worth five dollars*, the 'object' follows the adjective. And with *worthy* it follows and is characterized by *of*: *worthy of this nation*. It is not the purpose of this study to unravel all the details of the grammar of English and other languages with respect to such differences. It must suffice here to point out the parallels of polyadicity in other categories than surface structure verbs.

What is more directly relevant here is the treatment of quantifiers and connectives (co-ordinating conjunctions and negation). We shall deal with the quantifiers first. As is well known, every language has a large variety of quantifiers. Yet, they always seem to fall into two main classes, the *existential* and the *universal* quantifiers. (It is hardly a coincidence that standard logics distinguish precisely two quantifiers, the existential and the universal quantifier. Natural language does the same, but more subtly.)

Semantically, quantifiers are treated as predicates taking two arguments. The first argument must be a set-denoting term; the second argument is either a set-denoting term or a definite term, depending on the domain of quantification. Despite the variety of quantifiers found in different languages, we shall limit ourselves to simple existential and universal quantifiers, represented, respectively, by "∃" and "∀". Intuitively, the existential quantifier says that there is a non-empty intersection between the two sets denoted, and the universal quantifier expresses the claim that the set denoted by the object-term is included in the set denoted by the subject-term. (If the object-term is a definite term it denotes a set actually represented in the discourse domain; otherwise a set of potential addresses.) A few examples will help. Disregarding tense, (74a) has the SA (74b):

(74) a. Leo loves a lady.
    b. $\exists 1(\hat{x}(\text{love}(x: (\text{"Leo"}(x)), x)), \hat{x}(\text{lady}(x)))$

The SA is to be read intuitively as "there is a non-empty intersection (of one individual) between the set of any individuals Leo loves and the set of any individuals who are ladies". The semantic effect of the existential predicate is the setting up of a new address in the discourse (D), characterized by the predicates "lady(x)" and "love(d_n, x)", where d_n is the address denoted by the definite term *Leo*. (Note, incidentally, that proper names are analysed as ordinary definite descriptions, with the predicate ""N"" for any name N, to be read as "be called N" or "bear the name N". This analysis of proper names will be discussed in full in section 6.4.) The numeral "1" after the predicate "∃" indicates the number of addresses to be set up. Other possible additions would be "m" for "much" or "many", "sev" for "several", etc.

Now consider (75a) with the analysis (75b):

(75) a. Leo loves one of the ladies.
    b. $\exists 1(\hat{x}(\text{love}(x: (\text{"Leo"}(x)), x)), x: (\text{ladies}(x)))$

(We use the expedient of simply turning the predicate "lady" into the plural form of the corresponding noun in order to indicate the plurality of the sets denoted by the term in question. In the absence of any convincing analysis of plurality of nouns no further comment will be made on this aspect.) (75b) reads intuitively as "there is a non-empty intersection (of one individual) between the set of whatever individuals Leo loves and the set of individuals who are ladies and have been specified in the context". Again, the semantic effect consists in the setting up of a new address. However, this address does not increase the number of individuals referred to by the discourse. It is a 'provisional' address in the sense that it must, at some stage, be identified with one of the existing addresses characterized by the predicate "lady(x)". Addresses of this kind will be represented thus:

$$
\boxed{d_m}
$$
$$
x \in D\{\text{lady}(x)\}
$$
$$
\text{love}(d_n, x)
$$

The notation "$x \in D\{lady(x)\}$" is to be read as the instruction "this address must be identified with one member of the class of addresses characterized in the discourse domain D by the predicate 'lady(x)'". This analysis opens up the possibility of explaining why, after (75a), the question *Which one of the ladies does Leo love?* is a natural follow-up.

A sentence like (76a) is analysed as (76b):

(76) a. Leo loves a wealthy lady.

　　b. $\exists 1(\hat{}x(love(x:("Leo"(x)), x)), \hat{}x(lady(x)\,wealthy(x)))$

Note that the existential predicate still takes only two terms, both set-denoting terms. The truth-conditions would be satisfied if the predicate were to be given three set-denoting terms:

(76) c. $\exists 1(\hat{}x(love(x:("Leo"(x)), x), \hat{}x(lady(x)), \hat{}x(wealthy(x)))$

and it would not be difficult to adapt the SA Formation Rules to accommodate such structures systematically. Yet analyses like (76c) are considered incorrect for grammatical reasons. Later on in this chapter the grammatical transformation of structures like (74b), (75b) and (76b) to the corresponding (a)-sentences will be discussed in full. It must suffice here to point out that the subject-term of the quantifiers always represents the skeletal grammatical structure of the eventual sentence, while the second term represents the domain of quantification. In fact, a quantified noun phrase corresponding with the second term or object-term will eventually fill the position of the x ruled by $\hat{}x$ in the subject-term. Thus, e.g., the object-term of (74b), $\hat{}x(lady(x))$, will appear as the quantified noun phrase *a lady* in the position of the last x in the subject-term, thus giving love(x:("Leo"(x)), a lady), which, suitably treated, comes out as (74a). Likewise, the object-term of (76b) comes out as the quantified NP *a wealthy lady*, which then fills the same position as referred to in the preceding example, yielding (76a). It will be clear, globally speaking, that the regularity of this treatment would be disturbed if structures like (76c) were adopted, since the existential predicate there takes three arguments. It will now be clear why, in the SA Formation Rules, only one single S-structure is allowed under the SD-operator $\hat{}x$ in the subject-NP, whereas the corresponding option in the object-NP allows for an unlimited number of S_x-structures under $\hat{}x$. (The indirect-object-NP does not allow for set-denoting terms under the SD-operator at all, given the simple restriction that the quantifiers are two-term predicates, and given the fact that these set-denoting terms occur only with **quantifiers**.)

The universal quantifier receives an analogous treatment. Take (77a), with the SA (77b):

(77) a. All John's children are asleep.

　　b. $\forall(\hat{}x(asleep(x)), x:(John's\ children(x)))$ (where the complex predicate "John's child" is left unanalysed)

Note that the object-term stands under the DD-operator x:. This ensures that the semantic instruction that goes with the universal quantifiers applies to established discourse addresses only (or to discourse addresses that can be set up *post hoc*; see chapter 3 for details). The instruction is that all given discourse addresses characterized by "John's child(x)" will be extended with the further predicate "asleep(x)". It is also possible to have the object-term placed under the SD-operator. Then, however, the instruction does not apply to given addresses for specific individuals, but to what was called "super-addresses" in section 1.2, which act as discourse denotations for sets of individuals as defined by some predicate: "the set of all children", for example. This variant of *all* is expressed by placing *all* before its SA-object term without any determiner, such as *the*, *these* or *John's*. More will be said about this distinction in chapter 3, both from the point of view of truth-conditions and as regards the discourse machinery. In principle, this distinction accounts for the semantic difference between, e.g., (78a) and (78b):

(78) a. All children like playing.
    b. All the children like playing.

The informed reader will realize that the quantifying predicate *all* has the complication, like the definite article, of being somehow linked up with existential presuppositions. Sentence (77a), for example, is Strawson's classical example showing that universally quantified sentences carry existential presuppositions with respect to the term quantified over. We shall see (section 3.2.4) that this matter is not among the simplest in semantics, and that existential presuppositions depend more on the nature of the predicate or predicates involved than on *all*.

Multiple occurrences of quantifiers within the same sentence are auto-matically accommodated. Thus (79a) has the analysis (79b) – disregarding tense and the plural *children*:

(79) a. Some children have read all the books.
    b. $\exists(\hat{}x(\forall(\hat{}y(read(x, y)), y:(books(y)))), \hat{}x(child(x)))$

The quantified NP *some children*, originating from the object-term of the existential predicate, will occupy the bound-x-position in the subject-term:

$\forall(\hat{}y(read(some\ children, y)), y:(books(y)))$

Then the object-term of the universal predicate will result in *all the books*, which will subsequently occupy the bound-y-position in the subject-term:

read(some children, all the books)

It is interesting to note, in this connection, that a sentence like

(80) a. These are all John's children.

is ambiguous between a reading in which it is said that the entities referred to by *these* constitute the set of all and only John's children, and a reading implying that all the entities referred to are children of John's. The former reading is rendered by the corresponding SA:

(81) a. $\forall(\hat{}x(be(these, x)), x:(John's\ children(x)))$

The object-term is transformed into the NP *all John's children*, or *all of John's children*, and it is inserted into the S under the SD-operator of the subject-term, to yield (80a) or

(80) b. These are all of John's children.

which is not ambiguous the way (80a) is. The second reading, however, corresponds to:

(81) b. $\forall(\hat{}x(John's\ children(x)), x:(be(these, x)))$

which leads to either of the following:

(80) c. All these are John's children.
   d. All of these are John's children.

which are, again, not ambiguous. The ambiguity of (80a) arises through the application of the optional transformational rule of Quantifier Movement which, probably postcyclically, changes (80c) into (80a). (Cases such as (80a) contribute to the constituency argument against surface semantics, discussed in 2.1.5 above.)

We must end here the discussion of the SA Formation rules. A great deal more could be said, but it seems wise, for expository reasons, to avoid analyses that are too detailed for the time being, and to continue laying out the general features of our plan.

2.3 Some general principles of grammar

2.3.1 The overall architecture

The theory of grammar proposed here is a direct continuation of what was known as 'generative semantics' or 'semantic syntax' in the late 1960s and early 1970s. It assumes a Semantic Analysis as input to a set of transformational rules which map the SA onto a surface structure. There are, however, important differences and extensions with regard to the old theory of generative semantics. First, the rules of grammar are taken to be *really present and operative* in the mind. Or, put differently, the rules as presented on paper in linguistic descriptions are meant to approximate the computational procedures that really take place during production and comprehension of utterances. Although we still lack a precise specification of the formula of interpretation which defines exactly in what ways the written rules are implemented, there is no doubt that, contrary to the SA Formation Rules of the preceding section, the T-rules of the grammar are to be interpreted realistically. Traditional generative semantics, like its rivals in transformational grammar, has never been quite outspoken on this issue. Although the position of realism (mentalism) was proclaimed with some force, it remained non-committal in that no further consequences were drawn. This was to a large extent due to the overall negative results of psycholinguistic experiments carried out mainly in the 1960s and delivering results that seemed incompatible with transformational descriptions. Against this it must be observed, however, that the experiments in question were all based on certain implicit assumptions regarding the hardware implementation of the rules. The most damaging of these assumptions was that if T-rules are interpreted realistically, their implementation must be accessible to willed steering and intervention (see, e.g., Fodor et al. 1974: 229). It is now generally accepted, however, that a distinction must be made between those cognitive processes that are more or less open to introspection and awareness and whose results are recorded in what is called 'declarative knowledge' on the one hand, and routine procedures on the other. The latter are extremely rapid, automatic and inaccessible to any kind of introspection. If T-rules are regarded as formulations of routine procedures, the results of virtually all psycholinguistic experiments that proved negative for transformational grammar in principle can no longer be considered relevant (see Seuren 1978).

An important corollary of our reinforced realist position is that the grammar must now also specify *parsing procedures* in strict compatibility with the generative rules. In section 2.1.8 above an example was given of how such parsing procedure might be developed for the Dutch construction in its essential features. Traditional generative semantics, like its transformationalist rivals, has always been negligent about the parsing aspect.

The tradition of generative semantics, and especially the work of McCawley, has laid the foundations for an extremely interesting branch of grammar, so-called *prelexical syntax*. This resulted from the discovery that certain semantically complex lexical items, in particular verbs (predicates), are open to analyses which run crucially parallel to certain known rules and processes in 'open' syntax, i.e. the syntax of lexically given words. Owing to doctrinal competition and other external factors this promising approach was not adequately appreciated and there was no serious follow-up. In this book the old notions are taken up again and developed a little further. Our attempts in this area, however, are still tentative.

A much-heard objection to generative semantics in the 1970s was that it lacked sufficient *constraints*: given the mathematical laxity of the notion 'transformational grammar' it is necessary that sufficient non-mathematical restrictions should be formulated within which the grammar is taken to operate, on pain of the whole theory becoming unfalsifiable. It must be admitted that it was to a certain extent true that generative semantics was too free in the descriptive means employed.[12] Its critics, however, concluded that therefore generative semantics was objectionable in principle. This conclusion was illogical and flagrantly inconsistent. For what was said of generative semantics was equally applicable to virtually all developments in transformational grammar. Yet it was felt that 'constraints' should be formulated for other approaches and not for generative semantics, which was rejected as a whole, without it being in any way clear that the other approaches had more going for them to begin with. This situation will be redressed, at least in part, in the following pages, where a number of principles will be presented aiming at restricting the transformational processes postulated in significant ways. The restrictions apply mainly to the cyclic rules. The overall effect should be that, first, the theory of grammar presented should be falsifiable to a reasonable degree, and, secondly, that the conditions are preserved for sentential structures to be parsable. It must be observed, in this connection, that it seems a priori likely that language, being a product of nature, owes its functionality, in a very broad sense, less to general mathematical properties of the rule systems employed than to specific empirically detectable properties of systems which are lax from a mathematical point of view.

An area which is still riddled with problems is the interface between grammar and semantics, and in particular the question of the internal analysis of lexical predicates. The problems arise mainly from the fact that those analyses have many non-trivial features in common with grammatical analyses and are yet not clearly part of grammar. Two views have been developed in this respect. Some have proposed that a unique level of Semantic Analysis, with all complex predicates fully analysed, could be regarded as the input to the grammar. Lexical insertion was then thought to take place along with the transformational process. In the other view, a separate Deep Structure (DS) level was assumed, containing lexical predicates and not their analyses. The internal analysis of the complex items was taken to be provided within the lexicon. It appears, however, that both these positions are untenable.

The second theory runs into problems with cases such as:

(82) a. We lack a rudder.
　　　b. He refused her any money.
　　　c. Jack is ignorant of any corruption.

If DS-representations are considered to belong to some form of 'autonomous' syntax, which solely accounts for well-formedness (grammaticality) of

[12] See in particular Newmeyer 1980, ch. 5, and McCawley's reply (1980).

sentences (taking that to be a property which can be established on independent grounds), then these sentences need not themselves be problematic, but there will then be the serious objection that

(82) d. *He missed any train(s).

and vast numbers of similar sentences which are clearly ungrammatical escape the powers of the theory of autonomous syntax.[13] It will be clear anyway that any notion of autonomous syntax is entirely alien to the approach developed here – the main reason being that the notion of well-formedness or grammaticality is derivative of speakers' intuitions of what constitutes a proper expression of a given meaning. If, on the other hand, DS-representations are considered to contain a semantic analysis at any level of depth, and if internal semantic analyses of lexical items are kept away from the syntax, then there is no structural room to account for the fact that, in (82a) *a rudder* does not represent existential quantification over the whole remainder of the sentence. The sentence does not mean "there is a rudder we lack", but "we have no rudder", i.e. "it is not the case that there is a rudder which we have". Assuming then that *lack* is analysed as containing at least the bit "not have", and that this analysis *as a whole* is taken from the lexicon and placed in some DS structural position, there is no way left of weaving the existential quantifier into the internal analysis of *lack*. Similarly with (82b), which means "he was not willing for there to be any money he gave her", with the internal lexical analysis "not be willing to give" for *refuse*. (Note that *refuse* without an indirect object can also mean "not be willing to be given", with a passive embedded *give*.) In (82c) there is a similar problem, if it is accepted that *ignorant* stands for "not cognizant". The quantification of (82c) is woven into the internal lexical analysis of *ignorant*: "it is not the case that there is any corruption that Jack is cognizant of." No other quantificational analysis seems possible. It has been maintained that *any* in such cases should be analysed as representing the universal quantifier: "for all corruption it is the case that Jack is ignorant of it", but such an analysis is *ad hoc*, given the general limitations on the use of *any* as a universal quantifier, and given the fact that the indefinite article *a* must then also be treated as a universal quantifier:

(82) e. Jack is ignorant of a government imposing rules.

The first theory, which assumes a common SA-cum-DS level of representation as input to the transformational rules, will be happy with (82a–c), since

---

[13] See McCawley (1982: 59) for a discussion of these matters. He shows convincingly that any decision to speak of 'deviance' or 'unacceptability' in cases like (82d), and to relegate the problem to a semantics that need not bother the syntax, amounts to a mere terminological ploy which moreover undermines the empirical content of the theory.

it will now claim this as support for the thesis that prelexical analysis is required in syntax. Yet this theory then encounters problems with sentences like:

(83) a. We lack all the engine parts.
   b. He refused her two books.
   c. Jack is ignorant of one conspiracy.

In these cases the quantification clearly cannot penetrate into the internal structure of the lexical item. (83a) means "for all the engine parts it is the case that we lack them", and not "not for all engine parts is it the case that we have them", i.e. "we don't have all the engine parts". Similarly for (83b), which means "there are two books which he refused her", and not "he was not willing for there to be two books for him to give her". And (83c) means "there is one conspiracy that Jack is ignorant of", and not "there isn't one conspiracy that Jack is cognizant of". So in these cases the quantification clearly has to stay out of the internal lexical analysis, and this is something which the primitive prelexical hypothesis of generative semantics cannot explain other than by *ad hoc* means.

A distinction seems to be called for anyway between those complex items whose prelexical analysis is lexicalized to such an extent that no internal quantification is ever possible (the 'closed' items) and those that do allow for quantifier penetration (the 'open' class). Remarkably, if an open item incorporates negation, it lets in only existential quantifiers of a special class (*a, any, ever, the slightest*, etc.), the *any*-class we shall say.[14] Without negation they seem open to all quantifiers (see section 5.3.7). Causatives, though lexically complex, all seem to be 'closed', but the famous *look for* seems 'open' (5.3.7).

One might propose a combination of the two positions in the sense that an SA-level is assumed which is lexically analytic, at least for those predicates which allow for internal quantification, and which is input to a set of prelexical transformational rules. At DS-level these predicates replace their transformed lexical analysis. This creates the space required for a correct

---

[14] Similar phenomena are found in comparatives. For example, the following sentence:

(i) Jack is taller than no one.

can only be interpreted with large scope for *no one*: "there is no one that Jack is taller than." The same for all non-*any*-type quantifiers. *Any*-type quantifiers, however, require an internal analysis:

(ii) Jack is taller than anyone here.

The latter sentence can only be interpreted with small scope for *any*, and if *than* is analysed as "to/by which not" (Seuren 1973a, 1984), the structural room for such an interpretation is given: "Jack is tall to an extent to which not anyone here is tall."

quantificational analysis. (82a), for example, will have an SA containing the structure:

(82) a′.

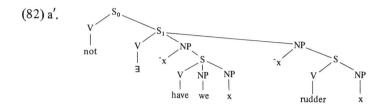

S_1 is then reduced to "have (we, a rudder)"; then the verb *have* is raised by prelexical Predicate Raising to the verb *not* on the S_0-cycle:

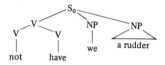

after which the verb [*not-have*] is replaced by the lexical predicate *lack*. Only now can open syntax begin to operate: the cycle starts anew, but now only with the rules defined for the open, i.e. postlexical, syntax of the language in question. In this conception there are thus two cycles, the prelexical cycle leading up to lexical insertions, and the postlexical or open cycle. The grammar that operates in either cycle does not need to be identical. The open syntax of English, for example, has Predicate Raising (PR), if at all, only for a small class of cases.[15] Yet PR is required prelexically on a large scale.

Such a theory, however, would require that the 'open' class of predicates, which would be inserted only at DS-level, would never carry extra semantic information on top of what is conveyed by their prelexical semantic analysis. There would be room for semantic 'extras' for the closed class of predicates, which are ready-given at SA-level: these would have a prelexical analysis entirely outside the transformational process, and would thus be free to assume extra semantic features. The English verb *assassinate*, for example, would have an internal analysis containing the structure "cause to die", but it is allowed to carry the extra information that the object must denote a person of public importance, that the killing takes place in connection with that public importance, etc. Since all the extras are stored in the lexicon, and

---

[15] It is eminently defensible to maintain that what is known in English syntax as *tough*-Movement (from *It is easy to fool Jack* to *Jack is easy to fool*) is in fact Predicate Raising, resulting in the verbal cluster [easy to fool]. Note, in particular, that such formations occur at times as single lexical items. For example, *gullible* is naturally analysed as "easy to fool", *tough* as "hard to defeat", etc. See section 2.4.5 below.

since such complex items are taken whole from the lexicon, there is, in principle, no problem for them. Nor should there be a problem for the 'open' items taken from the lexicon only at DS-level, as long as their prelexical analysis corresponds precisely with their lexical meaning. This seems to be so for, e.g., *lack*, which means "not-have", or *without*, which is "not having". But it is not always the case.

An example of a semantic predicate which has all the appearances of an 'open' item and yet does not seem to match its structural prelexical analysis semantically is *only* (widely known for its complications anyway). As is shown in section 3.5.2 below, *only* shows clear signs of an inbuilt negation which is active in its syntax. Thus there is subject–auxiliary inversion when an *only*-constituent is fronted (*Only then did he open the door*), and the occurrence of certain Negative Polarity Items (*Only you have the slightest idea*). Yet, the closest one gets to a satisfactory grammatical prelexical analysis is something like "the one who laughed is no one other than John" for *Only John laughed*, and the two are not entirely equivalent, since the latter does but the former does not presuppose that John laughed. The theory of a partial separation of SA and DS is thus not satisfactory.

One might also propose that the solution ought to be sought elsewhere, outside grammar proper. One might say that the fact that, e.g., *She lacks any charm* is good English but **He missed any train* is not, should be accounted for by provisions in the procedure of discourse incrementation. One would then say that the increment value associated with the verb *lack* is equal to or includes that of the composite structure "not-have", whereas the increment value of *miss* would not correspond to that of "not-catch" but would consist in the mere adding of the predicate "miss" to the addresses involved. This account will be needed anyway: the 'open' class of predicates will be assumed to increment according to their prelexical analysis, and the 'closed' items will increment as undivided wholes. But the question is whether this distinction should be integrated into the grammar in the form of some *grammatical* procedure of prelexical (de)composition. In spite of the impressive evidence (see, e.g., section 2.4.5 below) in favour of a theory establishing close links between syntax and prelexical analysis, the question as a whole is of such complexity that we must accept that it cannot be adequately answered here.

We will, therefore, not take a precise stand on issues of prelexical analysis, and leave it to later research to decide what the relations are between, on the one hand, whatever prelexical analysis seems justified for complex lexical items and, on the other, the grammar and rules of open syntax, where lexical items function as whole elements.

The other main elements in the overall structure of the grammar, as far as the generative rules are concerned, are on much firmer ground. They are not essentially different from what has been considered accepted wisdom in generative semantics for almost twenty years now. The following main division of a grammar into levels of representation and sets of rules can thus be given:

(84)

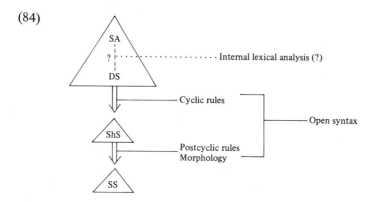

where "SA" stands for "Semantic Analysis", "DS" for "Deep Structure", "ShS" for "Shallow Structure", and "SS" for "Surface Structure".

The parsing is probably best conceived of as a set of rules reducing surface structures to shallow structures, and a subsequent procedure for setting up a Predicate-Arguments Inventory, as sketched in section 2.1.8 above. The generative rules can then be used to test, in a top-down fashion, the correctness of the resulting string given the parsing proposed.

2.3.2   The cyclic rules

The notion 'cyclic rule', or 'cyclic rule application' was developed in transformational grammar around or after 1965. It was an extremely elegant solution to certain conflicts in the ordering of rules if the rules were taken to apply serially. By and large, the concept of cyclicity still stands. It has not lost any of its explanatory power. The cyclic principle entails that the cyclic rules apply first to the most deeply embedded S, then to the next S up, and so forth, until the highest S is reached. After the last S-cycle (or simply: cycle), the resulting structure is the shallow structure of the sentence in question.

Every DS has associated with it a set of instructions determining the options left open to a given DS with regard to its treatment in the cycle (i.e. the whole of the procedure as defined by the cyclic rules). That is, for every DS it is given in advance which cyclic rules must or may apply. For most rules the instruction, or permission, to apply them originates with the predicate of each cycle: lexical predicates are defined in the lexicon for the rules they induce ('trigger'), optionally or obligatorily. But some rules must, or may, be applied as a result of specific semantic instructions associated with the sentence as a whole. In particular, SAs and DSs are regarded as carriers of possible specifications as to what part of the sentence stands for the *topic*.

When it is said of some structural part of a sentence that it stands for (or: is) topic, then this means, in terms of discourse semantics, that the part in question is already represented in the discourse domain D, and that, in addition, what is referred to by that part (and by its discourse representation) is singled out for special attention. It is, so to speak, highlighted, or made salient. Topic indication for a sentence part can have a direct bearing upon the cyclic rules to be used. It may also have a bearing on postcyclic rules, on morphology, or on intonational rules. An example of topic indication which is immediately felt in the cyclic rules is the class of English sentences where a subject-clause is topic. When a subject-clause is topic, it must either appear as a full clause in subject position in surface structure, or else the predicate of the sentence must be accented. If, on the other hand, a subject-clause is new, so that it is part of the increment added by the sentence to D, it cannot appear as a full clause in subject position in surface structure. Then it must either appear in object position with a dummy subject *it*, or its subject must be raised so that its eventual VP ends up after the main finite verb. For example, all three sentences in (85) are grammatical, but (85a) can be used appropriately only in contexts where the content of the subject-clause is already known and is being discussed. The other two sentences, on the contrary, are appropriate in contexts where the likelihood of John's winning is a new element in the discourse:

(85) a. That John will win is likely.

　　 b. It is likely that John will win.

　　 c. John is likely to win.

In the (b)-sentence the rule of *it*-Insertion has applied; in the (c)-sentence the subject of the subject-clause, *John*, has been raised to be the surface subject of *be likely*. It will be shown in a moment how these rules work. Here it is sufficient to see that initial rule specifications are sensitive to topic indications.

The cyclic rule applications of the grammar are subject to a few general constraining principles. To what extent these principles are universal is, of course, a question that can be asked but never conclusively answered. It seems good policy to posit their universality until proof to the contrary has come forth. Prominent among these principles are the following (the Ss are numbered top-down):

C-1 Predicates can be raised or lowered, but not deleted. Subjects can be raised or deleted, but not lowered. Other NP-arguments are not affected by any rule of cyclic syntax.

C-2 Whenever an S_n loses its V because of Raising, S_n disappears and all other material dominated by it is reattached to S_{n-1}.

C-3 Whenever an S_n loses its V because of Lowering, S_n remains and V is relabelled as an adverb, prepositional phrase, particle or affix, depending on lexical specification.

C-4 Whenever an S loses its subject, it is relabelled as VP.

C-5 Whenever a node X directly dominates an identically labelled node X and does not have other branches, it is pruned.

C-6 The domain of rule application is either the S_n under cyclic treatment or an embedded S_{n+1}.

C-7 The domain of rule effect is S_n, including any embedded S of any depth, or the immediate higher attachment of S_n.

C-8 The conditions of rule application depend on the predicate to which the rule in question is lexically attached, and/or the structure of the S_n under treatment and/or the structure of S_{n+1}, and/or higher tree structure.

The first constraint, C-1, restricts deletion of terminal material to forms of Secondary Subject Deletion (SSD). It also prevents Gapping (the form of Conjunction Reduction which typically deletes V in the second conjunct) from being a cyclic rule. The constraints C-2 to C-5 delimit relabellings and structural remodellings of trees as regular consequences of rule applications. C-6 to C-8 constrain rules with regard to their domains of application and effect, and their conditions. The domain of application is the segment of the tree with respect to which the rule is allowed to start operating. The domain of effect is the segment of the tree with respect to which the rule is allowed to bring about a change. The conditions of application are any set of sufficient conditions for the rule to operate.

It is useful, at this moment, to illustrate how the verb-first structures of SA and DS come out as NP-VP structures at ShS. The idea underlying this treatment derives directly from McCawley 1970 and 1971. In McCawley 1970 it is proposed that tense should be considered responsible for the structural change in question, and in McCawley 1971 the idea is launched that tenses are underlying predicates. The treatment proposed here is merely a refinement of those ideas.

I assume, in fact, in accordance with Reichenbach 1947 (§ 51) and Rigter 1980, that verbal tensing derives from two underlying tense verbs.[16] The highest tense, t_1, connects the sentence with some antecedently given time

---

[16] Reichenbach, of course, did not hold the view that tenses are underlying verbs. He did, however, posit three semantic elements: E (the point of the event), R (the point of reference), and F (the point of speech). The two tenses can be regarded as expressing R and E; F is always pragmatically defined.

denotation in the discourse D (see McCawley 1971: 110). It is to be understood intuitively as "at that time". The second tense, t_2, is probably best regarded as an existential quantification over either moments (aorist aspect) or extensions (durative aspect) of time.[17] In order to facilitate the exposition, I shall simply speak of t_1 and t_2. It is probably a universal feature of tense-predicates that they follow the lowering strategy that seems to go with all sentential operators: tenses are lowered into their argument-S and attached to the verb of that S. NP-VP languages have the extra feature that t_1 also induces Subject Raising. The NP-VP structure is now an automatic consequence. Without the Subject Raising the resulting ShS, and very often also the SS, will be of the verb-first type. An example will clarify this. Take the sentence (86a) with the SA (86b):

(86) a. Ben wrote the book.
  b.

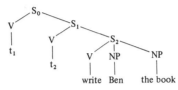

(It is assumed that there is a standard conversion of NP-structures of the type "$x:(F(x))$" into *the F*. Proper names, as has been said, are analysed analogously, with the name in quotes as the predicate: $x:(\text{"Ben"}(x))$, or "the one that is called 'Ben'".)

The S_2-cycle passes vacuously. On the S_1-cycle t_2 is lowered and left-adopted by $_V[\text{write}]$ of S_2 as an Affix:[18]

Then, on the S_0-cycle, the lower subject $_{NP}[\text{Ben}]$ is raised. This means (as will be repeated below) that the lower subject is detached and reattached to S_0

---

[17] An elaborate description in these terms of the tense system of Sranan is provided in Seuren 1981 and 1983.

[18] Adoption (cp. 2.1.6 above) is a standard procedure of transformational attachment: if node B is adopted by node A, then A forms a copy of itself above itself and B is attached to the higher, newly created, A to the left or to the right of the original A. If the attachment is to the right there is right-adoption; otherwise left-adoption.

in precisely the position of its own original S_2; S_2 is shifted to the right and relabelled "VP" because of C-4:

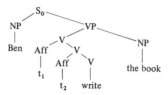

Now t_1 is lowered and left-adopted by the complex V of VP:

At this stage the NP–VP structure has come about. Note that on the S_0-cycle Subject Raising had to take place first because, if t_1-lowering had preceded, S_0 would have been pruned away due to C-5, and Subject Raising, though obligatorily imposed, could not have been put into effect. The verbal complex is then further treated in the morphology to yield the correct tense.

2.4 Some cyclic rules

2.4.1 *Secondary Subject Deletion*

At this point we may consider some of the 'great' rules of the cycle as they are known from the literature. The first to be discussed is the rule usually known as Equi-NP-Deletion. Here it is called Secondary Subject Deletion (SSD) mainly because it is not a question of 'equal' NPs but of a controlling antecedent (CA) in a primary clause and a variable in a secondary clause. Moreover, as we shall see, the central feature of the rule is precisely the deletion of the secondary subject.

SSD applies to Ss figuring[19] a predicate that is positively marked for SSD. All such predicates involve sentential terms. There are two main kinds of SSD. The first, to be called *vertical* SSD, occurs with a predicate P marked for SSD and taking a nominal subject-term besides a sentential object-term, and,

---

[19] The term *figure* is used in this book as a (somewhat) technical term to indicate the property of a predicate of being the highest predicate of an S, i.e. the V specified in SA Formation Rule (i) – see section 2.2.

possibly, a nominal indirect-object-term. The higher clause, which figures P, contains the antecedent NP controlling the deletion of the lower clause subject provided that subject is of the form $_{NP}[x]$ and NP is the antecedent of x. For some predicates it is the higher subject that controls the deletion; for others it is the indirect object. This point will be discussed in detail below. Vertical SSD is the form of SSD best studied in the literature (and known as Equi-NP-Deletion). It is found in sentences of the type *Harry wants to leave*, derived from a DS figuring the verb *want* that takes the sentential object-term $_S[$leave $_{NP}[x]]$. Owing to the lexical specification of *want* the lower subject $_{NP}[x]$ is deleted; S becomes VP; the verb *leave* becomes an infinitive preceded by the particle *to*.

Besides vertical SSD there is also *horizontal* SSD. It is found in sentences like:

(87) a. John died while eating the soup.

derived from an SA/DS of the form:

(87) b.

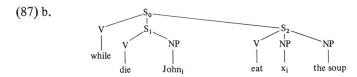

(The subscripts "i" indicate the anaphoric relation between the antecedent *John* and the pronominal *x*. The anaphoric relation must be given independently during production. In parsing it follows from the fact that SSD has occurred.) Object Incorporation (discussed below) combines $_V[$while] with S_2 into a complex derived predicate, later to be lowered into S_1 as an adverbial *while*-phrase. First, however, the subject of S_2 must be deleted by SSD associated with *while*. This form of SSD is called 'horizontal' since it operates between two sister-Ss. The verb *eat* is not turned into an infinitive here, due to the fact that *while*, after lowering, becomes a preposition requiring an argument NP. the VP *eat the soup* is thus nominalized into what is called a gerund.

We shall adopt the terminological convention of calling the higher clause in vertical SSD or the subject-clause in horizontal SSD the *primary clause*, and the lower or object-clause the *secondary clause*.

The predicate *while* takes optional SSD only if the leftmost argument of the primary clause is antecedent to the leftmost argument of the secondary clause. The rule is optional since, besides (87a), the following is also found:

(87) c. John died while he was eating the soup.

where no SSD has occurred. Horizontal SSD, as far as can be judged, always follows the *leftmost-to-leftmost principle* with regard to the antecedent condition. Its effect is invariably the deletion of the secondary grammatical subject.[20]

Matters are more complex with vertical SSD. First, as is well known, some SSD-verbs require anaphoric relatedness of the primary subject and the secondary subject; other such verbs require relatedness between the higher indirect object and the lower subject. Sometimes (but it is not clear how general this phenomenon is) the lower subject may refer to a group including the CA, as in:

(88) John proposed to let the fellow die.

This sentence can be used in a context where the semantic subject of *let die* is not given as an overt CA in the sentence itself but requires preceding discourse to be identified. Besides these relatively clear (and widely known) distinctions, there is, however, also the fact that vertical deletion under control is apparently subject to considerable individual variation, as became clear to me in discussions with Bernard Comrie on this topic. Acceptability judgements and possible interpretations seem to vary a great deal from speaker to speaker, and also according to lexical selection in constituents other than the verb triggering the deletion. The following analysis should, therefore, be looked upon as a first attempt to deal with phenomena (in English) that have, so far, not or hardly received adequate treatment but are nevertheless real. It may well be (and is to be hoped) that the distinctions made and the principles invoked can be simplified or eliminated in light of more systematic research into the real nature of the facts.

It seems that there are two subclasses of verbs taking vertical SSD with an internal antecedent. First there is the class of verbs where the controlling antecedent is either the semantic subject or the semantic indirect object, and the lower subject to be deleted under the condition of anaphoric relatedness is not the semantic subject but the grammatical subject of the secondary clause. For these verbs it does not matter in what grammatical position the semantically defined term occurs, provided it does not occur in a *by*-phrase. The indirect object may have become the grammatical subject by passivization, or the semantic subject may have been displaced by *there*-insertion (if that is a rule). In any case, it is the semantic function that counts in the primary clause, and the grammatical function in the secondary clause. This class of vertical SSD-verbs is the larger of the two. It comprises the classical cases *want, prefer, like, intend, expect*, etc., etc. for subject-bound deletion,

---

[20] That is, if either S_1, or S_2, or both, are passivized, thereby losing their semantic subject and putting up the next term in line, t_2, for grammatical subject-treatment, then t_2 is candidate for becoming controlling antecedent or for being deleted, depending on whether t_2 occurs in S_1 or S_2, respectively. Thus we have, besides the type of (87a):

    (i) Harry saved his skin by being arrested.
    (ii) Harry was saved by running as fast as he could.
    (iii) Harry was saved by being arrested.

and *persuade, order, prevail upon*, etc., etc. for indirect-object-bound deletion. Thus we have:

(89) a. Barry persuaded Sue to drive him home.
    b. Sue was persuaded (by Barry) to drive him home.
    c. Barry persuaded Sue to be driven home.
    d. Sue was persuaded (by Barry) to be driven home.

Note that the CA is always *Sue*, the semantic indirect object of *persuade*. The deleted secondary subject, however, is not always the *semantic* subject of the secondary clause. It is, however, always the *grammatical* subject of that clause. Let us call this type of SSD the *SC-to-leftmost type*, where "SC" stands for "semantic constituent", and "leftmost", again, for whatever term comes first as the cycle starts to operate. We shall reserve the terms "SU", "IO", "O" for the semantic constituents "subject", "indirect object", "object", respectively, and use "t_n" for the n-th term, starting from the left, as the cycle starts.

Besides the SC-to-leftmost type of vertical SSD, there is also a second type, which we shall call the *SC-to-SU type*. Here the CA is again SU or IO, but the deleted secondary subject must be the semantic subject (SU) of the secondary clause. That is, the secondary clause must not be passivized. This type of SSD, however, has a special escape clause. Let us first give a few examples, involving the verbs *ask* and *promise*, which are representatives of the SC-to-SU class:

(90) a. Barry asked Sue to drive him home.
    b. Sue was asked (by Barry) to drive him home.
    c. Barry asked Sue to be driven home.
    d. *Sue was asked (by Barry) to be driven home.

Clearly, *ask* is of the IO-to-SU type: the controlling antecedent is IO, and the deleted subject is the semantic subject, SU, of the secondary clause. This appears from (90a)–(90c), where there is denotational identity between the IO of the primary clause and the SU of the secondary clause (not the grammatical subject of the latter). There is, however, more. Whereas (90a) and (90b) are not problematic – their secondary clauses have not been passivized – (90c) and (90d) pose problems. First, in (90c) the deleted secondary subject is codenotational with *Barry*, the SU of the primary clause. Then, it must be explained why (90d) is ungrammatical.

Or take the following sentences:

(91) a. Barry promised Sue to drive her home.
    b. *Sue was promised (by Barry) to drive her/him home.
    c. *Barry promised Sue to be driven home.
    d. Sue was promised (by Barry) to be driven home.

The traditional view is that *promise* is of the SU-to-SU type, the governing antecedent being the primary SU, and the deleted subject being the secondary

SU. This is borne our by (91a) and (91c). But why is (91b) ungrammatical, and why is it that in (91d) *Sue* is the governing antecedent of the grammatical (deleted) subject of the secondary clause?

Clearly, there is a complication here. What seems to be going on with the SC-to-SU type of vertical SSD is the following. Besides the basic deletion process, which is regulated by the SC-to-SU principle, there is a secondary possibility of SSD with verbs of this class. *If the semantic subject of the secondary clause has been lost (mostly through passivization) and the grammatical subject is of the type $_{NP}[x]$, and if the grammatical subject has as anaphoric correlate the grammatical subject t_1 of the primary clause, t_1 being distinct from the original CA, then t_1 may take over as CA and delete the grammatical subject of the secondary clause.* Let us call this the *SSD-escape clause*.

Now consider (90c). The secondary clause has been passivized so that its SU has disappeared. Yet SSD has occurred, which means that the escape clause has been used. The fact that SSD has occurred requires the assumption that the deleted grammatical subject of the lower clause takes t_1 of the higher clause as anaphoric antecedent, i.e. *Barry*. This is exactly what the intuitive understanding of (90c) shows up. (90d) is impossible because t_1 is identical with the original CA. (91) now also falls into place. (91b) is ungrammatical because the primary SU occurs in a *by*-phrase, and it is never allowed that a governing antecedent occurs in a *by*-phrase. (91c) is ungrammatical because the escape clause must have been used, as appears from the passivized form of the secondary clause, but t_1 of the primary clause, *Barry*, is identical with the original CA. (91c) is thus seen to be ungrammatical for the same reason as (90d). In (91d) all conditions of the escape clause are satisfied: the grammatical subject of the secondary clause can be assumed to have the grammatical subject of the primary clause as antecedent. Hence the latter may take over as controlling antecedent, so that *Sue* is understood as the one to be driven home (by Barry).

All this may seem rather far-fetched. Yet the reader should take into consideration that the facts of (90) and (91) are also prima facie extravagant. There is very little serious discussion of them in the literature (see Růžička 1983), except for the relatively straightforward cases of vertical SSD. No convincing account exists of horizontal SSD, and the complications of vertical SSD have not even been signalled in any systematic way. It would seem that these complications should pose a challenge to any theory of grammar. We have met the challenge as best we can, which is not to say that all has been said. On the contrary, the analysis of SSD-phenomena given here still smacks too much of taxonomy and too little of explanation. Surely, there must be deep reasons why the facts are as they are. We must, however, be content with what we can achieve. We may be encouraged by the fact that the two cases in (90) and (91) where the SSD-escape clause is taken to have applied, viz. (90c) and (91d), seem to be less directly interpretable than the straightforward cases where the basic form of SSD has applied. Moreover, as we shall notice, the analysis given here fits in naturally with the whole of the grammatical theory being developed.

2.4.2 Subject Raising and it-*Insertion*

Subject Raising (SR) is the process whereby the subject of an embedded subject-clause or object-clause is raised into the higher clause, to become its grammatical subject or object, respectively. It is an extremely widespread rule of cyclic syntax. Some languages have SR only from subject-clauses, and not from object-clauses. Dutch, for example, has no (or hardly any) SR from object-clauses. (The few cases which are found, such as *Ik waande hem dood* ("I thought him dead"), never have an overt verbal form.) There seems to be a connection between SR and infinitival forms, in very much the same way as SSD seems connected with infinitives. As we have seen, SSD results in a *to*-infinitive in the lower clause, which thus becomes a VP. Likewise, SR (normally) results in a *to*-infinitive of the lower clause, i.e. VP. A language which has no infinitives, such as modern Greek, has no SSD and no SR. SR from subject-clauses is exemplified by:

(92) a. Harry is likely to win.
  b. John is rumoured to have failed.
  c. Hilary may be right.
  d. Max seems to have forgotten his wallet.

(Note that in (92c) the bare infinitive is found. This is due to a special rule for modal auxiliaries requiring a bare infinitive.) SR from object-clauses is found in, e.g.:

(93) a. She wants me to give up.
  b. That Harry was ill made Mary worry.
  c. I had expected him for many years to reach the top.
  d. That kept there from being a riot.
  e. She figured him out to be a goalgetter.[21]

---

[21] It has been proposed that SR into object position is not a rule of syntax, and that what looks like the derived grammatical object is, in fact, still the original subject. However, (93c)–(93e) show that this is not a viable analysis. See also Postal 1974 for a wealth of arguments showing that SR into object position is indeed a rule of syntax. Any claim to the effect that SR into object position is universally excluded from grammars of natural languages, not just from the grammar of English, is patently falsified by the vast numbers of languages where SR is undeniable on grounds of case assignment, word order, or a combination of both. Particularly instructive in this respect is Malagasy (Keenan 1976), which is a VOS-language. Keenan gives the example (p. 283):

Nanantena an-dRasoa ho   nanasa ny zaza Rabe.
hoped   acc.-Rasoa comp wash   the child Rabe
"Rabe hoped (for) Rasoa to wash the child"

Both the position and the case of *Rasoa* imply Raising.

In the earlier days of transformation grammar it was thought that SR into subject position and SR into object position were two different rules. Superficially this seems to be correct, since the structural movements are very different in either case as long as it is assumed that the initial structure is of the form NP-VP. SR into subject position then requires two movements, as shown in:

(92) a'.

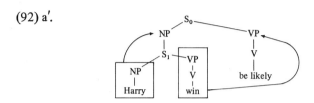

SR into object position likewise requires two movements, but their structural specifications seem rather divergent:

(93) a'.

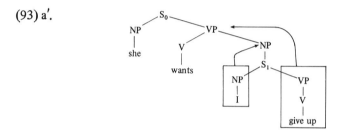

It was observed by McCawley (1970) that the structural differences between the two varieties of SR can be reduced drastically if it is assumed that the deep structure is not of the NP-VP type, but of the verb-first type. (It is, moreover, useful to drop the requirement that every embedded S be headed by an NP-node: verbs may take sentential terms that are not NPs.) In this new formulation we have *one rule*, which says that the lower subject is moved to the position of its own S, whereafter this S, now VP, is reattached on the immediate right:

(92) a''.

(93) a''.

Since it is a general fact for virtually all the rules of the cycle that they are simplified and streamlined by the verb-first hypothesis, this hypothesis has empirical advantages over the old NP–VP theory of SA/DS. The general form of SR is now as follows:

where "V_{SR}" stands for "subject-raising verb" and bracketed material is optional. Note that SR can only apply to the rightmost embedded S_{n+1} of S_n (which may have two S-arguments, as in (93b)). This is further support for the unity of SR: it need never be specified for a V_{SR} whether it takes subject-SR or object-SR since if it seems to have the choice it must take object-SR. If there is material, e.g., a *to*-dative, following the newly created VP, a post-cyclic rule moves the VP to the far right (see note 22):

(94) The phone call appeared to Clare to be a hoax.

SR is obligatory in English for modal verbs (*may, must, can, need, will,* etc.) and a few others.

Verbs that take optional SR usually have *it*-Insertion[22] as an alternative, at least for subject clauses. *It*-Insertion consists of the insertion of a dummy NP *it* just left of the embedded clause, which is processed as a fully tensed *that*-clause. *It*-Insertion, like SR, may apply to subject clauses as well as to object clauses. But unlike SR it always takes the leftmost embedded S if there seems to be a choice:

(95) a. It made Harry look guilty that he hid behind the curtains.
　　 b. *That he hid behind the curtains made it that Harry looked guilty.
　　 c. She took it that he was a goalgetter.

---

[22] The usual name for *it*-Insertion is Extraposition. It seems less suitable as a name since the extraposing movement to the right of the clause in question is only a marginal phenomenon in our theory, though it was more prominent in the NP–VP theory. In our theory the main feature is the insertion of the dummy subject *it* just left of S. Extraposition proper occurs only when the higher verb has an object, as in:

(i) It surprised Jenifer that Max had such good taste.
(ii) It takes courage to do that sort of thing.

But this extraposition seems an automatic consequence of the apparently universal principle, at least for non-verb-final languages (cp. Ross 1967), that subordinate Ss cannot occur internally but only at the far left or at the far right of the whole S. Note, by the way, that in argument Ss non-specific subjects can be deleted, as in (ii), leaving behind a VP.

It-Insertion (IT) has the following general form (but see also chapter 3, note 24):

$$\text{IT} \quad V_{IT} \underset{(NP)}{\big|} \overset{S_n}{(NP)} \; S_{n+1} \, (\dots) \quad \Rightarrow \quad V \; (NP) \; \underset{it}{NP} \; \overset{S_n}{(NP)} \; S_{n+1} \, (\dots)$$

where "V_{IT}" stands for "verb inducing *it*-Insertion", and bracketed material is optional. IT is relatively rare, in English, for object clauses. There the favourite alternative to SR is simple processing as a *that*-clause. One might perhaps surmise that for simple object *that*-clauses an underlying *it* has been deleted, but one might then also well ask what the point is of first introducing *it* transformationally only to delete it later. A possible argument in favour of such a treatment, however, is the fact that those verbs that take Ss as possible arguments for both the subject and the object never seem to allow for IT together with an object *that*-clause:

(96) a. *It proved that Harry was guilty that he hid behind the curtains.
    b. That he hid behind the curtains proved that Harry was guilty.

If object *that*-clauses involve a deleted *it*, then there is a rationale for this fact given the unity of IT as a cyclic rule and the concomitant corollary that a verb can take IT only once.

The reader will have noticed that in the general rule formulations of SR and IT the embedded S_{n+1} has an optional NP-node immediately dominating it. This is because it pays to distinguish between those predicates that take a non-nominal argument S and those that take a nominal argument S. The usefulness of this distinction is to be seen in the light of the following observations. It is often the case that those verbs which induce SR or *it*-Insertion with respect to the subject clause are free not to apply either rule. The subject clause then ends up at the beginning of the sentence in the canonical position for subjects:

(97) a. That Harry has won is likely/unbelievable/unproven/etc.
    b. That she gets firsts is a fact/feels good/stands to reason/etc.
    c. That he was foolhardy followed/transpired/showed/hurt/smelled/ etc.

(As has been pointed out earlier, this sentence form carries the additional semantic feature that the surface subject clause is topicalized.) There are, however, verbs which do not allow for the option of not applying either SR or IT:

(98) a. *That Harry has won seems/appears/turns out.
    b. *That she gets firsts threatens/tends.
    c. *That he was foolhardy began/continued/stopped.

Instead of the grossly ungrammatical sentences of (98) English has:

(99) a. Harry seems/appears/turns out to have won.
  b. She threatens/tends to get firsts.
  c. He began/continued/stopped being foolhardy.

In these sentences SR has applied. Application of IT is grammatical only for (100a), not for the (b) or (c) sentences:

(100) a. It seems/appears/turns out that Harry has won.
  b. *It threatens/tends that she gets firsts.
  c. *It began/continued/stopped that he was foolhardy.

The ungrammaticality of (100b) and (100c) must be accounted for by the purely lexical stipulation that the verbs occurring in these sentences take SR but not IT – whereas the verbs occurring in the (a)-sentence take both.

One could likewise stipulate for the verbs of the (a)-sentence in (98), (99), (100) that they *must* take either SR or IT, so that the option of not applying either is not open. This would be a purely lexical stipulation, and technically feasible. It would then have to be stipulated for the verbs in (97a) that they take either SR, or IT, or neither; and for the verbs in (97b) and (97c) that they take either IT or nothing.

It is also possible, however, to reduce these lexical stipulations drastically and let the consequences follow from the presence or absence of an NP immediately dominating the argument S in question. For if the argument S is not dominated by NP, tense processing cannot subject-raise the clause in question to make it the subject of an NP-VP structure:

(101)

This structure has been through the S_3-cycle (which was tensed). On the S_2-cycle SR may apply:

Or IT applies:

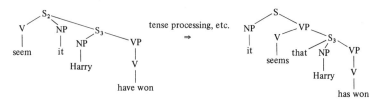

But if neither IT nor SR applies the derivation blocks on the S_0-cycle, when SR induced by t_1 must take place, since the raised subject must be an NP, not an S, and the unmodified S_2 contains no NP. If, however, *be likely* is used, or *be unbelievable*, or *be true*, or *stand to reason*, or *follow*, or *transpire*, or any other verb that allows for surface subject *that*-clauses, this difficulty does not arise, and the surface *that*-clause can come about. This explains at the same time why (102a) is ungrammatical whereas (102b) is well formed:

(102) a. *That Harry has won is likely to seem.
     b. That Harry has won seems to be likely.

This argument gains force in the light of other data. Thus, as has been observed by Lindholm (1969), a verb like *believe* pronominalizes its object clause by means of either *so* or *it*, depending on context:[23]

(103) a. Was Caesar a Jew? I believe so (*it).
     b. The evidence that Negative Raising is cyclic is so convincing that I now believe it (*so).
     c. I just saw John shoot Max, but people I inform of this don't believe it (*so).

The verb *think*, however, never allows for *it* as a propositional pro-form. Factive verbs, on the other hand, never allow for the *so* pro-form. All this accords well with the hypothesis that *believe* takes either a nominal or a sentential object clause, depending on context, that *think* takes only sentential object clauses, and that factives take only nominal lower clauses (which fits in well with their factive character).

But there is more. Structures of the type

$$V \diagdown S_n \diagdown S_{n+1}$$

are 'unstable' because they do not occur in surface structure and must therefore be transformed into a structure that can either occur in surface structure

---

[23] It seems that *so* is used for the expression of a belief held by the subject independently, on his own account, whereas *it* is appropriate in discourses where the subject is called upon to accept as true or reject as false a proposition or set of propositions already given.

or be further processed so that it becomes fit for surface structure. NP–VP languages seem to have an inbuilt guarantee in their grammars ensuring that such *unstable structures* are fitted out with an NP-subject or disappear. To the extent that the matter is clear, it seems that there is an obligation, at least in NP–VP languages, for such structures to undergo PR or SR or IT, or else to disappear as a result of the lowering of V into S_{n+1}. Since S_{n+1} has been through the cycle when S_n is up for treatment, the constraint in question will have ensured that S_{n+1} is itself not an unstable structure and has an NP-subject, whether lexically filled or zero (as with subjectless sentences). V-Lowering from S_n into S_{n+1} makes the unstable S_n disappear (C-5). SR is possible only with non-zero NP-subjects, so that a non-zero NP-subject is guaranteed for S_n with SR. Since NP–VP comes about as a result of SR on tense, and SR requires a non-zero lower subject, any NP–VP structure will have a non-zero subject NP.

Let us, therefore, assume there to be a constraint, operative during the transformational cycle, which we shall call the *NP-Subject-Constraint* (NPSC), which requires, at least for NP–VP languages, that unstable structures must undergo treatment resulting in there being a zero or non-zero NP-subject for the S being cycled. This means that some rule must operate that gives the unstable S an NP-subject or makes it disappear (V-Lowering). If no other rule is available to help the unstable S out of its predicament, a dummy *it* is inserted (by "brute force", as McCawley would say). NPSC will prove to be of considerable use in the explanation of passive constructions under PR in German and Dutch (sections 2.4.5 and 2.4.6).

Epistemic modal verbs, as well as intransitive occurrences of aspectual verbs like *begin, go on, stop, threaten* (Perlmutter 1970), are clear cases in English where Subject Raising is used to satisfy NPSC:

(104) a. That must be true. From: "That that is true, must"
b. Harry began to be rich in 1970. From: "That Harry was rich began in 1970"

2.4.3 *Lowering, scope, and co-ordination*

Predicate Lowering is a common procedure. The predicate in question loses its predicate status: it is recategorized into a quantifier, an adverbial, a tense, etc.[24] The most obvious class of lowering predicates consists of predicates that turn up as sentence adverbs (cp. (6) above, in Section 2.1.3):

[24] This is the constraint C-3 presented in section 2.3.2 above. This constraint is no doubt connected with a universal principle saying that there can only be one V per S or VP, at least in the cycle. This V may be complex, as with PR, but all verbal material is always united under a single V-node. This means that lowered tenses could retain verbal status, since they are attached to the lower V, probably by adoption, thus leading to a complex V. Since they must be recategorized anyhow, later in the derivation, into affixes, it seems best to recategorize them straight away. This enables us to formulate C-3 in a general way.

(105) a. Predictably, Leo let you down.

    b. Perhaps, Kate will return soon.

    c. She is reputedly very clever.

    d. The man was allegedly hanged.

    e. He gallantly fought till the end.

    f. She is arguably better equipped for the job than her husband.

As is well known, there often is an analogous sentence with an overt commanding predictate, i.e. a surface main verb:

(106) a. It was predictable that Leo would let you down.

    b. It is possible that Kate will return soon.

    c. It is said that she is very clever.

    d. It is alleged that the man was hanged.

    e. It was gallant of him to fight till the end.

    f. It can be argued that she is better equipped for the job than her husband.

It is equally well known, however, that there are often semantic differences between the sentences with adverbials and those with overt verbs. Thus, (105a) actually asserts that Leo let the addressee down, but (106a) does not entail that: it is possible to utter (106a) without implying that in fact Leo did what was predictable, as in *At that stage it was still predictable that Leo would let you down. Now, however, we know that he would never do such a thing.* Or take (105e) and (106e). The former provides the *new* information that he fought till the end, and it is said that that was a gallant thing to do. In the latter it is *presupposed* that the 'he' fought till the end, not new. We can account for such differences by enriching the lexical specification of the predicates in question. Thus, for *predictable* we stipulate that it lexically entails the truth of the argument S if it undergoes lowering and adverbializing, and that it lacks that entailment if it is lexicalized into a surface sentential adjective (with *be*). For *gallant* it is stipulated that, when used as a surface sentential adjective (plus *be*) it is factive (i.e. it presupposes the truth of its argument S), whereas it only entails the truth of the argument S when used adverbially.[25] (See chapter 3 for an analysis of presupposition and lexical

---

[25] It has been observed by many authors that sentences like (105a) and (105e) are paraphrasable by means of a conjunction or a non-restrictive relative clause:

    (i) Leo let you down, and that was predictable.

    (ii) Leo let you down, which was predictable.

    (iii) He fought till the end, and that was gallant.

    (iv) He fought till the end, which was gallant.

Although this observation is clearly correct, it does not entail that, therefore, such sentences should be grammatically derived from conjunctions (or relative clauses). In fact, though such a treatment would slightly simplify the lexicon, it would call for grotesque rules of syntax, violating every thinkable constraint. It therefore seems preferable to make use of lexical distinctions of a kind which is very familiar anyway. Note that the same argument applies to surface semantics: if that semantics is to be kept within reasonable constraints, it should not attempt to read sentences like (105a) and (105e) as semantic conjunctions.

entailment.) It is, in fact, very common to find that predicates show slight semantic differences according to the set of rules they follow in the syntax. Since these rules are associated with the semantic predicates in the lexicon, this is no argument at all against the principle of semantic syntax.

When a predicate is lowered into its argument S, it must be assigned a position. This position depends to a large extent on the kind of predicate that is being lowered and on the surface category to which it is to belong. Tenses, for example, are adopted by the lower verb (and are relabelled "Affix"). Quantifiers occupy the position of the variable quantified by them. In English, sentence adverbials have a specific set of possible positions. For negation the canonical landing site in English is best defined as a new node labelled "Aux" preceding the node V of the lower S. (Postcyclically, all Aux-nodes are checked on their dominating a verbal form; if an Aux-node does not, it gets *do*-support.) But other sites are possible as well, in particular in combination with quantifiers. In Dutch and German, negation is lowered to the far right, or else before any previously lowered operator.

This brings us to a central problem in the theory of lowering. The problem consists in the fact that, typically, the lowering predicates occurring in unstable structures (i.e. taking an S as their only argument) are *scope-bearing*. Their scope consists of their argument S. (Scope-bearing predicates with two argument Ss will be discussed in a moment: the two Ss are reduced or rearranged to become one single S, which is then the scope.) Semantically, as will be shown in the following chapter, there is nothing special to the status of being the scope or argument-S of a scope-bearing predicate. Grammatically, however, there is, in that the lowering of scope-bearing predicates seems subject to a constraint whose first formulation may be given as follows:

Scope Ordering Constraint (SOC)
Every semantic predicate P_1 which is lowered and then represented lexically, not morphologically, must stay to the left of any other semantic predicate P_2 that has been lowered on an earlier cycle.

This would mean that after lowering, but not necessarily in surface structure, semantic scope is represented by a strict left-to-right ordering of every lexical element that represents a scope-bearing semantic predicate. Since the constraint does not apply to purely morphological elements, tense is, in general, excluded from the constraint.

The Scope Ordering Constraint was discovered, in its essential features, in the period immediately following the publication of Katz and Postal 1964. In that book the authors proposed that transformational syntactic descriptions would be simpler and more adequate if the principle of *the semantic invariance of transformational rules* was observed. This meant that the propositional meaning of a sentence was accepted to be given at deep structure level, and that the transformations would not alter the meaning given. This hypothesis was soon revealed to be at variance with the actual deep structure analyses proposed in the literature till then. It required deep structures of a far more abstract nature. A popular T-rule such as Passive, in its current formulation, was inconsistent with the hypothesis of semantic invariance, as appears from cases such as:

(107) a. Nobody here knows two languages.
     b. Two languages are known by nobody here.

These two sentences differ in meaning. Yet they are the active and passive form, respectively, of what had to be one deep structure in the then current analyses. It also soon became clear that the offending elements tend to be either straightforwardly logical elements or at least to have a logical flavour: they all have *scope*. In the late 1960s it was found that there is a non-trivial correspondence between the scope of these logical or quasi-logical elements on the one hand, and the left-to-right ordering of their surface representatives on the other (Seuren 1967, 1969; Lakoff 1971a). This discovery underlies the Scope Ordering Constraint as it is formulated here.

The semantic predicates that fall under the Scope Ordering Constraint are typically the quantifiers, the truth-functional operators of negation, conjunction, and disjunction, and prepositional constructions and other sentence adverbials. As regards the latter, consider the difference between, e.g., *For five hours he did not work* and *He did not work for five hours* (the latter of which is ambiguous). Sentence adverbials that are derived from adjectives, such as those in (105a) and (105c)–(105f), tend to fall outside the constraint, a fact which is probably due to the general feature of adjectives that take sentential subjects that the subject S is dominated by an NP-node, so that the resulting structure is not unstable (see the discussion below in section 2.4.5 in connection with example (148)).

Some of the semantic predicates just mentioned do not occur, at SA-level, in unstable structures on account of the fact that they take two NP-terms (as with the quantifiers), or two S-terms (as with conjunction and disjunction), or an S-term and an NP-term (as with prepositions). In all these cases, however, the transformational derivation is such that an unstable structure occurs somewhere along the line. At that point NPSC applies.

It must be noted, in this connection, that some quantifiers, and also the conjunction operator, and perhaps other operators as well, allow for readings where scope is not at issue, but where a 'group reading' is appropriate: *Five policemen faced three hundred mobsters*, or *Many contestants are fighting for few prizes* are sentences containing quantifiers that do not, in their preferred readings, stand to each other in a relation of simple scope hierarchy, but involve a more complex logical relationship. It is not immediately clear what this more complex relationship is, and, in particular, what linguistic analysis captures this relationship in the empirically most adequate way. One might think of higher order predicate calculus analyses, whereby sets occur as individuals. The former of the two sentences just given would then read as something like "there is an overlap of one between the set of things x such that there are 300 mobsters whom x faces, and the set of things x such that x is a set of five policemen", and the latter sentence would read as "there is an overlap of one between the set of things x such that there are few prizes x is fighting for and the set of things x such that x is a set of many contestants". Similar phenomena occur, as is well known, with the conjunction operator: *Ian and Nancy are married* has the preferred reading that Ian and Nancy are a married couple, and not that both Ian and Nancy are married persons (though not necessarily married to each other). Here again, one thinks of an analysis whereby *Ian and Nancy* is a higher order definite description. It seems sensible, however, to disregard these phenomena here. They require analyses and apparatus that are beyond the scope of the present study. We shall restrict ourselves to ordinary scope-bearing quantifiers and ordinary distributive conjunction. These are in any case subject to some constraint regulating their occurrence in surface structures according to their scope hierarchy. What occupies us now is the fact that SOC as formulated above seems inadequate.

The regularity of the picture is disturbed by the fact that the correspondence in question is not perfect and can be **overridden in surface structure**:

(108) a. I visited two museums every week.
b. Joan may not have read two books.

Both these sentences are clearly ambiguous, and the ambiguity is one of scope. (108a) allows for the following two (approximate) analyses, expressed in something approaching the language of classical predicate calculus with restricted quantification:

(108) a'. $\forall x : \text{week} [\exists 2y : \text{museum} [\text{visit I } y]]$
a''. $\exists 2y : \text{museum} [\forall x : \text{week} [\text{visit I } y]]$

And (108b) corresponds to:

(108) b'. Poss [not [$\exists 2x : \text{book} [\text{read Joan } x]$]]
b''. Poss [$\exists 2x : \text{book} [\text{not} [\text{read Joan } x]$]]
b'''. $\exists 2x : \text{book} [\text{Poss} [\text{not} [\text{read Joan } x]]]$

(where "Poss" stands for the epistemic possibility operator). Note that there is no ambiguity in:

(109) a. Every week I visited two museums.
b. Joan may have read no two books.

The former can only have the reading (108a'), and the latter only (108b'). That is, they both obey the Scope Ordering Constraint with regard to their surface structure. Although a violation of the constraint can sometimes be connected with intonational phenomena, it never became clear how the non-trivial correspondence could be taken advantage of in a principled way. As a consequence, this line of research disappeared into relative obscurity.

This obscurity, however, is totally undeserved. It was due to a relatively defective knowledge of the logical and semantic aspects involved, as well as of the grammatical details. Thus, it was not realized with sufficient clarity that the Scope Ordering Constraint applies only to lowering predicates, not to raising predicates such as the modals when they are surface-verbal. This takes away some apparent irregularity, as we shall see presently. Then, on the positive side, it must be observed that cross-linguistic comparison strongly reinforces the status of SOC. Take, for example, the reading (108b''), and see how it is expressed in a few European languages – whereby only lowered operators are to be considered. *Poss*, $\exists$, and *not*, as expressed in the different surface structures, are subscripted 1, 2, and 3, respectively, to facilitate the detection of correspondence or lack of it between semantic scope and left-to-right ordering:

(110) a. *English:* (1) Joan has perhaps$_1$ not$_3$ read two books$_2$.

(2) ?*Perhaps$_1$, two books$_2$ Joan has not$_3$ read.

  b. *French:* (1) Il y a peut-être$_1$ deux livres$_2$ que Joan n$_3$'a pas lus.

(2) Il y a deux livres$_2$, peut-être$_1$, que Joan n$_3$'a pas lus.

  c. *Italian:* (1) Forse$_1$ ci sono due libri$_2$ che Joan non$_3$ ha letti.

(2) Ci sono due libri$_2$, forse$_1$, che Joan non$_3$ ha letti.

  d. *German:* (1) Joan hat vielleicht$_1$ zwei Bücher$_2$ nicht$_3$ gelesen.

(2) Vielleicht$_1$ hat Joan zwei Bücher$_2$ nicht$_3$ gelesen.

  e. *Dutch:* (1) Joan heeft misschien$_1$ twee boeken$_2$ niet$_3$ gelezen.

(2) Misschien$_1$ heeft Joan twee boeken$_2$ niet$_3$ gelezen.

Only in (110a1), (110b2), and (110c2) is the regular correspondence upset. But note that in (110a1) the NP *two books* must receive a reinforced accent if the intended reading is to be realized, and in the other two cases there very clearly is an intonational break. If we take intonational features to provide some sort of escape, the correspondence between semantic scope and surface ordering is very striking.

A second striking phenomenon is the fact, mentioned in note 2 of chapter 1, that newspaper headlines turn out to observe the Scope Ordering Constraint to the very letter. Relatively little attention has been paid, in the theoretical literature, to 'headlinese' (the only study I know of is Straumann 1935), but one tends to have the pretheoretical hunch that there is something skeletal to it. It seems quite plausible to hypothesize that many if not all postcyclic rules are not operative in the abbreviated form of language found in headlines. Given the lack of empirical studies, in the context of grammatical theory, of the language of newspaper headlines, however, this observation must remain suggestive and cannot be accounted for in a satisfactory way.

The same holds for the observation that the language of telegrams follows the Scope Ordering Constraint in total obedience. Ordinary language, however, takes certain liberties.

A third phenomenon to be observed is the fact, mentioned above, that it is only lowering operators that are subject to SOC. Subject-Raising operators, such as the English modal auxiliary verbs, or Predicate-Raising operators, such as the German and Dutch modal auxiliaries, are exempted on principle. It can thus be no problem for the theory that, for example, semantic "not possible" may result in English in the modal auxiliary construction *cannot*, and "possible not" in *may not*. Note that, although there is no violation of SOC, the interpretation is not free: *cannot* and *may not* are interpretatively fixed by specific rules of English grammar relating the former to "not possible", and the latter to "possible not", exclusively. Now consider the German and Dutch sentences:

(111) a. *German:*   Joan kann zwei Bücher nicht gelesen haben.
      b. *Dutch:*   Joan kan twee boeken niet gelezen hebben.

Both sentences have, besides the reading "it is possible that there are two books that Joan has not read", another perfectly natural reading "there are two books such that it is not possible that Joan has read them". This reading is entirely impossible for (110d) and (110e), where the adverb *vielleicht/ misschien* ("perhaps"), result of the lowering of the possibility operator, is used. When *Poss* is represented by the modal (Predicate-Raising) verb *können/ kunnen*, it is not subject to any constraint regarding scope and surface order. In addition, the sentences of (111) can have a third reading: "there are two books such that it is possible that Joan has not read them", a reading which is also possible, though not dominant, for (110d1) and (110e1), but not, or hardly, for (110d2) or (110e2).

These facts are of considerable significance. They not only support the analysis as a whole in that they bear out the distinction made between raising and lowering operators. They are also helpful towards finding a solution for the 'irregular' cases of scope representation. Let us compare the sentences of (111) and those of (110d) and (110e) - whereby we shall limit ourselves to the German sentences since there is no difference in the interpretative possibilities of the German and the Dutch sentences:

(111)   Joan *kann zwei Bücher nicht* gelesen haben - (1) Poss-∃-N
                                     (2) ∃-Poss-N
                NB: * N-∃   (3) ∃-N-Poss

(110d)   Joan hat *vielleicht zwei Bücher nicht* gelesen ⎱ - Poss-∃-N
        Vielleicht hat Joan *zwei Bücher nicht* gelesen ⎰

                NB: * N-∃
                    * ∃-Poss

Poss is the semantic counterpart of *kann/vielleicht*; ∃ of *zwei Bücher*; N of *nicht*. The orders listed on the right are the possible scope interpretations. Asterisked orders cover impossible interpretations. We note that in (111) *Poss* can stand in any position in the interpretation, but ∃ must precede N. That is, any interpretation in which N precedes ∃ is illegitimate. (110d) is more restricted: not only must ∃ precede N, but *Poss* must also precede ∃.

The interpretative freedom of *kann*, as far as scope is concerned, is explained by the fact that *kann* induces PR with regard to the lower V. It is not a lowering predicate and thus does not fall under SOC. *Vielleicht*, however, has been lowered and falls under SOC, which imposes extra interpretative restrictions. The interesting question now is: why is N-∃ excluded for (111) and both N-∃ and ∃-Poss for (110d)? In answering this question we observe that for the banned scope orderings there are perfectly viable alternatives which are generated directly in the cycle (*keine* = *nicht* + ∃):

(112)   Joan *kann keine zwei Bücher* gelesen haben -   (1) N-Poss-∃
                                                         (2) Poss-N-∃
       NB: * ∃ -N   (3) N-∃-Poss

(113)   Joan hat *vielleicht keine zwei Bücher* gelesen ⎫
       Vielleicht hat Joan *keine zwei Bücher* gelesen ⎬ - Poss-N-∃
                                                         ⎭

       NB: * ∃ -N
           * N-Poss

(114)   Joan hat *zwei Bücher vielleicht nicht* gelesen - ∃ -Poss-N

       NB: * N-Poss
           * Poss-∃

Sentence (112) represents the order N-∃, which is banned for (111). (112) is produced without any obstacle by the cycle of German syntax. The sentences (113) and (114) represent the banned scope orderings of (110d).[26] The existence of these alternatives suggests that whenever a shallow structure is generated according to SOC no later rule is permitted to change the order in which the elements representing operators occur. Only when the cycle 'blocks' in the lowering of operators is there an escape clause.

[26] Other representatives are:

(i)   Joan hat *nicht vielleicht zwei Bücher* gelesen - N-Poss-∃
(ii) *Joan hat *zwei Bücher nicht vielleicht* gelesen -∃-N-Poss

These sentences, however, present complications that are immaterial to the question at hand. Sentence (i) carries the well-known 'echo' effect that comes with sentences containing a Positive Polarity Item under negation. *Vielleicht*, like its English counterpart *perhaps*, is such an item: when it is in the scope of a negation there is an 'echo', as though the non-negated sentence has just been uttered and is then rejected as a sentence, not just for its lack of truth. In chapter 3 a great deal more is said about polarity items and their semantic and grammatical properties. It will be shown there that the negation which is allowed with Positive Polarity Items (and provokes the echo) is subject to certain grammatical restrictions, including the restriction that it must be the highest operator. This explains the ungrammaticality of (ii).

This is in need of some comment. Given the fact that lowered operators have a predefined landing site in the lower clause, and given the fact that, according to SOC, an operator P_1 must, when lowered, stay to the left of any other operator P_2 that has been lowered on an earlier cycle, it follows that it may occur that a P_1 cannot be lowered because its landing site is to the right of a P_2 lowered earlier. When such a situation occurs, the cycle blocks and there should be no output.[27] However, with the lowering of operators there are escapes (probably because otherwise language would be too poor in expressive means). First, SOC must be reformulated to apply to the final result of the cycle, i.e. shallow structure. We shall speak of *blocking* in a technical sense only if lowering violates the left-to-right correspondence in shallow structure of the scope hierarchy. In the case of blocking, the correspondence may be violated provided some postcyclic rule restores it or, failing that, a special intonational feature is placed on the operator that has been lowered 'illegitimately'. Moreover, all postcyclic rules are constrained in that they may not bring about an ordering of operators that would have resulted from the cycle without any blocking from any other SA than the one at hand. It seems that with these extra conditions SOC is adequate to the facts. Let us now reformulate SOC as follows:

Scope Ordering Constraint (SOC)
(a) Every semantic P_1 which is lowered and then represented lexically, not morphologically, must in shallow structure stay to the left of any other semantic predicate P_2 that has been lowered on an earlier cycle, provided the cycle does not block.
(b) If the cycle blocks, P_1 can still be lowered. But then some later rule *must* restore the order P_1-P_2, or else P_1 is marked intonationally.
(c) No postcyclic rule can move a lowered operator into a position that would have resulted form the cycle, i.e. in shallow structure, without blocking for any SA other than the SA at hand.

Intonational marking of P_1 is not always possible; it seems to depend on the grammatical possibility of moving P_1 postcyclically to a position preceding P_2. In this extended formulation SOC seems to be adequate, at least in principle.

Before we can review the cases discussed to see if and how SOC applies, it must be shown how quantified SAs are transformed into Surface Structures. An intermediate stage in this process, represented by (115e) below, is a struc-

[27] Just as there is no output, for example, when some SA requires relativization from the S of a complex NP or from, say, an embedded question: *This is the road that I don't know where leads to. The grammar of Standard English simply fails to deliver an output in such cases, and some other way must be found to express the thought in question. (A common, but not standard, way to get around the problem exemplified in the ungrammatical sentence just given is to leave a pronoun behind in the extraction site: This is the road that I don't know where it leads to.)*

ture corresponding to restricted quantification formulae, which are of the form $_S[V + S]$, and are thus unstable. According to the SA Formation Rules of section 2.2, quantified SAs consist of a quantifying predicate and two NP arguments, the first an SD-term, the second either an SD-term or a definite term.

Now consider, for example, (115a) with its Semantic Analysis (115b), or rather (115c):

(115) a. I see a house.
    b. $\exists 1(\hat{}x(see(I, x)), \hat{}x(house(x)))$
    c.

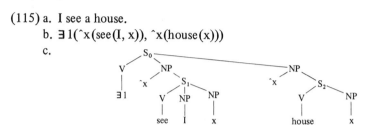

A special rule is assumed for the lowering of the SD-operator "$\hat{}x$" into its argument S: the SD-operator is lowered into the position of the lower x; the NP over $\hat{}x$ is deleted. This gives the following result:

(115) d.

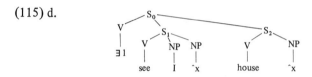

Then there is obligatory Object Incorporation, by which the object is made part of the main predicate. This rule is also found with prepositional predicates, and in surface lexical cases: *take advantage*, *keep tabs*, *take care*, *decapitate* (= cut off the head), *apologize* (= make apologies), etc. S_2 is right-adopted by the quantifier:

(115) e.

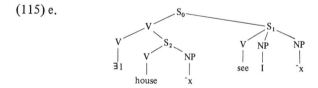

Quantifier Lowering now makes the complex quantifying predicate descend into S_1 to occupy the position of the bound variable $\hat{}x$. The complete V is restructured as an indefinite article plus noun:

(115) f.

Tense processing will turn this into (115a).

We can now proceed to look at the cases of operator lowering discussed above. Quantified Ss will be presented in the general form of (115e), i.e. in what amounts to predicate calculus with restricted quantification. The representations are linear, with square brackets enclosing cyclic Ss. The arrows indicate lowering.

Consider again (107a) and (107b):

(107) a. Nobody here knows two languages.
      b. Two languages are known by nobody here.

The former has the following derivation:

(107) a′.

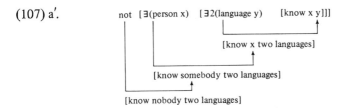

The derivation is simplified and only gives the essentials of the cycle. The variable y is eliminated first; then follows the variable x, whose replacement, *somebody*, nicely stays left of *two languages*. Finally, *not* is lowered, but not into the canonical position, i.e. left of the verb under a new Aux node. If the preceding operator (*somebody*) is existentially quantified, it may attract the negation with which it will then form a single negative surface quantifier. If *not* had been lowered into the canonical position for negation, the result would have been: [not know somebody two languages], which is against SOC(a), since tense processing will move the subject *somebody* to the left of *not*, resulting in (116a) with the underlying (116b):

(116) a. Somebody (here) does not know two languages.
      b. ∃ (person x) [not [∃2(language y) [know xy]]]

Here *not* must either be lowered canonically, or attracted by the second quantifier: *Somebody here knows no two languages.* For (107a), however, the canonical position is barred.

(107b) is derived thus:

(107) b′.

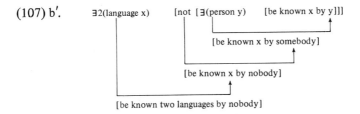

Again, SOC is observed without any complications: all lowered operators stay to the left of their predecessors. Note, however, that *not* could now have been lowered into its canonical position without any clash with SOC(a). The result of lowering *not* canonically is: [not be known x by somebody]. Now, on the next cycle, blocking occurs because the highest quantifier must land at the position of the variable *x*, which is to the right of *not*. Fortunately, however, *x* is subject, so that tense processing obligatorily makes it end up to the left of *not*, thus saving the derivation. The result of this process is: *Two languages are not known by anybody here* (with *some* replaced by *any*).

Note that (107a) is also derivable from:

(107) a″.

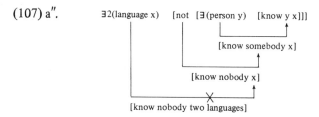

After tense processing this is identical with (107a). According to SOC(b) the order may remain unchanged, but then the offending quantifier, i.e. *two languages*, must receive a special intonation. (What the exact properties are of the marked accent or contour is a question not gone into here.) It seems reasonable to identify (107a′) with what was called the *dominant* reading of the sentence in section 1.1, example (8), and (107a″) with the *recessive* reading.

Likewise, (107b) is also derivable from (107b″):

(107) b″.

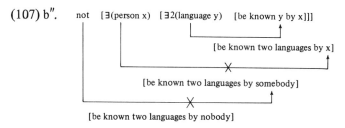

which then becomes identical with (107b). But owing to SOC(b) a special intonation is now required for *nobody*, which incorporates two offending operators. Again, we identify (107b″) with the recessive reading, and (107b′) with the dominant reading of (107b).

Now that we are at it, note that

(107) c. Two languages nobody here knows.

is ambiguous. One reading is (107a′), combined with optional preposing (topicalization) of the object-NP *two languages*. This preposing cannot be blocked by SOC(c) because no cycle can deliver a shallow structure with a preposed object. The other reading is (107a″), with postcyclic preposing of the object so as to restore the proper semantic ordering of operator representatives.

Let us now pass on to a discussion of (108a) and (109a), repeated here for convenience:

(108) a. I visited two museums every week.
(109) a. Every week I visited two museums.

As we have seen, (108a) is ambiguous between (108a′) and (108a″), but (109a) can only carry the meaning represented by (108a′). We will now see what explains this distribution of readings. ("$\mathcal{D}$" stands for the landing site of the class of adverbials to which the temporal adjunct *every week* belongs; this class consists, in general, of sentential adverbial operators of time, place, manner, modality. $\mathcal{D}$ and *not* are both left of V, in any order required by lowering without blocking.)

(108) a′.

Tense processing now yields a shallow structure *I every week visited two museums.* A postcyclic rule applying to adjuncts of place and time which are not surface adverbs[28] now obligatorily moves *every week* either to the left, giving (109a), or to the far right, giving (108a). Neither movement is disallowed: movement to the left does not disturb the semantic scope ordering. Movement to the right is allowed because it does not result in a scope ordering producible under SOC(a) for some other SA. This is so because (108a″), the other reading, leads to blocking, and hence falls under SOC(b):

(108) a″.

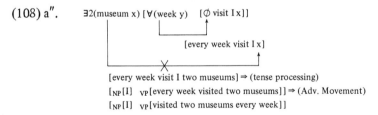

[28] For surface adverbs the position indicated by "ϕ" need not be changed:

(i) I usually visited the Louvre.
(ii) Usually I visited the Louvre.
(iii) I visited the Louvre, usually.

Leftward movement has taken place in (ii), and rightward movement in (iii). The movement rule in question will have to be formulated in such a way that it says that rightward movement for surface adverbs is possible only under specific discourse conditions – in this case the condition of "usually" being an afterthought.

This produces (108a) only. It cannot produce (109a) – by leftward movement of *every week* – because that would violate SOC(c): (109a) is directly generated in the cycle under observance of SOC(a) for the SA corresponding to (108a′), without any blocking. We thus see that the theory predicts that (108a′) produces (108a) as well as (109a), but that (108a″) produces only (108a). Hence (108a) is ambiguous between (108a′) and (108a″), but (109a) can only have the reading (108a′).

Note that it is a necessary requirement of the theory that the adverbial site ∅ precede V. If it were proposed that ∅ should stand, say, at the far right, the predictions turn out to be incorrect. Instead of (108a′) and (108a″) we would have (117a) and (117b), respectively:

(117) a.

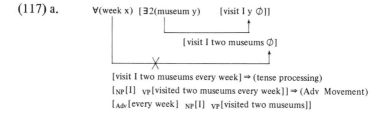

[visit I two museums every week] ⇒ (tense processing)
[NP[I] VP[visited two museums every week]] ⇒ (Adv Movement)
[Adv[every week] NP[I] VP[visited two museums]]

That is, (117a) leads to (109a). It can also lead to (108a) if *every week* is not moved to the far left. SOC(b) then requires a special intonation on *every week*.

(117) b.

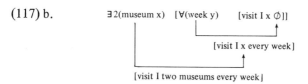

This leads to (108a), but it may also produce (109a), by optional Adv. Movement. This postcyclic movement rule can be applied here since it results in an ordering of operators that is not otherwise produced without blocking, i.e. by means of SOC(a) only. The only alternative is (117a), and that requires SOC(b), since otherwise there is blocking. Hence, both (117a) and (117b) lead to (108a) as well as to (109a), so that both these sentences should be similarly ambiguous. However, (109a) cannot possibly mean what is represented by (108″) or (117b). We are thus forced to accept that the site for adverbials in English, at least for the adverbials of the class that *every week* belongs to, is just left of V – which gives us the extra advantage that surface adverbs like *often, usually*, etc. are in fact found in that position in surface structures. This conclusion is of some relevance against the background of vociferous claims made in the past that what was known as generative semantics was an unconstrained theory that would fix any thinkable data. It is nearer the truth to say that masses of seemingly irregular or refractory data (mostly neglected in the literature) fall into place in the framework of semantic syntax.

Now consider (110a1): *Joan has perhaps not read two books*. This has the following three readings:

(108) b′.

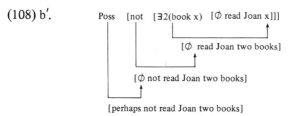

This reading is unproblematic: operator scope is reflected regularly in the left-to-right ordering of the operator representatives in surface structure.

(108) b″.

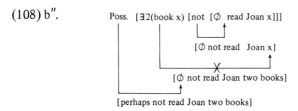

Here, however, the offending operator *two books* must either be removed by a later rule so that it will precede the negation, or it stays but with intonational marking. The former alternative is hardly realistic: the preposing needed can only lead, in English, to (110a2), but that sentence rather stretches the powers of English grammar, due to a conflict in preposing. So the second alternative seems best, as has been observed above.

(108) b‴.

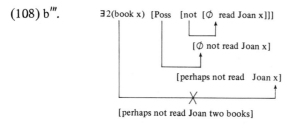

Now either *two books* must be **preposed**, or it receives special intonation. The former is fully possible given the postcyclic movement rules of English: *Two books Joan has perhaps not read*. The latter is found in (110a1).

The other three possible permutations are quickly dealt with. Two of them, N-∃-Poss and ∃-N-Poss, have Poss in third position. This is all right if the modal verb *can* is selected:

(118) a. Joan can't have read two books.

but not with the lowered adverbial *perhaps*. This is to do with the fact (note 26) that *perhaps* is a Positive Polarity Item, which means, in this case, that it must be either the first or the second operator. If the latter, there is an 'echo' unless the first operator is a variable binder:

> (118) b. Joan has not perhaps read two books.
>   c. Joan has always perhaps read two books.

Notice the slurred intonation invited by these two sentences on the part *perhaps read two books*. But *perhaps* cannot be a third or later operator: there is no way the readings N-∃-Poss or ∃-N-Poss can be rendered with *perhaps*. The only way is through the Subject-Raising modal *can*, as in (118a), which has both these readings, plus N-Poss-∃:

(108) b''''.

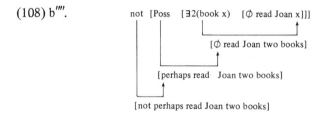

As appears from (108''''), a derivation with *perhaps* is possible, but only with the echo that has been mentioned a few times now. The result is (118b), just given above.

Finally, we go through (110d), (113) and (114). Here it must be kept in mind that in German (and Dutch), unlike English, the negation lands at the far right but before any operator lowered earlier, including quantifiers. The negation behaves like other adverbials in a large class, comprising also *vielleicht* ("perhaps"), *immer* ("always"), *schon* ("already"), *manchmal* ("often"), *selten* ("rarely") and many others. Quite a few of these (*vielleicht, schon, manchmal*, for example) are Positive Polarity Items.

> (110) d. (1) Joan hat vielleicht zwei Bücher nicht gelesen. ⎫
>   (2) Vielleicht hat Joan zwei Bücher nicht gelesen. ⎭
>   ("There may be two books Joan has not read")

d'.

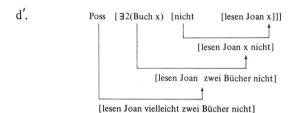

Given the positional flexibility of the three operators involved, there is no problem in their being lowered without any blocking. Tense processing and the postcyclic rule of Verb Final, which moves the non-finite part of V in main clauses, and the whole V in subordinate clauses, to the far right, now yields (110d1). Optional preposing of *vielleicht* gives (110d2).

(113) a. Joan hat vielleicht keine zwei Bücher gelesen. ⎱
     b. Vielleicht hat Joan keine zwei Bücher gelesen. ⎰

("Maybe there are no two books Joan has read")

c.
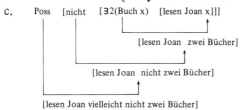

Again, predictably, no blocking occurs. The negation *nicht* is optionally (but preferably) changed into *keine* before the existential phrase *zwei Bücher*. Tense processing and Verb Final give (113a). Optional preposing of *vielleicht* yields (113b).

(114) Joan hat zwei Bücher vielleicht nicht gelesen.

("There are two books Joan may not have read")

(114′)
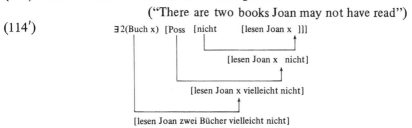

With tense processing and Verb Final we get (114). Note that here *vielleicht* cannot be moved to front position. This is forbidden by SOC(c): preposing of *vielleicht* would result in a sentence identical with (110d1) which, as has been shown, is derived in the cycle without any blocking. Postcyclic movement is heavily restricted in these sentences anyway, since any change in the relative order of the operators immediately leads to a sentence derivable without blocking from a different SA.

Clearly, the analysis of operator lowering presented here deserves a great deal more testing and discussion, but limitations of space forbid any further elaboration here. It is claimed, however, that none of the existing analyses of the Scope Ordering Constraint gets as close to the facts as the analysis presented here.

A few words must be said now about scope-bearing predicates with two argument Ss. It has been said, at the beginning of this section, that there always is a process whereby the two Ss are reduced to one S, which is then the scope. Something to this effect has been shown above, when (115) was discussed. The initial structure or SA (115c) has two NP arguments, but it does not take long for the structure to be one with two argument Ss: (115d). Since the existentially quantifying predicate must be lowered, the two Ss must be reduced to one S, which is done in (115e) by Object Incorporation. Lowering can now take place.

Another class of cases where this problem occurs is formed by *coordinating predicates*, in particular the truth-functional predicates *and* and *or*. They are represented in the theory as binary semantic predicates over sentential structures (more about this in the following chapter). That they are scope-bearing predicates is not widely recognized in the literature. Yet there can be no doubt that they are, as appears from:

(119) a. Some critics liked (both) the tenor and the soprano.
   b. (Both) the tenor and the soprano were liked by some critics.
(120) a. All critics liked (either) the tenor or the soprano.
   b. (Either) the tenor or the soprano was liked by all critics.

In the (a)-sentences the quantifier takes scope over the co-ordinating conjunction (*and, or*), whereas in the (b)-sentences either this (recessive reading) or the opposite (dominant reading) is the case. Note that *both* and *either* may help to delimit scope unambiguously. In (121a) and (122a) there is scope ambiguity between *thought* and *and/or*, but in the respective (b)-sentences and (c)-sentences the ambiguity is removed by the placement of *both/either*:

(121) a. The victim was thought to be Jewish and Italian.
   b. The victim was thought to be both Jewish and Italian.
   c. The victim was both thought to be Jewish and Italian.
(122) a. The victim was thought to be Spanish or Italian.
   b. The victim was thought to be either Spanish or Italian.
   c. The victim was either thought to be Spanish or Italian.

We shall see in a moment that the theory accounts for this fact quite naturally.

There is a vast literature on phenomena of conjunction reduction in its various forms. The literature is so vast that it would not be practical to even try and give an idea of what it amounts to within the limited scope of the few pages devoted to co-ordination here. One thing is clear, however: in spite of the vast amount of literature there is as yet no universally accepted solution which is equal to the facts. Given this, there can be no question of putting forward the irresponsible claim that the whole problem of conjunction reduction can be solved here and now. Yet the problem can be divided up to some extent. It seems that most problems are concentrated around cases where

surface *and* does not seem to be reducible to a conjunction of two propositions and where a form of reciprocity seems to be at play, as in *Harry and Sue*
are a lovely couple, and cases where two or more disjoint parts of the two
underlying sentences are different, i.e. cases of gapping, as in *John probably*
wants his steak rare, and Harry well done. If we limit ourselves to the relatively
simple cases where the underlying Ss differ in only one continuous part (not
necessarily one surface constituent), we can take advantage of a relatively
simple cyclic treatment whereby the two Ss are mapped onto each other and
are made to coalesce, except for the parts where the difference lies: these
parts are juxtaposed and connected with the co-ordinating variable "−"
defining the landing site for the co-ordinating conjunction to be lowered onto.

More precisely, a structure of the type:

a.

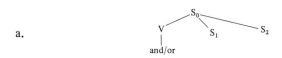

is changed first, on the S_0-cycle, to:

b.

where S' represents the result of mapping S_1 and S_2 on to each other. We shall
call this process *Conjunction Reduction Mapping* (CR-Mapping) – as opposed
to CR-Gapping. It identifies the two Ss at most to the extent that they are
repetitions of each other. The parts which differ, and in some cases even some
adjacent material, are juxtaposed and connected by "−". Then the co-
ordinating predicate is lowered onto "−". Note that the structure (b) given
above is unstable in the sense defined in section 2.4.2. The lowering is either
simple or *complex*. Simple lowering consists in no more than the lowering of
the conjunctive or disjunctive predicate onto the landing site that has been
prepared. Complex lowering involves simple lowering and, in addition, the
lowering of *both* (for *and*) or *either* (for *or*). These two reinforcers normally
join up with the split constituent and occupy its leftmost position. Only if
the split constituent stands under a lower S or VP with regard to S' will *both*
and *either* land at the position Φ (for adverbials) in S'. CR-Mapping applies
also to cases where two or more disjoint parts are different. In such cases
there is usually a choice between CR-Mapping with multiple splittings and the
preferred addition of the reinforcer *respectively* on the one hand, and CR-
Gapping on the other. For example, from the underlying conjunction (123a)
we get (123b) by CR-Mapping and (123c) by CT-Gapping:

(123) a. Harry likes his tea hot and Sue likes her coffee cold.
　　　b. Harry and Sue like their tea and coffee hot and cold, respectively.
　　　c. Harry likes his tea hot and Sue her coffee cold.

(whereby, of course, (123b) is more than a little stilted).

But let us consider a few examples, taking first a case of classical simplicity for the purpose of mere illustration:

(124) a. Otto loves (both) Liz and Eve.
　　　b.

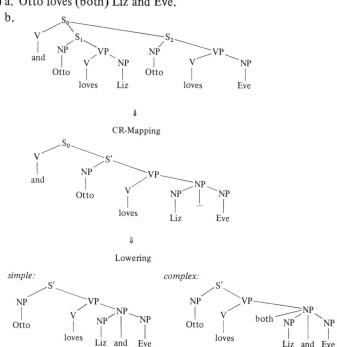

It is to be noted that the process is cyclic; the cycle in question is S_0. S_1 and S_2 are represented here in their Shallow Structure form of the NP-VP type – i.e. it has been assumed that S_1 and S_2 are themselves fully tensed. This is not unreasonable in this case, considering that there are analogous cases of conjunction reduction involving differing tenses:

(125) a. Otto loves and has always loved his family home.

Moreover, there are the well-known cases of successive conjunction, where two subsequent events are related in the order in which they occurred:

(125) b. The man drew a knife, pointed it at me, and said "Your life or
　　　　your money".

No need here, of course, to add, *in that order*. Since each sentence of this threefold conjunction refers to a separate event, occurring in the order in which they are presented, it would seem odd, from a semantic point of view, to withhold tense from the separate sentences and place tense over the whole conjunction. On the other hand, there is no necessity of any kind to tense the conjoined Ss separately. In other cases than the ones just discussed it has advantages to place tense over the conjunction:

(125) c. Otto has never praised both the tenor and the soprano.

In this respect there is no difference with quantified noun phrases:

(126) a. Some people love and have always loved their family home.
  b. Someone drew a knife, pointed it at me, and said "Your money or your life".
  c. Never has anyone praised both the tenor and the soprano.

It thus appears that tense can be in the scope of a co-ordinating conjunction, and vice versa.[29]

To return now to the scope differences pointed out earlier, let us consider (119):

(119) a. Some critics liked (both) the tenor and the soprano.
  b. (Both) the tenor and the soprano were liked by some critics.

Let the Ss that are conjoined not be tensed (either interpretation seems viable here). The derivation of (119a) is, in principle, as follows:

(119) a'.

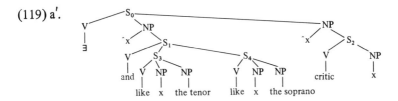

---

[29] Note that, again, the lowered conjunction (*and*, *or*) and any expression denoting tense and being the result of lowering, like *never*, observe SOC: in (125c) *never* precedes *and*, and takes scope over it ("there has never been a time when Otto praised both the tenor and the soprano"), out *and* takes scope over *never* in:

(i) Otto has never praised the tenor and Otto has never praised the soprano.

where *never* is a semantic part of each conjunct and *and* is not lowered into either of them. Note that (i) is equivalent with:

(ii) Otto has never praised either the tenor or the soprano.

where *never* again takes scope over the co-ordinating particle (*or*).

S_1-*cycle:*

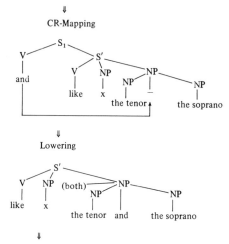

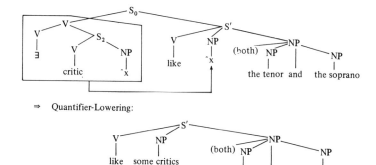

Note that the lowered quantifier stays to the left of *and* lowered earlier. No other reading is available. SOC(b) might be of help if *(both) the tenor and the soprano* could be intonationally marked. It seems, however, that this is difficult, given the harshness of:

(119) c. ?*(Both) the tenor and the soprano some critics liked.

That is, to the extent that English grammar bars this form of object preposing, the reading represented by (119b') is excluded.

Let us now consider (119b), with the following derivations:[30]

---

[30] As in (107b) above, Passive is taken to have applied and to have produced a *by*-phrase.

(119) b′.

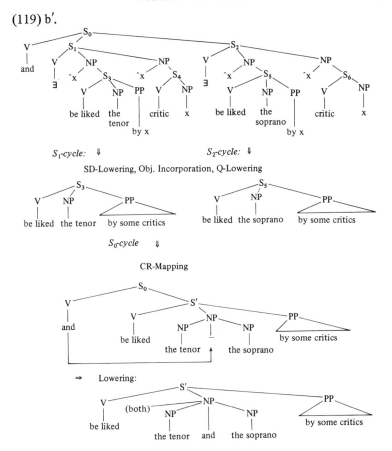

Again, the lowered operator *and* stays left of *some*, which has been lowered earlier. (119b′) represents the dominant reading of (119b). The recessive reading can be obtained from a structure which is similar to (119a′), the only difference being that all Ss with $_V$[like] are changed into passivized versions. Since ˆx then ends up in the *by*-phrase, Q-Lowering at the end violates SOC(a). The derivation is saved, however, by SOC(b), which allows for intonational amends. Contrary to (119a), this makes for a possible escape from the strict left-to-right correspondence requirement for lowered operators, since the *by*-phrase *by some critics* is easily preposed by a postcyclic rule:

(119) d. By some critics (both) the tenor and the soprano were liked.

In this sentence, the reading corresponding to (119a) is more readily felt to be present than in (119b).

Let us finally look at (122b) and (122c), given above and repeated here:

(122) b. The victim was thought to be either Spanish or Italian.
     c. The victim was either thought to be Spanish or Italian.

As we have seen, there is a semantic scope difference between the two. We can now account for that by observing the rule that in *complex lowering* the reinforcer (*both* or *either*) joins the split constituent as its leftmost member, as we have seen in (119a′) and (119b′), except when the split constituent stands under a lower VP with regard to S′. In that case the reinforcer lands at the position $\varnothing$ reserved for sentence adverbials in S′. The derivation of (122c) now runs, in principle, as follows:

(122) c′.

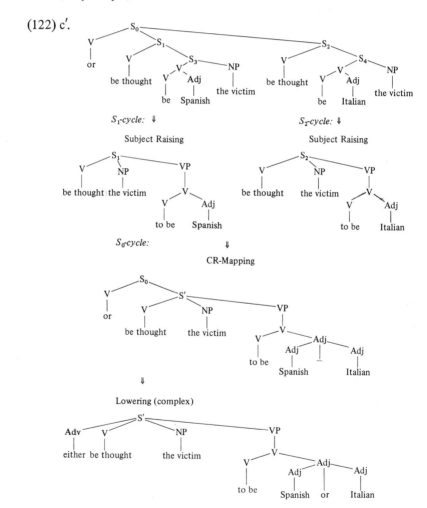

The reinforcer *either* now stays left of *be thought*, in the position of adverbials. If S_3 and S_4 had not been reduced to VPs, but had remained full Ss, mapped onto each other by CR-Mapping, lowering would still have taken place:

(122) d. It was either thought that the victim was Spanish or Italian.

Note that the constraining principle for cyclic rules C-7 as formulated in section 2.3.2, allows for lowering into embedded Ss whose cycle has already finished treatment: embedded Ss of any depth may be affected by a cyclic rule in the sense that material may be introduced into them. But C-6 restricts the removing of material to S_n or S_{n+1}: the domain of rule application is S_n or S_{n+1}, but the domain of rule effect extends to any depth of embedding. Note that lowering of quantifiers into more deeply embedded Ss is quite common:

(127) I assume that someone is warming up along the lines for that reason.

(said by a radio reporter of a football match, who was clearly referring to a specific individual).

(122b) is derived as follows:

(122) b'.

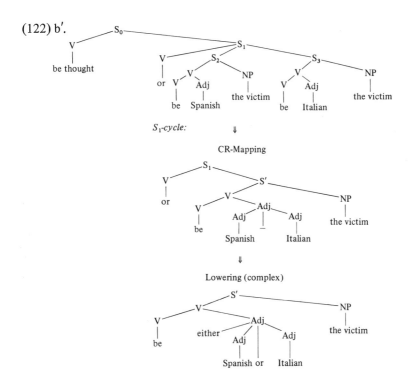

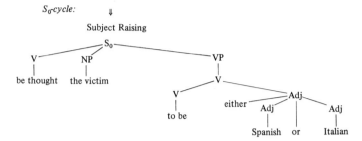

Note that the derivation would have been impossible if the whole CR-Mapping and Lowering process had not been cyclic. In particular the Subject Raising of *the victim* on the S_0-cycle would not have been possible if the disjunction of S_2 and S_3 had not first been reduced by Conjunction Reduction Mapping on the S_1-cycle.

2.4.4 Negative Raising

The negation, like the quantifiers, is a typical lowering predicate. It has associated with it in the lexicon the instruction, or rule, that it needs to be lowered into its (unstable) argument S. It appears, however, that the required lowering can be temporarily suspended under the influence of a higher predicate. If the first predicate higher up in the semantic tree is a predicate that induces the rule of Negative Raising (NR), then the negation is not lowered;[31] the (unstable) construction is left as it is until, on the next cycle, NR has applied. NR consists in the detaching of the negation in the first lower S and reattaching it (through left-adoption) to the S whose cycle is on. Let "P_{NR}" stand for a Negative Raising predicate, and "S_n" for the S whose cycle is on, then the rule can be formulated as follows:

The S_n-cycle can now be finished, and an extra S'-cycle is inserted. On the newly created S'-cycle the predicate *not* is finally lowered into S_n. This lowering is, of course, subject to the Scope Ordering Constraint (SOC) as formulated above. SOC is thus seen not necessarily to reflect the semantic hierarchy of lowering operators. It reflects the hierarchy of lowering operators as it

---

[31] Note that C-8 (section 2.3.2) allows for higher tree structure to play a part in the conditions of rule application.

comes about in the grammatical cycle. (It is phenomena of this nature that lend support to the view inherent in the whole of this work that grammar is but the totality of processes relating Semantic Analyses to Surface Structures, either way. Any theory claiming an independent status of grammar or syntax, definable without any reference to semantic facts, is deemed to be illusory.)

The existence of NR-predicates is a piece of traditional lore in linguistics. The fact that a sentence like (128a) should be taken to mean what is, in some sense, more literally expressed in (128b) has been recognized for a very long time:

(128) a. I don't think you are right there.
      b. I think you are not right there.

Early transformational literature immediately incorporated this old insight by postulating a transformation rule of Negative Raising, lifting the negation out of the embedded clause and putting it into the main clause. A few problems arose in that context. Thus it was problematic why (128a) and (128b) are related semantically the way they are while that correspondence is absent from, e.g., (129a) and (129b) but present in the pair (129a) and (129c):

(129) a. I don't think many voters will approve of that.
      b. I think many voters won't approve of that.
      c. I think not many voters will approve of that.

We now know that this is only an apparent problem: the negation can be raised only if, at the cycle where the raising is to take place, the negation is the highest embedded predicate. In (129b) the highest predicate of the embedded clause is *approve*, after the lowering of, first, *not* and, on the next cycle, *many*. In the lower clause of (129c), however, the negation takes scope over *many* and is thus the highest predicate of the embedded clause. The presence of the NR-verb *think* just above it prevents the lowering of *not*, which is thus the highest lower predicate, so that NR can apply. It was probably linguists' unfamiliarity with questions of scope and of logic in general, in those years, that kept them from seeing this regularity.

A further problem is that NR does not seem to operate freely whenever an NR-predicate occurs and *not* is the highest embedded predicate. NR seems somehow connected with the top of the tree, where it 'hooks' on to speech act properties. In fact, NR sits most comfortably with present tense indicative assertions with first person (singular) subject. Thus, (128a) and (129a) are paradigm cases. A sentence like (130a) is more a report of what the minister in question has said than of what the speaker thinks the minister thinks:

(130) a. The minister doesn't think that the plan will succeed.
      b. The minister thinks that the plan won't succeed.

In some kinds of embedding NR seems altogether out of place. A sentence like (130c) means what it says, not "I expect that the minister will think that the plan won't succeed":

(130) c. I expect the minister not to think that the plan will succeed.

However, the fact that NR-interpretations are limited to a class of cases that seems somehow connected with speech act properties of sentences is no sufficient reason to disclaim the reality of the rule. It is sufficient reason to try and investigate what exactly the conditions of application are. We will see in the next chapter that the radical negation is similarly bound up with speech act properties. Even though this aspect of grammatical and semantic analysis is still relatively misty, our defective insight into these questions is not a sufficient reason for abandoning the insight altogether.

Most of the problems, however, arising in the context of rules like Negative Raising, were not brought about by grammatical and semantic observations – the factual basis for linguistic theorizing – but rather by the fact that the formal properties of any adequate transformational rule of Negative Raising were at odds with theories that were being propagated. The problems, in other words, were of a purely theoretical making. Consequently, a publicity campaign was waged against rules like NR (in general against lowering and raising rules). The well-known observations of semantic correspondence between sentence pairs like (128a) and (128b), or (129a) and (129c), were dealt with by saying that the NR-interpretation must be seen as the result of 'pragmatic' factors of use. (128a) means linguistically what it says, but it is prone to being interpreted in use as an understatement or litotes, just as one can say, e.g., *That's not entirely satisfactory*, thereby meaning or intending to say *That's entirely unsatisfactory*.

This line of reasoning is entirely unsatisfactory. First, the formal properties of our fomulation of NR is not at all at odds with our theory of grammar. On the contrary, it fits perfectly well. Then, it must be stressed that there is no intrinsic opposition between the 'understatement' account and the grammatical account by means of NR. It is well known that what started off as a stylistic figure or a manner of speaking can be grammaticalized and become part of the language. It should not be excluded that such a process underlies cases of NR. But it is wrong to deny any grammaticalization to these cases. There are too many linguistic indications that point to a proper grammatical category to let them be accounted for in terms of creative, *ad hoc* understatement.

Thus there is the fact that the NR-predicates of the various languages are not always the same class. They clearly centre around prototypical cases like *think*, but languages differ as to which verbs are and which are not NR-predicates. The English verb *hope*, for example, is not a NR-predicate, but its Dutch counterpart *hopen* clearly is, just like its French counterpart *espérer*.

But Italian *sperare* is not. It is hardly thinkable that pragmatic understatements or other manners or speaking can be realized for sentence A in language L but not for A's exact counterpart A' in a language L'. But there are many more facts that militate against the 'understatement' account, inviting the inference that the embedded clause under an NR-predicate with negation raised, as in (128a), shows all the signs of a negated S. Thus, as is well known, all Negative Polarity Items that require to stand in the scope of negation freely occur in such clauses, whereas only some of them occur in subordinate clauses under non-NR-verbs:

(131) a. I don't think you need go yet.
     b. *I don't claim you need go yet.

Or consider the fact that, in English, epistemic possibility is expressed by means of the modal auxiliary verb *may*, unless the possibility operator stands directly under negation, in which case the expression is *cannot* ("not possible"). Thus we have:

(132) a. She may not have arrived yet.
     b. She can't have arrived yet.

The assumption of NR as a rule predicts that (132c) is a grammatical and normally interpretable sentence meaning "I believe that it is not possible that she has arrived already", whereas (132d) must be ungrammatical because it takes the embedded clause as having the possibility operator as the highest predicate, and *She may have arrived yet* is ungrammatical:

(132) c. I don't believe she can have arrived yet.
     d. *I don't believe she may have arrived yet.

Many more observations of this nature could be made.[32] Let it suffice, in this context, to add the observation that raising of this kind is by no means unique in the languages of the world. It is found in English, for example, in the well-known raising of *cannot* (only in the meaning of "not able", not "not possible" – see McCawley 1982: 58) under *seem*. Sentence (133) means "it seems that I cannot find it", not what it literally says:

(133) I can't seem to find it.

One wonders how any theory excluding this kind of raising as a matter of principle could ever be taken seriously.

There are, furthermore, definite advantages to the assignment of the rule property **NR** to predicates other than the well-known lexical ones and extending NR to certain abstract predicates, such as the conjunction *and*, the

---

[32] For a more elaborate discussion and more observations of this kind, see Seuren (1974: 184–6).

quantifier *all*, the necessity operator *must*. Often, but by no means universally, these predicates are converted into their logical counterparts *or*, *some*, and *can* respectively, when NR applies.[33] The applicability of NR to abstract (logical) predicates is, in fact, the point of Seuren 1974, to which the reader is referred for further details. One telling case will be discussed here. Consider the sentence:

(134) a. I don't believe that either Harry or Fred were late.

This sentence is remarkable for its plural form *were* in the subordinate clause, since **Either Harry or Fred were late* is an ungrammatical sentence, but *Neither Harry nor Fred were late* is well formed. Clearly, if we can derive (134a) from (134b), or rather if we can derive both from a common source, the status of NR as a rule of cyclic syntax is considerably reinforced:

(134) b. I believe that neither Harry nor Fred were late.

This derivation is unproblematic, given the machinery developed so far:[34]

(134) c.

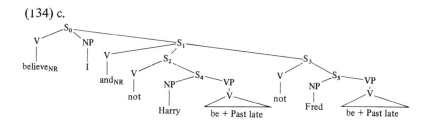

---

[33] Thus, for example, a natural expression in Standard English for "It is necessary that it is not so that that was very nice" is:

    (i) That can't have been very nice.

But in many dialects of English one finds:

    (ii) That mustn't have been very nice.

where the conversion from *must* to *can* has not taken place. The same phenomenon is observed in the French sentence:

    (iii) Ça ne doit pas être gai là-bas. ("That can't be very nice over there")

where (a) the position of *ne ... pas* proves that the negation is grammatically constructed with the modal auxiliary *doit*, and (b) the occurrence of *doit* ("must") shows that it cannot have its literal meaning. See (19e) above, in section 2.1.5, and the discussion of this example given there.

[34] As the reader will detect on careful examination, it is useful to assume, in this case, that S_4 and S_5 are tensed. The derivation starts at the point where S_4 and S_5 have been through tense processing and have thus acquired the NP–VP structure.

Since *and* is a NR-predicate, *not* on S_2 and S_3 is not lowered, and CR-Mapping applies on the S_1-cycle:

(134) d.

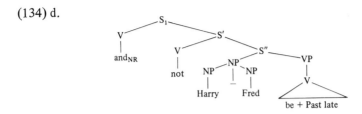

Now NR applies, still on the S_1-cycle, resulting in:

(134) e.

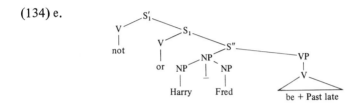

As specified in the rule, *and* has been converted into its logical counterpart *or*. Still on the S_1-cycle, *or* is now lowered (by complex lowering, in order to get (134a)):

(134) f.

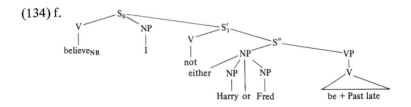

For the second time now *not* is prevented from being lowered, on account of the NR-verb *believe* this time. So the S_1'-cycle passes vacuously, and the S_0-cycle starts. Now NR applies, leading to:

(134) g.

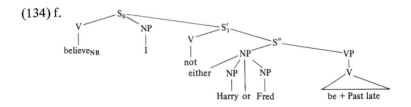

We now pass on to the newly created cycle of S'_0. Here, finally, *not* can be lowered into its argument S, whereby it attaches itself to *believe*, under an AUX-node just left of *believe*. A postcyclic rule of Number Assignment will now make the verb *be + Past* plural: *were*. This rule must be taken to be sensitive to earlier stages in the derivation (i.e. it must be a *global rule* in the sense of Lakoff 1970), as appears from a multitude of observations in English as well as in any other language that has verbal Number Assignment. The same rule of Number Assignment will thus account for the plural *were* in (134a) and in *Neither Harry nor Fred were late*.

A great deal more could be said about NR, but limitations of space keep us from indulging in too detailed analyses here.

2.4.5   Predicate Raising

At this point we can take up Predicate Raising (PR) again, now in a more systematic way than was possible in section 2.1.6. PR is defined as follows: a PR-verb or predicate, on its cycle, detaches the verb figured by its argument S and reattaches it by adoption to itself, either on the right or on the left. Schematically the transformational process is represented as:

$$V_{PR} \overset{S_n}{\diagdown} (NP) \quad \Rightarrow \quad V \overset{S_n}{\diagup \diagdown} (NP) \quad or \quad V \overset{S_n}{\diagup \diagdown} (NP)$$

right adoption   left adoption

C-2 dictates that all further material attached to S_{n+1} is reattached to S_n (or NP), since S_{n+1} disappears. V_1 remains verbal: only lowered Vs are relabelled (C-3). PR is lexically induced by the predicate figured by S_n.

PR is a widely attested rule of cyclical syntax. It occurs in a clear and straightforward way in French, Italian, Dutch, German (Seuren 1972a; Evers 1975), as well as in many other languages less directly known to the author, such as Uto-Aztecan (in particular Aztec, Yaqui, and Luiseño; Langacker 1970), Sre (Starosta 1971; Manley 1972), Tagalog (Starosta 1971), Japanese (Kuroda 1965), etc. In many languages it is especially causative predicates that take PR, but this does not seem to be a necessary requirement.

Let us, by way of example, take a cursory look at the French causative predicate *faire*, which clearly takes PR. It also gives rise to a derived dative:

(135) a. Je ferai   manger une pomme à Jules. ("I will get Jules to eat
         I will make eat   an apple to Jules   an apple")

This construction has a few peculiar properties, the most notable of which are the occurrence of the dative and the behaviour of clitic pronouns. Usually, in French, when the finite verb form is followed by an infinitive, clitic pronouns that represent arguments to the infinitive verb are placed between the finite and the infinitive verbs:

(136) a. Je veux le manger. ("I want to eat it")
       I   want it eat

Not so, however, with *faire* as the finite verb:[35]

(136) b. Je la lui   ferai   manger. ("I will make him eat it")
         I it to him will make eat
    c. *Je ferai la lui manger.

As appears from the few examples given, the subject of the embedded clause acquires dative status if the clause is transitive.[36] In (135a) and (136b) *Jules* or (dative) *lui* is the semantic subject of *manger* ("eat"). If the embedded clause is intransitive, the semantic subject regularly becomes accusative:

(137) a. Je ferai   partir Paul. ("I'll get Paul to leave")
      I   will make leave Paul
    b. Je le   ferai   partir. ("I will make him leave")
      I   him will make leave

It is, furthermore, noteworthy that a passive embedded clause does not take on any passive morphology. The passive appears from the possible addition of a *par*-phrase, the French equivalent of the English passive *by*-phrase:

(138) a. Je ferair   ouvrir la   porte par Jean. ("I will have the door
     I   will make open the door by Jean   opened by Jean")

Moreover, for reasons as yet entirely opaque, some subordinate clauses under *faire* must be passivized, while others cannot, and still others may. Thus, an

---

[35] There are very few exceptions to this rule of clitic placement in French. A notable exception is the behaviour of (clitic) reflexive pronouns. Thus (Martinon 1927: 302):

Nous les   ferons   se   retirer   d'ici.   ("We will make them with-
We   them will make themselves withdraw from here   draw from here")

Both the accusative *les* and the position of *se* are explained by the assumption that reflexives cliticize cyclically, as they do in Dutch and German.

[36] Grevisse (1969: 1064) notes a few examples (all from works by André Gide) of what appears to be Subject Raising, instead of PR, induced by *faire*. Thus (from *Journal 1942-1949*):

(i) ... ces quelques mots qu'il   fait   Nisus adresser à son Euryale...
    those few   words that he makes Nisus address to his Euryalus

(but note that the regular treatment would have resulted in two dative NPs). In the following sentence (from *La porte étroite*) PR must have applied but failed to yield a dative:

(ii) Des nouvelles un peu moins bonnes les   firent précipiter leur départ.
    News   a little less   good them made precipitate their departure
    ("Slightly less good news made them hasten their departure")

The position of the clitic pronoun *les* ("them") shows that PR has applied, but its accusative form is irregular. Such occurrences, however, are extremely rare.

underlying embedded clause like *Jean ouvre la porte* ("Jean opens the door") must be passivized under *faire*, as in (138a). The same sentence with *à* (dative "to"):

(138) b. Je ferai   ouvrir la   porte à   Jean. ("I will have the door
       I   will make open   the door   to Jean   opened to Jean")

is still a grammatical sentence, and still has a passive embedded clause, but without a *par*-phrase and with an extra dative. (138b) cannot mean "I will get Jean to open the door". (135a), on the other hand, may have its lower S passivized:

(135) b. Je ferai   manger une pomme par Jules. ("I'll make sure an
       I   will make eat   an   apple   by Jules   apple gets eaten by
                                            Jules")

The same semantic difference the reader notices between the English translation of (135a) and (135b) is found in the respective French originals. Passive is barred from embedded clauses figuring a verb of perception or cognition:[37]

(139) Je ferai   connaître ce   garçon à   (*par) Anne. ("I will make
      I   will make know   this boy   to (*by) Anne   Anne know
                                             this boy")

Both the lack of passive morphology and the tripartite division of obligatorily active, obligatorily passive lower clauses, and those that allow for both but with a subtle semantic difference, seem to be typical features of PR: they are found in other languages as well, as will be shown below.

The grammatical analysis of the *faire*-construction is relatively simple with PR as the central rule, and Dative plus postcyclic Clitic Movement as corollaries. The derivations of (136b) and (136a), respectively, will show this:

(136) b′.

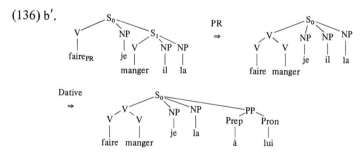

[37] Passive subordinate clauses under *faire* are barred in general when the verb figured by the clause prohibits passive:

   (i)   Paul sait la réponse juste. ("Paul knows the right answer")
  (ii)   *La réponse juste est sue par Paul. ("The right answer is known by Paul")
 (iii)   Je ferai savoir la réponse juste à Paul. ("I'll make Paul know the right answer")
 (iv)   *Je ferai savoir la réponse juste par Paul. ("I'll make sure the right answer is known by Paul")

Now tense processing turns this into:

Postcyclic Clitic Movement now moves all postverbal clitics (*la, lui*) to the position just left of the V of their own VP. There is some unclarity in the literature (Perlmutter 1971; Seuren 1976) regarding the rules governing the exact placement of clitics in preverbal position, and regarding the exact resulting structure. As to the former, I shall remain uncommitted here; as to the latter, I assume adoption by V:

(136) a'.

Tense processing:

Clitic Movement now moves (postcyclically) the clitic *le* to the position just left of the V of its own VP:

This describes, in essence, the French *faire*-construction. *Faire* is not the only verb inducing PR. Traditional French grammar has the list *faire* ("do", "make"), *laisser* ("let"), *voir* ("see"), *entendre* ("hear"), *envoyer* ("send"). Not usually mentioned is *donner à*, as in:

(140) a. J'ai   donné à boire ce vin   à Pierre. ("I gave Pierre this wine
       I have given to drink this wine to Pierre   to drink")
     b. Je le lui ai   donné à boire. ("I gave it him to drink")[38]
       I it him have given   to drink

The verb *laisser* takes PR optionally, with Subject Raising as the other option:

(141) a. Paul laissera tomber l'arme.   ("Paul will drop the weapon")
       Paul will let fall   the weapon
     b. Paul laissera l'arme   tomber. ("Paul will allow the weapon to
       Paul will let the weapon fall   fall")

The English translations render rather exactly the semantic difference that goes with the use of PR and SR: in (141a) PR has applied, and the verbal constituent *laissera tomber* corresponds with the one English verb *drop*. In the (b)-sentence, where SR has applied, Paul does not drop anything but allows that the weapon falls or continues to fall. *Voir* and *entendre* require passive lower clauses, except when the subject is pronominal:[39]

(142) a. J'ai   entendu jouer Mozart par Claire. ("I heard Mozart being
       I have heard   play Mozart by Claire   played by Claire")
     b. Je lui ai   entendu jouer Mozart. ("I heard her play Mozart")
       I her have heard   play Mozart

---

[38] Notice that Clitic Movement does not usually place the pronoun in front of the finite verb when this is followed by *à* + VP:

(i) Je tiens à l'écrire. ("I do wish to write it")
     I hold to it write
(ii) Il   procéda   à l'écrire. ("He proceeded to write it")
     He proceeded to it write

[39] It is not unusual in French grammar to find that pronominal constructions are possible where the analogous constructions with fully lexical NPs are not. Thus, e.g.:

(i) Il lui faut partir vite.   ("He must leave quickly")
     It him must leave quickly
(ii) *Il faut partir vite   à Paul. ("Paul must leave quickly")
     It must leave quickly to Paul

Also, surprisingly, although (138b) can only mean "I will have the door opened to Jean", as has been said, the following is ambiguous:

(iii) Je lui ferai   ouvrir la porte. ("I will make him open the door", or
      I him will make open   the door   "I will have the door opened to him")

Envoyer takes PR, but only in special collocations, and then the grammar is limited. A set expression is, e.g., *envoyer chercher* ("send for"), with PR or SR:

(143) a. J'ai   envoyé chercher Pierre. ("I have sent for Pierre")
       I have sent   seek   Pierre
    b. Je l'ai   envoyé chercher. ("I have sent for him")
       I   him have sent   seek
    c. J'ai   envoyé le   chercher. ("I have sent for him")
       I have sent   him seek

But note that no *par*-phrase is allowed:

(143) d. *Je l'ai envoyé chercher par le chauffeur.

Nor is a dative allowed. If the subordinate clause is transitive (and active), pronominal arguments cause no problem:

(143) e. Je l'enverrai   la   chercher. ("I will send him to look for her")
       I   him will send her seek

Other set expressions are *envoyer dire* ("send word"), *envoyer promener* ("send for a walk", "send one about his business"). These are used pretty much as single lexical items (see *Harrap's New Standard French and English Dictionary*, s.v. *envoyer*).

This brings us to a very important aspect of PR. As is well known, PR was proposed first by McCawley in the context of the prelexical analysis of causative verbs. His example (McCawley 1968) was the English verb *kill*, which he derived from "cause to die" by means of a rule which he had to invent for the purpose and which he dubbed "Predicate Raising". It does not appear, in that early publication, that McCawley was aware of the fact that that same rule of Predicate Raising is extremely common in the languages of the world. Its relative obscurity in the syntax of English is probably responsible for the belief, widely held and widely propagated in subsequent years, that PR was an irresponsible invention by adventurous generative semanticists, but without foundation in fact. This criticism is, however, entirely invalidated by the unusually firm status of the rule in universal syntax, and by the fact that it is precisely PR-constructions that tend to lexicalize. The expressions *envoyer chercher*, *envoyer dire*, *envoyer promener*, just mentioned, are only arbitrarily chosen examples of a very widely found class of cases. Another example is Dutch *leren kennen*, literally "learn know", which functions entirely as one single lexical item meaning "make the acquaintance of". The Dutch verb *leren* ("learn") is a prominent member of the class of Dutch PR verbs, as we shall see in a moment.

The only criticism levelled in those years against the principles of McCawley's analysis of *kill* as "cause to die" which needs a serious reply is Fodor (1970). A discussion of Fodor's point is given in section 2.5.2, when the phenomenon of lexical islands is dealt with. The result of the discussion there is that the principle of 'prelexical' analysis as first advanced by McCawley is reinforced rather than weakened. Besides Fodor's point, however, the available evidence points to some form of prelexical analysis as a potentially powerful source of insight. The fact that lexicalizations often acquire, or are characterized by, specific semantic properties that are absent from the prelexical analysis clearly is a complication, especially when there seem to be good reasons for incorporating the prelexical analysis in the syntax. On the other hand, these semantic extras illustrate the very point of lexicalization: complex meanings, though built up according to rules of syntax, are not compositional in that the meaning of the whole need not be a function of the meanings of the parts. Lexical items are often fitted out with special conditions, over and above the conditions presented by the prelexical analysis. Lexical items are thus enabled to be bearers of complex bits of meaning without the necessity of complex compositional constructions. Clearly, this device of lexicalization is an extra burden for memory, but it makes for rapid and efficient communication. Equally clearly, this device is put to use preferably whenever a bit of complex meaning is typically and frequently required given social and cultural conditions. When a new typical phenomenon occurs, a new lexical item will occur, or an existing item will modify its meaning to fit the new phenomenon. Thus, the English verb *frag* was coined during the period of American military intervention in Vietnam to denote specifically the killing of officers by soldiers. Such a verb is a causative, analysed as "cause to die" plus all the extra conditions characterizing the phenomenon.

The theory of prelexical analysis is reinforced further by the observation that many ditransitive causative verbs in many languages precisely follow the case assignments of the French *faire*-construction. The subject of the embedded clause in the prelexical analysis turns into a dative, and the object into a surface object. But when the underlying object is not expressed (very often the object is an optional argument), then what is dative in sentences with the full set of arguments becomes accusative. An example is the English verb *pay*: one pays the bill to the doctor, or one pays the bill, or one pays the doctor (not: *to* the doctor). Likewise *serve*: one serves dinner to the guests, or one serves dinner, or one serves the guests (not: *to* the guests). French is particularly rich in this kind of alternation:

(144) a. enseigner le latin aux enfants   ("teach Latin to the children")
        enseigner le latin   ("teach Latin")
        enseigner les enfants   ("teach the children")

b. servir le potage au client ("serve the soup to the customer")

   servir le potage ("serve the soup")

   servir le client ("serve the customer")

c. fournir du matériel à l'armée ("stock the army with goods")

   fournir du matériel ("provide goods")

   fournir l'armée ("stock the army")

d. conseiller du repos au malade ("advise the patient to take a rest")

   conseiller du repos ("advise rest")

   conseiller le malade ("advise the patient")

e. inspirer du courage aux troupes ("inspire the troops with courage")

   inspirer du courage ("inspire courage")

   inspirer les troupes ("inspire the troops")

f. payer cent francs aux médecin ("pay the doctor 100 francs")

   payer cent francs ("pay 100 francs")

   payer le médecin ("pay the doctor")

g. voler/dérober de l'argent à Paul ("steal money from Paul")

   voler/dérober de l'argent ("steal money")

   voler/dérober Paul ("rob Paul")

h. déléguer une tâche au secrétaire ("delegate a task to the secretary")

   déléguer une tâche ("delegate a task")

   déléguer le secrétaire ("delegate the secretary")

i. souffler le texte à l'acteur ("prompt the text to the actor")

   souffler le texte ("whisper the text")

   souffler l'acteur ("prompt the actor")

j. jouer un tour à Paul ("play a trick on Paul")

   jouer un tour ("play a trick")

   jouer Paul ("fool Paul")

Sometimes the active-passive distinction in the prelexical lower clause leads to an ambiguity:

(144) k. refuser une cigarette aux enfants ("refuse the children a cigarette")

   refuser une cigarette ("refuse (to give *or* be given) a cigarette")

   refuser les enfants ("refuse (to have) children")

l. défendre le vin aux enfants ("forbid the children to take wine")

   défendre le vin ("forbid wine" *or* "defend the wine")

   défendre les enfants ("defend the children")

Ditransitive *refuser* is analysed as "not allow to have". With just an object it can mean "not allow (oneself) to have", "not allow (oneself) to be given", or "not allow (oneself) to give". Ditransitive *défendre* is analysed as "not allow to take", but notice that with just an object it means either "not allow (anyone) to take" or "not allow to be taken", i.e. to defend. Both verbs have specific semantic additions. Thus, *refuser* generates the presupposition that, for active prelexical lower clauses, the subject of the lower clause has asked for what is expressed by the object, and, for passive lower clauses, that the grammatical subject of the lower clause has been offered. *Défendre* generates the presupposition that the semantic subject of "take" makes an effort at getting what is referred to by the object of "take".

Sometimes the paradigm is incomplete:

(144) m. épargner cette humiliation aux femmes ("spare the women this
　　　　　　　　　　　　　　　　　　　　　　　　humiliation")
　　　　épargner les femmes　　　　　("spare the women")
　　　　*épargner cette humiliation
　　n. persuader son innocence au juge ("persuade the judge of
　　　　　　　　　　　　　　　　　　　　　　one's innocence")
　　　　persuader le juge　　　　　　　("persuade the judge")
　　　　*persuader son innocence

Many more examples could be given, and it would then appear that there are often complications in the sense that certain constructions take on specialized meanings:

(144) o. subtiliser la bourse à Paul ("pinch Paul's purse")
　　　　subtiliser la bourse　　　("pinch the purse")
　　　　subtiliser Paul　　　　　("cheat Paul")

or that the paradigm is incomplete or partly irregular. It should be kept in mind, however, as was said at the end of section 1.3 above, that full prediction is an unattainable goal in lexical studies: we must be content with retrodiction so that we can spot the regularities when they are there, without being able to predict in each specific case if, and how, what will occur. The strength of the prelexical causative analysis of causative verbs lies precisely in the non-trivial parallels between the argument structure of these verbs and the phenomena observed with PR in open syntax.

The theory of prelexical analysis implies that there is much less content than is often thought to theories or notions that take as basic for semantic analysis the *case* of an argument NP. We have already observed (sections 2.1.7, 2.1.8) that certain dative intransitive verbs (DIVs) in Dutch and English – and many other languages – show the tendency of regrammaticalizing their argument structure in such a way that the old dative becomes subject and the old subject becomes accusative, i.e. object. Thus, obsolete English. *Me likes that* has become *I like that*, and Dutch wavers between *Mij mankeert niets* ("nothing ails me") and *Ik mankeer niets* (lit.: "I ail nothing"), both being standard and acceptable, and entirely synonymous. Here we see that datives and accusatives alternate, often without any semantic difference, according to whether there is or is not another object term. This means that if (deep or surface) cases have specific semantic characteristics, these have so far not come to light. In the present state of development of the theory it has not been possible to formulate semantic generalizations over cases at any level of description. We are thus reduced to specifying for each predicate separately what the semantic functions of its different arguments are. This is done, as will become clearer below, by means of a specification, for each predicate, of its predicate conditions, i.e. of the conditions that must be fulfilled by anything in the world if it is to be the referent of a term in a true sentence figuring the predicate in question.

As we have noted, PR in French does not always involve the Dative rule. Sentence (ii) in note 36 and sentence (143e) above show that PR can occur without a dative although the lower clause is transitive. The result is two accusative objects. In other languages which have PR as a prominent rule, this is more common. German, in particular, seems to have an inbuilt resistance to the Dative rule in open syntax. It is slightly more liberal with Dative in fully lexicalized items, though there, too, double accusative objects are more frequent than in more Dative-prone languages: *einen etwas lehren* ("teach someone something", with two accusatives). In open syntax, however, the Dative rule never occurs in the wake of PR: *Ich lasse ihn den Brief sehen* ("I let him see the letter", with two accusatives). Dutch takes Dative with PR in roughly the class of cases where French excludes the passive form of the lower clause: *Ik laat (aan) hem de brief zien* ("I let him see the letter", where the optional *aan* ("to") shows the dative character of the NP). We thus observe a number of highly characteristic phenomena all connected with PR, both in open syntax and in lexical argument structures. We clearly have now a potentially powerful instrument for retrodictive explanation of the phenomena in question. To what extent a predictive theory can be set up for them is still an open issue. Perhaps a detailed theory of implicative language universals can bring some light there.

PR never occurs in the literature as a rule of English cyclic syntax. This does not necessarily mean that it does not occur in English as a rule of cyclic syntax. As was adumbrated in note 15 above, the phenomena covered by what is known in the literature as *tough*-Movement are more adequately described by PR. Tough-Movement is generally formulated not as PR but as:

where "Adj_{t-M}" stands for "adjective inducing *tough*-Movement" and "V_{tr}" for "transitive verb". The subject of S_1 must be lexically empty. The status of the old S_1 is unclear, but it seems convenient to relabel it as VP. Thus we have:

(146) a. Jack is easy to fool
     b.

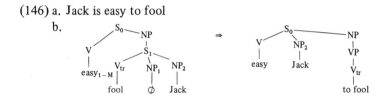

Some objections can be raised against this rule. Thus, the raising of NP_2 is problematic. If NP_2 is regarded as the *object* of S_1, then we have a unique case of object raising: all other known cases of NP-raising are instances of SR, as prescribed by C-1, which we cannot afford to lose. If, however, NP_2 is regarded as the grammatical *subject* of a passivized S_1, the fact that the verb appears in surface structure without any passive morphology is anomalous, since now *tough*-Movement would be nothing but SR from a passive lower clause. But in such cases there is a normal passive morphology: *John is likely to be cheated.* Here PR helps, given the fact that passive morphology can be avoided under PR.

Furthermore, it is remarkable that there are so many lexical items that lend themselves quite naturally to an analysis in terms of this particular construction: *gullible* ("easy to gull"), *tough* ("hard to defeat"), *excitable* ("easy to excite"), *readable* ("good to read"), *unreadable* ("not good to read"), *a pushover* ("easy to push over"), etc.

Then, it seems that there is a greater syntactic coherence in constructions of the type *easy to fool* (without passive morphology) than in those of the type *eager to fool* or *eager to be fooled* (i.e. with passive morphology):

(147) a. Difficult to erase as it was, the slogan remained visible for a long time.
          ?Difficult as it was to erase, the slogan remained visible for a long time.
     b. Anxious as Edith always was to please her son, he grew up a spoiled child.
          ?Anxious to please her son as Edith always was, he grew up a spoiled child.

It does appear that in (147a) the collocation *difficult to erase* coheres more strongly than the collocation *anxious to please* in (147b).

It is thus quite reasonable to propose that this particular construction in English syntax should be accounted for by a variety of PR. This has the additional advantage that no new rule of *tough*-Movement need be invented. Instead of (145) we thus have (with deletion of the empty NP):

(148)

Now the problem that an NP other than the subject is raised does not arise, since what is raised is V_{tr}, not NP_2. Moreover, as will be made clear in section 2.4.6, the PR-account of this construction makes it easier to understand the absence of passive morphology. Given the account of Passive given there, all we need to assume here is that PR-adjectives require a lower transitive clause with an unspecified subject, and that lexically empty nodes are shed under reattachment. The important point is that in the PR-account there is no need to raise the object, which would be against C-1.

It seems to be a feature of adjectives taking a sentential subject that the subject-S is dominated by NP. Adjectives do not seem to take purely sentential subject terms. In this case this has the important consequence that the input structure of (148) is not unstable, and does thus not require the insertion of an NP-subject or the lowering V of S_0. The presence of an NP-subject is ensured by the fact that the subject-S in these cases is already dominated by NP. NP_2 is reattached to this NP, which now pruned as a consequence of C-5 since it dominates no other material. We shall see in section 2.4.6 that this explains the absence of passive morphology for V_{tr}.

Let us now, to conclude, review the main facts of PR in Dutch. First a complete list is given of the verbs that induce PR, obligatorily or optionally, in Dutch, with their main rule features. Some of the verbs are marked for (vertical) SSD. In all cases the governing antecedent is the rightmost NP constituent of the S figuring V_{PR}: for a transitive V_{PR} it is the subject, for a ditransitive V_{PR} it is the indirect object that governs the deletion of the lower subject. All ditransitive PR-verbs take SSD. Many PR-verbs take the rule feature [+te], which means that the following infinitive in the cluster is always preceded by the particle *te*. Moreover, for every verb that induces PR optionally and SSD obligatorily, *te* is inserted whenever PR has not applied. The verbs in question are *durven*, ditransitive *helpen*, transitive and ditransitive *leren*. Finally, there is the rule feature IT, enabling the verb in question to take *it*-Insertion, which in Dutch is *het*-Insertion. When a verb is specified for optional PR and no other option is presented and no other rule is obligatory (as for transitive *zien, horen, voelen*), than non-application of PR leads to a *dat*-clause (= *that*-clause) for the lower S. *Dat*-clauses thus constitute a default option. When a verb is marked "opt/X" (where "X" is some rule feature), then X is an obligatory alternative for **PR**; a marking "opt, X" entails that whether or not **PR** applies, X applies anyway obligatorily. We thus have the following table:

INTRANSITIVE

1 lijken	(appear)	opt/IT	[+te]
2 schijnen	(seem)	opt/IT	[+te]
3 blijken	(turn out)	opt/IT	[+te]
4 heten	(be rumoured)	opt/IT	[+te]
5 plegen	(habitually)	obl	[+te]
6 zullen	(will)	obl	
7 moeten	(must$_{epist}$)	opt/IT	
8 kunnen	(may$_{epist}$)	opt/IT	
9 dienen	(must)	obl	[+te]
10 hoeven	(need$_{epist}$)	opt/IT	[+te]
11 moeten	(must$_{agent}$)	obl	
12 kunnen	(can$_{agent}$)	obl	
13 hoeven	(need$_{agent}$)	obl	[+te]
14 mogen	(be allowed)	obl	
15 beginnen	(begin)	opt/SR	[+te]
16 blijven	(continue)	obl	
17 gaan	(be going to)	obl	
18 dreigen	(threaten)	obl	[+te]

TRANSITIVE

1 weten	(manage)	obl, SSD [+te]
2 vermogen	(be able)	obl, SSD [+te]
3 durven	(dare)	opt, SSD [±te]
4 wagen	(dare)	opt, SSD [+te]
5 verlangen	(long)	opt, SSD [+te]
6 willen	(want, wish)	obl, SSD
7 weigeren	(refuse)	opt, SSD [+te]
8 proberen	(try)	opt, SSD [+te]
9 trachten	(try)	opt, SSD [+te]
10 leren	(learn)	opt, SSD
11 wezen	(have gone to)	obl, SSD
12 beginnen	(begin)	opt, SSD [+te]
13 blijven	(continue)	obl, SSD
14 gaan	(be going to)	obl, SSD
15 staan	(stand while...)	obl, SSD [±te]
16 zitten	(sit while...)	obl, SSD [±te]
17 liggen	(lie while...)	obl, SSD [±te]
18 lopen	(walk while...)	obl, SSD [±te]
19 komen	(come to)	obl, SSD [±te]
20 zien	(see)	opt
21 horen	(hear)	opt
22 voelen	(feel)	opt
23 denken	(intend)	opt, SSD [+te]
24 menen	(believe)	opt, SSD [+te]
25 doen	(make)	obl
26 laten	(let, allow, make)	obl
27 helpen	(help)	obl
28 vergeten	(forget)	opt, SSD [+te]

DITRANSITIVE

1 helpen	(assist)	opt, SSD
2 leren	(teach)	opt, SSD
3 zien	(see)	obl, SSD
4 horen	(hear)	obl, SSD
5 voelen	(feel)	obl, SSD
6 kijken	(look)	obl, SSD[40]
7 laten	(let, allow)	obl

A few verbs occur twice in this table, either as intransitive and transitive (*beginnen, blijven, gaan*), or as transitive and ditransitive, or even twice in the same column (the modals). In all cases a semantic difference is involved. The epistemic modals often take different rules from the agentive modals. (*Dienen*, equivalent with *moeten* ("must") takes obligatory PR whether it is epistemic or agentive.) *Leren* means "learn" when transitive, and "teach" when ditransitive. *Helpen*, when transitive, means "help" or "be instrumental in", but

---

[40] Only in the imperative (with possible morphological passive). I owe this observation to my Ph.D.-student Maurice Vliegen.

when ditransitive "assist". The perception verbs *zien, horen, voelen* show a subtle meaning difference according to whether they are transitive or ditransitive: when the former they simply express the fact of perception (whereby the object must be an event – see Vliegen, in prep.); when the latter they imply that the subject of the event perceived was actually perceived, besides the event. The difference shows up most clearly when the lower clause is passive (see section 2.4.6). *Laten* in transitive use implies non-interference with regard to an event or state of affairs; in ditransitive use it implies, in addition, non-interference with respect to the subject of the lower clause.

For some verbs the *te*-feature is optional: [+te]. For *durven* ("dare") the difference is a question of regional standard. For *komen* ("come to"), however, there is a semantic difference: with *te* it expresses an accident (*Hij kwam te sterven* – "It befell him that he died"), but without *te* it expresses ι purpose (*Hij kwam sterven* – "He came in order to die"). For the remaining verbs (*staan, zitten, liggen, lopen*) it is a question of tense: in the non-perfect tenses *te* is required; in the perfect tenses it is preferably left out.

Consistent applications of PR with these verbs leads to the typical 'Dutch construction' where the nominal arguments of the verbs are all strung together in left-to-right order reflecting the tree hierarchy (highest first), and where the verbs are strung together at the end of the clause (in main clauses the finite verb is in second position). Moreover, but for the finite verb form all verbs are purely infinitival (sometimes a passive infinitive may be used – see the following section). No past participles occur when the main verb is in a perfect tense: instead of the expected past participle, infinitives are found (see note 4). Only when the main verb is not followed by another verb can it occur in the shape of a past participle. There is no need here to go into derivational details, since those have been presented and illustrated above (section 2.1.6). A few examples will suffice of surface structure sentences, which the interested reader is invited to derive for himself. All examples are given as subordinate clauses, since these are less complex:

(149) a. ... dat ik Jan Marie het geld   heb zien overhandigen.
          that I Jan Marie the money have see hand over
                    ("... that I saw Jan hand over the money to Marie")
      b. ... dat ik dat heb gezien. ("... that I have seen that")
          that I that have seen
      c. ... dat ik Marie de deur heb proberen to leren verven.
          that I Marie the door have try   to teach paint
                    ("... that I have tried to teach Marie to paint the door")
      d. ... dat ik heb geprobeerd Marie de deur te leren verven. (id.)
          that I have tried   Marie the door to teach paint
      e. ... dat ik heb **geprobeerd** Marie te leren de deur te verven. (id.)
          that I have tried   Marie to teach the door to paint

f. ... *dat ik heb proberen Marie de deur te leren verven.
     that I have try   Marie the door to teach paint

g. ... *dat ik heb proberen Marie te leren de deur te verven.[41]
     that I have try   Marie to teach the door to paint

---

[41] Koster (1975) argues that the underlying word order in Dutch is SOV, rather than VSO (VSIO) as assumed here. He only argues, however, against undelying NP-VP structure; the possibility of VSO is not discussed (in spite of McCawley 1970 for English). Given the mathematical correspondences between VSO and SOV orders, it is always possible to keep up the one against the other while maintaining the dominating regularities. Any argument for or against either must therefore be based on universalist considerations, i.e. on considerations of typology. Here the VSO-theory seems to be the winner.

Koster's main argument in favour of SOV is the consideration that the verb in subordinate clauses need not be moved: it already occupies the position where it is found in surface structure. Movement of the verb is thus needed only for the finite verb in main clauses, according to Koster. There are, however, typological objections.

First, clitic pronouns in subordinate clauses gravitate towards the surface position just after the subject:

(i)   ... dat ik het Karel wilde   zeggen. ("... that I wanted to say it to Karel")
         that I it   Karel wanted say

In the SOV-theory Clitic Movement must thus be orientated towards the subject, which is an oddity, at least for European languages. Under VSO it can be said that the clitics gravitate towards the verb in shallow structure, which is the normal thing; later the verb is moved to the right. Furthermore, it is not true that SOV saves rules, since a (cyclic) rule of VP-extraposition is required, as can be seen from, e.g., (149e), which, without VP-extraposition, would look like (with NP-NP-S-V):

(ii) ... *dat ik Marie de deur te verven te leren heb geprobeerd.

or (with NP-S-NP-V):

(iii) ... *dat ik de deur te verven Marie te leren heb geprobeerd.

This rule of VP-extraposition is, again, an oddity. It would be no less of one if it were S-extraposition, since verb-final languages usually do not extrapose internal object clauses (see Greenberg 1963: 84 – Universal 13). But it cannot be S-extraposition, witness the word order of typical PR-sentences such as (149a), which, with (cyclic) S-extraposition, would have been:

(iv) ... *dat ik heb zien overhandigen Jan Marie het geld.

And if the extraposition is taken to be postcyclic, it is VP-extraposition anyway. So, in Koster's analysis VP-extraposition it must be. But VP-extraposition is not at all firmly established as a rule in universal syntax, especially not for languages that regularly place the object between the verb and the subject (see the Malagasy example in note 21, or Kuno (1978: 125-6) for the SOV-language Japanese).

There is, finally, the fact that there are stylistic variants in surface word order, such as:

(v) a. ... dat hij vaak aan zijn zoon zat te denken. ("... that he often sat thinking
      that he often to his son sat to think   of his son")
    b. ... dat hij vaak zat te denken aan zijn zoon. (id.)

The first of these two is more normal and more acceptable than the second. But the first is also the version which has the verb in final position, whereas for the second an optional movement rule must be assumed, in Koster's approach, shifting the verb away from its clause-final position. This being so, it would be strange if the language had an optional rule whose application resulted in a deterioration of the grammatical quality of the sentences affected by it. All in all, the verb-first theory seems preferable.

The PR description of the Dutch construction seems to be *crucially* correct: no unexpected snags have turned up so far and all the facts of word order and semantic predicate-argument structure fall into place quite naturally. In fact, the PR description of this construction is unusually successful, as syntactic descriptions go. It may therefore be considered to constitute by itself a forceful argument in favour of any theory of syntax that incorporates it. The argument is the more forceful since no alternative description has so far succeeded in getting all the facts crucially right, be it from the syntactic or the semantic angle. It thus speaks strongly against theories that exclude PR as a rule, in particular against surface semantics.

One serious problem, however, remains: the problem of passive morphology. Sometimes one does, and sometimes one does not find passive morphology under PR:

(150) a. De wagen moet gerepareerd worden door Jan.
          The car   must repaired   be   by Jan
                        ("The car must be repaired by Jan")
      b. *De wagen moet repareren door Jan.
          The car   must repair   by Jan
      c. Ik laat de wagen repareren door Jan. ("I have/let the car (be)
          I let the car   repair   by Jan   repaired by Jan")
      d. Ik laat de wagen gerepareerd worden door Jan.
          I let the car   repaired   be   by Jan
                        ("I allow the car to be repaired by Jan")
      e. De wagen moet gerepareerd kunnen   worden door Jan.
          The car   must repaired   can (inf) be   by Jan
                        ("It must be possible for the car to be repaired by Jan")
      f. *De wagen moet kunnen   repareren door Jan.
          The car   must can (inf) repair   by Jan
      g. Ik zag het varken slachten door Jan. ("I saw the pig being
          I saw the pig   slaughter by Jan   slaughtered by Jan")
      h. Ik zag het varken geslacht   worden door Jan. (id.)
          I saw the pig   slaughtered be   by Jan

The data of (150) are unambiguous: native speakers are remarkably unanimous in their agreement about grammaticality judgements. The problem is clear: why should it be that the infinitive of the lowest embedded clause must sometimes be passive, while in other cases where a passive meaning is unambiguously present the morphology has to be active, and in other cases again (notably where the PR-verb is a perception verb) there is a choice? Although the problem is obvious once the construction is looked at systematically, there does not seem to be any literature on it, either in the vast body of traditional grammar (of Dutch or German: the same problem occurs in German), or in the literature on theoretical grammar. The problem will be tackled in the following section, where the notion of *unstable structure*, introduced in section 2.4.2, will be seen to play a crucial role.

Other, minor, complications can be dealt with by lexical stipulation. Thus it appears that the PR-verbs *doen* and (transitive) *helpen*, on the one hand, do allow for object clauses requiring a passive interpretation, but not for the addition of a *door*-phrase (= *by*-phrase):

(151) a. Dat doet /helpt de rommel opruimen (*door Jan).
That makes/helps the mess   clear up   by   Jan
("That makes/helps the mess (to) be cleared up")

This in itself is an interesting fact, given the existence of many languages that do have a passive but lack any equivalent of a *by*-phrase. Then, a number of PR-verbs (*wezen, staan, zitten, liggen, lopen, komen*) are such that they do not allow for object clauses requiring a passive interpretation. They all take obligatory PR and obligatory SSD, but the subject to be deleted in the lower clauses cannot be the grammatical subject of a passive S:

(152) *Hij stond geplaagd te worden. ("He stood being teased")
He stood teased   to be

For these verbs, therefore, the question of passive or active morphology does not arise. (But even if it did, these verbs would not be problematic in our theory of syntax, together with the analysis of Passive presented in the following section.)

2.4.6 Passive

The idea that Passive is a rule of transformational syntax is as old as the notion of transformational grammar itself. It originated in work done by Harris in the 1950s (see, e.g., Harris 1957), and soon became the standard example for purposes of demonstration. When the notion of the syntactic cycle was introduced into the theory of grammar, around 1965, it became clear that if Passive was to be a rule of syntax it had to be in the cycle. It is something of an irony that this rule, once taken to be prototypical of transformational grammar, is now thought by many not to be a rule of syntax at all but a lexical variant (Bresnan 1978). The position advanced here is that passivization is essentially a fact of grammar, resulting from the selection of a lexical verb without a specified subject. Passive is thus considered a rule by which a passive auxiliary (*be*) is added, and the main verb is made into a past participle, and a new subject is chosen – at least in English and similar languages. This rule is cyclic.

The old idea is, in principle, that the semantic subject is turned into an optional *by*-phrase, and (in English) the next NP in line becomes the new (grammatical) subject of a passive sentence, augmented with the auxiliary verb *be* and the morphological past participle form of the old main verb. (In virtually all European languages the grammatical subject is not the first NP in line, from left to right, but the first NP from the right, i.e. the semantic object, but other than that the differences are insignificant.) Within the constraints imposed by the theory of semantic syntax, there are serious objections to such a notion of Passive. They centre mainly on two aspects: the purely grammatical definition of Passive in terms of subject and (direct, indirect, or prepositional) object, and the status of the *by*-phrase.

It is not true, in English or in any other language which has Passive, that passivization is automatically possible when the verb takes more than one NP-term:[42]

(153) a. (*)Many books are had by Mrs Miller.
b. (*)His shoulders were raised by Jonathan.
c. (*)This town has been slept in.
d. (*)The bridge was gone over by the car.

Contrast these with, e.g.:

(154) a. We have been had by Mrs Miller.
b. The flag was raised by Jonathan.
c. This bed has been slept in.
d. The bridge was gone over rather quickly by the committee.

These examples show that passivization is not automatically possible whenever the underlying form contains a suitable replacement for the semantic subject. Passive is anyhow conditioned by non-syntactic factors, and these are not simply attributable to the lexicon. With regard to the (a)-sentences one could maintain that two different verbs *have* are involved, and the (d)-sentences could be saved by a general stipulation with respect to metaphoric use of verbs of motion. But it is hard to maintain that different verbs *raise* or *sleep* are involved in (153b, c) and (154b, c), respectively.

What lies behind such phenomena is not at all clear. Apart from the (a)-sentences, which do seem to involve different verbs *have*, questions of semantic predicate-argument structure appear to play a role. (153b), for example, contains an object of inalienable possession and a reflexive possessive pronoun *his*. Note that the sentence becomes perfectly normal when *his* does not take *Jonathan* as antecedent but some third party to be inferred from the context. Note also that the ungrammaticality of (153b) in the reflexive sense cannot be accounted for by a theory of sentence-internal anaphora

---

[42] The bracketed asterisk is used here to indicate ungrammaticality on a reading, not just ungrammaticality *per se*, i.e. ungrammaticality on any reading whatsoever. Thus, (153a)–(153d) are grammatical if interpreted analogously to (154a)–(154d), respectively. The fact that such interpretations are implausible does not affect us, since the theory of grammar is independent of considerations of pragmatic plausibility.

forbidding an antecedent-anaphor relation of the kind exhibited in (153b), since the translation of this sentence into a language that does not use a possessive pronoun in cases of inalienable possession, but just the definite article, remains equally unacceptable. Take, e.g., French:

(155) (*)Les épaules   étaient levées par Jonathan.
      The shoulders were   raised by Jonathan

Probably, one would say, objects of inalienable possession form a closer unity, somehow, with the verb than ordinary objects. A verb with an object of inalienable possession seems to constitute more of a single predicate. The object could then be considered to be a part of a complex predicate, and would thus no longer be fit to stand in as grammatical subject after passivization. But, attractive as thoughts of this nature may be, there is as yet no semantic theory that could account for such phenomena.

Likewise for the (c)-sentences. Passivization of sentences figuring predicates like *eat*, *sleep*, *work*, and other intransitives combined with a prepositional phrase seems possible only if the prepositional phrase can be considered a semantic argument to the predicate. *Work at* is a well-known case in point:

(156) a.   This problem has been worked at for a long time.
      b. (*)The restaurant is worked at by Ben.

The (b)-sentence is ungrammatical if it is to mean that Ben works as an employee at the restaurant mentioned. Apparently, a locative prepositional phrase in English can attain the status of argument to the predicate if there is a sufficiently close connection between the activity denoted by the predicate and the place specified. Thus, there is a close connection between sleeping and the bed where the sleeping is done, but much less between sleeping and, say, the town where the sleeping takes place. If the link is close enough, then there seems to be sufficient argument status for the prepositional phrase to provide a stand-in subject for passive sentences, as in (154c). (153c) is acceptable only if it is clear that the sleeping was done all over town so that the effects are visible everywhere: *This town has been slept in by a whole division of infantry troops*. Whatever the explanation of these and related phenomena will prove to be, it is clear that Passive cannot be formulated adequately as a rule of syntax that is permitted to operate freely on underlying sentence structures which without Passive would turn out to be sentences with a direct or indirect object or a prepositional phrase. Passive must anyhow be made sensitive to semantic factors of the kind suggested, and it is not at all clear how this can be done. For the moment we must conclude that Passive is not an *ordinary* rule of syntax. Its roots seem to lie in the shady area where thoughts crystallize into linguistic structures, and since so little is known about those processes, Passive must accordingly remain a partly obscure phenomenon.

Then there is the question of the *by*-phrases, which are considered an optional part of the Passive rule in its common formulation. Closer observation quickly shows that this position is not very attractive. It is more attractive to consider the *by*-phrase a semantic addition expressing in an indirect way what the semantic subject is of the clause in question. More precisely, it seems that *by*-phrases are not part of any Passive rule, but independent sentential operators that can be missed, and sometimes must be missed.

In a first draft of a possible textbook on syntax, McCawley gives the examples (ch. 4):

(157) a. We have been outvoted (?by someone).
  b. The Earth was formed four billion years ago (?by someone).
  c. My brother was drowned in a boating accident (?by someone).
  d. Chomsky's *Syntactic Structures* was written in 1956 (?by someone).

This shows that some passive sentences really do not want any semantic subject specified. It should be noted, in this connection, that many languages which do have a passive lack anything resembling a *by*-phrase, or have various alternative forms for it, either in free variation or according to some semantic category. Thus, e.g., Latin has the preposition *ab* (with the ablative case) for personal agents, and the bare ablative for non-personal agents, and in some constructions it takes a bare dative to express the semantic subject. German has a distinction, which is neither entirely free not entirely bound by semantic factors, between the prepositions *von* and *durch*. Dutch has regular *door* besides isolated cases of *van* ("of"). English, likewise, has sporadic and archaic uses of *of* for *by*:

(158) a. Ben je nou helemaal *van* God verlaten?
    Are you now entirely *of* God abandoned
          ("Have you taken leave of your senses?")
  b. The gardens and parks were much beloved *of* Mary and her cousins.

Data of this kind are typical of *grammaticalization*: what starts out as a free, 'creative' semantic combination becomes a set collocation and gradually turns into a grammatical category. Yet the old origins keep shining through for a long time.

The historical origin of the *by*-phrase (or its equivalents in other languages) is that of a sentential operator formed by a preposition (*by*) and its object NP. Thus (159a) is considered to be derived, both historically and in transformational syntax, from (159b). Through the various stages of derivation it reaches the surface form of (159a):

(159) a. The thief has been arrested by the police.
       b.

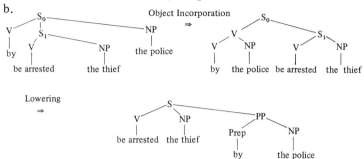

That this analysis is not entirely fanciful appears from the fact that *by*-phrases are sensitive to left-to-right order in exactly the way lowered operators are (see section 2.4.3). Consider the following pairs:

(160) a. The victim was thought to be Spanish or Italian.[43]
       b. The victim was thought by the police to be Spanish or Italian.
(161) a. It was thought that some of the mourners were members of the Mafia.
       b. It was thought by the police that some of the mourners were members of the Mafia.
(162) a. Some of the mourners were thought to be members of the Mafia.
       b. Some of the mourners were thought by the police to be members of the Mafia.

The (a)-sentences all have scope ambiguity. (160a) has the two readings "it was thought that the victim was Spanish or Italian", and "either it was thought that the victim was Spanish or it was thought that the victim was Italian". In (161a) and (162a) the existentially quantified NP *some of the mourners* either takes scope over the whole remainder of the sentence (specific reading) or it stands under *thought* (non-specific reading). In the (b)-sentences, however, one reading is systematically banned. (160b) can only have the first of the readings given for (160a); the second reading is not possible. (161b) can only have the reading where the existential quantifier has small scope, whereas (162b) requires the reading with large scope for the existentially quantified NP. The point is that the *by*-phrases in these sentences seem sensitive to left-to-right ordering in precisely the way logical elements like the truth-functional operators, the quantifiers and the (lowered) modals are. The *by*-phrase, in other words, seems to function in a system of senten-

---

[43] Note that the ambiguity of (160a) (=122a) is resolved by the placement of *either*, as was demonstrated above in connection with (122b) and (122c), in section 2.4.3.

tial operators whose scope expressions are subject to the Scope Ordering Constraint discussed in section 2.4.3. Note that the observations (160)–(162) are neither accounted for nor accountable for in any of the existing theories of grammar other than the theory of semantic syntax.

A last objection to the common formulation of the Passive rule is provided by PR-constructions in many languages that do have a morphological passive. As has been observed above repeatedly, it is a typical characteristic of PR-predicates that the embedded clause whose V is raised by PR may be passive to all intents and purposes without displaying any passive morphology or any trace of a passivizing auxiliary verb. It has been observed, (150a)–(150h), that in Dutch and German passive morphology in such cases is sometimes excluded, sometimes required, and sometimes optional. The commonly accepted version of Passive is inadequate for phenomena of this nature.

We must, therefore, provide an alternative analysis of passive sentences or clauses (whether they have or lack a passive morphology). The simplest analysis that fits both the facts and the theory set up so far seems to be the following. It is posited that all verbs (not necessarily all predicates) that take a semantic subject may occur without one.[44] This means that for verbs that regularly do take a subject, the subject position is filled by a 'dummy', which we symbolize with "$\emptyset$". That is, at SA-level structures may occur like the following:

(163) a.

Structures like this pose a problem for the grammars of those languages that require Subject Raising at some stage (say, the S_0-cycle), since there isn't a subject to be raised. Several ways out of this problem are found in these

---

[44] Some verbs, such as weather verbs, are lexically specified for the regular absence of a semantic subject. Semantically, there is a problem for subjectless propositions figuring an intransitive verb, in that it is not immediately clear how the truth-definition, which we wish to apply to all propositions, can be made to fit such propositions. The truth-definition, as was announced in chapter 1, and will be repeated in later chapters, amounts to the statement that a proposition is true just in case the reference values of the terms form an n-tuple that is within the extension of the predicate. Now, if there are no terms it is not clear how this definition can be satisfied. One answer to this question may be that subjectless intransitive sentences should be analysed as existential quantifications over events or states. Thus *It is raining* would be analysed as "there is raining", analogously to *There is shouting*. Note that German and Dutch have morphological passives for such cases: *Es wurde geschrieen Er werd geschreeuwd* ("there was shouting"). Otherwise, the *it* must be taken to have as its referent something as non-distinct as "the present situation".

languages. A dummy surface subject is sometimes inserted (English *they*, or French *on*), or the $\emptyset$-node is simply deleted and the object becomes the new subject, as in the numerous languages that have a non-morphological passive (a characteristic, it seems, of Creole languages). But some languages, in particular those of Indo-European stock, resort to a very special tactic. They not only delete the $\emptyset$-node and designate a new grammatical subject (usually the semantic object, but occasionally, as in English, the next NP in line), but they also provide the verb with morphological or other material that shows the passive character of the clause. Thus, in English as in many modern European languages, the verb is turned into a past participle and a new S-structure is inserted above the passive S, consisting of a passive auxiliary verb (*be*) and the passive S as subject. This new verb *be* (or its equivalent) then attracts the past participle on the newly created cycle, probably by PR, and a passive sentence is born.

Passive is thus regarded as one of a number of strategies developed in the languages of the world to get around the problem posed by the absence of a subject. Passive is thus not a lexical but a grammatical phenomenon. If we revert to (163a), we stipulate that, on the S_2-cycle, Passive takes place, leading to:

(163) b.

On the next cycle, *arrested* is raised by PR to form a complex V-node $_V$[be arrested], and standard tense processing takes care of the rest.

It has been widely observed that passivization is favoured when the semantic object refers to what is *topic* in the ongoing discourse. This probably explains why, in spite of a passive sentence form, nevertheless the semantic subject is sometimes expressed via a *by*-phrase. We can thus have, instead of (163a):

(164) a.

S_3 is now passivized, analogously to (163). At the end of the new S'-cycle we thus have:

(164) b.

S_2 now undergoes the treatment sketched above for (159b): Object Incorporation combines $_V$[by] with $_{NP}$[the police] to form a complex V, which is then to be lowered into S' to yield the result shown above for (159). Tense processing then delivers (159a), under the right t_1 and t_2.

Generally, we state that Passive requires an input structure, at SA-level, of a subjectless S-structure with (for English and most other passivizing languages, but not for, e.g., German and Dutch) at least one other nominal term which is not empty. The syntactic rule of Passive then deletes the empty subject and selects a new subject according to the way Passive functions in the language in question; a new higher S' is created, with the predicate *be* (or equivalent) inducing Predicate Raising. The original main verb is turned into a past participle. The whole complex of the Passive rule is put into effect on the cycle of the S-structure to be passivized.

The interesting thing to be noted here is that Passive is, apparently, a ploy or strategy used to circumvent the problem created by the absence of a lexically filled subject. For when the absence of a lexical subject does no harm and allows for a happy derivation, there is no morphological passive, in spite of the missing subject and the concomitant passive meaning. This explains the absence of a passive morphology in those adjectival constructions in English and many other languages usually accounted for by *tough*-Movement but better explained by way of Predicate Raising. If the reader looks again at (148) above, he will notice that the absence of a lexical subject in S_1 does no harm since S_0 of the input structure is not unstable and thus does not require SR or IT. PR yields the perfectly viable output structure shown in (148), where NP_2 automatically does the honours as the grammatical subject. The same applies to Dutch sentences like:

(165) a. Ik liet de wagen repareren. ("I had the car repaired")

(166) a. Ik zag het varken slachten. ("I saw the pig being slaughtered")

which have the underlying structures, respectively (neglecting tense):

(165) b.

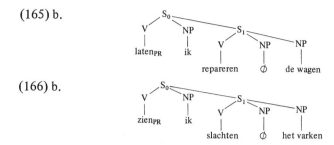

(166) b.

where PR results in the unproblematic:

Exactly the same analysis will do for, e.g., *Je ferai ouvrir la porte* ("I'll have the door opened") (cp. (138b) above). In all these cases a *by*-phrase may be inserted between S_0 and S_1, although for the PR-adjectives in question a *for*-phrase, i.e. a higher S with the predicate *for* and a specified NP-object, above S_0 seems a more natural way of indirectly expressing the subject of S_1.

Not so, however, for, e.g., a structure like:

(167) a. Ik zag het **varken** geslacht worden. ("I saw the pig being slaughtered")

b.

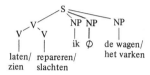

where the *ditransitive* verb *zien* is used, which requires not only PR but also SSD. Now, S_1 does contain a term filled by an anaphoric "x" taking *het varken* as antecedent, but this term is not subject and, therefore, cannot be deleted by (obligatory) SSD. No other way is left for a happy derivation than via Passive, which makes sure that $_{NP}[x_i]$ becomes the subject of a new S' under S_0, so that SSD can apply. But then passive morphology must be introduced, leading to (167a). The semantic difference with (166a) is that for the latter to be true it is not necessary that the speaker ("I") actually saw the pig in question, whereas for the truth of (167a) the actual visual perception is a necessary condition. This difference is hard to test for pragmatic reasons: it is difficult to be the eye-witness of the slaughtering of a pig without seeing the poor animal. For auditory perception, however, the difference is easier to evoke.

Likewise the following sentence (cp. (150a)):

(168) a. De wagen moet gerepareerd worden.

b.

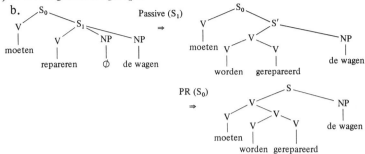

Tense processing turns this into the shallow structure:

(168) c.

The rule of Verb-Final in main clauses moves the non-finite part of the complex V to the far right:

(168) d.

whereupon an optional low level rearrangement rule, which moves a past participle to the front of its cluster, may change this into the preferred structure:[45]

(168) e.

---

[45] As regards this last rule, note that in subordinate clauses, where the whole cluster is moved to the far right, the preferred order is, predictaby:

... dat de wagen gerepareerd moet worden.
... that the car repaired   must be

The point is that (168b) is an unstable structure, directly under tense. If no passivization takes place on S_1 S_0 will have a zero NP-subject, which is forbidden by the NPSC (see p. 141). Only if S_1 is passivized will S_0 be provided with a non-zero NP-subject. The same applies to epistemic *moeten*, except that this allows for IT:

(169) Het moet dat Jan nog slaapt. ("It is necessary that Jan is still
       It   must that Jan still sleeps   asleep")

which, however, is not a very elegant sentence. Apart from this (marginal) possibility of applying IT with epistemic *moeten*, PR must apply, and thus Passive on S_1.

It will be noticed that the crucial part of the passive analysis is the subjectless SA-input structure and the application of the cyclic rule of Passive only if it is required for a happy derivation. It should be realized, with all this, that the literature contains no other motivated account for the absence or presence of passive morphology in the cases discussed and other similar cases (such as *the shooting of the deer by the hunters*). This does not mean, of course, that all questions around passivization phenomena have now been solved. Far from it: it is still entirely unknown, for example, why certain subordinate clauses under French *faire* require passivization (though always without passive morphology), others allow for it, and others again reject it. Nor is it known why in Dutch PR-constructions the subject of the lower active clause tends to become a dative in those cases where its French equivalent rejects a passive, whereas it tends to become an accusative where its French equivalent tends to require a passive. These are issues to be taken up in future research.

2.5 The lexicon

2.5.1 Regularity and irregularity

Only relatively recently has the world of theoretical linguistics begun to realize the central role of the lexicon in grammar and semantics. Naïve linguistic observers have always placed their hopes in the lexicon: speakers without a formal linguistic training often think that to know a language is to know its lexicon, with some morphology as a dispensable appendix. Bloomfield, however, in his extremely influential book *Language* of 1933, reversed this picture. For 40 or so years, his famous dictum "The lexicon is really an appendix of the grammar, a list of basic irregularities" (1933: 274) dominated and biased the theoretical linguists' attitude with regard to the lexicon. Nowadays we realize again, but on a more sophisticated level than the rustic linguist could attain, that the lexicon is much more than a list of basic irregularities, an appendix of the grammar. Yet, although Bloomfield no doubt underestimated the incredible dynamics of the lexicon of each natural language, he was right in relegating to it all irregularities found in the description of one single language or language variety: there seems to be no other receptacle for idiosyncrasies within one linguistic expressive system. But this does not mean that a lexicon is nothing but idiosyncrasies or irregularities. On the contrary, the lexicon of every language teems with regularities, but they all seem to be more or less arbitrarily restricted to subsections of the lexicon. As has been said above (section 1.3), the unpredictable extensions of lexical regularities have made it impossible for us, so far, to formulate *predictions* of lexical phenomena on any interesting scale. But we can formulate *retrodictions* nowadays in vastly more interesting ways than ever before. That is, we are beginning to find out what the regularities are in the lexicon when they occur.

Grammars are both different and similar in this respect. They are different in that predictions are the normal thing within the boundaries of one linguistic variety. But as soon as we widen our scope and look at the grammatical regularities across the various languages and language groups of the world we find ourselves in much the same situation as with the lexicon of one single language: there are all kinds of universal regularities but we are still not very good at predicting what the grammatical regularities of each particular language will be. It is probably fair to say that it is the main aim of present-day universalist linguistics to try and improve on this situation, so that the predictive powers of theoretical linguistics are increased. But even if this programme is successful, it will still remain far beyond the reach of linguistics to predict what grammatical regularities will be found where and when. And the reason for this unattainability of prediction (so that retrodiction is the best we can do) is the same here as it is with the lexicon of each particular language: there is no predicting of the multifarious social factors that determine what choice is made from the available inventory of linguistic means of expression. The study of the lexicon is thus similar to the universalist study of languages and grammars in that the aim is the setting up and definition of precisely the inventory of expressive means available to human speakers.

From a purely semantic point of view it has been known for a long time that the lexicon is a source of regularities. Since antiquity phenomena such as metaphor, metonymy, polysemy, catachresis ("the king was preceded by his followers", "the plane landed on the ocean", "a green blackboard", etc.), have been known and studied, though disappointingly little has come forth in the way of explanatory theory. Most of these and related phenomena are located in the border area of system and use, or 'langue' and 'parole', but to the extent that they are part of 'langue', or the linguistic system, they reflect linguistic regularities, retrodictively. However, the reason why we can say nowadays that so much progress has been made in our retrodictive insights into lexical phenomena is to be found not so much in these more semantic phenomena as in the relations between the lexicon and the theory of syntax. We are beginning to recognize reflexes of rules of (cyclic) syntax in the internal structure of lexical items in a number of extremely fruitful ways. We are even beginning to see that the distinction between grammar and lexicon is not as clearcut as Bloomfield wanted to have it. More and more evidence is coming to light which shows that there is a fluid line between grammar and lexicon. In the following section more will be said about this, in particular in connection with the notions of 'categorial island' and 'lexical island', and the rule of Predicate Raising, which has a special connection with the lexicon on account of its property of uniting verbal material under one category node labelled "V", just like ordinary lexical verbs.

Nominalizations, for example, are well known for their syntactic features. Secondary Subject Deletion (SSD) is rife: *Larry's wish to leave, Sue's ability to read palms, my hope to be promoted*. These nominalizations are not fully lexicalized, in that they involve nominalizations of the predicates *wish, able, hope*, but not of the syntactic constructions *wish to leave, able to read palms, hope to be promoted*. In some cases (but there is no predicting exactly which cases) the lexicon has full lexicalizations for such or similar constructions: *Sue's palmistry, my ambition*, but nothing like **Larry's eclipsophilia*, though no reason is known why such a word could not exist. What is remarkable is that nominalizations that are constructed with a VP never seem to involve any raising:

(170) a. *Harry's ability to be relied on
     b. *your appearance to lie
     c. *her certainty to win
     d. *our likeliness to be wrong
     e. *my belief you to be right
     f. *his ease to fool

It might be objected that a case like *your tendency to lie* is an example of SR as it occurs under the verb *tend*, but this objection is countered by the observation that the verb *tend* occurs in two constructions, one with a single subject-S (leading to an unstable structure), and one with a nominal NP and an object-S with obligatory SSD. Only in the latter construction is there a nominalization with a dependent VP. This explains why nominalizations such as **its tendency to rain, *there's tendency to be a riot* are not acceptable and cannot, in fact, occur. (170a)–(170e) all involve SR, the first four have SR into subject position, the fifth into object position. (170f) involves PR, as in (148) above.

Apparently, there is a constraint on nominalizations to the effect that *a nominalization can only contain lower cyclic material if it is based on a cycle whose non-cyclic material has not been affected by any cyclic rule.* "Cyclic material" stands for any amount of structure that consists of one or more

S-nodes or VP-nodes. The expression "based on" refers to the notion that there are lexical items (nominalizations) that have come about as a result of standard lexical procedures that operate in part in terms of syntactic structures, transformed or not.

Thus, (171b) is based on (171a):

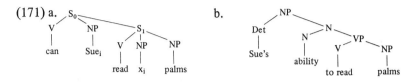

(171) a.

b.

via an intermediate structure where SSD has applied. But SSD has affected only S_1 (VP), not the non-cyclic material of S_0, i.e. $_V[can]$ and $_{NP}[Sue]$. If we compare this with, e.g.,

(170) a′.

a″.

we see that Passive has applied on S_1 (which is right because S_0 is an unstable structure and requires a raised subject), and that, subsequently, on the S_0-cycle SR has applied creating the NP-material for the Determiner node in the nominalization. But now the non-cyclic part of S_0 has been affected: it has been enriched with a new NP-subject, which bars it from being the input to a lexical nominalization rule. Similarly with, e.g.,

(170) f′.

f″

The nominalized form can only be based on a transformed structure where PR has applied. But PR affects both the V and the NP of S_0, so that the nominalization is barred.

Note that this constraint does not apply to nominalizations that do not contain lower cyclic structure. Consequently, formations like *Harry's reliability*, or *his gullibility* are perfectly acceptable, and formations involving Passive are also free to occur: *the city's destruction by bombers*.

The interesting point is that the lexicon, apparently, is not the static list of items it has long been thought to be, but is a highly dynamic structure with its own rules and principles. These rules and principles, however, are grafted on to the products of grammar so that the rules of grammar (cyclic syntax in particular) are found again in lexicalized combinations and structural properties of lexical items. In a trivial sense this has been known for a long time, given such combinations as, e.g., *tightrope-walker, forget-me-not* (Bloomfield's "synthetic compounds"; 1933: 231-4). We now see that this penetration of the syntax into the lexicon goes far deeper than the lexicalization of bits of surface structure. It crucially involves cyclical syntax, albeit with certain restrictions, such as the constraint just formulated. In a very general sense, this is strong confirmation for the overall correctness of the brand of syntax we are developing.

2.5.2 Islands and items

We have repeatedly, in the preceding pages, mentioned and defended the notion that certain verbs, in particular causative verbs, have an internal structure that reflects the working of the cyclic rule of Predicate Raising. This notion was mooted by McCawley in the late 1960s, in several publications, and has subsequently come under fierce attack from various quarters.

Originally, the idea of the 'internal' or 'prelexical' structure of a caustive verb was explicated in terms of lexical insertion somewhere down the derivational process from semantic deep structure to surface structure: a categorial V-island created by, say, PR, was thought to be replaced by a lexical verb with precisely the meaning of the complex V-island. For example, if in a derivation the complex V-island $_V[_V[\text{cause}]\ _V[\text{die}]]$ had come about, it was thought to be a matter of choice whether this V-island was left intact or replaced by a verb, say *kill*. In this analysis there should never be a semantic difference between a sentence containing the phrase *cause to die* and the otherwise identical sentence containing the verb *kill*. A slightly more sophisticated treatment would stipulate that if, in English, *cause* takes PR it must be lexicalized, but if it takes SR, as in

(172) a. The sniper caused the king to die.

then it cannot be lexicalized, owing to the fact that there is no categorial V-island. But even in this refined analysis there should never be a semantic difference between this sentence and:

(172) b. The sniper killed the king.

A flurry of publications then came about, showing or purporting to show that there often are indeed semantic differences between the 'analytic' and the 'lexical' versions. Linguists suddenly turned metaphysicists as they discussed the nature of causation, and many came up with case studies of sentence pairs where A can be said in truth to have caused B's death, but not to have killed B. For example, if I see that Mr B, who has a heart condition, reaches, by mistake, for a box containing lethal pills instead of the medicine prescribed for him, and I deliberately do not warn him, then I may, in some sense, have caused him to die, but I have not killed him. In much the same vein, Ruwet (1972: 142-3) gives some intriguing, and telling, examples (which are translated here into English) of differences between lexical and analytic causatives:[46]

> (173) a. The doctor caused her fever to go down.
>
> b. The doctor lowered her fever.
>
> (174) a. Alice caused Humpty Dumpty to get back on his wall.
>
> b. Alice put Humpty Dumpty back on his wall.

In all cases concerned it is possible to assert the analytic version while at the same time denying the lexical version without contradiction, *but never vice versa*. Thus, one can consistently assert that Alice caused Humpty Dumpty to get back on his wall but that she did not actually put him there, but one cannot assert consistently that Alice actually put Humpty Dumpty back on his wall without causing him to get there. And likewise for all the other cases. Which would suggest that the lexical versions are a special subclass of the analytic versions – a point of importance in our analysis.

Objections of this nature were cearly relevant with regard to the explication of the notion of prelexical structure presented in the early years, when these matters were hotly discussed. And they contributed to some considerable extent to the starkly contrasting silence surrounding issues of prelexical analysis in the following years. Clearly some rethinking was called for, in a number of different respects. But relatively few linguists thought it necessary to do so. Instead, most linguists preferred to take a derogatory attitude towards the whole notion of prelexical analysis and the application of rules of

---

[46] It is very interesting to note that only some of Ruwet's examples retain their force after translation into English. Thus, e.g., there is a very clear difference in French between:

> (i) Les pluies ont fait monter le niveau de la rivière.
> (ii) Les pluies ont monté le niveau de la rivière.

(his example (68)), the second of which is unacceptable in some pragmatic sense. But their English equivalents are both clearly acceptable, and do not show a clear semantic difference:

> (iii) The rains have caused the river level to rise.
> (iv) The rains have raised the river level.

This shows again how lexical items, in ways still largely unknown, differ subtly from language to language, despite an overall semantic identity.

syntax in the lexicon, thereby missing the opportunity of gaining important insights.

In spite of the many unsolved problems in the area of prelexical analysis, a few things can be established with reasonable confidence. One such thing is that, at least for a significant class of complex predicates, the old theory of lexical insertion as a possible option somewhere down the transformational derivation must be abandoned and replaced by an analysis involving fully lexicalized deep structures or semantic analyses. This applies in particular to those complex predicates which do not allow for 'penetration' by quantifiers and whose semantic description involves non-compositional elements, or 'extras' over and above the compositional part of their analysis. They are best assumed to enter syntax whole and undivided, so that their prelexical analysis would be a matter of semantics only. Thus, all English verbs denoting a form of killing (*kill, murder, assassinate, slaughter, frag, slay, execute, hang*, or whatever Roget's *Thesaurus* helps one to) are taken to contain the structure "cause-to-die" as part of their semantic description, but any notion of lexical substitution during the derivation is abandoned. The part "cause-to-die" plays a role only in the satisfaction conditions associated with these verbs. The relevant point is that such a V-node is indeed there, that it is a V-node of precisely the kind formed in open syntax by the cyclic rule of PR, and that it determines the argument structure of the verbs in question. The remaining semantic features of the verbs in question are extras, to be specified in the semantic conditions associated with each predicate for truth of any proposition figuring it. Clearly, this theory requires that truth of the analytic version is necessary for truth of the lexical version, but not vice versa.

Fodor (1970) contains three arguments against the idea that complex predicates are open to prelexical analysis, no matter in what form. They are different from the foregoing, and of considerable interest. His first argument is perhaps less relevant. It consists of the contrast between sentences like the following:

(175) a. Floyd melted the glass though it surprised me that it would do so.
     b. John killed Mary and it surprised me that she did so.

In the former, says Fodor, the *do so* anaphor takes *melt* as antecedent, in particular the *melt* that is incorporated as the intransitive part of the causative *melt*. But in (175b) it is entirely impossible to interpret the *do so* anaphor as taking an incorporated *die* as antecedent. It thus seems that Fodor accepts a prelexical causative analysis for *melt* but not for *kill*. This argument, however, seems less convincing if it is realized that anaphora to a semantically incorporated element gets easier to the extent that the incorporated element is phonologically present (though it remains quaint or stilted):

(176) a. Nicolai is a Stalinist, though he has never met him.
     b. Nicolai is a Christian, though he has never met him.

An interpretation for (176a) where *him* takes *Stalin* as antecedent is possible in much the same way as the *do so* interpretation of (175a). But in (176b) *him* cannot take *Christ* as antecedent, analogously to (175b). There thus seem to be independent factors of phonological identity at play, which do not seem to affect the prelexical argument directly.

The other two arguments, however, deserve more careful attention. First, Fodor observes that adverbial adjuncts can be distributed over *cause* and *die* independently, but not over the lexicalized *kill*, as appears from the pair:

(177) a. John caused Bill to die on Sunday by stabbing him on Saturday.
      b. John killed Bill on Sunday by stabbing him on Saturday.

the second of which is either odd or uninterpetable. This argument is clear and forceful, and it means that the original idea of lexical insertion somewhere along the derivation is untenable. The argument is neutralized, however, when open syntax is assumed to start operating on, in principle, fully lexicalized structures, as is assumed here for the items in question. (177a) takes the following DS/SA in our analysis:

(177) a′.

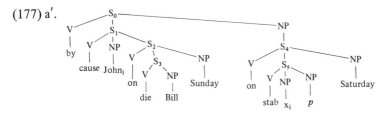

There are two subcycles, one leading up to S_4, and one leading up to S_1, after which the S_0-cycle applies. On the first subcycle, *Saturday* is adopted by $_V$[on] by adoption (Object Incorporation), after which the complex V-node is lowered into S_5, which then becomes: $_S$[stab x_ip on Saturday]. This is turned into a gerund: *stabbing x_ip on Saturday*, due to its nominal character as object to *by*. On the second subcycle S_3 becomes $_S$[die Bill on Sunday] by the same process. SR on the S_1-cycle yields:

There is a tree diagram here with nodes: S_1, V NP NP VP, V Prep Phr, cause John$_i$ Bill, to die, Prep NP, on Sunday.

Now, on the S_0-cycle, the subject of S_5, i.e. x_i, is deleted by horizontal SSD, as in (87b) above; the object-NP p is pronominalized into *him* (with *Bill* as antecedent). Now Object Incorporation attaches the object NP over S_5 to $_V$[by] by adoption; the complex V is then lowered into S_1 to yield the material for further treatment leading to (177a). Clearly, if instead of the two verbs *cause* and *die*, the one verb *kill* is used in deep structure, there is no way of letting a structure ₛ[die Bill] act as argument under *on Sunday*, and the only possible structure is then:

(177) b'.

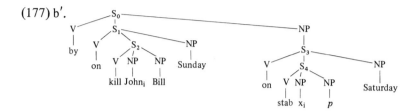

which is odd for semantic reasons, since any temporal operator over *kill* requires truth-conditionally that the whole killing process, including the causation, fall within the time span denoted by the temporal operator. In (177b'), however, a separate causal factor, denoted by *by stabbing him on Saturday*, is given, involving an event outside the time span denoted by *on Sunday*. This argument by Fodor thus reinforces our treatment of prelexical analysis for the cases at hand, by showing up a serious weakness of the old theory of prelexical analysis involving lexical insertion down the derivational path.

Fodor's third argument is again of a structural nature, and is to do with horizontal SSD. The following two sentences are contrasted:

(178) a. John caused Bill to die by igniting the charge.
     b. John killed Bill by igniting the charge.

Clearly, (178a) is ambiguous as to who did the igniting, whereas in (178b) it can only be John who did it. Again, the objection is countered by the assumption that there is no lexical insertion along the derivation, but only at deep structure level. (178b) then simply lacks the structural space for letting the *by*-operator take ₛ[die Bill] as argument. Although this suffices to counter Fodor's arguments, a few observations can be made in connection with this last argument, which show that even without the assumption of a fully lexicalized deep structure this argument has no force, owing to certain constraints that seem to exist for categorial islands that come about as a result of the application of cyclic rules.

In order to demonstrate this we shall look at the French *faire*-construction, discussed earlier in section 2.4.5. Consider the following French sentences:

(179) a. Jean a   fait   mourir Paul sans   dire un mot.
        Jean has made die   Paul without say a   word
                  ("Jean caused Paul to die without saying a word")
     b. Jean a fait mourir Paul en   ne   disant pas un mot. (id.)
                   while not saying   a   word

c. Jean a fait mourir Paul sans   un mot. ("Jean caused Paul to die
                      without a   word   without a word")

The first of these sentences is clearly not ambiguous the way its English translation is: the deleted subject of *dire* ("say") can only be an anaphor of *Jean*, not of *Paul*. In (179b) there is a very strong preference for the same reading, i.e. the reading in which it is Jean who did not say a word; but, it seems, a reading where Paul died silently is not altogether excluded. According to most speakers, e.g., a sentence like:

(180) L'officier   a   fait   marcher les soldats en   chantant.
        The officer has made march   the soldiers while singing

is ambiguous between the preferred reading where the officer sang, and a recessive but pragmatically perhaps more plausible reading where the soldiers sang. (179c), finally, is entirely ambiguous as to who remained silent, Jean or Paul. Note that if *fait mourir* in these three sentences is replaced by the single verb *tué* ("killed"), then all three sentences only have the reading where it is Jean who did not speak – but this is, of course, precisely what is predicted by the theory of fully lexicalized deep structure.

What the data of (179) suggest is that the categorial V-island $_V$[fait mourir], which has come about in the course of the syntactic derivation of the sentences in question, is subject to a *constraint* to the effect that *the object-S under* faire, *whose V is to be adopted by* faire *as a result of PR, is not allowed to contain lowered material containing a V*. Only if the V is a participial form (*disant*), can this constraint be overridden, albeit with some difficulty. (Note that participials or gerundives are not fully verbal, but share important properties with nominals.) Thus, if there is indeed such a constraint, or a more general constraint entailing it, then the following structure cannot lead to (179a) – where the quantified NP *un mot* ("a word") has already been lowered:

(179) a'.

The reason is that, after Object Incorporation on the S_1-cycle, the complex V *sans dire un mot* must be lowered into S_2. This in itself is not problematic, given the perfectly normal sentence:

(181) Paul est mort sans   dire un mot. ("Paul has died without saying
        Paul has died without say   a   word   a word")

but it is problematic here since S_2 now contains lowered material containing a V (*dire*), which prohibits PR on the S_0-cycle, according to the constraint. It is less problematic if, instead of $_V$[sans] the predicate of S_1 is $_V$[en], since *en* participializes the verb of its object clause (*disant*). Object Incorporation and Lowering on the S_1-cycle is not problematic at all if the object in S_1 is not an NP over S, but a simple NP, such as $_{NP}$[un mot]. Now nothing verbal need be lowered into S_2, and the derivation can go through.

   This shows that the mere ambiguity of (178a) against (178b) not only does not provide an argument against deriving *kill* from "cause to die", but also fails against a theory of lexical insertion somewhere down the derivation. For if it did, then *fait mourir* in (179a), which also lacks the reading which is absent from (178b), could not be considered derived from "fait mourir"! In general, Fodor's arguments have no force against the theory of prelexical analysis in so far as it maintains that important classes of semantically complex lexical items (verbs) are composed in ways that run strictly analogous to what is found in open syntax rules of languages. They do have some force against a theory of prelexical analysis that endorses insertion somewhere down the derivation, but they reinforce a prelexical analysis theory endorsing fully lexicalized deep structure, at least for the cases discussed.

   The facts of (179), moreover, suggest that categorial syntactic islands display properties fending them off from semantic penetration by material containing verbal forms. Thus, the categorial island $_V$[fair mourir] is impenetrable to *sans dire un mot*, i.e. the adverbial *sans dire un mot* cannot modify a proper subpart only of the categorial island, but must modify the whole island. Categorial islands are thus, if the constraint is real, more than just a syntactic construction. They show some degree of encapsulation, which increases in strength as the island becomes more lexicalized. Thus, the Dutch categorial V-island $_V$[leren kennen], likewise the product of syntactic Predicate Raising in the way normally found in Dutch syntactic constructions, and literally meaning "learn to know", has virtually acquired the status of a single lexical item meaning "make the acquaintance of". It is now no longer surprising to find that a sentence like

(182) Ik heb sommige mensen binnen twee minuten leren kennen.
       I have some   people within two minutes learn know
       ("I have made the acquaintance of some people within two minutes")

does not allow for a reading "I have learned how to get to know some people within two minutes", even though that reading is passed by the categorial constraint formulated above.

   It cannot be our purpose here to try and unravel all the details of the relation between grammar and lexicon. What we have presented here should be seen as samples of what is still there to be discovered, rather than an attempt at a complete theory. The important thing, in this context, is that the overall purpose of this long chapter can now be regarded as achieved. The present state of syntactic and lexical theory speaks strongly against any notion of surface semantics, and supports the view that a grammar is a mapping procedure between Semantic Analyses and Surface Structures of sentences. The facts and regularities unearthed in the preceding pages go far beyond the capacities of any existing variety of grammatical or lexical description married to a semantic calculus based on surface structures only. Most such descriptions suffer from a serious underestimation of the complexities of natural language and are exceedingly aprioristic, thus representing a modern form of analogism, while those that are linguistically more sophisticated have not, so far, been able to account for certain crucial facts.

3

The logic and semantics of presupposition

3.1 Logic and psychological reality

In this chapter, the notion of presupposition will first be investigated from a logical point of view. This will be found to be insufficient, and a discourse-semantic notion will be developed. Before, however, we can embark upon an investigation of the logical questions surrounding presuppositional phenomena, a few words must be said about the status of logic in the context of our theory.

In standardly accepted varieties of formal semantics, logic is not only the vehicle for the calculus of entailments, but also the prototype of procedures and calculi of semantic interpretation. Following works by Tarski, Carnap and others, it became accepted as something like a necessary truth that if a semantics is to be devised for natural language, it should be modelled after the truth-conditional, model-theoretic semantics devised by the great logical semanticists for logical languages. It is a basic contention of our theory that this second function of logic is based on a radical misconception about the nature and role of meaning in language. The great semanticization that has taken place in logic must not be transferred to the semantics of natural language. While Wittgenstein's and Tarski's dictum that the interpretation of an utterance implies a grasp of the conditions under which it is true is fully accepted and indeed used as an adequacy test for the theory, it is not our starting point, as it was for current forms of formal semantics. Our starting point is the notion that the interpretation of utterances is first and foremost a cognitive activity. Logic, in its capacity of the formal theory of entailments, is prima facie nothing but one of a number of tests for the correctness of the theory. If an assertive utterance is intuitively felt to be true in a given situation, and if that utterance is associated with an analysis enabling the formal derivation of entailments (i.e. if the analysis is an instance of logical form), then the test is that the entailments which are formally derived by means of the logic must likewise be judged to be true in the same situation.

This implies that not just utterances, but also the sentence types which they represent, be associated with a logical analysis. This analysis, in the theory presented, is identical with what we have called Semantic Analysis. Semantic Analysis is thus required to have a structure enabling the formal derivation of entailments. It must, moreover, be a syntactically motivated underlying form for well-formed sentences, and, finally, it must be a suitable input to a motivated and adequate procedure of semantic interpretation in terms of discourse incrementation.

In our approach, the question thus arises of the psychological status of logic. This question, as we saw in chapter 1, has never been treated with great enthusiasm by the world of formal semantics. But in our context it is central and inescapable. The answer is, in principle, that logic is psychologically real in so far as humans carry out logical operations as part of their cognitive behaviour. Any logic aiming at an adequate description of such cognitive processes is subject to empirical constraints. Otherwise, a logical calculus is merely epiphenomenal on whatever cognitive machinery is thought to be at work.

It is not our purpose, in this study, to work out a theory of natural, i.e. psychologically real, logic, though we do aim at a psychologically real semantics. It might thus seem that we could afford to work with a purely formal, and not necessarily psychologically plausible, logic to the extent that the derivation, or generation, of entailments is not involved in the *semantic* machinery postulated for the interpretation of linguistic utterances. But we shall see that there is an important part of (three-valued) logic which plays a direct and crucial role in linguistic interpretation. In the course of section 3.2 it will become clear that a separate class of *presuppositional entailments*, as opposed to classical entailments, must be recognized, and in section 3.3 it will be shown that these are *semantically* real and that their derivation is a semantically real process. The presuppositional entailments are actually generated (though at a sufficiently deep level, way below any possible threshold of awareness) and, as we shall say, "prejected" into preceding discourse if they are not already represented there. The "prejection" of presuppositions makes for what will be called "acceptable discourse" in some technical sense.

This means, among other things, that in so far as the logic must be assumed to be semantically real, it must not only simulate actual semantic processes as far as output is concerned, but the machinery used must also approximate the actual machinery as closely as possible. Whereas in an epiphenomenal interpretation of logic the question of notational variants is of no importance, it is here. Only to the extent that the logic is not directly relevant to the semantics can it still be said that it need not be subjected to these empirical constraints.

One thing is overwhelmingly clear: if the logic is to simulate natural cognitive processes of drawing inferences, assigning truth-values and interpreting utterances, it had better be three-valued and of the kind presented in section 3.2.4 and in the appendix by Weijters. This does not mean that classical logic is 'wrong' in any sense, but only that it is not sufficiently detailed. Presuppositional three-valued logic contains the classical calculus as a proper subpart. The appendix shows that the classical calculus is simply the two-valued representative of a hierarchy of n-valued calculi such that any i-valued system $(2 \leqslant i < n)$ is fully expressible in terms of the $i + 1$-valued system.

A few special words must be said now about the notion of entailment. Let us, in accordance with established usage, say that A *entails* B $(A \models B)$ just in case whenever an utterance of A is true, so is an utterance of B (but not necessarily vice versa). Contrary to established usage, however, this expression schema $(A \models B)$ will often be used as an observational statement. In logic, $A \models B$ is warranted only if the calculus ensures that truth of an utterance of A requires truth of an utterance of B. Here we shall say that $A \models B$ if there is a correct speaker's intuition that assertion of A together with the assertion of *not-B* leads to a contradiction. The term *entailment* by itself is thus reserved in principle for intuitive entailments as they are felt to be properties of sentences by native speakers. Judgements of entailment are thus similar to judgements of grammaticality: both are made of sentence types, and both imply generalizations over all possible occasions of utterance. When it is said that $A \models B$, this judgement implies that no occasion of utterance can occur where the utterance of A is true but the utterance of B is false. And when it is said that a sentence A is ungrammatical, this judgement implies that no occasion of utterance can occur where the utterance of A is acceptable as a proper expression, within the linguistic community concerned, of a possible meaning. Such judgements are hardly ever unshakeably certain: they are accepted as certain as long as they have not been disproved by some counter-example. (Yet they count as the empirical basis of linguistics and semantics. But we have learned to live with this paradox.)

When the term *logical entailment* is used, there is the implication that the entailment in question is accounted for by a logical calculus. *Semantic entailment* implies that the entailment in question follows from the conditions associated with the predicate figured by the entailing sentence, as when we say that a sentence *This is a tulip* entails that *This is a flower*. But since we shall follow the overall principle that the whole of the (deep) lexicon is incorporated into the logic and, vice versa, that the great truth-functional and other operators in logic are considered predicates in the (deep) lexicon, the distinction between logical and semantic entailments is not at all fundamental.

What is fundamental is that a distinction must be made between those entailments that are natural in the sense that they have the status of valid conclusions from given premises on the one hand, and, on the other, entailments that are mathematically valid, given the mathematical properties of the logical system at hand, but are not backed up by any intuitive feeling of validity. For example, in classical logic (and any n-valued extension of it) any logically true sentence, such as *Whoever is alive is not dead*, is entailed by any arbitrary sentence in the language, simply because whenever any arbitrary sentence (or its utterance) is true, the logically true sentence will be true. But from, e.g., *They all liked the performance* to *Whoever is alive is not dead* is not what we wish to call a "valid inference". And the reason why we don't want to call it that is that the entailment is not psychologically real. In other words, if a system of natural logic is to be set up, it must cut out those entailments that are not felt to be inferences, even though by mathematical necessity those entailments hold. This can only be done by changing the definition of entailment, or at least by defining a restricted class of entailments as "inferences". We now say that *inferences are entailments which follow from the conditions associated with each predicate of the language, including the logical predicates*, i.e. the truth-functional and other traditionally recognized logical operators. But entailments which follow from the mathematical properties of the field of valuations are, apparently, not psychologically real and are therefore not to be called "inferences". Typically, entailments based on 'field-of-valuations' properties, such as the fact that logically true sentences are entailed by all sentences, or that logically false sentences entail any sentence, do not play any role either in cognition or in semantic processing. They are thus not inferences. But the entailments derived from the truth-functional operators are highly functional in both general cognition and in semantics in particular, though in ways that either deviate slightly from or are richer than what is specified in the idealization of a logical calculus.

Against this background it will be clear that it makes good sense to let the psychological machinery of logical operations depend on the conditions associated with the predicates and on the discourse structures brought about by continuing incrementation. Since the classical logical operators are all treated as predicates in the language of Semantic Analysis, the entailments derived with their help are now all derived from the conditions associated with them. The predicate *or*, for example, as is demonstrated in section 3.2.4, is described as a semantic predicate over pairs of facts such that for all pairs of propositions referring to those facts the condition holds that at least one of them must be true. (In fact, the condition is somewhat more elaborate, given the trivalence of the logic, but these extras do not matter here.) Any entailment involving *or* will now be based not on the truth-table of *or* but on the predicate conditions associated with the predicate *or*. *Or*-entailments are also inferences in that they are psychologically real, except the much-discussed additive entailment that gives "*A* or *B*" from either just "*A*" or just "*B*". But this entailment is in jeopardy anyway in our system since most sentences of a natural language are not valued at all most of the time (our system is replete with truth-value gaps). Since the lack of a truth-value is 'infectious' in that it makes the whole (uttered) sentence truth-valueless, it is no longer possible to form a valid disjunctive entailment by simply picking out an arbitrary sentence of the language: it will almost certainly be without a truth-value in the given discourse. But even if the additive schema of disjunctive entailment is restricted to valued sentences only, the entailment, though valid, is not psychologically real in that it involves a generalization over the whole field of valuations and does not restrict itself to the material at hand. Some criterion of derivability from predicate conditions thus seems to work in distinguishing entailments from inferences.

Let us observe, finally, that, probably as a result of mere historical accident, logic has traditionally limited itself to the calculus of entailments resulting from the well-known truth-functional operators, the quantifiers of existence and universality, and the modalities of (metaphysical) necessity and possibility. Recently, no doubt under the influence of linguistic developments in analytic philosophy, logicians have made attempts at widening the scope of logical calculus. We have thus witnessed the birth of tense logic, deontic logic, belief logic, and what not. No attention will be paid, in this book, to these recent developments. The point of view taken is, mainly, that it is better to work out the semantics first; the logic can then be looked at later. Our interest in logic is limited, first, to the logic of presupposition – because this part of logic is also part of the semantics, and then to the traditional areas of logic, in particular the truth-functional operators, the quantifiers, and to some extent the verbs of modality.

3.2   The logical problem of presupposition

3.2.1   The Frege–Strawson notion

Frege's extensional notion of compositionality implied that if a part of a sentence lacks an extension, so does the sentence as a whole. In other words, if a definite term fails to refer, the sentence as a whole lacks a truth-value. Frege thus envisaged a (logically analysed) language with truth-value gaps – though he considered such gaps an abomination that should be avoided. The question is of a logical nature for two reasons. First, it is generally the case that a sentence containing definite terms as arguments to its main predicate entails the existence of what is denoted by these terms, and it is reasonable to require of logic that it should give a formal account of this entailment. Secondly, the notion of truth-value gaps is at variance with traditionally accepted views in logic, in particular with the Aristotelian view that a logical language obeys the Principle of the Excluded Third (PET). That is, if a logic is to be devised in accordance with Frege's principle of extensional composi-tionality, then a distinction must be made between those entailments whose falsity entails the falsity of the bearer sentence, and those entailments whose falsity results in a truth-value gap. In the tradition established by Frege and further developed by Strawson (1950; 1952; 1954), it has become customary to refer to those entailments whose falsity results in a truth-value gap for the bearer sentence as *presuppositions*. These presuppositions are all to do with the question of *existence* of the reference value of definite terms occurring in propositions. Later on, the term *presupposition* has come to be applied to a much wider range of phenomena, whereby it became questionable if these additions had not united incongruous and heterogeneous phenomena under one term. For the moment, we shall limit ourselves to the philosophically orientated existential notion of presupposition, as considered by Frege and Strawson.

Before we expand on the Frege–Strawson notion of (existential) presupposition, however, we must devote some attention to Bertrand Russell's brilliant attempt at shortcircuiting this notion altogether. In the classical study 'On denoting' Russell (1905) makes a valiant, and historically extremely influential, attempt at rescuing the classical Principle of the Excluded Third. It should be noted that PET expresses two independent properties of (logically analysed) languages. First, a language obeying PET is *fully valued*: all its sentences always have a truth-value; there is no truth-value gap ever at all. Secondly, there are *precisely two truth-values*, 'true' and 'false'. In other words, given a sentence of a PET-language, it is either true or false; *tertium non datur*. It was Russell's intention to show that natural language is a PET-language. Clearly, if Russell can be shown to be right, the whole Frege–Strawson construction collapses, and there is no longer any need to speak of presupposition in a logical sense. We shall see, however, that Russell was wrong, in spite of the brilliance and courage of his analysis.

Russell's analysis, his famous 'Theory of Descriptions', is to do with the *logical*, not necessarily the *grammatical*, analysis of definite terms, in particular definite descriptions, i.e. definite nominal terms built up with the help of lexical material, not proper names. His analysis was courageous in view of the fact that sentences with definite descriptions as terms often obviously lack truth-values when viewed as isolated sentences out of context. Take an arbitrary sentence of English, such as:

(1) The quick brown fox jumps over the lazy dog.

presented to you here and now. Clearly, it makes no sense to ask whether this sentence is true or false. Any question to that effect must be countered by the observation that the sentence as presented here and now simply has no truth-value, and that it will acquire one only if it is known, on independent or external grounds, what fox and what dog and what moment in time the sentence is about. It took Russellians quite some reasoning away to get around this all too obvious fact. Those who still defend his analysis in our days have extended Russell's analysis with extra ('pragmatic') apparatus meant to ensure that the Russellian quantifications are limited to predefined verification domains, provided on grounds of 'pragmatic' considerations. (How the 'pragmatics' defines the right verification domain for any given sentence containing definite descriptions is never made clear, but let us be charitable and gloss over such omissions.)

Russell's analysis, anyhow, amounted to the claim that what presents itself as a definite description in a 'surface' sentence, is dismantled in logical analysis, where it turns up as an existential quantification. Thus, sentence (1) should, according to Russell, be read as:

(2) There is one and only one x which is a fox, brown and quick, and one and only one y which is a dog and lazy, and x jumps over y.

Or, to take Russell's own celebrated example, sentence (3a) should be analysed logically as (3b) - using notational devices not yet developed in 1905:

(3) a. The present king of France is bald.
  b. $\exists x(Now(KoF(x)) \land Bald(x) \land \forall y(Now(KoF(y)) \supset x = y))$

This analysis has the advantage that the negation can be placed in various positions. If placed over the whole of (3b), we have logical sentence negation, and nothing is entailed with regard to the existence, now, of a king of France. This, Russell says, is one possible reading of the grammatical negation of (3a):

(3) c. The present king of France is not bald.

In another reading of (3c) the negation is placed before the predicate *Bald*. Now, the current existence of a king of France is entailed. This would represent the normal, unmarked reading of (3c). It would thus seem possible to save PET, as well as Frege's principle of extensional compositionality.

But there are problems. First, one wonders why there do not seem to be readings of (3c) with the negation in other logically possible positions, such as before *Now*, or before *KoF*, or before the universal operator. Why, in other words, should it be that (3c) has just the two readings specified by Russell? Other problems are to do with the intuitive fact that definite descriptions are not the same as existentially quantified terms. One might answer that Russell was not interested in the nature of human language or its grammatical systems, but only in the logic of sentences. Such an answer is probably fair to Russell, but not very relevant here, since *we* are indeed interested in the nature of language and grammar. And Russell's analysis has been used very widely in the past 80 years precisely for the purpose of linguistic analysis in some meaning of that term.

In the context of linguistic analysis with a view to grammatical and semantic processing by speakers the Russellian analysis is precariously off the mark. It has been noted in section 1.1 that there are salient systematic differences in grammatical and semantic behaviour between definite terms and quantified terms. The observations given there need not be repeated here.

But even from a purely truth-conditional point of view, the Russell analysis breaks down as soon as discourse phenomena are taken into account. Take, e.g.:

(4) a. Ed thought that there was a doctor around, and he hoped that *the doctor* would help.

A Russellian analysis for the definite term *the doctor* requires that the existential quantifier be placed somewhere in the total structure. But any of the available positions leads to incorrect truth-conditions:

(4) b. There was an x such that Ed thought ...
   c. Ed thought that there was an x such that there was a doctor around, and he hoped ...
   d. Ed thought that there was a doctor around, and there was an x such that he hoped ...
   e. Ed thought that there was a doctor around, and he hoped that there was an x such that ...

In other words, in none of the structurally possible Russellian analyses do we get the correct truth-conditions. The reason is, intuitively at least, that Russell's analysis leaves no way of identifying the referent of *the doctor* with the doctor existentially introduced in the first conjunct of (4a).

This type of analysis runs into other difficulties as well. Thus it fails to explain why of the following pair the first sentence is contradictory, but the second is not:

(5) a. There was a doctor, and he helped, and he did not help.
   b. There was a doctor and he helped, and there was a doctor and he did not help.

Admittedly, this type of sentence is troublesome for a variety of reasons (see section 4.1.1, where a full discussion is devoted to these sentences and the problem is solved in discourse semantics terms). Yet, if these conjunctions are troublesome for other reasons, we see that they are troublesome as well for this analysis. Analyses where they are not troublesome are, of course, to be preferred. In general, therefore, we conclude that Russell's analysis has little to offer for our theory.

As is well known, the Oxford philosopher Peter Strawson came to the same conclusion. In 1950 he published his famous attack on the Russellian analysis, in his article 'On referring', in the periodical *Mind*. Strawson's position is not essentially different from that taken by Frege in 1892, but Strawson adds some refinements. Strawson begins the article by stressing that it is not *sentences*, as linguistic type objects, that carry truth-values, but *utterances*, as linguistic token objects. Hence, the propositional variables of any logic for natural language should range over *utterance tokens* when truth-values are assigned, but over sets of identifiable utterance tokens, i.e. over *sentence types*, when entailments are specified.

Strawson's position on this matter is no doubt correct, and should be taken into account when logic is applied to language. We shall say that a language L is a set of sentences (i.e. types), and that each sentence is a (potentially infinite) set of realizations, or utterance tokens, or simply utterances, of that sentence. We shall adopt the notational convention of italicizing sentences or variables ranging over sentences, while utterances (or variables ranging over them) will be printed in roman. We shall systematically speak of sentences when we refer to elements of L, i.e. to linguistically defined objects, but of utterances (of sentences) when truth-values are assigned. More precisely, an utterance A of sentence A is a pair $\langle SA_i, D_j \rangle$, where SA_i is the Semantic Analysis of A and D_j is a discourse domain (cp. the beginning of section 1.2). If we split off the propositional part R_i of SA_i, then $\langle R_i, D_j \rangle$ is the proposition in A. Truth-values, then, are assigned to propositions (or sets of propositions in a discourse domain), not to sentences or SAs. If A is uttered in some D_j that is unfit for incrementation by R_i, then $\langle R_i, D_j \rangle$ has no truth-value (is undefined). Whenever we speak, below, of utterances having truth-values, the expression is short for propositions in utterances having truth-values.

At the end of the previous section we took care that entailment was defined as a property of (assertive) sentences, i.e. of types, not of tokens. (Strictly speaking, entailment is a property of the propositional representation R of a sentence A.) Thus, $A \models B$ just in case whenever (the proposition in) an utterance of A is true, so is (the proposition in) an utterance of B, in the same discourse domain D_j in which each A is true. Likewise, presupposition is treated as a property of sentence types, not of single utterance tokens, i.e. of pairs $\langle SA_i, D_j \rangle$. But the time has not come yet to define presupposition. Some further analysis is needed before a definition can be given.

Apart from this important distinction between types and tokens, Strawson's position is in principle identical with Frege's: if a definite term in (the proposition of) an utterance token fails to refer, i.e. if it has been decided that a particular definite term does not refer to an existing individual or set of individuals (or anything definable in terms of existing individuals), then, says Strawson, the utterance in question lacks a truth-value. (Strictly speaking, Strawson limits this rule to subject terms, but this may be considered a detail without further consequences.) Thus, given that at present France has no king, an utterance of (3a), but also of (3c), must remain without a truth-value. These sentences are said to presuppose the existence of a king of France. Logically, this should mean that both (3a) and (3c) entail:

(3) d. The king of France exists.

which is then a presupposition of these two sentences.

An avalanche of, sometimes angry, articles followed Strawson's publications in the early 1950s on presupposition. The main point in these reactions was not so much the observational inadequacy of Strawson's analysis (about which more below), as what was felt to be Strawson's tinkering with the principles of logic, in particular with PET. Perhaps the obvious irritation in some of the reactions to Strawson's presupposition analysis was a reflection of the unease that must have been felt (and deeply buried) by many philosophers of language at the intuitive inappropriateness of the Russell analysis. For there is not really any good reason for attacking Strawson on logical grounds. It may be objected that Strawson himself was, perhaps inexcusably, vague on logical matters, but there is no logical incoherence in his analysis. In fact, if the observational basis had been sound, his analysis would no doubt suffice as a logical account of the phenomenon of presupposition (though not as a semantic account).

Strawson's logical notion of presupposition can be made explicit in the following way. It must be noted in advance that Strawson sacrifices PET to some extent: he admits truth-value gaps, but he keeps the logic two-valued (bivalent). If, as has been said, a language L is a set of sentences (and each sentence a set of utterances), a distinction can be made between logically atomic and logically complex sentences. The latter are built up from the former, in recursive ways, by means of the truth-functional logical operators *not* ($\neg$), *and* ($\wedge$), *or* ($\vee$), and, if one wishes, the implication ($\supset$). Their truth-functional definition is as in standard propositional calculus. Any utterance of an atomic sentence of L can be valued 'true' (+), 'false' (−) or 'undefined' (U), i.e. without a truth-value. Note that a valuation 'U' for an utterance A does not mean that A has some third value. It means that A lacks a truth-value. This appears from the fact that any complex utterance containing A as a structural part must also be valued 'U': the truth-functions are defined for utterances or pairs of utterances with a value; they are undefined for anything lacking a truth-value. The Strawsonian tables for *not*, *and* and *or* are thus as follows:

Table 1

$\neg$A	A	$\wedge$ B			$\vee$ B		
		+	−	U	+	−	U
−	+	+	−	U	+	+	U
+	−	−	−	U	+	−	U
U	U	U	U	U	U	U	U

It is easily seen that all entailments of classical logic are preserved, except the so-called 'additive' entailments, where the entailment contains an arbitrary sentence of L, such as the well-known (and linguistically problematic) entailment schema $A \models A \lor B$. As can be read from table 1, it is possible for A to be true but for A $\lor$ B to be undefined; this occurs when B is undefined. The logic can be kept entirely classical if it is stipulated that it applies to valued utterances only. This, it seems, is the simplest and most straightforward interpretation in terms of propositional calculus of Strawson's notion of presupposition. All that has been given up is one half of PET, i.e. the condition that all elements constituting a language L (sentences, propositions, utterances) are always valued. Other than that, the logic is not, or need not be, affected.

The expression "*A* presupposes *B*", or "$A \gg B$", is now accounted for in the following way. $A \gg B$ just in case $A \models B$ and $\neg A \models B$. Whereas in a fully valued bivalent language this would mean that *B* is a logically necessary truth, in Strawson's system it means that if B fails to be true, A as well as $\neg$A are undefined. This is clearly demonstrated by table 2, where L = $\{A, B, C\}$ plus their logical compositions, some of which are listed. V is the set of admissible valuations $\{1, \ldots, 27\}$. Each valuation is a partial world description in which each atomic utterance of L is either assigned a truth-value, or left undefined. The logically complex utterances are valued in accordance with table 1. If *A*, *B*, and *C* are logically independent, there are the 27 possible valuations shown in table 2. If, however, there are entailment relations among *A*, *B*, or *C*, then some valuations become inadmissible. Thus, if, e.g., $A \models B$, then the valuations 4, 7, 13, 16, 22 and 25 are inadmissible. And if $\neg A \models B$, the valuations 5, 8, 14, 17, 23 and 26 are inadmissible. Consequently, if $A \gg B$, the sum of these two sets is inadmissible. In the remaining, admissible, valuations, whenever v(B) = U or v(B) = $-$, v(A) = U and v($\neg$A) = U.

One important question remains unanswered in this account of presupposition. The entailment relations, in terms of which presupposition is defined, are not part of the logical calculus. They are, therefore, not logical entailments, and the question arises in what way they can be computed or derived. As regards the truth-functional calculus, they are similar to what we have called semantic entailments, which can be attached to atomic utterances and are derived from the lexical satisfaction conditions of the predicates involved. Below, the position will be defended that presuppositions are indeed derived that way, whereby a separate set of lexical conditions is distinguished, the preconditions, which generate the presuppositions. In Strawson's account, however, the question of the 'origin' of presuppositions is not satisfactorily answered, and the same holds for practically the whole subsequent literature on presuppositions (with the exception of Katz and Langendoen 1976). The usual answer given is entirely *ad hoc*, and non-structural: one speaks of "presupposition inducers", and the definite article is considered to be an inducer

Table 2

V:	1	2	3	4	5	6	7	8	9	10	11	12	13	14	15	16	17	18	19	20	21	22	23	24	25	26	27
A	+	|	⊃	+	|	⊃	+	|	⊃	+	|	⊃	+	|	⊃	+	|	⊃	+	|	⊃	+	|	⊃	+	|	⊃
B	+	+	+	|	|	|	⊃	⊃	⊃	+	+	+	|	|	|	⊃	⊃	⊃	+	+	+	|	|	|	⊃	⊃	⊃
C	+	+	+	+	+	+	+	+	+	|	|	|	|	|	|	|	|	|	⊃	⊃	⊃	⊃	⊃	⊃	⊃	⊃	⊃
$\neg A$	|	+	⊃	|	+	⊃	|	+	⊃	|	+	⊃	|	+	⊃	|	+	⊃	|	+	⊃	|	+	⊃	|	+	⊃
$\neg B$	|	|	|	+	+	+	⊃	⊃	⊃	|	|	|	+	+	+	⊃	⊃	⊃	|	|	|	+	+	+	⊃	⊃	⊃
$\neg C$	|	|	|	|	|	|	|	|	|	+	+	+	+	+	+	+	+	+	⊃	⊃	⊃	⊃	⊃	⊃	⊃	⊃	⊃
$A \wedge B$	+	|	⊃	|	|	⊃	⊃	⊃	⊃	+	|	⊃	|	|	⊃	⊃	⊃	⊃	+	|	⊃	|	|	⊃	⊃	⊃	⊃
$A \wedge C$	+	|	⊃	+	|	⊃	+	|	⊃	|	|	⊃	|	|	⊃	|	|	⊃	⊃	⊃	⊃	⊃	⊃	⊃	⊃	⊃	⊃
$A \vee B$	+	+	⊃	+	|	⊃	⊃	⊃	⊃	+	+	⊃	+	|	⊃	⊃	⊃	⊃	+	+	⊃	+	|	⊃	⊃	⊃	⊃
$A \vee C$	+	+	⊃	+	+	⊃	+	+	⊃	+	|	⊃	+	|	⊃	+	|	⊃	⊃	⊃	⊃	⊃	⊃	⊃	⊃	⊃	⊃

of existential presuppositions. It should be noted that, as regards the definite article, this answer, besides being *ad hoc* and non-structural, is also factually incorrect, since there are verbs that are non-extensional with regard to some term. If there is a definite description in the position of that term, no exist-ence is entailed or presupposed. Take, e.g., the sentence (utterance):

(6) Edmund is looking for the catch in the contract.

This utterance may well be true even if there is no catch in the contract; there may even be no contract at all. What is required for the truth (or falsity) of the utterance is that it is contextually known what contract and what possible catch the utterance is about. Or, in our terms, the definite description *the catch in the contract* must denote, but it need not refer, for the utterance to have a truth-value. We now know that this is due to the lexical fact that the verb *look for* is non-extensional with respect to its object term, and the theory of discourse semantics provides a straightforward solution to pheno-mena of non-extensionality (intensionality). But it is anyhow clear that it is factually incorrect to say that the definite article is an inducer of existential presuppositions.

3.2.2 Supervaluations

Although, as we have seen, it is not difficult to interpret Strawson's notion of presupposition in a fairly straightforward way that minimally deviates from established classical logic, the logician Van Fraassen (1966; 1968; 1969; 1971) devised an interpretation which deviates dramatically from classical logic, although its primary purpose was the safeguarding of classical logic. This system, which has been acclaimed as extremely elegant (a judgement which the present author finds hard to understand), starts from a classical logical language L which is fully valued and has two truth-values, i.e. a PET-language. Supervaluations are then generated in the following manner. Take an arbitrary finite set of classical valuations C. If, for a given sentence p, $v(p) = +$ in all $v \in C$, then in the supervaluation to be constructed, the supervaluation value of p, $s(p)$, is also $+$: $s(p) = +$. Likewise, if for all $v \in C$, $v(p) = -$, then $s(p) = -$. But if p has no uniform value across the $v \in C$, then $s(p) = U$ ('undefined'). We thus associate with each supervaluation s a set of sentences X such that for each $p \in X$, $s(p) = +$ or $s(p) = -$. For all remaining sentences q in L, $s(q) = U$. It follows that each classical valuation is a supervaluation with the special property that the associated set X of sentences whose utter-ances are classically valued equals L.

Consider again a language L with the atomic sentences A, B, C. L is classi-cal, i.e. fully valued and bivalent. L has the usual syntax and truth-definitions for the truth-functional operators. Let v_1–v_8 in table 3 be the classical valua-tions in the classical valuation space V, and s_1–s_{10} be supervaluations in the

Table 3

V:	v1	v2	v3	v4	v5	v6	v7	v8	SV:	s1	s2	s3	s4	s5	s6	s7	s8	s9	s10
A	+	−	+	−	+	−	+	−		+	⊃	⊃	−	⊃	⊃	+	+	⊃	⊃
B	+	+	−	−	+	+	−	−		⊃	+	⊃	⊃	−	⊃	+	⊃	⊃	⊃
C	+	+	+	+	−	−	−	−		⊃	⊃	+	⊃	⊃	−	⊃	+	⊃	⊃
$\neg A$	−	+	−	+	−	+	−	+		−	⊃	⊃	+	⊃	⊃	−	−	⊃	⊃
$\neg B$	−	−	+	+	−	−	+	+		⊃	−	⊃	⊃	+	⊃	−	⊃	⊃	⊃
$\neg C$	−	−	−	−	+	+	+	+		⊃	⊃	−	⊃	⊃	+	⊃	−	⊃	⊃
$A \wedge B$	+	−	−	−	+	−	−	−		⊃	⊃	⊃	−	−	⊃	+	⊃	⊃	⊃
$A \wedge C$	+	−	+	−	−	−	−	−		⊃	⊃	⊃	−	⊃	−	⊃	+	⊃	⊃
$A \vee B$	+	+	+	−	+	+	+	−		+	+	⊃	⊃	⊃	⊃	+	+	+	⊃
$A \vee C$	+	+	+	+	+	−	+	−		+	⊃	+	⊃	⊃	⊃	+	+	⊃	+

supervaluation space **SV**, where s_1-s_{10} are associated with sets of classical valuations in the following way:

$$C(s_1) = \{v_1, v_3, v_5, v_7\} \qquad C(s_6) = \{v_5, v_6, v_7, v_8\}$$
$$C(s_2) = \{v_1, v_2, v_5, v_6\} \qquad C(s_7) = \{v_1, v_5\}$$
$$C(s_3) = \{v_1, v_2, v_3, v_4\} \qquad C(s_8) = \{v_1, v_3\}$$
$$C(s_4) = \{v_2, v_4, v_6, v_8\} \qquad C(s_9) = \{v_1, v_2, v_3, v_5, v_6, v_7\}$$
$$C(s_5) = \{v_3, v_4, v_7, v_8\} \qquad C(s_{10}) = \{v_1, v_2, v_3, v_4, v_5, v_7\}$$

It is easily shown that all classical entailments are saved in SV. In the classical calculus the entailment schema $A \models B$ can be defined in terms of valuations as follows: $A \models B$ iff for all valuations v where $v(A) = +$, $v(B) = +$. Let $T(p)$, for any sentence $p \in L$, be the set of valuations v where $v(p) = +$, then, if some supervaluation s_n gives truth for p, $C(s_n) \subseteq T(p)$. If $A \models B$, then, if for some s_n, $s_n(A) = +$, $C(s_n) \subseteq T(A) \subseteq T(B)$.

However, the truth-functional operators do not remain entirely truth-functional. Although truth-functionality is preserved in nearly all cases, conjunction and disjunction fail to be truth-functional for the values $\langle U, U \rangle$. In Van Fraassen's supervaluation system, the following truth-tables hold for negation, conjunction and disjunction:

Table 4

¬A	A	∧ B			∨ B		
		+	−	U	+	−	U
−	+	+	−	U	+	+	+
+	−	−	−	−	+	−	U
U	U	U	−	−/U	+	U	+/U

The lack of truth-functionality is apparent in the $\langle U, U \rangle$ combinations for conjunction and disjunction. As an example, note that A ∨ B in s_9 is valued as 'true', but in s_{10} as 'undefined', although in both cases both input values are 'U'. As for conjunction, no example occurs in table 3 of $\langle U, U \rangle$ yielding falsity. But if, say, s_{11} is added, with the associated set of classical valuations $C = \{v_3, v_4, v_5, v_6\}$, then $s_{11}(B) = U$ and $s_{11}(C) = U$, but $s_{11}(B \wedge C) = -$.

Note that table 4 is no longer bivalent, but trivalent (three-valued), since the value 'U' no longer automatically yields 'U' for the resulting utterance, as was the case in table 1. Here, 'U' plays its own role in the truth-value assignments, so that whatever function there is is no longer defined simply over '+' and '−'. The logic that comes with Van Fraassen's supervaluations is thus neither truth-functional nor bivalent, but a supervaluational language is fully valued.

For any system $\langle L, V \rangle$, where L is a classical language and V a classical valuation space, there is a system $\langle L, SV \rangle$, where SV is the set of all possible supervaluations for $\langle L, V \rangle$. We can now make a system $\langle L, SV \rangle$ reflect presupposition by restricting the admissible supervaluations in the following way. It is easily seen that for any set X of atomic sentences in L there is a set of supervaluations $S(X)$ such that for every $s \in S(X)$, and for every $p \in X$, $s(p) = +$ or $s(p) = -$, and for every $q \in L$ such that $q \notin X$, $s(q) = U$. $S(X)$ is generated by X in that each $s \in S(X)$ selects precisely those classical valuations for its associated set C where all utterances $p \in X$ have a uniform value. To give an example: if $X = \{A, B\}$ of language L in table 3, $S(X)$ is generated as follows:

$$
\begin{aligned}
C(s_1) &= \{v_1, v_5\} \quad - \quad s_1(A) = + \quad s_1(B) = + \quad s_1(C) = U \\
C(s_2) &= \{v_3, v_7\} \quad - \quad s_2(A) = + \quad s_2(B) = - \quad s_2(C) = U \\
C(s_3) &= \{v_2, v_6\} \quad - \quad s_3(A) = - \quad s_3(B) = + \quad s_3(C) = U \\
C(s_4) &= \{v_4, v_8\} \quad - \quad s_4(A) = - \quad s_4(B) = - \quad s_4(C) = U
\end{aligned}
$$

(Note that the cardinality of $S(X)$ is 2^n, where n is the number of sentences in X.) We now stipulate that for any set X of atomic sentences in L, if any $p \in X$ presupposes an atomic sentence q, then $q \in X$ and for all $s \in S(X)$, $s(q) = +$. Note that this does not *define* presupposition: the notion of presupposition is only *presupposed*. It does, however, ensure that all presuppositions of all sentences of X are in X and that their utterances are invariably valued '+' in $S(X)$.

Supervaluations complicate the notions of truth and falsity. Whereas in a classical valuation truth or falsity is predicted for those classes of states of affairs where the utterances of all sentences of L are true or false, as the case may be, in a supervaluation truth or falsity is predicated only for those classes of states of affairs where the classically valued utterances of the supervaluation in question (i.e. the utterances in its associated set of sentences X) are true or false. The difference is that for a classically valued language all utterances of all sentences always have a truth-value (true or false), whereas for a supervaluational language there are states of affairs where certain utterances of sentences of L are not valued (or not valued classically). In a supervaluational system truth and falsity are thus functions over classes of states of affairs and subsets of L, but in a classical system truth and falsity are functions over all states of affairs and all of L. It would seem that the supervaluational notion of truth and falsity is more realistic for natural language than the classical notion. But the question arises what role the classical valuations have to play. Looking again at table 3, let us imagine a state of affairs SA for which, say, v_1 holds. Utterance A is thus true in SA, as are B and C. But SA is also part of the class of states of affairs with respect to which truth and falsity are defined in, say, s_2. But in s_2 both A and C are valued 'U'. Does this mean that we are operating with two different notions of truth and falsity, so that in the same state of affairs an utterance is, say, true under one definition but undefined under the other? Or is it only the supervaluations that reflect truth and falsity? If the latter, the function of the classical valuations remains unclear.

One wonders, in fact, why the complex machinery of supervaluations should be activated if the same result, but with fully truth-functional conjunction and disjunction, and a strictly bivalent logic, can be achieved in the Strawsonian way, as demonstrated above. After all, it is merely the presence of a non-excluded third, be it a third value as with supervaluations, or the lack of a value as with Strawson, that creates the structural room for the Strawsonian notion of presupposition. That is, given a non-excluded *tertium*, it is possible for a sentence A to entail B while *not-A* also entails B, without B being a logically necessary truth. Both Strawson and Van Fraassen are free to restrict the set of admissible valuations (or supervaluations) in such a way that if an atomic sentence A presupposes B, non-truth of B always goes with the non-excluded third for A. This ensures automatically that a classical value for A always goes with truth for B. The Strawson system then has the advantages that it is considerably simpler, that it does not complicate the notions of truth and falsity, that it is bivalent, and that it is strictly truth-functional for the classical truth-functional operators. Since there is no independent evidence that natural languages fit supervaluational systems better than more classical systems, there seems to be no reason why a supervaluational logic or semantics should be adopted.

3.2.3 The entailment analysis

Our overall conclusion with regard to the Frege–Strawson notion of presupposition must be that logically speaking there is nothing amiss with it. The question remains, however, if it captures linguistic reality.

In one respect it badly fails to do so, and it will become clear that this is an inherent defect of all purely logical notions of presupposition. The problem is that a logically necessary truth is presupposed by any sentence. For no matter whether an utterance is valued 'true' or 'false', utterances of logically necessary sentences are always valued 'true'. If we let the language have an expression for the value 'undefined', then, for example, "A is either true or false or undefined" is necessarily true for any utterance of A, and it would be presupposed by any sentence of L. But it is, of course, absurd, from a linguistic descriptive point of view, to say that the sentence just given is presupposed by every sentence of English. We shall come back to this in section 3.3.

Another respect in which any logical notion of presupposition will fail to do justice to linguistic reality is shown up by the fact that presuppositions have been observed as properties not only of assertive sentences, which can have entailments, but also of other kinds of speech act, such as questions, commands, etc. But questions or commands have no entailments. Hence, if presupposition is explicated in terms of entailments there is no way of accounting for presuppositions of other sentence types. This point, too, will be discussed in section 3.3 below.

Within the limits, however, of a purely logical approach to presupposition it must be observed that the Frege-Strawson notion is observationally inadequate in one central respect. As was observed by Wilson (1975) and Boër and Lycan (1976), it is simply not true that presupposition failure results in a truth-value gap, or that a negated presupposition-carrying sentence still entails the presupposition. These authors maintain, with some justification, that presuppositions are nothing but (ordinary) entailments of the carrier sentences. They disappear under negation, and, generally, in all embeddings that generally cancel entailments; they are maintained in precisely those environments where entailments are preserved. What is special about the category of entailments we wish to call "presuppositions" is nothing to do with logical properties, but is of a pragmatic nature, and has to do with (Gricean) principles of co-operative behaviour. The authors who defend this *entailment analysis* of presupposition feel that natural language semantics should do without any notion of presupposition. If such a notion is to be used at all, it should be relegated to pragmatics. Both Wilson (1975) and Gazdar (1979) make attempts at setting up a formal framework for the pragmatics envisaged (contrary to virtually all other authors in pragmatics, who resort to suggestive statements and rhetoric rather than to rigorous analysis and description). We shall refrain from a critical discussion of Wilson's and Gazdar's formal approaches to pragmatics, first because this book is not about pragmatics, and secondly because their pragmatic accounts of presupposition are superfluous if the semantic theory of presupposition developed here is correct.

The defenders of the entailment analysis observe that the famous Russell sentence

(3) c. The present king of France is not bald.

does not entail the existence of the king of France, since it is possible to say without contradiction:

(3) e. The present king of France is NOT bald: there IS no king of France!

Admittedly, the negation needs to be heavily accented, and an explanation is called for and given of why the negation is heavily stressed. Yet it remains a fact that (3d) is not contradictory. Therefore, if it is maintained that

(3) d. There exists a king of France.

is a presupposition of

(3) a. The present king of France is bald.

we must conclude that presupposition failure, i.e. falsity of (3d), does not lead to a truth-value gap but to the falsity of (3a) and the truth of (3c). There is thus no reason to treat (alleged) presuppositions differently from the well-known entailments.

Due to the appearance of linguists on the presuppositional scene after the hue and cry raised in philosophy around the notion of presupposition, this notion had been widened to embrace also factive presuppositions (Kiparsky and Kiparsky (1971)),[1] and even purely lexical presuppositions (Fillmore 1971).[2] The factive presuppositions, in particular, have always counted, since Kiparsky and Kiparsky (1971), as prime examples of presupposition. It is thus not surprising that examples of factive presuppositions, besides examples of existential presuppositions, abound in the writings of the entailment analysts. These examples run exactly parallel to the existential ones:

(7) Hilary does NOT realize that he has lost: he HASN'T lost!

Again, (7) is not a contradiction. Hence, if one wishes to maintain that its first half (*Hilary does not realize that he has lost*) presupposes that Hilary has lost, one must abandon the claim that presuppositions are entailed by their carrier sentence.

Although no serious attempts were made by the entailment analysts to account for the fact that presuppositions are entailed by non-negated carrier sentences (apart from *ad hoc* invocations of "presupposition inducers"), the debunking of the notion of presupposition was now generally felt to be final and complete. From now on dominant trends in formal semantics felt secure in their total neglect of presupposition.

3.2.4 The three-valued analysis

The entailment analysis carried the day against the Frege–Strawson logical notion of presupposition on account of improved observations. Strawson

---

[1] For those who are unfamiliar with the notion of factive presupposition: a factive presupposition comes with certain complement-taking predicates, such as *realize*, *know*, *regret*, *scandalous*, *regrettable*, *wonderful*, etc. These have the property that a sentence figuring them has the presupposition that what is expressed in the complement (*that-*) clause is in fact true:

John has forgotten that today is my birthday.

presupposes the truth of *Today is my birthday* (and entails it), due to the fact that *have forgotten* is a factive predicate. Since the famous article by Kiparsky and Kiparsky (1971), called 'Fact', factive presuppositions have been prominent in the literature – although the primary purpose of the Kiparskys' article was not semantic but syntactic: they wanted to show that factive predicates are a separate *grammatical* category.

[2] The term "purely lexical presuppositions" is used informally here to refer to presuppositions that are associated, in the literature, with specific lexical items, such as *criticize* versus *accuse* (Fillmore 1971), or *only* and *even* (Horn 1969). It will be argued below that *all* presuppositions originate from the semantic properties of specific lexical items.

himself, in fact, had doubts about the truth-value gap in cases of presupposition failure. He admitted (1954) that we are inclined to speak of falsity, and not of a truth-value gap, when some bragger says:

(8) a. The king of France asked me for a ride.

(And in (Strawson 1964) he is prepared to admit that his account of presupposition may not be valid for all cases, but he refrains from attempting to characterize the class of cases where his account does apply.) Or take the case of a mother who is putting her young child to bed and tells the child a bedtime story. Unfortunately, the story is about the Abominable Snowman, and the child, instead of going to sleep, starts to cry and refuses to sleep because it is frightened. Now the mother understands her mistake, and in order to put things right she says:

(8) b. The Abominable Snowman WON'T come tonight: he doesn't exist!

If the Frege-Strawson account of presupposition were correct, the first half of (8b) would lack a truth-value on account of the truth of the second half, and the mother would forever be unable to soothe the child. Or, to take another example, often quoted in the literature, a sentence like

(9) God does not exist.

could be contradictory on the Frege-Strawson account since *God* is a definite term and would thus give rise to an existential presupposition. (Theologians would have too easy a go if the existence of God would thus prove to be analytically true!)

We must, therefore, grant the entailment analysis its point. Yet, although the entailment analysis sprang from improved observations compared with the Frege-Strawson analysis, this does not mean that the last word has been said. On the contrary, as we step up the level of observation the entailment analysis perishes and the Frege-Strawson analysis is returned to its previous position, though with a strengthened logical apparatus. The point is that the entailment analysts overlooked large classes of cases where the negation of a presupposition does indeed bring about a contradiction with the negated carrier sentence. The Frege-Strawson analysis thus applies in full force to these cases, even though it does not apply to the cases produced by Frege and Strawson themselves. Moreover, there are also cases where a negated presupposition combines quite easily with the negated carrier sentence, without there being even any suggestion that the presupposition obtains. One must, therefore, conclude that the picture is much more complex than has been thought. Language, again, turns out to harbour unexpected snags.

Some negations are *per se* presupposition-preserving. Without aiming at completeness we can mention the following classes of cases.

A *Morphologically incorporated negations*

Many lexical items contain a morphologically incorporated negation, expressed through a bound morpheme, usually a prefix: *un-*, *in-*, *a-*, *dis-*, etc., as in *uncooperative, indirect, asymmetrical, discontinuous*. These negations tend to preserve presuppositional entailments:

(10) a.   Harry is co-operative $\}$ $\models$ Harry exists
  b.   Harry is uncooperative
  c.   !Harry is UNcooperative: he doesn't exist!
  d. √Harry is NOT co-operative: he doesn't exist!

(The exclamation mark is used to indicate contradiction; the check sign stands for logical compatibility.)

The only exception found so far to this rule is the morphological incorporation of the negation into an existential quantifier: *nobody, never*. It does seem to be possible to say without contradiction, e.g.:

(11) a. √NOBODY realizes that the director is guilty: the director ISN'T guilty!
  b. √John has NEVER stopped drinking: he has never been a drinker at all!

(In (11b) the verb *stop* V-*ing* generates the presupposition that the subject was in the habit of V-ing.)

B *Negations in non-canonical positions*

By "canonical position" is meant, for English, the position occupied by the negation when it is in construction with the finite verb form. Negations often occur, however, in other positions, as when they are constructed with a quantifier in sentence-initial position. Negations in non-canonical positions always preserve the presuppositions of the negated clause:

(12) a.   All the doors were shut $\}$ $\models$ there were doors
  b.   Not all the doors were shut
  c.   !NOT all the doors were shut: there WERE no doors!
  d. √Tim did NOT shut all the doors: there WERE no doors!

C *Non-extraposed factive subject clauses*

This category of factive clauses was never taken into account by the entailment analysts. It thus escaped their notice that negation over the factive main verb does not affect presuppositions:

(13) a.   That Bill was guilty surprised her $\}$ $\models$ Bill was guilty
  b.   That Bill was guilty did not surprise her
  c.   !That Bill was guilty did NOT surprise her: he WASN'T guilty!
  d. √It did NOT surprise her that Bill was guilty: he WASN'T guilty!

(Note that (13c) is not contradictory with contrastive accent on the subject clause and parenthesis intonation on *he wasn't guilty*. It is, however, clearly contradictory with accents on *not* and *wasn't*, as in (13c).)

D *Cleft and pseudocleft constructions*
These preserve presuppositions under negation (but see section 3.5.1):

(14) a. What he said was "aargh!"
     b. What he said was not "aargh!" } $\models$ he said something
     c. !What he said was NOT "aargh!": he didn't say anything at all!
     d. √It is not true that what he said was "aargh!": he didn't say anything at all!

E *Contrastive accents*
(15) a, The WAITER started the argument
     b. The WAITER didn't start the argument
         (the customer did) } $\models$ somebody started the argument
     c. !The WAITER did NOT start the argument: NOBODY did!
     d. √It is not true that the WAITER started the argument: nobody did!

F *Negations in non-assertive clauses*
It seems that the use of negation whereby presuppositions are cancelled is limited to clauses that express a speech act of assertion. Typically, clauses that are subject or object to a predicate cannot express an assertive speech act. Consequently, the negation in such clauses always preserves presuppositions:

(16) a. √Harry has NOT been to his sister's funeral: he never HAD a sister!
     b. !Harry seems NOT to have been to his sister's funeral: he never HAD a sister!

Likewise, negations in that-clauses or under a quantifier preserve presuppositions:[3]

---

[3] It is in keeping with F that negations in questions, commands or other types of speech acts also preserve presuppositions:

  (i) !Don't stop eating now: you never started!
  (ii) !Did he NOT find his brother? He never had one!

It will be discussed in section 3.3, below, what it means for a non-assertive speech act to have a presupposition.

  Note that it would be incorrect to say generally that presupposition-cancelling *not* never allows for higher operators or for embeddings:

  (iii) In Ed's world of fancy, John's child is NOT asleep, because Ed thinks that John has no children.
  (iv) If indeed John's child is NOT asleep because he has no children, all is well.
  (v) If John has no children, then indeed his child is NOT asleep.

But in these cases one has to do with reports of what someone believes or has said.

(17) a. √John's child is NOT asleep: he HAS no children!
    b. √Mrs Whitehouse's gardener is NOT unreliable: she HAS no gardener!
    c. !Everyone of John's children is NOT asleep: he HAS no children!
    d. !Ed hopes Mrs Whitehouse's gardener is NOT unreliable: she HAS no gardener!

G *Negations with Negative Polarity Items*

Negative Polarity Items (NPIs) are lexical items, constructions or idioms that require a negation (or sometimes only a negative adverb, such as *hardly* or *only*, or a negative adjective such as *difficult*) in simple declarative sentences on pain of ungrammaticality. Any natural language has NPIs in large numbers. Subclasses of NPIs occur without (overt) negation in *if*-clauses, questions, after comparatives and superlatives, in complements of predicates containing an incorporated negation (*deny*, *refuse*, etc.), in relative clauses under some universal quantifiers (*every student who has done any work at all*, but **each student who has done any work at all*), and in quite a few more constructions.[4] English NPIs include:

can possibly	*budge*	*it's (no) use V-ing*
can help	*in the least*	*any – WH-soever*
can seem to	punctual *until*	*ever*
matter that	*the slightest*	*need/dare* + bare infinitive
mind that	*bat an eyelid*	*so – adjective – as*
give a damn that	*lift a finger*	*any more*
in weeks	*would hurt a fly*	*as much as* + VP
at all	*all that* + adj.	*half* + gradable adjective

Some NPIs, such as *mind that, matter that, give a damn that*, allow emphatic or contrastive accent to replace the negation. Some of these are, moreover, factive and thus presuppose the truth of their embedded *that*-clause. These provide clear examples of presupposition-preserving negations:

(18) a. Joe DOES mind that his boss is an alcoholic } ⊨ Joe's boss is an
    b. Joe doesn't mind that his boss is an alcoholic }   alcoholic
    c. !Joe does NOT mind that his boss is an alcoholic: the man ISN'T an alcoholic!

In all these cases and probably quite a few more (a systematic search will no doubt reveal many more cases than those listed above) negations preserve the presuppositions of the non-negated sentences in full force. Clearly, this makes the position defended by the entailment analysts untenable. There is obviously

---

[4] No systematic survey is available as yet of the precise behaviour of English NPIs in various constructions. For Dutch, see Hoppenbrouwers (1983).

more going on than meets the shortsighted eye. Consider, in contrast to the NPIs, the class of Positive Polarity Items (PPIs). These do not, as one might expect, refuse to stand in the scope of negation. They do admit of a higher negation, but when there is one, the so-called 'echo-effect' is produced, i.e. there is the feeling that the non-negated sentence has been uttered just before, and the negation is felt to have the function of indicating that there is something radically amiss with that sentence as a whole. From the point of view of strict observation, therefore, PPIs are not symmetrically opposed to NPIs. Whereas the latter require negation (in simple assertive sentences) on pain of ungrammaticality, the former do not reject negation on pain of ungrammaticality. (We shall see below that in our analysis there *is* a symmetrical opposition between NPIs and PPIs.) PPIs are extremely numerous in any language. In English the class of PPIs includes:

relatively	*staunch*	*even*	*swarm with*
reasonably	*confirmed (bachelor)*	*each*	*bristle with*
rather $\Big\} +$ adj.	*as fit as a fiddle*	*both*	*teem with*
pretty	*at most*	*most*	*forever + be*
far from	*at least*	*few*	*the whole bloody lot*
hardly	*perhaps*	*still*	*yet have to*
splendid	*certainly*	*some*	*already*
decent	*surely*	*not*	*always +* progressive
(metaphorical)	*awful*	*several*	*be delighted that*
terrific			

The striking feature of PPIs, in this context, is that when they are placed under negation the presuppositions are entirely cancelled: not even a suggestion or a hint of the old presupposition remains. Under PPIs, therefore, presuppositions behave as if they were ordinary entailments. Consider, for example, the contrast between the following two pairs of sentences:

(19) a. !Harold doesn't live in Paris any more: he has never set foot in France!

b. √Harold does NOT still live in Paris: he has never set foot in France!

Both *any more* (as an NPI) and *still* (as a PPI) induce the presupposition that what is expressed in the clause that forms their scope used to be the case. Their assertive properties are opposed in that *any more* (with *not*) induces the assertion that what is expressed in the clause that forms its scope does not obtain at the time expressed by the tense of the main verb, whereas *still* induces the assertion that what is expressed in that clause (still) obtains at the relevant time. Now note that in the negative sentence (19a) that presupposition cannot be cancelled, while in the negated sentence (19b) the cancelling of the presupposition is a matter of course. We conclude, therefore, that the negation in (19a) is presupposition-preserving while the negation in (19b) is presupposition-cancelling.

Notice, in particular, the difference between those factive verbs that are NPIs, such as *matter that, mind that, give a damn that, interest that*, etc., and those factive verbs that are PPIs, such *be delighted that, be overjoyed that*, etc. The former, as we saw in example (18), lead to stark contradiction when the factive presupposition is denied together with the negative carrier. But the latter show little more than the usual echo that goes with negated PPIs. There clearly is no contradiction:

(20) √She was NOT delighted that Jim had been saved: Jim had NOT been saved!

Or take the pair of sentences:

(21) a. Few people did not recognize the teacher's good intentions.
    b. The teacher's good intentions were not recognized by few people.

Although (21b) looks nothing but the passive of (21a), our intuitive understanding of these sentences quite clearly tells us that *not* in (21a) is presupposition-preserving, while *not* in (21b) is presupposition-cancelling. Logically, these sentences are different, in that (21b) is compatible with "the teacher's intentions were not at all good", whereas (21a) is not. This difference is not accounted for simply by the scope differences resulting from the different left-to-right orderings of the scope-bearing operators in the two sentences. It is accounted for, however, by the systematic rule that a negation under a quantifier preserves presupposition (see F above), so that the *not* in (21a) is presupposition-preserving, and that a negation over a PPI (note that *few* is a PPI) cancels presupposition, so that the *not* in (21b) is presupposition-cancelling.

The minimal conclusion from all this is that there are at least two ways of using the negative operator in language: a presupposition-preserving way and a presupposition-cancelling way. The question now is: what is the optimal formal account of this difference: two truth-functionally distinct negation operators, two possible structural positions of the same negative operator, or some third alternative? We shall now argue for the first option, mainly on grounds of simplicity and because no reasonable alternative has been presented so far. In any case, no matter what solution is preferred or proposed, it now seems no longer reasonable to support any notion of presupposition whereby Gricean principles of 'co-operative behaviour' are put forward as the causal factors underlying what we recognize as being typically presuppositional in some entailments (as in Kempson 1975). If such principles are to give the answer, it remains entirely opaque why in the cases discussed under B to G above presuppositions should necessarily be retained under negation, while they vanish under negation when the sentence contains a PPI. Why, for example, should (18c) be contradictory but should (20) be consistent, if Gricean pragmatics is to give the answer? We are clearly in the territory of entailments, not of 'co-operative behaviour' rules. (This does not mean that presupposition is primarily a logical notion. As will be shown below, the notion of presupposition cannot be captured adequately by any logic. All that logic can do is describe the logical properties of presupposition, not define it. Presupposition is a semantic phenomenon, directly related to discourse factors. For the moment, however, we shall limit ourselves to the logical properties of presupposition.)

Let us now review some proposals to the effect that natural language has only one negative operator, closely corresponding to the bivalent operator in classical propositional calculus, but that this operator can occur in structurally different positions, some of which are such that what we see as presuppositions disappear. The commonest view, in this respect, is still that the Russell analysis of definite descriptions does the job. We have already had occasion to reject this analysis (section 3.2.1, examples (4) and (5)). Now we can add the objection that Russell's analysis, if it were tenable, would account only for existential presuppositions, and not for factive and other (lexical) types of presupposition.

An improvement on Russell's analysis would consist in analysing presupposition-carrying sentences always as a conjunction, the first conjunct expressing the presupposition, the second the more strictly assertive contents of the sentence. The negation can then be positioned over the whole conjunction, or over just the second conjunct. Thus (22a) would read as either (22b) or (22c):

(22) a. It did not surprise her that Bill was guilty.
  b. Bill was guilty and ⌐ (that surprised her)
  c. ⌐ (Bill was guilty and that surprised her)

This seems an improvement, since the analysis would now appear not to be limited to just existential presuppositions but to include other classes of presupposition (such as factive presupposition) as well. But this is not so, for the original existential presuppositions resist this treatment because of failure of variable binding. Take again the old example:

(3) a. The present king of France is bald.

This would now have to be analysed as a conjunction of the presupposition and the carrier sentence (without the presupposition). This, however, is not possible unless free variables are allowed:

(3) f. $\exists x(\text{Now}(\text{KoF}(x)) \land \forall y(\text{Now}(\text{KoF}(y)) \supset x = y)) \land \text{Bald}(x)$

But free variables are really the same as anaphoric definite pronouns, in this case *he*. However, the sentence *He is bald* has again the presupposition that the *he* exists. Hence, in an analysis of the type (3f) there is an infinite regress of presupposition renderings. And if we make sure that the variables are all properly bound, we pay the price that the account of presupposition is not uniform.

Then, the same problem that was spotted with the Russell analysis turns up again here: why should it be that the negation is restricted to just the two positions mentioned, i.e. over the whole negation or over the second conjunct. Why not over just the first conjunct?

Moreover, what on earth could be the grammatical justification for the analysis of (22a) as either (22b) or (22c), or of (3a) as, say (3f)? It would seem that such analyses violate just about every constraint on grammatical derivations or analyses that exists. They furthermore violate the general methodological principle that analyses must capture regularities. Even Russell, who was very little of a grammarian, recognized this principle when he discussed the two phrases *the king of England* and *the king of France*, and observed that *the king of France is bald* "by parity of form ... ought to be about the denotation of the phrase 'the King of France'" (1905: 483). Thus, the conjunction analysis requires that the internal negation should be presupposition-preserving, and the external negation should be presupposition-cancelling. But if this is so, how can it be that in, e.g., (12b) the negation is presupposition-preserving and yet occurs in the most external position possible in the English sentence?

Finally, the conjunction analysis stumbles again over the examples (5a) and (5b), used above against Russell. That is, it fails to explain why (5a) is contradictory but (5b) is not, since (5a) and (5b) would amount to the same.

We must conclude that the conjunction analysis of presupposition will not do either, even though it has elements in common with the presupposition analysis proposed here. (The position will be defended below that presuppositions must be represented in previous discourse for a sentence carrying that presupposition to be interpretable and thus to have a truth-value. But the conjunctive juxtaposition resulting from a discourse that has the presupposition and then the carrier sentence represented in it does not count as the analysis of the carrier sentence. On the contrary, the carrier is not separated from its presupposition at all; it only requires that the presupposition be represented in previous discourse.)

Another proposal often heard to account for the difference between presupposition-preserving and presupposition-cancelling negation amounts to a distinction between sentence negation and verb-phrase negation, where the former does not preserve presuppositions but the latter does. The two forms of negation are logically identical, but they are used in different positions. The sentence negation is a general logical operator taking whole propositions or propositional functions as its scope. The verb-phrase negation does the same but in lambda-formulae, where it operates on the propositional function forming the lambda-predicate. Here again, however, there are serious obstacles of a grammatical nature, i.e. violations of the principle of "parity of form" as formulated by Russell. Thus, if *not* in (12b) is verb-phrase negation, since it is presupposition-preserving, how can it be in construction with *all* as part of the subject at the beginning of the sentence?

Gabbay and Moravcsik (1978) contains a more sophisticated proposal. A distinction is made between sentence negation, which is presupposition-cancelling, and constituent negation or "denial", which would have to be seen as presupposition-preserving. For example,

(23) N_{John} (John eats fish)

should be read with "denial" on the constituent *John*: "it is not John who eats fish". Truth is brought about for (23) if there is an element other than John, to be taken from a pre-defined complement class, eating fish. Ordinary (bivalent) sentence negation, on the other hand, would be the classical formula where "John eats fish" is placed under the sentential negation operator.

While a proposal of this nature might bring some relief for cases such as (10b), (12b), and perhaps, under some suitable analysis, for (14b), it fails to account for (13b), as well as for all cases resulting from the presence of an NPI. Moreover, if the concept of "constituent negation" is viable at all, constituents with built-in negation, as exemplified in A above, will be prime cases. Yet there often are morphologically incorporated negations which do not "deny" the constituent they form a structural part of. For example:

(24) Nobody left because the play was boring. (Those who left did so because they had a train to catch.)

The constituent which is semantically "denied", in Gabbay and Moravcsik's sense, is the subordinate clause *because the play was boring*, as appears from the paraphrase "it is not because the play was boring that some people left". Yet the negation is incorporated in the word *nobody*, and would thus be expected to "deny" *somebody*. (Note that this example is not far-fetched or against the spirit of the proposal in question: on p. 254 the authors themselves give an example of a *because*-clause under constituent negation.) In the same way, *not* in (25) should "deny" *until yesterday*, with which it is strongly connected, but it clearly fails to do so:

(25) Not until yesterday did he post the letter.

There is no interpretation of this sentence in which *until yesterday* should be replaced by another phrase in its complement class, say, *until today*, for the sentence to become true. A sentence like:

(26) He posted the letter until today.

is only interpretable in an iterative sense (so that each day there is a letter to be posted), and does not make (25) true.

Nor can another constituent of (25) be considered negated by *not*. There is no possible reading for (25) of the kind:

(27) It is not the letter that he posted until yesterday (but the parcel).

So the negation in (25) is not constituent negation. But neither is it sentence negation in Gabbay and Moravcsik's sense, for the presuppositions of (25) are not cancelled: (25) is incompatible with, e.g., "there WAS no letter". The right answer, it seems, is to regard *not until yesterday* as a grammatical transform of *until yesterday not* (by Negative Raising), and to assign to (25) the meaning of its Semantic Analysis: "until yesterday [it was not the case that [he posted the letter]]", where the negation (in keeping with F above) preserves presupposition.

Other proposals can no doubt be devised, or may have been devised already, which circumvent the problems raised and still do not assume two truth-functionally distinct negations in a three-valued logic. But no such alternative solution has come to my notice so far which satisfies the requirement of descriptive adequacy. In this situation it seems reasonable to propose a solution in terms of two distinct negation operators and a three-valued propositional calculus. This is what we will now argue for.

In fact, we now have a cogent argument, based on the observations made, that three truth-values are needed. This *trivalence argument* runs as follows. Given that there are non-necessary sentences A and B such that $A \models B$ and not-$A \models B$, as we have seen there are, and given that not-B does not lead to A lacking a truth-value altogether (as has been demonstrated by the entailment analysts who argued against the Frege–Strawson notion of presupposition), *it follows that a third value is needed*. Consider a two-valued valuation space with truth-value gaps, as in table 2 above. Here, if $A \in L$ and $B \in L$, and $A \models B$ and not-$A \models B$, then when B is false, A must be unvalued. But, as we have seen, normally non-truth of the uttered presupposition B does not lead to an utterance of its carrier sentence A being without a value. The value that A has, in that case, however, cannot be 'true', for $A \models B$; nor can it be just 'false', since not-$A \models B$. There must, therefore, be a third value, assigned to A when its presupposition fails to be true.

The three truth-values in our presuppositional propositional calculus (PPC) are *'true'*, represented by "1", *'minimally false'* (or just *'false'*), represented by "2", and *'radically false'*, represented by "3". Two negations are defined: the *minimal negation* ($\sim$), which preserves presuppositions, and the *radical negation* ($\simeq$), which cancels presuppositions. The following truth-functions are defined:[5]

---

[5] See the appendix in this book for a full formal account of the three-valued PPC.

Table 5

$\neg A$	$\simeq A$	$\sim A$	A	$\wedge B$			$\vee B$		
				1	2	3	1	2	3
2	2	2	1	1	2	3	1	1	1
1	2	1	2	2	2	3	1	2	2
1	1	3	3	3	3	3	1	2	3

For the sake of completeness, the classical negation ($\neg$) has been added, although it is not reckoned to be represented in natural language. It is easily seen that the classical negation is the disjunction (union) of the minimal and the radical negations: $\neg A \equiv \sim A \vee \simeq A$.

Provided the classical negation is used and no truth-value gaps occur, all entailments of classical propositional calculus are preserved, even though PPC is three-valued. This is true generally: the logical system $(\vee, \wedge, \neg)$ is independent of the number of values, provided the operator "$\vee$" is defined as a truth-functional propositional connective selecting the lowest of the component values (for an n-valued system, "1" designates truth, and any value i $(1 < i \leqslant n)$ designates some kind of falsity); "$\wedge$" is a truth-functional connective selecting the highest of the component values; and "$\neg$" is a unary propositional operator turning 1 into 2, and all other values into 1. Under these definitions the theorems of the classical bivalent system $(\vee, \wedge, \neg)$ remain unchanged for any number of truth-values. It is mainly for this reason that the tables for conjunction and disjunction have been chosen as in table 5.

The tables for minimal and radical negation are not arbitrary either. Apart from their property of giving a logical account of presupposition, as will be shown in a moment, they fit into a hierarchy of n-valued propositional calculi in the following way (but see the appendix for further details). For any n-valued system, $n-1$ negations can be defined in such a way that each negation yields truth for exactly one value of the proposition in its scope. Moreover, if $\tilde{1}, \tilde{2}, \ldots, n\tilde{-}1$ are the negations in question, then $\tilde{1}A \vee \tilde{2}A \vee, \ldots,$ $n\tilde{-}1A \equiv \neg A$. PPC contains the negations "$\sim$" $(=\tilde{1})$ and "$\simeq$" $(=\tilde{2})$, where the former yields truth only when A is minimally false (we shall say: $\varphi(A) = 2$), and the latter yields truth only when A is radically false $(\varphi(A) = 3)$. PPC is the three-valued member of a family of systems characterized by the properties just given. (For the other values of the negations $\tilde{1}, \ldots, n\tilde{-}1$ see section 6.3 of the appendix, where the family of n-valued presuppositional propositional calculi is defined.) Given the specific properties of the $n-1$ negations defined for each n-valued system, each n-valued system contains the classical calculus as a proper subpart, since the union of all the specific negations results in the classical negation. The same holds for PPC: since the bivalent classical negation is defined as the union of the minimal and the radical negations, classical propositional calculus is a proper subpart of the trivalent PPC.

The logical property of presupposition can now be defined as follows:

(28) In a partially valued trivalent propositional calculus, if A and B are assertions: IF $A \gg B$ THEN $A \models B$ AND $\sim A \models B$.

This is not a definition of presupposition: presupposition is a, or probably the, central notion in discourse semantics, and its definition lies there. But as a semantic phenomenon it has the logical property (28). This property imposes an admissibility condition on valuation spaces for partially valued trivalent propositional languages: assuming that for all entailments B from A, if A is undefined (U), so is B, and vice versa (this is a necessary consequence of the conditions for being valued, as will be shown in section 3.3), the following valuation space for atomic sentences A, B, C, where $A \gg B$, is admissible:

Table 6

V:	v_1	v_2	v_3	v_4	v_5	v_6	...
A	1	2	3	3	3	U	
B	1	1	1	2	3	U	
C	1	2	3	U	1	2	

(The values for utterances of logically compound sentences can be filled in on the basis of the truth-tables.) The logical property (28) excludes any valuation where $\varphi(B) = 2$ or $\varphi(B) = 3$, and $\varphi(A) \neq 3$. The availability of the third value makes it possible for B to be (minimally or radically) false without the necessity for A to be unvalued. In this way justice is done to the observations made by the entailment analysts.

(One sometimes finds the term "metalinguistic negation" for what is here called "radical negation". Although this term has an intuitive appeal (since sentences with radical negation have a decidedly metalinguistic touch about them), it can easily be misleading. It might suggest that in cases like:

(29) a. I wasn't "invited for dinner": I was summoned to help finish the enormous pike he had caught!
   b. He isn't just "well off": he is damned rich!

the negation is radical. Yet it is not, although it is metalinguistic. It is not radical, because these sentences do have presuppositions: (29a) presupposes that something happened to the speaker, and it asserts that what happened was not that he was invited for dinner, but that he was summoned to help eat a fish. And (29b) presupposes that the "he" occupies a position on the wealth scale, whereas it asserts that what he is is not just "well off", but rather "damned rich". We thus have minimal negation used in a special kind of underlying cleft or pseudocleft sentence. Note, furthermore, that even if the term "metalinguistic" were more appropriate, it would still have little theoretical import as long as no separate level of metalinguistic analysis has been formally defined.)

It is now clear that the minimal negation is presupposition-preserving. For it follows from (28) that if $A \gg B$, then also $\sim A \gg B$, and vice versa. But the radical negation cancels presuppositions in precisely the same way as classical negation cancels entailments. The observations made in A–G above now show that in all those cases, for some reason or other, only the minimal negation can be used. Or, in other words, the radical negation is allowed only in the canonical position for negation in the sentence, provided the grammatical subject is not a factive clause, the sentence is not a cleft or pseudocleft, the sentence does not bear contrastive accent, it occurs as a direct or indirect assertion, and provided there is no NPI around.[6] Thus, the negation which is required for NPIs must be the minimal negation, but the negation which is allowed for PPIs can only be the radical negation. The behaviour of NPIs and PPIs is thus seen to be more symmetrical than seemed to be the case in a two-valued system with one negation: NPIs require minimal negation[7] and exclude radical negation, whereas PPIs allow for radical negation and exclude minimal negation.

All predicates of the language in question, i.e. its whole semantic lexicon, are incorporated into the logic. That is, the logic of a natural language is best

---

[6] Radical negation is excluded also with PPIs and *double* negation (see Baker 1970a):

There is nobody here who would not rather be in Montpellier.

The PPI *rather* does allow for a single negation (and echo), provided the negation is radical. Baker observed, however, that PPIs stop being PPIs when under a double negation of certain structural kinds.

[7] That is, NPIs require minimal negation when they occur in simple assertive sentences (whereby the negation may be morphologically or lexically incorporated, as in *lack*, *hardly*, *scarcely*). As is well known, most NPIs, in addition, occur in a variety of other constructions (questions; *if*-clauses; under 'negative' predicates such as *deny*, *be surprised*, *fail*; after *than* in the comparative, etc.). Some recent work (Ladusaw 1979; Zwarts 1981; Hoeksema 1983) suggests or asserts that the occurrence of NPIs is bound up with 'downward entailing' contexts, and excluded in 'upward entailing' contexts. Although there is no doubt a strong correlation between direction of entailment and the possibility of occurrence of polarity items, it remains to be seen to what extent the direction of entailment provides a (partial) explanation for these occurrences. Counter-examples remain a serious problem. Thus, relative clauses under *each* are downward entailing but do not allow for NPIs; *that*-clauses under *surprise* are not downward entailing, yet they do allow for NPIs. It would seem that the hypothesis of an underlying negation for many classes of NPI occurrences is still of high explanatory value. See also the discussion in sections 4.1.1, 4.1.3 and 4.1.5. The downward entailing property of many NPI contexts seems epiphenomenal on such contexts, rather than explanatory.

defined as not containing predicate variables but only individual predicate constants. Each predicate constant has associated with it a set of conditions which, when satisfied, make an utterance of the sentence figuring that predicate true. These conditions will be called *predicate conditions*. Very often, predicate conditions can be formulated only in cognitive descriptive terms (according to some, in terms of prototypes). It is not our business here to try and develop the terminology and the criteria for adequate formulations of predicate conditions. In particular, it is not our business here to go into the well-known questions of extensional vagueness of predicates with fuzzy extensional boundaries. As was said in section 1.1, the point of view taken here is that semantic processing is a yes/no system applied to a world full of continuums, so that threshold values are unavoidable. We shall proceed, for the moment, as though the predicate conditions for each predicate had been sorted out satisfactorily. The reader is asked, therefore, not to put too fine a comb through the predicate conditions as they are stated in the examples given throughout the remainder of this book.

More to the point is the distinction which is made between two kinds of predicate conditions, the *preconditions* and the *satisfaction conditions*. This distinction is directly related to the two kinds of falsity in our system: if the n-tuple of term extensions under the predicate in question fails to satisfy the preconditions, radical falsity ensues; if the preconditions are satisfied, but not the satisfaction conditions, then minimal falsity ensues; truth ensues only if all predicate conditions are fulfilled by the term extensions. For the predicate *drunk*, for example, the satisfaction conditions include the condition that the subject (i.e. the extension of the subject term) be intoxicated with alcohol, and the preconditions stipulate, among other things, that the subject extension be non-null (i.e. the subject exists), and that it be an animate being (flowers, stones, tabletops, or the square root of 4 may or may not be affected by alcohol, they cannot ever be drunk). The first precondition, stipulating existence, is caught under the general label 'extensional': *drunk* is extensional with respect to its subject (and since it is a one-place predicate, it is just extensional). Thus, if an utterance of the sentence:

(30) The man was drunk.

is true, then it is entailed that there was a man (and thus an animate being), and that this man was intoxicated with alcohol, at the time referred to by the simple past tense of the utterance in question. However, an utterance of

(31) The Cadillac was drunk.

stands very little chance of being true if it is about a motor car. In fact, if it is about a motor car, the sentence is radically false, since one of the preconditions of the main predicate is not fulfilled. Sentences like (31) are commonly said to harbour a *category mistake*.

Category mistakes are often corrected, in actual discourses, by means of a *metaphorical interpretation*. The stylistic figure of metaphor (a paramount foe of formal semantics) consists, in principle, in a (necessarily radically false) category mistake, but one that has a tantalizing effect on listeners because of the highly applicable satisfaction conditions, besides the failure of the pre-conditions. If only the preconditions could be fulfilled, the satisfaction conditions would make for a highly informative discourse increment. Take the example:

(32) The volcano was asleep, not dead.

Clearly, the predicate *asleep* requires, as a precondition, animate beings as subjects, in particular, animate beings that alternate sleeping hours with waking hours, and the predicate *dead*, likewise, requires animate subjects (or subjects that *were* animate: either will do for truth or minimal falsity). Equally clearly, anything properly called *a volcano* will not be an animate being. Now all that is needed to make sense, in some appropriate context, of (32) is that the listener's cognitive faculty be numbed into accepting, for the momentary purpose of interpreting, that the addition to the discourse of the proposition that the volcano in question was an animate being, does not lead to contradiction with available knowledge. For this it is necessary that the bit of knowledge that volcanoes are lifeless be made inoperative. It seems that the human species makes a quick and natural use of the faculty to bar certain bits of knowledge from functioning if an utterance is to be interpreted whose satisfaction conditions are applicable and informative, but whose precondi-tions (or rather: the preconditions of whose predicate) fail to apply owing to available knowledge. Metaphors, in fact, seem to come to life precisely to the extent that the satisfaction conditions of the predicate in question would apply splendidly, were it not that the preconditions stand in the way.[8] We

[8] If this account of metaphor is, at least in principle, correct, it shows why there is no need to reckon with a separate truth-value for the case that the satisfaction conditions are met but the preconditions fail. Two-dimensional logic (Herzberger 1973; Bergmann 1981) provides for the logical space to cover such cases. From an empirical point of view, however, that particular eventuality does not seem to need to be covered. Under literal interpretation, the value 'radically false' is assigned when the satisfaction condi-tions are satisfied but not the preconditions. Thus, although the sandy or light brown colour that is called *fawn* for animal furs falls under the predicate *blond* for human hair, the sentence *Fido is blond* is radically false when uttered about a dog called "Fido", and

(i) Fido is NOT blond: he is fawn-coloured.

is true with radical *not*. Or take the transitive verb *equal*, and let it have the satisfaction condition that its subject and object extensions attain equal values on some (presupposed) scale, together with a precondition that the subject attained lesser values in the past, then we can understand why a sentence like

(ii) Harry does NOT equal Max in productivity; Max equals Harry!

is natural and perfectly understandable, and can be true while the same sentence with *Harry* and *Max* interchanged is false. In general, there seems no need for a further, fourth truth-value to account for utterances whose preconditions are not satisfied but whose satisfaction conditions are.

must, however, let this matter rest here, first because stylistic devices are beyond the scope of this book (and generally too difficult for formal semantics), and secondly because we are already invoking processes that have not been incorporated into the theory yet.

What is directly relevant here, however, is that we have, more or less surreptitiously, introduced a further kind of presupposition. We are familiar with existential and factive presuppositions. Now we have *categorial* presuppositions. Given the blanket requirement that for truth all conditions of the predicate in question must be fulfilled, both preconditions and satisfaction conditions, it follows that a sentence, in all its utterances, always entails its presuppositions as well as its other entailments. Predicate conditions thus *generate* entailments, including presuppositions. If a predicate is extensional with respect to some term, then any sentence figuring that predicate entails, in fact presupposes, the existence of that term's extension in any utterance of the sentence. If a predicate requires, by way of precondition, that, say, its subject be animate, then any sentence figuring that predicate entails, in fact presupposes, that that subject is animate. If a predicate is factive, i.e. it requires by way of precondition that a subject or object clause be true, then any sentence figuring that predicate entails, and presupposes, that the lower clause is true.

This enables us to set off the large and varied class of *presuppositions* against *denotational entailments*. Presuppositions are derived from the preconditions associated with the predicates in the semantic lexicon. A sentence figuring a predicate with some precondition will have as a presupposition the application of the precondition in question to the term or terms in question. Existential presuppositions are thus lexically derived, just as the categorial and the factive ones.

Denotational entailments are induced by the definite determiners, in particular by the definite article *the*. They are in our theory what the entailment of 'existential generalization' is in standard logic. Existential generalization is the entailment from a sentence containing a definite term "$x: + S_x$" that there is some x such that S_x, and such that what is predicated of the definite term is predicated of x. Thus, *The prisoner escaped* has the entailment of existential generalization that there is an x such that x was a prisoner and x escaped. This entailment is valid, but it is improperly called "existential". For only in some cases is the entailment one of real existence; in many other cases all that is entailed is that "there *is* an x...", not that "there *exists* an x...". For example, when it is said that *Harry dreamt of the Abominable Snowman*, then it follows that there is something that Harry dreamt of, but not that what Harry dreamt of actually exists. We conclude that there are things which do not exist, a conclusion which is both central and crucial to our theory.

The distinction between being and existence is, of course, ancient and hotly debated in philosophy. We maintain the distinction (against, e.g., Quine in his famous essay 'On what there is': Quine 1953: 1-19). But we stipulate that the things which are there but do not exist are defined by some discourse domain. Thus, the Abominable Snowman is defined by the set of stories in which he figures. And if the whole village believes that some unicorn rampaged through the local supermarket last Saturday (see (33) below), then there *is* a unicorn believed by the village to have rampaged through the local supermarket, though it does not *exist*. If it is then said that Billy, one of the villagers, is looking for that unicorn, then, if what is said is true, there is something which is a unicorn believed by the village to have wreaked havoc in the supermarket and which Billy is looking for. Existence of that unicorn, of course, does not follow.

In our theory this 'existential' entailment, which is not existential but one of being, and therefore better called 'denotational', is induced by the definite determiner. It is accounted for by the fact that definite terms need a denotation or an address to 'land at'. Failing such an address, the sentence in which the definite term occurs is uninterpretable in the given discourse. If the address is available, the (uttered) sentence is interpretable (all other conditions being fulfilled), but not necessarily true. For the truth of the utterance each term must have its extension (really existing or not), and the n-tuple of term extensions must be a member of the extension set of the predicate. But all term extensions are mediated by discourse addresses, and, as will be shown in chapter 6, the extensions vary according to whether the discourse is or is not true. If D is true, then the addresses in the truth-domain correspond to (refer to) really existing entities, and the addresses in intensional subdomains correspond to intensional entities. If D is false, then all or some addresses correspond to intensional entities defined under the operator "in the discourse D".

These matters cannot be satisfactorily discussed until more is said about the machinery of discourse domains and their truth-conditional aspects. This will be done in later chapters, especially in chapter 6, where questions of truth and reference are broached. Here it suffices to say that the availability of those portions of the discourse domain that are involved in the interpretation of a sentence S is a prerequisite for the truth of S. Or, in other words, S needs the addresses and fact-denotations required for an utterance of S to be interpreted. And for an utterance of S to have a truth-value, it must be interpreted. Hence, S needs domain structures to be denoted by its terms for an utterance of S to have a truth-value. For example, if the uttered sentence

(33) Billy is looking for the unicorn.

has a truth-value, then D must contain an address d_n for the term *the unicorn*. This d_n may be in the truth-domain (see section 5.3). If the truth-domain is true, then d_n corresponds to a real unicorn. If (33) is true, then indeed the real unicorn corresponding to d_n is what Billy is looking for. But if the domain is false in that d_n, though in the truth-domain, fails to correspond to a real unicorn, then (33) may still be true (Billy may believe that the domain is true), but what he is looking for then cannot be caught and displayed because it is an intensional object. Likewise, if d_n is in a subdomain defined by what Billy and the other villagers believe about what happened over the weekend in the supermarket, (33) may be true but then Billy is looking for something which cannot be found and caught because it is an intensional object. In any case, our theory requires that for truth or falsity every term in a sentential structure has a domain denotation, and that every domain denotation has an extension in some given verification domain. And it seems that these assumptions are not just required by our theory, but that some theory containing far-reaching assumptions about intensional objects is called for anyway in view of the facts of language.

Present-day philosophy of language, broadly speaking, has not succeeded in developing an adequate account of intensional objects. It has been dominated by positivistic, antimentalist tendencies, which blocked the way towards the development of necessary mentalist concepts and theories. A notion like "discourse-defined intensional object" has, since the days of Russell's earlier work, been looked upon as an abomination in philosophy, but without sufficient grounds. Moreover, the tenacity with which, again since the days of Russell's earlier writings, the Aristotelian Principle of the Excluded Third has been upheld has prevented an adequate insight into the role of discourse in semantics. It now looks, however, as though with discourse taken into due account, no philosophical problems will arise, and the facts of language can be better respected. But the machinery seen to underlie linguistic processes turns out quite a bit more complex than has been anticipated. More about this, however, in chapter 6.

Although existential, categorial and factive presuppositions are all treated alike in that they are considered presuppositions, i.e. derived from lexical preconditions, it does not follow that they have equal status in all respects. In fact, they do not. It is immediately obvious that the fulfilment of existential and factive presuppositions depends on the verification domain against which truth is checked: in most cases existence or non-existence of certain entities, or truth or non-truth of certain propositions, are contingent properties of the verification domain. The fulfilment of categorial presuppositions, however, is directly checked against a fund of generalized background knowledge: we need not inspect the world in order to find out if a stone can be drunk, or if a volcano is an animate being so that it can properly be said to be asleep or awake. This means that a text some or all of whose existential or factive presuppositions are not fulfilled can still be a coherent and perfectly intelligible text. But a text with categorial presuppositions unfulfilled will soon become gibberish. Metaphor will not always help out. A psycholinguistic experiment conducted by Reichgelt (1979) shows up the difference between existential presuppositions on the one hand and categorial presuppositions on the other. In this experiment seven subjects gave truth-ratings ("likely to be true", "could be true", "could not possibly be true", "true", "not true but could be true", etc.) to 15 sentences, five of which were indifferent to the test, but the remaining ten of which contained existential or categorial presuppositions. These ten critical sentences were offered in pairs: in one presentation the presupposition was fulfilled, but in the other presentation the presupposition was not fulfilled. Where the presuppositions were not fulfilled, there was a clear discrepancy in judgements. If the presupposition was categorial, subjects tended towards "could not possibly be true", but for existential presuppositions the ratings were rather of the "not true but could be true" type. One would expect factive presuppositions to behave like the existential ones.

The distinction between preconditions and satisfaction conditions of predicates makes for a much refined apparatus for lexicographic description compared with standard practice. Many distinctions between pairs of particular lexical items, often felt to be 'subtle' and not fitting any general theory, can now be regarded as being of a preconditional nature. Consider, for example, the English verbs *discover* or *assassinate*. Both carry the preconditions that the object is somehow important, whereby the importance associated with *assassinate* must be derived from public life. Or take the English predicate *bald*, which carries the precondition that the subject is of a kind usually covered with hair or pile. It differs from its nearest equivalent in, say, German (*kahl*) or Dutch (*kaal*), which have the precondition that the subject be of a kind usually covered with growth or ornaments. Thus, *ein kahler Baum* is good German, but *a bald tree* is not good English. In English, *bare* takes over some of the functions of *kahl/kaal*.[9]

We have seen that predicates frequently carry preconditions of existence with respect to some specified term (subject, indirect object, object). When they do, we say that they are *extensional* with regard to that term. It is important to note that the entailment of existence should be a presuppositional entailment, not one derived from the satisfaction conditions. There is one predicate in particular that generates an existential entailment but not an existential presupposition, the predicate *exist*. It has been observed in the past that under Strawson's notion of presupposition (where both the affirmative and the negated carrier sentence entail the presupposition), a sentence like

(34) God does not exist.

must have contradictory entailments: it entails that God does not exist, but also, presuppositionally, that he does. This all too easy proof for the existence

[9] Remarkably, the English collocation *a bald tyre* is entirely normal. This is probably a case of conventionalized metaphor.

of God is dismantled in the three-valued calculus, but there (34) is doomed to be radically negated (since the minimal negation still has contradictory entailments) if the subject term carries a precondition of existence. And it is strongly counterintuitive to consider the *not* in (34) the radical negation. On the contrary, it has all the marks of an ordinary minimal negation. But then *exist* cannot have a precondition of existence, so that (34) does not presuppose the existence of God. It only classically entails the existence of God. It will be shown in section 5.3.4 that the specific increment function of the predicate *exist* consists in taking a subject term denotation from some subdomain and placing it in the truth-domain. It would seem that this simple and elegant solution to the old presuppositional riddle of sentences like (34) should speak in favour of the present analysis of presuppositional phenomena in terms of a three-valued calculus, preconditions and satisfaction conditions on predicates. We conclude that extensionality with respect to an argument term is attributed to a predicate only if it is felt that there are descriptive and theoretical advantages in fitting that predicate out with a *precondition* of existence with respect to that argument term, not when existence follows for that term's extension on account of the satisfaction conditions.

Most predicates are extensional with respect to their terms. And if they are not, it is usually the object term which is non-extensional (intensional). Few predicates are non-extensional with respect to their subject term. *Exist* is one of these, and so is the identity predicate *be* (*identical with*). And, of course, predicates that lexically incorporate these also lack existential preconditions. Thus, the predicates *imaginary*, (= "non-existent but only thought up"), or *real* (= "actually existing") are likewise non-extensional (with respect to their subject term). Below, when formal notations are introduced for predicate extensions, extensionality with respect to some term will not be specially marked. Only if a predicate is non-extensional with respect to some term will there be a notation. The notation used is an asterisk over the non-extensional term extension – more or less like the "heavy parentheses" in Katz (1972: 167) are used to characterize extensional extensions.

Formally, the extension of a predicate is represented as a set of n-tuples of term extensions, characterized by comprehension, not by enumeration. The conditions of the set characterization are divided into two classes, the preconditions and the satisfaction conditions. The preconditions are stated first and are preceded by a colon. They are followed by the satisfaction conditions, which are preceded by a vertical line. The extension set of a predicate is the value of a function "σ" providing a unique extension set for each predicate in the real world. It will be remembered that the function "ρ" yields extensions for terms, and the function "φ" yields truth-values for propositions.

Depending on the predicate in question, sentential terms sometimes take facts as extensions, and sometimes propositions. (It is a matter of descriptive adequacy which option is chosen in the description of each given predicate.)

The term *fact* is used here to refer to whatever it is in the, or a, world that makes a proposition true: facts are truth-makers, no matter in which world. If a fact is a truth-maker in the real world, it is an extensional fact, if it is a truth-maker in a non-real world, it is an intensional fact. (We don't mind falling into the philosophical idiom of "worlds", as long as we refrain from incorporating this intuitive notion into our semantics.) Facts cannot be individuated other than by means of a proposition. In fact, their existence depends on the occurrence of propositions made true by them. Facts are not countable in the real world. They are not part of any sound ontology but are projected onto the world by humans dealing in propositions. We thus disagree fundamentally with Wittgenstein's dictum (*Tractatus* 1.1): "The world is the totality of facts, not of things". We are also forced to disagree, though on a different level, with the Fregean notion that the extensions of S-structures are truth-values. Apart from being somewhat counterintuitive, this notion cannot be used in our theory because we need a clear distinction between ρ-values (extensions) of S-structures, and their φ-values or truth-values.

Different variables are used for different kinds of term extensions. Individuals as term extensions are indicated by the variables i, j, k ... A subclass of these are the extensions of definite mass terms (*the air, the wine*) or of intrinsically plural definite terms (such as the object term of *be among*). These take the variables I, J, K ... Their discourse representations would typically be the superaddresses of section 1.2. Facts as term extensions take the variables e, f, g ..., whereas propositions as term extensions are indicated by p, q, r ... The variables T, U, V ..., finally, are reserved for the extensions of set-denoting terms (SD-terms). The choice of variable category does not reflect a precondition whose non-fulfilment leads to radical falsity. Thus, it is not considered a precondition of the predicate *bald* that it takes individuals as subject term extensions, and not, say, propositions. The choice of variable category is to do more with well-formedness conditions on SAs than with preconditions. If, for example, the predicate *bald* were to be given a sentential subject term, the result would be an ungrammatical sentence, rather than a radically false (utterance of a) sentence:

(35) a. *That the cat is on the mat is bald.
     b. *It is bald that the cat is on the mat.

By way of example, the extension sets of the predicates *bald, blond* and *kill* can now be characterized roughly[10] in the following way:

---

[10] The reader is called upon to be indulgent in evaluating the details of the predicate conditions, especially of those predicates that reflect 'facts of life' rather than philosophical positions (as with *exist, identical, true*). For an elaborate treatment of a section of the Dutch and German lexicon, i.e. the section of predicates of auditory perception, see Vliegen (in preparation), which is a specimen of lexicography in terms of preconditions and satisfaction conditions.

(36) a. $\sigma(bald) = \{$i: i standardly has hair or pile | lacks hair or pile$\}$

b. $\sigma(blond) = \{$i: is human (hair) | i is light-pigmented/has light-pigmented hair$\}$[11]

c. $\sigma(kill) = \{\langle i, j \rangle$: j is animate | i causes j to die$\}$

Note that the existential presuppositions that go with all terms involved with these predicates are not expressed separately: they follow from the absence of asterisks with the is and js. The same device can be used for factive predicates. Thus, for the predicate *know* no special precondition need be given requiring the truth of the object-clause. We reckon factive verbs to take facts as extensions of their factive clauses. By leaving out the asterisk we make it clear that real, i.e. extensional, facts are required for a classical truth-value. (The satisfaction conditions are, again, approximate and may well have to be replaced by more adequate formulations in a serious lexicographic description of this verb.) Thus, the extension set of *know* can be presented (roughly) as follows:

(36) d. $\sigma(know) = \{\langle i, e \rangle$: i is animate | i has established on the basis of reliable information that for all propositions p such that $\rho(p) = e$, $\varphi(p) = 1\}$

The fixing of extensions is discourse-dependent for individual terms, for definite mass or definite intrinsically plural terms, and for propositions or propositional terms taking facts as extensions. That reference fixing for definite terms, such as *the man*, *the men* and *the water*, is discourse-dependent is, of course, a truism that has been known (but not always respected) for a long time. The fixing of fact-extensions is likewise discourse-dependent. This follows from the definition of a fact as whatever it is in the world that makes a proposition true. Facts are real only by virtue of the propositions requiring them for truth, and thus their fixation is as discourse-dependent as the propositions expressing them are. But note, again, that though individuals and quantities (extensions of definite mass terms or definite plural terms) are safely assumed to exist independently of any term referring to them, facts have no such independent 'existence'. Yet they are considered to be in, or part of, the world, inasmuch as they are 'talked about'.

Propositions as extensions of propositional terms need not be fixed separately: they are themselves discourse-dependent entities, being defined as pairs of SAs and discourse domains (for which they define an increment). They are not 'in the world', but are part of the interpretative process. When it is said that a propositional (sentential) term of some predicate takes propositions as extensions (and not facts), then for each such proposition extension the first element of the pair defining the proposition, i.e. the SA, is given by the

[11] Again, as with *bald* (see note 9), there are special collocations, such as *blond beer*, *blond walnut*, probably interpretable as conventionalized metaphors.

sentence under interpretation, either because the sentence contains the SA or because the sentence contains an anaphoric expression with a referral to an SA-antecedent. Thus, the sentence *It is true that the cat is on the mat*, with the predicate *true* whose subject term takes propositions as extensions, contains the actual SA of the subject term extension. And *That is true* contains an anaphor for the SA in the subject term extension. The second element of the pair, the discourse domain D_j to which the proposition is to be incremented, must be given in the discourse. It is either the discourse itself as it is being developed, which we call the *truth-domain*, or some *subdomain* defined within the truth-domain as an 'attachment'. If, for example, the truth-domain contains a denotation for a man called "John" and a specification that this man believes certain things, then there is a subdomain containing the propositional increments of what the man believes. A new sentence *John believes that p* will now have the increment of *p* added to the subdomain in question, while the increment of the proposition of the whole sentence is, of course, added to the truth-domain.

SD-terms, as will be remembered, have the grammatical structure "$^{\wedge}x + S_x^{**}$". Their extensions are the sets denoted. More precisely, set-denoting terms can be represented as being of the general syntactic form $^{\wedge}x(P_1(x), \ldots, P_n(x))$, where each P_i is a unary predicate, either given as such in the semantic lexicon or constructed from a binary, ternary, etc., lexical predicate by extracting the x-term and making it the subject of a complex predicate formed with the help of the lambda-operator. The reference value of a set-denoting term is identical with the intersection of the extension sets of $P_1, \ldots, P_n$, or:

$$\rho(^{\wedge}x(P_1(x), \ldots, P_n(x))) = \cap\, \sigma(P), \text{ where } \sigma(P) = \{\sigma(P_1), \ldots, \sigma(P_n)\}$$

For example, if the SD-term is $^{\wedge}x(car(x).\ \lambda x(own(x: \text{"Bill"}(x), x))(x))$, or: "the set of cars that Bill owns", then the extension of this term is the intersection of $\sigma(car)$ and $\sigma(\lambda x(own(x: \text{"Bill"}(x), x)))$, i.e. the intersection of the extension sets of the predicates *car* and *owned by Bill*. (This is sufficient for exclusively extensional extensions. Below, in particular in section 5.3.6, provisions will be built in to cope with intensional extensions.)

If no context-dependent term occurs in S_x^{**}, the extensions of $^{\wedge}x + S_x^{**}$ is determined independently of discourse factors. Thus, e.g., $^{\wedge}x(human(x))$ takes as its extension the set of all humans in the real world. But an SD-term like $^{\wedge}x(car(x), \lambda x(own(x: \text{"Bill"}(x), x))(x))$, or "the set of cars that Bill owns", must have its extension fixed in association with the extension of the definite term x: "Bill"(x)". SD-terms may have a null extension, as with $^{\wedge}x(mermaid(x))$, since the set of all mermaids in this world is empty.

Since SD-terms occur under quantifiers, and since the increment value associated with quantifiers never makes a direct use of the SD-terms occurring under them but is always formulated in terms of addresses (or superaddresses) or instructions for the further development of the discourse domain, it is not necessary to define a discourse value for SD-terms.

The issue of term extensions and their fixation is important because it leads up to a discussion of intensionality phenomena. Any semantic theory that is worth its salt must give an adequate account of intensionality phenomena. It was these, together with the a posteriori nature of identity statements with unequal terms, that led Frege to draw his classical distinction between *Sinn* (sense) and *Bedeutung* (reference). Frege's notion of intensionality, embodied in his *Sinn*, was later formalized in the framework of possible worlds where intensionality is treated as extensionality with respect to all possible worlds. In our theory an entirely different account of intensionality is given, based on the distinction between truth-domains and subdomains. A full discussion of these matters must wait till chapter 5, since not enough notions have been developed yet to make an exposé of our account of intensionality possible. Here, however, some preliminary remarks can be made and some central definitions can be given or prepared.

Terms whose extension is in the world and is discourse-dependent may have *intensional extensions*. For example, let Russell's famous sentence *The present king of France is bald* be uttered in a discourse where a denotation is provided for the definite term *the present king of France*, despite the fact that, in reality, no such king exists. Instead of saying, as is the custom, that this term fails to refer and thus has no extension (or a null extension), we say that it has an intensional extension, i.e. the intensional object "king of France" defined by the present discourse. We are thus committed, as has been said, to the assumption of intensional objects (and facts), *pace* Quine and a powerful tradition in empiricist philosophy (see section 6.5).

If a predicate P is extensional with respect to a term t, and $\rho(t)$, in some token occurrence of the sentence S figuring P, is an intensional object, then $\varphi(S) = 3$. (If $\rho(t)$, is undefined for lack of sufficient contextual clues, $\varphi(S)$ is undefined.) There are, however, also predicates that are not extensional with respect to one or more of their terms. We will say that a predicate P is intensional with respect to a term t just in case it does not automatically follow that $\varphi(S) = 3$ whenever $\rho(t)$ is an intensional object. That is, intensional terms do not carry an existential precondition. An example of a predicate which is intensional with respect to its object term is the well-known *look for*:[12]

(36) e. $\sigma(look\ for) = \{\langle i, j^* \rangle : i$ is animate | i tries if i can find j$\}$

---

[12] Note that *look for* is a verb that allows for quantifier penetration provided the quantifier belongs to the *any*-class, and not to the open class (see section 2.3.1):

Jack is looking for any traces.

is to be analysed as "Jack is trying if there are any traces he can find" at SA-level. Only at DS-level will the bit of structure corresponding to "try if x can find" be replaced by *look for*. For the definition of the extension set of this verb this syntactic property makes no difference, however.

The asterisk over j, as was announced earlier, indicates the intensional character of the second term of this predicate, which thus lacks an existential precondition. Take the case, discussed above, of the village believing that what caused the mess in the local supermarket over the weekend was a unicorn. Now consider again:

(33) Billy is looking for the unicorn.

If indeed this Billy is trying to find the unicorn believed by the whole village to have rampaged through the supermarket over the weekend, and not some other possible thought-up unicorn, then $\varphi(33) = 1$, despite the fact that the object term 'fails to refer'. Although the term *the unicorn* 'fails to refer', it has an extension: ρ (the unicorn) is the intensional object "unicorn", defined by the discourse domain characterizing what the villagers believe in respect of this intensional animal. (33) thus does not carry an existential presupposition with regard to its object term. But, of course, the denotational entailment that there is a, possibly intensionally defined, unicorn, remains untouched.

The assumption of intensional objects makes it possible, among other things, to maintain the uniform truth-definition for all propositions in uttered sentences. Let P^n be an n-ary predicate followed by n terms t, then:

$P^n(t_1, \ldots, t_n)$ is true just in case $< \rho(t_1), \ldots, \rho(t_n) > \in \sigma(P^n)$.

This definition now applies not only to purely extensional cases, but also to sentences involving intensional terms.

Analogously, real facts are extensional, but there are also intensional facts. These are extensions of (minimally or radically) false propositions or propositional terms. Intensional facts are, again, defined with the help of whatever discourse the proposition is uttered in. The assumption of intensional facts makes it possible to define the extension sets of the truth-functional predicates of negation, conjunction and disjunction:

(37) a. $\sigma(\sim) = \{e^*$ such that for all p, if $\rho(p) = e$, then : $\varphi(p) \neq 3 \mid \varphi(p) = 2\}$
b. $\sigma(\approx) = \{e^*$ such that for all p, if $\rho(p) = e$, then $\mid \varphi(p) = 3\}$
c. $\sigma(\wedge) = \{\langle e^*, f^* \rangle$ s.t. for all p, q, if $\rho(p) = e$ and $\rho(q) = f$, then :
$\varphi(p) \neq 3$ and $\varphi(q) \neq 3 \mid \varphi(p) = 1$ and $\varphi(q) = 1\}$
d. $\sigma(\vee) = \{\langle e^*, f^* \rangle$ s.t. for all p, q, if $\rho(p) = e$ and $\rho(q) = f$, then : not
$(\varphi(p) = \varphi(q) = 3) \mid$ not $(\varphi(\neg p) = \varphi(\neg q) = 1)\}$

We may add the extension of the classical negation, although it does not occur in language:

(37) e. $\sigma(\neg) = \{e^*$ such that for all p, if $\rho(p) = e$, then $\mid \varphi(p) \neq 1\}$

The reader will quickly check that these extension set definitions correspond exactly to the truth-functions given in table 5 above. It is also clear that the general truth-definition applies without problems to propositions figuring a truth-functional predicate.

Intensional objects or facts are *per se* discourse-defined. It makes no sense to speak of intensional objects or facts outside any specific discourse. Their reality is dependent upon the discourse at hand, a property they share with propositions and extensional facts. They are, moreover, not part of the real world. Their ontological status (or "category of being") is restricted to the fact that they are being talked about. Ontologically, they have nothing but 'aboutness' of a given discourse, which limits their shadowy being to the class of counterfactual situations of which the discourse in question would be true. A fuller discussion of these questions is given below, in chapter 5, when the semantic machinery of intensionality and subdomains is presented. Here, the reader is merely invited to follow the analysis, even if he feels that he has no adequate grasp of all aspects involved.

We can set up a matrix for the different kinds of term extensions, marking them for the following ontological and semantic properties: being part of the real world, being part of what is talked about, being discourse-determined (i.e. depending on discourse domains for their determination), and being discourse-dependent (i.e. without any ontological status in the absence of a discourse domain). As appears from this matrix, shown in table 7, we speak of intensional objects or facts only when the objects or facts in question are discourse-dependent for their ontological status, not part of the real world, but part of what is being talked about.

Table 7

properties term extensions	part of real world	talked about	discourse- determined	discourse- dependent
SD-term extensions	+/−	+	+/−	−
extensional objects	+	+	+	−
extensional facts	+	+	+	+
intensional $\begin{Bmatrix} \text{objects} \\ \text{facts} \end{Bmatrix}$	−	+	+	+
propositions	−	−	+	+

SD-term extensions sometimes are, and sometimes are not, or are partially, in the real world. This depends on the extension set associated with the predicate $\lambda x(S_x^{**})$ that corresponds with $\hat{x} + S_x^{**}$. If the variable x stands in the position of an intensional term, then $\sigma(\lambda x(S_x^{**}))$ need not be made up entirely, or at all, of extensional objects. Thus, the extension of the SD term $\hat{\ }x(\text{human}(x))$, as has been said, consists of all real humans and is, in this world, not empty. But the extension of, e.g., $\hat{\ }x(\lambda x(\text{look for}(x: \text{"Henry"}(x),x)))$ consists of all the things Henry looks for, and, provided it is known who is referred to by *Henry*, this set may well contain non-existing things. Or, in other words, the extension of the predicate $\lambda x(\text{look for}(x: \text{"Henry"}(x), x))$ may comprise intensional objects defined by the discourse subdomain of what Henry has in mind while searching, due to the fact that x stands in the position of the intensional object term of *look for*. The extension of $\hat{\ }x(\text{fictitious}(x))$, on the other hand, must consist entirely of intensional objects: this SD term's extension, $\sigma(\lambda x(\text{fictitious}(x)))$, consists of the set of all fictitious things, which, due to the nature of the predicate *fictitious* are perforce intensional objects. Each one of these fictitious things owes its ontology to some discourse domain somewhere in the world, but not to the discourse domain of the proposition in which the SD term in question is used. The set of all fictitious things is, therefore, not discourse-dependent, although each of its members is. (See section 6.2 for a more complete discussion.)

We can now define a few more predicate extensions:

(36) f. $\sigma(exist) = \{i^* \mid i \text{ is real}\}$

    g. $\sigma(identical) = \{\langle i^*, j^* \rangle \mid \rho(i) = \rho(j)\}$

    h. $\sigma(true) = \{p: \varphi(p) \neq 3 \mid \varphi(p) = 1\}$

    i. $\sigma(false) = \{p \mid \varphi(p) \neq 1\}$

Exist is intensional with respect to its subject term. Hence, if of a non-existing intensional object it is said that it exists, the utterance is minimally false. The identity predicate, *identical*, is intensional with respect to both its terms. Thus, when I say *Zeus is identical with Jupiter*, my utterance is true just in case there is a class of discourses where both names are about the same (intensional) individual. The predicates *true* and *false* are analysed as taking propositions as extensions of their subject clauses, not facts. This is done because it is normal to say, e.g., *What you said is true (false)*, and not *That fact is true (false)*. (The reason for the precondition of *true* will be discussed in the following section.)

Other predicates over propositions, rather than facts, are, e.g.:

(36) j. $\sigma(believe) = \{\langle i, p \rangle: i \text{ is animate} \mid i \text{ has established as near certain}$
                that $\varphi(p) = 1\}$

   k. $\sigma(be\ convinced) = \{\langle i, p \rangle: i \text{ is animate} \mid i \text{ has established as abso-}$
                    lutely certain that $\varphi(p) = 1\}$

In section 2.4.2 the difference was mentioned between the anaphors *it* and *so* as objects of *believe*. This difference does not seem to be truth-conditional, but only discourse-semantic: if the proposition that is the extension of the object term is a new increment to i's belief-subdomain, the anaphor is *so* (and the SA has no NP over the object-S). But if the object clause represents an old increment to i's belief-subdomain, then the anaphor is *it*, and the SA has an NP over the object-S. Both *believe* and *be convinced* are taken as ranging over propositions, not facts, in object position, on grounds of naturalness of expressions like *I don't believe what you said*, or *I believe that information*, whereas it is unnatural or inappropriate to say *I believe those facts*.

The existential predicate ∃ can now be given its extension set:

(38) a. $\sigma(\exists) = \{\langle T, U/I^* \rangle$: for some term t, $\rho(t) \in I$ (if applicable) and
$\varphi(S^T_{x/t}) \neq 3 \mid T \cap U/I \neq \emptyset\}$
("$S^T_{x/t}$" stands for the S_x of the subject SD term (with the extension T), but with t replacing the variable x.)

That is, the existential predicate ∃ is two-termed, and takes as subject an SD term and as object either an SD term or a definite quantity term (a mass term or a definite plural term), in accordance with the specifications in section 2.2.

The precondition ensures that radical falsity is assigned when some term other than the one quantified over violates a precondition of the predicate P of S^T_x, as in:

(39) a. The Prime Minister's speech sold a car to the President.

We want such a sentence to be radically false when uttered in an appropriate discourse on account of the fact that the predicate *sell* has the categorial precondition that the subject term must refer to a human, or at any rate animate, being. The assignment of radical falsity in cases such as (39a) is a result of the condition that for some term t $S^T_{x/t}$ must have a classical value. This condition is not fulfilled since for no term t will "The Prime Minister's speech sold t to the President" have a classical value. Radical falsity is assigned, moreover, when the object-term in Semantic Analysis is not a set-denoter but a definite quantity term, with an extension of type I, and any term t referring to any member of I causes $S^T_{x/t}$ to be radically false, either because of category failure or because a precondition of existence is violated, or for any other reason that may cause radical falsity. Thus, of the following two sentences (uttered in an appropriate discourse)

(39) b. John met a mermaid.
c. John met one of the mermaids.

the former will be minimally false given that no mermaids exist, but the latter will be radically false since any term t referring to any discourse-defined intensional mermaid (given the absence of real mermaids) will make $S^T_{x/t}$ radically false. If, however, the world were such that there were indeed a few really existing mermaids, then there would be a term t referring to one of the real mermaids and $S_{x/t}^T$ would then be either true or minimally false, and so would (39b) be.

As regards the satisfaction condition it can be observed that if both T and U or I are entirely made up of extensional objects, any non-empty intersection must also consist exclusively of extensional objects. In such cases actual existence is entailed, as when I assert that *Some wine is red*. The set of all red things is extensional, and the set of all quantities of wine (or the total quantity of wine) is likewise extensional. Hence the actual existence of some red wine is entailed by this sentence. Actual existence is also entailed if only one of the two sets involved is fully extensional, since any non-empty intersection of an extensional and an intensional (or not entirely extensional) set must itself be entirely extensional. Thus the sentence *There is some wine*, expressing the fact that there is a non-empty intersection between the set of things that are there and the set of all quantities of wine, entails the actual existence of some wine, even though the set of things that are there is non-extensional since, as we have seen, there are many things that do not exist. On the other hand, if both sets involved are non-extensional, there is no guarantee of actual existence and hence no entailment to that effect. Thus the utterance *James is looking for some ghosts* may be true even though there *exist* no ghosts that James is looking for.

It is possible to add to the existential predicate (which, as we now realize, is inappropriately named) a specification of the cardinality or, less precisely, of the size of the non-empty intersection between the subject set and the object set, required for truth by the satisfaction condition. We can say that there are 1, 2, 3 ... barrels of wine, or that there are few, many, some of them. The formal and technical details, however, of such additions will not be gone into here.

The universal predicate *all* ($\forall$) is quite a bit more complex than $\exists$. (Other universal predicates, such as *every*, *each*, universal *any*, are probably even more complex, but they are not discussed here.) First, as has been said (section 2.2), there is a difference between *all* with and without the definite article or some other definite determiner. Thus, there is a difference between *All children like playing*, where extensions are not dependent on discourse for their fixing (apart from, of course, the present tense), and *All the children like playing*, where *the children* needs context to have its extension fixed. Grammatically, this is expressed by allowing the predicate $\forall$ to take either as SD term as object, or a (mass or plural) definite term. This difference is expressed in the characterization of the extension set, i.e. in (38b), by leaving the universal predicate the choice between an SD-term extension in object position (indicated by the variable U) or a definite mass or plural term extension (indicated by the variable I), in that position. The most serious problem, however, consists in getting entailments and truth-values right in all cases, including those where non-existent entities are involved, or empty sets, with extensional and intensional predicates. The following specification seems to do the job:

(38) b. $\sigma(\forall) = \{\langle T, U/I^* \rangle$: for all terms t such that $\rho(t) \in U/I$, $\varphi(S_{x/t}^T) \neq$
$$3 \mid \varphi(S_{x/t}^T) = 1\}$$

("$S_{x/t}^T$" is defined as for (38a).)

Let us try this out on a number of cases. A simple one is:

(40) a. All kings have huge bank accounts.
  b. All these kings have huge bank accounts.

For both sentences, T is the set of individuals with huge bank accounts, a non-empty set of extensional (real) individuals. In (40a), U is the (non-empty extensional) set of all kings. The precondition is fulfilled, since any name N of a real king in $S_{x/N}^T$, i.e. "N has a huge bank account", yields a sentence whose utterances (in the right Ds) will always have a classical value and will never be radically false because the king in question fulfils the preconditions of "have a huge bank account". (40a) is then true just in case each one of the real kings is a member of T and therefore has a huge bank account. Note that both (40a) and its minimal negation entail that there are really existing kings, the reason of this entailment being that "have a huge bank account" is an extensional predicate expression whose subject must refer to an existing individual for truth or minimal falsity. Note that if U is empty, radical falsity ensues on account of precondition failure. Utterances of the sentence

(40) c. All Australian kings have huge bank accounts.

are doomed to be radically false in this world, simply because the set of all Australian kings is empty.

Now consider (40b), whose SA-object term is not a set-denoter but a definite plural term, with a discourse-defined extension. (This SA-object term *these kings* ends up as part of the surface subject, due to the grammatical treatment of quantifying predicates and the position of the variable in the SD term acting as SA subject.) Depending on the discourse, the term *these kings* has an extensional extension, or an intensional one, or a mixed extension consisting of real and imagined kings. It is, furthermore, possible that the discourse is such that it provides no clues as to the identity of "these kings", in which case this term has no extension. This is not a violation of the precondition in (38b) or in any $S_{x/t}^T$. The absence of an extension only means that no reference can take place in any $S_{x/t}^T$, and that the second element in the pair $\langle T, I \rangle$ is not provided: there is no I for this discourse. It follows, given the truth definition, that in those cases utterances of (40b) are undefined and fall into the truth-value gap. If, on the other hand, I is defined, some truth-value is assigned. When I comprises only real kings, then an utterance of (40b) is either true or minimally false, not because ∀ is extensional with regard to I (which it is not), but because each name N of such a king in "N has a huge bank account" yields a classically valued (utterance of a) sentence. When I is mixed or entirely intensional, radical falsity ensues, because it is now not so that for all names N of the kings denoted "N has a huge bank account" yields a sentence whose utterances are guaranteed to be classically valued.

Likewise, utterances of

(40) d. All fictional characters in literature have huge bank accounts.

can only be radically false in this world, where fictional characters abound in literature, but where every utterance of "N has a huge bank account", where "N" is a definite term taking a fictional character in literature as its extension, is inevitably radically false.

Utterances of

(40) e. All kings exist.

are bound to be true in virtue of the semantics of this sentence together with the fact that the set of all kings (i.e. U) happens not to be empty. This is so because the set T of existing things is *per se* extensional due to the extension of *exist* (given in (36f)), and comprises everything that is real in this world. It must, therefore, include the set of all kings, which is purely extensional due to the predicate *king* being extensional with respect to its subject term, and non-empty. On the other hand,

(40) f. All Australian kings exist.

is bound to be minimally false since any term extension deserving the name "Australian king" is bound to be intensional, and intensional entities do not exist. For the same reason,

(40) g. All Australian kings are fictitious.

is bound to be true, as are utterances of

(40) h. All these Australian kings are fictitious.

in discourses where an (intensional) Australian king has been defined, given that the predicate *fictitious* has the extention set $\{i^* \mid i \text{ is not real}\}$. Discourses that do not allow for an Australian-king-denotation or address will make (40h) undefined. We note again, as with the definite article, that it is incorrect to regard the universal quantifier *all* as an inducer of existential presuppositions: if it were, (40h) could never be uttered in truth. Nor could an utterance of, e.g.,

(40) i. All things that John looks for exist.

be minimally false on account of the fact that John only looks for non-existing things. Yet, if John does indeed only look for non-existent things, the extension U of the SD term "$^x +_S$[look for(John,x)]" is non-empty (though intensional), and every utterance of a sentence "N exists", where "N" is a definite term for something John looks for, will be minimally false (given (36f)), but not radically false. Now, since no member of U is in the extension of *exist*, the satisfaction condition of ∀ is not fulfilled, and (40i) is minimally false – which is the way we want it to be.

It seems, generally, that the above account of the universal quantifier as expressed by English *all* satisfies speakers' intuitions reasonably enough. It is, in any case, far more sensitive to speakers' semantic intuitions than any of the existing analyses of natural language quantifiers.

3.2.5 The ambiguity of not

Several authors have raised objections against the assumption of an ambiguous *not* in English. It is perhaps useful, at this point, to look at their arguments in detail.

Kempson (1975) presents four arguments against the ambiguity of negation. First (pp. 82-3), we find the argument that a sentence cannot possibly both presuppose and entail another sentence. A reference is made to Wilson (1975) where "proof" is said to be given for this assertion, but Wilson (1975) contains no such proof. Apart from this reference, however, the argument runs (ibid.): "This is so because for any two sentences S_1 and S_2, the falsity of S_1 cannot both be a necessary condition for the truth of S_2 and not a necessary condition for the truth of S_2. So the analysis of negative sentences as ambiguous cannot be correct." This is a curious argument. For if it appears that in some cases the falsity of S_1 is required for the truth of S_2 and in other cases it is not, then surely a solution is provided by any theory that claims that the expression "falsity" is ambiguous. It is unclear how Kempson could conclude that the ambiguity solution *cannot* be correct.

The remaining arguments in Kempson (1975) still fail to establish the non-ambiguity of negation. On pp. 95-100, three further arguments are presented: an argument against internal versus external negation, an argument based on multiple negation, and an argument based on what is called "standard tests of ambiguity".

The first of these need not concern us here: if it is correct, it reinforces what has been concluded above. Moreover, the concepts of "internal" and "external" negation are ill defined (as so often in the literature; cp. Karttunen and Peters 1979: 47), so that a discussion risks being fruitless. The argument based on multiple negations first sets up a man of straw then to shoot it down. It is said, first, that emphatic accents, as in *He HAS passed his exams*, are to be analysed as denials of negated sentences. If then an interlocutor says: *No, he has NOT*, and the first again: *Yes he HAS!* then negations are accumulated in a way no longer congruous with intuitive understanding. In particular, Kempson says, the distinction between the two alleged negation operators (ill defined as they are) would be lost. However, the argument, if it is one, collapses if emphatic accent is not analysed as double negation. Moreover, real double negations all have the property that the highest negation is radical, since *not* is a Positive Polarity Item.

Finally, the argument based on "standard tests for ambiguity" is deficient for two reasons. First, the notion of standard test, in Kempson (1975), appears to be limited to what was or could be considered standard in *linguistic* theory of the early 1970s. In fact, only one test is applied, that of preservation of ambiguity across VP-pronominalization (Lakoff 1970), and what is presented as "evidence" (p. 100) is nothing but a not very convincing acceptability judgement made by the author. In general, when applied to *not*, arguments of this nature prove inconclusive, whether they aim at establishing ambiguity (Martin 1982) or at showing the absence of it (Atlas 1977). But secondly, if more widely accepted tests for ambiguity are applied, the case for the ambiguity of *not* would seem to be strengthened rather than weakened.

A widely accepted test is: "Vague terms are only dubiously applicable to marginal objects, but an ambiguous term such as *light* may be at once clearly true of various objects (such as dark feathers) and clearly false of them" (Quine 1960: 129). This test appeals to judgements of truth or falsity, given a particular state of affairs. It would seem that in a situation where a new law on immigration has been passed,

(41) The new law on immigration is not bald.

can be considered (trivially) true, but also false. It will be considered false in a context, say, where entities that are not bald are to be listed so that their hair can be shaven off. "Not bald" is then to be read as "unbald", i.e. "having hair".

Another widely accepted test for ambiguity is given by the criterion of non-truth resulting from non-truth of an entailment. If, at the same time and given the same state of affairs, an utterance A cannot be true if another utterance B is not true, and also may be true even though B is not true, then A must be ambiguous, or B must be ambiguous. Consider, for example:

(42) Bill has not forgotten that we have a meeting at two.

Let it not be so that we have a meeting at two. Now, in one sense (42) cannot be true – in the sense, that is, in which (42) entails that Bill knows full well that we have a meeting at two. But in another sense (and with another intonation) (42) is clearly true: how could he have forgotten that we have a meeting at two, if there isn't even a meeting at that time! And if we do have a meeting at two, the same duplicity of meaning is observed. Suppose Bill does not know about the meeting, then, in one sense, (42) cannot be true. But in another sense (42) may well be true: he may never have known about the meeting anyway.[13] Or take:

(43) Harry did not lock all the gates.

This entails that there is at least one gate, under the standard analysis cherished by Kempson. Yet (43) is compatible, under certain emphatic intonational patterns, with there not being any gates at all: of course he did not lock all the gates – there WERE no gates!

We will, therefore, regard Kempson's crusade against the ambiguity of *not* as unsuccessful. The same applies to all but one of Gazdar's arguments (1979: 65-6). He writes (p. 65): "We have no independent reason for believing that all or any of the surface negative morphemes in English are homonymous." Here he overplays his hand, since, if we take other negative morphemes than just *not* into account, assuming that in all cases concerned there is just one kind of negation, the "sentential negation operator definable on a standard bivalent semantics" (p. 66), it is easily established that this semantic negation is homonymous, and that bivalence is at serious risk.

Take the two sentences:

(44) a. The new law on immigration is not married.
     b. The new law on immigration is unmarried.

If there is only one negation, the ordinary bivalent sentential negation, these two sentences ought to have exactly the same truth-conditions. Yet (Allwood 1977: 30), the former "is barely acceptable as a true sentence", while the latter "is both unacceptable and false". It is clear why Allwood regards the former as only "barely" acceptable as a true sentence: emphatic tone on *not* is needed, so that it is the radical, presupposition-cancelling negation. In (44b), however, the negation has been lexically incorporated, and such negations, as we have seen, are always minimal, or, as Allwood puts it (p. 28), "the negative terms seem to be interpreted with categorial presuppositions". Therefore, if we take other negative morphemes than just *not* into account, we hardly seem to have any other choice left than to accept that there is more than one negation in natural language.

One wonders, anyway, how Allwood reconciles his observations just quoted with his assertion (1977: 43): "We have in all cases taken negation to be the same basic semantic operation indicating that a certain state of affairs

---

[13] Cp. Shakespeare, *The Taming of the Shrew* (v.i.49):

Vincentio: Come hither, you rogue. What, have you forgot me?
Biondello: Forgot you! No, Sir: I could not forget you, for I never saw you before in all my life.

quoted by De Rijk (1974: 64) in a similar context).

is not a fact. We have taken negation to have exactly the properties of logical negation: always giving the predication it operates on an opposite truth-value." Allwood's position thus seems to be inconsistent. This is worth mentioning since there has been a tendency in the literature on presupposition (Karttunen and Peters 1979: 47; Kempson 1975, to mention just a couple of cases) to be inconsistent in precisely this way. On the one hand two different negations are accepted, whose differences clearly seem to involve truth-conditions; on the other, lip-service is paid to the monument of classical bivalent logic, which seems to inspire so much awe that authors are often obviously reluctant to depart from it, even though they themselves implicitly admit that one must.

Gazdar (1979: 65–6) falls back on Allwood (1972), Atlas (1975), and Kempson (1975) in support of his position. These "have produced a series of arguments which show that natural language negation is unambiguous ... None of them ... have been challenged in the literature, so that we are entitled to assume their validity." (This author, again, does not seem too bent on challenging classical logic: the alleged absence of challenges in the literature suffices as an argument, for him, that all is well; he feels no urge, apparently, to probe for himself.) But it was said too soon. Allwood (1972) was republished, in a slightly revised version, as Allwood (1977) (from which we have just quoted). In that publication there is not so much a stringent argument as a position taken and illustrated. We have just seen that that position is inconsistent. Atlas (1975) was disowned in Atlas (1979: 275): "However congenial this strategy in 1975 I ultimately regarded it as unsatisfying." Kempson (1975) has just been discussed.

A further argument put forward by Gazdar runs as follows (p. 66):

The proponent of a nonbivalent semantics is faced with a dilemma. If he chooses a negation operator which predicts the presuppositions in (11) [= *John doesn't regret having failed*], then he loses the ability to account for the possible TRUTH of (13) [= *John doesn't regret having failed, because, in fact, he passed*]. But if he chooses a negation operator which allows for the TRUTH of (13), then he loses the ability to predict the presupposition of (11), which is what his nonbivalent semantics was introduced to do in the first place.

This argument, however, is based on a defective understanding of non-bivalent logics. As shown in the Appendix to this book by Weijters, it is not only possible but also natural to have n-valued logics with $n-1$ negations. A three-valued logic has room for two negations. This argument, which is really an argument against non-bivalence, is based on the misapprehension that n-valued logics will still have to do with one negation.

Gazdar, furthermore, seems insensitive to intonational features. He refers (p. 66) to Hausser (1976: 253), who observes that "a certain ironic intonation" may cancel presuppositions of negative sentences. Gazdar's comment is that other intonations may cancel presuppositions as well, and that "almost any sentence in this book can be pronounced with a certain ironic intonation if one so chooses". This reaction is unsubtle, to say the least. Intonational phenomena are known to be difficult to analyse and to handle theoretically in a precise way, due, in part, to the absence of an adequate notational system. Yet phoneticians know very well that intonation, though hard to catch, is extremely delicate and is in many ways intimately connected with central semantic distinctions. The mere coincidence that semantically orientated linguists tend to have little or no training in phonetics and work in a tradition of massive indifference towards phonetic facts, is no justification for a facile dismissal of intonational features as a factor to be reckoned with in semantic analyses. Hausser's expression "a certain ironic intonation" may not have been the happiest possible choice, but one should not try to win an argument on account of one's opponent's less luckily chosen terminology.

It thus seems that just one serious objection remains with regard to the ambiguity of *not*: if *not* is ambiguous in English, then why is it that we do not find it disambiguated in other languages? Ordinary homonyms, such as *board* or *bank*, tend not to be homonymous in other languages. Yet *not* never seems to be represented in other languages by distinct forms according to whether it is the minimal or the radical negation. There are many languages with more than one negation (Arabic, Blackfoot, Latin, Greek, French, Irish, etc.), but the differences found are to do with modality, emphasis, morpheme environment and what not, but, as far as can be seen, not with minimal and radical negation. Even if tomorrow a language were to be found that does express the two negations by means of different lexical material, it remains a remarkable fact that a distinction that seems so well motivated from a semantic point of view, is so weakly represented on the lexical or morphological level in the languages of the world. Gazdar (1979: 65) mentions this point, and he deserves an adequate answer.

First of all, it must be observed that the postulated ambiguity of *not* is not a purely accidental, idiosyncratic fact of the lexicon of some language, like ordinary cases of lexical ambiguity. If *not* is ambiguous in English or in any other language, it is so between two closely related logico-semantic operators and not between a random pair of meanings, as in the case of *board* or *bank*. As ambiguities go, therefore, the ambiguity of *not*, if real, is highly idiosyncratic. Then, it must not be forgotten that we do not really claim that *not* is ambiguous or homonymous, for what is to be regarded as radical *not* is invariably marked by a special intonation on itself as well as on the surrounding verbal material. Thirdly, and this is the crucial part of the defence, given the principles and structures involved in the discourse-bound semantic processing of utterances of natural language, there is no need for any natural language to distinguish the two negations formally. The discourse is always such that it does the disambiguating for you, so to speak.

The radical negation, as has been said (see example (29) above), has a metalinguistic touch about it. In fact, a radically negated utterance of a sentence has an 'echo' suggesting that the argument proposition of the negation has been uttered, or at least is 'on everybody's lips', in preceding discourse. (And when the negation stands over a PPI, the negation must be radical so that the echo becomes a property of the sentence type.) The radical negation thus requires that the negated proposition is already, somehow, part of the discourse domain D. Example (29) showed that this is not an exclusive property of radical negation: minimal negation can do the same, under certain conditions. But it is a distinctive property. Moreover, radical negation seems not to work unless it is specified what exactly is wrong with D so that the negated argument proposition is radically false (necessarily false given the falsity of some proposition in D). It will be noticed that whenever a radical negation occurs, it is accompanied by an explanation of what is wrong in D and thus has to be put right. The quote from Shakespeare in note 13 bears clear testimony to this. Radical negation, requiring as it does a repair in D, is highly marked (as is witnessed by its intonational features) with respect to the unmarked minimal negation. It is metalinguistic and, moreover, wants a specification of the D-repair called for. All these factors may well be taken to contribute to a situation where it does not 'pay' to have two lexically distinct negations: the discourse does the sorting out anyway. The conditions of use for radical *not* always make it stand out and be recognized. Moreover, as will be remembered, radical *not* can only occur as speech-act negation, so that embedded *not*s are exempt from possible confusion anyway.

A naïve reply would be that it is possible, therefore, to do with one single negation, the classical bivalent negation " ⌐ ", since whatever extra is needed is supplied by the discourse or is deducible from the grammatical position of the negation. This reply is naïve in the light of the arguments for the ambiguity of negation adduced above. It should be noted, in particular, that if one single negation is envisaged it cannot be truth-functional because of cases where a negated (utterance of a) sentence can be both true and not true of a given state of affairs, as demonstrated above in connection with (42). Double negation, likewise, shows this up. Suppose someone is accused of not stopping in front of a red traffic light. Yet the accused never was there at all: it's all a case of mistaken identity. So he says, in truth: *I did NOT not stop there.* Now, clearly, the conclusion that he did stop is unwarranted. Yet under truth-functional classical negation this conclusion is inescapable. So whoever advocates one single negation must give up its truth-functionality, which is likely to be a higher price than he is prepared to pay. Moreover, it does not help him if he does pay the price, because even so the negation must be deemed ambiguous in the light of the examples given. It seems sensible to keep up truth-functionality and accept an unmessy but ambiguous negation.

There is another consideration as well that deserves attention here. As has been observed, the radical negation represents the marked case versus the unmarked minimal negation, as appears from the special intonational features and the restricted usage that are associated with radical *not*. This feature of markedness is accounted for by the postulation of an eminently reasonable functional principle, the *principle of minimum effort* in discourse domain construction. This principle implies that there will be a preference to select readings of (utterances of) sentences that are maximally consistent with the domain as it has been built up so far. This preference is especially manifest in the interpretation of clauses embedded under intensional predicates, such as *believe*. When a sentence like:

(45) a. Harry believes that his son lives in Kentucky.

is uttered in a context where no son of Harry's has been mentioned yet, there is an 'invited inference' or 'suggestion' that Harry has a son. In other words, the unsuspecting listener will take it that Harry has a son (whom Harry believes to live in Kentucky). If the listener is then told that Harry has, in fact, no son but only believes that he has one, he cannot complain that he has been falsely informed because strictly speaking (45a) does not entail that Harry has a son. But he has some right to say that he has been led up the garden path. This is because an interpretation where Harry actually has a son (so that a denotation or address for Harry's son is in the truth-domain), whom he believes to live in Kentucky, yields a simpler and more coherent domain than an interpretation where Harry has no son but only believes to have one. This issue will be returned to in the following section, and in chapter 5, when intensional phenomena are explicitly discussed.

The principle of minimum effort is equally manifest in the case of negation. An utterance *not*-A requires less interpretative effort when *not* is minimal than when it is radical, simply because the minimal negation requires no *post hoc* revisions in D, whereas the radical negation does: when *not* is radical, D will be warranted for truth only if it is revised in such a way that A no longer fits onto it. It is because of this principle of minimum effort, which seems very reasonable in the light of general considerations of cognitive functionality, that men like Frege, Strawson, Van Fraassen and many others fell victim to the misapprehension that when $A \geqslant B$, A, as well as not-A, entails B: when a sentence is presented in isolation, outside any precise context of discourse, the unmarked reading will be taken to be the 'right' one, and the marked reading will tend to pass unnoticed.

3.3 The definition of presupposition as a semantic notion

It is high time now to pass on to the discourse properties of presupposition. So far, only the logical property of presupposition has been investigated in detail, but we still lack a definition of presupposition, nor has it been made clear how precisely presuppositions are to be recognized. In this section we shall concentrate on the question of the real nature, and the definition, of presupposition. The conclusion will be that presupposition finds its definition in the discourse machinery of semantics: presupposition is primarily and by definition a discourse phenomenon. Together with anaphora, one might say, it makes up the 'cement' of discourse structures. It should be noted that this point of view does not brand presupposition as a "pragmatic" phenomenon. In rather large sections of the literature it is customary to regard anything to do with discourse as "pragmatic". Although one may not wish to quarrel over a term, one must also realize that terms provoke associations and expectations. Since "semantics" for us is the theory of interpretation of sentences in use on account of their systematic structural properties, and since it is a central contention of the theory that discourse plays a systematic role in interpretation, it would be strange if the term 'pragmatic" were used, as it often is in the literature, for all things to do with discourse. So when it is said here that presupposition is primarily a semantic and not primarily a logical notion, what is implied is that the nature of what we wish to recognize as presuppositions lies in their discourse properties, not in their logic.

There are some good reasons why it is not desirable to define presupposition in a purely logical way. That is, one might propose that presupposition should be defined as follows (cp. (28) above):

(46) $A \gg B =_{\text{Def}} A \models B$ AND $\sim A \models B$.

Such a definition, however, has too many drawbacks for it to be considered adequate. First, according to this definition, a logically true sentence, i.e. a sentence whose utterances cannot but be true, such as

(47) Either all mermaids exist, or there are no mermaids.

would be presupposed by any other sentence of the language, and a sentence which is necessarily radically false would presuppose any sentence of the language except itself. This is serious (protestations to the contrary in Seuren 1979 notwithstanding), since if, say,

(48) We were all packed in an ancient Cadillac.

(to take just an arbitrary sentence of English) were said to presuppose, say, (47), not only the intuitive notion of presupposition would be done an injustice, but, worse, it would no longer be possible to apply any general observational criteria for the diagnosis of presuppositions.

Then, the preconditions of the truth-functional predicates and of *all*, as in (38) and (39b), would give rise to quaint 'presuppositions'. Thus it would follow that, e.g.,

(49) a. That Harold was guilty did not surprise me.

presupposes the following sentence

(49) b. The sentence "That Harold was guilty surprised me" is not radically false.

on account of the definition of the extension set of the minimal negation as given in (38a). Note that the negation in (49a) must be minimal given that there is a factive clause in the position of the grammatical subject. But such a presupposition goes against the intuitive grain. We are happy to say that (49a) presupposes:

(49) c. Harold was guilty.

but not (49b). And our intuition is not entirely arbitrary, for it is a fact that a coherent discourse comes about when (49c) is uttered first and then (49a), but not when (49b) is uttered first and then (49a). Or at least, a discourse such as the latter would be frowned upon as being somewhat extraordinary. In other words, if it is accepted, as seems reasonable in the light of the intuitive notion of presupposition, that whenever $A \gg B$, an utterance of B followed by an utterance of A (preferably connected by *and* or *but*, and granting anaphoric devices) makes for a good and normal discourse fragment, then the preconditions of the truth-functional predicates and of *all* do not generate presuppositions directly, even though they have the normal logical properties of preconditions that do generate presuppositions. The idea (central in Van der Sandt 1982) that it should be a condition for presupposition that an utterance of a presupposition followed by an utterance of the carrier sentence must in all cases deliver a natural and coherent piece of discourse, is not to be discarded lightheartedly, since it is not only highly satisfactory from an intuitive point of view but it is also a precious observational criterion for the spotting of presuppositions.

Finally, it is a remarkable fact, noticed by a variety of authors, that in some valid intuitive sense one can say that questions, commands, wishes and indeed any kind of speech act have presuppositions, but there is no satisfactory construal of the term "entailment" that would ascribe entailments to questions, commands, wishes, etc. In other words, if presupposition is defined as a particular constellation of entailments, as in (46), it is unclear why questions etc. are not plausibly said to have entailments, but are plausibly said to have presuppositions, as appears from the famous example:

(50) When did you stop beating your wife?

which undeniably carries the presupposition that the addressee was in the habit of beating his wife. A purely logical account of presupposition is unable to deal with presuppositions of speech acts other than assertions, which is empirically inadequate.

It seems inevitable, therefore, to conclude that a definition like (46) is untenable. The formulation of the logical property of presupposition, as given in (28) above, may be correct, but it cannot be transformed into a definition. A distinction must be made between preconditions that do and preconditions that do not generate presuppositions. That is, not all preconditions of predicates generate presuppositions in the proper semantic sense of the term. The question is: which do and which do not?

The correct general answer to this question seems to be that, in principle, *all entailments derived from preconditions are presuppositions except those which are truth-value statements and are thus on a metalevel with respect to the ongoing discourse.*

Thus (49b), though directly derived from the precondition of the minimal negation as formulated in (38a), cannot be a presupposition because (49b) is a truth-value statement. But then, (49b) entails (49c), since if the sentence mentioned in (49b), i.e. "That Harold was guilty surprised me" has a classical truth-value, the preconditions of its highest predicate, the factive verb *surprise*, must be fulfilled and (49c), "Harold was guilty", follows. This can then safely be considered a presupposition of (49a). Or take a similar example involving the universal quantifier *all*. Utterances of, e.g.,

(51) a. All committees are married to Parliament.

must be considered radically false (in its literal meaning) because of failure of the first precondition of *all* as in (39b): let *the finance committee* be a term referring to some real committee, then utterances of:

(51) b. The finance committee is married to Parliament.

are bound to be radically false because of precondition failure of *married*. However, the immediate formulation of the precondition of (51a):

(51) c. The sentence "The finance committee is married to Parliament" is not radically false.[14]

cannot be a presupposition because it is a truth-value statement. But non-metastatements following from the preconditions of (51a) are again presuppositions. Thus, e.g.,

(51) d. All committees are human individuals.

can be regarded as a presupposition of (51a). It is bound to be false, of course, which reinforces the case for the radical falsity of (51a). This rules

---

[14] Strictly speaking, (51c) is not an entailment of (51a), since it involves the reference relation between the term *the finance committee* and some real committee, and reference relations cannot be introduced by entailment. Strictly speaking, the following is a proper entailment derived from the preconditions of *all*:

All utterances of sentences of the form "x is married to Parliament" with a term t for x referring to a real committee are classically valued.

(51c), however, will do for expository purposes.

out the troublesome cases presented by the preconditions of the truth-functional predicates and of *all*.

The difficulty mentioned above, that a logically true sentence would be presupposed by any other sentence of the language if presupposition is defined as in (46), and that a logically radically false sentence would presuppose all other sentences in the language, is eliminated by the stipulation that all presuppositions must be derived from the preconditions of the highest predicate of the carrier sentence. Clearly, no such relation exists between, say, (47) and (48) above.

We are thus left only with the last problem mentioned, the problem that presuppositions adhere not only to assertions but also to other speech act types. And here we come to the heart of the matter. For the central characterizing feature of presuppositions is that they are required in preceding discourse, before the carrier sentence can be interpreted. If the propositional part of a sentence S generates a presupposition P under the constraints just described, S cannot be interpreted unless its presuppositions have been added to the discourse D. Now, if S is an assertion, P is entailed because truth of S in D means that $i(S)$, i.e. the increment of S in D, brings about no falsity in D. If $i(P)$ is required for $i(S)$, $i(P)$ cannot bring about a falsity in D either. But if S is a question, P is not entailed because questions have no entailments. Yet P is a presupposition of S, which means that $i(P)$ is required in D if S is to be interpretable so that $i(S)$ can be added to D. This discourse property of presuppositions is considered here to be axiomatic in the sense that no formal account or explanation is sought for the fact that non-meta-level entailments derived from preconditions are required in preceding discourse. Informally or intuitively one understands that this special property of this class of preconditional entailments is to do with economy of expression in coherent discourse, but although such a notion is undoubtedly essentially correct, no formal analysis will be attempted for it.

The discourse property of presupposition has been noted by a variety of authors, but Van der Sandt (1982) was the first to incorporate discourse acceptability conditions systematically into the theory of presupposition. If $S \gg P$, then invariably P followed by S, and preferably connected with *and* or *but* on account of the internal link between S and P,[15] makes for an acceptable, coherent or well-formed bit of discourse. We shall use this typical feature of presupposition as the prime testing criterion and observational basis for pressupositionhood. The test takes a double form. First, as has been said, "P (and/but) S" must make for an acceptable discourse bit. This is so because (a) P is entailed by S so that the truth-domain D must be such that

---

[15] Cp. McCawley (1981: 80): "Conjoining is normal only when the conjuncts are instances of the same general proposition, and conjunction reduction is sensitive to the understood general proposition." It should be added that conjoining is normal also when the conjuncts contribute to one overall proposition, as when the first is a presupposition of the second.

it excludes $\sim P$ and $\simeq P$, and (b) because the typical presuppositional property of the entailment is that P must precede S. Secondly, and for the same reasons, a discourse which explicitly does not exclude the falsity of P together with the truth of S must be inconsistent: "perhaps not-P but S" must be a contradiction. (In most cases, the test "not-P but S" suffices, but the possibility operator over not-P is sometimes crucial (see section 5.4)):[16]

(52) a. Joan has come back.
    b. Joan has been away.
    c. Joan has been away, but she has come back.
    d. !Joan may not have been away, but she has come back.

On the other hand, (53b) is not a presupposition of (53a) (though cases of this kind are usually thought to be presuppositions), because although (53c) is a natural bit of discourse, (53d) is not a contradiction:

(53) a. Lady Fortune neighed.
    b. Lady Fortune was a horse.
    c. Lady Fortune was a horse, and she neighed.
    d. Lady Fortune may not have been a horse, but she neighed.

In general, predicates of animal sounds (*bleat, bray, bark, neigh, mew*, etc.) do not have the precondition that the subject be of the appropriate species: the link between the species and the verb is partly one of biologically determined sound quality, and partly one of general knowledge of nature.

This observational test for presuppositionhood is positive also for factive presuppositions. Take the following:

(54) a. Bill is delighted that he was elected to the board of directors.
    b. Bill was elected to the board of directors.
    c. Bill was elected to the board of electors, and he is delighted that he was.
    d. !Bill may not have been elected to the board of directors, but he is delighted that he was.

Likewise, the presuppositions that go with cleft or pseudocleft sentences, and with sentences with contrastively or emphatically accented constituents, satisfy the test, as will be shown in sections 3.5.1.

[16] Note that entailments that are not presuppositions fail the test: if $S \models E$ but $S \not\Rrightarrow E$, than "E (and/but) S" is not an acceptable bit of discourse:

    (i) Harry bought tulips.
    (ii) Harry bought flowers.
    (iii) !Harry bought flowers, and/but he bought tulips.
    (iv) !Harry may not have bought flowers, but he bought tulips.

With *and*, (iii) is acceptable only if read as "Harry bought flowers, and what he bought was tulips". With *but* one feels the need to read "Although Harry bought flowers, what he bought was tulips". In any reading that is possible for (iii), however, the effortless interpretation and naturalness found with truly presuppositional cases is absent.

Presuppositions of clauses that are embedded in such a way in a larger sentence that the clause in question is not entailed, are not presuppositions. There is a great deal of confusion on this matter in the literature on presupposition, sometimes only of a terminological nature, but more often due to insufficient attention being paid to the logical properties of presupposition. Here we shall be ruthless, and say that there is a presupposition only if the alleged presupposition is entailed by the assertive form of the sentence in question. This fits in with the discourse test. Thus, (45a) does not presuppose (45b), because, although (45c) is all right, so is (45d):

(45) a. Harry believes that his son lives in Kentucky.
   b. Harry has a son.
   c. Harry has a son, and he believes that his son lives in Kentucky.
   d. Harry may not have a son, but he believes that his son lives in Kentucky.

The confusion over this matter is similar to the Strawsonian misapprehension that presuppositions are preserved under negation. In both cases, what remains of the embedded presupposition is a suggestion or 'invited inference'. Where they differ is that with negation there are wide categories of cases where, contrary to the general rule, presuppositions of the embedded argument clause are fully preserved. Moreover, as we have seen, there are also many cases, in particular those where a PPI is placed under negation, where not even a suggestion remains of the embedded presupposition. These observations made us distinguish between the minimal and the radical negation. In the case of *believe* and other entailment-cancelling embedding predicates, however, it never happens that embedded presuppositions are fully preserved, though it does happen that they disappear without a trace, leaving behind not even a suggestion or invited inference.

The whole complex of problems around the fate of embedded presuppositions is known in the literature as the *projection problem of presupposition*. For reasons that are not entirely clear, this problem has dominated the presupposition literature perhaps more than is warranted by its intrinsic interest. In any case, remarkably little has come of the various treatments found in the relevant literature (mostly in the 1970s), and it would seem that this is the inevitable result of a somewhat myopic preoccupation with the question of how to formulate 'rules' for the stopping, filtering or letting through of embedded presuppositions (as in Langendoen and Savin 1971; Karttunen 1973, 1974; Karttunen and Peters 1979; Gazdar 1979), whereas the more basic question of the nature and the logical property of presupposition was neglected. The projection problem of presupposition will be returned to below, when the machinery of subdomains will have been introduced. It will then become clear that no separate 'projection rules' need be formulated, since the machinery set up for independent reasons will automatically explain and account for the projection observations as they are found in the literature (and for others as well).

The notion of presupposition is thus seen to be analysable in terms of entailment and the property of being required in preceding discourse for the interpretability of the carrier sentence. This latter property will from now on be called *prejection*. In general:

S projects P ($S > P$) just in case (a) P is entailed by S or by some (possibly non-entailed) clause embedded in S by virtue of the preconditions of the predicate figured by S or its embedded clause, and (b) P is not a truth-value statement, and (c) "P (and/but) S" is an acceptable discourse.

What is needed now is an independent definition of the notion of *acceptable discourse*. The first systematic attempt at defining discourse acceptability conditions, and at the same time the first demonstration of the relevance of discourse acceptability as an independent criterion in presuppositional semantics is found in Van der Sandt 1982 (esp. ch. 5).[17] It is shown there that the notion of presupposition is directly related to discourse acceptability conditions. The central condition on acceptability in Van der Sandt (1982: 185) is the requirement that the discourse D must entail neither the sentence to be added nor its negation. Other, subsidiary conditions are then stated which are seen to account for presuppositional behaviour. Thus, for example, a modal sentence (under a modal operator of possibility or necessity) is acceptable only if the embedded clause is acceptable. Or if a disjunction is to be added, both disjuncts must be acceptable separately. A conditional is acceptable only if the antecedent is acceptable and the consequent is accept-able, or at least a combination of both in either order is acceptable. We can thus draw up a list of acceptability conditions, more or less like the following:

For any sentence A, $i(A)$ is acceptable in a discourse D, if

(a) A is non-complex, or under a negation operator, and $D \not\models A$ and $D \not\models \neg A$.

(b) A is of the form $Poss(B)$ or $Nec(B)$ (i.e. B under a modality of possi-bility or necessity), and $i(B)$ fulfils the relevant acceptability condi-tions.

(c) A is of the form B *or* C, and $i(B)$ and $i(C)$ fulfil the relevant accept-ability conditions.

(d) A is of the form *if* B *then* C, and $i(B)$ and $i(C)$ fulfil the relevant acceptability conditions, either separately or in some ordered com-bination.

.
.
.

[17] I refer to the original Dutch version of Van der Sandt 1982, and not the revised English version (forthcoming), that not being available for reference at the time of writing.

Such a list, however, as is recognized by Van der Sandt, is not easily made complete. It is, moreover, more taxonomic than explanatory (for further discussion see section 5.4).

It would seem that a simple explanatory principle can be formulated in the following way. Increments to a discourse all have the typical effect (or function) of either restricting the class of possible verification domains in which the incremented discourse is true, or, at least, of increasing the available knowledge of the class of verification domains in which the discourse is true. Let a discourse D be true in the class of verification domains V, then $D + i(A)$, for any given acceptable sentence A, is true in V' where $V' \subseteq V$. If $V' = V$, then $D + i(A)$ is more informative about V than just D.

For example, if D is true for all $V \in V$ where John is ill, then the addition of, say, *John has measles* restricts V to V' where John is ill with measles. This increment is thus restrictive with respect to V. Increments under entailing predicates, such as *entail, infer, apparently, therefore, so* and *follow*, are not restrictive in this sense: if D is true for all $V \in V$ where, say, all humans are mortal and John is a human, then the addition of *Therefore, John is mortal* does not restrict V but leaves it as it is. In this case, however, the knowledge available about V and expressed in D is increased.

We subsume the disjunctive condition of V-restrictiveness or informativeness under the cover-term of *informativeness*, since that is what it is all about. *The single general condition of discourse acceptability is thus given by the functional criterion of informativeness.* This criterion ensures that $D \not\models A$ and $D \not\models \neg A$, except for entailing statements, and thus replaces condition (a) above. That is, it rules out repetitions (*Today is Friday and today is Friday*), since as soon as D contains i(today is Friday) and repetition will fail to either restrict V or provide more information about V. The criterion will also exclude contradictions if it is stipulated that the restriction of V to V' does not result in an empty V': no addition to any given D may be such that the class of possible verification domains in which D is true is reduced to the null set.

It should be observed here that a violation of the constraint against repetitions is less serious than a violation of the constraint against contradictions. In fact, language has certain means at its disposal to override the non-repetition constraint, in particular the emphasis of the finite verb form (with *do*-support and accent, in English, for all verbs except the modals and the other auxiliaries, which simply receive emphatic accent). It is thus possible to have, e.g., a discourse like:

Kate has been away. Richard doesn't know that she has been away. In fact, he is absolutely convinced that she has nót been away. Still, she hás been away.

Apart, however, from minor complications and escape clauses, we can now formulate as an overall principle the *informativeness criterion* for acceptable additions to a given discourse D as follows:

For any sentence A, i(A) is acceptable in D just in case either i(A) restricts V to V' (V' $\subset$ V; V' $\neq \emptyset$), or i(A) contains information about V that has not so far been made available in D.

As regards complex sentences, their conditions of acceptability must now be seen to follow from the general criterion plus the mechanics of discourse semantics. For conjunctions the answer is now simple: *B and C* is acceptable in D just in case i(B) is acceptable in D and i(C) is acceptable in D + i(A). Modal statements are looked at in detail in chapter 5, disjunctions and conditionals in chapter 4, and there will be many other occasions throughout to consider complex sentential structures from this point of view.

This account of acceptability in discourse, in so far as it is adequate, must be considered minimal. It is reasonable to expect more from a discourse than is warranted by these conditions. For example, a discourse like: *John came barging into the room. His upper wheel, however, wouldn't start, and he couldn't manage to lift it*, would qualify as 'acceptable', but for it to be acceptable in an intuitively satisfactory sense more is needed than the fulfilment of the acceptability condition(s) developed above. What is needed on top of that is the availability of some information about what it is for John to have an upper wheel, what it is for that thing to be started or to be lifted, and why one would try to lift it. In other words, background information is indispensable for a proper interpretation so that the listener knows what is the case when the discourse is true. The above conditions are, if correct, necessary requirements for discourse acceptability. They can be considered sufficient (if properly elaborated) only if sufficient background information is available. It is perhaps correct to say that they are (or can be made to be) sufficient in the sense that it is always possible to think up a background story so that a discourse meeting the conditions is not only acceptable but also fully interpretable. We thus distinguish between acceptability and full interpretability of a discourse.

Thus, all presuppositions of a sentence S are, besides entailments of S, also projections of S. And all projections of S are either presuppositions of S or of some clause embedded in S. When S projects P without presupposing it, we say that P is a *mere projection* of S. Mere projections give rise to what we have so far called "suggestions" or "invited inferences".

They are recognized by the following criterion: P must be a presupposition (and thus fulfil the observational criterion formulated above for presuppositions) of some clause embedded in S, and the discourse "P (and/but) S" must be acceptable. It is not required that "perhaps not-P but S" be inconsistent (it will usually not be). Thus, (45b) is a mere prejection of (45a), but (53b) is not a (mere) prejection of (53a) since it is not presupposed by any clause embedded in (53a) or by (53a) itself. (55b) is not a (mere) prejection of (55a), nor (55e) of (55d), because acceptability condition (d) is not met:

(55) a. If Harry has a son, his son lives in Kentucky.
 b. Harry has a son.
 c. !Harry has a son, and if he has a son, his son lives in Kentucky.
 d. If Harry's son lives in Kentucky, Harry has a son.
 e. Harry has a son.
 f. !Harry has a son, and if his son lives in Kentucky, he has a son.

As will be shown in the chapters to follow, observations such as these are immediately interpretable in terms of a machinery of domains and subdomains. We say that if S presupposes P, P is projected into the truth-domain (and entailed if S is an assertion). If S merely prejects P, then i(P) can be added to the truth-domain as far as S itself is concerned. The truth-domain may be such that i(P) is excluded (for example when D already contains i($\sim P$)), but P will be prejected as long as the isolated bit of discourse "P and/ but S" is acceptable. That is, prejection is a semantic property, independent of *actual* context or discourse. What counts is that there is nothing in S itself that blocks the addition of i(P) to D. In (55a), for example, the blocking is caused by the fact that the antecedent of the conditional is itself a presupposition of the consequent. Given the general discourse acceptability condition for conditional constructions, (55a) is unacceptable in any domain that already contains i(Harry has a son), since in any such discourse domain the antecedent is unacceptable on account of the condition which forbids repetition. Generally, as was pointed out at the end of the previous section, the principle of minimum effort will ensure that i(P) is added to the truth-domain if nothing in S or D is in its way. This is what underlies the suggestive force of mere prejections. If P is an embedded presupposition but i(P) is blocked from entering D because of a structural property of S, then S neither presupposes nor prejects P, and no suggestion or invited inference remains. The embedded presupposition is "cancelled" or "neutralized", as the literature calls it. Instead of being added to the truth-domain D, i(P) is then added to, or prejected into, some subdomain under D.

As has been said, the projection problem of presuppositions will solve itself gradually in the following chapters. Here we can say something about embedded presuppositions that 'make it to the surface', i.e. that are neither blocked nor reduced to being mere prejections. All such presuppositions are entailed by S (if S is an assertion), and are presuppositions of S. And vice versa, if a clause C embedded in S is entailed by S, then all presuppositions of C are presuppositions of S. *In general this means that a prejection is a pre-*

supposition just in case it is entailed. The central underlying property is prejection. When coupled with entailment, it generates presupposition. Questions, imperatives, etc., which do not have entailments, can still have presuppositions: all speech act types are assumed to be analysable in terms of a speech act component and a propositional component, as part of their Semantic Analysis (and thus at type-level). Although the question, command, wish, etc. as a whole does not have entailments, the propositional component does. It is these that are operative in the definition of presupposition.

Let us consider a few examples. (56a) presupposes (56b), which in turn presupposes (56c):

(56) a. Harry realizes that his son lives in Kentucky.
   b. Harry's son lives in Kentucky.
   c. Harry has a son.

Presupposition and prejection are thus seen to be transitive relations. (57a) is somewhat different, in that (57a) entails (57b) but does not presuppose it. (57b) presupposes (57c), which is thus presupposed by (57a). And likewise with (58):

(57) a. She managed to put the bird back in the cage.
   b. She put the bird back in the cage.
   c. The bird had been in the cage.
(58) a. She must have put the bird back in the cage.
   b. She put the bird back in the cage.
   c. The bird had been in the cage.

Both (57c) and (58c) pass the observational testing criterion for presuppositions:

(57) d. The bird had been in the cage, and she managed to put it back there.
   e. !The bird may not have been in the cage, but she managed to put it back there.
(58) d. The bird had been in the cage, and she must have put it back there.
   e. !The bird may not have been in the cage, but she must have put it back there.

Moreover, if (58c) is negated, (58a) must be radically false and can therefore be made true only by means of the radical negation. The normal, i.e. minimal, negation for *must* is *needn't* followed by a bare infinitive. But, as we have seen, *need* + bare infinitive is an NPI and thus requires the minimal negation while excluding the radical one. Hence

(58) f. !The bird had not been in the cage, so she needn't have put it back there.

is still contradictory. What is needed to eliminate the contradiction is a radical negation as in (58g) or (58h):

(58) g. The bird had not been in the cage, so she must NOT have put it back there!

h. The bird had not been in the cage, so it does NOT follow that she put it back there!

All this confirms our analysis. Yet there is a problem, or at least there appears to be one. The (apparent) problem is that the logical property of presupposition, as given in (28) above, does explain cases like (56) but fails to explain cases like (57) and (58). That is, although it follows from the logical property (repeated here for convenience)

(28) IF $A \gg B$ THEN $A \models B$ AND $\sim A \models B$

that

(59) a. IF $A \gg B$ AND $B \gg C$, THEN $A \models C$ AND $\sim A \models C$,

it does not follow that:

(59) b. IF $A \models B$ AND $B \gg C$, THEN $A \models C$ AND $\sim A \models C$.

Yet what is said in (59b) is correct. (59a) follows from (28) because if the truth or minimal falsity of A requires the truth of B, and if the truth or minimal falsity of B requires the truth of C, then the truth or minimal falsity of A requires the truth of C. Moreover, given the definition of prejection, if $A > B$ and $B > C$, then $A > C$. Hence, we may strengthen (59a) to:

(59) c. IF $A \gg B$ AND $B \gg C$, THEN $A \gg C$.

But (59b) does not follow from (28), since if the truth of A requires the truth of B and the truth or minimal falsity of B requires the truth of C, it follows that the truth of A requires the truth of C but nothing follows with regard to what is required by the minimal falsity of A. Yet, not only is (59b) correct, it can also be strengthened to:

(59) d. IF $A \models B$ AND $B \gg C$, THEN $A \gg C$.

Note that (59d) does follow from the definition of presupposition as the combination of prejection and entailment, i.e.

(59) e. IF $A \models B$ AND $B \gg C$ AND $A > C$, THEN $A \gg C$.

This is so because the entailment of B from A ensures contradiction when the discourse D contains both i(A) and i(not-B), and the prejection of C by A ensures that nothing in A prevents i(C) from being added to D previous to i(A), provided there is nothing in D blocking i(C). But since C is entailed by

B and hence by A, there can be nothing in D blocking i(C) if i(A) is acceptable in D. Hence both i(C) and i(A), in that order, are added to D, so that $A \geqslant C$.

So far there is not really a problem: all that has been shown is, again, that a purely logical definition of presupposition, as in (46), fails to do justice to the facts, and that the semantic definition is more adequate. Yet, it has also been stipulated that the only source of radical falsity is precondition failure. Now, if (59b) or (59d) is correct, then $\neg C \models\, \simeq A$. But since all that is given with respect to A is that A entails B, there is no guarantee that the radical falsity of A that is entailed by the non-truth of C is indeed the result of precondition failure of the highest predicate in A. This is the (apparent) problem we are facing. Or, in other words, we must make sure that (59b) holds even though the logic fails to warrant the conclusion that C follows from $\sim A$. Yet, again, we need this conclusion because if C is both projected and entailed by A, there is no way of keeping i(C) from the truth-domain.

Since the solution does not come from the logic, it must come from the semantics. The semantics now requires, on pain of inconsistency, that if a sentence A entails an embedded sentence (clause) B (so that all presuppositions of B are projected by A), then the highest predicate of A has the precondition that the entailed embedded clause has a classical truth-value and thus does not suffer from precondition failure. This requirement is imposed by the logic and the machinery of discourse semantics, if the source of radical falsity is not to be complicated.

Let us see if our observations confirm this requirement. First, factive predicates trivially fulfil the requirement: they require truth for the factive clause, and hence a classical value. The crucial cases are those where an embedded clause is entailed but not presupposed. The class of these predicates is limited. First, there are the 'logical' predicates for entailment or truth: *true, follow, prove, entail*, and also the predicate of epistemic necessity *must*. Then there are the verbs often called 'implicative", such as *manage, pull off, succeed*; the causative verbs such as *cause, make, induce, persuade*; aspectuals such as *begin, continue, stop*; and perhaps a few others. All such verbs must be fitted out with the precondition that the entailed embedded clause has a classical value. This ensures that any D in which a sentence figuring one of these predicates is uttered allows for the increment of the entailed embedded clause by itself. Given the general principle that if $A \models B$, then, if i(A) is a possible increment to some D without requiring any retrospective change in D, so are i(B) and i($\sim B$), but not i($\simeq B$). This preconditional requirement on entailing verbs is an automatic consequence of the theory. When the predicate extension of *true* was given above, in (36h), this precondition was added explicitly, but one might just as well regard such explicit formulation as redundant since it follows automatically from the fact that if i(*B*) can be added to D, so can i(~*B*), but not i(≃*B*). The verb *manage*, to give another example, could be specified as follows:

(60) σ(*manage*) = {⟨i, e⟩: i is animate; i tries to achieve e; for all p, if ρ(p) = e, then φ(p) ≠ 3 | φ(p) = 1}

A special case is the semantic predicate *and*. It is special in that it does not obey the general rule that presuppositions of entailed lower clauses are presupposed by the whole sentence. Thus, as has been observed many times in the literature, a sentence like

(61) a. Harry has been away and he is back now.

must not be said to presuppose that Harry has been away. Usually, the only motivation given is that it is "absurd" to accept that a sentence is both asserted and presupposed, and that "Harry has been away" is asserted and therefore not presupposed. (It is generally assumed (and turned into a formal principle in Gazdar 1979) that assertion takes priority over presupposition.) We must recognize the problem because the observational discourse test is not passed successfully. In fact, acceptability condition (a) is violated:

(61) b. !Harry has been away, and he has been away and he is back now.

is not a good enough bit of discourse. Yet "Harry is back now" is entailed by (61a) and it presupposes that Harry has been away. Moreover, if it is not true that Harry has been away, the second conjunct "he is back now" is radically false so that the whole conjunction is radically false. It would thus seem that the first conjunct, "Harry has been away" simply has to be a presupposition of (61a), but it can't be.

The answer lies in the definition of the concept of 'embedding'. We shall say that, at SA-level, a clause *B* is embedded in a superordinate structure *A* if *B* is an argument of the predicate figured by *A*, or if there is a superordinate structure *C* such that *B* is embedded in *C* and *C* is embedded in *A – and if* i(*A*) *involves one single incrementation procedure*. This means, as will become clear below, that an embedded clause is always added as an increment to some subdomain (and in some cases to the truth-domain as well). *And*, however, is different in that its constituent clauses are not added to any subdomain but only to its own domain. Its discourse effect is, moreover, defined by the stipulation that the two conjuncts are to be added separately, and in the order of presentation. There are thus as many separate incrementation procedures as there are conjuncts, and in their order. Ordinary, sentential conjunctive *and* (as opposed to, e.g., the reciprocal or symmetrical *and* of *Bob and Angela are a nice couple*) is, in fact, nothing but a link between successive increments. The conjuncts *A* and *B* in the conjunction *A and B* are thus not embedded but are separate incrementation units, though 'offered as a package'. Prejection must therefore be defined in terms of single consecutive increment units. It should be noted that it is not only *and* that involves separate increment units, but also *if*: *if* involves a potential consecutive package deal. Note, moreover, that both conjunction and implication refuse ordinary grammatical minimal negation. It would thus seem that grammatical minimal negation is also restricted to single increment units.

It is interesting to note, in this connection, that the truth-table for three-valued *and*, as given in table 5 above, is a direct consequence of the simple increment-linking function of *and*. Let a conjunction A *and* B be a 'package deal' P, consisting of two separate increment units, A and B. For any increment unit S to yield a truth-value, the domain D in question must be connected with a verification domain V, and i(S) must be non-empty, i.e. there must be an actual representation of S in D, or the function i must be defined for S in D. For S to yield truth or minimal falsity in D, the presuppositions of S must be both represented in D and true. If $\varphi(S) = 3$, then the presuppositions of S are represented in D but they are not all of them true. Hence, if D is to preserve truth, at least one of the presuppositions of S must be eliminated from D, so that i(S) will be undefined for D. For S to yield truth in D, not only must its presuppositions both be represented in D and be true, but i(S) itself must both be represented in D and be true. If the presuppositions are both represented and true, but i(S), though represented, is not true, S yields minimal falsity in D, i.e. $\varphi(S) = 2$.

Now apply this to the package deal P. For any package deal P to yield a truth-value, D must be connected with a verification domain V, and i(S), for any increment unit S in P, must be non-empty, i.e. must yield a representaton in D. For P to yield radical falsity in D, the presuppositions of each S in P are represented in D but are not all of them true. Hence, if truth is restored for D, some i(S) will be undefined. For P to yield truth or minimal falsity in D, all presuppositions of all S in P must be both represented in D and true. If, then, for each S in P i(S) is true, P yields truth in D. If, however, for some S in P i(S) is not true in D, then P yields minimal falsity in D. It is easy to see that this corresponds precisely to the truth-table of *and* in table 5.

(It may be noted, in this connection, that the well-known 'successive' *and*, occurring in conjunctions each of whose conjuncts has an event reference in its tense (has an aorist tense), is likely to fit naturally into this theory. Successive *and* implies that the event described in the first conjunct actually preceded the event described in the second conjunct. There is thus a clear truth-conditional difference between, e.g.:

(62) He went to Spain and made a fortune.

(63) He made a fortune and went to Spain.

Existing standard theories of meaning have always had to consider such cases troublesome, due to their strict adherence to the symmetrical *and* in classical logic. For us, however, *and* is primarily a link between successive increments, and its logical properties are derived. Its description in propositional calculus abstracts from prejections and from tense movements. Although, as has been said, tenses will be left out of account in this book, it is intuitively plausible that the aorist (past) tense has the discourse effect of changing the verification domain V to V', where V' differs from V only in that the event described in the clause at hand has taken place. In (62) the second conjunct "he made a fortune" is thus interpreted in a domain that is connected with V', where the "he" has laready gone to Spain, whereas in (63) the opposite is the case.)

Meanwhile, the machinery is beginning to show some of the complexity it is bound to have if it is to be an adequate rendering of what must be assumed to be actually going on during the interpretation of utterances. In particular the interplay between logical and (discourse-)semantic properties needs to be made clear. Let us therefore summarize our findings.

All entailments of sentences, including presuppositions, are derived from the conditions associated with the highest predicate.[18] 'Ordinary' entailments follow from the fulfilment of the satisfaction conditions; presuppositions follow either from the preconditions of the highest predicate, or from those of the predicate of some embedded and entailed clause – provided they are not truth-value statements. Presuppositions have the specific and distinctive semantic property that their increments are required in preceding discourse for the carrier sentence (of any speech act type) to be interpretable. That is, they are prejected as well as entailed. Accordingly, presupposition is defined as follows:

(64) $A \gg B =_{\text{Def}} A \models B$ AND $A > B$.

where A is the SA of a proposition and one increment unit. The entailment means that $i(B)$ is prejected into A's domain D^n, since its upward path to D^n cannot be blocked on pain of inconsistency. If just $A > B$, without the guarantee that $i(B)$ is prejected into D^n, but with the upward movement into D^n not blocked by any element in A, we have *mere prejection*, i.e., a suggested inference. If the path to A's domain is blocked by a structural property of A, $i(B)$ will never make it to D^n. Then $A \not> B$: there is no prejection, at least not into D^n, and hence no suggested inference.

The semantic effect of prejection is thus as follows: $A > B$ ensures that $i(B)$ is added to the highest possible (sub)domain prior to $i(A)$. If no (sub)-

---

[18] A caveat must be inserted here. What is meant is "all psychologically real entailments", i.e. all entailments that correspond to inferences drawn by cognitively functioning humans. There are also entailments based on the mathematical properties of the logical system at hand. In section 3.1 above they were characterized as being based on the mathematics of the field of valuations (i.e. a three-valued field with gaps). They include entailments involving universally quantified statements over sentences of the kind "every logically true sentence is entailed by all sentences in L". These entailments are valid but not psychologically real since they transcend the limitations of what is presented in the form of linguistic and/or cognitive material in the discourse at hand.

domain accepts i(B), i.e. if the addition of i(B) to any of the available (sub)domains is unacceptable, i(A) is empty, and A is uninterpretable, and lacks a truth-value. The single increment condition ensures that 'package deals' or, for that matter, stretches of discourse, do not presuppose anything, in the technical sense of presupposition.

A guarantee must now be provided to ensure that if $A \gg B$, then not only $A \models B$, but also $\sim A \models B$, so that the logical property (28) is saved. No extra provisions are needed when $A \models_{\overline{p}} B$ (i.e., $A \models B$ on account of the preconditions of A's predicate), since by definition, if $A \models_{\overline{p}} B$, then $\sim A \models_{\overline{p}} B$, hence $\sim A \models B$. Also, if $A \not\models_{\overline{p}} B$ but there is an embedded clause C such that $A \models_{\overline{p}} C$ and $C \models_{\overline{p}} B$, no extra provisions are needed, since now $\sim A \models_{\overline{p}} C$, hence $\sim A \models C$, and $C \models B$, so that $\sim A \models B$. However, in cases where $A \not\models_{\overline{p}} B$ and there is an embedded clause C such that $A \not\models_{\overline{p}} C$ but $A \models C$, and $C \models_{\overline{p}} B$, it does not follow that $\sim A \models B$, nor is it excluded. To make it follow that, in such cases, $\sim A \models B$ we stipulate that whenever A entails an embedded clause C, the highest predicate of A has the precondition that $\varphi(C) \neq 3$. This ensures that $A \models_{\overline{p}} C \vee \sim C$, hence $\sim A \models_{\overline{p}} C \vee \sim C$. Since $C \models_{\overline{p}} B$ and hence $\sim C \models_{\overline{p}} B$, $C \vee \sim C \models_{\overline{p}} B$, and hence $C \vee \sim C \models B$. Given that $\sim A \models_{\overline{p}} C \vee \sim C$ and hence $\sim A \models C \vee \sim C$, it follows that $\sim A \models B$, which is what had to be shown. This extra stipulation is arbitrary from a purely logical point of view, but it follows directly from the general principle that if $A \models B$, any D accepting i(A) must accept i(B), and hence i($\sim B$). The extra stipulation is, moreover, fully supported on the observational level, which shows rather neatly the epiphenomenal character of logic in the whole of semantics and the crucial role of discourse domain machinery in the interpretation of utterances.

Note that it is theoretically possible to have a predicate that takes an embedded clause C as argument without causing the entailment of C but with the precondition that $\varphi(C) \neq 3$, so that any presuppositions of C are entailed but not C itself. Semantically, such a predicate would force all presuppositions of C into the truth-domain D, so that any uttered sentence figuring it would be unacceptable if D were to refuse the presuppositions of C, but i(C) itself might be kept out of the truth-domain and relegated to the appropriate subdomain. The subdomain would thus be saddled with the constraint that it, in its entirety, can at most be minimally false if the truth-domain D is true and that it must share all presuppositions of its increments with the truth-domain. Such a predicate has not so far been found, which might mean that subdomains must, as matter of principle, be free to develop radical falsity while the truth-domain is true, or else they must be entailed. But they cannot be not entailed and yet be limited to minimal falsity or truth, if this constraint holds.

The only predicates which are exceptions to the rule that all presuppositions of their entailed embedded clauses are inherited by the whole sentence figuring them are the predicates of conjunction and implication. No exception need be formulated if it is stipulated that, in presuppositional theory, the notion of embedding is restricted to single consecutive increment units. As has been stated above, conjunction and implication involve separate consecutive increment procedures, for each of their component sentences or clauses. They are 'package deals'.

3.4 Background knowledge and backward suppletion

If semantics is, as we maintain, the empirical study of how humans come to understand or interpret uttered sentences the way they do, there is no escaping from the fact that semantics is part of cognitive science. This is clear not only because of the trivial fact that 'understanding' or 'interpreting' utterances is a cognitive function, but also because no formal account of semantic interpretation is possible without the assumption of a store of background knowledge, whether generalized or particular. The theory of discourse domains as either developed or suggested so far may be helpful with respect to a large number of observational and other considerations, but it cannot be the ultimate answer to the question of actual interpretation of utterances. We must accept that actual processes of understanding or interpretation are heavily dependent not only on explicit verbal discourse and context of utterance, but also on the availability of background knowledge.

This dependence is probably not 'essential'. That is, it seems sensible to assume that it is probably possible to build up a store of background knowledge by storing discourse domain upon discourse domain, so that one should be able to construct an idealized discourse not needing any appeal to background knowledge in order to be fully interpretable (in the sense that no question arises as to the meaning or relevance of newly added propositions or utterances). However, whether this is possible, or thinkable, or not, is largely an academic question, since in actual fact that which we wish to call "background knowledge" is built up in the course of an individual's life on the basis not only of linguistic utterances but also of cognitively interpreted perceptions other than linguistic ones. Thus, visual perceptions may well contribute to what we like to regard as background knowledge. And perceptions through sensory organs other than the eyes are, in practice, equally powerful as a source of knowledge. Therefore, there is little point in making it a central claim that background knowledge as it exists and is operational in human linguistic communication is, in principle, entirely derivable from linguistic input. The claim may be justified, but it is of little relevance, because, in fact, that which we call "background knowledge" and is required for the real understanding of utterances derives from a variety of modal inputs (where the term *modal* is a variable for the different channels of sensory input that the human race is equipped with).

What is essential is that, in all sorts of ways, speakers can allow themselves to rely heavily on what they expect their listeners to know already, apart from what they offer them in the way of explicit linguistic material. Or, put differently, the construction of discourse domains by listeners can be made heavily dependent on available knowledge taken for granted by speakers. Such heavy dependence is absolutely standard in actual speech situations, and natural language possesses all kinds of standardized means for such appeals to available knowledge.

In fact, the whole concept of discourse domain can be seen in this light: it captures the idea that discourse domains are stores of available knowledge arising out of coherent linguistic material that has been offered. These stores are organized in such a way that they can be called upon systematically in proceeding discourse, as new material is offered by a speaker who, reasonably enough, expects his previous messages to have been heeded. A very central structural means made available by language is the device of definite terms: they hark back to specific bits of information or knowledge stored in discourse domains. Seen from this perspective, of course, the availability of 'background' knowledge is as essential for semantic theory as is the notion of discourse domains. Yet, what is usually meant when it is stressed that linguistic interpretation depends on available or background knowledge is the dependence on knowledge (or beliefs) not arising out of the material explicitly presented, but arising or being available 'non-verbally'.

The knowledge, presumed by speakers to be available 'non-verbally', is of different kinds, ranging from the very general to the very particular. Thus there are constant appeals to *generalized categorial knowledge*. This is the fundamental element in human knowledge where ontological categories are assigned. For example, the knowledge that adults and children of both sexes are humans, that trees are plants, that sounds are not visible, etc., is all generalized categorial knowledge. This kind of non-factual, heavily a priori, knowledge is not plausibly assumed to be stored in any kind of memory. Rather, it is an integral part of the complex fabric of concept and concept formation. Conceptual analysis should be able to isolate a number of general categories and define concepts in terms of combinations of these. Each category and/or concept can be regarded as being defined by a set of truth-criteria or satisfaction conditions, and is potentially linked up or associated with a linguistic expression of the grammatical category "predicate". Ideally, a 'grammar' of categories should be formulated, with a finite set of axiomatic or primitive categories, and a finite set of production rules defining a potentially infinite set of new categories, much in the way of well-known mathematical production systems.

This programme of conceptual analysis laid down in the shape of an axiomatically ordered system of production rules is, in principle, as old as Aristotle. But unlike some other age-old programmes, conceptual analysis has not, so far, benefited from modern insights developed in the mathematical theory of rule systems on the one hand, and cognitive psychology on the other. There has been no twentieth-century boom in conceptual analysis, as there has been one in grammar, in intelligence research, and in other areas pertaining to cognitive functions. All we can do, therefore, is formulate a few (unsatisfactory) generalities.

Little of substance can be said on the question, interesting and important though it is, of the relation between conceptual and lexical analysis. There seems to be some 'contract' between these two in the sense that some complex concepts are associated with non-complex lexical items, whereas other complex concepts reflect their complexity, at least to some extent, in the internal analysis of the predicates that express them. Moreover, there are complex lexical items (such as *waistcoat*) that no longer express or reflect the analytic composition of the associated concept. If any value is attached to the idea of realistic cognitive modelling, it is imperative that greater clarity be achieved in this particular area.

Many presuppositions are statements directly derivable from generalized categorial knowledge. Examples have been given: the categories "human" or "animate" abound in the lexical descriptions presented above (sketchy though they are), and these and other basic categories are found all over the lexicon. If something is said to have weight, or height, or girth, or tallness, it must be material and not, say, an idea or a mathematical entity. (The building up of mathematics has led to the setting up of new categories and new categorial attributions: in mathematics, lines can have length and circles can have diameters and circumferences even though lines and circles are not material objects. But mathematical objects, whatever they are, have no weight, height, girth, etc., unless these properties are mathematically defined for them.) If something is said to be a room, it both occupies and contains space so that anything solid cannot be a room. And one could go on stating truisms of this kind.

It would be fastidious to require that presuppositions of this kind, derivable, that is, from generalized categorial knowledge, should all be represented as separate increments in discourse domains preceding an utterance of the carrier sentence. The requirement of their presence in any given D can be met in a simpler way. The preconditions of the generalized categorial kind as they are associated with predicates are satisfiable by the extensions of the terms with which they are associated. That is, if the predicate *kill* has the precondition that its object term refers to an animate being (as in (36c) above), then, clearly, this precondition is satisfiable by anything referred to by the object term of the verb *kill* whenever this verb is used in an utterance. Reference, however, cannot take place unless mediated by a discourse address (or, as in the case of facts, of a larger bit of discourse structure). Discourse addresses tend to be sortally characterized: they tend to carry sortal specifications of the type "man(x)", "woman(x)", "box(x)", "city(x)". The sortal specification may be wide or not very specific, but it is usually there. In some cases the description "going on(x)" will do, or "inauspicious process(x)", or "nondistinct threat(x)". Such sortal descriptions carry their generalized categorial entailments with them, as a result of their conceptual composition. It is thus superfluous to require that the generalized categorial entailments in question are all represented separately in D: the sortal descriptions entailing them deputize for them, and they are immediately accessible for discourse purposes by virtue of their being an integral part of the conceptual make-up of the concepts expressed by the sortal descriptions in question.

Less general, and less abstract, is what we may call *generalized factual knowledge*. This is generalized *a posteriori* knowledge about the ways the world is, or happens to be, organized. That a mountain has height, or has a top, is probably generalized categorial knowledge, but that a mountain worthy of that name has cliffs is generalized factual knowledge. Consequently, no contradiction arises when it is said that a mountain somewhere in this world has no cliffs. But to say that some mountain has no top, or no height, comes close to attributing contrary properties to an object. Thus the knowledge that groups of people can form tribes or states, and can live together in villages, towns or cities, that tribes and states tend to have heads (tribal heads or heads of state), that motor cars have brakes, that rooms have no steering wheels, etc. – all such knowledge is generalized factual knowledge. Unlike generalized categorial knowledge, this is clearly stored in long-term memory. And like generalized categorial knowledge, it plays a crucial role in the interpretation of utterances, though its role is quite different.

Generalized factual knowledge does not seem to be presuppositional in any sense. That is, unavailability of such knowledge does not seem to be profitably regarded as some kind of presupposition failure. Presupposition failure causes radical falsity, but unavailability of generalized factual knowledge causes perplexity. An example was given above, when acceptability of discourses was contrasted with uninterpretability:

(65) John came barging into the room. His upper wheel, however, wouldn't start, and he couldn't manage to lift it.

Technically speaking, a perfect discourse domain can be built up on the basis of (65): it will contain addresses for *John, the room, John's upper wheel*, and these will be characterized by means of the predicates as they are distributed in (65). Yet (65) makes no sense in that it is not clear precisely what must be the case for (65) to be true. We do not want to say that presuppositions are violated or anything of that kind, since presuppositions are linguistic or semantic properties of sentences, and the factual knowledge required for the full interpretation of stretches of text (and absent in the case of (65)) is not linguistic knowledge. Or, in other words, suppose the world were to be or to become such that (65) is perfectly normal and fully interpretable, then what has changed is the world, not the language. After all, the world has done nothing but change rapidly over the past 150 years in ways that made utterances that were uninterpretable 50 years earlier perfectly interpretable 50 years later. These changes may be reflected in an up-to-date encyclopaedia, they must not be reflected in a dictionary, not immediately at any rate. Of course, languages change, too, and linguistic changes often reflect in certain ways changes in cultural environment. And since such culture-induced changes very rarely affect anything outside the lexicon, the proper place to look for them is a good dictionary which will tell you, for example, that the word *engine* in modern English is properly used for machines that generate power, in particular locomotive power, and even more in particular for the great machines on steel wheels that pull trains, the railroad engines. In earlier days, however, this word was used, first, for ingenuity or trickery, then for products of ingenuity, i.e. any kind of plot or set-up, and any kind of mechanical contrivance or gadget. But a good knowledge of modern English will not help you to understand what engines tend to be used for in late twentieth-century Western life. It is rather the other way around: some basic familiarity with modern patterns and ways of life is indispensable for a good knowledge of a modern language. What is at issue here is not culture-induced linguistic changes but world changes, while the language stays constant. If we were to be told a story about John and why he has an upper wheel and about what upper wheels do and what it is for them to be started or lifted, etc., then we would have learned something about some fancy world, but we would not have improved or updated our knowledge of English.

It seems that languages contrive to have certain words that make a direct appeal, by virtue of their meaning, to background knowledge of the generalized factual kind. The English word *have* is a case in point. It really is, in its normal sense, an existential quantifier introducing a new element in the discourse. (It has been noted by many authors that *have* shows a strong preference for indefinite objects.) However, it introduces a new element always with respect to someone or something, and the relation between that someone or something on the one hand, and the newly introduced item on the other, *is assumed to be known*.[19] Moreover, grammars are often sensitive to the nature of the relation implicitly assumed to be known: often, for example, a grammatical distinction is based on whether the relation is one that can be severed or changed ('alienable') or is unchangeable ('inalienable'), given the practical circumstances and material limitations of our lives. Possessive and dative constructions tend to share with *have* the semantic property that they make an implicit appeal to a relation assumed to be known. Some-

---

[19] This "relation implicitly assumed to be known" is the central element in Janssen's thesis (1976) on the verb *have* and indirect object constructions, where cases like (66) are amply discussed.

times, more than two elements are involved in such a relation. Thus, it is normal to say, for example, not only (66a) but also (66b); not, however, (66c):

(66) a. This car has a dent in its front bumper.
    b. John has a dent in his front bumper.
    c. !Mary has a dent in John's front bumper.[20]

The precise structures, processes and conditions involved in such cases are far from clear, but it seems profitable to look at such phenomena in the light of a dependency with regard to available background knowledge.

Implicit appeals to factual background knowledge presumed to be available in the listener are extremely frequent, and they have invariably caused embarrassment in semantic theories that are not psychologically orientated – as is the case with most. The connective *but*, for example, is like *and* (just as *have* is like the existential quantifier), but with the extra element that it is used by a speaker to correct an opinion or an expectation that might be held by his listener. These opinions or expectations often derive from generalized factual knowledge (or belief) which the speaker attributes to his interlocutor. Misuse of *but*, again, is not a linguistic mistake but a failure of realism:

(67) !Harry was happy but healthy.

requires a very special context to be acceptable.

Besides generalized factual knowledge, there is also *particular factual knowledge*, to do with particular situations, events and individuals. The boundary lines between the general and the particular variety of factual knowledge are fluid: it is probably more appropriate to speak of a gradient scale rather than a clear dichotomy. At one extreme, there is very general knowledge based on broad inductive processes; at the other there is highly incidental knowledge of either the actual speech situation or the actual things and situations being talked about. Deictic expressions typically rely on elements in the actual speech situation for their interpretation – though their use may be transferred to the situation related, to enhance vividness, as is the case with *over there* in:

(68) There it was, *over there*, right in front of me: an enormous hound.

---

[20] The reason for the unacceptability or oddness of (66c) is probably not only the presumed absence of a close enough relation between Mary and John's car, but also the fact that an animate being (i.e. John) is an intermediate link in the relational chain. Compare the following:

   (i) This horse has a nail in its hoof.
   (ii) !John has a nail in his hoof.

Clearly, the latter sentence cannot be used to say that John's horse has a nail in its hoof, in the way (66b) can be used to express that John's car has a dent in its front bumper.

So-called 'comparison classes' for gradable adjectives depend on a presumed sense of proportion. There are many attempts in the literature to derive the comparison classes from the linguistic material presented, as one may justifiably say that a big mouse is a small animal: what is "big" for the comparison class of mice, is "small" for the comparison class of animals (prototypical animals, that is, not simply animals, for the majority of animal species as well as individuals are smaller than mice). As a general principle, however, it is not so that the comparison classes in question are derived from linguistic material. They are derived from available factual knowledge, and their determination can be ambiguous, as in the following exchange between father (F) and daughter (D):

(69) F: What is that huge model of Westminster Abbey doing in my study?
   D: It isn't huge! You know what models can be like.
   F: OK, but it's huge in my study, and I don't want it there.

Or, in other words, an enormous ship can be but a tiny speck in the ocean, or what is a vast amount of money for me can be only a small amount for someone else who is either richer or doesn't care so much about money as I do. What is expensive in Tibet may be cheap in Arizona, though the nominal value and the objects bought are the same. And so forth. Such comparison classes are based in cognition, not in the language.

The availability of such comparison classes is a necessary requirement for a truth-value, and the comparison class available is crucial for the actual truth-value an utterance has. In the situation in which (69) was supposed to be uttered, the model was both huge and not huge, depending on the comparison class. If Quine's criterion (1960: 129) that "an ambiguous term ... may be at once clearly true of various objects ... and clearly false of them" were complete, then the term *huge* in (69) should be considered ambiguous. But if we let in this kind of ambiguity, any natural language will stop being describable on type-level, i.e. as a linguistic system usable in actual contexts and situations. So the Quinean criterion must be refined by means of a *ceteris paribus* clause: if all other factors, including the comparison class inolved, are kept constant, then, if a term is at once clearly true and clearly false of the same objects, we assume ambiguity. The difference in truth-value is then brought about precisely by the other meaning being applied.

If no comparison class is available at all, then there is no truth-value. When I point to a carton box containing a TV-set, and say: *This is a large box*, the comparison class is suggested to be the set of all carton boxes, and there would be some justification in branding this utterance as true (due allowance being made for vagueness). Situations are thinkable, however, where the same utterance, made of the same box, would be clearly false, owing to a different comparison class being at play. But when I point at the same box and say:

This is large, then no comparison class is possibly suggested, and no truth-value can be assigned. If it were the case that the latter utterance should clearly be valued as radically false, so that its radical negation would bear the mark of truth, then the availability of a comparison class would have to be made a precondition of the predicate *large*, so that the existence of a comparison class would be presupposed. But this would be empirically inadequate. A better description results when the availability of a comparison class is treated on a par with the availability of extensions for definite terms in utterances: lacking these, the utterance is truth-valueless. The proposal, often found in the literature, to treat predicates such as *large* as two-place predicates thus makes a great deal of sense. *Large* is then described semantically as "large with respect to", where the object term is an implicit, contextually given, definite description referring to a comparison class.

The availability of factual background knowledge is, likewise, a condition for what we have called *backward suppletion* (or: *suppletion post hoc*) of missing addresses or larger bits of discourse. Backward suppletion is a standard device for filling in, *post hoc*, missing prejections. This filling in is subject to two main conditions. First, if the prejection is a presupposition, the discourse set up so far must be compatible with the presupposition to be supplied. If this condition is violated, the sentence carrying the presupposition is unacceptable in that discourse, according to the acceptability condition (b) in the previous section, and it will have no truth-value as long as the discourse is not modified so as to accept the sentence. If what is to be supplied is a mere prejection, then some (sub)domain, i.e. either the truth-domain or some appropriate embedded subdomain, must accept the prejection, on pain of the whole sentence being unacceptable. Secondly, the prejection to be filled in, whether in the truth-domain or in some subdomain, must 'make good sense' in the light of available factual background knowledge. This condition must of necessity remain vague and informal as long as no explicit theory of cognitive modelling is available. Any such theory will have to show in inductively generalized terms what conditions must be fulfilled for a cognitive datum (such as a discourse address or a bit of discourse structure) to be part of an integrated cognitive whole, the sort of thing sometimes called "scenario" in the literature on Artificial Intelligence. (But actual knowledge of things and facts is incomparably more complex than the structures worked with in scenario-like approaches in Artificial Intelligence.)

If this second condition is not fulfilled, i.e. if the background knowledge required is not available, then there is perplexity, rather than unacceptability, and only the possibility of a truth-value. This is one of the typical situations in which *questions* arise. Thus, the little discourse (65), given above, raises eyebrows as well as questions. "Wait a minute", one imagines someone saying on hearing (65), "I'm not with you. What does it mean to have an upper wheel? What does it mean to start it, and why should one want to lift it?" Only after the required answers are given can it be decided whether (65) is true or (minimally or radically) false.

Backward suppletion of addresses occurs typically when the speaker expects the hearer to be in possession of the factual background knowledge required for full interpretation. When a fairy tale starts out about a faraway country it is not necessary for the story to contain the explicit information that that country had a king. It may do so, especially since it is a fairy tale (fairy tales are known for their minimal reliance on background knowledge), but it may also simply go on with *The king of that country*, whereupon any minimally knowledgeable reader or listener will supply the missing king-address, since it is well known that countries sometimes have kings as heads of state. That the suppletion of missing addresses implies an appeal to the listener's knowledge appears from conversational exchanges where the speaker wants an address to be supplied *post hoc*, without, however, being fully apprised of the means for optimal reference. The listener is then called upon to supply the information that can be used for unique reference. Take, for example:[21]

> (70) A: I was there with ehh – what's her name, you know, the cellist I mean.
> B: You mean Betty Nichols?
> A: Yes, Betty Nichols, the cellist.

Since speaker A expects his interlocutor B to know the person he wants to talk about by name, he is free to rely on backward suppletion of the missing address. This reliance is almost imperative in this case, where A expects B to know the person in question better than he himself does. A could have said, e.g.:

> (70) I was there with someone who is a cellist and whose name I can't remember just now.

But then there would not be the presumption that B knows that person very well. If B then says what he said in (70), A will be surprised at B's being so well informed.

Backward suppletion of missing addresses takes place only as a last resort, when none of the addresses already available will do. It is excluded when the lexical material in the definite description unambiguously selects an address available in D. Thus, in (71a) the term *the banker* simply denotes the address set up for a Swiss banker in the preceding utterance:

> (71) a. Yesterday, a Swiss banker was arrested at Heathrow Airport. *The banker* declared that he had come to Britain to kidnap the Queen.

[21] I owe this consideration, and the example (70), to Herb Clark.

Personal pronouns, as well as non-deictically used demonstrative pronouns, prohibit backward suppletion. They require the presence of an appropriate address:

(71) b. Yesterday a Swiss banker was arrested at Heathrow Airport. *He* declared he had come to Britain to kidnap the Queen.

c. Yesterday a Swiss banker was arrested at Heathrow Airport. *That man* declared that he had come to Britain to kidnap the Queen.

Only non-demonstrative definite terms allow for backward suppletion, but even then the suppletion does not occur unless it is necessary for the making of good sense by the utterance. Thus, the definite term *the 53-year-old bachelor* does not lead to backward suppletion in (71d), because it makes perfect sense for a Swiss banker to be a 53-year-old bachelor. Hence, the term in question safely 'lands' at the address set up for the Swiss banker:

(71) d. Yesterday a Swiss banker was arrested at Heathrow Airport. *The 53-year-old bachelor* declared that he had come to Britain to kidnap the Queen.

Suppletion does occur when background knowledge tells us that an identification of whatever is denoted by the definite term and any of the available addresses is ruled out:

(71) e. Yesterday, a Swiss banker was arrested at Heathrow Airport. *The customs officer* declared that he had come to Britain to kidnap the Queen.

Here, the *presumption of good sense* that steers the interpretation of every utterance dictates that *the customs officer* is not to be identified with the Swiss banker, and, moreover, that the *he* is not the customs officer but the Swiss banker. The reason being, of course, that standard socialization in modern Western ways of life brings along the knowledge that customs officers check foreigners arriving at airports, and may even cause an arrest to be made, while Swiss bankers arriving at Heathrow Airport are unlikely to be customs officers as well. Observe that the discourse becomes hard to follow when the definite term is changed to *that customs officer*, precisely because the use of the (non-deictic) *that* requires that an appropriate address be available without backward suppletion:

(71) f. Yesterday a Swiss banker was arrested at Heathrow Airport. !*That customs officer* declared that he had come to Britain to kidnap the Queen.

These examples illustrate the crucial role of background knowledge in the interpretation of utterances, and at the same time the delicate interplay of linguistic and cognitive constraints.

Karttunen (1974: 191) noted the phenomenon of backward suppletion. He gives the examples (72a)–(72c), which are easily imagined used in a context where the presuppositions (or, in the case of (72b), the mere prejection) have not been incremented explicitly prior to the carrier sentence (in Karttunen's terminology, where the context does not satisfy the presuppositions):

> (72) a. We regret *that children cannot accompany their parents to commencement exercises.*
> b. I would like to introduce you to *my wife.*
> c. John lives in *the third brick house down the street from the post office.*

(The italicized constituents represent the presuppositions in the carrier sentences.) Karttunen's comment is:

> I think the best way to look at this problem is to recognize that ordinary conversation does not always proceed in the ideal orderly fashion described earlier. People do make leaps and shortcuts by using sentences whose presuppositions are not satisfied in the conversational context. This is the rule rather than the exception, and we should not base our notion of presupposition on the false premiss that it does not or should not happen. But granting that ordinary discourse is not always fully explicit in the above sense, I think we can maintain that a sentence is always taken to be an increment to a context that satisfies its presuppositions. If the current conversational context does not suffice, the listener is entitled and expected to extend it as required. He must determine for himself what context he is supposed to be in on the basis of what was said and, if he is willing to go along with it, make the same tacit extension that his interlocutor appears to have made. This is one way in which we communicate indirectly, convey matters without discussing them.

This, in a nutshell, is the principle of backward suppletion of presuppositions and mere prejections. It implies that "the ideal and orderly fashion described earlier" will not do as a theory, but also that backward suppletion is warranted only if the speaker may assume that the hearer has the background knowledge required for the suppletion. This shows how useful backward suppletion is for good communication. The reliance on knowledge shared by speaker and hearer makes for an enormous saving in communicative effort. One may even argue that without such reliance linguistic communication to the extent that it is practised by *Homo sapiens* would be impossible. It would not be feasible to add increments of all generalized categorial presuppositions to the discourse, and to specify for each little discourse all over again whatever is needed in the way of background knowledge. As was said at the beginning of this section, it is probably possible to build up a discourse exclusively on the basis of linguistic input, without any reliance on background knowledge of any kind. But if such discourses were the only ones possible, who would ever want to say anything? It is, after all, a truism that linguistic modelling is not possible without cognitive modelling. Yet, this truism has been badly neglected in theoretical linguistics and formal semantics.

3.5 Some special cases of presupposition

3.5.1 Cleft and pseudocleft sentences

A well-known class of presuppositions is generated by cleft and pseudocleft constructions as, respectively:

(73) a. It is the letter that John wrote.
b. What John wrote was the letter.

The typical presupposition associated or induced by this construction is not, as is often said, the *existence* of what is denoted by the WH-clause constituent but rather the *truth of the discourse address* denoted by the WH-clause constituent. In (73) it is the existence of something written by John that is presupposed, but in, e.g.,

(74) a. It is the Abominable Snowman that Mrs Prendergast is trying to shoot.
b. What Mrs Prendergast is trying to shoot is the Abominable Snowman.

what is presupposed is not the existence of what Mrs Prendergast is trying to shoot, but that *there is something* that Mrs Prendergast is trying to shoot, or, in other words, that it is true that Mrs Prendergast has gone out with the idea of shooting something. This, of course, may be true even if what she intends to shoot does not actually exist. We say that the term "that which Mrs Prendergast is trying to shoot" denotes an address either in the truth-domain or in some subdomain (or else (74) is uninterpretable), and that the bit of discourse constituted by this address and its link with the truth-domain is presuppositionally required to be true. Thus, for example, the address for what Mrs Prendergast is trying to shoot is likely to be anchored in a subdomain defined by what Mrs Prendergast intends to do. If it is in fact true that Mrs Prendergast intends to do the things that are specified in the subdomain (after all, the discourse domain may attribute to Mrs Prendergast intentions she does not have), then the presupposition associated with (74) is satisfied: then there is indeed something which Mrs Prendergast is trying to shoot. In (73), on the other hand, the address required for the term "the thing that John wrote" must be in the truth-domain since *write* is extensional with respect to both its terms. This being so, if the address required is true, there must actually exist something that John wrote. The common denominator for both classes of cases is that "there is something/someone such that...", whereby the expression "there is" does not entail actual existence but only the availability of an extension, be it extensional (i.e. actually existing) or intensional (i.e. discourse-defined). The term *cleft presupposition* will be used to refer to this typical presupposition of clefts and pseudoclefts.

It is the cleft presupposition that cannot be eliminated by (radical) negation, as was illustrated above in section 3.2.4 (example (14)). Other presuppositions can be eliminated freely by the use of the radical negation:

(75) a. It is NOT John who wrote the letter: John doesn't exist!
   b. What Mrs Prendergast is trying to shoot is NOT Shakespeare's *Hamlet*: *Hamlet* is a play, not a person, and Mrs Prendergast knows that!

From a grammatical point of view clefts and pseudoclefts must be distinguished from other constructions that are structurally similar. In particular, (73a) and (73b) must be distinguished from cases like:

(76) a. It is expensive what Henry sells.
   b. What Henry sells is expensive.

which are not cleft or pseudocleft sentences, despite the structural similarities. The difference shows up when one looks at other, synonymous, sentences whose well-formedness and conditions of use correspond regularly with the (pseudo)clefts. Thus, clefts like (73a) always have an alternative with *that* for the relative pronoun (*who*), but non-clefts lack this possibility:

(77) a. It is John who/that wrote the letter.
   b. *It is expensive that Henry sells.

Pseudoclefts have no corresponding sentence form with *-ever* attached to the relative pronoun, but sentences with ordinary relative subject clauses do:

(78) a. *Whoever wrote the letter was John.
   b. Whatever Henry sells is expensive.

The former is either just ungrammatical, or if it is taken to be interpretable, it has lost its semantic correspondence with (77a) and must mean something like "for any x, if x wrote the letter, x = John". Both clefts and pseudoclefts, at least in English (but not, e.g., in French), have the peculiarity that they invariably correspond with non-cleft or non-pseudocleft sentences, where the focused (accented) constituent takes the place of the relative pronoun, while retaining contrastive accent. Thus, (73a) and (73b), and (74a) and (74b) correspond to, respectively:

(79) a. John wrote THE LETTER.
   b. Mrs Prendergast is trying to shoot THE ABOMINABLE SNOWMAN.

Moreover, pseudoclefts have the extra peculiarity that they correspond, in spoken language, with a pseudocleft form where the focused constituent is replaced by the non-pseudocleft form as in (79):

(80) a. What John wrote is John wrote THE LETTER.
b. What Mrs Prendergast is trying to shoot is she is trying to shoot the ABOMINABLE SNOWMAN.

(This construction type is extremely common in spoken English of all socio-linguistic levels, even though some who frequently use it will hotly deny that they do.) Clearly, both the sentence form instantiated in (79) and the one shown in (80) are not available for, e.g., (76b):

(81) a. *Henry sells EXPENSIVE.
b. *What Henry sells is Henry sells EXPENSIVE.

And other grammatical differences could be pointed out.

Semantically, the observation can be made that the focused constituent in clefts and pseudoclefts, and the accented constituent in non-(pseudo)clefts, are typically appropriate answers to questions implicit in the topic constituent (the WH-clause constituent) of (pseudo)clefts. Thus, an appropriate answer to the question *Who wrote the letter?* is: *John*; and likewise, *The Abominable Snowman* is an appropriate answer to the question *What is Mrs Prendergast trying to shoot?* But *Expensive* is not an appropriate answer to the question *What does Henry sell?* Accordingly, ambiguities may arise, as in:

(82) Who wrote the letter was an idiot.

which means either that the predicate "idiot" befits whoever wrote the letter, or that the question *What sort of man wrote the letter?* is (veridically) answered by *An idiot*.

The relation between question–answer pairs and (pseudo)clefts is systematic. Compare, for example, the following pairs:

(83) a-1. What Henry sold was a postcard.
a-2. What did Henry sell? A postcard.
b-1. What Henry sold was a few postcards.
b-2. What did Henry sell? A few postcards.
c-1. *What Henry sold was few postcards.
c-2. *What did Henry sell? Few postcards.
d-1. *What Henry sold was many postcards.
d-2. *What did Henry sell? Many postcards.
e-1. *What Henry sold was most postcards.
e-2. *What did Henry sell? Most postcards.

Apparently, a distinction must be made between straightforward quantification, as in

(84) a. Henry sold a postcard.
 b. Henry sold a few postcards.
 c. Henry sold few postcards.
 d. Henry sold many postcards.
 e. Henry sold most postcards.

on the one hand, and predicative (quasi-quantificational) use, as in (83a)–(83e), or:[22]

(85) a.   Henry sold A POSTCARD.
 b.   Henry sold A FEW POSTCARDS.
 c. (*)Henry sold FEW POSTCARDS.
 d. (*)Henry sold MANY POSTCARDS.
 e. (*)Henry sold MOST POSTCARDS.

(The examples (85c)–(85e) are marked with a bracketed asterisk because they are grammatical in one specific reading – which is not at issue here and which has no cleft or pseudocleft counterpart – the reading, that is, where the accented constituents are to be interpreted as quoted elements. (85c), for example, is well formed and appropriate in the following context:

(86) No, you've got it all wrong, Henry didn't sell "lewd photographs"; he sold "few postcards". You misheard because of the bad quality of the loudspeakers.

Since we are concentrating on (pseudo)clefts, and since neither the grammar nor the semantics of quoted elements has been written, we shall leave such cases out of account.)

Why it should be that some (quasi-quantificational) indefinite NP-types, such as *a postcard, a few postcards, all postcards, some postcard* (in a specific sense), *some postcards*, freely occur as predicates, while other forms of quantification do not, is a question that still awaits an appropriate answer.[23] But we need not answer it here. The point here is simply that clefts, pseudoclefts and sentences with emphatically or contrastively accented constituents

---

[22] It is perhaps interesting to note that modern Greek makes a distinction between straightforward existential singular quantification, as in

(i) O Leonídas agórase ena vivlío ("Leo bought a book")

and predicative use, as in:

(ii) O Leonídas agórase VIVLÍO. ("Leo bought A BOOK")
(iii) Aftó pou agórase o Leonídas ítan vivlío. ("What Leo bought was a book")

The difference is that with ordinary quantification the indefinite article *ena* ("a") is used, but is left out in predicative use.

[23] Richard Montague, who was linguistically naïve, was entirely unaware of the distinction. He proposed to analyse *John is an American* as "there is an x such that x is John and x is American". This analysis has been rightly found too poor by the linguistic world.

(in so far as the accent is not to do with getting the sentence form right) show a significant correlation with pairs of specific (WH-) questions and appropriate answers. To give just another illustration of this principle, consider:

(87) a-1.   What the captain is is an idiot.
     a-2.   What is the captain? An idiot.
     b-1.   *What an idiot is is the captain.
     b-2.   *What is an idiot? The captain.
     c-1.   Who is an idiot is the captain.
     c-2.   Who is an idiot? The captain.

The question now is how these phenomena are to be accounted for grammatically and semantically. Let us begin by distinguishing a separate verb *be*, distinct from the ordinary predicative *be* as in: *The minister is a troublemaker* or *The ambassador was corrupt*, and distinct also from the *be* of identity as in *The Morning Star is the Evening Star*, from the locative *be* as in *I was in Paris*, etc. This *be* will be called the "specifying *be*", or *be*$_{sp}$.[24]

This verb *be*$_{sp}$ takes as subject term a question-raising NP of the form "$x: + S_x$". S_x must be such that it 'raises a question', i.e. it expresses a property which in the given discourse domain and the given verification domain is insufficient to pick out unambiguously one specific referent, and it thus gives rise to a question of who or what. It is the denotational entailment going with this subject term which is identified as the cleft presupposition. Since denotational entailments are not presuppositional, a separate precondition of *be*$_{sp}$ must be formulated. It can be expressed as follows, with

---

[24] We take it for granted that any grammatical analysis taking as basic the 'straight' form of the sentence and generating (pseudo)clefts or emphatic/contrastive accents out of these is misguided. The main grammatical argument against such an approach is based on the observation that certain surface forms do not allow for all of their constituents to be clefted out or accented for contrast. Take, for example:

  (i) (a) I don't think John has arrived yet.
       (b) *I don't think JOHN has arrived yet, but HARRY.
       (c) *It isn't John that I think has arrived yet, but Harry.
  (ii) (a) He didn't post the letter until yesterday.
       (b) *He didn't post THE LETTER until yesterday, but THE PARCEL.
       (c) *It isn't the letter he posted until yesterday, but the parcel.

The reason for the ungrammaticality of the (b)- and (c)-sentences is clear: they involve structures that are ungrammatical for independent reasons that will have to be stipulated in the grammar anyhow. (ic), for example, involves *I think x has arrived yet*, and (iic) involves *he posted x until yesterday*. Both these ungrammatical structures require the negation in the position in which it occurs in the 'straight' sentence to be grammatical. The negation in the (c)-sentences is in a different position and does not help. The conclusion is obvious that the (b)-sentences are related with or derived from the (c)-sentences and that the (c)-sentences are not based on the 'straight' (a)-sentences but have a different source involving structures without the negation. The generalization that *I think x has arrived yet* and *he posted x until yesterday* are ungrammatical for the same reasons as the (b)- and (c)-sentences is thus captured.

"a" as the extension of the subject term: "for all terms t such that $\rho(t) = a$, $d(t) = 1$", where "$d(t)$" stands for the discourse address (denotation) of t. Truth of an address d in the truth-domain means that there exists a real world referent with the properties specified in d; truth of an address d in a sub-domain means that the subdomain is true (i.e. the subdomain functions as an address and must have a real world counterpart) at least in so far as its ascribed property of containing the intensional address d is concerned.

The cleft presupposition makes for certain truth-conditional differences with respect to 'straight' sentences. For example, if in a situation where nobody laughed (88a) is uttered it will simply be (minimally) false and its negation (89a) will be true, but if (88b) is uttered it will be (radically) false and its negation (89b) will still fail to be true:

(88) a. Harry laughed.
  b. The one who laughed was Harry.
(89) a. Harry didn't laugh.
  b. The one who laughed wasn't Harry.

This shows that it is mistaken to say that whatever difference there is between (pseudo)cleft and 'straight' sentences is merely pragmatic and not truth-conditional. The differences are in part truth-conditional and in part to do with discourse semantics, in that (pseudo)clefts fit into a different class of discourses than 'straight' sentences.

The main question remaining now is how to specify the second term of be_{sp}, the question-answering term. This is a difficult question given the variety of forms that can be used to answer a question. To take a simple example, consider:

(90) a. Who laughed?   Peter.
                                        The man with the grey coat.
                                        Someone from the audience.
                                        A few hoodlums.
                                        Nobody other than Jeremy.
                                        Only Jeremy.
                                        Just about everyone.

     b. What does he write?   A novel.
                                          Novels.
                                          That he wants the job.
                                          A few poems.
                                          Only poems.

Not only is there the problem, not further discussed here, of what constitutes an appropriate answer to a WH-question. There is also the purely grammatical difficulty of how to capture question-answering terms under a common SA-specification, and the semantic question of how to give a proper specification of the sort of thing that can be the extension of the question-answering term. It seems that this is either impossible or achievable only at the cost of serious loss of generalizations.

There is, however, a different solution to this problem,[25] which consists in taking as the second term of be_{sp} not the question-answering term but the question-answering sentence. Deletion of material under identity with the S_x of the subject-NP will then leave the question-answering constituent under an NP-node. For example, let (91) underlie (77a):

(91)

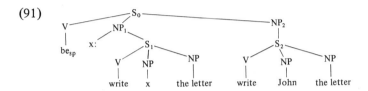

The first thing to be done on the be_{sp}-cycle is the reduction of S_2 to just the material differing from S_1.[26] S_2 thus becomes just $_{NP}[John]$. This deletion thus provides the question-answering constituent while no grammatical or semantic generalization over this constituent need be formulated. S_2 under NP_2 can be quite complex. It may contain negations, quantifications, and other operators. But for S_2 to be an appropriate answer to the question raised by S_1 an identity requirement must be fulfilled between the material of S_1 and the material of some specific S_n embedded under S_2 or of S_2 itself.

This identity requirement can be formulated as follows. The material of S_x of NP_1 must re-occur in identical form (except that the variable x may be replaced by a constant form) in some S containing (or identical with) the nuclear S of S_2 under NP_2. A nuclear S is the S whose V will be the main verb of the Surface Structure. That is, if the superordinate S contains operators to be lowered, the nuclear S is the S into which the operators are lowered. All operator material that is lowered will thus land at the position of the variable x, so that S_2 will eventually differ from S_x only in that x is replaced by some, possibly elaborate, non-variable constituent. There is, furthermore, the requirement that the grammatical (transformational) treatment of S_x and the nuclear S under S_2 be identical.

---

[25] This proposal originates from Léon Stassen at Nijmegen University, whose (unpublished) work on clefts and pseudoclefts made me see the point of this analysis.

[26] This reduction of identical material is obligatory in standard English, but only optional in colloquial English, such as the sentences of (80). In this variety, if the reduction does not take place, NP_1 becomes a WH-clause constituent and S_2 remains in full. The two are connected by the surface verb *be*.

To give another example:

(92)

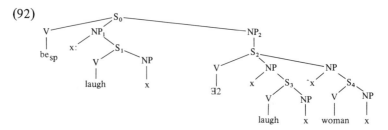

Here the identity requirement holds between the material in S_1 and in S_3, which is the nuclear S under S_2. In this case the identity is complete owing to the existential quantification in S_2, which leaves its nuclear S with a variable constituent. Cyclic treatment of S_2 now gives S_3[laugh(two women)], which answers the question raised by S_x. Deletion under identity leaves only the subject *two women* as NP_2, which is thus the question-answering constituent.

The subsequent grammatical treatment is relatively unproblematic. First, $V[be_{sp}]$ incorporates NP_2 (like the incorporation of S_2 by the quantifier – see section 2.4.3 above). Then there is optional *Predicate Lowering* (PL), a simple variant of Lowering (see 2.4.3): NP_2 is lowered to the position of x in S_1, whereby it carries strong accent (a falling tone starting from a high rise). S_1 is now the main clause and all higher structure is deleted:

(93) a.   b.   c.

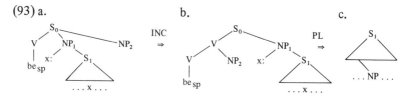

PL generates the lowered sentence form as exemplified in (79). If PL is not applied, there are two options. Either NP_1 comes out as *what/who ...* (or *that which/the one who ...*), thus leading, via tense processing, to a pseudo-cleft. Or *it*-insertion applies (see section 2.4.2),[27] so that a new subject-NP *it* is formed and S_1 becomes a WH-clause or *that*-clause. This leads to the cleft form.[28]

---

[27] Strictly speaking, "x:" of NP_1 is translated as *it* and made into a separate new subject-NP to the left of NP_1, which thus dominates only S_1. It should not be excluded that *it*-insertion as described in section 2.4.2 is indeed precisely this: *it* translates an underlying "x:" and becomes a separate new subject-NP.

[28] Note that, in English, Number Agreement follows the insertion of *it*, so that the verb be_{sp} is always singular:

(i) It *is* (*are) the students who want an end to military involvement.

One additional point needs to be discussed in connection with the grammatical analysis. It is a direct result of PL that non-cleft surface sentences are often derivable from underlying cleft structures formed with be_{sp}, and that they are derivable in many different ways according to the intonational pattern of the sentence in question. This can be considered a free bonus of the analysis, since it shows at least one way in which intonational patterns in particular express contextual or discourse functions of utterances. It is a well-known fact that intonation is a highly sensitive indicator of the role of an utterance in a given discourse and speech situation, and it has often been observed that, besides a host of other factors, a distinction between *topic* and *comment* stands out prominently. Intonational differences often correspond to differences of what, in the given discourse, is being talked about (the topic), and what is said of it (the comment). It seems that, typically, the predicate be_{sp} serves to separate the topic-denoting constituent from the comment constituent. The question-raising subject term is typically the topic-denoter, whilst the comment is embodied in the question–answering S. When PL applies, the difference is expressed solely by the intonational pattern of the sentence.

The (pseudo)cleft analysis given here provides a straightforward link between the well-known topic-comment distinction and the theory of grammar. It was pointed out in section 2.1.2 above that attempts to use lambda-formulae for the grammatical expression of the semantic features felt to inhere in (pseudo)clefts are misguided in so far as they are thought to be compatible with surface semantics. If, however, lambda-formulae are regarded as underlying grammatical structures (so that surface semantics is given up), then some form of transformational grammar has been adopted, and then the

---

In German, Dutch, Standard French, etc., Number Agreement precedes the insertion of *it* (or rather, its equivalents), at least in 3rd person plural cases:

(ii) Es *sind* (*ist) die Studenten, die die militärische Einmischung beenden wollen.
(iii) Het *zijn* (*is) de studenten die de militaire inmenging willen stoppen.
(iv) Ce *sont* (*est) les étudiants qui veulent terminer l'intervention militaire.

In normal colloquial French, however, the order is as in English, and the singular is used:

(v) C'*est* les étudiants qui veulent terminer l'intervention militaire.

French, by the way, does not have P-Lowering. There is no possible lowered sentence form with strong accent on the lowered NP_2. Only for non-NP constituents does French have contrastively or emphatically accented elements:

(vi) Il a VOLÉ la voiture; il ne l'a pas ACHETÉE. ("He STOLE the car; he didn't BUY it")
(vii) Dieu DISpose; il ne PROpose pas. ("God DISposes; he doesn't PROpose")

There are many (especially West African) languages where clefting of verbs and adjectives in predicate nominal position is a standard grammatical procedure. These languages have equivalents of "It's steal he stole the car", or "It's big your feet are big". Invariably, in these cases, the verb of adjective is repeated in the *that*-clause.

proposal had better fit in with the demands posed by grammatical theory. In this perspective lambda-formulae are strikingly *ad hoc*, in contrast to the be_{sp}-analysis, which is a natural part of the theory of grammar.

What remains is the definition of the extension set of the predicate be_{sp}. The following might be proposed:

(94) $\sigma(be_{sp}) = \{\langle a^*, e^* \rangle$: for all terms t such that $e^{(t)} = a$, $d(t) = 1$; for all S such that $\rho(S) = e$, $\varphi(S) \neq 3 \mid S$ is a true answer to the question $WHx(S_x)\}$

The variable "a" chosen for the subject term extension implies that it is not restricted to any specific ontological category: the subject may refer to (intensional) individuals, sets, facts and propositions, as long as it has the grammatical form of a definite term. The variable "e" stands, as usual, for facts. "$WHx(S_x)$" stands for "who/what x is such that S_x?". As has been said, the denotational entailment linked with the subject term ensures that it is presupposed that "there is some x such that S_x", i.e. the cleft presupposition. The precondition explicitly given ensures the radical falsity of sentences like those of (75) above – a radical falsity that can be made good by the radical negation.

3.5.2 Only

The semantic predicate *only*, or, as we shall say, *be only* is in many ways similar to be_{sp}. The presuppositional properties of *(be) only* have been discussed in the literature (e.g., Horn 1969; Keenan 1971), and there seems general agreement that a sentence like

(95) a. Only John laughed.

presupposes that John laughed and asserts that no one else did.

It must be noted that, besides (95a), there are alternative sentence forms with the same semantic properties (including, by and large, discourse properties), and with the grammatical structure of clefts or pseudoclefts:

(95) b. It was only John that laughed.
c. Who laughed was only John.

All three forms (95a)–(95c) satisfy the discourse acceptability test for presuppositions in the same way. We shall try out both (95) and its minimal negation (note that the negation of (95a) is obligatorily minimal due to its non-canonical position):

(96) a. John laughed, and ⎧ only John did so.
⎨ it was only John that did so.
⎩ who did so was only John.

b. !John may not have laughed, but $\begin{cases} \text{only John did so.} \\ \text{it was only John that did so.} \\ \text{who did so was only John.} \end{cases}$

(97) a. John laughed, but $\begin{cases} \text{not only John did so.} \\ \text{it wasn't only John that did so.} \\ \text{who did so wasn't only John.} \end{cases}$

b. !John may not have laughed, but $\begin{cases} \text{not only John did so.} \\ \text{it wasn't only John that did so.} \\ \text{who did so wasn't only John.} \end{cases}$

We shall treat *only* as an internally complex lexical item whose decomposition consists of a specific form of be_{sp} construction:

(98)

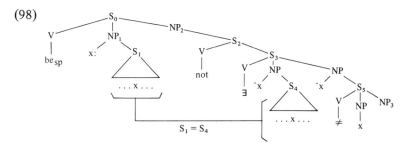

where the predicate "$\neq$" stands for "not identical with". NP_2 reduces to "no x other than NP_3", which is then incorporated under $_V[be_{sp}]$ by adoption. The part "no x other than" is replaced lexically by *only*, which is then right-adopted again by $_V[be_{sp}]$ and becomes adverbial:

(99)

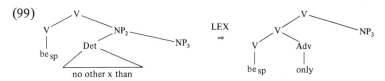

There is a certain amount of unclarity about the prelexical analysis of *only*. This unclarity has become apparent only as a result of the greater explicitness, as compared with other approaches, of our theory of presupposition and our analysis of the problems connected with prelexical analysis. It arises from the fact, mentioned in section 2.3.1 above, that *only* is internally complex in a way that clearly affects the syntax of the constructions in which it occurs, yet the closest grammatically adequate internal analysis differs somewhat in meaning from *only* itself. This combination is slightly perplexing if it is assumed that only 'closed' items, whose internal analysis has no syntactic effects, can carry semantic extras with regard to their analysis. In other words, it is not clear how the prelexical analysis of *only* can be taken to underlie grammatically *only*-sentences if that prelexical analysis is semantically different from the word itself. The semantic difference is easily grasped if the definition of the extension set of *only* is compared with the compositional meaning of the analysis given ιιι (98).

The extension set of *only* can be given as follows:

(100) $\sigma(be\ only) = \{\langle a^*, e \rangle$: for all terms t such that $e^{(t)} = a$, $d(t) = 1$, for all S such that $\rho(S) = e$, S is a true answer to the question $WHx(S_x)$ | there is no fact $f \neq e$ in the verification domain V such that for all $S^a_{x/\alpha}$ such that $\rho(S^a_{x/\alpha}) = f$, $\varphi(S^a_{x/\alpha}) = 1\}$

("a" and "e" are as in (94) above; "$S^a_{x/\alpha}$" is S_x of the subject-NP (with the extension a), but with some material α substituted for the variable x.)

Again, any term referring to *a* is a question-raising (topic-denoting) term, and any term $_{NP}[S]$ referring to *e* is a question–answering S (containing the comment). The main respect in which the semantics of *be only* is not straight-forwardly derivable from that of be_{sp} is that what is satisfaction condition for be_{sp} is precondition for *be only*, namely that any S referring to *e* be a true answer to the question $WH_x(S_x)$. In other words, whereas all three sentences of (95) presuppose that John laughed, the analysis "the one who laughed was no one other than John" carries no such presupposition but presupposes only that there was someone who laughed.

If it were possible to formulate a prelexical analysis for *only* which would do full justice to its meaning and at the same time would satisfy the requirements of syntax, there would be no problem. However, such an analysis has not been found. The semantic discrepancy suggests that *only* belongs to the 'closed' class, but the possibility of *only* occurring with *any*, as in (102a) below, suggests that it belongs to the closed class. The occurrence of *any* suggests, moreover, that the discourse increment value associated with *only* should be formulated in terms of the negation prohibiting the subsequent introduction of any address, apart from the one already given, characterized by the material of S_1 in (98). For (95) this means that *only* should place an embargo on any subsequent address characterized by "laugh(x)" besides the address for *John* already characterized that way. In light of the possible principle that Negative Polarity Items of the *any*-class can occur only in constituents denoting or setting up V-relaxing addresses, such an embargo is indispensable if the occurrence of *any* (and members of its class, such as *the slightest* in (102c)) with *only* is to be explained (see sections 4.1.1 and 4.1.3 for further comment).

Grammatically speaking, the negation plays a prominent role in the prelexical analysis of *only*. In traditional English grammar, *only* counts as a "negative adverb", for two good reasons. First, it brings about the subject-auxiliary inversion which is typical for sentences opening with a negative non-subject constituent:

(101) a. Never in his lifetime had he seen such a mess.
    b. Not one of his friends could he persuade to participate in the scheme.
    c. Not until five o'clock did he open the door.
    d. Hardly ever did he forget to bring an umbrella.
    e. Only then did he open the door.

And, secondly, as we have seen, *only* creates an environment for some Negative Polarity Items, including those of the *any*-class:

(102) a. Only then did he show *any* courage.
    b. Only Harry *need* worry about that.
    c. Only you have *the slightest* idea.
    d. Only I *can seem to* get *any*where.

The assignment of a prelexical analysis containing the negation, as in (98) and (99) above, seems a straightforward way of accounting for the clear negativity built into the internal structure of *only*.

In this description and analysis of *only* we shall take the unclarity connected with its prelexical analysis for granted and proceed on the assumption that matters will be cleared up later. To the extent that the analysis given here is successful, it may contribute to a more definitive solution.

Grammatically and lexically, *be only* is a one-term predicate with the question-raising NP as subject. But it is a complex predicate in that it involves, besides $v[be_{sp} + only]$, also NP_3 under the higher V, as is illustrated in (99). Truth-conditionally it is defined for the formal structure of its prelexical analysis, i.e. (98). The Semantic Analysis of, e.g., (95a) is thus:

(103)

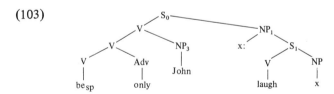

But note that the syntactic restrictions on what can fill NP_3 can be formulated only with the help of the prelexical analysis (98) together with the specification that S_2 must be an appropriate answer to $WHx(S_x)$. This is a further motivation for the prelexical analysis.

It is clear that in this analysis the presupposition that there is an x who laughed remains untouched. Consider the following examples:

(104) a. Someone laughed, and it was John who laughed, and only he did so.

b. !Maybe no one laughed, but it was John who laughed, and only he did so.

c. !Someone laughed, but maybe it wasn't John who laughed, and only he did so.

Although (104a) may sound a little tedious because all presuppositions have been spelled out, it sounds coherent. But (104b) and (104c) are straightforwardly contradictory. In the former the contradiction arises between the first and the second presupposition. In the latter it is between the second presupposition and the carrier sentence.

The grammatical treatment of *be only* runs closely parallel to that of *be*$_{sp}$, after NP$_2$-incorporation. Predicate Lowering makes *only* + NP$_3$ descend into S$_x$ of the subject-NP to the position of the variable x. All higher structure is deleted:

(105) a.

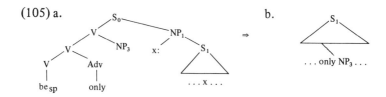

As with *be*$_{sp}$, the material lowered by PL carries along a strong accent, whose more subtle modulations depend on discourse factors. If, e.g., the presupposition that the question-answering S is true must be supplied *post hoc*, while it is given explicitly in the discourse that the denotational entailment is fulfilled, then there is a marked high-low contour on both *only* and NP$_3$ – the latter more marked than the former. But if both presuppositions are overtly present in the discourse, as in (104a), then *only* carries its high-low contour, but not NP$_3$.

PL is, again, optional. If it is not used, then there is either *it*-insertion, leading to a cleft form as in (95b), or NP$_1$ remains the surface subject, and a pseudocleft comes about, as in (95c).

This analysis makes for a straightforward description of the derivation of a sentence like:

(106) a. Only two women laughed.

which has the Semantic Analysis

(106) b.

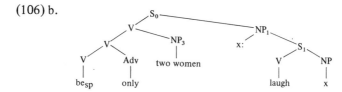

and the corresponding semantically analytic structure

(106) c.

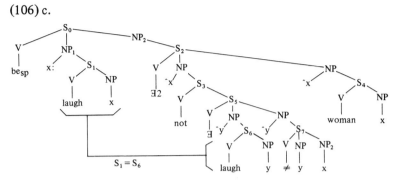

This may look formidable, but what it says is only: "who laughed is nobody other than two women." The reader will easily check that S_3 is reduced to $_S$[laugh nobody other than x], and hence S_2 to $_S$[laugh nobody other than two women]. Deletion under identity with S_1 leaves $_{NP}$[nobody other than two women], which can then be lexicalized as *only two women*, as in (106b). PL gives (106a).

Similarly, we can derive, e.g.,

(107) a. Only John said something.

with the SA

(107) b.

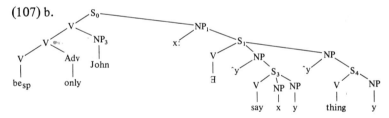

and the semantically analytic structure

(107) c.

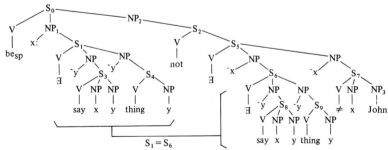

S_6 is reduced to $_S$[say x something]. Then S_5 is reduced to $_S$[say somebody other than John something], and S_2 to $_S$[say nobody other than John something]. Now S_2 differs from S_1 only in that S_2 contains the question-answering NP *nobody other than John* where S_1 contains *x*. Deletion under identity now leaves only $_{NP}$[nobody other than John] of S_2. From here on, the derivation of (107a) is straightforward.

3.5.3 Too *and* even

Similarly notorious, in the literature on presupposition, as (pseudo)clefts and *only* are *too* and *even* (Horn 1969; Fraser 1971; Keenan 1971; Fauconnier 1975; Karttunen and Peters 1979, and many more). Here, too, it is commonplace to assert that sentences with *too* or *even* do not differ truth-conditionally from the sentences without them (Fauconnier 1975: 364; Karttunen and Peters 1979: 33). Yet, this assertion runs counter to intuition. If, in a situation where only Nancy laughed, (108a) or (109a) is uttered, the utterance can hardly be said to be true. More convincingly, in such a situation (108b) or (109b) will have legitimate claims to truth, whereas, of course neither (108c) nor (109c) will then possibly be called true:

(108) a. NANCY laughed, too.
     b. It is not true that NANCY laughed, too.
     c. Nancy did not laugh.
(109) a. Even NANCY laughed.
     b. It is not true that even NANCY laughed.
     c. Nancy did not laugh.

We shall, therefore, conclude that both *too* and *even* have a truth-conditional contribution to make to the sentences in which they occur, besides the special discourse features which they bring along.

Too is analysed as a semantic predicate (which, through Lowering, becomes adverbial) taking either a set-denoting term or a definite quantity term as subject-NP, and a definite NP (with the usual structure "x: + S_x") as its second or object-NP. The latter is unrestricted from the point of view of ontological category, and its extension is therefore represented, again, as "a". The extension set of *too* can be given as follows:

(110) $\sigma(too) = \{\langle T/I^*, a^* \rangle$: there is some b $\neq$ a such that for all terms t such that $\rho(t) = b$, $\varphi(S_{x/t}^{T/I}) = 1$; for all terms u such that $\rho(u) = a$, $\varphi(S_{x/u}^{T/I}) \neq 3 \mid \varphi(S_{x/u}^{T/I}) = 1\}$

("$S_{x/\alpha}^{T/I}$" stands for S_x of the first NP-term (with T or I as its extension), but with the material α replacing the variable x.)

The SA-form of a *too*-sentence is as follows:

(111)

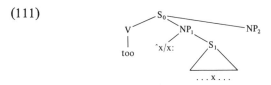

The further grammatical treatment is, again, strongly analogous to that of be_{sp}: NP_2-Incorporation brings NP_2 under $_V$[too] by adoption. Then obligatory PL lowers *too* + NP_2 to the position of the variable x in S_1. All higher structure is deleted, and the lowered constituent is marked by accent. (Later, postcyclic, rules may move *too* to a small number of other possible sites in the sentence, as has happened in (108a).)

Given this description, it is explained why the following bits of discourse are unacceptable:

(112) a. !Nobody else laughed, but Nancy laughed, too.
   b. !Nancy doesn't exist, but she laughed, too.

Both bits of discourse are unacceptable on account of the first sentence contradicting a presupposition of the second. (112a) violates the first precondition of *too*, and (112b) the second. The observational test for presupposition yields a positive result:

(113) a. Somebody else laughed, and Nancy laughed, too.
   b. !Maybe nobody else laughed, but Nancy, too, laughed.
   c. Nancy exists, and she, too, laughed.
   d. !Maybe Nancy doesn't exist, but she, too, laughed.

Note, moreover, that *too* is a Positive Polarity Item and thus does not allow for the minimal negation. The only negation it admits is the radical negation:

(114) a. Nancy did NOT laugh, too: she was the only one who laughed!
   b. Nancy did NOT laugh, too: she doesn't even exist!

The semantic predicate *even* is much like *too*, but with some extra features. Its most striking feature is the involvement of an implicit, understood property that must be supplied from context or background knowledge on pain of the sentence being uninterpretable. The tacitly assumed property, to be supplied from context or background knowledge, is a precise analogue of the comparison class tacitly assumed for gradable adjectives or of the "relation assumed to be known" of the verb *have* – as has been shown in section 3.4. Accordingly, *even* is specified for three terms, not just for the two terms involved in the predicate *too*. Its extension set is specified as follows:

312   *The logic and semantics of presupposition*

(115) $\sigma(even) = \{\langle T/I^*, a^*, P\rangle$: there is some $b \neq a$ such that for all terms t such that $\rho(t) = b, \varphi(S_{x/t}^{T/I}) = 1$; for all terms u such that $\rho(u) = a, \varphi(S_{x/u}^{T/I}) \neq 3$; a has P to such an extent that one would not expect that $\varphi(S_{x/u}^{T/I}) = 1 \mid \varphi(S_{x/u}^{T/I}) = 1\}$

The third term has no corresponding expression in the grammatical SA-form of *even*-sentences. This form is strictly analogous to that of *too*, and is precisely as in (111), but with *even* for *too*. The grammatical treatment is also precisely like that of *too*, at least as far as the cyclic rules are concerned (*even* does not have the freedom of movement, in English, that *too* has).

Of the three preconditions the first two are identical to those of *too*. Since both *too* and *even* also have the same satisfaction condition, *even*-sentences entail *too*-sentences – a fact that can be confirmed by observation. The third precondition is special for *even* and involves the understood property P. For (109a), for example, a property like "impervious to humour", or "despondent":

(116) Nancy was so impervious to humour that one would not expect her to laugh. But even SHE laughed.

If the context or discourse, or background knowledge, provides no clue whatsoever regarding the property to be understood, the utterance will fail to be interpreted.[29]

Even is, like *too*, a Positive Polarity Item, and therefore admits only the radical negation over itself. This might seem in contradiction with the fact that sentences like

(117) a. Not even BILL laughed.

are good English and have the negation in a non-canonical position, so that this negation must be minimal. This is correct: the *not* in (117a) is indeed the minimal negation, but it does not have *even* in its semantic scope. What (117a) means is not "it is not so that even Bill laughed", but "it is even so that BILL didn't laugh", and the PPI-status of *even* has consequences only for a higher negation, not for a lower one. The question is, however, how the *not* in (117a) comes to occupy the position it has, given the grammar of Lowering and the Scope Ordering Constraint (section 2.4.3). The answer is that, in English, *even* is an optional Negative Raiser (section 2.4.4). (Most other languages do not have this rule feature for their equivalents of *even*, as the reader who is familiar with one or more other languages will quickly detect.) The rule of Negative Raising prevents *not* from being lowered into

[29] *Even* is some sort of cross between *too* and *yet*, incorporating the properties of both. *Yet* is like *even*, but without the understood property and with only one sentential term. Its precondition is that "one would not expect that the fact referred to by the sentential term is true", and its satisfaction condition is that that sentential term is, in fact, true. *Even*-sentences thus entail *yet*-sentences.

its argument-S and raises it (on the *even*-cycle) to immediately above the S figuring *even*. Then, on the next cycle, which is the cycle of the newly created S, *not* is lowered and must stay left of *even* according to the Scope Ordering Constraint. Negative Raising is optional, given the alternative but roughly equivalent form:

(117) b. Even BILL didn't laugh.

Facts like these are strong confirmation for the reality of the rule of Negative Raising.

4

Incrementation and denotation

4.1 The construction of discourse domains

4.1.1 Some general principles

Discourse domains are cognitive 'working spaces' set up for the specific purpose of interpreting successive utterances. The grammatical and semantic systems of any natural language are organized in such a way that they fit on naturally to discourse domains. No theory of grammar or meaning can convey an adequate picture of linguistic reality unless it is geared, in specific ways, to the necessary presence of discourse domains. These domains are intermediate between utterances and 'the world' in those cases where the discourse is about things that are or are not the case. The (propositions in the) utterances of such discourses have truth-values, but there are many discourse domains built up by speakers where the question of truth-values does not arise. Yet in these cases, too, the utterances are as readily interpreted as if they did have a truth-value. Apparently, truth-values are not necessary for the interpretation of a coherent set of successive utterances.

Discourse domains are set up as a result of the *increment value* associated with each predicate in the semantic lexicon. These predicates fall into two classes, the purely *lexical* and the *technical* predicates. The lexical ones are relatively straightforward (the complications are taken care of in section 4.2.5): their terms select addresses in the domain D, and the predicate is stored under the addresses in the appropriate form. Thus, for

(1) $eat(x:(child(x)), x:(biscuit(x)))$

in a D where the address d_1 is characterized by "child(x)" and d_2 by "biscuit(x)", the increment value of the proposition $\langle(1), D\rangle$ consists in the addition to d_1 of the material "eat(x, d_2)", and to d_2 of "eat(d_1, x)", since *eat* is a purely lexical predicate.

The technical predicates have as a specific property that their increment value consists at least in part in an *instruction* other than the simple addition of the predicate to the appropriate addresses. This instruction may be "set up a new address", as in the case of the existential quantifier, or to set up a new subdomain, as with intensional predicates, or to ban a particular increment from D, as with minimal negation. Some technical predicates are mixed (such as the intensional predicate *believe*), in that their increment value involves both the standard addition to the appropriate addresses and some technical instruction. Strictly speaking, therefore, the distinction between "lexical" and "technical" applies to the incremental instructions associated with each predicate: some such instructions are standard or lexical, others are technical. Predicates have increment values which are either entirely lexical, or entirely technical, or mixed.

The increment of a proposition whose Semantic Analysis has the existential quantifier as its highest predicate consists in the setting up of a new address, characterized by the predicates figuring in the two set-denoting terms – at least if the SA in question has two SD terms under $\exists$ and not a (plural) definite description as its second NP term. Thus, the SA (disregarding tense)

(2) a. $\exists 1(\hat{\ }x(\text{meet}(I, x)), \hat{\ }x(\text{man}(x)))$

(where "I" stands for the speaker – though it is not syntactically defined in the SA formation rules of section 2.2), in a discourse where time and place parameters have been filled in, will lead to the following increment:

(2) b.

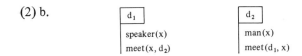

$$\boxed{d_1}$$
speaker(x)
meet(x, d_2)

$$\boxed{d_2}$$
man(x)
meet(d_1, x)

Speaker and listener are pragmatic elements in every discourse, and the use of the appropriate pronoun is sufficient to bring about (by backward suppletion) the addresses required. The point here is that the address d_2 is set up as a result of the technical instruction that goes with the existential quantifier (here limited to a single address) to open a new address characterized by the predicates in the two terms of the existential predicate, i.e. *man* and *meet*, and to ensure that possible other addresses (such as d_1 here) mentioned in the specification of the new address are updated in the appropriate way. Here, d_1 is mentioned in "meet(d_1, x)" under d_2, so that "meet(x, d_2)" must be added to d_1.

Both (2a) and (2b) are made true by at least one entity satisfying the conditions specified in the new address d_2. The existence of more such entities is not ruled out, but not required for truth. We use the symbol "1" to indicate the singular character of an existential quantifier, just as we use "2", "3", etc., or the adjective *many/much, few/little*, or other modifications, to indicate quantification involving at least two, three, etc., elements or large or small quantities. The problem of singularity versus plurality, as is widely recognized, is of great complexity, and it would be overoptimistic if it were hoped that this problem could be solved in any satisfactory manner in this study. Therefore, no serious claim is involved in the addition of modifications like "1" to the existential predicate: such notation serves to mask our ignorance in this respect rather than to clear up a complex problem area.

If the second term under the existential predicate is a definite description, as in

(3) a. $\exists 1(\hat{\ }x(\text{meet}(I, x)), x: \text{men}(x))$

then, likewise, a new address is set up, but in a slightly more complex way. Now, instead of d_2 in (2b), an address is opened whose truth requires not just any man met by the speaker but one of a given set of men, i.e. those men who, together, form the extension of the term *the men* in the given discourse. In section 2.2 the notation

(3) b.

$$\boxed{\begin{array}{l} d_2 \\ \hline x \in D\{\,\text{man}(x)\} \\ \text{meet}(d_1, x) \end{array}}$$

was introduced for such addresses, where "$x \in D\{\text{man}(x)\}$" stands for something like "this address must be identifiable with one of the addresses defined in the discourse as 'man(x)'". (Addresses of this kind naturally give rise to the question "Which of the men did you meet?", so that an identification can take place, and d_2 can be eliminated – whereby the material "meet(d_1, x)" is added to the address that d_2 is identified with. But such further elaborations will be left out of account here.)

Now a definite description in a subsequent utterance containing the lexical specification "man(x)" and "meet(I, x)" will inevitably select d_2, either as in (2b) or as in (3b), as its denotation. Thus, if (2a) – *I met a man* – or (3a) – *I met one of the men* – is followed by (4a) – *The man I met was drunk* – or

(4) a. drunk(x : man(x), meet(I, x))

the term x : man(x), meet(I, x) scans the discourse domain D first for any address set up for the speaker (i.e. d_1), and then for any address characterized by the material "man(x)" and "meet(d_1, x)". If there is only one such address, the term has found its denotation and the interpretation of the utterance can proceed. If there are more such addresses there is no unique denotation for the term in question, with the result that the utterance is uninterpretable. Provided that d_2 in (2b) or (3b) is the only address in D thus characterized, the subject term of (4a) does indeed find its denotation, d_2, and the increment of (4a) now involves the addition to d_2 of "drunk(x)":

(4) b-1.   b-2.

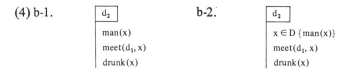

This is not the whole story, however. If the incremental result of (4a) were simply the addition of the relevant material to the relevant address, as in (4b), a truth-conditional and referential snag would creep in. Both addresses d_2 in (4b) are *open* addresses, i.e. they are made true by the existence of at least some entity in the verification domain V associated with D, which answers to the description given in either of the d_2s. Their truth conditions thus do not differ in any way from those of, respectively:

(5) a. I met a drunken man.
   b. I met one of the men, who was drunk.

For (5b) this is not serious. In fact, one may well maintain that the truth-conditions of *I met one of the men. The man I met was drunk* and (5b) are identical, and are adequately rendered by (4b-2). but there are problems with (4b-1) and

(6) I met a man. The man I met was drunk.

The truth conditions of this succession of two utterances are not identical to those of (5a). The difference is, in principle, that for (5a) to be true it is simply sufficient that there be at least one person whom the speaker met, who was a man, and who was drunk, at the time referrred to by the simple past tense used. However, for (6) to be true it is required, in addition, that one specific person be singled out to whom it applies. If there was, in fact, more than one man who the speaker met and who was drunk, at the time referred to, then (5a) is clearly true, but (6) can only be called true on condition that a unique referent be assigned to the definite description *the man I met*.

Take the case of the English Department at Nijmegen University. It so happens that there are two professors of English language, both of them **Dutch nationals. Now an utterance of**

(7) a. There is a professor of English language at Nijmegen University who is a Dutchman.

is clearly true, but how about:

(7) b. The professor of English language at Nijmegen University is a Dutchman.

What can one say if one is asked whether (7b) is true, given the state of affairs as specified above? One's natural reaction would be to say something like "Which of the two do you mean?". If one simply says that (7b) is true, then what would be the correct answer to the question "Does he wear glasses?", given that only one of them does?

Or, more clearly perhaps, take the whole English Department at Nijmegen ᵀJniversity, which has, besides the two professors mentioned, a third professor, for English literature, who is a British national. Given this state of affairs, an utterance of

(8) a. There is a professor of English at Nijmegen University who is British.

is clearly true, and in no way in conflict with (7a). But

(8) b. The professor of English at Nijmegen University is British.

is not so clearly true, and might be taken to be contrary to (7b). What is missing in the (b)-sentences is additional information as to which of the professors is meant. What is needed is the fixing of a referent. Only then is it clear whether the utterances in question are or are not true.

An adequate solution to this complication seems to be provided by the device of *referential closure* of open addresses. We say that *an open address is closed as soon as, in a subsequent increment unit, the address is selected as the denotational target for a definite term*. The notation used for referential closure of an open address is a horizontal line where the closure takes place. The semantic consequence of closure is that the extension of the address in question is no longer any arbitrary individual answering to the description but one specific individual rigidly locked onto the address for the duration of the discourse. (But see section 6.2 for further discussion.) Now the result of (4a) is not (4b) but:

(4) c-1.

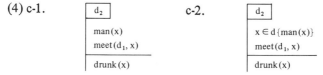

$$
\begin{array}{ll}
\boxed{d_2} & \\
\text{man}(x) & \\
\text{meet}(d_1, x) & \\
\hline
\text{drunk}(x) &
\end{array}
\qquad
c\text{-}2.
\qquad
\begin{array}{ll}
\boxed{d_2} & \\
x \in d\{\text{man}(x)\} & \\
\text{meet}(d_1, x) & \\
\hline
\text{drunk}(x) &
\end{array}
$$

And it is now part of the truth-conditions that a specific individual be singled out as the reference value in V of either (4c-1) or (4c-2). (It would seem dangerously inappropriate not to let the (2)-cases partake in the referential closure operation.)

Whenever referential closure is involved, there is a necessity that the definite term and its closed address in question have their uniquely determined reference value or ρ-value before the discourse is brought to an end. Often, and perhaps usually, referent fixing is simultaneous with referential closure of the address in question. If, after existential introduction of a new address in D, it appears that the verification domain V contains one and only one exemplar answering to the description of the new address, reference fixing is unproblematic: after closure the new address can only have that one exemplar as its reference value. But it may be the case that V contains more than one instance of the type defined by the address to be closed, as in:

(9) There is a professor of English at Nijmegen University. He is British.

Now, at the point where the newly introduced address for the Professor of English at Nijmegen University is to be closed, no unique referent is determined, and closure has to take place even though no unique referent is available. We say that in such cases closure takes place and that referent fixing is achieved as soon as the material added by subsequent increments suffices to single out one specific individual. In (9), for example, the new address opened by the first utterance does not have a uniquely determined p-value when it is closed as a result of the second utterance. Yet for (9) as a whole to have a truth-value the address for the English professor must have a p-value. This p-value is fixed, we say, if after the addition of the increment of *He is British* V does indeed contain one and only one individual who is professor of English at Nijmegen University, and is British. In such cases reference fixing takes place after referential closure of the address in question. Yet no harm is done as long as, at the end of the discourse, the definite term in question, and its discourse address, have a uniquely determined reference value.

That this analysis corresponds to psychological reality appears from the fact that hearers, who take speakers to present stories which have at least the merit of having a truth-value (one of the three), are entitled to infer that unique p-values are to be assigned to definite descriptions occurring in the utterances presented – provided it is expected that the story in question is about real things and has a truth-value at all. It is, in other words, a natural feeling that justice is done to truth only if, at the end of the discourse, every definite term has its unique p-value. Suppose I hear someone say:

(10) Last year I was at a conference. At that conference someone said that Wittgenstein is the most overrated philosopher of the century.

Then, accepting that the speaker has said what he wanted to say and that what he said is true, I infer that of the possibly many conferences the speaker went to last year there was precisely one where it was said (or where the speaker was aware that it was said) that Wittgenstein is the most overrated philosopher of the century. As long as the initial existential introduction was done through "$\exists 1$", and not "$\exists 2$", "$\exists 3$" or whatever other plural existential quantification, subsequent reference fixing requires one and precisely one reference object for truth. This condition is expressed by referential closure of open addresses. (In chapter 6 it will become clear that referential closure is an indispensable ingredient in the solution of certain potentially nasty referential and truth-conditional problems arising with natural language sentences whose utterances are *per se* discourse-dependent.)

This machinery provides the solution to an apparent problem spotted by Geach (1972: 115–27). It concerns the apparent contradiction between his examples (11a) and (11b):

(11) a. Socrates owned a dog and it bit Socrates.

b. Socrates owned a dog and it did not bite Socrates.

These, Geach proposes, are not conjunctions of the form "*A* and *B*" or "*A* and not-*B*", since a pair of such conjunctions is incompatible but (11a) and (11b) are not incompatible because Socrates may have had more than one dog. Geach's solution consists in letting one single existential quantifier bind the dog-variable in both conjoined propositional functions. In Geach's restricted quantification analysis, (11a) and (11b) would be analysed as follows:

(12) a. $\exists$x: dog (Socrates owned x $\wedge$ x bit Socrates)
     b. $\exists$x: dog (Socrates owned x $\wedge$ $\neg$(x bit Socrates))

Now there is no contradiction between the two. Hence, Geach concludes, existential binding over both conjuncts is the correct analytical solution. (He takes this to be a confirmation of Quine's analytic approach to natural language.)

However, apart from the observational objection that one would expect analyses like (12a) and (12b) to read, respectively

(13) a. Socrates owned a dog which bit him.
     b. Socrates owned a dog which did not bite him.

the solution proposed by Geach is inadequate since it lacks in generality (see Seuren 1977). While it is undeniably so that (11a) and (11b) cannot be juxtaposed under the contrary analysis "*A* and *B*, ánd *A* and not-*B*", the analysis proposed by Geach will not do either. This is clear when one considers that the same problem as was spotted by Geach in relation to (11a) and (11b) turns up in sentence pairs like:

(14) a. Socrates must have owned a dog, and it may have bitten Socrates.
     b. Socrates must have owned a dog, and it cannot have bitten Socrates.
(15) a. I know that Socrates owned a dog, and I hope that it bit Socrates.
     b. I know that Socrates owned a dog, and I do not hope that it bit Socrates.

Yet here the proposed solution fails owing to scope problems. The normal readings of these sentences have the existential *a dog* in the scope of, respectively, the *must*-operator and the *know*-operator. But then, if the *it* in the second conjunct is to be bound by the existential quantifier in the normal way, the *may*-operator, or the *hope*-operator, will necessarily fall in the scope of *must* or *know*, respectively, which is absurd in view of what the sentences in question mean. The only way in which this can be avoided is to place the existential quantifier over the lot, so that *must* and *may*, and *know* and *hope*, are on a par. But this again grossly violates the normal readings of the sentences involved. We are thus forced to conclude that Geach's solution is *ad hoc*, and hence insufficient.

In our analysis, however, the problem does not arise (or is immediately solved), provided the pronominal *it* attaches to the address just introduced.

Let D contain a previously given address for *Socrates*. The utterance of (11a) will then result in two successive increments, the first adding a dog-address, the second closing this address and adding the information that the newly introduced dog bit Socrates:

(16) a.

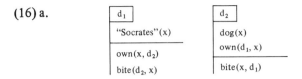

If Socrates owns just one dog, d_2 has found its ρ-value at the moment of closure. But if Socrates owns more than one dog, closure takes place as soon as *it* is used, but no uniquely determined reference value is yet available. It will be available if Socrates owns just one dog which bit him. And since the availability of a reference value is a necessary requirement for (11a) to have a truth-value, it follows that, if (11a) is true, then Socrates cannot have had more than one dog biting him.

Now add (11b). The result is that a second dog-address is opened for a dog not biting Socrates (negative increments are marked by the asterisk):

(16) b.

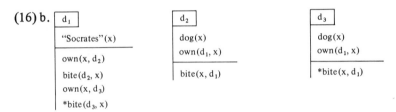

This discourse domain as represented in (16b) contains nothing that would prevent it from being true in some verification domain. There is no contradiction or contrariness. Nor is it based on a Geach-type analysis for (11). On the contrary, (11a) and (11b) have been treated as ordinary conjunctions, and nothing exceptional was called for to get (16b). But the second conjunct of (11b) is not, in this analysis, the negation of the second conjunct of (11a). The concatenation of (11a) and (11b) is analysed as "a and b, ánd a and not-c", where a, b and c are propositions. The proposition negated in (11b) is different from the proposition asserted in (11a) because the *it* in both cases goes to different addresses. (A proposition, it will be remembered, is an ordered pair of a Semantic Analysis and a discourse D, and defines the increment brought about in D by the utterance of the sentence corresponding to the Semantic Analysis.)

It is an interesting corollary of this analysis that if (11a) and (11b) are both true, and hence (16b) is true, Socrates had exactly two dogs. This follows from the fact that both d_2 and d_3 must have a unique dog as referent, each dog being uniquely characterized by the predicate material in the respective addresses. If Socrates had a third dog d_4, then d_4 either bit Socrates or it did not do so. If the former, d_2 lacks a uniquely determined referent; if the latter, d_3 lacks one. Hence Socrates cannot have had a little dog, if both (11a) and (11b) are true. No such conclusion follows, of course, from the combined truth of (13a) and (13b).

Contrary to Geach's analysis, this analysis is not *ad hoc*. It will become clear in the next chapter that (14) and (15), and similar cases, are treated in precisely analogous ways. This analysis is, furthermore, the first step towards a solution for a nasty referential problem not noticed, apparently, by Geach. It presents itself in a situation where Socrates has two dogs, one biting him and the other one not – i.e., a situation like the one given earlier – and where the following sentence is uttered:

(17) Either Socrates owned no dog, or he owned a dog and it bit him.

According to all known treatments of the disjunction, a disjunction is true if at least one of the disjuncts is true. Now, given the situation described, the second disjunct must be considered true. Yet, our intuition says clearly that (17) is false in the situation described. It is falsified by the dog not biting Socrates. We shall not, however, discuss this problem here. It will come up for ample discussion in section 6.3.

There is one property of discourse domains which is reminiscent of human memory in general: there is a recency effect, and a gradual integration of specific information into the vast fund of generalized knowledge. Incoming information is retained for a relatively short period in a form which is still closely bound up with contingent properties of form and of mode, time, manner, etc., of presentation and reception. The contingent properties tend to disappear from memory as time goes by, and the information received passes through a process of integration, whereby particulars tend to fade into what gives the impression of being a more or less indistinct mass of generalized knowledge, with very few real particulars left. The loss of contingents and particulars is rapid at first, and then slows down considerably until hardly any change is noticed over a long period of time. In a small way, discourse domains have the same tendency. Fresh increments are not only 'salient' in a sense often found in the psychological literature. They also retain, for a little while, information about the order in which they have been introduced, as appears from expressions like *the former, the latter, in that order*, and also from phenomena found in the study of sentence-external anaphora. Soon, however, the order of introduction is 'forgotten', and consequently no appeal can be made any more to the ordering of increments beyond a certain threshold of remoteness in time. (I am not acquainted with any empirical investigation with regard to this threshold. I would not be surprised, however, if it were to be found that humans behave rather uniformly in this respect.)

Given the linguistic relevance of some form of recency in the construction of discourse domains, it is probably useful to mark increments as to their order of introduction, in so far as the order is not already apparent from the notation used. This marking for ordei would then have to be discontinued beyond a certain threshold, when it may be assumed that the order of introduction is no longer relevant. Such marking, however, will not be used in this book, mainly because any decision as to where to discontinue the marking would be arbitrary given the absence of empirical data on this score, and because the study of discourse domains, in so far as it is carried out in this book, is, apparently, still so elementary or primitive that this device is not called for.

Another feature of discourse domains that shows the parallel with general memory is the fading of exact numbers into plural sets. If, in a discourse, information is given about, say, 25 individuals or events, hardly any listener will be able to recall the specific information associated with each of the 25 individuals or events. What happens is that generalizations are made over the information provided. If the information is very different for each individual or event, the result is an indistinct and blurred picture of things being the case or things happening. If the information is systematic and similar, more precise generalizations are made. But even then the exact number 25 is not recalled, unless the listener has made it his business to count.

Other such features can no doubt be spotted. All we can say about such phenomena, however, is that they are as yet beyond our powers of analysis and modelling. The discourse domains presented in the sequel are stiff and static, and show nothing of the internal dynamics typical for real cognitive and other psychological processes.

Meanwhile, the problem of plurality remains. The denotation of singular individual addresses (i.e. potentially or actually referring to real or intensional individuals) is, as has been shown, relatively simple – not reckoning cases of the Swiss banker type (section 3.4) where additional principles are called upon. In ordinary, straightforward cases the predicate material contained in the singular definite description must single out a unique individual address. The increment function then adds the highest predicate of the incremented clause to the address in question, for all individual addresses denoted by a definite description under that predicate. Denoting pronouns and pronominally used definite descriptions ("epithets") require an auxiliary procedure where the denotation is mediated via an antecedent. This auxiliary Assignment Procedure is the subject of further discussion in section 4.2 below.

For plural definite terms, however, the situation is not so simple. It must be said again that no satisfactory theory is available yet accounting for plurality, either in terms of discourse semantics or, for that matter, in terms of any other theory. We have, as a crude makeshift device, spoken of "superaddresses", without, however, defining them properly. All we can do here is point to some of the problems, and only in a cursory way.

The simplest case is that of a discourse domain where a small number of distinct individual addresses has been set up with some predicate material common to all of them. Plurality of a definite description or a pronoun can then simply be accounted for as an instruction to repeat for each of these addresses what would be specified for one in the singular case:

(18) There were three students. The students (they) were drinking.

No superaddresses need be invoked for such cases.

The matter is not so simple, however, for either larger or indefinite numbers of given individuals. (Larger numbers quickly recede in memory, and one expects also in discourse domains, to become indefinite numbers, a phenomenon just commented upon.) Here some special provision, different in kind from a simple grouping of individual addresses, is called for, a conclusion which is amply supported by grammatical and semantic observations. The problem is, however, that it is not at all clear what that provision will have to look like. The superaddresses are nothing but a, probably temporary, home for plural denotations other than simple collections of individual addresses.

One particular aspect of this complex issue may be mentioned here. It is to do with the relation of plural denotations (superaddresses) to individual instantiations. Take the following two cases:

(19) a. Lots of students were taking the exam. Those who had done some work passed.
   b. Lots of students were taking the exam. Those who had done any work passed.

There is a subtle non-truth-conditional semantic difference between the two: the latter has an implicit conditionality about it which the former lacks – something like "for any arbitrary individual i from the set of students taking the exam, if i had done any work i passed". It would seem that a partial and provisional account for this difference might be given by drawing the following distinction. In (19a) the second sentence prejects "some of the students had done some work", thereby creating *post hoc* a superaddress for its subject term. In (19b), however, such a prejection is inappropriate, as appears from the diminished acceptability of:

(19) c. ?Lots of students were taking the exam. Some of them had done some work, and those who had done any work passed.

We thus say that in cases like (19b) no new superaddress is set up (*post hoc*). The definite description *those who had done any work* 'lands' at the super-address which was set up for the students taking the exam by the first sentence. However, the incrementation does not consist in the adding of further predicate material to this superaddress, but in the imposing of an instruction to the effect that any individual address to be introduced in subsequent discourse with the predicate material "student(x)", "take the exam(x)", and "do some work(x)" must be further characterized by "pass(x)". It is not clear, at this stage, what should be considered the conveyor, in Semantic Analysis, of this instruction. Perhaps a separate abstract predicate of conditional plurality should be postulated ranging over the whole sentence. We do not know. All we know now, with some degree of confidence, is that the occurrence of *any*, as opposed to *some*, calls for a special provision which is non-trivially analogous to what must be supposed to take place with conditional constructions.

If this account is viable in principle, there is the beginning of an explanation for the occurrence of *any* in (19b). The explanation envisaged is to do with the requirement, commented upon in section 3.3, that increments, in order to be acceptable in a discourse D, must be *informative* in a technical sense (i.e. each new increment must, if it is to be acceptable, either restrict the class of possible verification domains V in which D is true, or else add new information (entailments) about D). A distinction can now be made between V-restricting and V-relaxing addresses. A V-restricting address is an address d_r which is so positioned in D that further addition of predicate material to d_r leads to further restriction of the class of possible Vs in which D is true. A V-relaxing address, on the other hand, is an address d_1 which is so positioned in D that further addition of predicate material to d_1 leads to a widening of the class of possible Vs in which D is true (and is thus unacceptable). The former are the normal addresses occurring in domains and subdomains. The latter are addresses which are not added to D but specified in some instruction associated with a technical predicate that places an 'embargo' on the address in question.

A clear example is the negation over an existential predicate: "There are no ghosts." As we shall see, the negation has the effect of an instruction barring the incrementation of its argument proposition from D. In this case any address characterized by "ghost(x)" is barred from being added to D. If further predicate material is added to the address type specified in the instruction, the effect will be that the class of possible Vs in which D is true is widened, not restricted. Thus, if the ban is not just on addresses characterized by "ghost(x)", but on addresses characterized by "ghost(x)" and, say, "in the tower(x)", then a V where there are ghosts in the graveyard still stands a chance of being one for which D is true, whereas this is not so if D contains a ban on ghosts generally.

It is an interesting thought that this distinction is bound up with the conditions of occurrence of Negative Polarity Items, in particular those of the *any*-class (existential *any, ever, the slightest, a red cent*, etc.), in the sense that these NPIs are allowed only in material leading to the setting up or to the denotation of a V-relaxing address, i.e. an address under some restrictive embargo. We shall come back to this suggestion in section 4.1.3 below.

In the following sections some technical predicates will be investigated from the point of view of the instructions associated with them with regard to the building of discourse domains.

4.1.2 The existential predicate

The use of the existential predicate in a discourse leads inevitably to the setting up of a new address (unless, of course, the utterance in question is presented as a repetition of an earlier utterance). The address is then characterized by $P_1, \ldots, P_n$ of $S_{x_1}, \ldots, S_{x_n}$ of the object term and P of S_x of the subject term. Some material, though present in the SA of existentially quantified sentences, is not represented in D. For example:

(20) a. $\exists 1(\hat{}x(be\ there(x)), \hat{}x(man(x)))$
     b. $\exists 1(\hat{}x(love(x:\text{“Mary”}(x),x)), \hat{}x(man(x), other(x)))$

corresponding to, respectively (using the simple past tense):

(21) a. There was a man.
     b. Mary loved another man.

(The grammatical treatment of (20a) is not problematic. At the end of the $\exists$-cycle, the S-structure $_S[be\ there(a\ man)]$ has come about, as described in section 2.4.3. Then, as a result of an idiosyncratic rule associated with a small class of predicates including *be there*, the element *there* is optionally detached from the predicate and placed just left of the subject-NP, under the category node “NP”, thus creating a new *there*-subject. This new subject can be raised again, as in: *I expected there to be a man.* The rule is optional, since, besides (21a), there is also: *A man was there.* Other predicates in this class are, e.g., *exist, come, come about, go*, which optionally insert a new $_{NP}[there]$ instead of detaching it from the predicate. They form pairs like:

(22) a. There existed an ancient belief.
     b. An ancient belief existed.)

The incremental result of (20a) should be, if all material were to be represented, as in (23a), and (20b) would result in (23b):

(23) a.   b.

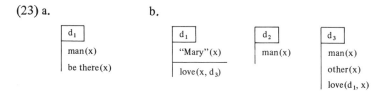

However, the predicate material "be there" in (23a), and "other" under d_3 in (23b) is superfluous. "Be there" means simply that the address is in D, which is self-evident, and "other" means that the address in question is distinct from any other address in D, which is also self-evident. It is probably correct to say that *other* in (21b) gives rise to the presupposition that there is a man different from the man introduced by (21b), but that presupposition only needs to be fulfilled (as it is in (23b)). It does not require that the lexical material giving rise to it be represented in D. On grounds of descriptive economy we are, therefore, entitled to stipulate that predicates such as *be there* or *other* are not represented in D.

4.1.3 The universal predicates

The universal quantifier occurs in a number of different guises in every natural language. In English we have *all*, *every*, *each*, universal *any*, and perhaps a few more, which are far from identical. Since, however, an analysis of universal quantification in English would by itself fill a sizeable monograph, we shall limit ourselves to some uses of *all*, and to some aspects of universal *any* and of *each*.

The universally quantifying predicate *all*, represented by "∀", occurs in two different constructions, as we have seen (section 2.2). In one construction it takes two SD-terms; in the other its subject is an SD-term, but the object is a definite description:

(24) a. ∀(ˆx(mortal(x)), ˆx(man(x)))
 b. ∀(ˆx(mortal(x)), x:(men(x)))

corresponding to, respectively:

(25) a. All men are mortal.
 b. All the men are mortal.

We stipulate that in cases of type (24b) the second term, "x:(men(x))", denotes a superaddress *sd* potentially corresponding to a plurality of men in the world. Now, as with plural definite terms specifying larger or indefinite numbers, there are two possibilities, which are truth-conditionally equivalent but semantically different. Either the material of the first term, "mortal(x)", is simply added to *sd*, or a technical instruction is attached to the effect that any address to be introduced in the sequel of the discourse domain at hand and characterized by "x∈D{man(x)}" must be further enriched with "mortal(x)". The former type of increment is of a lexical, the latter of a technical nature.

The situation is different for cases of the type (24a), where the second term is a set-denoting term. Here no superaddress is involved, but there is only a technical instruction, applying to a wider set of discourse domains, to add the material "mortal(x)" to any V-restricting address containing the material "man(x)". (Neither here, nor in the previous case, can the instruction apply to V-relaxing addresses, since that would be an instruction to add an unacceptable increment – see section 3.3.) The "wider set of discourse domains" is probably best defined as the set of all possible discourse domains under the same parameter of time and associated with the same discourse domain, except that, when the universal present is used, the verification domain is unrestricted. Thus, given (25a), with its universal present, the instruction to add the material "mortal(x)" to any V-restricting address containing "man(x)" applies to the unrestricted set of all possible discourse domains. But for a sentence like

(26) All students passed.

the instruction is best restricted to all V-restricting addresses in any discourse related to the time referred to by the simple past in *passed*, and related to the verification domain associated with (26). This instruction is technical, and not lexical, or at least not purely lexical, since it affects also other Ds than the D under construction now and thus places an 'embargo' or restriction on other Ds besides the present one.

Let universal *any* have the same syntax as *all*, i.e. it takes two terms, the first of which is an SD term, and the second either an SD term or a definite description for a plurality or a quantity. We may even suppose that the extension set of *any* is identical, in main outline at least, to that of *all* (i.e. (38b) in section 3.2.4). Whatever truth-conditional differences there may be between *all* and universal *any* may be ignored here. What counts is a difference in the increment value associated with universal *any* as compared with that of *all*. The difference is mainly that in cases where the second term is a definite quantity term, with the predicate material $P(x)$, *any* lacks the possibility of simply adding the predicate material $Q(x)$ of the first (set-denoting) term to the superaddress *sd* denoted by the second term. It only allows for the technical instruction that $Q(x)$ be added to any singular individual address characterized by "$x \in D\{P(x)\}$" to be singled out for further incrementation in subsequent discourse. When the second term under *any* is a set-denoting term, with the predicate material $P(x)$, the instruction is that $Q(x)$ of the first term be added to whatever address characterized by $P(x)$ is newly introduced in subsequent discourse. This latter instruction is very similar to that attached to *all* in the same syntactic construction. There is probably some difference with respect to the class of discourse domains to which the instruction applies.

Each, finally, may be considered to take an SD term in first position, like the others, but to differ from these in that the second term must be a definite plural term (not a quantity term, so that no definite mass term can occur in that position). The plural term denotes either a small number of definite singular addresses, or a superaddress of indefinite or large plurality. In either case the instruction is purely lexical: add $Q(x)$ of the first term to the addresses or the superaddress denoted by the second term and thus characterized by $P(x)$.

If we now assume, as was suggested earlier, that Negative Polarity Items of the *any*-class can occur only in grammatical material selecting or setting up V-relaxing addresses, and not V-restricting ones, we have a basis for the understanding of the following observations, which are highly troublesome for all existing theories of quantification or of NPI-occurrence conditions (including Ladusaw 1979):

(27) a. All students who had done some/any work passed.
    b. All (of) the students who had done some/any work passed.
    c. All of these students who had done some/any work passed.
(28) a. Any student who has done some/any work will pass.
    b. Any of the students who has done some/any work will pass.
    c. Any of these students who has done some/any work will pass.
(29) a. Each student who had done some/*any work passed.
    b. Each of the students who had done some/*any work passed.
    c. Each of these students who had done some/*any work passed.

Any is allowed in the relative clause of all of (27) and (28), the reason being, it would seem, that in all these cases there is an interpretation whereby the relative clause serves to help select a V-relaxing address. Not so, however, with (29a)–(29c), where *each* is the highest semantic predicate. Here the only option is lexical addition of material to V-restricting addresses, so that (existential) *any* is excluded.

It would seem, on the basis of some further preliminary investigations along these lines, that this approach is worth pursuing. It provides, in particular, a possible basis for the explanation of phenomena of 'polarity inversion' under double negation (cp. Baker 1970a) or other forms of embargo on embargo. Consider, for example, the well-formed occurrence of *any* under *only*, as in:

(30) a. Only Wilma said anything.

This can be explained, in principle, by letting *only* induce an embargo on any address to be identified by means of the material "say anything". Such an embargo would naturally follow from the semantic definition of the extension set of *only*, as given under (100) in section 3.5.2. If, however, the embargo is nullified, as in

(30) b. Not only Wilma said something.

the class of addresses specified is no longer V-relaxing but has become V-restricting. As a consequence, the following must be ungrammatical, as indeed it is:

(30) c. *Not only Wilma said anything.

Again, however, we must refrain from further forays into this promising area, given limitations of size and time.

4.1.4 The predicates of negation

The minimal and the radical negation are technical predicates in that they place an embargo on their argument proposition. For the minimal negation ($\sim$) the embargo is as follows: if A is the Semantic Analysis of the argument proposition, then $i(A)$ is excluded from D. We shall use the single asterisk to indicate minimal negation in D-representations. If $i(A)$ consists in the setting up of a new address (i.e. if A is an existentially quantified sentence), then the address will be set up but it will be asterisked. If $i(A)$ consists in the addition to one or more addresses of further predicate material, then the additions in question will be asterisked, as in (16b) above.

Note that there is no discourse-acceptable way of closing an asterisked (negated) address. Since any address of the type specified by the negated existential is excluded from D, no such address can serve as the denotation for a definite term, and hence no closure can take place if all additions to D are to be acceptable. We shall see in a moment that the radical negation makes it possible to close an asterisked address, but the closure will be marked as unacceptable and will therefore play no further role.

The radical negation ($\approx$) has an instruction which not only excludes its argument proposition from D but requires a change in D such that $i(A)$ is unacceptable on account of presupposition failure. That is, the instruction is: if A is the Semantic Analysis of the argument proposition, then $i(A)$ is excluded from D in virtue of some *post hoc* change in D excluding some presupposition of A, so that $i(A)$ is unacceptable and uninterpretable. The notation in D-representations will consist of a double asterisk, requiring at least a single asterisk for one of the presuppositions of the radically negated incremented sentence. For example, the effect of

(31) a. Lady Fortune did NOT promise you a ring: Lady Fortune is a horse!

in an appropriate D containing an address for an individual called "Lady Fortune" will be:

(31) b
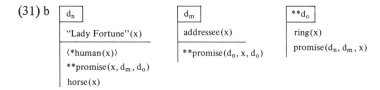

(The material "human(x)" is placed between angled brackets because it represents generalized categorial knowledge (see section 3.4), which is preferably not represented explicitly under each address in full but nevertheless functions as though it was.) The address d_0 for the ring that Lady Fortune is radically denied to have promised the addressee is marked with a double asterisk since it is the intended increment of the proposition under the radical *not* of (31a). It requires the cancellation of at least one presupposition of *Lady Fortune promised you a ring*, which is that Lady Fortune is human. The assertion that Lady Fortunate is of equine nature entails the negation of "human(x)" under d_n, which is thus marked with a single asterisk. The doublets of "promise(d_n, d_m, x)" of d_0 under d_m and d_n are also marked with a double asterisk in accordance with the marking for d_0. The radical falsity marking for d_0 results straightforwardly from the predicate conditions associated with the existential predicate as given in (38a) of section 3.2.4, and the fact that *promise* places a precondition of being human on its subject.

Russell's case of

(32) a. The king of France is NOT bald: there is no king of France!

is incremented in the following way:

(32) b

$*d_n$
KoF(x)
$**$bald(x)

where the address d_n for the king of France is negated. This prevents it from being referentially closed, as we have seen, except when the predicate material added after the closure is marked for radical falsity.

It might seem that the principle preventing (acceptable) closure of negated addresses is contradicted by cases such as:

(33) a. There are no ghosts. All the ghosts are fictitious.

This is not so, however. The (super)address required by *all the ghosts* cannot be the (super)address barred from D by the first sentence. Instead, it *must* be a (super)address in some intensional subdomain of D. For example, if there has been talk of a number of presumed ghosts by speaker A, then the (super)address is located in the subdomain of what A has been saying. The predicate *fictitious*, as will be shown in section 5.3.4 below, ensures that its subject denotation is excluded from the truth-domain of D, to which the exclusion of any ghost-address applies. The address or address type excluded does therefore not function as a denotation for any subsequent definite term in a proposition which is not radically negated.

Typically, predicates associated with a technical increment value involving an embargo on possible future developments of the discourse domain D seem to resist minimal negation. Thus, there is no grammatically integrated form (other than the periphrastic "it is not true that ...") to negate disjunctions or conditionals, which, as will be shown in the following section, both involve such embargos. It might seem as though sentences like

(34) a. Joe doesn't like coffee or tea.

would be instances of a canonically negated disjunction. It was shown, however, in section 2.4.3 above that the SA of (34a) corresponds to "Joe does not like coffee and Joe does not like tea", which is a conjunction of two negative clauses and not a negated disjunction. It will be remembered that the semantic relation between (34a) and its proposed SA is intuitively obvious. However, no such obvious link exists between, e.g.,

(34) b. Joe doesn't like coffee and tea.

and the analysis "Either Joe doesn't like coffee or Joe doesn't like tea" – which would suggest that the SA of (34b) is indeed a grammatically regular (but radical) negation of a conjunction. Moreover, if no conjunctive underlying structure is assumed for sentences like

(35) I don't think either Harry or Leo were late.

it would be difficult to find an explanation for the plural *were*. We assume, therefore, as long as no counter-evidence comes to light, that technical instructions with regard to future D-developments do not allow for ordinary negation.

This is confirmed by the behaviour of the universal quantifiers in this respect. (The existential quantifier does allow for a higher negation, but then the surface representative of the quantifier must be of the *any*-class. Note that *some* is a Positive Polarity Item and can thus stand only under the radical negation.) The universal quantifier *all* can stand under the ordinary minimal negation, but not when its increment consists of a technical instruction relating to possible D-developments. Only when *all* leads to an ordinary addition of predicate material to the addresses specified can it be negated, as appears from the ungrammaticality of those negated *all*-sentences where the occurrence of a quantifier of the *any*-class in the relative clause quantified over makes it clear that such a technical instruction relating to D-developments is involved:

(36) a. *Not all students who had done any work passed.
     b. *Not all students who aroused the slightest suspicion were arrested.

Note that these sentences are fully grammatical when *any* or *the slightest* is replaced by *some*. But with *some* in the relative clause the increment is of the ordinary additive type.

Since *each* is of that ordinary type where predicate material is added to the addresses involved, one would expect that sentences like the following should be grammatical:

(37) *Not each student who had done some work passed.

However, *each* is a Postive Polarity Item and thus does not allow for the minimal negation, and the negation in (37) must be minimal due to its non-canonical position. If the principle is correct that Positive Polarity Items are never allowed to set up or select V-relaxing addresses and are restricted to V-restricting addresses, then there is a rationale for the fact that *each* is a PPI: it is by definition excluded from any position in which it helps to select a V-relaxing address, and is thus restricted to the selection of V-restricting addresses.

4.1.5 Conjunction, disjunction and conditionals

Little need be said about *and*, given the discussions in section 3.3. Ordinary S-conjoining *and*, as opposed to the symmetrical *and* of *Ben and Ruth form a nice couple*, or the *and* of, e.g., *ham and eggs*, is, from an incremental point of view, an instruction applying to two (or more) consecutive increments. If the conjunction is "*A* and *B*", then the incremental result is the addition of, first i(*A*) and, after that, i(*B*). Conjunctions are thus incremental 'package deals', involving two or more increment units. Since presuppositions are defined for single increment units, conjunctions do not presuppose anything, although as a semantic predicate *and* has its preconditions.

More must be said about the disjunction and the conditional implication. Let us discuss disjunction first. The discussion will be limited to sentential disjunction. That is, although a sentence like

(38) The paper was grey or white.

is ambiguous between a reading where the colour of the paper is said to be vaguely greyish or whitish, and one where it is said that the colour of the paper was either grey or white, only the latter, sententially disjunctive, reading will be considered. Note that sentential disjunction includes cases like:

(39) All our students are Belgian or French.

in the ordinary meaning "for every student it is so that he or she is either Belgian or French" – and not in the possible but far-fetched meaning that the students in question are vaguely Gallic.

An old, and still unsolved, riddle in the history of disjunction studies is the fact that natural language disjunction has a tendency to be interpreted 'exclusively' and not, as the logical operator *or*, 'inclusively'. That is, a sentence like

(40) Harry or Jeanette found the solution.

will preferably be taken to mean that only one of the two can have found the solution, not both. In recent times, attempts have been undertaken to account for this exclusive character of natural language *or* on grounds of pragmatic principles of communicative good behaviour: in those communicative situations where I am supposed to give information to the best of my knowledge (and not, as befits a quiz-master or a school teacher, to withhold information), I will be considered shifty or devious if, knowing that both Harry and Jeanette found the solution, I say (40). However, even if the principles involved are correct, they fail to account for the exclusive character of *or*. All that such an account can deliver is some understanding of the trust put by listeners in the words of speakers, but nothing relating to truth-value judgements can be inferred from such an account.

In many logic textbooks the truth-conditional aspect of the question is recognized, and the standard answer found is that, in many cases, natural language prefers a truth-conditionally different *or* which is like classical inclusive *or* except that falsity results when both disjuncts are true. It has been shown, however (McCawley 1981: 76–8), that a truth-functional exclusive *or*-operator has such strange properties that it could not possibly be considered as a candidate for the logical analysis of natural language *or*. The strangeness of this operator appears when more than two disjuncts are connected by exclusive *or*. A little experimenting with the truth-tables (whether classical or trivalent) soon shows that when the number of disjuncts is even falsity ensues when both disjuncts are true (as stipulated for the even number 2), but that when the number of disjuncts is odd, truth, and not falsity, ensues when all disjuncts are true. Clearly, this makes a truth-functional exclusive *or* entirely unfit to act as the logical counterpart of natural language (exclusive) *or*, and the castaway observation about exclusive *or* found in current textbooks on logic must therefore be considered thoughtless. It might be added that, in both classical and trivalent calculus, with or_i for inclusive, and or_e for exclusive *or*, "$A \; or_i \; (\text{not-}A \text{ and } B)$" is equivalent with "$A \; or_e \; (\text{not-}A \text{ and } B)$", although the *or* used in such cases is a prima-facie case of exclusive *or*. It seems wise, therefore, to leave *or* inclusive, as it has always been in logic.

But then, how does the undeniable exclusive character of *or* come about? It is not language-specific but universal, and must therefore have to do with universal, probably semantic, principles and procedures. We shall, in fact, propose that it is a direct consequence of the principles of discourse semantics and, in particular, of the increment value associated with *or*, combined with a topic condition of uniqueness.

It must be remarked first that often *or* cannot but be exclusive, due to the way the world is, or to metaphysical or other forms of necessity. When I say *This liquid is either water or alcohol*, the liquid cannot be both since water cannot be alcohol. Or when I say *Either you or I will be the one to die first*, that may be radically false (if, for example, we both die at the same moment) but metaphysical necessity keeps us from both being the one to die first. For these cases no problem of exclusive *or* exists, and if all instances of exclusive interpretation of *or* could be handled this way we could stop here. But, as we know, this is not so. When I say *Either it was raining or the sun was shining*, there is no metaphysical, epistemic, or other necessity preventing both disjuncts from being true. Yet we feel that this sentence is inappropriately used when describing a situation where it is both raining and the sun is shining.

Natural language *or* has a remarkable, but little observed, feature which we shall call the *true alternatives condition* (TAC). This condition requires that of two disjuncts the one may not entail the other. If there is a relation of entailment between the one and the other, the disjunction as a whole is unacceptable (though logically faultless). Consider the following examples (where the exclamation mark is used to indicate **unacceptability**):

(41) a. !Either Mr Twiddle is dead, or he has been killed.
   b. !Charlie laughed, or only Charlie laughed.
   c. !Bruce is dead, or Jack knows that Bruce is dead.
   d. !Either the children were unhappy, or the whole family was.

and contrast them with:

(42) a. Either Mr Twiddle died of natural causes, or he has been killed.
   b. Either Charlie and some others laughed, or only Charlie laughed.
   c. Either Bruce is dead and Jack does not know it, or Jack knows it.
   d. Either just the children were unhappy, or the whole family was.

In the latter cases care has been taken that the entailment relation is cut, and the disjunctions have suddenly become fully acceptable.

This means that natural language disjunctions are subject to the following acceptability test: for a disjunction "*A* or *B*" to be acceptable it is necessary that "(*A* and not-*B*) or (*B* and not-*A*)" can be said without any contradiction in either of the disjuncts. Clearly, if either $A \models B$ or $B \models A$, the disjunction is rejected. The form "(*A* and not-*B*) or (*B* and not-*A*)" will be called the *expanded version* of "*A* or *B*". Note, by the way, that (as expected) the test applies only when psychologically real entailments are taken into consideration, i.e. inferences, and not mathematically valid entailments which do not correspond to natural intuitions of entailment (cp. section 3.1). Thus, a disjunction like

(43) Either that man is a swindler, or I am not who I am.

is fully acceptable (and will amount to a strong affirmation that the man in question is a swindler given the impossibility of the second disjunct), in spite of the fact that the second disjunct is contradictory in all appropriate Ds and should therefore be taken to entail any sentence of the language that can be uttered appropriately in the D at hand. This is further confirmation of the importance of psychological reality of entailments in the semantics of natural language.

The **expanded version of a disjunction is formed from the unexpanded** version by conjoining each disjunct with the negation of the other disjunct. This negation is minimal in normal cases, but sometimes the minimal negation is excluded and the radical negation must be used. For example, the expansion of

(44) a. It will be either terrific or awful.

will have to be, with A for "it will be terrific", and B for "it will be awful",

(44) b. $(A \wedge \simeq B) \vee (B \wedge \simeq A)$

since both *terrific* and *awful* are Positive Polarity Items and thus allow only for the radical negation. The same occurs when there are conflicting presuppositions, as in

(45) a. Either he still loves his wife, or he never loved her.

which is expanded as (with A for the first, and $\sim B$ for the second disjunct)

(45) b. $(B \wedge A) \vee (\sim B \wedge \simeq A)$

or "either he has loved his wife in the past and he still loves her, or he never loved her and (therefore) does NOT still love her". Note that discourse principles require that the order of the sentences in the first expanded disjunct is "B and A", and not vice versa, because B is a presupposition of A. For the same reason, the negation of A in the second expanded disjunct can only be the radical negation, given the preceding negated presupposition.

Truth-functionally, the expanded version is different from the unexpanded version of a disjunction, as is easily checked. The effect of expansion is, in fact, that *or* is made exclusive by logical necessity: it is impossible for both expanded disjuncts to be true simultaneously.

TAC is accounted for by a proper formulation of the increment value associated with *or*. Let this value be an instruction applying to disjunctions "A or B", to add at least $i(A)$ or $i(B)$, and a permission to add $i(\neg B)$, if found true, only with $i(A)$, or to add $i(\neg A)$, if found true, only with $i(B)$. Hence, if one of the disjuncts is negated, then the other disjunct must be added. The incrementation of "A or B" thus 'splits up' D in the sense that two possible additions to D are defined, one with $i(A)$ added, and one with $i(B)$ added. The two additions must both be acceptable, according to the normal acceptability conditions for the construction of any D (see section 3.3). They must, furthermore, represent real alternatives, which implies that the one may not entail the other. If D_A is the discourse as it is with i(A) added, and D_B the discourse as it is with i(B) added, then the true alternatives condition requires that neither must D_A entail B, or D_B entail A.

This brings us to the question of exclusive *or*. The TAC is insufficient to explain this, since there is, strictly speaking, no embargo on i(B) given D_A, or vice versa. If the requirement that $D_A \not\models B$ and $D_B \not\models A$ is extended over the whole further development of D, then *or* is exclusive, but this extension is not provided for by the TAC alone. The 'extra' needed for exclusive *or* seems to depend on what is the *topic* in the ongoing discourse: if the topic (which might be seen as arising out of a question) is a uniquely determinable entity, event or state of affairs, then one answer only can be given and *or* is exclusive. But it is not when no topic is involved, as in *All our students are over 16 or very bright* (where *or* takes scope under *all*), or when the topic does not involve uniqueness, as in: *What does she do for a living? She writes or translates.*

It is natural for speakers to supply the missing parts of the full TAC-expansion if they are not already given explicitly, provided the radical negation is not involved as in (44) and (45) above. This suppletion is often functional, in particular when it provides an antecedent for an externally anaphoric pronoun in a disjunction which lacks the antecedent required, as in:

(46) a. Either Socrates owned no dog, or *it* bit him.

The second disjunct needs not only suppletion *post hoc* of the presupposition that whatever is denoted by *it* is animate in D_B, it also needs a proper antecedent for *it*, or the presupposition to be prejected cannot be formulated at all. The suppletion provided by the true alternatives condition kills both birds with one stone:[1]

(46) b. (= 17) Either Socrates owned no dog, or he owned a dog and it bit him.

(The first disjunct is not so naturally expanded since that expansion requires the use of the radical negation: it did NOT bite him".)

Let us, finally, turn to the conditional construction "if A then B". We shall not discuss counterfactuals ("if A were/had been true, then B would be/have been true") or other varieties, such as the potential ("if A were to

---

[1] The same suppletion helps out on other presuppositions in the second disjunct as well. Compare, for example, the following sentence,

Either Harry hasn't left, or Jane has left too.

where the *post hoc* suppletion of the presupposition induced by *too* requires the positive of the negative first disjunct.

be (found to be) true, then *B* will be true"), and confine our attention to straightforward conditionals. This means that we shall leave out of account also cases of 'performative implication', as in

(47) There's food in the oven, if you are hungry.

which ask for an analysis involving a performative expression: "if you are hungry, I inform you that there is food in the oven" (where it is understood that "if you are not hungry, then I have said nothing").[2]

It has long been recognized that natural language conditional implication does not match its traditional logical analysis in terms of the material implication. The material implication is truth-functional and is, in classical logic, simply defined in terms of the disjunction: $A \supset B \equiv \neg A \lor B$. In our trivalent presuppositional logic, the analysis in terms of the truth-table for $\sim A \lor B$ would be badly off the mark. This truth-table is as follows:

(48) $A \supset B \equiv \sim A \lor B$

		B		
	$\supset$	1	2	3
A	1	1	2	2
	2	1	1	1
	3	1	2	3

If a conditional of the form "if *A* then *B*" were to follow the truth-value assignments as prescribed by this table, the following absurd argument would be valid:

(49) a. A: If the king of France has any dignity left, France is safe.
　　　 B: But there is no king of France.
　　　 A: All right, then France is safe.

The conclusion should follow since if the conditional as a whole is true and the antecedent clause (*A*) is radically false, the consequent clause (*B*) must be true. Note that the same argument expressed in disjunctive terms is impeccable:

(49) b. A: Either the king of France has no dignity left, or France is safe.
　　　 B: But there is no king of France.
　　　 A: All right, then France is safe.

---

[2] Mainly for reasons of convenience we shall also leave out of account those (very common) conditional sentences with a future or modal *will* in the consequent clause and either a deleted or an overt *will* in the antecedent clause. The inconvenience caused by this type of conditional arises from the complications associated with the future/modal *will*. It is more sensible to let these cases rest till they can be dealt with in a comprehensive study of futuricity and epistemic prediction, the more so since prima facie there seems to be nothing in these conditionals that would directly contradict the analysis given here – apart from the obvious fact that the epistemic necessity operator as presented in (52) below cannot apply in these cases.

This shows that (48) will in any case not do as an analysis of the natural language conditional construction. A better analysis is:

(50) $A \supset_L B \equiv \neg A \vee B$

		B		
	$\supset_L$	1	2	3
A	1	1	2	2
	2	1	1	1
	3	1	1	1

Now the inconvenience of (49a) has been removed.

This does not mean, however, that we now have an adequate solution to the problem of natural language *if*-constructions. No matter what truth-table we come up with for these constructions, the question remains whether *if* is truth-functional or not. It seems that we must resign ourselves to the idea that it is not. This appears most clearly when we think up a situation where a conditional is denied, as in:

(51) a. A: If your husband is drinking tea, he is not feeling well.
B: Not at all! He often drinks tea while he is as fit as a fiddle.

b. A: If God does not exist, everything is permitted.
B: Not at all! God is not the ultimate source of all moral rules. God may well not exist while there is still a distinction between good and evil.

Whether the speakers B are right or wrong in their respective replies, one cannot say that they are incoherent or 'illogical' in any sense. The speakers A, on the other hand, would clearly violate the rules of natural logic if they said, in reply to (51a), "Ah, so your husband is now drinking tea", or to (51b), "Ah, you have just asserted that God does not exist". Yet, if natural language *if* followed table (50), A's conclusions would be correct since falsity of the conditional occurs only in the row of (50) where the antecedent is true. Other tables can be tried, such as the table corresponding to $\sim A \vee (A \wedge B)$, but this has the drawback that all presuppositions of A are preserved as entailments. And this is wrong because truth-functionally A_C (A presupposing C) $\equiv A \wedge C$, and, whatever one may think of "if A_C then B", clearly "if C and A, then B" does not entail C.

Another observation (made by our student Bart Geurts), strikingly reinforcing our suspicions with regard to the truth-functionality of natural language conditionals, is the following: (51c) should, on any truth-functional account, be equivalent with (51d), but surely, few speakers will agree that they are:

(51) c. If Harold goes to the party then Sue does not go.
d. If Sue goes to the party then Harold does not go.

To speak of "equivalence" in such cases is to show little regard for the semantic reality of natural language (and a little too much for its logical aspects).

There is thus no escaping from the fact that natural language *if* is not truth-functional. This conclusion is reinforced by the observation that natural language conditionals (in so far as they are discussed here) do not change their meaning when prefixed by something like "It is a valid inference that..." Thus, for example, the sentence uttered by A in (51a) is equivalent with "It is a valid inference that if your husband is drinking tea he is not feeling well". Now, B's reply means: "That is not at all a valid inference", and B can then quote cases of her husband drinking tea while he was as fit as a fiddle, thus invalidating the (inductive) inference made by A. Clearly, the prefixing of "It is a valid inference that..." takes away truth-functionality from whatever is represented by the dots: not all true propositions are valid inferences from whatever is given in some discourse. We can capture this notion of valid (deductive or inductive) inference truth-conditionally by stipulating that "if *A* then *B*" is true just in case the truth of *A* guarantees the falsity of $\neg B$. The true assertion of *A* thus licenses the true assertion of *B*. The guarantee is based on logic, induction or factual knowledge. More precisely, we define the extension of *if* as follows:

(52) $\sigma(if) = \{\langle e^*, f^* \rangle | \text{ for all p, q, if } \rho(p) = e \text{ and } \rho(q) = f,$
  $\text{then } Nec(\neg(p \wedge \neg q))\}$

Without the necessity operator *Nec*, which is epistemic necessity (and will be discussed in chapter 5), *if* would be truth-functional and would correspond exactly to the truth-table given in (50).

A well-known feature of natural language conditional constructions which cannot be accounted for in terms of truth-functional material implication is the fact that some connection must exist between the two clauses for the whole to be acceptable. This feature is also found in conjunctions

(53) a. If two and two makes five, New York is a large city.
  b. Two and two makes five, and New York is a large city.

and the usual answer given is that this is a feature which does not affect the logic of the construction. Though this answer is correct, it does not make the question of the relatedness required uninteresting. The relatedness in question is clearly discourse-dependent. A sufficient condition for coherence or relatedness in the case of conjunctions is that both conjunctions are answers to questions that have come up in the discourse. For conditionals this condition must be fulfilled, and there must be an epistemic justification for establishing an inference from the antecedent clause to the consequent clause. But quite apart from the nature and the function of this relatedness criterion, there is the interesting fact that conditionals share this property with conjunctions. This fact is interesting because it is matched by other such parallels.

Thus, conditionals and conjunctions show a certain similarity in behaviour with respect to presuppositions and prejections (cp. Karttunen 1974), and discourse acceptability conditions (see section 3.3):

> (54) a. If Socrates owned a dog, it bit him.
> b. Socrates owned a dog, and it bit him.
> c. If Socrates' dog barked, the children became nervous.
> d. Socrates' dog barked, and the children became nervous.

(54a) and (54b) are unacceptable when it has been said that Socrates owned a dog, but (54c) and (54d) are fully acceptable in such a context.

Moreover, there is an intuition of stark contradiction in conditionals where the antecedent entails the falsity of the consequences, as in (55a), precisely as with conjunctions, as in (55b). But although logic accounts for the latter (provided it is rich enough to capture the entailment), no such account is available for (55a):

> (55) a. !If Charlie is alive, he has been killed.
> b. !Charlie is alive, and he has been killed.

If intuitions of contradiction are to be accounted for by a demonstration of the logical impossibility of truth, then one would expect that logic should show that (55a) can never be true. If the analysis of (55a) is given in terms of the material implication, however, there is no contradiction, for in that analysis (55a) is false when Charlie is alive (and has therefore not been killed), and true when Charlie is dead. In terms of this analysis nothing is amiss with (55a). It would simply be a roundabout way of saying that Charlie is dead.

In reality, however, (55a) is not a roundabout way of saying that Charlie is not alive. Such roundabout assertions by means of conditionals do exist, as can be seen from:

> (56) a. If Charlie is alive, I am not who I am.
> b. If Charlie is alive, I am a Dutchman.

From (56a) it is immediately inferred that Charlie is not alive, for the assertion of "Charlie is alive" licenses a contradictory statement, i.e. a statement which is necessarily false. And likewise, from (56b) it is quickly inferred that Charlie is not alive (as long as it is taken for granted that the speaker is not a Dutchman). (55a), however, given the truth-condition that the assertion of "Charlie is alive" licenses the assertion of "he has been killed", can never be true since under no adequate account of the cognitive machinery of drawing valid conclusions can the assertion of A license the assertion of B if $A \models \neg B$.

The fact that in conditionals the antecedent clause must not entail the falsity of the consequent clause is reminiscent of the true alternatives condition found with disjunctions. The conditions in question, however, are not identical. Suppose we try to analyse "if A then B" as $\neg A \vee B$, i.e. as (50), we would expect, given the true alternatives condition for disjunctions, not only that "A and B" is non-contradictory – an expectation which is fulfilled by conditionals – but also that "not-A and not-B" should be free of contradiction. But this condition does not apply to conditionals, as is seen from the full acceptability of sentences like:

(57) If Charlie is dead, he has not been killed.

If this is analysed as "either Charlie is not dead, or he has not been killed", we would expect (57) to be unacceptable, since although "he is dead and he has not been killed" is without contradiction, "he is not dead and he has been killed" is not. Moreover, TAC as applied to disjunctions only gives an account of acceptability phenomena. But in the case of conditionals what we have to do with is not just acceptability conditions, but straightforward judgements of truth and falsity.

There is thus a cumulation of arguments all leading to the conclusion that *if* in natural language is not a truth-functional predicate explicable in terms of the disjunction, one way or another, even though there are non-trivial similarities with disjunction. We must accept that any semantic description of *if* must be given in terms of inferencing, and the similarities with conjunctive *and* as well as those with disjunctive *or* must be accounted for in the semantics, truth-conditional and discourse-defined, of *if* without positing identity with either a conjunctive or a disjunctive analysis.

A further complicating fact is the following. A sentence like

(58) a. If Socrates owned a dog, it bit him.

must be considered false in a situation where Socrates had, say, two dogs, one that bit him and one that did not bite him. Natural intuitions are quite clear on this count. Yet, under any classical or near-classical analysis of *if* this should not be so, since

(58) b. Socrates owned a dog, and it bit him.

is true in such a situation, which should be sufficient for (58a) to be true if the natural language conditional is truth-functional. If, as we maintain, the conditional is not truth-functional but subject to conditions of epistemic necessity (as specified in (52) above), the problem is still that the presence of a dog owned by Socrates and not biting him must be seen to falsify (58a). A full discussion of this problem, together with the related problem, mentioned earlier in section 4.1.1, of

(17) Either Socrates owned no dog, or he owned a dog and it bit him.

which is likewise falsified, intuitively, by the presence of a dog owned by Socrates and not biting him, will be postponed till chapter 6, in the context of questions of truth and reference. Here we can remark that the solution to (58a) will be found in the stipulation of (52) that the antecedent and the negated consequent must be inferred not to be both true. Hence, if (58a) is true, then there must be good reason for inferring that "Socrates owned a dog and it did not bite him" is false, which excludes the presence in the verification domain of a dog owned by Socrates and not biting him.

Then we must observe (as it has been observed widely in the literature) that *if*-clauses allow for the occurrence of some Negative Polarity Items:

(59) a. If he is *any good at all*, he has scraped through.

b. If he is *in the least* troublesome, he has been drinking.

c. If he *bats and eyelid*, John registers.

d. If he *as much as lifted a finger*, everybody was saved.

e. If he has shown *the slightest* interest, he has got through.

The following, however, are ungrammatical, despite the occurrence of an NPI:

(60) a. *If you *can possibly* help me, I can help you.

b. *If he *can seem to* remember what happened, he isn't all that dumb after all.

c. *If he *gives a damn* about his daughter, he is rushing up here before she dies.

These sentences are well formed (or better formed) only if the *if*-clause is in the morphological past tense, indicating a counterfactual or potential condition. (What determines the conditions of occurrence of an NPI in *if*-clauses of non-counterfactural conditionals is totally unknown.)

Positive Polarity Items, on the other hand, can also occur in *if*-clauses, but then there is an echo:

(61) a. If there is *plenty* of money around, they must be rich.

b. If he has said *some*thing, it has been recorded.

c. If he drank *the whole bloody lot*, he must be drunk by now.

Notice that these sentences are even more natural with the echoing *indeed* in the *if*-clause. For PPIs there seem to be no restrictions on occurrence within *if*-clauses, as there are with NPIs, except (a fact not noted at all in the literature) that PPIs and NPIs do not mix in *if*-clauses:

(62) a. *If he has said *some*thing *at all*, it has been recorded.

b. *If it *as much as swarms with* cops, he can't leave the house.

Recapitulating, we say that *if*, in the conditional construction-type under analysis, is not truth-functional but involves an element of epistemic necessity or of valid inference with regard to truth-conditions that seem adequately expressed by table (50). The truth-conditions of *if* are given in (52), which reflects the close relation between "if *A* then *B*" and "either not-*A* or (*A* and) *B*". Besides the similarities with disjunction, *if* also shows similarities with conjunction, as appears from (54), where the prejection behaviour is seen to be similar, and from (55), where contradictions arise under similar conditions. Furthermore, we have observed that conditionals share with disjunctions the awkward referential and truth-conditional problem that sentences like (17) or (58a) are falsified by the presence of a 'gatecrash' reference object of which no mention occurs in the sentence itself. Finally, we have observed that a restricted class of NPIs is allowed to occur in (non-counterfactual) *if*-clauses, and also the whole class of PPIs, but that they do not mix. What is needed now is a formulation of the increment value associated with *if* which does maximal justice to these observations.

Let us try the following. We say that the increment value associated with sentences of the type "if *A* then *B*" is a permission to add i(*A*), if found true, but only if i(Nec(*B*)) is also added,[3] either after i(*A*), or, if discourse acceptability conditions require the inverse order, before i(*A*). Both additions must be acceptable given preceding discourse. That is, if i(*A*) is added first, it must be acceptable in D, allowing for the normal machinery of backward suppletion of missing presuppositions, and i(Nec(*B*)) must be acceptable in D + i(*A*). And vice versa if the order is reversed. Moreover, *A* must not entail the falsity (radical or minimal) of *B* – understandably since what would be the use of an instruction to set up a contradictory discourse while claiming truth?[4]

This account of the increment value associated with *if* gets us a little further. It ensures that conditionals (of the type analysed) are not truth-functional, since the consquent is processed as a modal structure. The conditional instruction (or permission) to add i(*A*) in case it is found to be true shows up the similarity with disjunctive *or*, whereas the instruction to add i(Nec(*B*)) in case i(*A*) is added smacks of conjunction. The problem of 'the gatecrash falsifier', as exemplified in (58a) (and (17)) is helped by the fact that i(*B*) *must* be added if i(*A*) is, so that no room is left for any addition of a negation of *B*. The occurrence of some NPIs – including those of the *any-*

---

[3] With other types of conditionals, in particular those which involve a future or modal *will*, the modality of epistemic necessity will probably have to be replaced by that of epistemic prediction.

[4] It may be observed, in this connection, that it is a striking feature of disjunction as well as of conditionals that they do not occur in fictional stories other than as part of what a character in the story says, knows, thinks, expects, hopes, etc. In other words, they only occur in stories under some intensional operator of epistemic 'attitude'. This is intuitively understandable since disjunctions and conditionals express uncertainty on the part of the speaker, and a story-teller is not meant to be uncertain, mainly because there is nothing to be uncertain about, the story being fictional. The uncertainty, of course, is expressed in the increment instructions of both *or* and *if*.

class – fits in with the distinction between V-restricting and V-relaxing bits of discourse structure which we introduced above and have used a few times with relative success. The bit of discourse structure defined by i(A) is V-relaxing because further addition of material to the discourse structure under the *if*-instruction, instead of restricting the class of verification domains in which the conditional in question is true, relaxes it: i(Nec(B)) is then subject to a condition applying less widely than without the addition. This would account for the occurrence of (some) NPIs. But it does not account for the possible occurrence of PPIs in *if*-clauses. That account, however, is easily found: it may be the case that i(A) is already part of some intensional sub-domain in the preceding discourse. That is, it may have been suggested, or it may be believed, hoped, expected, etc., that A. If subsequently i(if A then B) is added, i(A) is copied whole from its subdomain and made the object of the permission embodied in the *if*-instruction. Thus, in

(63) Maybe Jack has eaten *some*thing bad. If he has (indeed) eaten *some*thing bad, that is why he is feeling ill now.

the bit of domain structure introduced first under the operator *maybe* is copied whole in the conditional structure, and so is the linguistic material. This bit of discourse structure is originally, i.e. under the *maybe* operator, V-restricting and hence allows for PPIs. What is needed in the theory is an adequate provision to allow for wholesale copying of V-restricting bits of D-structure under instructions bringing about V-relaxing bit of D-structure. Mixing of NPIs and PPIs in the same *if*-clause is now excluded since a bit of D-structure cannot both be new and old.

The reader may have wondered why in the *if*-instruction the order of i(A) and i(B) is left free, or at least constrained only, or mainly, by discourse acceptability criteria. This relative freedom is motivated by cases like the following:

(64) a. If he was there, she was there, too.
    b. He was there, if she was there, too.
(65) a. If he has been away, he has come back.
    b. He has been away, if he has come back.
(66) a. If Joe plans a divorce, his psychiatrist knows about it.
    b. If his psychiatrist knows that Joe plans a divorce, then Joe plans a divorce.

Clearly, if i(A) were always to precede i(B), then the (b)-sentences would lead to unacceptable D-structures when i(A) is added owing to the pre-supposition following the carrier sentence. In the (b)-sentences, the consequent clauses satisfy the presuppositional requirements of the antecedent clauses. Inevitably, therefore, in any actual incrementation procedure involving the two, the consequent must precede the antecedent, despite their names. (It seems, in any case, that in those cases where the consequent must precede the antecedent in the event of actual incrementation, it also prefers to precede the antecedent in surface structure, but this regularity is not absolute, as appears from (66b).)

4.2 Anaphora

4.2.1 Introductory remarks

A special problem in the theory of reference and denotation is presented by pronominal anaphora. We speak of anaphora when a term reaches its denotation (address) not by virtue of its own lexical material but by virtue of the lexical material of another term, which is called the *antecedent*. The anaphoric term then takes over the denotation of the antecedent, at least in principle. In some cases, known in the literature as cases of 'sloppy' anaphora, the pronoun does not take over the denotation of the antecedent term, but has its own denotation with a closely parallel cognitive role in the discourse. The classic example is (Karttunen 1969):

(67) a. The man who gives his pay-cheque to his wife is wiser than the man who gives it to his mistress.

where the *it* will normally not denote the same address as its antecedent term *his pay-cheque*. Another, less well-known example is:

(67) b. In the old days I used to remember the names of my students, but nowadays I no longer remember them.

where in one reading the pronoun *them* denotes an address referring to the speaker's present students' names, not those of the students of yore. What the conditions are under which sloppy anaphora functions is not very well understood. In some cases, such as (67a), the conditions are likely to be derived from a combination of grammatical and cognitive factors. In (67b) and similar cases, the conditions appear to be of a purely grammatical and lexical nature. Compare, for example (see De Rijk 1974):

(67) c. In the old days I used to remember the names of my students, but nowadays I have forgotten them.

which does not allow for sloppy anaphora and only has the straight anaphoric reading.

We shall speak of anaphora only in cases of overtly occurring pronouns or epithets (the notion of 'epithet' will be discussed in a moment), and not in cases of term-deletion. as, for example, under Secondary Subject Deletion, Co-ordination Reduction or Comparative Reduction. It is quite likely that there is a relation of give-and-take between phenomena of anaphora and phenomena of deletion in the languages of the world, but the two classes of phenomena appear to obey different principles and can thus not be handled in one single theory. Attempts at unifying pronominal anaphora and facts of Secondary Subject Deletion have not been convincing. This does not mean that the notion of 'zero anaphor' is without content: one cannot exclude the possibility that, in certain languages, there is a rule deleting anaphoric pronouns under specific conditions. If a form of deletion clearly falls within the theory of anaphora as it has been set up on the basis of clear cases of anaphora, there is no good reason why it should be kept outside that theory. But it is misguided to regard all cases of deletion involving terms automatically as cases of zero anaphora. In English, no zero anaphors have so far been detected.

There are cases of pronominal reference and denotation without an overt linguistic antecedent. In such cases the missing antecedent must be supplied *post hoc* on the basis of available background knowledge, usually knowledge derived from the *hic et nunc* circumstances surrounding the utterance. On the basis of observations of English and French pronominal anaphora made by Tasmowski-De Ryck and Verluyten (1982), one is inclined to conclude that this *post hoc* suppletion is psychologically mediated by tacit linguistic forms, at least for personal pronouns – not for demonstratives. Tasmowski-De Ryck and Verluyten observe, for example, (1982: 328) that number and gender agreement work in accordance with the linguistic representation of the object or objects referred to:

(68) a. (John wants his pants that are on a chair and he says to Mary:)

Could you hand $\left\{ \begin{matrix} \text{them} \\ \text{*it} \end{matrix} \right\}$ to me, please?

b. (Same situation, but with a shirt:)

Could you hand $\left\{ \begin{matrix} \text{it} \\ \text{*them} \end{matrix} \right\}$ to me, please?

(69) a. (John is trying to stuff a large table (French: *la table*, fem.) in the trunk of his car; Mary says:)

Tu n'arriveras jamais à $\left\{ \begin{matrix} \text{la} \\ \text{*le} \end{matrix} \right\}$ faire entrer dans la voiture.

("You will never manage to get $\left\{ \begin{matrix} \text{it(fem.)} \\ \text{*it(masc.)} \end{matrix} \right\}$ into the car")

b. (Same situation, but with a desk (*le bureau*, masc.):)

Tu n'arriveras jamais à $\left\{ \begin{matrix} \text{le} \\ \text{*la} \end{matrix} \right\}$ faire entrer dans la voiture.

("You will never manage to get $\left\{ \begin{matrix} \text{it(masc.)} \\ \text{*it(fem.)} \end{matrix} \right\}$ into the car")

Assuming that the conclusion that deictic or other anaphora without overt antecedent is mediated by tacit linguistic forms (at least for anaphora by means of ordinary personal pronouns) is correct, we can uphold the general rule that anaphoric denotation and reference is mediated by fully lexical antecedents.

It has been widely observed in the linguistic literature that pronouns in anaphoric use can sometimes be replaced by lexical definite terms called "epithets". These have the peculiarity that the lexical material used is in no way useful for the proper identification of the discourse address denoted and hence the intended reference object (if one is intended). Moreover, such quasi-lexical definite terms must always be unaccented. Usually, the lexical material used expresses an opinion held by the speaker about the intended reference object:

(70) a. A: Have you seen John?
     B: No, and I don't want to see that idiot either.
   b. The policeman who arrested Harry thought the little runt was pilfering money.

Epithet anaphora differs from Swiss banker cases (as in (71d) of section 3.4) in that the latter are necessarily accented (probably because they add new and informative material to the address denoted), whereas the former are hardly informative and have the character of a speech act: "and I hereby call him an idiot/a little runt." Not all forms of pronominal anaphora, however, allow for the epithetic variant, as will become clear below.

In this section we shall look at a number of anaphora phenomena and see how they can be seen to fit in with the general theory of discourse semantics. We shall limit the discussion to anaphora by definite personal or possessive pronouns or by epithets (and not indefinite anaphora by means of indefinite pronouns such as English *one*), and to cases of strict denotational identity with the antecedent (and not the 'sloppy' identity mentioned above). The gist of the enterprise will be an attempt to provide a unified theory for sentence-internal and sentence-external anaphora.

The discussion of anaphora here must be seen against the background of a somewhat frustrating history of anaphora studies in circles of transformational grammarians over the past 20 or so years. It has proved extraordinarily difficult to provide a faultless account of the principles by which sentence-internal antecedents are selected by pronoun occurrences in English sentences – other languages have been studied, if at all, on a vastly inferior level of detail and accuracy in this regard. A fair number of proposals have been formulated in this period, all trying to capture the structural constraints limiting the possible choice of sentence-internal antecedents, and the net result has been, so far, that none of these proposals remain free from counter-examples of a serious nature. On the other hand, one cannot escape from the distinct impression that such constraints exist. Yet they have so far eluded a precise formulation. Against this background it would be foolhardy to pretend to be able to provide the ultimate solution to this problem in this one section. What we can achieve, however, is something less ambitious. By taking into account the many interesting observations that have been made over the past years by a large variety of authors, and reconsidering the classifications that have been set up, we may be able to add a new and helpful element to the state of anaphora theory, at least in so far as it applies to English.

The strategy followed is this. As in all existing theories, different kinds of pronoun uses (or, as we shall say, pronouns) will be distinguished, but, although our classification will be reminiscent of those more traditionally accepted, the lines will be drawn rather differently. In particular, the class of reflexive pronouns will be dramatically enlarged and the class of 'ordinary' antecedent-bound internally anaphoric pronouns will accordingly be restricted. It will then appear that the structural constraints sought after are probably more easily formulated for the newly delimited classes. Discourse semantics will be seen to be relevant in this context mainly for two reasons. First, the class of pronouns now widely known as "E-type" pronouns (Evans 1980) will find its solution in the machinery of discourse incrementation which provides an antecedent for straightforward cases of sentence-external anaphora of the type

(71) a. Socrates owned a dog, and it bit Socrates.

(unrevealingly called "pronouns of laziness' in Geach 1962). In principle we shall say that the first conjunct of (71a) introduces a new address characterized by the properties of being a dog and being owned by Socrates, and that this address, by virtue of its immediately preceding introduction, is salient enough for it to be the natural landing site for the pronoun *it* in the second conjunct. The same mechanism will be invoked for pronouns in 'donkey'-sentences or E-type pronouns, as in:

(71) b. If Socrates owned a dog, it bit him.
    c. Everyone who owns a dog feeds it.

And secondly, external anaphora generally, not just cases like (71a), will be seen to fit in naturally with the apparatus of discourse semantics as so far developed. Moreover, anaphora through denoting pronouns in general will tentatively be considered from the point of view that such anaphora is a natural consequence of a process whereby an address is first either introduced or denoted and then denoted again very soon afterwards. The sheer recency of the previous address activation is perhaps the general rationale behind the semantic poverty and the denotational sufficiency of denoting pronouns, whether internal or external.

It is a remarkable fact in anaphora research that sentence-internal anaphora is dealt with almost exclusively by linguists, whereas sentence-external anaphora seems a hunting ground for psycholinguists. The formal semanticists have shown an interest only in highly specific cases (such as the 'donkey'-sentences first discussed in Geach 1962: 128-9). This curious division of labour is no doubt due to the fact that linguists feel ill at ease outside the sentence and are much more at home in trees, while psycholinguistics has been characterized, at least till recently, by a tendency to eschew the abstract formal structures of linguistics if they did not lend themselves to experiments. Psycholinguistic experiments are hard to devise for internal anaphora, but for external anaphora controlled experiments are a great deal more natural. We shall try here to bridge the gap and propose an integrated theory, or, more precisely, the beginnings of an integrated theory, of anaphora, external as well as internal. An algorithm will be developed for the interpretation of definite pronouns or epithets.

The algorithm, or Assignment Procedure (AP), occupies an intermediate position between the grammar and the discourse semantics. The proper selection of an antecedent is neither strict grammar nor strict discourse semantics. Before the discourse semantics can start to operate, the pronouns must have found their antecedent, so that the predicate material of the sentence in question will be added to the proper addresses. For the grammar, which is a transformational mapping system between Semantic Analyses and Surface Structures, pronouns have no special status: they are treated according to the rules of grammar for the language in question (and most languages have special grammatical rules for pronouns), but only rarely is the grammatical rule system sensitive to the relation between a pronoun and its antecedent (reflexivity is a case in point). This intermediate position of AP between grammar and semantics shows up in the fact that antecedent assignment to pronouns often depends on levels of syntactic representation other than SA. The Assignment Procedure can therefore not be constrained to operate exclusively on the basis of information contained in Semantic Analysis: other derivational stages must be considered relevant.

The analysis is based on a distinction of three kinds of (personal or possessive) pronouns: *reflexive pronouns, bound variable pronouns* and *denoting pronouns*. The first and second category are obligatorily pronominal, whereby the reflexive pronouns are sometimes, but by no means always, morphologically marked as reflexives. The third category, that of the denoting pronouns, are rather different from the other two. Thus, only denoting pronouns can have a sentence-external antecedent. Moreover, only denoting pronouns may be represented, *salva veritate*, by an epithet. This fact, first noted by Bosch (1983: 49), is particularly interesting and important because it can be used as a test: pronouns which can be replaced, *salva veritate*, by an epithet must be crucially different from pronouns that do not allow for such a substitution. This test will be used repeatedly in the discussions and analyses of the following sections.

4.2.2 Reflexive pronouns

The class of reflexive pronouns does not coincide with the class of pronouns with overt morphological marking for reflexivity, the *marked reflexives*. A pronoun is reflexive just in case it is co-denotational with (or is the same variable as) the subject of either the same clause or of a higher clause to which its own clause is subordinated, at some stage of analysis. If the pronoun is related to the subject of its own clause, it is a *direct reflexive*. If it is related to the subject of a higher clause it is an *indirect reflexive*.

Languages differ considerably in their ways of marking reflexivity morphologically. In many languages, including English, indirect reflexivity is never marked morphologically. For these languages a category of 'hidden' or 'tacit' reflexives must be assumed. On the basis of Japanese data, Kuno (1972) came to the same conclusion, and he could point at a number of facts in the behaviour of English indirect reflexives showing them up to be different from 'ordinary' (denoting) pronouns. We shall follow this line of thought.

An example of a language with special marking for indirect reflexives is Attic Greek, which uses the direct descendants of the Indo-European reflexives (genitive: *hou*; dative: *hoi*; accusative: *he*) for this purpose. Latin uses ordinary reflexive marking also for indirect reflexives:

(72) a. <u>Sibi</u> Asterigem mitti <u>Caesar</u> iussit.
("<u>Caesar</u> ordered for Asterix to be sent to <u>him</u>")
b. <u>Caesar</u> Asterigi imperavit ut <u>sibi</u> nuntium mitteret.
("<u>Caesar</u> ordered Asterix that he sent <u>him</u> a messenger")

Latin (like Swedish) also has a separate third person reflexive possessive pronoun *suus* (Swedish: *sin*), besides the non-reflexive personal pronoun genitive *eius* (Swedish: *hans*). Dutch has three different forms for the marked third person reflexive: *zich, zichzelf, hemzelf* (with parallel forms for differences in number and/or gender) where English has only one: *himself*. The conditions of use for the three Dutch marked reflexives differ from each other (and from English) in fairly complex ways, as is shown by the following examples:

(73) a. <u>Ben</u> toonde Josef een foto van <u>zichzelf</u>.
("<u>Ben</u> showed Josef a picture of <u>himself</u>")
b. Ben toonde <u>Josef</u> een foto van <u>hemzelf</u>.
("Ben showed <u>Josef</u> a picture of <u>himself</u>")
c. <u>Karel</u> liet <u>zich</u> het pakje bezorgen.
("<u>Karel</u> let the parcel be delivered to <u>him</u>")
d. <u>Karel</u> liet Ben <u>hem</u> het pakje bezorgen.
("<u>Karel</u> let Ben deliver the parcel to <u>him</u>")

e. Karel liet voor zich werken.
("Karel made (people) work for him")
f. Karel liet Ben voor zich werken.
("Karel made Ben work for him")
g. Karel liet Ben voor zichzelf werken.
("Karel made Ben work for himself")

The obvious differences between Dutch and English in this respect come about as a result of differences in the grammar of complementation (Dutch *laten*, as we have seen (section 2.4.5) takes obligatory Predicate Raising), and of differences in reflexive marking rules. Restrictions of space forbid an adequate discussion of the rules of Dutch grammar in this respect (but see note 7), but even so it will be clear that languages differ considerably in the ways and conditions of morphological marking of reflexives. A corollary to this conclusion is that we may expect to find many cases of unmarked reflexives, and that the category of reflexives is defined by 'deeper' criteria than just the morphology. This is borne out by a number of observations that systematically point in the same direction. Unmarked reflexives differ from the 'ordinary' denoting pronouns in that they cannot be replaced by epithets, and also in that they do not obey the antecedent rules of denoting pronouns. Thus, the much quoted case of *his* in (74a) is profitably regarded as a 'tacit' reflexive, as appears from the disrupted anaphora (indicated by an exclamation mark) in (74b) and (74c)

(74) a. In his studio Graham paints.
b. !In the poor kid's studio Graham paints.
c. !In Graham's studio, he paints.

Indirect reflexivity is as alive in English as it is in Latin, although English does not mark indirect reflexive pronouns for reflexivity:

(75) a. That she was clever, Mary knew very well.
b. !That the old girl was clever, Mary knew very well.
c. !That Mary was clever, she knew very well.

If no account were taken of reflexivity it would be difficult to explain why co-denotation is disturbed in the (b)-sentences of (74) and (75) by the use of the epithets, or why there is no anaphora (co-denotation) in the (c)-sentences. The latter point is remarkable (and has been remarked upon by Akmajian and Jackendoff 1970), since one of the outstanding features of denoting pronouns is that they always take *preceding* NPs as possible antecedents. If *his* in (74a), or *she* in (75a) were ordinary denoting pronouns, then (74c) and (75c), respectively, should in any case be admissible variants. But they clearly are not.

What seems to lie behind these facts is the following. In the search for a, or the, proper address for a pronoun, the first question to be asked and answered is whether or not the pronoun in question is reflexive. If it is marked for reflexivity, the answer is greatly facilitated. But in any case, whether marked or not, pronouns are subject to a principle which we shall call the *Reflexive Principle*, and whose proper formulation is approximated by the following:

(76) The *Reflexive Principle*:

> Whenever a *subject* of equal or higher rank is involved, at any stage of analysis, in a co-denotation or co-variable relation between two terms, then that subject must be the antecedent and the other NP will be reflexive, marked if the grammar of the language requires marking, and otherwise unmarked (or null).

The expression "subject of equal or higher rank" is meant to cover clause-mate subjects (equal rank), as well as subjects of higher clauses (i.e. clauses to which the clause in question is subordinate, except relative clauses). The Reflexive Principle ensures not only that the proper configuration and, helped by the grammar, also the proper reflexive morphology are selected in production, but also that, in perception, the first thing to be checked is whether the pronoun in question can, within the limits admitted by the grammar of the language, be co-denotational with (or can be a co-variable of) a subject of equal or higher rank. If the answer is in the affirmative, then that is the preferred interpretation, to be overridden only by strong cognitive factors or by factors of discourse construction (including a distinction between topic and comment).

It has just been said that the proper formulation of the Reflexive Principle is "approximated" by (76). This caveat is necessary because there seem to be gliding norms for reflexivity in subordinate clauses that are further removed from the nuclear predicate argument structure of the sentence. The principle as formulated in (76) seems to apply happily to subordinate clauses that are sentential arguments to the main predicate:

(77) a. Harold said that he/!the poor kid was bored.
  b. !He said that Harold was bored.
  c. Harold has told Sue that she/?!the old girl has inherited all of her father's estate.
  d. !Harold has told her/the old girl that Sue has inherited all of her father's estate.
  e. Sue promised John that she would help the creep.

Epithets are excluded because they cannot stand in for reflexives. (77c) is marginal in this respect, probably because there is a stage of (prelexical) analysis at which *Sue* is the subject of a prelexical "know" (if *tell* contains the structure "cause-to-know"). (77e), on the other hand, is a great deal better, again probably because *John* does not seem to be a subject at any level of analysis, no matter how abstract. (77b) and (77d) are excluded anyway because they violate the conditions for internally anaphoric denoting pronouns, which is what they must be if they are not reflexive.

It is different, however, for subordinate clauses that are not arguments but derive from other sources. Consider, for example, the following sentences:

> (78) a. Harold left because he/! the poor kid was bored.[5]
> b. Because Harold was bored, he/the poor kid left.

There is no problem in (78a). The Reflexive Principle as formulated in (76) has simply been applied: the higher subject is the antecedent, and the pronoun is reflexive and can thus not be replaced by an epithet. But (78b) is somewhat problematic in that it should not be allowed at all if (76) was the last word. The fact that an epithet is usable in the position of the pronoun shows that we have a denoting pronoun here and thus not a reflexive. Given that, the position of the antecedent is regular: the antecedent NP *Harold* precedes the anaphor. The only difficulty is that the use of a denoting pronoun is allowed at all. Some provision must therefore be built into (76) specifying more precisely the conditions under which reflexivity is mandatory and those under which it is possible. It may well be that distinctions as between topic and comment, or given and new, are relevant here. Intuitively, one would say that in (78a) the reason for Harold's leaving is topic, while "because he was bored" is the comment (and thus 'new'). The fact that Harold left is 'given'. In (78b), however, "Harold was bored" is 'given', and "he left" is 'new', while there does not seem to be a clear topic-comment structure.

Note also that there is a point in regarding (78a), but not (78b), as built up, at some level of analysis, of a subject "Harold" and a complex predicate "left because he was bored", as is proposed in Evans 1980. This is brought out by the fact that the addition of *and so did Fred* to (78a) implies that Fred, too, left because he was bored. But if the same addition is made to (78b), the implication is merely that Fred, too, left, whatever Fred's reasons for leaving were. Our analytic machinery, however, is not sufficiently developed, as yet, to handle such differences adequately. It is relatively easy, of course, to propose that an analysis must be given in terms of complex predicates (Evans 1980), but if such a proposal is to be taken seriously, it must be integrated in the theory of grammar and in the theory of discourse incrementation. The strong intuitive appeal of the proposal suggests that such an undertaking is likely to be successful and to yield important new insights. It must, however, be left to future research.

---

[5] It would seem that an epithet in the *because*-clause is less abhorrent when there is a clear intonational break between it and the main clause:

Harold left – because the poor kid was bored.

But apart from the complications brought about by non-nuclear subordinate clauses, the Reflexive Principle works rather well.[6] It applies at any stage of generation or parsing between Semantic Analysis and Surface Structure, not necessarily at a well-defined level or representation (Surface Structure, Shallow Structure, Deep Structure, Semantic Analysis), which are defined by the kind of rules to which they are input or output.

If a language has reflexive marking only when the antecedent subject is a clause-mate of the pronoun, at any stage of analysis, it is possible to have marked reflexives that are not co-denotational with the surface subject but with the semantic or some intermediate subject. Thus we find in English and Dutch, which do require reflexive marking for clause-mates:

(79) a. Ben had wanted <u>Graham</u> for a long time to look after <u>himself</u>.
   b. Ben told <u>Graham</u> a story about <u>himself</u>.
(80) a. Karel gelastte <u>Ben</u> voor <u>zichzelf</u> te werken.
   ("Karel ordered <u>Ben</u> to work for <u>himself</u>")

---

[6] Bosch (1983: 169) is unique in accepting anaphoric relations of the following type:

   (i) <u>He</u>'s unbearable when <u>Stan</u> gets one of his tantrums.
   (ii) <u>He</u> usually flunked when <u>John</u> cheated in his exams.
   (iii) <u>He</u> was quite improved when <u>John</u> paid us another visit.

But he joins the fold of linguists again in rejecting:

   (iv) <u>He</u>'s unbearable when <u>Stan</u> talks.
   (v) <u>He</u> flunked when <u>John</u> cheated.
   (vi) <u>He</u> was improved when <u>John</u> paid us a visit.

It would seem, however, that, far from being "unproblematic" (p. 170), these judgements lack the factual basis necessary for sound theory. It is probably so that under very special contextual conditions, and with a highly marked intonational pattern, all of these sentences have marginally acceptable occurrences. But before any use of such possibilities is made in theory building, the precise conditions should be empirically investigated and formulated adequately. Cases like (Bosch 1983: 165; Reinhart 1983: 34; Lakoff 1976; 289):

   (vii) Mary hit <u>him</u> before <u>Max</u> left.
   (viii) I saw <u>him</u> when <u>John</u> arrived.

tend to be rejected in the literature, though much less clearly than (i)–(vi). Their longer counterparts

   (ix) Mary hit <u>him</u> before <u>Max</u> left in his Rolls Royce for a dinner engagement at the Ritz.
   (x) I briefly saw <u>him</u> when <u>John</u> arrived home from hospital.

are, on the whole, accepted, and thus deserve the predicate "unproblematic" with greater justice than (i)–(iii) in Bosch's view. We observe here that (i)–(vi) violate the Reflexive Principle, but (vii)–(x) do not. The problem with (vii)–(x), as will become clear below, is that they run counter to a highly prized principle for denoting pronouns with a definite antecedent, which says that the pronoun may precede the antecedent only if it does not command it (Langacker 1969). Apparently, this condition is attenuated to the extent that the clause containing the antecedent gets 'heavier'. This point will be taken up below.

b. Ik gelastte <u>Karel</u> Ben voor <u>zich</u> te laten werken.
 ("I ordered <u>Karel</u> to make Ben work for <u>him</u>")
c. <u>Karel</u> vertelde Ben een verhaal over <u>zichzelf</u>.
 ("<u>Karel</u> told Ben a story about <u>himself</u>")
d. Karel vertelde <u>Ben</u> een verhaal over <u>hemzelf</u>.
 ("Karel told <u>Ben</u> a story about <u>himself</u>")

The reflexive marking in (79a), as has been the traditional account in transformational grammar from the beginning, is due to the fact that Graham is the subject of the object-clause under *want* at the stage before Subject Raising is applied. At that stage the reflexive marking is applied. Cases of the type (79b) seem solvable only in the light of a theory of prelexical analysis providing a stage of analysis which shows up *Graham* as the subject of a lexically incorporated abstract verb of knowing.

The Dutch sentences are more interesting, mainly because reflexive marking is more complex in Dutch than in English. (80a) is immediately obvious: at SA-level *Ben* is the subject of the object-clause under *gelasten* ("order"). The selection of the form *zichzelf* results from the rule that at SA-level all clitic reflexives are *zich*, and all non-clitic reflexives, such as those in preposition phrases, are *zichzelf*. (80b) derives from the SA:

(80) b'.

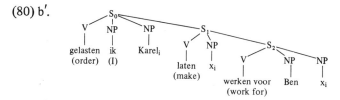

The verb *laten* (section 2.4.5) takes obligatory Predicate Raising:

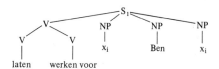

At this intermediate level the reflexive pronoun x_i in object-position is clausemate with its antecedent, x_i in subject-position. It reflexivizes into *zich* (not *zichzelf*) by virtue of the rule that reflexive marking at derived levels is always *zich*, never *zichzelf*.[7] (This rule thus excludes a reading where Ben

---

[7] More precisely, the rule for Dutch reflexive marking at derived stages is that the marking is always by means of *zich* except if *zich* could have manifested itself at earlier stages. In that case no reflexive marking is assigned, and the pronoun is of the ordinary personal kind:

 (i) <u>Karel</u> liet Ben <u>hem</u> het pakje terugbezorgen.
 ("<u>Karel</u> made Ben return the parcel to <u>him</u>")

works for himself.) (80c) is explained on the basis of the rule that SA-reflexive marking is *zichzelf* for preposition phrases. And *hemzelf* in (80d) is due to the rule that marking by means of the addition of *zelf* ("self") to the ordinary personal pronouns *hem, haar, het, hen* ("him", "her", "it", "them") is restricted to prelexical cases. (The regularities observed in this respect are, of course, powerful further confirmation for the grammatical theory espoused in chapter 2.)

A few observations are in order here. First, the fact that (79a) does not allow for a reading in which *Ben*, the surface subject, is co-denotational with *himself* shows that the assignment of morphological reflexive marking takes place 'top-down': the marking is assigned at the earliest opportunity in the generative process, not in the parsing process. The same conclusion follows, even more strongly, from the rules of reflexive marking in Dutch (see in particular note 7). This has interesting consequences for psycholinguistic theories of parsing and comprehension: it means in any case that a considerable amount of top-down checking is required. In Dutch, for example, the occurrence of the reflexive pronoun *zich* requires that its subject-antecedent is located at the earliest possible stage of derivation, i.e. top-down. And the same goes for all English marked reflexives.[8]

Secondly, it is clear from the cases discussed that the rules will be unable to operate without a separate and independently given indexing, i.e. a marking of the 'empty' cases of $_{NP}[x]$ whether they are co-denotational with any of the higher NPs and if so with which. It will be remembered that the same requirement holds for Secondary Subject Deletion (see (87b) in section 2.4.1): identity of index is a necessary condition for deletion under SSD. We

---

Zich is impossible here. With *zich* the sentence unambiguously means that Ben returns the parcel to himself.

Dutch also has a case of non-reflexive marking, at least in slightly formal, written style. In cases where the reflexive interpretation of a third person singular masculine pronoun would be possible but is not intended, the normal form *zijn* ("his") may be replaced by *diens* ("that one's"):

   (ii) <u>Karel</u> bracht <u>Leo</u> om in zijn woning. ("<u>Karel</u> killed <u>Leo</u> in his apartment")
   (iii) <u>Karel</u> bracht <u>Leo</u> om in <u>diens</u> woning. ("<u>Karel</u> killed <u>Leo</u> in his apartment")

For the feminine or plural third person possessive pronouns (*haar* ("her") and *hun* ("their")), no such alternatives exist.

[8] Note that morphological marking of reflexive pronouns in English is not simply conditional on a co-denotation (or co-variable) relation with the subject of the same clause. The pronoun in question must also not be in a secondary VP, as in:

   (i) <u>Ben</u> wanted the parcel to be delivered to <u>him</u> before noon.

When the secondary VP is 'weakened' by the deletion of the infinitive, as in

   (ii) <u>Ben</u> had the parcel delivered to <u>him(self)</u> before noon.

morphological marking seems optional. In any case, however, the pronouns in (i) and (ii) are reflexive, in our sense, witness the impossibility of e.g.:

   (iii) !<u>Ben</u> wanted the parcel to be delivered to <u>the old rascal</u> before noon.

shall see that the same applies to the bound variable pronouns. Only denoting pronouns can do without independently given indexing.

4.2.3 Bound variable pronouns

Bound variable pronouns are so-called because they function logically and semantically as the well-known variables bound by quantifiers in classical predicate calculus. If a pronoun belongs to this category it is normally and preferably preceded, in Surface Structure, by a quantified NP. It must anyway be commanded by it in Surface Structure, or be commanded by the quantifying predicate in SA, according to the traditional definition of 'command':[9]

(81) In a constituent tree structure, a node A *commands* a node B just in case A does not dominate B, B does not dominate A, and the first S-node in the tree up from A also dominates B.[10]

[9] Evans (1980: 341), following Reinhart 1976, poses a more stringent condition for quantifier-controlled pronouns. In his view the antecedent must both precede and c-command the pronoun, where the notion of c-command is defined as follows:

A node A c-commands a node B just in case B is dominated by the first branching node dominating A.

That this condition is too stringent is quickly shown. First, the precede-condition does not seem to be absolutely necessary, as has been widely noted and appears again from the examples (82c) and (82e) below. More seriously, the notion of c-command misses the point in that there are many perfectly straightforward cases of quantifier-controlled pronouns where the antecedent does not c-command the pronoun, though, of course, it commands the pronoun. Besides (82b) below, one has, for example:

(i) I won't believe rumours about anyone that he is playing tricks on me.
(ii) There is a story about everyone that he has done something heroic.
(iii) I don't ask of anybody that he betrays his principles.

[10] In view of the many problems arising with constituents in determiner positions, it is probably wise to ensure that the definition of the command-relation does not extend to determiner positions. That is, if we stipulate that a constituent in determiner position does not command either its head nor anything else in the sentence, we have rid ourselves of awkward cases like the following:

(i) !Everyone's mother thinks he is a genius. (Reinhart 1983: 177)
(ii) !Gossip about every businesssman harmed his career. (ib.: 118)

There is obviously a great deal to be sorted out yet in this respect, but it seems relevant that (ii) allows only for a paraphrase "Gossip that is about every businessman...", and not for a paraphrase "For every businessman it is the case that gossip about him harmed his career". Contrast this with, e.g., (ii) in note 9, which clearly does allow for a reading "For everyone there is a story about him that he has done something heroic", and not, or hardly, "There is a story which is about everyone, that..." What is behind these phenomena is simply not known, and any satisfactory answer must be postponed till sufficient work has been done on these cases.

Note, incidentally, that if determiner positions are excluded from the command relation, no problems arise for cases like

(iii) His mother loves Oscar.

which are widely quoted in the literature and would seem to contradict the principle that a denoting pronoun may precede its antecedent only if it does not command it.

Thus, for a pronoun to fulfil the role of a bound variable as they are known in classical predicate calculus, its antecedent, i.e. its quantifying phrase, will normally precede and must command the pronoun, as appears from the following examples:

(82) a. Nobody had been told that he had to pay in advance.
    b. I'll hold it against everybody if he plays a bad trick on me.
    c. ?In his garden everyone likes to relax.
    d. Everyone likes to relax in his garden.
    e. ?The he was going to win surprised none of the contestants.
    f. Nobody left because he was tired.
    g. !Nobody left – because he was tired.
    h. !Because nobody was tired, he left.

(82a) and (82b) are standard cases of quantifier control of pronouns. (82c) is less felicitous than (82d), due to non-compliance with the preferred order principle, and likewise for (82e). (82f) and (82g) have different intonational patterns, and it is commonly, and no doubt correctly, assumed in transformational linguistics that this difference corresponds to a different surface tree structure:

(82) f'.   (82) g'.

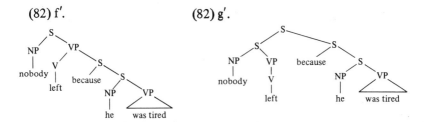

Under this assumption it is clear why the pronoun in (82f) is preferably interpreted as quantifier-controlled, whereas this interpretation is impossible for (82g).[11] No tree need be drawn to show that the quantifier expression in (82h) does not command the pronoun and can thus not control it.

The case quoted in Reinhart 1983: 130

    (iv) Every daughter of every professor in some small college town wishes she could leave it.

does not contradict the exclusion of determiner positions from the command relation, since, in this case, we have to do with a denoting pronoun, and not with a bound variable pronoun, as is seen from the fact that the pronoun *it* in (iv) is easily replaced by an epithet like *the bloody place*. This shows that the pronoun in question is not quantifier-controlled but is a denoting pronoun with indefinite antecedent, or, in Evans's (1980) terminology, an E-type pronoun.

  [11] Note that *since*, unlike *because*, must be assumed to occur only in structures of the form (82g'), and not in structures like (82f'). This accounts for the fact that (i) is impossible and (ii) is allowed only if there is no anaphoric relation between the

It is interesting to note that what is expressed by the command relation in surface structure is likewise expressed in Semantic Analysis by the variable binding relation (see section 2.2). The last three sentences of (82) correspond, respectively, to the following three SAs: [12]

(83) a. $\sim\exists$ (^{x}(because(leave(x), be tired(x))), ^{x}(person(x)))
   b. because ($\sim\exists$ (^{x}(leave(x)), ^{x}(person(x))), be tired(p))
   c. because (leave(p), $\sim\exists$ (^{x}(be tired(x)), person(x)))

The occurrences of *p* in (83b) and (83c) are unproblematic: they are not in a binding position and can therefore not be replaced by *x*, i.e. the bound variable. The corresponding pronoun *he* in both sentences can therefore not be interpreted as a bound variable pronoun. But in (83a) all argument positions must be filled by the bound variable *x*, except in the first SD term under the quantifier where one bound variable would suffice. That is, nothing in the semantics prevents the subject term of either *leave* or *be tired* from being *p* instead of *x*, *p* then being a denoting pronoun with an external antecedent (for lack of an internal one). The preferred reading is that both arguments are bound variables (the preference being due to the Assignment Procedure, as will be shown), but there is a possible reading with a denoting pronoun as subject of *be tired*. Not, however, as subject of *leave*.

The question now arises why it should be that the subject of *be tired* in (83a) can be pulled away from underneath the quantifier, but not the subject of *leave*. The grammar of *because*-clauses and of the quantifiers, if applied according to the principles of grammatical transformation as exposed in chapter 2, would yield an impeccably grammatical sentence, namely (82h), where indeed the subject of *left* is not quantifier-controlled. Yet (82h) does not mean what (83a) means with the subject of *leave* not bound, namely, "there is no x such that y left because x was tired". In fact, this meaning cannot be expressed at all in an English sentence, which must be due to a constraint on Quantifier Lowering whereby the quantifier may not be lowered into an S which is not either nuclear itself or an argument of the nuclear S. Whatever its proper formulation, some such constraint must exist, which is a curious and intriguing fact. It would seem that the notion of command plays a crucial role here: if the subject of *leave* in (83a) is replaced

---

quantifier and the pronoun:

(i) *Nobody left since he was tired.
(ii) !Nobody left – since he was tired.

(This assumption eliminates (22b) in Reinhart 1983: 118, which would otherwise be problematic.)

[12] The semantic predicate *because* is taken to require two sentential terms as arguments. The first term is nuclear in that it will become the main clause; the second term is first adopted (by Object Incorporation) by $_V$[because], and subsequently the complex new verb is lowered into the first (nuclear) S.

by *p*, the grammar generates (82h), where *he* is not commanded by the existential quantifier, whereas in (83a) it is. Apparently, the grammar, despite all its drastic transformational changes, manages to avoid scope confusions as between (83a) and (83c). The fact that the command-condition in Surface Structure works not too badly for quantifier-controlled pronouns may well turn out to find its rationale in a functional principle throughout the grammar ensuring that command relations of semantic predicates within the same complex sentence remain unchanged (or if they are changed, that the change is compensated for by secondary means). A similar tendency to what is found here is seen in the Scope Ordering Constraint for quantifiers, discussed above in section 2.4.3.

The question remains, however, whether the conditions for possible anaphoric relations between controlling quantifiers and bound variable pronouns should be read off from Surface Structure or from Semantic Analysis, since both look as if they will do. It is not necessary for us to decide this issue here, but it may be observed that there is some evidence (Reinhart 1983: 118, and examples (110) and (111) below) which would seem to favour the view that, despite the practical (and psycholinguistic) convenience of Surface Structure conditions, it is indeed the SA-level representation which is, in the last resort, responsible for the possible anaphoric relations of bound variable pronouns. If this conclusion proves to be correct, we see again that the full reality of language is a great deal richer and more surprising than those who are keen on formalization are happy to give it credit for.

As with the reflexive pronouns, indexing of the variable *x*s is necessary with quantifier-controlled pronouns. In chapter 2 (section 2.2 and elsewhere) different variables (x, y) were used to distinguish binding by different quantifiers within the same sentence. Thus, (84a) $(= (79a)$ in chapter 2) is analysed as (84b) $(= (79b)$ in chapter 2):

(84) a. Some children have read all the books.
   b. $\exists(\hat{}x(\forall(\hat{}y(read(x, y)), y:(books(y)))), \hat{}x(child(x)))$

The device of using different variables is not essentially different from indexing by means of subscripts (or whatever), so that "x" in (84b) is replaced by "x_i", and "y" by "x_j". Denoting pronouns will not be indexed at all but simply rendered by the bare variable "p".[13] We thus express the crucial fact that reflexive and quantifier-controlled pronouns are structurally bound up with their antecedents and that certain rules of grammar are sensitive to that binding, whereas denoting pronouns are much freer in their search for an antecedent.

---

[13] We leave out of account the minimal lexical characterization found with most, if not all, pronouns and consisting of very broad category indications such as "human", "female", "male", "non-personal" and the like.

We can now, in principle, understand the threefold ambiguity of a sentence like

(85) a. No one told everyone that he would win.

where the pronoun *he* can be bound either by the quantifier *no one* or by the quantifier *everyone*, but may also not be bound at all and be a denoting pronoun controlled by an external antecedent. The first reading is captured by the use of "x_i" in (85b), the second by "x_j", and the third by the bare variable "p":

(85) b. $\sim\exists\,(\hat{}x_i(\forall(\hat{}x_j(\text{tell}(x_i, x_j, (\text{will win}(x_i/x_j/p)))), \hat{}x_j(\text{person}(x_j))),$
$\hat{}x_i(\text{person}(x_i))))$

Note that there is no objection to the lowering of the universal quantifier, which binds x_j, into the object-clause of *tell*, since this clause, though not itself nuclear, is an argument of the predicate of the nuclear clause, so that command relations and scope orderings are not disturbed.

4.2.4 Denoting pronouns

The third category of pronouns distinguished, the denoting pronouns, has traditionally attracted most attention in anaphora research. They have always been considered more or less prototypical of pronouns, from the first endeavours at their analysis in antiquity up to early transformational work. The very term "pronoun", and its Greek model "antōnymía", signify this fact: they mean literally "substitute for a noun", and are thus properly used only for denoting pronouns, since the other two categories lack this substitution feature.[14] This traditional tendency of regarding denoting pronouns as pronouns proper is still found in the contemporary literature on anaphora and pronouns, which is characterized by a relatively late recognition of bound variable pronouns as a separate category and by the failure to recognize unmarked reflexive pronouns for what they are. It is hardly surprising, therefore, that attempts to account for (sentence-internal) anaphoric relations with the help of one principle only were bound to fail, and that more sophisticated attempts still failed because the category of denoting pronouns was not sufficiently restricted. With a more strictly limited class of denoting pronouns and a suitably extended class of reflexives, we may expect that the problem of sentence-internal anaphora will be less refractory than it has so far proved to be.

Langacker (1969), still, with Lakoff (1968), among the most inspired and fruitful studies on anaphora in recent grammatical literature, formulated the

---

[14] This point is discussed in detail in Bosch 1983, where our denoting pronouns are called "referential", and the reflexive and bound variable pronouns are lumped together under the term "syntactic pronouns".

principle that antecedents have a *primacy* over their anaphors. The most directly statable conditions for primacy (1969: 167-8) are that the antecedent A must precede the pronoun P in "conjoined structures", or, as we will say, in subsequent increment units, and, in so far as internal anaphora is concerned, that P may precede A only if P does not command A. Let us call the former the *discourse precede condition*, and the latter the *precede and not-command condition* (PNCC).

Both conditions have their problems. The discourse precede condition seems at variance with cases like (Reinhart 1983: 55):

(86) a. She has the whole city at her disposal and Rosa just sits at home.

b. He hasn't contacted me, but I'm sure John is back.

Yet, even though cases like those in (86) are no doubt acceptable, there can be no doubt that the general rule for unmarked external anaphora is that A precedes P in discourse. Sentences like (86a) and (86b) require a special context to be naturally used. A reasonable guess would be to say that the second conjunct in such cases has an 'echo' of what has already been said or suggested in previous discourse. One might surmise that what happens then is that the echoed sentence is taken whole from the discourse and repeated – a process reminiscent of what has been found with Positive Polarity Items (section 4.1.5). Interesting though Reinhart's observations are, it does not look as if they should be taken as a serious threat to Langacker's discourse precede condition.

The more serious problems arise in connection with PNCC. In fact, the indubitable insufficiency of this condition for all internal pronominal anaphora has given rise to the vast body on literature on the subject since 1969. A well-known problem was presented by sentences of the type (74a), repeated here for convenience:

(74) a. In his studio Graham paints.

where A and P cannot swap places without disrupting the anaphoric relation, and where P both precedes and commands A. (If we follow the suggestion of note 10 that no command relation holds from determiner positions, then P does not command A, and anaphora should thus be permitted. But even then it is not clear why A and P cannot swap places.) We have removed this difficulty by observing that P in (74a) is not a denoting but a reflexive pronoun, so that A must be in subject position. Consequently, if we want to save something like PNCC, it cannot apply to reflexive pronouns.

A similar but less severe problem for PNCC is posed by cases like

(87) a. His mother loves Graham.

which is accepted by most authors as a legitimate case of anaphora. Note, however, that here the pronoun is not reflexive, but a denoting pronoun, given the possibility of

(87) b. Graham's mother loves him.
    c. The poor thing's mother loves Graham.
    d. Graham's mother loves the poor thing.

Therefore, what remains to be explained is the possibility of anaphoric relatedness in (87a) and (87c). If, as is suggested in note 10, indeed no command relation holds from determiner positions, this problem is removed as well.

Problems arise also when PNCC is applied to quantifier-controlled pronouns. Thus, for example, although the passive sentence (88a) is impeccable, the active (88b) is not:

(88) a. Everyone is loved by his mother.
    b. !His mother loves everyone.

This shows that the pronoun *his* in (88) is of a different class than the *his* in (87a) – in fact, epithet substitution is ruled out in (88a). Accordingly, since bound variable pronouns have been seen to be subject to their own conditions, *PNCC should not be taken to apply to this class of pronouns, but only to denoting pronouns.*

This restriction, however, of the applicability of PNCC is not sufficient yet. It misfires on 'donkey-sentences':

(89) a. If Harry owns a donkey, he beats it/the poor animal.
    b. Everyone who owns a donkey beats it/ the poor animal.
    c. !If Harry owns it, he beats a donkey.
    d. !Everyone who owns it beats a donkey.

If PNCC applied here, (89c) and (89d) should be all right, but they clearly are not. And again, the sensible solution seems to be *to restrict PNCC further to denoting pronouns with definite antecedents*, and account for (89) by means of separate principles. Now PNCC is safe as far as (89) is concerned, because if *a donkey* is replaced by a definite NP, such as *this donkey*, all four sentences, with or without epithets, are acceptable, and comply with PNCC.

Even within this further restriction, however, some problematic cases remain. Thus, as was observed by Akmajian and Jackendoff (1970), NPs under contrastive or emphatic accent are prevented from being antecedents for pronouns not commanded by them:

(90) a. !That JIM was going to be Harry's supervisor surprised him.
    b. That JIM was going to be Harry's supervisor surprised him.
    c. !That Jim was going to be HARRY's supervisor surprised him.
    d. That Jim was going to be HARRY's supervisor surprised him.

If, however, P is commanded by a contrastively or emphatically accented A, and preferably follows A, then anaphora is unproblematic:

(91) People dislike JIM because he is abrasive, not HARRY.

Note, moreover, that epithet substitution is allowed in (90b) and (90d), but not in (91):

(92) a. That JIM was going to be Harry's supervisor surprised the creep.
 b. That Jim was going to be HARRY's supervisor surprised the old maniac.
 c. !People dislike JIM because the fellow is abrasive, not HARRY.

These observations look perplexing, and they have perplexed most authors. Yet in our analysis everything falls into place if it is assumed that NPs under emphatic or contrastive accent behave like the quantifiers and bind variables. Then (90a) and (90c) are ruled out because A does not command P, and (91) is found to be in order. The *him* in (90b) and (90d) are not controlled by the accented NPs but by the unaccented ones, and they are, accordingly, ordinary denoting pronouns, as appears from (92a) and (92b), and also from the fact that in these sentences P and A may swap places:

(93) a. That JIM was going to be his supervisor surprised Harry.
 b. That he was going to be HARRY's supervisor surprised Jim.

We shall not work out here the suggestion that accented NPs behave like quantifiers. Only a few suggestive remarks can be made. First, the quantifiers are in any case not unique in controlling bound variable pronouns. WH-constituents do the same:

(94) a. Whom do people dislike because he/!the fellow is abrasive?
 b. Whom did you tell that he/?!the fellow had won a million dollar prize?

Moreover, WH-constituents and accented NPs both share common traits with quantifiers. Like the quantifiers, WH-constituents and accented NPs naturally allow for a Lowering analysis. For WH-constituents, see Baker (1970b); for accented NPs and their relation with cleft and pseudocleft sentences, see section 3.5.1 above. Then, accented NPs seem to play their part in the system of scope hierarchies in much the same way as quantifiers, negation and the logical connectives do. Note, for example, the difference between (95a) (=(122a) in section 2.4.3) and (95b):

(95) a. The victim was thought to be Spanish or Italian.
 b. The victim was thought to be SPANISH or Italian, not GREEK or Italian.

The former has a scope ambiguity, which the latter lacks: (95a) means either "Either the victim was thought to be Spanish, or the victim was thought to be Italian", or "It was thought that the victim was either Spanish or Italian". However, (95b) can only mean "The thing such that the victim was thought to be either it or Italian is SPANISH, not GREEK", and not "Either what the victim was thought to be is SPANISH, not GREEK, or the victim was thought to be Italian". In other words, *SPANISH*, in (95b) takes higher scope over *or*, and this is probably connected with the fact that it precedes *or*. We will, however, not pursue the question of the quantifier status of accented NPs here.

Another class of difficult cases is provided by sentences containing anaphora to an antecedent NP, not, however, taking over its denoting function but making reference to its mere occurring as a word:

(95) a. You've lived in <u>Dnepropetrovsk</u> for 20 years, and you still find *it* an impossible name to pronounce.

Note that there are special restrictions on anaphora involving hypostasis (or 'quote reference') one way or another. Thus (96b) seems impossible, but (96c) is all right:

(96) b. !"<u>Volapük</u>" means "world speak" in it.
    c. It is called "<u>Punch</u>" because it has <u>it</u>.

Given our almost total ignorance regarding the grammar of quotation, we can do little else than let such cases rest.

The only significant class of problematic cases now left for PNCC, restricted as it is to denoting pronouns with a definite antecedent, is presented by sentences like (ix) and (x) in note 6 above, or (Reinhart 1983: 34):

(97) a. The chairman hit <u>him</u> on the head before the <u>lecturer</u> had a chance to say anything.
    b. We'll just have to fire <u>him</u>, whether <u>McIntosh</u> likes it or not.

It has been observed (Lakoff 1968) that the clauses containing the offending A must be of more than minimal length: the shorter they are the less acceptable the anaphoric relation. Here the answer may be that the length of the clause could be a means of increasing the primacy status discussed by Langacker (1969). It is to be noted anyway that backward pronominalization ("cataphora" in traditional grammar) seems to be connected with the topicality of the antecedent: only when A denotes (refers to) the topic of the ongoing discourse can it follow P. And this condition may well be another manifestation of a phenomenon we have tentatively identified on a couple of occasions earlier on: sometimes preceding bits of discourse, or bits of discourse that have been suggested, asserted, questioned or what not, are taken up whole and re-used in a different incrementational complex. In any case, more than a tentative or suggestive answer cannot be given now.

Special mention must also be made of cleft and pseudocleft sentences, whose anaphoric behaviour accords with the non-cleft forms of the sentences in question, as is widely known, not only for denoting pronouns but for pronouns generally:

(98) a. !What he said was that Peter was out of his mind.

    b. !He said that Peter was out of his mind.

(99) a. What everyone expected was that he would win.

    b. Everyone expected that he would win.

(100) a. !It was in Harold's room that he wrote the paper.

    b. !In Harold's room he wrote the paper.

(101) a. What I have against Peter is that the fellow is out of his mind.

    b. I have against Peter that the fellow is out of his mind.

(102) a. !What I gave him was the story that you wanted to see Ed.

    b. !I gave him the story that you wanted to see Ed.

There is no accepted view in theoretical grammar why this should be so, though the facts are perfectly straightforward. If the idea mentioned in section 3.5.1 (and attributed to Leon Stassen) holds water, the explanation will not be far to seek: the idea is that clefts and pseudoclefts derive from full non-cleft sentences as predicate nominal under a verb *be*, more or less as in:

(103) a. What everyone expected was everyone expected that he would win.

    b. Where Harold wrote the paper is Harold wrote the paper in his room.

Any solution to this complication will require anyway that more than just surface structure is brought into account. We shall, however, regard this more as a problem of clefts and pseudoclefts than as a problem of anaphora proper.

A proposal to improve on Langacker's PNCC, which has gained some notoriety in recent years, is Reinhart (1976), and, in a revised version, Reinhart (1983). Reinhart's aim is to provide a constraint on anaphoric relations in so far as they are restricted to a *domain*. (In discussing Reinhart's proposal I shall ignore the 1976 version and concentrate on the revised version of 1983.) A *domain* is defined as follows (1983: 41): "The domain of a node A consists of all and only the nodes c-commanded by A." And the notion of c-command is defined thus:[15] "A node A c-commands a node B iff the branching node α_1 most immediately dominating A either dominates

---

[15] This definition is meant to be more precise than but still equivalent with the 'easier' definition as given in note 9 above. The 'precise' version corresponds with 'precise' tree structures, whereas the 'easy' version corresponds with 'simplified' trees. We shall ignore the simplifications here and work with the precise notions and structures.

B or is immediately dominated by a node α_2 which dominates B, and α_2 is of the same category type as α_1."

"Sameness of category type" is postulated to cover cases of $\bar{S}$ over S or $\overline{VP}$ over VP (p. 23), where "$\bar{S}$" consists of the complementizer and the sentential structure proper, and "$\overline{VP}$" is assumed for cases where the Verb Phrase contains, besides the verb and one or two nominal arguments, also prepositional or sentential material. Reflexive (and reciprocal) pronouns are considered subject to special extra constraints, and they will play no part in the appraisal given here. Apart from reflexives, however, the constraint presented is (p. 42): "If a rule assigns node A some kind of prominence over node B, A must be a D(omain)-head of the domain containing B."

Here a "D-head" is the node c-commanding its domain, and the notion of prominence is relevant in so far as an antecedent is considered more prominent than a pronoun. Thus, in simple words, A must c-command P, or else P is not in the domain of A.

For anaphoric relations within domains, order is considered largely irrelevant: its relevance is restricted to what is (vaguely) termed as "pragmatics", and this means that forward anaphora is more normal than backward anaphora, but the possibility of anaphoric relatedness never depends crucially on order. For anaphora outside domains the pragmatic principle that A precedes P is a little stronger, but, again, not mandatory, as is shown by examples like (86) above. This would imply that, although (104a) is "pragmatically" preferable, (104b) is not altogether excluded (p. 42), while the two remain synonymous. This is not supported by intuitions in this regard:

(104) a. If Pepito owns a donkey, he feeds it.
      b. If Pepito owns it, he feeds a donkey.

Likewise, (105a) would have to be considered "pragmatically" preferable, and (105b), though less preferable, should be possible:

(105) a. It came as a surprise to Harry that he had won.
      b. It came as a surprise to him that Harry had won.

Few speakers of English, however, would agree that (105b) is acceptable with the anaphoric relation as indicated. (We would say that (105a) is acceptable because A precedes P, and that (105b) is unacceptable because P precedes A and also commands A.) Likewise, both of the following should be permitted:

(106) a. She hit Joe when he laughed.
      b. She hit him when Joe laughed.

because A and P are not in each other's domain. Note that for us (106b) is excluded, which seems supported by intuition. However, intuition supports Reinhart for lengthier clauses, as in (97) above, where the same structural relations hold. Reinhart thus cuts into intuitions (even if special allowance is made for 'donkey'-cases as in (104)), whereas what *we* need is a supplementary provision for longer clauses.

The most serious objections, however, to Reinhart's theory of anaphora stem from the plentiful cases of bound variable control without the antecedent (i.e. the quantifier) c-commanding the bound variable pronoun. Justifiably, Reinhart is concerned to rule out impossible cases like:

(107) a. ! Because everybody laughed, he felt happy.
      b. ! If Joe laughs, I'll curse himself.

which would be allowed if no special provision were made to prevent them: read *John* for *everybody*, and *him* (or: *the bastard*) for *himself*, and (107a) and (107b) are both right. In order to achieve this, two supplementary principles are formulated (Reinhart 1983: 136–7), one for reflexive (and reciprocal) pronouns, and one for bound variable pronouns:

> A reflexive or reciprocal pronoun (an R-pronoun) must be interpreted as coreferential with (and only with) a c-commanding NP within a specified syntactic domain... A non-R-pronoun must be interpreted as non-coreferential with any c-commanding NP in the syntactic domain which is specified for ⟨R-pronouns⟩.

> Quantified NPs... can have anaphoric relations only with pronouns in their c-command domain.

Whereas the extra provision made for R-pronouns seems to do its work, Reinhart has been overzealous with regard to bound variable pronouns, because here the counter-examples march in in such numbers that the theory collapses on this front. And the breach is so serious that the whole theory is in direct jeopardy.

Short shrift was given to Evans on this count in note 9, but he only followed Reinhart – uncritically, one fears, because the counter-examples abound. It is simply untenable to say that bound variable pronouns must be in the (Reinhart-)domain of the binding quantifier. Besides the few cases quoted in note 9, consider, e.g.:

(108) a. I will send a reply to everyone if he returns the form.
      b. That he wasn't elected surprised nobody.

Anxious, no doubt, to keep counter-examples away, Reinhart declares certain cases impossible which are, in fact, entirely normal. The following, for example, are unexceptionable, although Reinhart (1983: 118) declares them out of bounds:

(109) a. We changed the carpets in each of the flats to make it look more cheerful.
      b. I placed the scores in front of each of the pianists before his performance.

An interesting case is (ibid.):

(110) So many patients called a p̲s̲y̲c̲h̲i̲a̲t̲r̲i̲s̲t̲ that h̲e̲ couldn't handle them all.

This is, again, ruled out as impossible by Reinhart. Yet it must be observed that there is one reading in which it is acceptable: if *a psychiatrist* is given widest scope, then (110) is impeccable. However, in the preferred reading, with narrow scope for *a psychiatrist*, the sentence is indeed inadmissible. If we wish to preserve the principle that bound variable pronouns are bound by their quantifiers, which has served us so well, then it would appear that Surface Structure is not reliable enough as a guide towards the proper identification of the conditions for bound variable anaphora, since in Surface Structure *a psychiatrist* commands the pronoun *he*, and anaphora should be possible no matter which of the possible readings is taken. In Semantic Analysis, however, which disambiguates structurally between the two possible readings, the quantifier binds what is to become the bound variable pronoun in the acceptable reading, and it does not do so in the reading which is to be rejected. One would therefore feel inclined to formulate the conditions for bound variable anaphora in terms of Semantic Analysis, and not in terms of a Surface Structure relation of command. Problems of this nature, however, transcend the limits imposed on this study by considerations of space and of available expertise. We shall, therefore, let them rest, for the moment – the more so since a decision, one way or another, will not crucially influence the theory of discourse semantics.

The converse of (110) is:

(111) a. The secretary who worked for e̲a̲c̲h̲ o̲f̲ t̲h̲e̲ m̲a̲n̲a̲g̲e̲r̲s̲ despised h̲i̲m̲.

Reinhart (1983: 113) lets this pass as acceptable. However, if (111) is acceptable (which is doubtful) it is so only in the reading "For each of the managers, the secretary who worked for him despised him", and not in any reading in which *each of the managers* is part of the relative clause under *the secretary*. In this latter reading, the pronoun must be plural

(111) b. The secretary who worked for e̲a̲c̲h̲ o̲f̲ t̲h̲e̲ m̲a̲n̲a̲g̲e̲r̲s̲ despised t̲h̲e̲m̲.

and is an ordinary denoting pronoun, as appears from the possible substitution of an epithet:

(111) c. The secretary who worked for e̲a̲c̲h̲ o̲f̲ t̲h̲e̲ m̲a̲n̲a̲g̲e̲r̲s̲ despised t̲h̲e̲ m̲a̲l̲e̲ c̲h̲a̲u̲v̲i̲n̲i̲s̲t̲ p̲i̲g̲s̲.

Note that, if, in the appropriate reading, (111a) is acceptable, it requires that the command-rule for quantifier-controlled pronouns be formulated for Semantic Analysis, and not for Surface Structure.

On the whole, it seems that little is gained and much is lost by Reinhart's proposed solution to the problem of sentence-internal anaphora. A proper demarcation of the class of reflexive (and reciprocal) pronouns as against the denoting pronouns, and a return to the old notion of command, yield a better net result. We must, however, be prepared to add a few supplementary principles to get the facts straight. Thus, PNCC must be supplemented by the principle that A can follow P only if A denotes or refers to the topic of the discourse at hand. If A is made topical in the sentence itself, as, for example, by means of a phrase like *as regards* . . . , then A must precede P: P cannot be used to establish a new topic:

(112) a. As regards Henry, I believe he will support the opposition.
     b. ! As regards him, I believe Henry will support the opposition.

And other further refinements will no doubt be called for in light of the vast amount of often perplexing facts.

What remains now is a discussion of the denoting pronouns with an existentially quantified antecedent (more or less the 'E-type' pronouns of Evans 1980, or the 'donkey'-cases). These pronouns do not follow the PNCC-rule given above for denoting pronouns with definite antecedent, as appears from:

(113) a. If John bought a car, he drives it.
     b. ! If John bought it, he drives a car.
     c. If John bought the car, he drives it.
     d. If John bought it, he drives the car.
(114) a. Everyone who bought a car drives it.
     b. ?! Everyone who bought it drives a car.
     c. Everyone who bought the car drives it.
     d. Everyone who bought it drives the car.

The sentences (113a), (113b), (114a) and (114b) are not cases of quantifier-controlled pronominalization (except (114b), but only in a clearly non-preferred reading where *a car* takes highest scope). This appears, amongst other things, from the fact that negated existentials are impossible here:

(115) a. ! If John bought no car, he drives it.
     b. ! Everyone who bought no car drives it.
     c. ! If no one speaks up, he will be rebuffed.

Contrast this with, for example

(116) No one will be rebuffed if he speaks up.

where quantifier-control is evident.

The fact that negated existentials are impossible in the cases at hand, together with the fact that these cases are limited to *existential* quantification, strongly suggests that what we have to do with here is a special case of discourse or sentence-external anaphora, where subsequent increment units are involved. These cases would thus fall under the *discourse precede condition* (DPC), mentioned above in connection with Langacker 1969. Note also that the pronouns in question admit epithet substitution:

(117) If John bought a̲ c̲a̲r̲, he drives t̲h̲e̲ t̲h̲i̲n̲g̲.

and that pronominalization of *every* takes the plural form, as in discourse pronominalization, and not the singular, as in variable binding constructions:

(118) a. If e̲v̲e̲r̲y̲o̲n̲e̲ leaves after eleven, t̲h̲e̲y̲ will a̲l̲l̲ miss the ferry.
b. ! If e̲v̲e̲r̲y̲o̲n̲e̲ leaves after eleven, h̲e̲ will miss the ferry.

Furthermore, the constructions at hand allow for *too* in much the same way as in conjunctions:

(119) a. John bought a̲ c̲a̲r̲ and he drives i̲t̲ too.
b. If John bought a̲ c̲a̲r̲, he drives i̲t̲ too.
c. Everyone who bought a̲ c̲a̲r̲ drives i̲t̲ too.

We may thus safely conclude that we have to do here with subsequent incrementations, as in normal discourse, and not with variable binding.

In principle, the theory of discourse semantics offers an immediate explanation for these cases. As we have seen (section 4.1.5), the increment value associated with sentences of the type "if A then B" is a permission to add $i(A)$, if found true, but only if $i(\text{Nec}(B))$ is also added. That is, the instruction associated with *if* involves the possible setting up of a bit of discourse structure resulting from the linguistic sequence "A and $\text{Nec}(B)$". It is this bit of discourse which accounts for the phenomena of anaphoric pronominalization in *if*-constructions.

A similar account is given for pronouns whose antecedent is an existentially quantified NP in the relative clause under a universally quantified NP, as in (114a), or under an ordinary definite description, as in:

(120) a.   The man who bought a̲ c̲a̲r̲ drives i̲t̲.
b. ?! The man who bought i̲t̲ drives a̲ c̲a̲r̲.
c.   The man who bought a̲ c̲a̲r̲ drives t̲h̲e̲ b̲l̲o̲o̲d̲y̲ t̲h̲i̲n̲g̲.

In so far as the universal quantifier carries the instruction to add the material of the first term to any address, already in D or to be introduced later, characterized by the material of the second term (see section 4.1.3), there is again the specification of a bit of discourse structure as resulting from a linguistic sequence of conjoined sentences: "x bought *a car* and drives *it*." And in so far as ordinary lexical incrementation is concerned (with super-addresses for the universal quantifier), the situation does not change in principle: there is an instruction to look for a specific bit of discourse structure in D, and to add what is newly given. Thus, in (120a), the instruction is to look for an address (i.e. a bit of discourse structure) answering to the description "man who bought a car", and to add the increment value of "he drives it".

It must be observed that this account requires that the subject term of a lexical predicate is located first, then the direct object and then the other arguments. We shall see that this is a general principle (and possibly a defining feature for the notion of "subject") for all lexical predicates. Technical predicates behave differently in this respect. The quantifiers, for example, require that the second term is processed first. This will explain the impossibility of the sentences in (121) while those in (122) are unproblematic:

> (121) a. !It was bought by the man who had seen a car.
>   b. !I sold the man who had seen a car it.
>   c. !I sold it to the man who had seen a car.
> (122) a. The man who had seen a car bought it.
>   b. I sold the car that someone had seen to him.
>   c. I sold him the car that someone had seen.

(Admittedly, (122c) sounds less felicitous than (122b). Whether this is to do with a Surface Structure left-to-right constraint for this kind of anaphora, or whether the bare dative without preposition is restricted to cases where it is part of the topic description while the object represents the comment – which would rule our (122c) – is a question that must remain unanswered here.)

It has often been observed that existentially quantified NPs in *if*-clauses may assume a 'generic' character. The condition for this to happen seems to be, at first sight, that the *if*-clause in question does not contain another non-existential quantifier with higher scope than the existential, and that there is no definite NP in subject-position:

> (123) a. If a man runs a business, he tends to be respected.
>   b. If a linguist works with that theory, he is crazy.
>   c. If a shopkeeper abuses all his customers, he will soon go bankrupt.

The italicized NPs are all naturally interpreted generically. (123a) contains two such generic NPs. What they all have in common is that they represent the opening of a new address without first being tied up with another address, either already in D or hypothetical, i.e. under an instruction with respect to future developments of D, and that this opening of a new address is not actually carried out in D but made subject to a general embargo that if any address of the type specified by the existentially quantified NP in question is opened, the material of the consequent clause must be added. In other words, a generic NP of this type represents not a single opening of a new address, actual or hypothetical, but an almost unrestricted class of possible (hypothetical) address openings of a certain *kind*. And this seems to be precisely the reason why such existentials are interpreted generically.

That is, we venture the principle that genericity is the result of increment instructions that apply not to one or two or three possible future increments but to a *kind* (i.e. *genus*) of increment whose exemplars can be multiplied at will. For example, the possible future increment specified by the *if*-clause in

(124) a. If John loves his wife he won't leave her.

is restricted to one possible future occurrence: once D contains i(John loves his wife), there is no room for another increment i(John loves his wife) since repetitions are considered unacceptable (acceptability condition (a) in section 3.3). It is a little different with, for example,

(124) b. If John has a car, he will take good care of it.

where i(John has a car) may be added more than once without D becoming unacceptable. Thus the use of the existential *a car* opens up, in principle, the possibility of a generic interpretation. Yet, for most ordinary mortals in this day and age the fact that he or she owns one or more cars does not establish a *kind* of cars owned by that person. Even if we think up an outlandish story about some A who turns out to own car after car, the story will not, or at any rate need not, give rise to a notion of "kind of car owned by A". Only if it is made clear that A has a special preference for a specific kind of car and buys those cars in large quantities can one begin to think of "the kind of car owned by A".

The crucial question is whether the material provided by the *if*-clause suffices to characterize what is known as a *kind* or *type*. This is a psychological, and not a logical question. Consequently, attempts at defining a separate quantifier of genericity truth-conditionally distinct from other quantifiers are, as far as natural language semantics is concerned, entirely misguided: the solution lies in the mechanics of discourse semantics plus the psychology of types (stereotypes, prototypes). Thus, the embargo associated with *if* with respect to the opening of a new address for a linguist taking a careful look at "that" theory is not an embargo covering the introduction of addresses referring to linguists of a special *kind*

(124) c. If that theory is looked at carefully by a linguist, it will collapse.

since linguists are not primarily characterized by whether or not they look at certain theories. But the linguists covered by the embargo associated with, e.g., (123b) do form a certain type, since the typology of linguists proceeds primarily by the criterion of what theories they work with.

The question of genericity thus seems to be solvable, in principle, in terms of the theory of discourse incrementation, in close connection with more general cognitive theory about the formation of concepts of kind. No separate truth-conditional operator of genericity need be invented. The reader will understand, however, that this matter cannot be pursued here.

4.2.5 *The Assignment Procedure*

Having reviewed the question of internally anaphoric pronouns in some detail we conclude that, though we may have succeeded in clearing up some puzzles and in bringing about a relative improvement in our insight into these matters, we are still far removed from victory. For even if we succeed in setting up a correct classification and in formulating correct conditions of use and anaphoric relatedness, there still is the question of the rationale behind pronominal behaviour. We have only the beginning of an answer to the question of what the various types of pronoun have in common so that they behave in exactly the ways that they are found to behave. Part of the answer must lie in the general principles of grammars of human languages. Thus, the great question of the relation between semantic scope and Surface Structure properties of precedence and/or command relations, which is of a very general nature and extends well beyond the realm of pronouns and anaphora, certainly has a direct bearing on questions of bound variable pronominal anaphora. But in part the answer will also be seen to lie in the fact that pronouns do not denote their addresses directly, i.e. through the (always minimal and woefully insufficient) semantic material stored in them, as fully lexical definite terms do, but indirectly, i.e. via a separate auxiliary procedure whereby the appropriate address is reached with the help of structural information from within the clause or the whole sentence and/or information based on recency, intonation and other, strictly cognitive, factors in the discourse.

In this section this auxiliary procedure is presented as part of the *Assignment Procedure* (AP), which assigns addresses to definite terms in SA-representations. The pronominal part of AP is an algorithm for anaphora resolution. It is based on the observations made in the preceding sections on the different classes of internally anaphoric pronouns, and will be extended to cover sentence-external anaphora as well, at least in principle. It will be seen that AP proceeds by elimination. It checks first on reflexivity, then on possible quantifier control, then on possible sentence-internal control by a definite antecedent, and after that on possible control by a clause-external but still sentence-internal indefinite (existential) antecedent, to end up with the last option, that of sentence-external anaphora. There is thus a step-by-step transition from the most rigid structural control within the smallest domain (reflexives) to the least rigid structural control within the widest manageable domain (external anaphora).

Recent work, mainly by psychologists,[16] has made it clear that external anaphora is not entirely unstructured and simply dependent on discourse recency (and, of course, on conditions of gender, number, natural sex and other possible general semantic categories expressed in pronouns). Although there is, in a sense, greater freedom in antecedent selection in external anaphora than in internal anaphora, there still are clear restricting conditions. An overriding principle seems to be that external antecedents are assigned according to the greatest cognitive plausibility, which is a non-structural condition.[17] But other, structural, factors play a role as well. Similarity of syntactic function is a determining factor:

(125) a. John looked at Bill, but he did not hit him.

Here subject (*he*) goes to subject (*John*), and object (*him*) to object (*Bill*). But this condition of similarity of syntactic function can be overridden by contrastive intonation (Akmajian and Jackendoff 1970). Thus, in the following sentences,

(125) b. Harry kicked Sam, and then HE shot at HIM.
     c. John looked at Bill, but HE did not hit HIM.

subject goes, or may go, to object, and vice versa. This inversion of syntactic function is clearly facilitated if there is identity or similarity of the remaining (verbal) material, as appears from the widely known cases (Lakoff 1971b: 333):

(125) d. Harry kicked Sam, and then HE kicked HIM.
     e. John called Mary a lexicalist, and then SHE insulted HIM.

(where the implication is that calling someone, or calling Mary, a lexicalist is an insult).

Another feature of AP, besides its gradual progress from the structurally constrained and small domains of control to the less constrained and wider domains, is the procedure of provisional assignments, to be confirmed and made definitive later in the procedure. This element in AP is necessary in view of the so-called *Bach-Peters paradox* in pronominalization. This paradox occurs when P_1 has an antecedent A_1 which, in turn, contains a pronoun P_2

---

[16] See, for example, Sanford and Garrod 1981; Tyler and Marslen-Wilson 1982, and literature cited there.
[17] Consider, for example, the following three external pronominal pick-ups from a sentence:

Audrey asked Sue to drive Helen to the station.
    (a) She didn't want her daughter to miss the train.
    (b) But if she didn't have time, Jeeves could do it.
    (c) Otherwise she would miss her train.

The *she* in (a), (b), and (c) are most naturally interpreted as taking, respectively, *Audrey*, *Sue*, and *Helen* as external antecedents, for no other than cognitive reasons.

whose antecedent A_2 contains P_1. Then to say that the denotation of A_1 must be found first so that P_1 can take it over will not work because in order to fix $d[A_1]$ all material under A_1 must be interpreted and this material contains P_2 whose denotation depends on A_2, but A_2 contains P_1 again. We are thus caught in a vicious circle and no interpretation will get off the ground at all. For example:

(126) The girl who got them liked the flowers that were sent her.

This apparent paradox is solved if it is assumed (as we do) that pronouns appear in Semantic Analysis as empty terms and not as their antecedents (pronouns are not a 'laziness' phenomenon), and, furthermore, that AP contains the provisions for tentative assignments of addresses to pronouns and to full lexical definite terms, whereby the tentative or provisional denotations are confirmed if consistency is achieved.

This is illustrated as follows. We have assumed that lexical definite NPs denote addresses that have either been set up in previous discourse or can be supplied *post hoc* on grounds of background knowledge. They select the right address on the basis of their lexical material. Thus, taking (126) as an example, there must be a discourse address d_1 characterized at least by the predicates "girl" and "got the flowers that were sent her". Likewise, there must be an address d_2 characterized at least by the predicates "flower" and "were sent to d_1". More precisely:

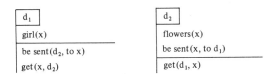

One can imagine these addresses having been set up on the basis of some preceding discourse such as:

(127) There was a girl. She was sent flowers. She got the flowers.

However, neither of the two main NPs in (126) matches either of the addresses completely: *the girl who got them* matches d_1 but for the pronoun *them*, which does not match d_2 in any lexical sense. If the pronoun can be made to denote d_2, however, then indeed there is no obstacle left to letting *the girl who got them* denote d_1. So we provisionally assign d_1 to *the girl who got them*, and, likewise, d_2 is provisionally assigned to *them*. Now take the other main NP: *the flowers that were sent her*. Here an analogous complication arises: *her* does not match d_1 lexically, but could still denote d_1, and we provisionally assign d_2 to *the flowers that were sent her*. Now we are in a quandary since neither of the two NPs is assigned a definitive address. But if *them* is made to denote d_2 and *her* d_1, all is well.

So why don't we cut the knot and make the assignments definitive? This is precisely what we will do, but we must first ascertain if such assignments do not violate any structural condition on anaphoric relatedness between the pronouns in question and their antecedents. In this case there is no worry: *the girl who got them* precedes (and commands) its anaphor *her*, and *the flowers that were sent her*, though it follows its anaphor *them*, is not commanded by it. The pronouns in question are of the denoting kind, as appears from the possibility of epithet substitution:

(128) The girl who got the ruddy things liked the flowers that were sent the creature.

Note that the Bach–Peters paradox does not occur in cases where, unlike (126) or (128), the pronoun is part of its own antecedent, as is the case with *her* in:

(129) a. The girl who got the flowers that were sent her, liked them.

or with *he* in:

(129) b. The man for whom Ann bought the book he liked was ungrateful.

Here the pronouns in question are the surface representatives of the *ruled variable* under the DD-operator of the term in question. And they occur in *indirect relative clauses*, i.e. relative clauses attached to an antecedent t′ which is part of the lexical material of a term t. As was shown in section 2.2, ruled variables in indirect relative clauses manifest themselves as overt pronouns, and, if they are unaccented, they *must* be interpreted as ruled variables, and cannot be interpreted as 'loose' denoting pronouns (represented in SA as "p"). Thus, *the girl who got the flowers that were sent her* corresponds to the SA-term:

(130) $x_i : {}_S[girl(x_i)], {}_S[get(x_i, x_j : {}_S[flowers(x_j)], {}_S[be\ sent(x_j, to\ x_i)])]$

The italicized x_i must, if the corresponding surface pronoun is unaccented, be a ruled variable, ruled by the DD-operator x_i heading the whole term. It cannot be x_j, since if it were, the surface pronoun would be a marked reflexive (*themselves*). So it must be ruled by the x_i-operator.

It should be noted that such pronouns, representing ruled variables in indirect relative clauses, are denoting pronouns, unlike their bound counterparts in indirect relative clauses under a quantified term. This appears, again, from the possibility of epithet substitution:

(129) c. The man for whom Ann bought the book the nitwit liked was ungrateful.

Here again, the only reading admitted if *the nitwit* is unaccented is the reading where *the nitwit* functions as a ruled variable within the definite NP headed by *the man*.

Note, likewise, that in SA-representations the symbol "p" is used only for denoting pronouns but that, on the other hand, not all denoting pronouns are represented by "p". Ruled variable pronouns, i.e. pronouns in indirect relative clauses (or reduced indirect relative clauses) in definite NPs, are denoting pronouns but they are not represented by "p", obviously, precisely because they correspond with ruled variables.

The resolution of the anaphora relation of ruled variable pronouns is now simple. Since unstressed pronouns in indirect relative clauses under definite NPs *must* be interpreted as ruled variable pronouns, the anaphora resolution is thereby given: their antecedent is their own variable ruler, i.e. the definite NP within which they are ruled. Their interpretation is an automatic part in the denotation function for lexical NPs. Thus, the complex definite NP *the girl who got the flowers that were sent her* will automatically denote the address d_1 set up as a result of the little discourse (127). No separate procedure of anaphora resolution is required. It is for this reason that cases like (129a)–(c) are not instances of the Bach–Peters paradox, at least not in our treatment of pronouns, and the provision in AP for tentative assignments is not needed here.

We can now proceed towards a formulation of the Assignment Procedure proper. It starts with an initial instruction I, to decide whether the lexical or the pronominal procedure is to be followed for any given definite term t under treatment. It ends with the final instruction F assigning the proper address, unless the procedure has ended in "BLOCK", which indicates that no assignment is made and t remains uninterpreted, with the result that its whole sentence remains uninterpreted.

AP takes as input SA-representations of sentences, but with the pronominal terms unspecified. In the examples given below to illustrate the working of AP the pronominal terms are represented by the symbol α, indexed if necessary. The result of AP is then twofold: not only will every occurrence of α be replaced by a (ruled or bound) variable or by "p"; every occurrence of "p" will also be assigned a discourse address. The total result of AP on t is indicated by "AP[t]"; the assignment of an address to t is indicated as "d[t]".

Although the input of AP is SA-representations, AP itself can 'look into' the grammar of the language concerned, and it will have to do so at various stages. In particular, occurrences of α where α corresponds to an unaccented non-reflexive pronoun in a surface structure indirect relative clause (or relative adjunct) under a definite or quantified term, and agreeing in gender and number with the head of that term, will immediately be replaced by a ruled or bound variable (as the case may be), so that any problem of address assignment for such αs is eliminated forthwith. This element of AP is prefixed to the main body of AP under the name of *Immediate Variable Interpretation*. These pronouns thus do not stand in the way of immediate definitive lexical address assignment. For example, the surface sentence (131a), with its unfinished SA (131b):

(131) a. A man who bought the book he liked paid for it.

b. $\exists 1(\hat{} x_1(pay(x_1, for \alpha_1)), \hat{} x_1(man(x_1), buy(x_1, x_2:(book(x_2),$
    $like(\alpha_2, x_2)))))$

will immediately have its α_2 replaced by the bound variable x_1 since it corresponds to the unaccented pronoun *he* in the indirect relative clause (*that*) *he liked* under the existentially quantified term headed by *a man*, and *he* agrees in gender and number with *a man*. Now only α_1 need be processed by AP.

We say that a term t *matches* an address d_n *lexically* if the predicate material of t, $P(t)$, agrees with what is found under d_n, with all ruled variables in the proper places. We say that a term t *matches* d_n *provisionally* if $P(t)$ contains one or more terms t_u which do not match d_n though all other material does. In the position corresponding to t_u, d_n will be found to contain either its own ruled variable or an address name, d_k. If the former, AP checks if t_u can be made to denote d_n; if the latter, AP checks if t_u can be made or seen to denote d_k. For example, in (129c) above, assuming the presence of an address d_n containing the information "$man(x)$, $buy(d_k, d_m, for x)$", an address d_k for the person called "Ann", and an address d_m with "$book(x)$, $like(d_n, x)$", the expression *the nitwit* prevents the term *the book the nitwit liked* from matching immediately the address d_m. But it matches d_m provisionally. AP now checks if the expression *the nitwit* can be made to denote the address d_n, which is mentioned under d_m in the appropriate place. Rule L-2 enables the interpreter to do so, provided there is sufficient cognitive backing for the addition of "$nitwit(x)$" to the provisionally assigned d_n. Provisional assignments are crucial in the solution of Bach–Peters paradox cases. Provisional address assignments are marked thus: $d[t] =_p d_n$.

The term *lexical* is used in connection with pronouns to cover conditions of gender and number agreement, and other possible general category indications carried by the pronoun.

Whenever the symbol "t" is used in AP, it refers to the definite NP-term under treatment. "D" stands for the domain in question. "G" stands for the grammar of the language in question. The instruction "→" is a traffic direction of the "go-to" kind. The order in which AP proceeds corresponds to the order of preference in the interpretation of pronouns. That is, the first option is always the preferred one. Only if cognitive factors are allowed to override an option, is there another possible, but less preferred, interpretation.

AP applies to the terms of a sentence (S-structure) in a hierarchical order, starting with the terms of the highest predicate that has one or more definite terms as arguments, and descending to the embedded predicates, always in the order: subject, object, indirect object. Track is kept of assignments made, so that terms that have already been interpreted because of cross-references (in particular anaphoric cross-references) can be skipped. The *Assignment Procedure* (AP) now runs as follows:[18]

Preliminary: Apply the *Immediate Variable Interpretation Procedure:* any occurrence of α which corresponds to an unaccented non-reflexive pronoun in a surface structure indirect relative clause or relative adjunct under a definite or quantified term and agreeing in gender and number with the head of that term is replaced by the variable ruled or bound by the term in question.

I: Check if t is *Lexical* → L-1
                  Pronominal → P-1

L-1: Check if some d_n (or the provisional d_n) is matched by $P(t)$.
       If *Yes* → F
       If *No* → L-2
       If *Provisionally* → L-4

L-2: Check if for some d_n (or the provisional d_n) cognitive backing of D allows for further characterization of d_n by whatever lexical material in $P(t)$ fails to match d_n.
       If *Yes* → F
       If *No* → L-3

L-3: Check if cognitive backing of D allows for the insertion *post hoc* of a d_n matching $P(t)$.
       If *Yes* → F
       If *No* → BLOCK

L-4: Provisionally assign d_n to t. Take the uninterpreted term t_u and provisionally assign any corresponding address d_k (where d_k may be identical with d_n) to t_u:
       $d[t] =_p d_n$; $d[t_u] =_p d_k$. Apply I to t_u if $d_k \neq d_n$; if $d_k = d_n$ → P-2

P-1: Check if there is a d_n such that $d[t] =_p d_n$.
       If *Yes* → P-4
       If *No* → P-2

P-2: Check if t is *reflexive*. A pronominal t is reflexive just in case:
      (a) t is marked for reflexivity and required to be thus marked by G if P-2 yields "Yes" for an appropriate direct or indirect subject term t_s, and lexical conditions are fulfilled with respect to t_s, OR:

---

[18] I am indebted to Wietske Vonk, Leo Noordman, and Ton Weijters for thorough discussions of earlier versions of AP.

(b) t is not marked for reflexivity and not required by G to be thus marked if P-2 yields "Yes" for an appropriate direct or indirect subject term t_s, and lexical conditions are fulfilled with respect to t_s.

If *Yes*, then $AP[t] = AP[t_s]; \rightarrow F_2$
If *No* $\rightarrow$ P-3

P-3: Check if t is a *bound variable*. A pronominal t is a bound variable just in case:

(a) t is the only non-lexical term in an S_x of a set-denoting term, and lexical conditions are fulfilled with respect to the head of the quantified term in Surface Structure, OR:

(b) t is a term in any S-structure under a set-denoting term, and lexical conditions are fulfilled with respect to the head of the quantified term in Surface Structure, and cognitive backing of D allows for this path to be followed.

If *Yes*, then $AP[t] = AP[x_i]; \rightarrow F_2$
If *No* $\rightarrow$ P-4

P-4: Check if there is a possible *internal definite antecedent* term A_{id}. A pronominal t may take a term u as its A_{id} just in case:

(a) u is a definite term, AND:

(b) t does not both precede and command u in Surface Structure (or u is primary with respect to t because u represents the topic and occurs in a heavy clause) and lexical conditions are fulfilled with respect to u, AND:

(c) cognitive backing of D allows for this path to be followed.

If *Yes*, apply I to A_{id}, if necessary. Now if there is a d_n such that $d[t] =_p d_n \rightarrow$ P-7. Otherwise, for any d_n such that $d[A_{id}] = d_n$ or $d[A_{id}] =_p d_n \rightarrow F$
If *No* $\rightarrow$ P-5

P-5: Check if there is a possible *internal existentially quantified antecedent* term A_{ie}. A pronominal t may take a surface term u as its A_{ie} just in case:

(a) u is existentially quantified, AND:

(b) u precedes and does not command t in Surface Structure, AND:

(c) u is part of an increment unit i(S) immediately preceding the increment unit of t, and lexical conditions are fulfilled with respect to u, AND:

(d) cognitive backing of D allows for this path to be followed.

If *Yes*, then for any d_n such that $i(S) = d_n \rightarrow F$
If *No* $\rightarrow$ P-6

P-6: Check if there is a possible *external antecedent* term A_e. A pronominal t may take a term u as its A_e just in case:

(a) u is a definite term, or u is an existentially quantified surface term, AND:

(b) u is part of an increment unit i(S) which is very recent in D, AND:

(c) cognitive backing of D allows for this path to be followed.

If *Yes*, then for any d_n such that $d[A_e] = d_n$ or $i(S) = d_n \to F$

If *No* $\to$ BLOCK

P-7: Check if $d[A_{id}] = d_n$ or $d[A_{id}] =_p d_n$.

If *Yes* $\to$ F

If *No* $\to$ BLOCK

F: F_1: Assign d_n to t.

F_2: Confirm any previous provisional assignments. CLOSE.

Let us, for the sake of illustration, consider a few examples. We take first sentence (132a) with its (unfinished) SA (132b), in a D containing d_1 and d_2 as follows:[19]

d_1		d_2	
girl(x)		flowers(x)	
be sent(d_2, to x)		be sent(x, to d_1)	

(132) a. The girl got the flowers that were sent to her.

  b. get(x_1: girl(x_1), x_2: flowers(x_2), be sent(x_2, to α))

AP: $t = x_1$ I   -   Lexical $\to$ L-1

  L-1   -   Yes (d_1) $\to$ F

  F   - $d[x_1] = d_1$ CLOSE

  $t = x_2$ I   -   Lexical $\to$ L-1

  L-1   -   Provisionally (d_2) $\to$ L-4

  L-4   - $d[x_2] =_p d_2$

    $d[\alpha] =_p d_1$

  $t = \alpha$ I   -   Pronominal $\to$ P-1

  P-1   -   Yes $\to$ P-4

  P-4   -   Yes: $A_{id} = x_1$; $d[x_1] = d_1 \to F$

  F_1 - $d[\alpha] = d_1$

  F_2 - $d[x_2] = d_2$ CLOSE

NB: "α" in (132b) is replaced by "p" since it is a denoting pronoun which is not a ruled variable.

---

[19] In following up AP through the illustrative examples, definite NPs which are not represented in the (unfinished) SAs as α are named by the *ruling variable* (the ruled variables need no special mention or treatment). Thus, in (132), "x_1" stands for the whole definite NP "x_1: girl(x_1)", i.e. *the girl*.

Now try the Bach-Peters paradox case (126) above, repeated here as (133a), and based on the addresses d_1 and d_2 as given there, i.e. d_1 and d_2 as given for (132) but with "get(x, d_2)" added to d_1, and closure plus "get(d_1, x)" added to d_2:

(133) a. The girl who got them liked the flowers that were sent her.

     b. like(x_1: girl(x_1), get(x_1, α_1), x_2: flowers(x_2, be sent(x_2, to α_2)))

$$\begin{aligned}
&\text{AP: } t = x_1 \quad \text{I} \quad - \quad \text{Lexical} \to \text{L-1} \\
&\qquad\qquad\quad \text{L-1} \; - \; \text{Provisionally } (d_1) \to \text{L-4} \\
&\qquad\qquad\quad \text{L-4} \; - \; d[x_1] =_p d_1 \\
&\qquad\qquad\qquad\qquad\quad d[\alpha_1] =_p d_2
\end{aligned}$$

$$\begin{aligned}
&t = \alpha_1 \quad \text{I} \quad - \quad \text{Pronominal} \to \text{P-1} \\
&\qquad\qquad \text{P-1} \; - \; \text{Yes} \to \text{P-4} \\
&\qquad\qquad \text{P-4} \; - \; \text{Yes: } A_{id} = x_2
\end{aligned}$$

$$\begin{aligned}
&t = x_2 \quad \text{I} \quad - \quad \text{Lexical} \to \text{L-1} \\
&\qquad\qquad \text{L-1} \; - \; \text{Provisionally } (d_2) \to \text{L-4} \\
&\qquad\qquad \text{L-4} \; - \; d[x_2] =_p d_2 \\
&\qquad\qquad\qquad\qquad d[\alpha_2] =_p d_1
\end{aligned}$$

$$\begin{aligned}
&t = \alpha_2 \quad \text{I} \quad - \quad \text{Pronominal} \to \text{P-1} \\
&\qquad\qquad \text{P-1} \; - \; \text{Yes} \to \text{P-4} \\
&\qquad\qquad \text{P-4} \; - \; \text{Yes: } A_{id} = x_1; d[x_1] \\
&\qquad\qquad\qquad\qquad\qquad =_p d[\alpha_2] = d_1 \to \text{P-7} \\
&\qquad\qquad \text{P-7} \; - \; \text{Yes} \to \text{F} \\
&\qquad\qquad F_1 \quad - \; d[\alpha_2] = d_1 \\
&\qquad\qquad F_2 \quad - \; d[x_2] = d_2 \\
&\qquad\qquad\qquad\qquad\quad d[\alpha_1] = d_2 \\
&\qquad\qquad\qquad\qquad\quad d[x_1] = d_1 \text{ CLOSE}
\end{aligned}$$

NB: "α_1" and "α_2" are replaced by "p_1" and "p_2", respectively, in (133b).

Now consider:

(134) a. The man who loved himself was vain.

     b. vain(x_1: man(x_1), love(x_1, α))

with the given address:

$$\begin{aligned}
&\text{AP: } t = x_1 \quad \text{I} \quad - \quad \text{Lexical} \to \text{L-1} \\
&\qquad\qquad\quad \text{L-1} \; - \; \text{Provisionally } (d_3) \to \text{L-4} \\
&\qquad\qquad\quad \text{L-4} \; - \; d[x_1] =_p d_3 \\
&\qquad\qquad\qquad\qquad\quad d[\alpha] =_p d_3 \to \text{P-2}
\end{aligned}$$

P-2 - Yes. So $d[\alpha] = d[x_1] \rightarrow F_2$
F_2 - $d[\alpha] = d_3$
$d[x_1] = d_3$ CLOSE ("α" is rewritten as "x_1")

Suppose that, instead of (134a), the sentence had been:

(134) c. The man who loved it was vain.

Its unfinished SA would be identical to that of (134a), i.e. (134b). Let the given D consist of d_3 as given above, and not contain anything that would count as an external antecedent for *it*. Now the application of AP is identical to the one just given up to P-2. The answer to P-2 is "No": *it* is not marked for reflexivity whereas it should be, given the presence of d_3 and the absence of any address, real or to be supplied *post hoc*, identical to d_3 but for the second predicate, which would have to be "love(x, d_i)", where d_i would be a proper address for *it*. In other words, the "appropriate direct subject term t_s" mentioned in P-2 is, in this case, obligatory for proper interpretation: it must be the relative pronoun *who* heading the relative clause of (134a) or (134c). Now, from P-2 onwards, AP runs as follows:

P-2 - No $\rightarrow$ P-3
P-3 - No $\rightarrow$ P-4
P-4 - No $\rightarrow$ P-5
P-5 - No $\rightarrow$ P-6
P-6 - No $\rightarrow$ BLOCK

Hence, in a D as specified, (134c) is not interpretable.

For the following sentence AP has little work to do:

(135) a. Everyone who loves himself is vain.
b. $\forall(\hat{\ }x_1(vain(x_1)), \hat{\ }x_1(love(x_1, \alpha)))$

This is interpretable without any specific D (i.e. it is an 'eternal' sentence). The only term to be processed by AP is α, since all other terms are either set-denoting terms or bound variables not overtly represented by a pronoun.

AP: $t = \alpha$ I - Pronominal $\rightarrow$ P-1
P-1 - No $\rightarrow$ P-2
P-2 - Yes. So $AP[\alpha] = AP[x_1] \rightarrow F_2$
F_2 - CLOSE ("α" is rewritten as "x_1")

The "appropriate" subject term t_s, required by P-2 for the answer "Yes", can only be x_1, and the surface form of α, *himself*, fulfils the morphological and lexical conditions for being the reflexive of x_1.

Finally, consider:

(136) a. Some American expects that he will win.
b. $\exists 1(\hat{\ }x_1(expect(x_1, win(\alpha))), \hat{\ }x_1(American(x_1)))$

No specific D is presupposed (at least not for the interpretation of the pronoun). Again, the only term to be processed is α, all other terms being bound variables or set-denoting terms.

AP: $t = \alpha$ I   –   Pronominal $\rightarrow$ P-1
                   P-1 –   No $\rightarrow$ P-2
                   P-2 –   Yes (indir. refl.). So AP$[\alpha]$ = AP$[x_1]$ $\rightarrow$ F$_2$
                   F$_2$ –   CLOSE ("α" is rewritten as "x_1")

The semantics can now do its work, and the following address will be set up:

$$d_4$$
$$American(x)$$
$$expect(x, win(x))$$

As regards the psycholinguistic aspects of AP we may remark the following. Clearly, AP only gives half of the picture, since it sketches a procedure for the comprehension of pronouns, not for their production. This choice is not entirely arbitrary. Let it be accepted that the question of how speakers go about actually formulating their thoughts so that these can be cast in the format of an appropriate SA to be transformed into a regular sentence, is still so far beyond our powers of description and explanation that it is wise to let it rest for the moment. Assuming, however, that a speaker has actually cast a thought in the format of a proper SA to be transformed into a surface sentence, there will be no α-occurrence in the SA in question, assuming the speaker is not puzzled by the very words he is going to utter. Moreover, in so far as the SA contains p-occurrences, these have all been assigned the proper denotations in the discourse domain that is being built up. Given all this, the grammar can function without a hitch and no separate problem area is in sight.

Not so, however, for the comprehension side. Here the listener must reconstruct, as closely as possible, what the speaker intended. He must build up, in his own mind, the bit of domain structure that the speaker has just given expression to. Now pronouns can be puzzling, and often guesses have to be made, especially when the speaker has not been too careful to take the listener's interpretative problems into account. (It is a well-known fact that children often need some time to acquire the skill and the (cultural) habit of expressing themselves in such a fashion that their listeners can interpret the messages sent out by the children with minimal ambiguity. In particular, it is well known that children tend to overuse pronouns with external antecedents, thereby creating massive interpretative ambiguity in their speech. They for themselves, of course, know precisely what they mean.) It is thus clear that there is a special problem area of pronoun comprehension, as distinct from production. It is this problem area that the Assignment Procedure is intended to broach.

5
Intensionality and subdomains

5.1 Intensionality revisited

So far we have occupied ourselves in principle only with presuppositions and anaphoric relations within one single domain, the truth-domain. We shall now turn to the question of subdomains and the phenomenon of suggested or invited references, or, as we have called them, mere prejections. We shall do so in the context of the notion of intensionality, because this notion plays a central part in the theories of meaning and reference that have been developed to date, and also because the related facts, the facts of intensionality, are both centrally important and inadequately described and observed in these theories.

Frege discovered that there are contexts where co-extensive definite terms cannot freely stand in for each other *salva veritate*. That is, Leibniz's principle of substitution of co-extensive terms *salva veritate* seems to break down in these cases. This is troublesome, since if truth comes about as a result of the n-tuple of term extensions being a member of the extension set of the predicate, then it should never make any difference whether some given extension is called by this or by that name. Frege was the first (1892) to see that Leibniz's substitution principle was not a priori but testable, and he found that, on the face of it, it failed. It fails in particular whenever a definite term occurs in a clause describing a *thought* entertained by a person mentioned in the text or the sentence, as in:

(1) Helen believes that Jack L. is a spy.

Let the person described as *Jack L*, be identical with the person listed in the telephone directory as *J. Lewis*, and known to the world as such, or as Jack Lewis. Helen, however, has never heard of Jack Lewis, but she has read in the morning paper that some Jack L. has been arrested on a national security charge. Now, although (1) may be true, it is highly unlikely that (2) is also true:

(2) Helen believes that J. Lewis is a spy.

Yet the terms *Jack L.* and *J. Lewis* refer to the same person and are thus co-extensive. If Leibniz's principle were valid in so simple a way, (1) and (2) should always have the same truth-value.

Frege's answer consisted in adopting the old distinction between extension and intension, in his terms "Bedeutung" or reference, and "Sinn" or sense, and subsequently applying it systematically to (utterances of) sentences as well as to terms. The Sinn, sense or intension of a sentence is the thought schema underlying it. The Bedeutung, reference or extension of an utterance of a sentence is its truth-value, in Frege's analysis. As regards terms, their Sinn, sense or intension is the procedure whereby their Bedeutung, reference or extension is to be located. However, says Frege, when a sentence does not stand on itself but is a term under a thought-describing predicate, then the extension of that sentence is not its truth-value but the actual thought underlying its utterance. (The distinction made here between utterance tokens and sentence-types is not, or hardly, made by Frege himself. It is, however, entirely legitimate since senses, being defined for a language, must be defined linguistically, but references only in some context of actual use. If this is so, then Frege's "thought" underlying a sentence as its sense can only be a thought schema, a type, that is, not a token. But the "thought" which is the extension of a sentence embedded under a thought-relating predicate cannot but be a thought token, i.e. an actual thought.)

The solution now consists in the fact that if substitution of co-extensive terms is made in a sentential structure embedded as a term under a thought-relating predicate, then the underlying thought has changed for that sentential term, and hence its extension has changed. The sentential term before the substitution has a different extension from that term after the substitution. Hence, we have not carried out Leibnizian substitution of co-extensive terms at all. No wonder that truth-values change. (The assumption is that extensions of sentences are built up from the extensions of the component parts, and that likewise the intensions of sentences are built up from the intensions of the component parts: Frege's celebrated compositionality principle.)

Frege's solution has proved very powerful. He meant it to apply to contexts created by *thought-relating* predicates (1892: 37). By the time, however, that his analysis began to attract the attention of the philosophical world, it was decidedly unfashionable to operate with such mentalistic notions as thoughts. Consequently, this element in Frege's thinking was simply discarded as being a nineteenth-century blemish, and whatever formal underpinnings were constructed to elaborate Frege's system (Carnap 1947; Montague 1974) were based on a theoretical construct 'intensional contexts', meant simply to cover all contexts where substitutivity fails and where existential entailment[1] is

---

[1] The normal term is "existential generalization". We have, however, already used this term (section 3.2.4), and reinterpreted it as "denotational entailment" induced by the occurrence of the definite determiner, and entailing 'being', not necessarily existence. In order to avoid confusion we speak of "existential entailment" when real existence is involved.

blocked, i.e. the entailment "there exists an x such that F(x)" from a sentence of the type "the x such that F(x) Gs" (F and G are predicates). These intensional contexts comprise, besides the Fregean ones, a few more, in particular those under modals, added by Quine (1953):[2]

(3) a. 9 is necessarily greater than 7.
   b. The number of planets is necessarily greater than 7.
(4) a. Necessarily if there is life on the evening star, there is life on the morning star.
   b. Necessarily if there is life on the evening star, there is life on the evening star.

Although, says Quine, *The number of planets is 9* is a true statement, substitution of *the number of planets* for *9* turns the true (3a) into the false (3b). Moreover, says Quine, from (3a) or (3b) it does not follow that there is a number which is necessarily greater than 7. Likewise for (4): although the evening star is in fact identical with the morning star, substitution turns (4a), which according to Quine is false, into the true (4b). And neither (4a) nor (4b) license the entailment that there is an evening star such that necessarily, if there is life on it, there is life on it (or the morning star).

Since Quine's paper (1953) was published, it has been universally accepted that modal contexts block free substitution of co-extensive terms. A closer look at the facts, however, quickly reveals that matters are not that simple. Quine's observations on the intensional character of the modalities of necessity and possibility are erroneous, and this cannot fail to have consequences for semantic theory.

It must be said, in fairness to Quine, that he limits his pronouncements on the referentially opaque character of the modalities to what he calls "strict" necessity (1953: 143), with a reference to Lewis (1918). He then says, still on p. 143:

> The general idea of strict modalities is based on the putative notion of *analyticity* as follows: a statement of the form 'Necessarily...' is true if and only if the component statement which 'necessarily' governs is analytic, and a statement of the form 'Possibly...' is false if and only if the negation of the component statement which 'possibly' governs is analytic.

Thus, in this sense of necessity, (3a) is equivalent with: "9 > 7" *is analytic*. In terms of possible world semantics one says: "9 > 7" *is true in all possible worlds*.

Yet this is not the sense of any natural language necessity operator. As is well known, the natural language modalities of possibility and necessity fall

---

[2] Surprisingly, Dowty, Wall and Peters (1981: 142) attribute the view that modal contexts are intensional to Frege 1892 – erroneously dated 1893 by the authors. Frege, however, never touched modalities. It was Quine (1953) who brought them into the intensionality picture.

apart in two main classes, the class of *epistemic* modalities and that of *agentive* modalities (the latter are known by a variety of names: *root modals* being the commonest in linguistics). Agentive modalities semantically contain a 'hidden agent' bringing about the necessity, as in *You must leave now*, where either the speaker or some other person imposes his will on the addressee. Epistemic necessity expresses the speaker's insight that a given proposition A follows deductively or inductively from a set of known facts: given these facts it cannot but be the case that A. Roughly speaking, if A's truth has not been established or accepted yet, the modal verb *must* is appropriate in English (besides the use of *necessarily*), as in:

(5) Harry must be at home by now./Harry is necessarily at home by now.

But if the truth of A has been established, and the comment is that A is a necessary truth, then only the sentence adverb *necessarily* is appropriate; the use of *must* is then quaint:

(6) !9 must be greater than 7.

In these cases, some theory is presupposed that generates necessity statements for statements (propositions) expressed in some object language. For (3a) this theory is (meta-)arithmetic, according to which arithmetic equations, when true, are necessarily true. There is no natural language sense of either *must* or *necessarily*, however, whereby the proposition in the scope of the operator is said to be 'analytic' (or true in all possible worlds). This analysis is a philosophical artefact, and is thus irrelevant for natural language semantics.

In fact, modal statements are not true or false *per se*, as Quine has it, but contingently, like most other statements in language. If we take (3a) to be true *tout court*, it is because we have some (perhaps not too explicit) notion that arithmetic is to do with a priori necessity, and that its truths are necessary truths in that sense. But there is no comparable way in which (4a) can be said to be true or false. It is no doubt so that the component proposition in (4a) is not analytic, nor true in all possible worlds (trusting that that notion is clear enough); nor is there any general theory of heavenly bodies generating necessity statements about them. But (4a) is perfectly interpretable under the ordinary epistemic necessity operator, and it is true, for example, for all cases where it is known that the morning star is the evening star: that being so, if there is life on the one, there must be life on the other. For us, therefore, who know that the two names refer to the same planet, (4a) is true, and not false, as Quine has it.

Moreover, the expression *the number of planets* in (3b) is not at all co-extensive with the expression *9*. And the statement *The number of planets is 9* is not at all an identity statement, but a statement assigning a value to a parameter, as in *The temperature is 90 degrees*. A little linguistic experimenting soon shows the difference with identity statements like *Jack L. is J. Lewis*.

One says naturally *90 degrees is a lot for those plants*, but not **The temperature is a lot for those plants*, or *9 is correct as the number of planets*, but not **The number of planets is correct as the number of planets*. Or, although we say naturally *Jack L. is identical with J. Lewis*, we do not say naturally **The number of planets is identical with 9*. Many more examples of linguistic differences between identity statements and value-assigning statements can be given.

Quine has, moreover, fallen victim to an ambiguity in the word *number*, an ambiguity which it shares with the Latin *numerus* and the Greek ἀριθμόσ. It has been known traditionally (Aristotle, *Physics* IV.219.b; Buridan, *Tractatus de Infinito*, 59 verso, Minerva, Frankfurt 1964) that *number* denotes either a unit in arithmetic ("a mental faculty of separation by which we count things so that we know how many there are" – Buridan), or the things themselves that are counted, as in *A number of people laughed*. There is a third sense, not known or distinguished traditionally, viz. "cardinality of a set". Some languages disambiguate, at least in part. German *Zahl*, Dutch *getal*, or Swedish *tal* mean "unit of arithmetic"; these languages have the words *Anzahl, aantal* and *antal*, respectively for reference to either the cardinality of a set or the set itself. Quine's confusion is between the sense "cardinality of a set" and "unit of arithmetic". His pair of examples (3a) and (3b) thus lacks relevance in the context of substitution of co-extensive terms.

We must conclude, on the basis of impartial inspection of linguistic facts, that substitutivity holds for the epistemic modalities when it is known that the terms in question are co-extensive.[3] On the other hand, possibility blocks existential entailment. Although a sentence like:

(7) Harry's dog may be ill./Harry's dog is possibly ill.

strongly suggests that Harry has a dog, and although we have a strong intuition of contradiction when it is said that,

(8) a. !Harry has no dog, but his dog may be ill.

the conclusion that (7) licenses the entailment that Harry has a dog would be too strong, in view of examples like:

(8) b. Harry may have a dog, and his dog may be ill.

---

[3] Notice that substitutivity never holds when the embedded clause is itself an identity statement. The sentence

(i) William M. must be W. Murphy.

is true under very different conditions from those that make

(ii) William M. must be William M.

true. This fact will be commented upon amply below.

where the second conjunct, which is semantically identical with (7), clearly does not entail that Harry has a dog. (What might be taken to underlie this curious behaviour of the possibility operator in natural language, will be discussed in section 5.2.)

It is not our business here to investigate to what extent Quine's argument, which is ontological and not linguistic, suffers from these objections. If we have pulled a rug from underneath his (intensional) feet it was not to trip him: what we want is the rug, not the destruction of his argument. Our quarrel is more with the tradition of formal semantics, where Quine's observations have become the stock-in-trade of any exposé on intensionality, and not so much with Quine's own plea against quantifying into modal contexts – although, in a wider perspective, it is difficult to see why such a ban should be enforced.

In our theory, existential entailment correlates straightforwardly with the extensional character of the predicate in question: if a definite description is a term under a predicate which is extensional with respect to terms in that position, then existential entailment is an entailment of any sentence figuring this predicate, and of any sentence entailed by such a sentence. But if a definite description occurs in a non-extensional position, such as the position of object under to the verb *look for*, then the entailment is blocked (though the entailment of "existential generalization", which is really an entailment of being and is induced by the very fact that a definite term is used, remains unaffected – see section 3.2.4 above):

(9) Simon is looking for the man who killed his cat.

neither entails that Simon has (had) a cat, nor does it entail that anyone killed the animal, if animal there was.

In general, our theory has no problems with the notion of extensionality: a predicate is extensional with respect to a term-position t_i just in case it has a precondition of existence for any referent of a definite term in position t_i. This accounts for the validity of existential entailment (which is nothing but the formulation of the presupposition of existence generated by the existential precondition). The general definition of truth, moreover (i.e. $P(t_1, \ldots, t_n)$ is true just in case $\langle \rho(t_1), \ldots, \rho(t_n) \rangle \in \sigma(P)$ – see section 3.2.4 above, in particular p. 253), guarantees the validity of substitution of co-extensive terms *salva veritate*, trivially, for all cases where there really is a $\rho(t_i)$. The standard notion of intensionality, however, cannot be used. This is because standard theories of formal semantics oversimplify the facts. It is clearly not the case that all contexts where substitutivity holds are extensional. Nor is the set of contexts where substitutivity holds co-extensive with the set of contexts where existential entailment holds. On the contrary, there is a set of contexts where both substitutivity and existential entailment hold. These are the extensional contexts. But outside this set we have contexts where substitutivity holds but not existential entailment; we have contexts where existential entailment holds but not substitutivity; and we have contexts where neither holds. Thus, if we take substitutivity and existential entailment as criteria, we have a complete matrix on the binary features "S" (substitutivity) and "E" (existential entailment), which are thus seen to be independent properties:

$$\alpha: [+S, +E] \qquad \beta: [+S, -E] \qquad \gamma: [-S, +E] \qquad \delta: [-S, -E]$$

The contexts involved, other than those of α, will normally be created by predicates which take an embedded clause as one of their terms. The "context" in question consists of the whole remainder of the sentence around the definite term in question. We thus face the problem of accounting for the fact that definite terms occurring in embedded clauses sometimes preserve their properties of substitutivity and existential generalization, and sometimes do not. It is clear that this problem is similar to the well-known projection problem for presuppositions. That problem consists in accounting for the fact that presuppositions generated in embedded clauses sometimes survive as presuppositions of the whole sentence, and sometimes do not (or survive in a weakened form as what we call "mere prejections"). The problem here is to do with the survival of the properties of substitutivity and of existential entailment. The two problems are linked up in that in all cases where existential entailment survives, so does existential presupposition (except for the verb *exist*), and hence all presuppositions. But let us take a look at the material first.

The set of contexts α is extensional, and the other sets are not. It would be too simple, however, to label them all "intensional". Moreover, some predicates, in particular the epistemic modalities, wander from one category to another, depending on certain conditions of use.

Let us give a few illustrations. The set α contains all contexts of predicates with respect to the terms with regard to which they are extensional. The predicate *hit*, for example, creates an extensional context for its subject as well as for its object. But the predicate *adore* creates an extensional context only for its subject; its object does not stand in an extensional context. Moreover, α contains those contexts created by the epistemic necessity predicate *must* where the embedded clause taken by itself creates an extensional context and an identity statement is known to be true for the term in question (except when the embedded clause is itself an identity statement; this, however, will be seen to follow from the condition that the embedded clause by itself must create an extensional context: the identity predicate is non-extensional with respect to both its terms).

A special problem is created by the verb *exist*, which seems, according to the criteria adopted so far, to be extensional with respect to its only term, its subject. We have already, in section 3.2.4, had occasion to point out that this cannot be so: if it were, then the minimal negation of *exist* with respect to a subject term *a* would *entail* that *a* does not exist but *presuppose* that *a* exists, which is not compatible with our theory. We have, therefore, defined *exist* as a predicate which is non-extensional with respect to its subject term (see (36f) in section 3.2.4). However, under the definition given of existential entailment - "G(the x such that F(x))" $\models$ "there exists an x such that F(x)" - *exist* should be marked [+ E] since, e.g., *The conspirator exists* does indeed entail *There is an x such that x is a conspirator*. This means that if we accept *exist* as a verb marked [+ S, + E], i.e. as fully extensional, we can no longer say that [+ E] coincides with the inducing of existential presupposition, and we complicate our notion of extensionality.

This complication, however, is naturally avoided when we apply the three-valued apparatus developed in chapter 3. This is done by redefining the notion of existential entailment as follows, thereby making it a technical term specific to our theory:

If both "G⟨the x such that F(x)⟩" and "∼G⟨the x such that F(x)⟩" entail "there exists an x such that F(x)", then, and only then, the predi-cate "G" is said to induce an *existential entailment* with regard to the term "the x such that F(x)". (The angled brackets indicate "context".)[4]

Now we have eliminated *exist* from the class α, as we should, since it now has the feature [− E]. It also has the feature [+ S], so that it will fall under β.

The set β contains, besides *exist*, the identity predicate "=". We have known since Frege that this predicate allows for substitution *salva veritate*, though what is contingent truth when the terms are different becomes necessary truth when the terms are the same as a result of substitution. Yet it does not allow for existential entailment, as is clear from cases like

(10) Zeus is Jupiter.

which is true although the deity in question is unlikely to exist. The set β contains, moreover, those contexts created by epistemic possibility (*may*), where the embedded clause taken by itself creates an extensional context and an identity statement is known to be true involving the term in question.

The category β contains, moreover, all those predicates that are non-extensional, or intensional, with respect to one or more individual-denoting

---

[4] We should be a little more precise here. In fact, the definition of "context" must be made recursive: the angled brackets indicate (a) the context created by the term *t* being an argument to G, and (b) the context created by *t* being an argument to a predicate "H" in a sentential term under G, but only if H licenses an existential entailment with respect to *t*. The notion of existential entailment now coincides essentially with that of existential presupposition (the odd case out being conjunction: "*B and A_B*" may license an existential entailment (if *B* is an existential statement), but, as has been shown in section 3.3 above, it will not presuppose anything). It is important now that it be ensured that wherever presuppositions are preserved (or weakened into mere prejections), so are existential entailments.

terms, such as *look for, covet, discuss* (see section 5.3.5). These preserve substitutivity for the terms in question because (contrary to much of current philosophical opinion) they refer to uniquely identifiable individuals even when those individuals do not exist but are defined in some thought-domain. They do, of course, not allow for existential entailment with respect to the terms in question, precisely because they are non-existensional with respect to these terms.

The set γ contains the factive predicates, with respect to their factive clauses, as well as entailing predicates such as *imply, entail, therefore, so*. The factive predicates were spotted by Frege (1892: 37), who must have been the first to spot them. He gives the following, rather circumstantial, example (1892: 47):

(11) Bebel is under the illusion that the return of Alsace-Lorraine will appease France's lust for revenge.

(The predicate *be under the illusion that* (German: *wähnen, dass*) can be termed "antifactive" – like other predicates such as *pretend that, lie that* – in that it presupposes not the truth but the falsity of the lower clause.) In (11), Frege says, two thoughts are expressed:

(12) a. Bebel believes that the return of Alsace-Lorraine will appease France's lust for revenge.
  b. The return of Alsace-Lorraine will not appease France's lust for revenge.[5]

In (12a), he continues, the lower clause has the thought inherent in the belief as its extension, but in (12b) the extension is the truth-value, as normally. Thus, the lower clause of (11) really has a double function (1892: 48), with different extensions. And, since the truth-value is not the entire extension of the *that*-clause but only part of it, simple substitution by another proposition with the same truth-value is not possible *salva veritate*. Likewise, he says, with

---

[5] In the translation of Frege 1892 in Geach and Black 1952, the point is missed. Black (ib: 76) translates Frege's example given as (11) above as

(i) Bebel fancies that the return of Alsace-Lorraine would appease France's desire for revenge.

and the sentence corresponding to (12a) as

(ii) Bebel believes that the return of Alsace-Lorraine would appease France's desire for revenge.

These are not very apt translations of the German, since English factive predicates do not take a subjunctive (*would*) in the subordinate clause. The use of *would* in Black's translation is obviously meant to get across the idea that what is said in the lower clause is not true. It is, however, doubtful that *would* can fulfil that function in the sentences given. And even if it can, it does not convey the (anti)factive character of the predicate of the main clause. *Fancy* is not (anti)factive, but *be under the illusion that* is, and it requires no subjunctive in the lower clause.

know, acknowledge, be known that. It is indeed true that substitutivity is blocked under a factive predicate:

(13) a. Don realizes that the Eiffel Tower is in Paris.
b. Don realizes that the highest tower of Europe is in Paris.

Of these, the former may be true and the latter false, of the same Don at the same time.

What struck Frege as peculiar was the fact that, although in extensional contexts truth or falsity is preserved under substitution of co-extensive terms, the status of being an entailment is not. The truth or falsity of a proposition A is not affected by substitution of co-extensive terms in extensional positions, but the fact that A is an entailment of a set of propositions P is affected. In fact, if P entails A, and A differs from B only in that in some extensional position A contains the term a and B has the term b, a and b being co-extensive, then P also entails B provided P contains the identity statement "$a = b$". Otherwise, B will generally not be entailed. Frege did not elaborate this point, however. Had he done so, he would have noticed that entailing predicates like *therefore, so, apparently, entail* block substitutivity in the same way as the factive predicates do. Take the sentence:

(14) Therefore, W. Murphy is Irish.

Let W. Murphy be the same person as some William M. Now, in some discourse, (14) may be true, yet

(15) Therefore, William M. is Irish.

false. The sentential predicate "therefore" has a satisfaction condition for the truth of a sentence *therefore (A)* that A must be entailed by the preceding discourse. If the discourse does not contain the identity statement *William M. is W. Murphy*, it may entail that W. Murphy is Irish, but not that William M. is Irish. In that case, (14) is true, but (15) is false, even though it is true that William M. is Irish. Analogous analyses can be given for *so* and *apparently*.

The set δ (which may be called fully intensional) contains all non-factive thought-relating and volitional predicates (*believe, hope, assume, want, try*), as well as predicates like *promise, say, suggest,* and *probably,* and the logical predicates *or* and *if.* As regards the latter, their lack of substitutivity appears from cases like:

(16) a. Either the morning star is the evening star, or there are ten planets./ If the morning star is not the evening star, there are ten planets.
b. Either the morning star is the morning star, or there are ten planets./ If the morning star is not the morning star, there are ten planets.
(17) a. Either W. Murphy has not been on the phone with William M., or we have a problem./If W. Murphy has been on the phone with William M., we have a problem.

b. Either W. Murphy has not been on the phone with W. Murphy, or we have a problem./If W. Murphy has been on the phone with W. Murphy, we have a problem.

A context need not be too far-fetched for the (a)-sentences to be true and the (b)-sentences to be false. Existential entailment, moreover, fails, as appears from ordinary cases like

(18) a. Either Rupert has no dog, or his dog is called Nero.
b. If Rupert has a dog it is called Nero.

neither of which, clearly, entails that Rupert has a dog. In general, existential generalization holds for disjunctions only if the entailment in question is shared by *both* disjuncts. In most cases this will be because both disjuncts share the same existential presupposition, as in

(19) Rupert's dog is called either Nero or Fido.

which entails that Rupert has a dog, and, as will be shown in section 5.4, also presupposes that Rupert has a dog (since it will be seen to preject "Rupert has a dog").

Note that in this respect disjunction does not run parallel to conditionals. It is not so that if the negation of the antecedent clause of a conditional structure and the (non-negated) consequent share an existential entailment or presupposition, then the whole conditional has that entailment or presupposition. Take the sentence:

(20) a. If Rupert's dog has any tail at all, it is a very short one.

The negated antecedent presupposes, and thus entails, that Rupert has a dog, and so does the consequent. However, (20a) does not entail that Rupert has a dog, because one can say without contradiction, e.g.,

(20) b. Maybe Rupert has no dog. But if he has one, and if his dog has any tail at all, it is a very short one.

It will become clear that all these and related facts follow from the structuring of discourse domains into truth-domains and subdomains. It will also become clear why, although (20a) does not strictly presuppose that Rupert has a dog, it certainly strongly suggests that he has one.

It thus appears that the notion of intensionality is quite a bit more complex than appears from standard treatments in formal semantics. It will also appear that the phenomena observed are naturally interpretable in terms of a system of truth-domains and subdomains. Before, however, we proceed to developing the machinery of subdomains in greater detail, we must take stock of what we have done so far.

The category α, characterized by the features $[+S, +E]$, comprises all normal fully extensional predicates that take denoting terms, but not *exist*.

It also comprises implicative predicates with a sentential object, such as *manage*, *cause*: for any fully extensional clause embedded under these predicates full extensionality is preserved. I.e. for all the definite terms there is substitutivity as well as existential entailment (= presupposition). Moreover, the minimal negation (~) as well as the conjunction *and* fall under α, since they preserve substitutivity for fully extensional embedded sentential terms, and also existential entailment since both preserve presuppositional entailments. Likewise, the predicate of epistemic necessity (*must*) belongs to this class, provided it has been established in the discourse that $a = b$ if a is to stand in for b *salva veritate*. (But epistemic modalities will be discussed in the following section.) The predicate *true* also falls into category α since, clearly, it preserves substitutivity, and also existential entailment: its extension set is formulated in such a way (see (36h) in section 3.2.4) that it preserves the presuppositions of its embedded clause.

We have seen that the category β comprises the identity predicate as well as *exist*. It contains, moreover, the radical negation (≈), which, being presupposition-cancelling, does not preserve existential entailment, though it does preserve substitutivity. It contains, moreover, all predicates that are intensional with respect to one or more individual-denoting terms, as well as the predicate *may*, i.e. epistemic possibility, provided the discourse contains the identity statement "$a = b$" for any pair of co-extensive terms a and b to stand in for each other *salva veritate*. Strictly speaking, therefore, *may* (and *must*) do not belong to β (and α, respectively), but to δ (and γ). But this matter will be looked at in greater detail in the following sections.

The category γ, i.e. [−S, + E], comprises, as we have seen, the entailing predicates (e.g. *imply, entail, so, therefore, apparently*), as well as the factive predicates, and epistemic necessity (*must*). δ consists of all thought-denoting predicates, epistemic possibility (*may*), *or* and *if*.

5.2 The modals

We shall now investigate the seemingly erratic behaviour of the predicates of epistemic necessity and epistemic possibility. Their main representatives in English are the predicates *must* and *necessarily* for necessity, and *may* and *possibly* for possibility. There are other, grammatically conditioned, forms, such as *need* for necessity, or *can* or *can possibly* for possibility, constructed with the bare infinitive and requiring a negative context, being Negative Polarity Items.[6] Moreover, the adjectival predicates *necessary* and *possible* differ from

---

[6] Note that *must* and *may* are Positive Polarity Items. When constructed with minimal negation *must* becomes *need not*, and *may* becomes *can*. When constructed with radical negation (*John must NOT be drunk by now: he hasn't touched a drop the whole day!*) their forms do not change.

the others in that they come closest to what the philosophical tradition wants them to be, but, as we shall see, they continue to differ from that tradition on essential points. We saw in section 5.1 that the predicates of epistemic modality as they occur in language display substitutivity in all cases where the embedded clause does and where it is known that the term in question occurs in a true identity statement, except when that identity statement itself stands under a modal predicate (see note 3 of this chapter). We shall see that these properties adhere to *possible* and *necessary* as well. Thus, in all cases where it is true to say

(21) W. Murphy must be guilty of embezzlement.

it is also true to say

(22) William M. must be guilty of embezzlement.

provided the statement

(23) W. Murphy is William M.

is known to be true. And whenever (21) is false, so is (22), provided (23) is known to be true. The reason, intuitively speaking, is simple: if William M. is known to be the same person as W. Murphy, then if there are compelling reasons to accept that the one is guilty of embezzlement, there are compelling reasons to accept that the other is, precisely because it is known that the one is identical with the other. Or if no such reasons are available with respect to the one, there will be none with respect to the other, for the same reason.

We may extend this observation to the modality of epistemic possibility. If there is justification for saying

(24) W. Murphy may be guilty of embezzlement.

then there is equal justification for saying

(25) William M. may be guilty of embezzlement.

provided (23) is known to be true. And, if (23) is known to be true, then, if there is no justification for saying (24), there is none for saying (25) either.

Remarkably, however, if the embedded clause is an identity statement, as in

(26) William M. must be W. Murphy.

there is a clear intuition that substitutivity does not hold. This goes together with the intuition that if (26) is true it cannot have been established and known yet that the embedded identity statement (23), needed for substitutivity, is true. And when substitution is carried out, so that identical names are used,

(27) William M. must be William M.

the resulting sentence is somehow odd, presumably because, since of course it is true that William M. is William M. (for any x, x = x), there seems no need to say that it *must* be true. Notice that this oddness disappears when we use the more philosophical predicate *necessarily*:

(28) Necessarily, William M. is William M.

We furthermore noticed, in section 5.1, that although existential entail-ment seems licensed from necessity statements, provided the embedded clause licenses this entailment, it must be considered blocked generally from possibility statements. That is, from

(29) Harry's dog must be ill.

one feels entitled to conclude that

(30) Harry has a dog.

But when we take

(31) Harry's dog may be ill.

although there is a strong suggestion that (30) holds true, it would be wrong to conclude that (30) must be considered to follow logically from it. The suggestion (mere prejection) is very strong, also because we have a clear intuition of contradiction when one says

(32) !Harry has no dog, but his dog may be ill.

Yet, it is also possible and quite natural to say

(33) Harry may have a dog, and it may be ill.

which shows that the second conjunct, which is equivalent to (31), cannot have (30) as a logical consequence.

These observations are, for the most part, new and have, therefore, not been taken into account in existing semantic treatments of the modalities. We shall now attempt to give an analysis of the epistemic modalities of neces-sity and possibility in natural language which accounts naturally for the observations made, in terms of the general theory of discourse domains and three-valued presuppositional semantics.

The observations made with respect to *may* and *must* have made it clear that these predicates make reference in their satisfaction conditions to a known set of true statements **T**. For *must*, the assertion is that the embedded proposition p follows from **T**, and for *may* that p is not excluded by **T**. However, **T** is not expressed overtly in a statement of epistemic modality. Its availability is only presupposed in the technical sense of presupposition. This is not an unusual situation. Compare our analysis of *even* given in (115) of section 3.5.3. There is also a great deal of literature about the implicit term with so-called 'vague' gradable adjectives (*big*, *old*, *small*, etc., see section 3.4), which require an implicit reference or comparison class for their truth or falsity with respect to their overt subject term denotation. The same can be said of the agentive modals: when someone is told *You must leave in half an hour*, there is an understood 'agent' or 'factor' causing the obligation. This 'missing agent' (Kraak 1968) cannot be expressed as a Surface Structure term to the modal predicate in question (at least not in English; Dutch expresses the 'hidden agent' effortlessly in a prepositional *van*-phrase, indicating that the agentive modal is originally a passive, with the semantic subject unexpressed in English, but expressed in an agent-phrase in Dutch). Given facts such as these, it makes sense to provide for semantic terms for certain predicates even though these terms are not expressed in the grammatical constructions taken by the predicates in question when they function grammatically as verbs. This is what we shall do with the epistemic modals. Accordingly, the following extension sets can be specified for *must* and *may*, where p ranges over propositions, and T over sets of statements:

(34) $\sigma(must) = \{\langle p, T \rangle$: T is known to be true; T gives rise to the question of the truth-value of p; there is no $T' \supset T$ known to be true and containing p or $\neg p \mid T \models p\}$

(35) $\sigma(may) = \{\langle p, T \rangle$: T is known to be true; T gives rise to the question of the truth-value of p; there is no $T' \supset T$ known to be true and containing p or $\neg p \mid T \not\models \neg p\}$

(For these definitions to be entirely explicit, an account must be provided of what it is for a set of statements to give rise to a question. Such an account, however, transcends the limits of this study: in this respect the analysis remains incomplete. A natural condition for T to give rise to the question of the truth-value of p is that p, $\neg p \notin T$. The last precondition ensures, in addition, that the truth-value of p is also unknown.)

According to (34) and (35), an epistemic modal statement has truth-conditions which include the *availability* of truth-values for certain other statements. This is precisely what makes these modalities *epistemic*: what counts is not so much that there *is* a set of true statements T as that T is known, and thus available. Intuitive judgements (virtually our only empirical basis) seem to support this analysis. It is quite natural, for example, to deny a *must*-statement on grounds of insufficient knowledge:

(36) A: It's eight o'clock. Jim must be in safety now.

B: No, we don't know if he managed to catch the five o'clock plane.

Or a *may*-statement may be true even though there are lots of true statements to be made which entail the falsity of the embedded clause, as long as these statements are not known. Clearly also, a denial of a *must*-statement can be rectified by revealing new information:

(37) A: Alex needn't be guilty. We have no convincing proof yet.
B: I've just heard that he lied about his alibi.
A: Ah well, if that is correct, he must be guilty.

The precondition which specifies that there is no set of known true statements T' such that either p or *not-p* is part of T' explains why it is inappropriate or unacceptable (in the technical sense of discourse acceptability discussed in section 3.3 above) to make a modal statement about something which is already known to be true or false. A discourse of the type exemplified in (38)

(38) a. !W. Murphy is guilty of embezzlement, and he must be guilty of it.
b. !W. Murphy is guilty of embezzlement, and he may be guilty of it.
c. !W. Murphy is not guilty of embezzlement, but he may be guilty of it.

is unacceptable, a fact often noted in the literature, and connected with the similarly unacceptable type of sequence:

(38) d. !W. Murphy is guilty of embezzlement, and he is guilty of that or of manslaughter.

Not much is improved when, instead of *and*, the entailing predicate *therefore* is used, even though (39b) and (39d) represent valid inferences:

(39) a. !W. Murphy is guilty of embezzlement. Therefore, he must be guilty of it.
b. !W. Murphy is guilty of embezzlement. Therefore, he may be guilty of it.
c. !W. Murphy is not guilty of embezzlement. Therefore, he may be guilty of it.
d. !W. Murphy is guilty of embezzlement. Therefore, he is guilty of that or of manslaughter.

No other ploy will help to save such sequences. Thus, (39c) remains unacceptable even if *therefore* is replaced by *yet*. McCawley (1981: 33) makes this observation about disjunction (i.e. the inferential validity but the discourse unacceptability of the additive disjunctive entailment exemplified in (38d) or (39d)), and attributes the "fishiness" of the argument to "the fact that the conclusions that it leads to, while true, are less informative than the premises to which it was applied, and it is misleading to assert something which takes more words to say but is less informative than another thing that you were in a position to assert".

We agree with McCawley only in part. Clearly, the validity of the additive disjunctive entailment, or of the rule *ab esse ad posse*, is not disputed. What is at issue is only the acceptability of the sequences of sentences in question, and we agree that a discourse sequence of premises and a conclusion, where the conclusion is less informative than the one or more premises, is unacceptable. We disagree, however, on the "misleading" character of being less informative than one could be (a line of explanation that smacks rather too much of Grice). As has been said in section 3.3, the criterion of informativeness can be regarded as the most general criterion for discourse acceptability, and it falls into two alternative criteria: the new discourse addition either restricts the set of possible verification domains (Vs) in which the discourse is true, or it provides new information about the V at hand, not yet contained in D. This criterion rules out repetitions as well as contradictions (provided the V-restriction is required to keep the set of Vs for which D is true nonempty). It also provides the rationale for the unacceptability of bits of discourse such as those in (38) or (39).

For *or* the solution is simple: given the discourse increment instruction associated with *or* (section 4.1.5), which says that, for "*A* or *B*", if *B* is excluded then *A* must be added, and vice versa, it follows that both i(*A*) and i(*B*) must be acceptable increments to any D to which i(*A or B*) is added. Hence, if i(*A*) or i(*B*), or i($\neg A$) or i($\neg B$), is already part of D, i(*A*) and i(*B*) are unacceptable. For the modals *may* and *must*, the explanation is similar but not identical. If it is accepted that these modals (but not all others) are specifically designed to help the discourse on towards an answer to the question of the actual truth-value of the embedded proposition, so that either that proposition or its negation can be added, it follows that D must be such that, for "must(*A*)" or "may(*A*)", i(*A*) is an acceptable addition to D, which implies that D must not already contain either i(*A*) or i($\neg A$). This is what is expressed in the preconditions of (34) and (35): if D already contains either *p* or *not-p* (for any proposition *p* under an epistemic modal operator), then there is a set T' ($\supset T$) which contains *p* or *not-p*, and the precondition is violated. Since the precondition requires of D that it does not contain *p*, or *not-p*, D is unfit to accept the increment of the modal statement in question. It is now clear how a speaker who knows for a fact that W. Murphy is guilty of embezzlement can say: "No, he is guilty." to anyone who has just uttered (21) or (24).

There is a further reason, applying especially to *must*, why the provision is needed that the truth-value of the embedded clause is not known, at the moment of utterance. Since, logically speaking, every sentence entails itself, it would follow, without this provision, that as soon as it has been established for some proposition A that it is true, *must*(*A*) would be automatically true as well, which would make the notion of epistemic necessity vacuous. To

avoid this a provision is needed to the effect that **T** in (34) should not contain
A - or else entailment must be defined as a non-reflexive relation.

The analysis given makes us understand why substitutivity is freely applicable under the modals, provided **T** contains the identity statement for the
terms to be substituted. Given (23), for example, whatever is necessary for
William M. is necessary for W. Murphy, and whatever is possible for the one is
possible for the other. If, however, (23) is true but not known to be true,
these modalities do not carry over from one name to another.[7] Nor do they
when (23) is false, even though it is thought to be true. It also follows that
substitutivity fails to hold when the embedded clause is itself an identity
statement, as in (26). For in order that there be substitutivity it is necessary
that the identity statement is known to be true. But it is precisely a precondition of these modalities that the embedded clause should not be known
to be true, or false, so that it can never be part of **T**. Therefore, whenever
(26) is true, it is so without it being known that William M. is the same person
as W. Murphy. The oddness of (27) is now also explained: it can hardly fail to
be known, given it is known who the expression *William M.* refers to, that
William M. is William M. is true. But that makes (27) both radically false and
unacceptable in virtually every discourse.

Then, the intuitions observed above in regard of existential entailment
now also fall into place. All existential entailments that follow from A are
preserved under $must(A)$, for the simple reason that if T entails A, so that
$must(A)$ is true, it also entails all entailments of A, entailment being a transitive relation. *Must* is, therefore, classified as $[-S, +E]$. But *may* blocks
existential entailments because, given $may(A)$, there is nothing in the lexical
conditions of *may* which ensures that A is entailed if $may(A)$ is true. Hence
may is classified as $[-S, -E]$.

It also follows that although (31) does not entail that Harry has a dog,
the discourse (32) is still unacceptable. The feeling of contradiction arising
with (32), apparently, does not originate from an ordinary conflict of entailments, but from the fact that given the assertion of the truth of the first
sentence, *Harry has no dog*, the precondition of the second sentence, *his dog*

---

[7] The matter is, in fact, slightly more complex (and thus more interesting). For
substitutivity to hold under a *must*-statement what is required is either a true identity
statement (as has been said), or a true statement entailing a true identity statement, as,
e.g., an identity statement under *must*:

    (i) a. William M. must be guilty.
       b. William M. must be W. Murphy.
       c. Hence, W. Murphy must be guilty.

For *may*, what is required is *at least possible truth* of the identity statement.

    (ii) a. William M. may be guilty.
       b. William M. may be W. Murphy.
       c. Hence, W. Murphy may be guilty.

See the following section for an ample discussion of these matters.

may be ill, that the truth-value of the embedded clause must be unknown, is not fulfilled: if it is known that Harry has no dog, it is also known that the truth-value of *his dog is ill* is "radically false". The contradiction is thus based on the conclusion that if a proposition is asserted and added to D, it is known to be true, or at least accepted as being true as long as it is accepted that D is true. In any case, the second sentence is not informative, in that it neither restricts the class of possible verification domains in which D is true, nor does it provide information about D not already available.

It is interesting to note, in this connection, that the following equivalences hold: $\sim must(\neg A) \equiv may(A)$; $\sim may(\neg A) \equiv must(A)$. This is quickly shown. First, *must* and *may* have the same preconditions; hence, the minimal negation cannot make any difference of a preconditional nature, these being fulfilled in all cases concerned. If we now look at the satisfaction conditions, we see that $\sim must(\neg A)$ entails $T \not\models \neg A$ (note that the crossed entailment of (35) represents minimal negation, since all preconditions for entailment are fulfilled and only the satisfaction condition remains unfulfilled). This, however, is precisely the satisfaction condition of $may(A)$, so that the first equivalence is established. As regards the second equivalence, $\sim may(\neg A)$ entails, following (35), $\sim T \not\models \neg\neg A$, i.e. $T \models A$ (see table 5 in section 3.2.4), which is the same as $must(A)$. And $must(A)$, or $T \models A$, entails $\sim\sim T \models \neg\neg A$, since both minimal and classical negations cancel each other.

As was adumbrated at the outset of this section, there are various ways in English, as in most natural languages, to express modalities, especially those of necessity and possibility. We have *need* and *can*, or *can possibly* as negative polarity variants for the positively polar *must* and *may* (note 6 above). *Have to* can also be used epistemically, and many more variants exist, often with subtle differences in meaning or conditions of use (cp., e.g., Leech 1971, ch. 5; Palmer 1974, ch. 5; Coates 1983). Anyone only superficially familiar with the grammar of English will know that this part of the language is complex and full of unexpected variations and pitfalls. But it cannot be our purpose, in this chapter, to present a complete treatment of this part of English grammar. Although most of the examples are taken from English, the theory is meant to be language-independent, and English is used only as a specimen of the species "natural language". Yet, it is interesting to consider two variants a little more closely, the adjectival predicates *possible* and *necessary*, both of which were mentioned at the outset of this section as coming closest to the philosophical notions of necessity and possibility.

Notice that the metaphysical rule *ab esse ad posse*, which establishes possibility from reality, can be expressed in coherent discourse by means of the adjectival predicate *possible*:[8]

---

[8] The emphatic predicate *can* may also fulfil this role:
Alex is out of his mind. Therefore, he cán be out of his mind.

(40) a. Alex is out of his mind. Therefore it is possible that he is out of his
mind.

Notice also, as was observed in the previous section, that (41a) and (41b) are
natural and acceptable, but that (41c) is not:

(41) a. It is necessary that 9 is greater than 7.
  b. Necessarily, 9 is greater than 7.
  c. !9 must be greater than 7.

Likewise, the oddness of (27) disappears under the predicates *necessary* or
necessarily:

(42) a. It is necessary that William M. is William M.
  b. Necessarily, William M is William M.
  c. !William M. must be William M.

The adverb *possibly*, on the other hand, does not seem to substitute for *be
possible* the way *necessarily* does for *be necessary* The variant

(40) b. !Alex is out of his mind. Therefore, he is possibly out of his mind.

is still an unacceptable discourse. Notice, furthermore, that (32) above is not
at all improved when *possible* is used:

(43) !Harry has no dog, but it is possible that his dog is ill.

All this indicates that *possible* and *necessary* differ from (most of) the
other modal predicates in the preconditions, not in the satisfaction conditions, and that the adverb *necessarily* can function both as *must* and as *necessary*, but *possibly*, although it functions as *may*, does not do the work of
possible.

In the light of these observations we may make the following attempt at
defining the extension sets of *necessary* and *possible*:

(44) $\sigma(necessary) = \{\langle p, T \rangle$: T is true; T is a set of ϕ statements (p $\notin$ T);
  p is a ϕ statement; $\varphi(p) \neq 3 \mid T \models p\}$
(45) $\sigma(possible) = \quad \{\langle p, T \rangle$: T is the set of all true ϕ statements; p is a ϕ
  statement $\mid T \not\models \neg p\}$

These modalities are not epistemic, since no requirement obtains for **T** to
be known to be true. The variable "ϕ" stands for adjectives pertaining to
systematic investigations of any kind: mathematical, linguistic, logical, metaphysical, epistemological, police work ... (If ϕ is "metaphysical", the modality
is *de re*; if it is "epistemological" or "linguistic", the modality is *de dicto*.)
For *necessary* the extra specification in the preconditional part that p $\notin$ T is
needed to avoid a vacuous notion of necessity according to which every true
statement (within a discipline) is also a necessary truth. We must avoid the

spurious rule *ab esse ad necesse esse*. For *possible*, however, this extra specification is uncalled for, since we do wish to preserve the rule *ab esse ad posse*, for this predicate. (It should be noted that this undeniably inelegant feature of the analysis is avoided if the relation of entailment is defined non-reflexively. Then, if $T \models p$, by definition $p \notin T$. And no harm is done for *possible*, since for non-reflexive entailment, $p \not\models \neg p$, for any proposition *p*. The attractive aspect of this thought is that the natural meaning of "entail" or of "logical consequence" would also favour a non-reflexive analysis.)

It now follows that (40a) is an acceptable bit of discourse, provided some investigation is specified in terms of which it is said. It also follows that

(46) 9 is greater than 7, and it is necessary that 9 is greater than 7.

is acceptable: the set **T** of true ϕ statements required preconditionally is independent of the discourse at hand and may have to be found elsewhere, or even be unknown. However, given the implicit reference to some **T**, it is natural that either the speaker of (46) goes on to give his reasons for the necessity statement or the listener asks for them. The unacceptability of (43) follows for the following reason. If it is established (as part of the set **T** of all true ϕ statements) that Harry has no dog, then **T** entails the minimal falsity of *It is possible that Harry's dog is ill*. (43) is thus contradictory: the first conjunct entails the falsity of the second. In fact, the following discourse is perfectly acceptable:

(47) Harry has no dog. Therefore it is impossible that his dog is ill.

In the same way we exclude:

(48) !Harry's dog is not ill, but it is possible that his dog is ill.[9]

For if the first conjunct is true it belongs to **T**, and $\sim$(*Harry's dog is ill*) entails $\neg$(*Harry's dog is ill*), so that the satisfaction condition of *possible* is violated. Likewise, the following is correct:

(49) Harry's dog is not ill. Therefore it is impossible that it is ill.

Existing systems of modal logic would accept (48) as correct and reject (49) as false, given normal assumptions. In language, however, the judgements are different. (Care must be taken, of course, that the same tense is attached to *is ill* in both conjuncts. If Harry's dog is healthy *now* it cannot be ill *now*, though it is presumably possible for the animal to be ill at another time.)

[9] Of course, a sentence like

Harry's dog is not ill, but it could/might have been ill.

is fully acceptable. But the double selection of the simple past tense (one for *could/might*, and one for *have been ill*) carries the presupposition that the embedded clause is or was not true. Hence the acceptability of the sentence.

In summary, it is clear that the epistemic modalities in natural discourse are totally incompatible with the philosophical notions of necessity and possibility. The philosophical modalities have to some extent been standardized in natural English through the adjectival predicates *necessary* and *possible*. But there is no question that the modal auxiliary verbs *must* and *may*, the English prototypes of epistemic modality, do not at all follow the patterns set out by philosophical analysis. And even *necessary* and *possible* deviate from philosophically defined rules in significant ways. Yet formal semantics has, by and large, treated the natural language modalities as though they are adequately represented in philosophical analysis. There are few areas in semantics where the vitiating effect of philosophical analysis has become more apparent.

5.3 Subdomains

5.3.1 Some machinery

So far we have spoken of subdomains in an intuitive way. It is time now to be a little more explicit about them. The explanatory load of the notion of subdomains is considerable: all **intensional** phenomena are to be accounted for by them (it might be remembered that it was mainly phenomena of intensionality that gave rise to modern formal semantics), and, less spectacular perhaps but still significant, the projection problem of presupposition is to find its solution here.

A subdomain is the result of the addition to the domain D, henceforth the truth-domain or D^0, of a sentence figuring a predicate of the classes γ, i.e. $[-S, +E]$ or δ, i.e. $[-S, -E]$. The new subdomain corresponds to the sentential term under the predicate in question.

Some predicates of the classes γ and δ take two sentential terms. If they are lexical predicates, such as *prove, mean, suggest,*

(50) a. That the man is nervous suggests that he is guilty.
   b. That Joan is not at home does not mean that nobody else is there.
   c. That the rioting has now become massive proves that the government has failed.

the subject clause is invariably factive (a fact which has hitherto remained without explanation, but seems nevertheless to be universal). These predicates introduce two subdomains, one for each clause, but they always imply an incrementation, necessary or possible, or excluded under negation, in the truth-domain D^0, in the most natural order. (50d), for example, is ambiguous as to the temporal ordering of the events mentioned:

(50) d. That Andy went to Spain means that he got rich.

We have here the same type of ordering indeterminacy found with the two clauses under *if* in section 4.1.5 above. Other than these lexical predicates with two sentential terms, there are *or* and *if* (both belonging to class δ). Of these, *or* gives rise to two separate subdomains, and *if* to only one, where both clauses are housed in the order that makes best sense.

When, for the predicates in question and in conjunction with the same term denotations, a subdomain has already been set up in the discourse at hand, the subordinate clauses that correspond to subdomains (let us say: the intensional clauses) are added to the subdomain already created.

The point of subdomains is that they form autonomous increment spaces: just as 'ordinary' assertive utterances are added to D^0, any D^n is incremented by whatever is asserted of it in the discourse. Moreover, just as 'ordinary' prejections are made within the truth-domain D^0, prejections arising from presuppositions of embedded intensional clauses are prejectable into the subdomain to which the clause in question belongs. As regards prejections, however, a special proviso is to be built in: prejections from embedded intensional clauses are preferably made into the highest possible domain; only if prejection into the highest possible domain is blocked or refused, on account of it being unacceptable in the technical sense described in section 3.3, is it made into a lower domain, until, finally, it is added to its own intensional subdomain. Moreover, for a prejection properly belonging to a subdomain D^n to be added to a higher domain $D^{n-m}(1 \leqslant m \leqslant n)$, it must be an acceptable increment not only to D^{n-m} but also to every $D^{n-k}(1 \leqslant k < m)$ between D^n and D^{n-m}. Failing this condition, addition to a higher (sub)domain is blocked. If addition to the proper subdomain D^n is also blocked, the whole sentence is unacceptable in the given discourse. The acceptability criterion of section 3.3, which is fundamentally a functional criterion of informativeness, is thus generalized over subdomains. In this way, the machinery of prejection, the application of the acceptability criterion (generalized over subdomains), and what we may call the *principle of ambition* ascribed to prejections, whereby they aspire towards addition to the highest possible domain, are jointly responsible for the widely observed fact that presuppositions of embedded clauses sometimes 'make it to the surface' as effectively entailed presuppositions, sometimes remain in a weakened form as strong suggestions or, as we have called them, mere prejections, and sometimes disappear, or are cancelled, entirely – in other words, for projection phenomena of presuppositions.

A few examples will illustrate this. Sentence (51a) carries the mere prejection that Harry has a son:

(51) a. Harry believes that his son lives in Kentucky.

The proposition "Harry has a son" is not entailed, because no contradiction arises when it is also asserted that Harry has no son. Yet there is a suggestion, or invited inference, that Harry has a son. And this is a linguistic property of the sentence, not a result of some specific context or discourse. Discourses such as

(51) b. Harry has no son, but he believes that his son lives in Kentucky.

are marked in this respect, as against the unmarked cases where the discourse allows for a son of Harry's in the truth-domain D^0. (Mere prejections differ from presuppositions, obviously, in that the latter do not allow for contextual 'cancelling' in the way of (51b), that leading immediately to contradiction.) If D^0 is such that it accepts the prejection from the intensional clause, but the intensional clause is itself part of an intermediate intensional clause, then, for the prejection to be added, as a mere prejection, to D^0 it is necessary that it be acceptable also in the intermediate D^1. Thus, (51c) is interpretable in terms of the truth-domain D^0, the subdomain D^1 of what Harry believes, and the subdomain D^2 of what Mary is believed by Harry to hope:

(51) c. Harry believes that Mary hopes that his son lives in Kentucky.

For this sentence to be interpreted in such a way that Harry has, in fact, a son, D^0 must allow for that addition, but also D^1 and D^2. That is, in that interpretation Mary must be believed by Harry to believe that Harry has a son (hope-domains submerge into belief-domains, as will be made clear below), and Harry himself must believe that he has son. In other words, in a discourse of the type

(51) d. Harry is convinced he has no children, but he thinks that Mary thinks he has a son, and that she hopes that his son lives in Kentucky.

the prejection of "Harry has a son" is blocked for D^0 because of its unacceptability in D^1. (51d) carries no suggestion or invited inference that Harry has a son. The prejection remains restricted to D^2. Clearly, if the existence of a son of Harry's is explicitly given in D^0, so that there is no question of *post hoc* suppletion, the prejection finds its way across the intermediate D^1:

(51) e. Harry has a grown-up son, but he is convinced that he has no children, and he thinks that Mary thinks he has a son, and that she hopes that his son lives in Kentucky.

As a sentence in isolation, i.e. as a linguistic object, (51c) prejects, but does not entail, that Harry has a son. As a linguistic object, again, the discourse (51d) neither prejects nor entails that Harry has a son, and (51e) entails but does not preject that Harry has a son.

It will not come as a surprise that non-entailed prejection into a domain or subdomain is blocked not only when the structural acceptability conditions are violated but also when background knowledge makes the prejection impossible or improbable. Thus, when speaking of a patient in a mental hospital in London I say,

(51) f. He believes that the Queen will receive him tomorrow, and that his chauffeur will drive him to the palace in his Rolls.

it is clear which definite descriptions 'survive' as corresponding to real entities, i.e. their denotations are prejected into D^0, and which are lost, i.e. their denotations remain stuck in the patient's belief-world: the Queen and the palace are safe, but there will be little inclination to believe in the existence of the chauffeur and the Rolls – although one never can tell. As a linguistic object, however, (51f) is independent of contingencies of context or the way the world happens to be. As a linguistic object, (51f) prejects, but does not entail, that there is a Queen, a palace, a chauffeur and a Rolls for the subject of *believe*.

Before, however, we take a look at further cases, let us first introduce some of the machinery involved. After that we can see in detail how intensionality phenomena as well as projection phenomena fall into place. The machinery is perhaps best illustrated with the classical example of the intensional predicate *believe*, which is extensional with respect to its subject-term, but its object-term is sentential and intensional. Let D^0 contain an address d_1^0 for *John*, then the increment of (52a) is (53), in the primary reading with small scope for the existential quantifier, i.e. as (52b) – the non-specific reading – but it will be as in (54) in the specific reading with large scope for the quantifier:

(52) a. John believes that he owns a house.
   b. believe (x: "John"(x), $\exists 1$ [ˆy(own(x, y)), ˆy(house(y))])
   c. $\exists 1$ [ˆy(believe (x: "John"(x), own(x, y))), ˆy(house(y))]

(53)

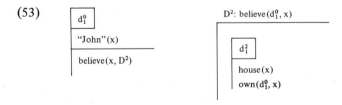

The first term under "believe" maps onto d_1^0, the address for *John*. The second term is intensional and sentential, and opens up a subdomain D^2 (the superscript "2" will be explained in a moment). In D^2 the sentential term is incremented in the standard way, except that the address d_1^0 from the superordinate domain D^0 is involved. In effect, D^2 is an address of a special kind: it is an address – characterized, first by "believe(d_1^0, x)", and subsequently by its further contents – which contains sentential increments and not term increments.

If, however, (52a) is analysed as (52c), the increment will be:[10]

(54)

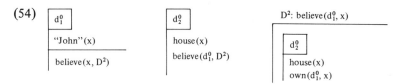

Now D^0 contains two term-addresses, one for John and one for the house John believes he owns, and one subdomain D^2, which represents John's belief. Under d_2^0, the house address, the material "believe(d_1^0, D^2)" is added, without the familiar variable "x" tying it up to the address. This is to be interpreted as saying that d_2^0 occurs in D^2: the house is believed by John to be owned by him. In D^2, d_1^0 occurs again (perhaps some reflexive variable could be used, indicating that it relates to the subject of the belief domain in question). And likewise, d_2^0 occurs again, and is in fact copied. It might be thought that a more economical representation would suffice, in which d_2^0 would not be copied in D^2 but D^2 would simply contain the information "own(d_1^0, d_2^0)". In view, however, of phenomena of opaque and transparent reference within belief-domains, this cannot be good enough: it must in fact be specified precisely what John believes, and that includes that there is a house.

Once D^2 has been established as whatever John believes, any later sentence in the same discourse (and under the same tense) containing further information about what John believes is simply added to D^2. Thus, if instead of (52a) we have

(55) John believes that he owns a house and that it is valuable.

the increment value will be as in (53), but with d_1^2 as follows:

(56)

Note that the existentially quantified phrase *a house* in (55) cannot have large scope. That is, (55) does not have the paraphrase "there is a house which John believes he owns and believes to be valuable". The explanation for this observation is well known: the *Co-ordinate Structure Constraint* (Ross

---

[10] In order not to complicate the exposé unduly at this stage, we shall take it for granted here that the specific reading involves the existence of a real house. As will be shown below (section 5.3.6), this is not necessarily so: there may be a specific non-existing house (e.g., a house described in a fiction story) which John believes to be his. At this stage the theory is not affected by this simplification. Until we come to section 5.3.6 we will assume that the address d_2^0 in (54) is an address of D^0.

1967) forbids extraction from or introduction into just one conjunct of a co-ordinate structure of any lexical material by any rule of the grammar of a natural language. In this case, the rule of Operator Lowering would introduce the existential *a house*, over the predicate "believe", into just one conjunct of the conjunction under "believe", in contravention of the Co-ordinate Structure Constraint:

(57)
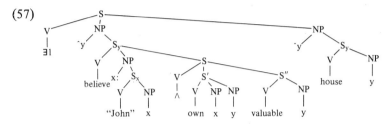

(see section 2.4.3). Although (57) is well formed from the point of view of the syntax of Semantic Analysis (see the Formation Rules of section 2.2), it cannot issue in any surface structure of English – other than the extremely stilted and logic-ridden *There is a house such that John believes that he owns it and that it is valuable*. (But note that in this sentence no Operator Lowering has taken place.) What makes (57) an impossible structure for the grammar of English to process is the fact that Operator Lowering on *a house* conflicts with the Co-ordinate Structure Constraint. First we get (see (115) in section 2.4.3):

(58)
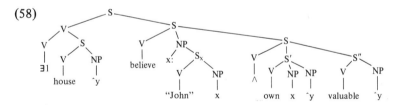

For Operator Lowering to apply on the highest S, the lexical material *a house* must now be introduced into the first conjunct of the object-S of "believe", viz. S′, but not into the second conjunct S″, which contravenes the Co-ordinate Structure Constraint.[11]

---

[11] We thus have an additional ground for rejecting a Geach-type solution to sentences like (11a) and (11b) in section 4.1.1 (repeated here for convenience):

(i) Socrates owned a dog and it bit Socrates.
(ii) Socrates owned a dog and it did not bite Socrates.

According to Geach (1972: 115–27) the existential quantifier binds the variable in both conjuncts. We saw in section 4.1.1 that this analysis runs into scope trouble. Here we see that it also runs into grammatical trouble: the lexical material *a dog* cannot be introduced into just one conjunct and picked up anaphorically in the second. (The epithet replacement test (section 4.2.1) also shows that the *it* in both sentences is not a bound variable pronoun but a denoting pronoun.)

If we want to express in ordinary English what (57) says, a different but equivalent structure is needed, for example:

(59)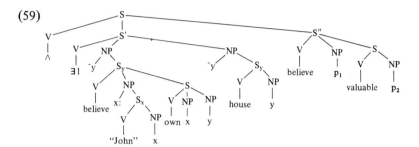

or:

(60) John believes that he owns a/some house, and he believes that it is valuable.

Now Operator Lowering need not violate the Co-ordinate Structure Constraint, and the *it* of the second conjunct is an internally anaphoric, and not a bound variable, pronoun. The increment-value of the first conjunct, S', is as given above in (54). When the second conjunct, S'', is added to (54), D^2 will close d_2^0 and add the predication "valuable (x)". But a closure operation will also have to be carried out on d_2^0 in D^0, since a referential commitment has been established by the second conjunct. We therefore close the address d_2^0 in D^0 (which was left open in (54)), thereby securing closure of d_2^0 in both its occurrences. The result is now as follows (cp. (54)):

(61)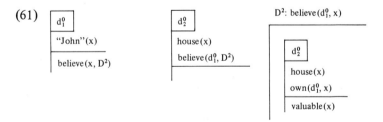

(Note that without the double closure of d_2^0 the domain corresponds to what it would have been after the addition of (57) and its contorted Surface Structure counterpart which does not involve Operator Lowering.)

Now consider the sentence:

(62) John believes that the house he owns is valuable.

analysed as:

(63) $\text{believe}(x_1: \text{"John"}(x_1), \text{valuable}(x_2: \text{house}(x_2), \text{own}(x_1, x_2)))$

Let D^0, again, contain d_1^0, i.e. the address for the subject-term. The increment of the object-term will be housed, as before, in the subdomain D^2, characterized as being believed by John. The question now is: what will the increment of the object-term in D^2 look like? The question arises because the subject-term of "valuable" is in search of an address to map onto, and we have allowed addresses from the higher domain D^0 to be used in increments in the lower domain D^2. If the domain contains no address as yet of the desired description, suppletion *post hoc* is called for, and the question is, therefore, will this suppletion be implemented in D^0, or in D^2, or in some intermediate domain?

If the suppletion is implemented in D^2, the result is:

(64)

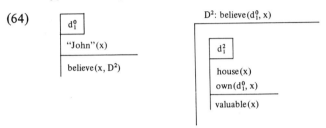

That is, the result, in this case, is identical to that of (55). (We might wish to make it clear, in the domain structure, what the difference is between (55) and (62) incremented as (64). That can be done by introducing a system of numbering successive increments. The numbering will then show up what has been introduced by a previous utterance and what has been introduced by *post hoc* suppletion. But this aspect of the theory is immaterial here.)

If, on the other hand, the suppletion is carried out in D^0, the result is:

(65) a.

but not:

(65) b.

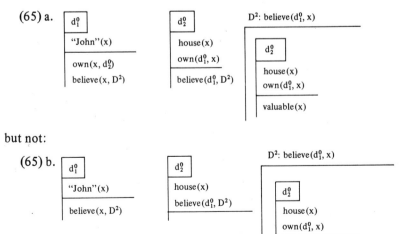

In (64) the backward suppletion is entirely limited to the subdomain D^2, which means that something in D^0 blocked the addition to it of an address for the house owned by John. (64) expresses what is said by:

(66) a. John believes that he owns a house, and he believes that the house he owns is valuable.

In (65a) the backward suppletion is not blocked by D^0 and is hence carried through in D^0. It expresses what is said by:

(66) b. John owns a house, and he believes that the house he owns is valuable.

However, (65b) reads as:

(66) c. There is a house that John believes he owns, and he believes that the house he believes he owns is valuable.

Or, in other words, the subject term of "valuable" in (63) cannot denote d_2^0 in (65b), the reason being that the D^0-address d_2^0 does not match the description given in (63). Its copy in D^2 does match the description, but the predication "own(d_1^0, x)" crucially needed for the denotation is unique to the belief-subdomain D^2. We must stipulate, therefore, that the procedure of address denotation by definite terms must select possible candidates in their own domain or subdomain: the description provided in the definite term must match any address d^n it is to denote in D^n.

Clearly, if no backward suppletion (by virtue of the mechanism of prejection) is called for because D already contains an address properly matching the definite term *the house he owns*, either as a D^0-address, or as a D^2-address, or, possibly, as some D^1-address, then the term will denote that address directly, and the result will be the same as it is with backward suppletion, and (65b) will still remain excluded.

The case of (62) with its analysis (63) shows that the increment function i cannot be formulated as a binary relation taking Semantic Analyses to increments. As was said in section 1.2, i is a relation which takes ordered pairs of Semantic Analyses and given domain structures (i.e. propositions) as input and yields incremented domains. Moreover, it shows that Semantic Analyses can be vague in a way in which their increments are not, a fact which illustrates vividly the dependence of language as a means of communication on presupposed discourse domains. Thus, (62) must be considered vague between the presence or absence of existential entailment for the house John (believes he) owns. But once the increment function i has worked, this vagueness is eliminated, since the discourse domain must specify whether the address corresponding to the NP *the house he owns* is in D^0 or in D^2. If the domain does not already contain an address for *the house he owns*, it must be supplied *post hoc*, either in D^0 or in D^2, or, as we shall see presently, in an intermediate D^1. As has been said, there is a preference for the highest possible domain, i.e. D^0, by virtue of the principle of ambition – which is nothing but a functional principle of minimum effort (see also the end of section 3.2.5): restrict as much as possible the number of presuppositions that are specific to one single subdomain, and let as many presuppositions as possible be shared by all (sub)domains in D. Only if D^0 refuses the *post hoc* increment of an address for a house owned by John will the increment have to be made in a subdomain of lower rank. And, of course, if none of the subdomains that qualify for the increment accept it, the whole sentence is unacceptable in D.

5.3.2 Intensional scales

But there is more. Apart from (66a)–(66c) we can also have:

(67) a. John knows that he owns a house, and he believes that it is valuable.

This means that the missing address for the x_2-term of (63) can be retrieved also from (and hence, if need be, prejected into) another domain than D^0 or the domain of John's beliefs. Here we need a structure like (67b) – whereby it should be noted that factive verbs (such as *know* here) do not allow for any additions to their subdomain which are not copies from the domain in which the factive verb (*know*) is interpreted:

(67) b.

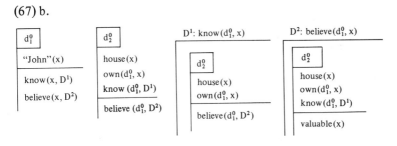

A little systematic observation soon shows that there is a hierarchy in thought-relating predicates. The hierarchy is formed by the fact that a definite description occurring in an embedded sentential structure can map onto an address in its own subdomain or in a subdomain of a higher order, but never in a subdomain of a lower order. There seem to be scales of predicates, which we shall call *intensional scales*. One such scale is the following:

(68)	0	1	2	3
	true	*know*	*believe*	*hope*
		realize	*think*	*wish*
		regret	(*regret*)	*want*
		. . .	. . .	*try*
				. . .

Thus, although we can say (67a), we cannot say, e.g.,

(67) c. *John hopes that he owns a house, and he believes that it is valuable.

   d. *John thinks that he owns a house, and he realizes that it is valuable.[12]

But we can say:

(67) e. John believes he owns a house, and he hopes that it is valuable.

It might be objected that we, though perhaps marginally, say:

(67) f. John knows that he owns a house, and it is (true that it is) valuable.

This, however, is only an apparent difficulty, since the verbs of category 1 are factive, and thus presuppose their factive clauses, so that whatever address is introduced into a D^1 is retrievable from D^0 on account of the prejection relation inherent in presupposition.

It is now clear why the superscript "2" was attached to belief-subdomains. Knowledge-subdomains are assigned "1", and hope-subdomains, as well as volitional and conative subdomains, are assigned "3".

The category 0 represents all that is found in D^0. The only overt predicate in this category is *true*, which, though thought-relating, is not domain-introducing. Category 1 contains the factive predicates with an animate (thinking) subject. Category 2 contains verbs or belief. For some speakers, *regret* belongs to this category, together with all other 'emotive' factives, such as *be delighted, rejoice*. They accept sentences like:

(67) g. John believes that he owns a house, and he regrets that it is valuable.

The third category, as has been said, contains verbs of hoping, wishing and trying.

It must be noted that for a subdomain D^n ($n \geqslant 2$) to pick up an address from, or insert an address into, a subdomain D^1, D^n and D^1 need not be tied to the same subject. We can have

(67) h. Ann knows that John owns a house, and Pete hopes that it is valuable.

---

[12] Dinsmore (1981: 53) erroneously lets (i) presuppose (ii):

(i) Fred knows that George has stopped smoking.
(ii) Fred believes that George used to smoke.

Note that a discourse formed by "(ii) and (i)" is unacceptable, but

(iii) Fred knows that George used to smoke, and he believes that George has stopped smoking.

is a well-interpretable discourse.

but not, e.g.,

(67) i. *Ann believes that John owns a house, and Pete hopes that it is valuable.

This is no doubt to do with the fact that the verbs of category 1 presuppose their argument-clauses, so that the argument-clause increments are added to D^0 by prejection, if need be. Now D^0 is the truth-domain and is not tied up with any particular thinking subject to whom it is attributed. The verbs of category 2 and 3, however, do not presuppose their argument-clauses, which, therefore, do not end up in D^0, unless especially asserted. Their increments stay within the subdomain in question. We can thus state as a general rule that whenever a thought-relating subdomain D^n picks up an address from, or inserts an address into, a thought-relating subdomain D^{n-m} ($n-1>m\geqslant 0$), D^n and D^{n-m} must be tied to the same cognitive subject. The rule does not hold when $D^{n-m} = D^1$, because, as we have seen, all D^1 clauses are either factive or otherwise entailed, and are thus copied in D^0.

Let us call scale (68) *epistemic-volitional*. Besides this, there are others, such as the *modal scale*:

(69)	0	1	2	3
	true	*must*	*probably*	*may*
		necessarily	*likely*	*possibly*
		. . .	. . .	*or*
				if[13]
				. . .

or the *inferential scale*:

(70)	0	1	2	3
	true	*entail*	*clearly*	*suggest*
		imply	*obviously*	. . .
		therefore/so	. . .	
		explain		
		apparently		
		. . .		

In scale (70) the verbs *entail, imply, explain* and *suggest* take sentential subjects as well as sentential objects. We have seen (example (50)) that in such cases the subject clause is invariably factive, and thus falls into class 1.

---

[13] We saw in section 5.1, examples (16)–(18), that the logical predicates *or* and *if* are intensional: they block both substitutivity and existential generalization (category δ). These two predicates are seen to belong to the modal scale, as appears from cases like:

Harry has either a son or a daughter. So it is possible that his son is at College.

The ordering given in (70) is made according to the status of the object clauses with these verbs.[14]

There seems to be, moreover, a *phatic scale*:

(71) 0   1   2   3   4   5   6

    true   *inform*   *report*   *say*   *assure*   *promise*   *suggest*

    . . .   . . .   *tell*   *guarantee* . . .   . . .

        assert   . . .

        . . .

(all with animate subjects, except, of course, *true*). More such intensional scales will no doubt be found on a little more research, and the scales given will no doubt have to be expanded and revised. What all have in common is a root in D^0, and the fact that in all cases category 1 consists of verbs entailing the embedded clause.

We are now in a position to gain a better insight into the fact, signalled in section 5.1, that of the predicates that take sentential arguments, some allow for both substitution of co-extensive terms *salva veritate* and existential entailment with respect to definite terms in their embedded argument clauses, while others block substitutivity but license existential entailment, others again do the opposite, and a last category block both. We can now formulate a general principle of an explanatory nature for all embedded argument clauses[15] linking up the increment-value of their commanding predicate with their behaviour under the criteria or substitutivity and existential entailment. This principle, which we may dub the *Principle of Substitutivity and Existential Entailment* (PSE) runs as follows:

(72) Given a predicate P as the highest predicate of an assertive sentence A, and given an embedded argument clause S which is itself fully extensional, then,

    (a) A licenses *existential entailment* (i.e. P is classsified as [+ E]) just in case S is either directly incremented in D^0 or required in D^0 because it is presupposed or otherwise entailed, and A preserves the presuppositions of S;

    (b) A licenses *substitutivity* for definite terms in S just in case S is directly incremented in D^0 and not in any subdomain.

The linking of existential entailment with D^0 is natural since D^0 is the truth-domain: whatever ends up in D^0 is true if D^0 is true. Here it does not

---

[14] Natural language use of predicates like *entail* or *imply* thus differs from the technical use made of these verbs in logic. In logic, their subject clauses are not factive, since logic is not concerned with truth, but with conservation of truth through an argument.

[15] This principle does not apply to embedded questions: sentential question terms are not taken into account here at all.

matter if what ends up in D^0 also ends up in some non-extensional sub-domain. For substitutivity, too, the link with D^0 is natural. But in this case it is required that the clause in question be directly incremented to D^0, and not to some subdomain D^1, to be copied (by prejection *post hoc*) in D^0 if it was not already there. Truth of a domain D requires rigid reference relations between addresses in D and entities in the verification domain V, so that it can make no difference for the truth-value of any sentence incremented in D by what name an address is called. Or more specifically, substitutivity results from the fact that an address d may be characterized by a number of predicates, more than one of which may characterize d uniquely. Substitutivity is thus a consequence of the state of a domain D^n and the truth-value of D^n. If an address d_m^0 is characterized uniquely by a predicate P^1 as well as a predicate P^2, and if d_m^0 is true, then it can make no difference for an assertive utterance's truth-value whether a term t^1 is used with predicate P^1, or a term t^2 with predicate P^2. And given an address d_m^n likewise uniquely characterized both by P^1 and by P^2, and if $I(d_m^n)$ is true – where "I" is any operator or complex of operators linking D^n with D^0 – then, again, it can make no difference for the truth-value of an utterance of the form $I(S)$, where S is intensionally embedded under I and S is incremented into D^n, whether S contains a definite term t^1 with predicate P^1, or a term t^2 with predicate P^2. Thus, if Harry believes that William M. and W. Murphy are the same person, then, if he believes that William M. is a crook, he believes that W. Murphy is a crook, and vice versa.

The problem, however, is presented by substitutivity across domains. If t^1 and t^2 land at the same address d_m^0 in D^0, but at different addresses in the D^2 of Harry's beliefs, then t^1 is not substitutable *salva veritate* for t^2 in an S to be added to D^2. And since in general there is no guarantee that sameness of address in the truth-domain D^0 corresponds to sameness of address in a sub-domain $D^{>0}$, substitutivity is generally blocked when S is incremented in a domain $D^{>0}$. But this is substitution of terms which are really co-extensive, i.e. denoting the same address d_m^0 in a true domain D^0, carried out in a sub-domain $D^{>0}$. It is not difficult to see why such substitutivity should be blocked.

Let us consider a few examples. The predicate *cause*, as in

(73) The short-circuit caused the fire to start.

or the predicate *manage*, as in

(74) Jack managed to free himself.

which increment their object clauses into their own domains, are marked [+ S, + E]. Note that these predicates, since they entail their object clauses, carry the precondition that the embedded clause is not radically false (see the discussion in section 3.3, and the extension set (60) of the predicate *manage* in section 3.3). The predicate *and* is likewise positively marked, for both its clauses, for substitutivity as well as existential entailment. And so is minimal *not*, being presupposition-preserving. The same goes for *true*, which is [+ S] since it directly increments its argument clause into D^0 (more properly: into its own domain), and it is marked [+ E] because it, too, is presupposition-preserving (see (36h) in section 3.2.4). The radical negation falls under category β: it takes [+ S] as expected, but it is marked [−E] because it cancels presuppositions. The predicates *or* and *if*, which, according to (69) above, increment their clauses into some D^3 on the modal scale, are normally marked [−S, −E], precisely because they fail to fulfil both conditions of PSE as given in (72).

The predicates listed under "1" of one of the scales (68)–(71) are marked [−S, +E], since the embedded S is incremented in some D^1 but the increment is required in D^0 as well, as we have seen, whereby care has been taken that presuppositions are always preserved (section 3.3). The presence of i[S] in D^0 ensures existential entailment, but the fact that S is incremented in D^1 blocks substitutivity. Predicates which increment their embedded clauses in subdomains deeper than rank 1 are marked [−S, −E]: they have no guaranteed link with D^0, and thus fail to fulfil both conditions of PSE.

It is clear now that category β, marked [+ S, −E], must be very thinly represented as far as sentential terms are concerned: the [+ S] feature requires that S is directly incremented in D^0, but the feature [−E] forbids direct or indirect incrementation in D^0, unless presuppositions are cancelled for S. Thus only predicates whose embedded clause S is directly incremented in D^0 but which cancel the presuppositions of S are allowed into category β. Now all lexical predicates whose embedded clause S is incremented in D^0, and which therefore entail S, are required to preserve the presuppositions of S and thus cannot enter β. The only possible candidates, as far as predicates with embedded Ss (and not definite terms) are concerned, are thus technical presupposition-cancelling predicates which increment their argument S directly in D^0. Only one such predicate is known, i.e. the radical negation.

5.3.3 Opaque and transparent reference

Especially since Quine's famous essay "Reference and modality" (1953: 139-59), the distinction between opaque and transparent reference has been well known and very widely commented upon in philosophical semantics. The distinction applies to definite descriptions, i.e. definite terms with a lexical descriptive content P, occurring in thought-relating intensional contexts. It amounts to the following. Given two (or more) definite descriptions, t_1 and t_2, with the lexical content P_1 and P_2, respectively, and given that t_1 and t_2 are co-extensional, i.e. refer to the same individual i, then, in a thought-relating intensional context C, t_1 and t_2 may be substituted *salva veritate*, even though the subject of C is not aware that t_1 and t_2 both refer to the same individual *i*. It must be added immediately that such substitution is not permitted, *salva veritate*, if the subject of C holds the belief that t_1 and t_2 are not co-extensional. In that case truth can be achieved only by using the opaquely referring term. Opaque reference is made by means of the term whose lexical content corresponds with *i*'s description within C, whereas transparent reference is made by means of the term whose lexical content corresponds with one or more real properties of *i* but not necessarily with *i*'s description in C. In that case the description is attributable to the speaker, and not to the subject of C.

For example, let the terms *W. Murphy* and *William M.* (t_1 and t_2, respectively) refer to the same individual, Mr William Murphy of O'Connor Street, who, to paraphrase Quine, is a pillar of society.[16] Shirley, who knows Mr Murphy very well but has no idea of his double life, reads in the morning paper that one William M. has been arrested on a spying charge. The newspaper article gives a few details, and there is no doubt in Shirley's mind that the man is, in fact, a dangerous spy. It is therefore true to say

(75) a. Shirley thinks that William M. is a spy.

It does not occur to her at all that this William M. is, in fact, the same person as the respectable Mr William Murphy of O'Connor Street. Yet, in spite of that, it is also true to say

(75) b. Shirley thinks that W. Murphy is a spy.

even though Shirley herself would hotly deny that that is what she thinks. Imagine a situation in the local police station, where Mr Murphy is being held, and where a police sergeant, who knows Shirley and has spoken with her about the newspaper article but without revealing William M.'s real identity, says sentence (75b) to a colleague, using a description that will directly refer to the man who finds himself behind bars a few doors away. The reference made in (75a) by means of the term *William M.* is now said to be opaque, while the reference made in (75b) by means of the term *W. Murphy* is transparent.

Note, however – a fact not mentioned in the literature (to my knowledge) – that (75b) cannot be uttered in truth if Shirley is explicitly convinced that William M. is *not* the same person as W. Murphy. Then Shirley's friend, the police sergeant, *must* use an opaquely referring description if he wants to be truthful. This catch in the charter of transparent reference is important because, without it, substitutivity would simply apply to all thought-relating

---

[16] As we have silently done so far, we treat proper names as definite descriptions, with the lexical content "be called 'NN' ", or just "NN". In chapter 6 more will be said about this analysis of proper names. It will be shown there that Kripke's analysis of proper names as "rigid designators", forever linked with their reference object through a causal chain originating in some original "baptism", is both inadequate and unnecessary.

intensional contexts and would lose its status of distinguishing feature for intensional contexts. Now we can maintain that status for substitutivity, and state that substitutivity is *also* allowed in intensional contexts **C** if it is given within **C** that $\rho(t_1) = \rho(t_2)$, and even if this referential identity is not given in **C** provided **C** does not contain the information that $\rho(t_1) \neq \rho(t_2)$. Then substitutivity still applies, albeit with a distinction between opaque and transparent reference.

The catch in the charter of transparent reference is important for another reason as well, a reason widely discussed in the philosophical literature on the subject (e.g. Quine 1966: 183-94; Kaplan 1969: 206-14). If opaque and transparent readings were freely applicable in intensional (thought-relating) contexts, then both (75b) and its negation (75c) would be true, the former in the transparent reading, and the latter opaquely:

(75) c. Shirley does not think that W. Murphy is a spy.

This would make it necessary to say that all definite descriptions in intensional contexts of this kind are ambiguous in the strict, technical sense of ambiguity by which an expression is ambiguous if the smallest truth-value bearing expression in which it occurs is both true and false in some one situation. But we do not want to invoke the heavy notion of ambiguity here. What we need is a distinction between ways of referring, nothing more. We can now say that, as long as Shirley does not actually think that William M. and W. Murphy (of O'Connor Street) are not the same person, both (75a) and (75b) are true, and (75c) is false. But (75c) becomes true, and (75b) false, as soon as Shirley actually entertains the thought that the William M. she read about in the paper and the W. Murphy she knows from O'Connor Street are different persons.

It seems anyway that, generally, transparent readings of definite descriptions in thought-relating intensional contexts are marked, or less preferred, compared with opaque readings. Usually, a special context is required for a transparent reading to be seen to be applicable, just as it was felt to be helpful above to describe a specific situation, the police sergeant and the rest, in order that the transparent reading of (75b) could be seen to be possible.

The machinery of intensional subdomains as described above seems, in principle, to account automatically for the facts of opaque and transparent reference. Let the situation be as described for (75a) and (75b), corresponding with a discourse domain D prior to the addition of either (75a) or (75b):

(76) a.

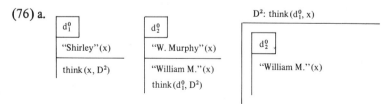

The address established in Shirley's belief-domain D^2, d_2^0, has been identified with the D^0-address for the actual Mr Murphy, not because Shirley is aware of this identification (which she is not) but because you, the reader, who have been told about the fact that the person arrested is Mr W. Murphy, are aware of it, just as, in the story, the police sergeant is. We may also say that in a 'God's eye view', or (Shadbolt 1983) from the point of view of an 'Omniscient Observer', the identification of the two d_2^0-addresses is justified, and since we are concerned with questions of truth and falsity, which are metaphysical notions, we are justified in adopting this grandiose perspective. In any case, when now (75a) is added, the SA-term corresponding to *William M.* immediately finds a proper denotation in Shirley's belief-domain D^2, so that d_2^0 in D^2 is closed and the predication "spy(x)" is added:

The opaque reading is thus unproblematic. When, instead of (75a), (75b) is added – and we must remember that it is uttered by a person, the police sergeant, who is aware of the identity of both W. Murphy and William M. – then again the SA-term corresponding to *W. Murphy* immediately locates its denotation, d_2^0 in D^0, and since d_2^0 also occurs in D^2, the same predication as before can now be added to d_2^0 in D^2, and the result is identical with that of (75a), though the procedure for obtaining this incremental result is different from that followed for (75a).

Now suppose that Shirley has heard it said that the person she read about in the morning paper is in fact the respectable Mr Murphy of O'Connor Street, but she refuses to believe that. Now her belief-domain D^2, for those who are in the know (including any metaphysically present Omniscient Observer), looks as follows:

(76) b.

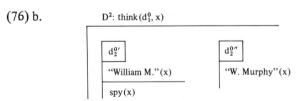

Now d_2^0 has been positively disidentified in D^2, and any SA-term corresponding to *W. Murphy* occurring in a clause under the predicate "think" with Shirley as the person entertaining the thoughts in question will denote $d_2^{0''}$ in D^2, and not d_2^0 in D^0. We must stipulate, therefore, in addition to what was stipulated with regard to (65b) and (66c) in the preceding section, that, although the description of any D^m-term must match the d^n-address in its own D^n, the search for a denotation concentrates on D^m first, and only when

D^m yields no answer will the search pass on to D^n, for any D^n ($0 \leqslant n < m$) above D^m. In this case this means that, given (76a), the SA-term corresponding to *W. Murphy* in (75b) will scan D^2 first for a denotation, but in vain. It then scans D^0 and finds d_2^0, which is partially copied in D^2. Now the predication "spy(x)" can be added to d_2^0 in D^2. If, however, D^2 is as specified in (76b), then the SA-term corresponding to *W. Murphy* in (75b) will select $d_2^{0''}$ of D^2 and add "spy(x)" to that. But now D is no longer true because Shirley emphatically thinks that Mr W. Murphy is *not* a spy. That is, given (76b), (75c) is true, and (75b) is false. But (75c) can only be true because the denotation function applied to the term *W. Murphy* scans D^2 first. The addition of "spy(x)" to $d_2^{0''}$ results in falsity because Shirley clearly does not hold the view that Mr Murphy is a spy. The result of incrementing (75c) to (76a) is an embargo of the form "*spy(d_2^0)" on D^2. But this makes D false since Shirley does think of the person referred to by d_2^0 (though unbeknownst to her this person is Mr Murphy whom she knows and respects) that he is a spy. However, the result of incrementing (75c) to (76b) is an embargo of the form "*spy($d_2^{0''}$)" on D^2, which preserves truth for D since, though Shirley thinks that her William M. is a spy, she does not think that her W. Murphy is one.

As the analysis proceeded, the denotation procedure whereby definite descriptions find their discourse addresses has gathered a few extras. We now say that a definite description t with the lexical material **P** in a context **C**^{n} corresponding to a (sub)domain D^n ($0 \leqslant n$), will scan D^n first for a fitting address $d(t)$. If a matching $d(t)$ is found in D^n then, if $d(t)$ is superscripted "n", the denotation procedure is closed successfully. But if $d(t)$ has a superscript of value $n - m$ ($0 < m \leqslant n$), then, although t matches $d(t)$ lexically in D^n, it must be checked if t also matches $d(t)$ in D^{n-m}. If it does, the procedure is closed; if it does not, no denotation is made (as in (62) and (65b) above). Furthermore, if no matching $d(t)$ is found in D^n (or if D^n does not exist yet because it is being set up with the sentence being processed), D^{n-1} is scanned (if any), then D^{n-2} (if any), etc., until D^0 is scanned. If a fitting $d(t)$ is located in any D^{n-m} ($0 < m \leqslant n$), it is copied in D^n provided D^n allows for the introduction of $d(t)$. If not, the procedure is blocked and no denotation is made. If no D^{n-m} contains a fitting $d(t)$, backward suppletion is applied and a $d(t)$ is prejected into the highest possible D^i ($0 \leqslant i \leqslant n$).

It seems that if this procedure is followed maximum justice is done to the observations made so far. It will be shown now, however, that the procedure is not yet quite complete.

5.3.4 *Identity*, exist, true

The identity predicate "=" (or "be$_{id}$") is non-extensional with respect to both its terms. That is, it is free to let its terms search lower domains than the one in which the predicate itself occurs. If a clause "$=(t_1, t_2)$" occurs in a context of depth n, then the denotation procedure will scan first D^n, as with normal extensional predicates. But if D^n does not yield the $d(t)$ looked for, any other (sub)domain in D is allowed to provide a fitting $d(t)$. (Backward suppletion, however, remains upward-directed and follows the principle of ambition of section 5.3.1.) The increment-value of the identity predicate consists in the setting up of a new address d^i in D^i assembling the lexical material of $d(t_1)$ and $d(t_2)$, where i is the lowest value j of the superscripts of $d(t_1)$ and $d(t_2)$ provided $n \leqslant j$, and $i = n$ if $n > j$. $d(t_1)$ and $d(t_2)$ can no longer be used as denotation targets for increments to D^i but they remain the first choice for terms in increments to some D^j ($j \neq i$).

Thus Frege's example

(77) The Morning Star is the Evening Star.

given a D containing as yet no star-addresses, is processed in the following way. By backward suppletion (which follows the principle of ambition) two d^0-addresses are prejected into D^0, d_1^0 with "Morning Star(x)" and d_2^0 with "Evening Star(x)". The incrementation of (77) now results in the merging of d_1^0 and d_2^0 into a new d_3^0 characterized by "Morning Star(x); Evening Star(x)".[17]

A slightly more complex case is

(78) Zeus is Jupiter.

where the context of occurrence is C^0 and hence the corresponding domain is D^0, but both terms are to be found in an intensional subdomain under the operator "in Classical mythology" or something of that nature. Now D^0 does not contain any address for either term to denote, but a presupposed (i.e. discourse-given) subdomain D^i does, for both terms. Let us say that *Zeus*

---

[17] Strawson (1974: 55-6) expresses pre-theoretical intuitions in this respect in the following illuminating way (having first compared a man's knowledge with a map that has dots for individuals and lines for relations):

> When he learns something from an ordinary predication, new lines inscribe themselves on his map, attached to the appropriate dot or joining two different dots. When he learns from an identity statement, the two appropriate dots approach each other and merge, or coalesce, into one, any duplicating lines merging or coalescing at the same time.
>
> The model helps us to see what was troubling us. Our eyes were too firmly fixed on the case of the ordinary predication. So we were inclined to think that the only way in which a statement including a reference already on the map could be informative for all audiences informed by it would be by adding detail, and the same detail, to each of their maps – by adding lines, and the same lines, to each of their maps. But we see there is another way – the same in general for all audiences informed by it – in which an identity statement can change the knowledge state of all audiences informed by it.

It will be obvious that our theory of discourse domains is an attempt at providing a precise elaboration of Strawson's notion of a man's knowledge map with its dots and lines.

denotes d_1^i and *Jupiter* d_2^i, where $0 < i$. The lowest value of d_1^i and d_2^i is, trivially, i, so that both addresses are merged into a new address d_3^i assembling all information available about Zeus and Jupiter.

Or consider

(79) Judy thinks that a man has been following her for the past few weeks, and she thinks that this man is Mr Murphy of O'Connor Street.

where, in fact, no man has been following Judy, least of all the really existing Mr Murphy of O'Connor Street. The identity clause in the second conjunct of (79) occurs in the context of what Judy thinks and is thus interpretable in the D^2 of Judy's thoughts. The two terms of the identity, *this man* and *Mr Murphy*, each denote an address without problems: *this man* denotes, say, d_1^2 in D^2, and *Mr Murphy* denotes, say, d_5^0 in D^0. A new address assembling d_1^2 and d_5^0 must now be set up of depth i. The lowest value of the superscripts of the two addresses is "0", of d_5^0, so that $j = 0$. Since $n = 2$, $n > j$, and therefore $i = n = 2$: the new address will be located in the D^2 of Judy's thoughts. This is correct since it is in D^2 that the identification is made, and not in the D^0 that corresponds (if all goes well) to the verification domain at hand in the real world. It is easily checked that exactly the same result obtains when the following sentence is uttered

(80) Judy thinks that Mr Murphy has been following her for the past few weeks, and she thinks that Mr Murphy is the man who made an obscene phone call last night.

where Mr Murphy, as always, really exists and Judy did in fact receive one of those phone calls on the evening before the utterance of (80). Now both the address for Mr Murphy and that for the unsavoury caller are d^0-addresses, but because the identification is made in D^2, the new address is set up in D^2.

Let the incremental result of (77) and (78) be represented as (81a) and (81b), respectively:

(81) a.   b.

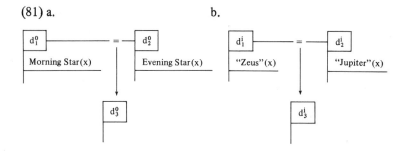

(where it is understood that the new addresses take over the lexical contents of their predecessors). Then the incremental result of (79) can be represented as follows:

(82)

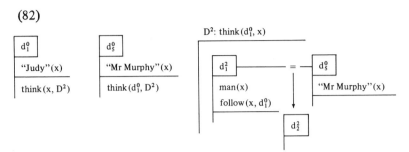

And for (80) the incremented D will be:

(83)

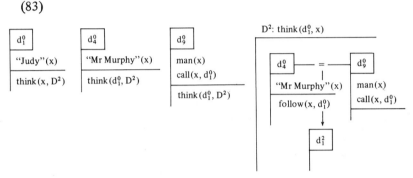

The predicate *exist* is likewise non-extensional with respect to its subject term. That is, its subject term is free to search any (sub)domain in D for a possible denotation. In fact, if D is to remain informative, the denotation of the subject term of *exist* should not be found in D^0 (or at any rate the D^n in which *exist* is to be incremented), but in a domain of lower rank. The incremental effect of *exist* consists in the introduction of a copy of the subject denotation in the lower subdomain into the D^n in which *exist* is incremented. Thus, if it is said that

(84) The man that Judy thinks has been following her really exists.

then, taking (82) as the domain in which (84) is to be incremented, the subject term has to denote d_1^2. (Note that for (84) d_1^2 can still act as a denotation target because (84) is to be incremented into D^0 and not into D^2.) The address d_1^2 is now copied in D^0, say as d_8^0, and d_1^2 is accordingly relabelled as d_8^0. d_1^0 is enriched with "follow(d_8^0, x)".

The predicate *fictitious* is somehow the opposite of *exist*. Like *exist* it takes its subject term denotation from any available (sub)domain in D, including, this time, D^0. Its incremental effect consists in banning the denotation address from D^0: if the subject term has an already existing address d_n^0 (i.e. in D^0) as its denotation, then a search is made in suitable available intensional subdomains (for example, the subdomain of what Judy thinks if the sentence is *Mr Murphy is fictitious*, against the background of (82)), and if an intensional copy of d_n^0 is found, say in some D^2, then d_n^0 in D^0 is erased and the d_n^0 copy in D^2 is relabelled d_m^2. If no suitable and plausible subdomain contains a copy of d_n^0, a special intensional subdomain under "fictitious" is set up and d_n^0 is copied in it and relabelled accordingly, after its erasure from D^0.

It is essential that the subject term of (84) should denote d_1^2 in (82), and not d_2^2, although the latter, too, matches the term description lexically, since given (79) and (84) it does not follow that the man who has been following Judy is the same person as Mr Murphy. No contradiction arises when, after (79) and (84), it is said that he is not Mr Murphy. A provision is therefore required to ensure that the subject term of (84) denotes d_1^2 and not d_2^2. For our present purposes this provision is afforded by the stipulation made above for the identity predicate that an address d^i which has been identified with another address to yield a new address assembling the material of both, can no longer be used as a denotation target for increments in D^i but remains the primary target for terms in propositions to be incremented to some D^j where $j \neq i$. Since (84) is to be incremented to D^0 but its subject term denotes an address in D^2, this term will denote d_1^2 and not d_2^2. It remains to be seen, however, if a provision of a more general nature should not be made and incorporated into the denotation procedure for definite descriptions, i.e. the lexical part of the Assignment Procedure of section 4.2.5.

The predicate *true* is a little like *exist*, in that it lifts bits of structure in lower domains up to its own domain. For example, if, given the domain as in (82), the following sentence is uttered

(85) It is true that a man has been following Judy for the past few weeks.

we want the result to be virtually identical to that of (84) (the only difference being that the new D^0-address d_8^0 for the man in question is closed after (84) but not after (85)). That is, we want the sentential subject term of *true* to pick up the propositional increment of "a man has been following Judy" from D^2 and insert it in D^0.

In order to let the machinery do this properly we need to stipulate that *true* requires that the material corresponding to its sentential subject term is already present in D, in particular in a subdomain lower than the D^n to which the proposition figuring *true* is to be incremented. The subject term of *true* does not bring in new propositional information not yet stored anywhere in D, as, e.g., *believe* or *think* or *hope* do or may do. It acts more like a definite term than like a sentential term in that it induces the denotational entailment common to all definite terms and finding its origin in the fact that definite terms need an address to land at for interpretation to take place at all (see section 3.2.4). In the same way *true* requires its subject term to denote not an address but a propositional increment in some subdomain. The simplest way to achieve this is probably to specify *true* syntactically as taking as subject a definite term (i.e. under the DD-operator of section 2.2) of the form "the proposition that S", where the grammar then allows for the deletion of the part "the proposition", just as the grammar allows for the deletion of "the fact" in the underlying "the fact that S" for most factive verbs.[18] These 'content-noun descriptions' do not denote addresses in (sub)domains but bits of domain structure: they select those bits of domain structure that are lexically represented in the description. Fact-descriptions are limited to a search in the (sub)domain to which the proposition figuring the factive verb is to be incremented; intensional proposition descriptions, such as occur in subject position to the predicate *true*, are free to search any (sub)domain.

5.3.5 More on intensional terms

Although most predicates in natural language are such that they require extensional reference values for their terms if true (or minimal falsity) is to be achieved, some do not have that requirement for some or all of their terms. We have already looked at the identity predicate and at *exist*, but we may add, e.g., *look for, want, hunt for, search, covet, suggest, represent, talk about, think about, adore, worship, pray to, love, resemble* and *look alike*. All these predicates belong to category β of section 5.1, i.e. they are marked $[+S, -E]$. Substitutivity is preserved simply because the intensional terms refer just like extensional terms, except that the reference object may be an intensional, i.e. thought-created, object (see the following chapter for a discussion of the philosophical points involved). *Represent*, for example, is intensional with respect to its object term, which means that truth (or minimal falsity) can be achieved even when the reference-value of the object term is intensional. Intuitively speaking, there is, of course, nothing strange or outlandish in the notion of a relation between, say, a person and a thought-object created by himself or by someone else, or a relation between thought-objects (as may be the case under the identity predicate).

In section 3.2.4 the notational convention was introduced of asterisking term variables in the extension set definition of the predicates in question when the predicate is intensional with respect to that term position. For the denotation procedure this means that the address for the intensional term is

---

[18] All factive verbs except *know* allow for substitution of the complementizer *that* introducing the factive clause by *the fact that*:

(i) Rosalind regretted (the fact) that her husband was an alcoholic.
(ii) *Rosalind knows the fact that her husband is an alcoholic.

to be found either in D^0 or in any available D^n of the proper kind. For the object term of *look for*, for example, it must be specified that if $n > 0$, D^n must be linked up with the belief-domain of the subject denotation. To pick up again the example (33) of section 3.2.4, repeated here as

(86) Billy is looking for the unicorn.

where D contains the information that Billy is one of the villagers and that the whole village believes that a unicorn rampaged through the local supermarket over the weekend, the object term *the unicorn* will denote precisely the address for the intensional unicorn believed by Billy and the other villagers to have made a mess of the supermarket.

After (86) the discourse domain D will contain the following structure:

(87)

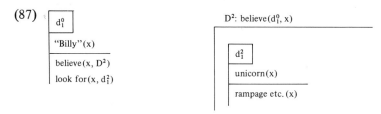

Note that the predication "look for(x, d_1^2)" is added to d_1^0, but there is no counterpart "look for(d_1^0, x)" under d_1^2. The reason is simply that, though the information is that Billy is looking for the unicorn, it is not that Billy believes that he is looking for the unicorn, and since anything added to d_1^2 under D^2 represents what Billy believes it would be improper to add "look for(d_1^0, x)" to d_1^2. Truth-conditional purity thus requires a special provision in the increment function for verbs of the category under discussion, to the effect that the predication is added only to the extensional addresses but not to the intensional ones. Thus, if a predicate incrementable in a D^n relates two addresses d^n and d^m and if $m > n$, then the predication is added to d^n only and not to d^m. (Clearly, if the object term of (86) denotes a really existing unicorn, whose address is in D^0, then the predication is added to both addresses.)

Truth is established for (86) just in case, at the relevant time, Billy is trying if he can find the implementation of the entity as it is defined in the (sub)domain where the denotation of the object term is located.

5.3.6 *Intensional quantification*

We must now make a provision for existential quantification over intensional term referents. For this it is necessary to define extension sets of predicates which, besides extensional entities, may also contain intensional entities. So far, set-denoting terms of the form $\hat{}x(P_1(x), \ldots, P_n(x))$ have implicitly been taken as taking extensional sets as their reference-value, i.e. the set of things e such that $e \in \sigma(P_1) \cap \ldots \cap \sigma(P_n)$ – see section 3.2.4. But clearly, if a unary predicate P^1 is intensional (is defined in the lexicon as being intensional with respect to its subject term), then $\sigma(P^1)$ may contain extensional as well as intensional entities, as long as the σ-function over P^1 yields the set of all things that have the property denoted by P^1.

Non-extensional sets are automatically denoted by intensional predicates. If a predicate P^n is intensional with respect to one of its n terms, say t_i, then lambda extraction of t_i yields a unary predicate which is simply intensional. Thus the derived predicate $\lambda x(\text{speak about}(y: \text{"Leo"}(y), x))$, or "be something Leo speaks about", is intensional by virtue of the fact that *speak about* is marked in the lexicon as being intensional with respect to its object term. Likewise, a derived predicate like $\lambda x(\text{think}(y: \text{"Leo"}(y), \text{red}(x)))$, or "be something that Leo thinks is red", is also intensional: Leo may think of something that it is red even though it does not exist. Formally we say that, since *think that A* is intensional with respect to the sentential term A, any predicate formed by lambda extraction for some term t_i in A is intensional, by virtue of the fact that any predicate which is intensional with respect to a sentential term is likewise intensional with respect to any term in the sentential term in question. The λ-derived predicate, however, allows for substitution *salva veritate* (is marked $[+S]$), even though the basic predicate may not.

Apart from the predicates which are intensional by virtue of the lexicon, we can make intensional predicates out of extensional ones. Given the extensional predicate *dog*, we can make the intensional predicate **dog*, whose extension set consists of all dogs, either really existing or somehow thought up. Let P_e^1 be a unary extensional predicate over individual-denoting subject terms, let "t(i)" stand for any term referentially related to the individual i, and "I" for any predicate or complex of predicates that is intensional with respect to a sentential term, then from P_e^1 with the extension set schema

(88) a. $\sigma(P_e^1) = \{i \mid P_e^1(t(i)) \text{ is true}\}$

the intensional predicate **P_e^1* can be formed with the extension set schema:

(88) b. $\sigma(*P_e^1) = \{i* \mid P_e^1(t(i)) \text{ is true or } I(P_e^1(t(i))) \text{ is true}\}$

This procedure will be called *intensionalization* of an extensional predicate. Intensionalized predicates are asterisked. Correspondingly, intensional set-denoting terms formed with an intensionalized predicate have the predicate marked by an asterisk. Whereas $\hat{}x(\text{dog}(x))$ denotes the set of all real dogs, $\hat{}x(*\text{dog}(x))$ denotes the set of all real or imagined dogs.

We add to the syntax of the semantic language the requirement that if in a set-denoting term $\hat{}x(P_1(x), \ldots, P_n(x))$ some $P_i(1 \leqslant i \leqslant n)$ is intensional, then all Ps in the term must be intensional. If a P_j in the term is extensional, it is intensionalized. Thus the set of all dogs, real or imagined, that Leo talks about is denoted by the term ˆx(*dog(x), λx(talk about(y: "Leo"(y), x))(x)). This is an intensional set-denoting term since all predicates in the term are intensional. The requirement that all predicates of a set-denoting term must be intensional if the term is to be intensional follows directly from the simple fact that if one of the predicates is extensional, i.e. denotes only real individuals, then the intersection of the extension sets of all the predicates involved can only comprise real individuals and is thus not the extension of an intensional set-denoting term.

For the same reason we add the further requirement that if a set-denoting term *t* is matched under a quantifier by an intensional set-denoting or definite term, then *t* must be intensional, i.e. its extensional predicates are intensionalized. Without this stipulation a sentence like

(89) a. Harry is thinking of a ship.

could not have an interpretation whereby there is a specific ship that Harry is thinking of, yet that ship does not really exist but has just been ordered at some yard and is defined only, for the moment, by the plans and specifications. For this interpretation to be obtainable (89a) must be analysed as:

(89) b. ∃1(ˆx(think of(y : "Harry"(y), x)), ˆx(*ship(x)))

i.e. "the set of things that Harry thinks of (which includes intensional entities), and the set of *real or imagined* ships have a non-empty intersection". Without the asterisk over the predicate *ship* in (89b) the sentence would state that the intersection of the set of things Harry thinks of and the set of *real* ships is non-empty, which would leave us with a real ship that Harry is thinking of. The same consideration holds for universal quantification: a sentence like

(90) a. Harry remembers all ships.

has a possible interpretation whereby Harry remembers all real and imagined ships (within some verification domain). This requires an analysis

(90) b. ∀(ˆx(remember(y : "Harry"(y), x)), ˆx(*ship(x)))

or "the set of real or imagined ships is included in the set of things Harry remembers" (and Harry may well remember intensional entities). We stipulate, therefore, that if one SD-term under a quantifier is intensional, so is the other.

In the light of what has been said already about the incrementation of terms in intensional positions, the question of the increment-value of intensional existential quantification is relatively straightforward. Take again (89a) with its analysis (89b), i.e. in its specific reading with the existential quantifier as the highest operator. Instead of an address denotation in the domain of Harry's thoughts, as was required for the cases discussed in the preceding section, we now need the introduction of a new address in Harry's thought-domain. Given that D contains an address for *Harry* and a subdomain D^2 of what Harry thinks, the address d_1^2 can be introduced for the ship Harry is thinking of, and the Harry-address will contain the new predication "think of(x, d_1^2)":

(89) c.

Similarly, cases like

(91) a. This picture represents a dog.
     b. Howard was referring to a lady.

increment the new, existentially introduced, addresses in some subdomain defined for the subject. Special provisions must be made in the lexicon to ensure that the proper relations are established between the subdomains in question and the addresses to be introduced. For *represent*, as in (91a), a subdomain is required representing whatever can be seen to be the case in the picture referred to. For *refer*, as in (91b), a subdomain is required for whatever Howard said on the occasion referred to by the past tense. It is a question of proper lexicography to formulate the relations in question in an adequate way.

Increments of this nature do not entail the real existence of an entity answering the description of the new address, nor do they exclude it. The sentences in question, in their SA-forms with the existential quantifier as the highest predicate, are vague in this respect, not ambiguous. That no ambiguity is involved, but only vagueness, appears when the standard tests are applied. If we apply the verb-phrase pronominalization test (Lakoff 1970) to, e.g.,

(92) This picture represents a dog, and that picture does too. But the dog represented on the latter really exists, whereas the other dog does not.

we see that vagueness, and not ambiguity results: if the pronominalization *does too* had been unacceptable, unnatural or 'funny', there would have been an argument for ambiguity. Likewise, Quine's philosophical test (1960: 129) yields ambiguity, not vagueness. A sentence like (91a) is not "at once clearly true" of the picture in question, "and clearly false". It thus seems justified to treat the specific existential readings of the sentences under discussion as vague between there being and there not being real existence for the object quantified over.

5.3.7 Specific and non-specific intensional readings

Some sentences involving intensional existential quantification allow for a non-specific reading in spite of the fact that the highest surface predicate is a single lexical verb. Thus, sentence (89a) allows for a non-specific reading (in fact, as we shall see, a number of them), besides the specific reading which has been analysed. A non-specific reading is actualized, for example, in a context where a group of people are deliberating about the question of a suitable means of transport for certain goods. Various proposals are made, and Harry is thinking of the possibility of using a ship. Equally ambiguous is, e.g.,

> (91) c. Billy is looking for a unicorn.

but not, for example, (91b) or (91a), where the quantified expressions can only be interpreted specifically. Sentence (91c), however, also allows for an interpretation where Billy's search is satisfied by an arbitrary unicorn found by him.

A general criterion for deciding whether an intensional predicate allows for non-specific readings besides the specific ones when it has an existential expression in its intensional term position is not easy to get by. It is much simpler to formulate criteria for specific readings. Thus, for example, there is a specific reading when such a sentence can be followed acceptably by the demonstrative pronoun *that* followed by an appropriate term description. Thus, (91c) has a specific reading because it is possible to carry on saying: "That unicorn, however, left the country days ago." And likewise for (89a), (91a) and (91b). But this test is less interesting because there is no reason to doubt that all cases of this class allow for a specific reading. What is needed is a test for the availability of non-specific readings. We may forge one by using the test just given for specific readings but applying it differently. Let us say that in case speaker A uses the sentence that is to be tested and speaker B carries on saying "That ship/dog/lady/unicorn ...", a non-specific reading is available when it is possible for speaker A to correct speaker B by saying, "I don't mean that; I mean just any ship/dog/lady/unicorn." If we apply this test to (89a) and (91c), the result is clearly positive. It makes perfect sense for A to say "Harry is thinking of a ship", then for B to say "That ship, is it large enough?", and for A to correct B by saying, "I don't mean that. Harry is thinking of just any ship, not one in particular." And likewise for (91c). But applied to (91a) or (91b) the result is negative:

> (93) a. A: This picture represents a dog.
> B: That dog, does it have a long tail?
> !A: I don't mean that. It represents just any dog.
> b. A: Howard was referring to a lady.
> B: That lady, does she live in High Street?
> !A: I don't mean that. He was referring to just any lady.

We shall, therefore, take it that, of the sentences under discussion, (89a) and (91c) are ambiguous between a specific and one or more non-specific readings, whereas (91a) and (91b) only have specific readings.

In general, non-specific readings for existentially quantified expressions come about as a result of the existential quantifier in question standing under a higher (non-existential) operator. Thus, for example, the normal interpretation of (94a) is non-specific for the dog believed to have been saved; (94b) is non-specific, in the normal reading, for the politician Leo must have talked to; (94c) for the flag everybody was holding:

(94) a. Harry thinks he has saved a dog.
  b. Leo must have talked to a politician.
  c. Everybody was holding a flag.

Specific readings, on the other hand, come about as a result of the existential quantifier having largest scope. We would naturally wish to extend this account of non-specific readings to the cases at hand. The problem is, however, that they leave no structural room for scope differences if they are analysed with one single semantic predicate "look for" or "think of" corresponding with the surface verbs. The problem is solved if we can argue that these predicates are not semantically primitive but complex, and that they belong to the 'open' class of complex lexical items, discussed in section 2.3.1, which allow for quantifier penetration. It seems that we can indeed argue for such a solution, on the grounds that the predicates that allow for non-specific readings are naturally paraphrasable in terms of a syntactic construction.

Let us assume that the verb *look for* is represented in the lexicon as a replacement of the syntactic structure

(95)

             V
       /   \
    V   V
    | |
   try find

Let sentence (91c) be analysed in the following two ways:

(96) a. $\exists 1[\hat{}x(try(y:\text{"Billy"}(y), find(y, x))), \hat{}x(*unicorn(x))]$
  b. $try(y:\text{"Billy"}(y), \exists 1[\hat{}x(find(y, x), \hat{}x(unicorn(x))])$

Analysis (a) represents the specific reading; (b) represents the non-specific reading. The syntactic tree corresponding to (96b) is:

(96) c.

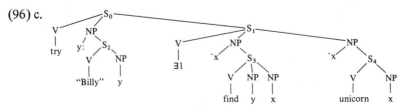

Reducing the subject-NP of *try* and the two set-denoting NP-terms of S_1 (by SD-Operator Lowering; see section 2.4.3) to, respectively,

we get

(96) d.

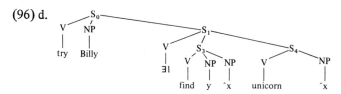

Object Incorporation on S_1 yields

(96) e.

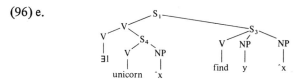

After Operator Lowering on S_1, S_0 looks like:

(96) f.

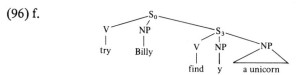

The S_1-cycle has now been terminated. On the S_0-cycle we apply Prelexical Predicate Raising (after the deletion of the subject of S_3 under co-referentiality with *Billy*):

(96) g.

Now the V of S_0 can be replaced by *look for*, giving its syntactic representation (95):[19]

[19] Note that if the distinction tentatively drawn in Section 2.3.1 between Semantic Analysis and Deep Structure is applied here, all rule applications from (96c) to (96h) are prelexical and thus pre-DS. Only at (96h) is a DS-representation reached. The same goes for the derivation of (96a).

(96) h.

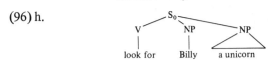

It is easily shown that the derivation of (96a) leads to the same structure (96h). From

(96) i.

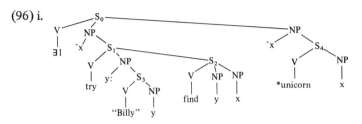

via

(96) j.

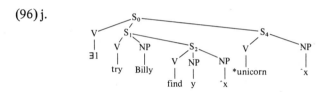

and

(96) k.

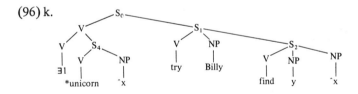

Operator Lowering yields (96f), from which point onwards the derivation is as before.

The verb *think of*, as in (89a), is slightly more complex. It does not seem that there is one single prelexical analysis which would cover all the possible readings of (89a), repeated here for convenience:

(89) a. Harry is thinking of a ship.

The most straightforward reading is represented as (89b): it is specific and the verb *think of* is unanalysed. In this reading the sentence is true just in case there is a ship, real or imagined, passing through Harry's thoughts. However, as was adumbrated at the outset of this section, *think of* can also be interpreted in terms of "think that may be suitable", or

(97)

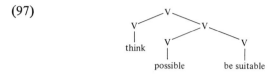

This leaves structural room for an existential quantifier in three positions: highest scope (i.e. specific), intermediate scope and narrow scope (between *possible* and *be suitable*). Close observation shows that these three readings are indeed available. The specific reading is actualized, for example, when certain special goods have to be transported and there is a specific ship that Harry thinks might be suitable for the job. Sentence (89a) is now appropriate. It is likewise appropriate when Harry thinks that there is a ship that might be suitable for the job: he has been falsely informed that Mr Onassis owns a ship of possibly the right description. Finally, (89a) is usable when Harry is just considering the possibility of there being a ship that would be all right.

A similar case is presented by the verb *dream of*. Let Harry be dreaming of a ship this time, then, if what is meant is simply that a ship occurs in Harry's dream there is only a specific interpretation and no non-specific ones. But the verb *dream of* can also be used in the sense that Harry indulges in dreams that he hopes will be fulfilled. Then suddenly one or more non-specific readings come to the fore, as is easily checked.

There are many more such verbs, which are non-extensional with respect to one or more terms, and moreover allow for non-specific readings in spite of their being non-complex at the surface. Examples are *resemble, look like, suggest* or *covet*, as in:

(98) a. She resembles a purring cat.
    b. He looked like a drunken gnome.
    c. This suggests a miracle.
    d. Nancy has always coveted a Norwegian husband.

In all such cases an analysis in terms of prelexical analysis would seem to be called for, so that the required non-specific readings can be accounted for by an appeal to scope differences. Which precise prelexical analyses will be preferable, in each case, so that justice is done to all observations and, moreover, the syntactic processes invoked are 'natural' in the sense that they fall within universal constraints and are independently motivated in syntactic theory (as Predicate Raising certainly is), is a matter of theoretical lexicography. Let us hope that it will not let us down.

5.3.8 *Modal increments*

In the light of the foregoing we may now specify the incremental effects of the modals. The modal predicates introduce subdomains for their embedded clauses, and according to the modal scale (69) as given in 5.3.2, modalities of necessity introduce subdomains of depth 1, but those of possibility of depth 3, depth 2 being taken by subdomains introduced by modalities of probability. The increment-value of a sentence like (31) above

(31) Harry's dog may be ill.

in a domain which already contains the addresses d_1^0 for *Harry* and d_2^0 for *Harry's dog*, is[20]

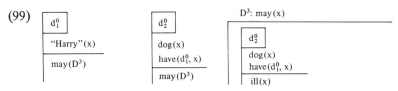

(99)

If, however, the domain does not contain d_2^0 for *Harry's dog*, then one would expect there to be two possibilities for the prejecting of the required sentence *Harry has a dog*: it can be prejected in D^0 or in D^3, with a preference for D^0. And the expectation is fully borne out, even more than fully, since the preference for preposing in D^0 is exceptionally strong in this case, due to the semantics of *may*, as given in (35) above. The satisfaction condition of *may* requires that, for (31), whatever is available in the way of knowledge must not include that Harry has no dog, since, if that is available knowledge, (31) is false: the statement that Harry has no dog will then be part of some set of known true statements **T** entailing "Harry's dog is not ill" (with radical negation). Therefore, if the increment of (31) is to be added to some D^0, and D^0 is to be consistent with available knowledge, then neither D^0 nor available knowledge can contain whatever corresponds to the proposition "Harry has no dog". This effectively precludes the blocking of i[Harry had a dog] in D^0: D^0 *must be free to receive* that increment, if it hasn't got it already. Yet, as has been observed, it would be a mistake to think that D^0 *must receive* i[Harry has a dog]. This is because, although "Harry has no dog" cannot be part of available knowledge, there is no guarantee that Harry has a dog when (31) is true: it may simply not be known whether he has or hasn't a dog, as in (33) above:

(33) Harry may have a dog, and it may be ill.

---

[20] The reader will notice that the copied address d_2^0 under D^3 in (99) is only partly identical with the original address in D^0. Where the latter has a reference to D^3 the former has "ill(x)". It is this extra predication under the copied D^3-address which falls under the possibility operator: it is said of Harry's dog that it is possibly ill. Clearly, if the D^3-copy had no extra predication compared with the D^0-original, nothing would be said to be possible about the individual referred to by d_2^0 which had not already been said to be true. This would be in violation of the preconditions of *may* as specified in (35) of section 5.2, where it is required that what is predicated under *may* is not known to be either true or false.

The increment of (33), in a D^0 which contains an address for *Harry*, is:

(100)

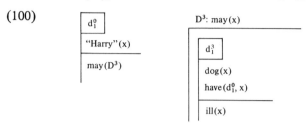

That is, in the normal reading in which *may* has larger scope than *a dog*. In the not so natural reading where *a dog* takes scope over *may*, the increment-value is:

(101)

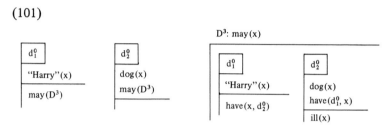

Although D^0 is not allowed to contain the increment of the argument clause of *must* or *may* before a modal statement is made, the argument clause as such must be acceptable in D^0. In fact, with "must(A)", A is immediately added as a consequence of the addition of "must(A)", since A is entailed, and entailment automatically leads to addition in D^0. "Must (A) and A" is not acceptable because after "must(A)" i(A) has been added, and the second conjunct thus repeats what is already in D^0 and is not informative. It is unacceptable for a second reason as well, which appears more clearly with *may*.

With "may(A)", as we have seen, A must be acceptable in D^0 but D^0 may not already contain i(A). Hence "A and may(A)" is unacceptable. After i(may(A)) A must remain acceptable in D^0, yet "may(A) and A" is not acceptable (nor is "may(not-A) and A"). This might look strange, since if A is acceptable in D^0 containing i(may(A)) why is "may(A) and A", or "may(not-A) and A", not an acceptable sequence? The answer lies, it seems, in the fact that the conjunction *and* makes the two conjuncts be asserted, so to speak, 'in one breath'. Since, as has been stipulated for the modals *may* and *must*, the truth-value of the argument clause must not be known at the time of utterance, and hence cannot be recorded in D^0 if D^0 is what is being asserted to be true, one cannot assert "may(A)" and "A" in one breath: that would show that the speaker both knows the truth-value of A and does not know it. If A is to be added to D^0 there must be a break, or some time must elapse, and when A, or not-A, is added, the modal increment must be erased from D.

Another point which deserves mention is the fact that *may*, in virtue of its predicate conditions, leaves room in D for a further *may*-statement with the negation of its argument clause: "may (A) and may (not-A)" is a well-formed sequence. Note, however, that "may$(A$ and not-$A)$" is not acceptable. This shows that *may*-statements are, in principle, housed in one D^3-subdomain, until an addition is made which is unacceptable in D^3, on account of contradiction or otherwise. Then a second D^3 is opened under *may*, strictly separate from the first D^3. Apparently, the grammar prohibits Conjunction Reduction in such cases.

Many more things could be said about the modals in natural language, modality being among the more complex areas of grammar and semantics. For an adequate understanding of the machinery at this stage of the enquiry, however, it seems that this will suffice.

5.4 The projection problem and discourse acceptability

The so-called projection problem for presuppositions has, for some time, dominated the systematic study of presupposition phenomena, especially through the influence of the writings of Karttunen in the 1970s. A satisfactory solution, however, was not found, and it would seem that this is because the rationale of the projection behaviour of presuppositions was not brought into focus.

The problem is posed by the fact that when a clause carrying a presupposition (i.e. an elementary presupposition) is embedded in a larger sentential structure, then sometimes the whole superordinate sentence maintains the elementary presupposition as a full presuppositional entailment, sometimes the presupposition is weakened in the sense that it is no longer entailed but it 'survives' as a suggestion, of varying strength, i.e. as what we have called a mere prejection, and sometimes it disappears altogether so that not even a trace of a suggestion remains. Take, for example, the simple clause *Kate has come back*, with the elementary presupposition *Kate has been away*, and embed it in the following ways:

(102) a. Barry knows that Kate has come back.
     b. This entails that Kate has come back.
     c. If Kate has come back, Richard will be pleased.
     d. Maybe Kate has come back.
     e. Richard hopes that Kate has come back.
     f. If Kate has been away, she has come back.
     g. If Kate has come back, she has been away.

The problem now is to explain why in (102a) and (102b) the elementary presupposition *Kate has been away* is preserved, while in (102c) and (102d) it survives as a slightly weakened presupposition, i.e. as a strong suggestion, but in (102e) as a mere suggestion, with less strength than in (102c) and (102d), and not even a trace of a suggestion is left in (102f) and (102g).

Karttunen, as is well known, proposed a system of 'plugs' or predicates blocking all presuppositional percolation (such as the predicate *say*), 'holes' or predicates letting through elementary presuppositions either as full presuppositions, as with factives and other entailing predicates, or as mere prejections of any degree of strength, as with predicates of propositional attitude (*believe*, *hope*, etc.) or the modals, and, finally, 'filters' or predicates that let elementary presuppositions through (in full or just as mere prejections) only under certain conditions. But although Karttunen put in more and more refinements into this classification and the formulation of the filtering conditions, counter-examples continued to plague the proposals (as is clearly demonstrated, for example, in Van der Sandt 1982). Especially the category of 'filters' proved troublesome. Now, with some hindsight, one feels tempted to say "no wonder", because Karttunen's analysis was, in fact, nothing but a taxonomy of the facts without any explanatory principles that could provide an insight into the rationale behind this projection behaviour of presuppositions.

Van der Sandt (1982) was the first to propose that the projection phenomena of presuppositions follow from independently given conditions of discourse acceptability. As has been said (section 3.3), he proposes a set of discourse acceptability conditions and proceeds to show that elementary presuppositions are cancelled when their prejection into the truth-domain (or "context", in Van der Sandt's terminology) would make the carrier sentence unacceptable. Thus, given the following acceptability conditions (1982: 185),

(103) A sentence A is considered an acceptable addition to a context C if:

  a. C does not entail A.
  b. A is logically consistent with C.
  c. If A contains an embedded clause D which is not itself an elementary presupposition of A, then A is acceptable in C only if D is acceptable in C – except when A is of the form $B \wedge C$, or $B \vee C$, or $B \supset C$, or when D is complement to a verb of propositional attitude.
  d. If A is of the form $B \wedge C$, then A is acceptable in C only if B is acceptable in C and C is acceptable in C', where $C' = C + B$.
  e. If A is of the form $B \vee C$ or $B \supset C$, then A is acceptable in C only if B and C are both acceptable in C.

one sees immediately, for example, that a sentence of the form "if A_B then B", or "if B then A_B" (where "A_B" is to be read as "A presupposing B") must cancel the elementary presupposition B. For according to (103e) an implication is acceptable only if both the antecedent and the consequent clauses are acceptable in the context. But if B is prejected into C (or, as we say, into D^0), then $i(B)$ is no longer acceptable. Thus for the whole conditional of the form "if B then A_B" or "if A_B then B" to be acceptable, the elementary presupposition B must be cancelled and not even a suggestion of the truth of B remains.

Van der Sandt does not provide the formal means for deriving either elementary presuppositions or the entailments that go with them if the carrier sentence is non-complex. He simply postulates these properties for certain sentences, a feature which his theory has in common with virtually all treatments of the presupposition or the projection problem. It must be said, however, that Van der Sandt's theory is entirely compatible with the system generating (elementary) presuppositions as unfolded in chapter 3. Furthermore, Van der Sandt's acceptability conditions are not complete (and not presented as such): they do not cover sentences containing verbs of propositional attitude (= categories 2 and 3 in scale (68) of section 5.3.2), and thus no account is presented by Van der Sandt for the behaviour of presuppositions embedded under such verbs. However, to the extent that the acceptability relation is elaborated, the empirical predictions are essentially correct (one small blemish will be discussed in a moment). Then, no distinction is made, in Van der Sandt's projection system, between full, i.e. entailed, presuppositions and mere prejections. But besides these and perhaps other such possible critical notes, the main feature about this theory is its taxonomic character: even if the conditions formulated are made complete and entirely adequate in the observational sense, the theory still lacks an explanatory element since it is not clear why the conditions should be as they are. It fails to show how the various, carefully formulated conditions can be seen to follow from a cognitive mechanism such as the construction of discourse domains. In fact, as we shall see, all elements in Van der Sandt's theory to do with contextual acceptability and the projection behaviour of presuppositions are immediately derivable from, and make a great deal more sense in the context of, the cognitive theory of domains and subdomains.

Elementary presuppositions must always be prejectable into the D^n to which the clause in question is to be incremented. If in a given D^n such a prejection would lead to the unacceptability of D^n as a discourse structure in its own right, then the whole sentence containing the elementary presupposition is rejected as unacceptable in the D in question and is uninterpretable in D. This puts a constraint on the whole of natural language: it is impossible for a sentence A_B to be itself acceptable in a class of discourses D while, in all Ds, the prejection of B into any D^n to which A is to be incremented automatically makes A unacceptable.

This constraint would be violated if the increment-value of the conjunction *and* did not consist of a separate increment unit for each conjunct. Take the conjunction (104a), which is acceptable in a large class of domains, just like virtually all normal sentences:

(104) a. Kate has been away, and Harry knows that Kate has come back.[21]

which is of the form "*A* and B_{C_A}". If the factive presupposition under *know*, i.e. C_A, were prejectable into the position immediately preceding the whole conjunction, the resulting discourse would be unacceptable:

(104) b. !Kate has come back, and Kate has been away, and Harry knows that Kate has come back.

Since there is no subdomain for C_A to take refuge in, (104a) should be unacceptable by definition for any discourse on earth, which it clearly is not. The solution is, clearly, that the second conjunct *B* is a separate increment unit and prejects its presupposition C_A into the position immediately preceding *B* itself. Then again, C_A prejects *A* into the position immediately preceding the prejected *C*, but without practical effect because *A* is already there:

(104) c. Kate has been away, and she has come back, and Harry knows that she has come back.

(In fact, (104a) is a counter-example to Van der Sandt's theory since in his theory prejection of (elementary) presuppositions is made into the position immediately preceding the whole complex sentence in all cases, including conjunctions. Since for (104a) such prejection makes the whole sentence unacceptable, C_A should be cancelled as a presupposition in (104a), which it clearly is not. This blemish can be removed by postulating, as is done in our theory, that conjunctions constitute separate increment units for each conjunct.)

For sentences that are complex in ways other than through conjunction, a distinction must be made between those which entail the embedded clause that carries the elementary presupposition, and those that do not. That is, if a sentence *S* embeds a clause *B* with the elementary presupposition *A*, or $S\langle B_A \rangle$, then either $S \models B$ or $S \not\models B$. If $S \models B$. as we have seen (section 3.3), then also $S \gg B$, and hence $S \gg A$. Then if *S* is to be incremented to a domain D^n both *B* and *A* must be incrementable to D^n (unless they have already been incremented) and rejection of either *B* or *A* by D^n makes *S* unacceptable, as well as any larger sentential structure of which *S* may be a part. For these cases presuppositional projection phenomena are relatively straightforward

---

[21] This example (and its significance in the context of projection phenomena of presuppositions and acceptability conditions) was found by our student Bart Geurts.

and unproblematic. The complications arise predominantly with embedded presupposition-carrying clauses that are not entailed by the superordinate S, i.e. $S \not\models B$.

In general, embedded clauses not entailed by the superordinate S are incremented to a properly defined and properly ranked intensional subdomain, following the scale classification outlined in section 5.3.2. The only exceptions are the argument clauses under the logical predicates of minimal or radical negation (section 4.1.4). For a sentence of the form $\sim(B_A)$ to be incremented to, say, D^0, it is required, as part of the increment conditions for minimal negation, that B_A forms an acceptable increment to D^0, which implies that all presuppositions of B must be prejectable into D^0 if they are not already represented there. In fact, although $\sim(B_A)$ does not entail B, it entails all presuppositions of B. Since it also projects all presuppositions of B, $\sim(B_A) \geqslant A$, and no special problem remains. For a sentence $\simeq(B_A)$ to be incremented to D^0, it is required, as part of the increment conditions for the radical negation, that B_A be acceptable in D^0, just like minimally negated sentences. It follows, likewise, that all presuppositions of B are either already represented in D^0 or prejectable into it. However, other than with the minimal negation, there is the further requirement that at least one presupposition of B be blocked, *post hoc*, from D^0 so that B_A is no longer acceptable in D^0 and hence uninterpretable in the new D^0. Now not only $\simeq(B_A) \not\geqslant A$, it is even so that $\simeq(B_A) \not> A$: the elementary presupposition is cancelled.

Apart, however, from the rather special cases of minimal and radical negation, embedded non-entailed clauses have their own intensional subdomain D^m. A minimum requirement for the acceptability of the whole superordinate S is that B_A is acceptable in D^m. But if $m > 1$ this does not guarantee mere projection into D^0, i.e. the suggestion of truth for A. As we have seen (section 5.3.1), non-entailed presuppositions tend to make themselves incremented to all possible higher domains as well, apart from D^m, up to D^0, by virtue of the functional *principle of ambition*: the less subdomains differ from D^0, the more economical the cognitive processing. $i(A)$ will therefore be added to all higher domains above D^m unless it is stopped by some D^n ($n < m$) either on grounds of discourse unacceptability or on grounds of background knowledge. Stoppage on account of background knowledge does not interest us here since we are now concerned with sentences as linguistic objects and these are independent of encyclopaedic cognitive contingencies. Nor are we interested here in cases where some contingent D^n blocks the incrementation of $i(A)$, again because we are concentrating on sentences as linguistic objects: if some $S\langle B_A \rangle$ is incremented to, say, a D^0 already containing, say, $i(\sim A)$, then A is not projected into this D^0 and it will have to take refuge in its own D^m or some intermediate D^n. But this leaves untouched the possibility that this S, as a linguistic object, still merely prejects A and thus carries the suggestion that A. The projection problem is to formulate the conditions under which complex sentences, as linguistic objects, continue to preject presuppositions of embedded non-entailed clauses into their own domain, *nullo obstante*.

The general answer now is that $S\langle B_A \rangle$ with non-entailed B (and non-entailed A) will always preject A into D^0 (if S is incrementable in D^0) unless such D^0-prejection makes S unacceptable in D^0 on account of the increment instructions associated with S.[22] This answer is generally valid and without exceptions. The discovery of this principle is due to Van der Sandt (1982), but in his formulation it is not a functional principle. In the context of discourse semantics this principle is seen to be functional (in so far as the theory of discourse domains is functional) and to follow directly from the machinery of discourse domain construction.

Let us now look at a few cases. A simple case, discussed a number of times in previous chapters, is

(105) a. Harry believes that his son lives in Kentucky.

where "Harry's son lives in Kentucky" is B and "Harry has a son" is A. B is incremented to the D^2 of Harry's beliefs, and A is prejected into this D^2. But, provided D^0 allows for the addition of $i(A)$ because $i(A)$ is not blocked either by what is already in D^0 or by background knowledge – we speak of the condition *nullo obstante* for D^0 - A is also prejected into D^0, since

(105) b. Harry has a son, and he believes that his son lives in Kentucky.

is a perfectly acceptable bit of discourse. This accounts for the semantic fact that (105a), as a linguistic object, carries the suggestion that Harry has a son.

A more complex case is

(106) a. Harry's son may live in Kentucky.

where B and A are as in the previous example. Sentence (106a) does not entail B, of course, but it does not entail A either, even though a feeling of contradiction is provoked by a conjunction of the negation of A and (106a):

(106) b. !Harry has no son, but his son may live in Kentucky.

The intuition of contradiction provoked by such conjunctions, however, is not a sufficient test for entailment since the intuition may also arise from the fact that the conjunction is unacceptable in a discourse-technical sense. And

---

[22] Here and later, the term "increment instructions" is meant to include the truth-conditional description of the extension set of the highest predicate in S. This follows, of course, from the mere fact that entailment relations are involved.

this is what underlies the rejection of (106b). That (106a) does not entail A appears from

(106) c. Harry may have a son, and his son may live in Kentucky.

which does not entail that Harry has a son, i.e. A, though it entails (106a). If (106a) did entail A, then, since (106c) entails (106a), (106c) would have to entail A, which it clearly does not do. But (106b) can be seen to be rejected on different grounds than logical contradiction. The extension set of *may*, as given in (35) above (section 5.2), requires that, at the moment of utterance, the truth-value of the clause under *may*, i.e. B_A, is not known. But if the discourse already contains the incremental representation of $\sim A$, i.e. "Harry has no son", then by definition the truth-value of A is known, and since A is given as false in D^0, B_A must be radically false, and hence the truth-value of the clause under *may*, B_A, is known, which is against the preconditions of *may* and makes the whole of (106b) unacceptable under any discourse conditions.

The conclusion must be that (106a) strongly suggests (more than just 'merely' prejects) that Harry has a son. The mere prejection is particularly strong here because a negation of it is unacceptable in the discourse. Yet it does not presuppose that Harry has a son. In fact, if we apply the observational test used in section 3.3, we see that the conclusion is borne out:

(106) a. Harry's son may live in Kentucky.

    d. Harry has a son.

    e. Harry has a son and his son may live in Kentucky.

    f. Harry may not have a son, but his son may also live in Kentucky.

As will be remembered, the embedded elementary presupposition, i.e. (106d), must make for an acceptable bit of discourse when prefixed to the sentence in question, (106a), which it does, as appears from (106e). This means that (106a) prejects (106d). Now, since the negation of (106d) under the possibility operator, prefixed to (106a), also yields an acceptable bit of discourse we must conclude that (106a) does not presuppose (106d) but merely prejects it.

We are now in a position to understand why this observational test should work the way it does. A naïve procedure would be to test presupposition-hood by prefixing the negated prospective presupposition to the carrier sentence and see if a contradiction arises: for every B_A, a discourse "not-A and/but B" must be contradictory since if $B \gg A$, also $B \models A$. It has just been shown, however, that such a test would be naïve, since it is possible for B not to presuppose A and a discourse "not-A and/but B" still to be unacceptable in such a way that an intuition of contradiction arises. This complication is avoided when the presupposition under scrutiny is negated and placed under the operator of epistemic possibility *may*. The reason is that a bit of discourse of the form "may(not-*A*) and/but *B*" is acceptable only if $B \not\models A$. For if $B \models A$, the second conjunct, "*B*", ensures the truth of *A*; but the first conjunct, "may(not-*A*)", requires that the truth-value of *A* should not be known, and hence not be recorded as being known by addition to the truth-domain, at the time of utterance. If, in one breath, both "may(not-*A*)" is uttered and "*B*", while $B \models A$, clearly, no speaker can maintain that he knows both to be true, which is what he does when he asserts them, so to speak, in one breath. It is possible for one speaker to utter both "may(not-*A*)" and "*B*" consistently (where $B \models A$), but some time must pass between the former and the latter, and anyway D must be revised. So,

(106) g. ! Harry may not have a son, but his son lives in Kentucky.

is unacceptable because one cannot both be consistent and utter (106g) in one breath. A speaker can only claim consistency when asserting both conjuncts of (106g) if there is a clear break between the two conjuncts and, as a result of the second conjunct, the first is withdrawn. Moreover, if $B \not\models A$, the bit of discourse "may(not-*A*) and/but *B*" is always acceptable (provided the contingencies of background knowledge do not put an obstacle in the way and the discourse has given rise to the question of the truth-value of *A*), since there is nothing in the increment instructions (including the predicate conditions) of *may* that stands in the way.

So a discourse of the form "may(not-*A*) and/but $S\langle B_A \rangle$", where $S \not\models A$, is acceptable in principle, but *A* is prejected into the subdomain associated with *B*, not into D^0. Thus, if we apply the test to (105a),

(105) c. Harry may not have a son but he believes that his son lives in Kentucky.

we see that (105a) does not presuppose that Harry has a son but merely prejects it. (Note that the other half of the test, the acceptability of "*A* and/but $S\langle B_A \rangle$", is fulfilled by (105b).)

Let us now look at (102a)–(102g) and see how the projection behaviour of the embedded presuppositions is correctly predicted. In all cases, "*B*" stands for "Kate has come back", and "*A*" for "Kate has been away", and "*S*" for the sentence under scrutiny. For (102a),

(102) a. Barry knows that Kate has come back.

the observational test shows that $(102a) \gg B$ and $(102a) \gg A$. This is predicted by the theory since *know* is factive and thus requires a fact-denotation in D^0 (to which *S* is incremented) for *B*. If no such fact-denotation is there in D^0 it must be inserted *post hoc*, on pain of *S* being unacceptable and uninterpretable. Likewise for A. D^0 must therefore contain or accept both A and B, in that order. Hence (102a) $\gg B \gg A$. For (102b),

(102) b. This entails that Kate has come back.

observation shows that (102b) $\gg A$. Moreover, (102b) $\models B$. The increment instructions associated with *entail* result in the addition to D^0 of B, but not by way of prejection (or backward suppletion). B is added after S. The predicate conditions of *entail* require a set of true statements T as the subject term referent. T must therefore be represented in D^0 (without that, no reference can take place). Since by virtue of the satisfaction condition of *entail* T must prove B, T must contain all presuppositions of B, including A. Hence, A must be represented in D^0 before S is added, i.e. (102b) $\gg A$.

Now consider

(102) c. If Kate has come back, Richard will be pleased.

The observational test shows that the embedded presupposition A of the antecedent clause B is prejected but not presupposed by (102c):

(102) c'. Kate has been away, and if she has come back, Richard will be pleased.
　　　c''. Kate may not have been away, but if she has come back, Richard will be pleased.

Note that the naïve test would give the incorrect result that (102c) $\gg A$:

(102) c'''. !Kate has not been away, but if she has come back, Richard will be pleased.

As with (106a) and (106b), the unacceptability of (102c''') is not due to logical contradiction but to the specific increment instructions associated with *if*. As was stipulated in section 4.1.5, *if* requires that both the antecedent and the consequent clause are acceptable in D^0. But if D^0 already contains $i(\sim A)$, then $i(B_A)$ is unacceptable. (102c'') shows that (102c) $\ngg A$, which is correct because (102c) $\not\models A$. (102c') shows that (102c) $> A$. The interpretation of (102c'') now prevents A from being inserted into D^0; A is confined to the subdomain defined for *if* by the (technical) increment instruction associated with it. (102c'') will thus be read as:[23]

---

[23] Note that the second conjunct of (102c'''')

If Kate has been away and has come back, Richard will be pleased.

no longer prejects "Kate has been away". This follows from the theory because this antecedent clause, *Kate has been away and she has come back*, is not acceptable in a D which already contains i(Kate has been away).

(102) c''''. Kate may not have been away, but if she has been away and has come back, Richard will be pleased.

We can skip (102d) and (102e) because they run exactly parallel to (106) and (105), respectively. (102f) and (102g) are more interesting:

(102) f. If Kate has been away, she has come back.
g. If Kate has come back, she has been away.

For both, the observation test shows that $S \not> A$ and hence $S \not\gg A$:

(102) f'. !Kate has been away, and if Kate has been away she has come back.
f''. Kate may not have been away, but if she hás been away she has come back.
g'. !Kate has been away, and if she has come back she has been away.
g''. Kate may not have been away, but if she has come back she hás been away.

Interestingly, (102f'') and (102g'') are acceptable (which does not show that $S > A$ because one other condition for mere prejection, the acceptability of (102f') and (102g'), is not fulfilled). It might be expected that (102f'') and (102g'') are not acceptable since

(107) !Kate may not have been away, and/but she hás been away.

is as grossly unacceptable as (106g) above. But, as has been said, although cases such as (106g) or (107) are unacceptable 'in one breath', modal increments do not preclude the later addition of the embedded clause. In fact, as we have seen (section 5.3.8), *must* requires immediate addition of its argument clause to D^0, while *may* allows for either its argument clause or its negated argument clause to be added any time later, in which case the modal increment is removed. It must, therefore, be understood that when acceptability is required for a possible addition any time later in the development of D, as with both clauses of *if*, or of *or* for that matter, this does not necessarily mean that *and*-conjunction with the existing D is always acceptable.[24]

The disjunction *or*, given its increment instruction (section 4.1.5), including its predicate conditions ((37d) of section 3.2.4), now behaves entirely predictably as regards the projection of embedded presuppositions. Disjunctions of the form "B_A or C_A" maintain the presupposition A. This accords with the truth-table of trivalent *or* (i.e. table 5 in section 3.2.4), or, equivalently, with the extension set definition (37d) in section 3.2.4: if A

---

[24] It would seem that the accent which is naturally placed on *has* in (102f'') and (102g'') is to do with the fact that, although (107) is unacceptable, the second conjunct, *Kate has been away* can still be added, either now but by a different speaker, or later (by any speaker). When it is added, the accent on *has* seems natural.

is (minimally or radically) false, then both disjuncts are radically false, and hence the whole disjunction is radically false. Since all other conditions for presuppositional status for A are fulfilled, $S \gg A$. This is confirmed by the observation test:

(108) a. Either Harry's son lives way out in Kentucky, or he is at school.
     b. Harry has a son.
     c. Harry has a son, and either his son lives way out in Kentucky or he is at school.
     d. !Harry may not have a son, but either his son lives way out in Kentucky, or he is at school.

Since the embedded presupposition (108b) is entailed, it must be added to D^0 if D^0 does not already contain it, and it must be added as a prejection. The unacceptability of (108d) follows from the incompatibility of *Harry has a son* with *Harry may not have a son* 'in one breath'.

A disjunction of the form "B_A or C" (or: "C or B_A"), where C is logically independent of B_A, as in

(109) a. Either Harry's son lives in Kentucky, or Mr Bathwater got the flight-number wrong.

does not presuppose (108b) ($=A$) but merely prejects it. A, of course is not entailed by (109a). Acceptability observations support the analysis:

(109) b. Harry has a son, and either his son lives in Kentucky or Mr Bathwater got the flight-number wrong.
     c. Harry may have no son, but either his son lives in Kentucky or Mr Bathwater got the flight-number wrong.

For the interpretation of (109c) it is necessary that the prejection of "Harry has a son" be limited to the subdomain associated with the first disjunct of (109a), *Harry's son lives in Kentucky*, so that it reads as:

(109) d. Harry may have no son, but either he has a son and his son lives in Kentucky, or Mr Bathwater got the flight-number wrong.

Disjunctions of the form "B_A or A" cannot occur because they violate the True Alternatives Condition for disjunctions (section 4.1.5) which forbids that one disjunct entails the other. But we can have "$\sim A$ or B_A", as in

(110) Kate has not been away, or she has come back.

This neither presupposes nor merely prejects the embedded presupposition ($=A$) "Kate has been away", for the simple reason that A is not entailed, which rules out presupposition, and A is not projected into D^0 because if it were, the first disjunct, *Kate has not been away*, would be unacceptable in

D^0 beyond redemption. The first disjunct thus stops the elementary presupposition of the other disjunct from being prejected into D^0.

A similar case is presented by disjunctions of the form "B_A or C_{not-A}". as in

(111)   Either Rosalind lied about Kate having been away, or Kate has come back.

where the first disjunct presupposes that Kate has not been away, and the second that Kate has been away. Clearly these two embedded presuppositions cannot both be incremented to D^0. In fact, neither can, since addition of one would make the carrier clause of the other unacceptable. Both prejections are thus limited to their own subdomain, and nothing percolates to D^0.

Many more examples could be given. It would seem, however, that the machinery of domains and subdomains, in conjunction with an acceptability theory for discourse additions, will have to make the right predictions in all cases. If, possibly, cases are found where the theory fails to make predictions, it must be extended to cover the missing cases. Any possible incorrect predictions must be remedied. But one may feel confident that the remedy will be found in specific formulations of predicate conditions for extension sets, or in the technical aspects of increment instructions. It seems unlikely that the counter-evidence will be so massive that the whole notion of projection of elementary presuppositions through the machinery of domains and subdomains will have to be abandoned.

6
Truth and reference

6.1 Uniform truth and simple reference

As has been said repeatedly in earlier chapters, we are using throughout one uniform definition of truth for utterances of assertive sentences:

(1) An utterance $P^n(t_1, \ldots, t_n)$ is true just in case $\langle \rho(t_1), \ldots, \rho(t_n) \rangle \in \sigma(P^n)$.

This definition is a straightforward version of the ancient correspondence theory of truth, which, despite many subtle philosophical arguments and distinctions, still seems the most solid metaphysical view of what truth and falsity amount to. The formal semantics programme initiated by Tarski is also based on a correspondence view of truth, but in a rather different way. In the Tarskian programme, something like our definition (1) is applied to atomic sentential structures, and then a recursive syntax is defined for complex sentential structures while for each recursive syntactic rule a separate truth-definition is added. The whole complex of syntactic rules and associated truth-definitions thus forms a massive truth-definition for the whole language that is analysed in this way. Our tactic is very different. Instead of using the theory itself as a means for making the notion of truth explicit, we make the notion explicit beforehand: its explicit definition is given in (1). We then make sure that all sentences, simple or complex, are of the form $P^n(t_1, \ldots, t_n)$, and that all terms have a properly defined extension or ρ-value for truth to be testable (for those discourses where truth is testable, i.e. which have a verification domain and are not simply fictional). That is, we too have a programme on our hands, but of a different kind. We must show that grammatical analysis gains by assuming that all sentences have the predicate-term structure given, and, moreover, that semantic analysis benefits from this assumption plus the imposition of a uniform truth definition.

This programme has the advantage of implying a general and severe constraint on both grammatical and semantic theories. Chapter 2 is a sustained attempt at showing that, far from being a bothersome constraint in any limitative sense, the grammatical aspects of the programme are extremely fruitful and helpful, in myriad ways – liberating rather than strait-jacketing. In the semantics, too, we have made ample use of the advantages afforded by the decision to treat all lexical material, including the well-known logical operators of classical propositional and predicate calculus, as predicates. In other words, hardly a pinch was felt as a result of the constraint imposed by this programme. It is time now to pay some attention to the burdens inherent in the programme.

They are largely to do with questions of reference. Since some of the predicates P^n are 'abstract' in the sense that they do not appear in Surface Structure as verbs or even as items with a lexical meaning, their terms can be different from what terms are in traditional grammatical anaysis. In particular, the set-denoting terms that are postulated with quantifying predicates need special attention. Then, definition (1) requires that all terms have an **extension for the sentence** (or rather, uttered sentence) to have a truth-value. This makes it necessary to define extensions also for terms that do not refer to existing things. For example, if an utterance of *The girl Leo dreams of does not exist* has a truth-value, then the subject-term must have an extension in the world, or, more modestly, the verification domain at hand. Even when the utterance is true, so that the girl in question does not exist, there must be a non-existing girl. And many other complications arise.

But let us consider the straightforward cases first. We have stipulated that a term cannot refer other than via the intermediate role of a discourse domain. For a term t to refer to a really existing object r, t must first denote an address d_n^0 in the truth-domain D^0 of some D at hand. Then, d_n^0 must be the mental representation of r, or, as we shall say, d_n^0 must *designate r*. If t denotes d_n^0 and d_n^0 designates r, then t refers to r.

We have devoted a fair bit of attention to the denotation relation, but far less to the designation relation. For an address d_n^0 to designate anything in the world there must, first, be a verification domain V and, second, a truth-value for d_n^0. The requirement of a verification domain is justified by the trivial fact that most natural language assertive utterances are not about the whole existing universe, and even less about all possible universes. On the contrary, it is normal to limit truth-value assignments to utterances made with regard to some predefined portion of the world. How this portion is delimited, in each case, is not an easy question to answer. Deictic means are often used, so that an appeal is made to data provided by knowledge presumed to be present about the setting in which an utterance is made. Place and time parameters to delimit V are often filled in by linguistic material (locatives, verbal tenses) in conjunction with background knowledge presumed available. In general, it seems, verification domains are fixed by the use of expressions in the linguistic material which latch on to available (background or situational) knowledge. This knowledge directs the listener who shares it with the speaker to the verification domain intended. Since this process is distinct from the mechanics of denotation and designation once a V has been established, and since we are concentrating on the latter, we shall not attempt a further elaboration of this matter here.

One distinction, however, must be made. A discourse domain D can have either a *specific* or a *non-specific* V (besides, of course, no V at all). V is specific when both speakers and hearer know what precise things are being referred to. V is non-specific when all they know is that there are things and situations for which D is true although they do not know precisely where and when. This distinction is closely parallel to that between specific and non-specific reference discussed in the following section.

We have repeatedly spoken, in earlier chapters, about domains having truth-values. It is time to say more about this notion. Obviously, the truth-definition (1) does not apply here, since domains do not have the predicate-term structure of uttered sentences. We say that a domain D is true just in case all addresses in D^0 designate really existing things (or complexes of things) or, depending on the address category, designate real facts, and all predications under each D^0-address are true of the things or facts designated, i.e. represent real properties or facts. Open addresses are satisfied by any entity satisfying the description; closed addresses must be true of their specific designations. Moreover, all instructions or embargoes attached to D must be such that their observance keeps D true in the sense just given. Subdomains count as addresses: whatever is represented as being believed by Judy in some D is stacked in the D^2 of Judy's beliefs, which counts as an address. Subdomains not attached to some other address in D, such as sub-domains of modality, count as addresses as well. Subdomains designate (complexes of) facts, not things. An address D^i (i.e. a subdomain) is true in D just in case the (complex of) facts designated is indeed an element, in the appropriate position, in an n-tuple which is a member of the extensions set of the intensional predicate. An intensional individual address d_j^i in a subdomain D^i is true just in case D^i is true for the intensional designation of d_j^i.

One may wonder whether domains are bivalent, i.e. just either true or false, or whether they also allow for minimal and radical falsity. The question applies only to Ds requiring a specific V, such as a D introduced with an utterance of "Yesterday, at four in the afternoon...", and not to Ds made for non-specific Vs ("Once upon a time there was..."). The latter have a V if they are true and because of their truth, and they are false just in case there is no fitting V. One might say that such Ds take the whole universe with all its history as their specific V and are true as soon as an appropriate set of things and circumstances is found fulfilling all conditions posed by the addresses and predications in D, just as open addresses are true as soon as any individual in V is available answering to their description. But for Ds with a specific V one may indeed ask whether they are bivalent or trivalent. It seems that, besides truth, minimal and radical falsity are indeed definable for such Ds. One might say that falsity ensues when not all addresses have proper designations or not all predications tit the designations. And one might then proceed to specify that the falsity is radical if not all closed addresses have designations according to the predications before closure, or when some predication of some address after closure violates an ontological category constraint, and that the falsity is minimal in all remaining cases. But however that may be, the question is likely to be just academic because no calculus is involved, logic operating with sentential formulae and not with domain structures.

What counts is whether a given D is true or not true, because that is what matters for the fixing of reference values for terms. Simple reference is (relatively) unproblematic: the term t denotes the address d_n^0, and d_n^0 designates some really existing thing r in V. Now t refers to r. But this takes it for granted that d_n^0 is true, i.e. designates a really existing thing, in this case r, and contains only predications that are true of r. But what if d_n^0 is not true, say, because there is nothing in V answering the descriptions under d_n^0? Then the designation of d_n^0 is fictitious. We still need a designation for d_n^0, since d_n^0 can be denoted by a term t in some utterance with a truth-value, for example "t is fictitious". Now the utterance is true, and hence t must have a reference value, which means that d_n^0 must have a designation. But the same holds for ordinary extensional sentences: "t was hit by a bullet" is radically false if $\rho(t)$ does not *exist*, but there must *be* a $\rho(t)$ if the utterance is to have a truth-value at all. We say that if a d_n^0 fails to designate a real thing, and is thus false, it designates an intensional thing, defined by the D at hand. The extensions of addresses thus depend on the truth-value of the addresses and, therefore, of D.

According to some, semantics consists in the precise formulation of truth-conditions for sentences. This is not the position defended here: here, truth-conditional purity is one of a number of criteria of correctness for a theory of semantic analysis. But anyway, in so far as semantics is about truth-conditions it is important that the truth-conditions of discourse domains should be formulated precisely. As long as the theory is at the relatively primitive level at which we are operating now, truth-definitions for discourse domains are relatively unproblematic and straightforward, if not trivial. This point is of some relevance, since at the same relatively primitive level of operation defining truth for sentences without the intermediary of discourse domains is far from the trivial matter it is with discourse domains. Discourse domains are thus seen to simplify the aspect of truth-definitions in a non-trivial way.

However, beyond the relatively primitive level at which we have been operating so far the truth-conditional aspects of discourse domains may well prove to be thornier. In particular, the relation between definite terms and their denotation addresses in discourse domains on the one hand, and the entities referred to on the other, is in reality far from the straightforward matter it has been depicted to be. In section 4.2.1 brief mention was made of 'sloppy identity' pronouns. They are a complicating factor to be reckoned with – although it would seem that there it is not a question of identical addresses that stand in complex designation relations to their designata, but rather of different addresses with analogous roles. There are also cases, however, where it does seem that identical addresses are involved but where the ontological status of the designatum (reference object) is a matter of some complexity. For example, a proper analysis of phrases like *the average Englishman, the country as a whole, the majority* and *the nature of language* will involve non-trivial machinery applying to the relation between discourse domains and verification domains. Such questions are not touched upon here, but it must be stressed that standard forms of formal semantics have hardly touched upon such problems either.

6.2 Specific and non-specific reference

In section 4.1.1 the operation of closure of an open address was described and argued for. An open address is the result of address introduction by means of an existentially quantified sentence. A sentence like *I bought a motorcycle*, added to an appropriate D, results in the establishment of a new open address characterized by "motorcycle(x)" and "buy(d_n^0, x)" where d_n^0 is the address denoted by the term *I*. An open address is satisfied, or made true, by any individual in V answering to that double description. But as soon as the new address is denoted by some definite term it is closed (in our notation by a horizontal line), indicating that it is now part of the truth-conditions for both the utterance in which the definite term occurred and the address in question that a specific individual be singled out as the reference value of the term, or the designation of the address. This relation is 'rigid', in some Kripkean sense, in that it is in principle unchangeable for the duration of the discourse: from now on the address is the mental representation of that individual, and all mental processes involving this address also involve this individual in so far as things are involved in what is said about them.

This operation of closure was seen, in principle, to provide an answer to a puzzle formulated by Geach (1972: 115-27), but not adequately solved. The puzzle, it will be remembered, is that there is no contradiction between two sentences like the following

(2) a. Ted has a dog, and it is fierce.
    b. Ted has a dog, and it is not fierce.

uttered in the same D with respect to the same V. This is, as we have seen, because each new existential statement introduces a new address, which is subsequently closed, and rigidly linked up with an individual, if there is one in V, uniquely characterized by the predications in the open address. Now, if Ted has exactly two dogs, one fierce and one not fierce, the first conjunct of (2a) will fix upon the former, and the *it* in the second conjunct will refer to that dog. But in (2b) the first conjunct will open a second dog-address fixing upon the meek dog, and the *it* there will close the second dog-address and refer to the meek dog. The "it is fierce" in (2a) and – negated – in (2b) are thus different propositions, because they involve different addresses, and the apparent logical problem vanishes.[1]

It was seen, moreover, in 4.1.1, that the actual establishment of a rigid reference relation may, in some cases, be posterior to the closure of the address. This was demonstrated with the help of the example of an English Department with three professors, one of whom is a British national. Now the sentence

(3) The professor of English is British.

can be considered true provided the term *the professor of English* has not already been rigidly linked up with one of the two other professors in the department, who are Dutch nationals.

In this section we shall enlarge somewhat on this notion of address closure, and add certain refinements of a truth-conditional and referential nature. In the process, we shall take a critical look at Donnellan's widely known (1966) distinction between *referential, attributive,* and *denoting* use of a definite description.

What was not brought out in explicit words in section 4.1.1 is that address closure and the establishment of a relation of rigid reference do not necessarily have to coincide. It is possible for a definite term to close an open address without there being yet a unique individual for the address to fix on to. This occurs when the address, while still open, was satisfied by more than one individual answering to the description. When this address is closed by the subsequent use of a definite term, a pronoun or a definite description containing no new information, the address has been closed but the scanning of V still yields more than one possible reference value. We have stipulated that no truth-value can be assigned unless the terms have a uniquely determined extension or ρ-value. Yet utterances with such terms which fail to refer uniquely are often used and assigned truth-values. Our answer is that, as long as the required unique referent is not available, the truth-value of the utterance is held in abeyance until it is clear, on account of further predications made about the intended referent, which precise individual must be the referent.

A rigid reference relation comes about as a result of the function ρ over a term t finding in V a unique individual by checking all the predications previously assigned to the address denoted by t. This may happen after closure

---

[1] Of course, a sentence like

Ted has a dog, and it is fierce, and it is not fierce.

must be contradictory in any context, since there is only one occurrence of an existential statement introducing a dog-address. Now both *it*s denote this one address, thus giving it contradictory properties.

of the address, but such a procedure is 'marked' or 'non-standard', because a truth-value has to be withheld until sufficient information is available.

We now define *specific reference* as follows: a term t refers specifically to an individual r just in case a relation of rigid designation has been established for the address d denoted by t, or is established by the use of t. *Non-specific reference* is defined as follows: a term t refers non-specifically to an individual r just in case, at the time of utterance, the address d denoted by t has been closed but does not yet uniquely designate r.

It should be noted that the establishment of a rigid designation relation between an address d and a term t by the use of the term t can take two different forms. First, if t is a pronoun used just after the existential introduction of d, as in (2a), or if t is a definite description whose lexical material matches the newly established open address uniquely, and V contains just one individual of the desired description, then the use of t both closes d and establishes rigid designation and rigid reference. But there is also another way, the way of the Swiss banker (discussed as example (71) in section 3.4):

(4) Yesterday a Swiss banker was arrested at Heathrow Airport. The 53-year-old bachelor declared that he had come to Britain to kidnap the Queen.

Now suppose two Swiss bankers were arrested at Heathrow Airport yesterday, one a 35-year-old married man and one a 53-year-old bachelor. By the principles of economy and the presumption of good sense, as was shown in 3.4, the definite description *the 53-year-old bachelor* denotes the Swiss banker address just set up, thereby closing it. Now although the lexical material of the address before closure was insufficient to pick out a unique referent, there being two arrested Swiss bankers, the 'surreptitious' addition of the material "53-year-old bachelor" suddenly fixes reference.

We thus see that an utterance of (2a) can be true in two ways: either Ted has just one dog, and that animal is fierce, or he has more than one dog but only one fierce specimen. In the latter case, *it* refers non-specifically, and room is left for a dog owned by Ted and meek, making (2b) true. But then the qualification "it is not fierce" is added to another dog-address in D, and the semantic analysis of "it is fierce" under the negation represents a different proposition from the first occurrence. If both (2a) and (2b) are true simultaneously, both *its* must refer non-specifically. If Ted owns precisely two dogs, one fierce and one meek, then after (2a) the first dog-address has its fixed designatum, and after (2b) likewise for the second dog-address. But suppose Ted has three dogs, two of them fierce, and the third meek, and let one fierce dog be white and the other black. Now (2a) will be seen to be true in retrospect only if the first dog-address can be fixed upon one of the two fierce dogs, as, for example, when (2a) is followed by:

(5) The animal is black, too.

Our distinction between specific and non-specific reference is strongly reminiscent of Donnellan's theory (1966) that definite terms can be used in three ways, *referentially* and *attributively*, with a *denoting use* as a neutral third. A term is used *referentially* in Donnellan's theory, but couched in term of discourse semantics, when it is, for the duration of the discourse, rigidly linked up with an entity in V, just as is postulated for specifically referring terms in our analysis. A term is used *attributively* when *any* individual satisfying the description can satisfy it. This occurs, says Donnellan, when I, on finding my friend Smith brutally murdered, say *Smith's murderer is insane*, thereby not referring, according to Donnellan, to any specific person but to whoever committed the murder. In either case a description may *denote*, depending on whether there actually is an entity referred to or satisfying the description. A referentially used description is also a denoting expression; an attributively used description is a denoting expression just in case there is an entity satisfying the description. Thus, if I say *The first man to land on the planet Venus will be a Frenchman*, the phrase *the first man to land on the planet Venus* is denoting if it will indeed happen that a man lands on Venus, and otherwise it will not be denoting. (Needless to say this criterion had better turn out to be useless in semantics: how could we ever hope to explain the fact that we understand each other's utterances and interpret them if it had to be decided whether a phrase is denoting or not!) But if it is denoting, Donnellan is unwilling to say that I have referred to, mentioned or talked about that person: "I feel these terms would be out of place." Referential use should be restricted to reference to entities known by acquaintance. This is why it does not matter much for Donnellan if a referentially used description does not truly fit the reference object, as long as it is known that it is that object which is being talked about, whereas such an incorrectness in an attributively used description should be fatal.

Donnellan's almost proverbial example (1966: 103–4) is about a person seen to hold a martini glass which, however, contains only plain water, and referred to by the phrase *the man drinking a martini*. As long as this person is clearly identified, the reference will still be successful, in spite of the incorrect description. Then Donnellan goes on to consider the case of a chairman of a temperance society who has just been told that a man is drinking a martini at the annual party:

> He responds by asking his informant, "Who is the man drinking a martini?" In asking the question the chairman does not have some particular person in mind about whom he asks the question; if no one is drinking a martini, if the information is wrong, no person can be singled out as the person about whom the question was asked. Unlike the first case, the attribute of being the man drinking a martini is all-important, because if it is the attribute of no one, the chairman's question has no straightforward answer.

This, however, can hardly be correct. It seems that, if a description is used incorrectly whereas the reference is still successful, it makes no difference whether the entity referred to is known by acquaintance or not. Take the case of Australia, where the whole country has a Prime Minister, but the states have Premiers. An ill-informed speaker using the expression *the Prime Minister of Queensland* will clearly be understood as referring to the Premier of that state. There seems to be no essential difference with the man thought to hold a martini but in fact holding a glass filled with plain water. If a reference is successful in spite of an incorrect description, it is thanks to idiosyncratic conditions of use, which allow the correction of a descriptive mistake to be made without too much fuss. The matter seems of marginal interest only, in this context.

In our perspective it does not matter very much whether a reference object is known by acquaintance or arrived at by following the description as a search guide. In either case the description is a referring phrase, even if the thing in question is not or will not be part of the existing world. In that case, as we have seen, the description or definite term refers to an intensional object. We use the term *refer* for those cases where a definite term, or its corresponding address, takes a well-defined individual, really existing or intensionally defined, as the touchstone for truth of the utterance involved. It need not be at hand for us to clip the description on to, and it does not matter for our understanding and interpretation whether we know or do not know if it really exists or which individual it is. When we do not know whether it exists or which individual it is, we may be unable to assign an actual truth-value to a given utterance, but why should that worry us? We are not concerned with actual truth-values, but at most with truth-conditions. It is no concern of semantics to find out whether, indeed, there will ever be a first man to land on Venus and whether he will be a Frenchman. But it is our concern to be able to specify our reasons for calling the sentence in question false when nobody will ever land on Venus. We must then assign an extension to the definite term in question, in order to be in a position to compute the truth-value. As has been said, we assign it an intensional object as extension when a real object fails to turn up, and the value "false", or more precisely, "radically false", results by virtue of the fact that the predicate "be a Frenchman" requires existing entities, not intensional ones, for its subject-term if truth is to ensue.

What does matter, however, is Donnellan's claim that there are uses of definite terms in which any entity of the kind described will do to help make the utterance (proposition) true. Even if we feel that some of Donnellan's examples of alleged attributive use are perhaps better analysed as referential cases, we may still propose that there is attributive use in the definite term *it* in (2a) and (2b). Or, in other words, we can accept Donnellan's distinction between referential and attributive use provided the criterion of knowledge by acquaintance is dropped: we let a definite term refer specifically, or we let it be used referentially, when the reference function has settled on one unique individual, and we let a term refer non-specifically, or be used attributively, when no one unique individual has been singled out yet but has to be for the utterance in which the term occurs to have a truth-value.

6.3   Gatecrash falsifiers

Let us recapitulate. The general form of a Geach-type conjunction is

(6) a. $\exists 1(\hat{x}(F(x)), \hat{x}(G(x))) \wedge H(p)$

where "p" is a pronoun denoting the address d_n^0 set up by the first conjunct and characterized by "$F(x)$" and "$G(x)$". The increment schema of (6) is

(7) a.

$H(p)$ is true just in case $\rho(p) \in \sigma(H)$. $\rho(p)$ is defined if there is precisely one entity in V satisfying $F(x)$ and $G(x)$, or if there is precisely one entity in V satisfying $F(x)$, $G(x)$ and $H(x)$. If there is an entity r in V uniquely satisfying $F(x)$ and $G(x)$, the term p refers specifically, and it refers to r. If the predications $F(x)$ and $G(x)$ fail to select a unique individual but are successful in doing so in conjunction with $H(x)$, then the subject term of H refers non-specifically, and it refers to the entity isolated jointly by $F(x)$, $G(x)$ and $H(x)$. Likewise for Geach-type conjunctions with a negated second conjunct:

(6) b. $\exists 1(\hat{x}(F(x)), \hat{x}(G(x))) \wedge \sim H(p)$

Here, $\sim H(p)$ is true just in case $\rho(p) \notin \sigma(H)$, where $\rho(p)$ is defined if there is precisely one entity in V satisfying $F(x)$ and $G(x)$, or if there is precisely one entity in V satisfying $F(x)$, $G(x)$ and $\sim H(x)$. In the former case, p refers specifically; in the latter, p refers non-specifically. The increment schema of (6b) is as (7a) but with $H(x)$ asterisked:

(7) b.

$$\begin{array}{|l}
\hline
d_n^0 \\
\hline
F(x) \\
G(x) \\
\hline
*H(x) \\
\end{array}$$

No problems seem to be in sight yet.

But now suppose that H(p) in (6a) has proved to be false. It follows from the definitions given that *p* can now refer only specifically: non-specific reference is ruled out. For non-specific reference it would be necessary that the individual uniquely satisfying F(x), H(x) and H(x) does not satisfy H(x), which is impossible. The only way for H(p) to be false, when it occurs in an utterance of the form (6a), is for *p* to refer specifically, so that there is only one individual satisfying F(x) and G(x). Thus, if I say *Ted has a dog and it is fierce*, and you reply *Oh no, Ted has a dog all right, but it is not fierce*, then, if you are right, it follows that Ted has precisely one dog and that this animal is not fierce. This entailment of uniqueness follows from the falsity of H(p) in (6a), but not from the truth of ~ H(p) in (6b). Yet, in both cases, H(p) is the same proposition, since *p* denotes the same address in both cases.

Likewise with ~ H(p) in (6b). If, in (6b), ~ H(p) is false, then *p* refers specifically and V contains just one entity satisfying F(x) and G(x), and this entity also satisfies H(x).

Now we do have a problem, for it appears that to say that H(p) is false is not the same as saying that ~ H(p) is true. If we say that ~ H(p) is true than it is possible for V to contain more than one individual satisfying the descriptions F(x) and G(x), though only one individual must satisfy F(x), G(x) and ~ H(x). But if we say that H(p) is false then V must contain precisely one individual satisfying F(x) and G(x), and this individual must not have the property expressed by H(x). If V contains more individuals satisfying F(x) and G(x), then H(p) cannot be false: it is either true (when there is one entity for which F(x), G(x) and H(x) hold), or it remains without a truth-value. Analogously, to say that ~ H(p) is false is not the same as to say that H(p) is true. If H(p) is true, then V may contain more than one entity that is both F and G, though it must contain exactly one entity that is F, G and H. But if ~ H(p) is false, then V must contain just one individual that is both F and G (and this individual must have the property H). If there is more than one individual that is F and G, then ~ H(p) cannot be false. It must either be true (with one individual that is H) or without a truth-value (when all individuals that are F and G are also H). This is the gremlin in the logical works which is responsible for the problem of gatecrash falsifiers to which we turn now.

The problem occurs in disjunctions of the type (8a) or (8b), and conditionals of the type (8c):

(8) a. Either Ted has no dog, or it is fierce.
  b. Either Ted has no dog, or he has a dog and it is fierce.
  c. If Ted has a dog it is fierce.

The problem is that, according to indubitable natural intuition, these sentences are uttered falsely in any V where Ted has two dogs, one fierce and one meek. In such a V the first disjunct of (8a) and (8b) is false, so that the second disjunct must be true if the whole disjunction is to be true. Now the second disjunct is true, in both cases, and yet no intuition of truth arises. As for (8c), there the antecedent clause is true, so that, for truth of (8c), the conjunction *Ted has a dog and it is fierce* (= (2a)) must also be true. We now see that although (2a) is true in this V, (8c) is not. All three sentences are, apparently, falsified by the presence in V of the meek dog, the gatecrash falsifier that meddles in sentences whose truth-conditions should not be affected by it.

We are, meanwhile, saddled with a paradox. If "*A*" stands for "Ted has a dog" and "*B*" for "it is fierce", then (8a), (8b) and (8c) correspond, in standard analysis, to:

(9) a. $\neg A \lor B$
   b. $\neg A \lor (A \land B)$
   c. $A \supset B$

respectively. Now if, given the verification domain just described, the truth-values for (9a), (9b) and (9c) are computed then, since "$A \land B$" is true, all three should be true. But since in this V, which contains Ted's meek dog, "$A \land \sim B$" is also true, all three should be false. Note that now we cannot say that "*B*" in "$A \land B$" and "*B*" in "$A \land \sim B$" are two different propositions because we are considering the two as alternative additions to the same D, so that in either case i(*A*) is identical and the *it* of *B* denotes, in both cases, the address introduced by *A*. We may seek refuge in our trivalent logic and our reanalysis of *if*, as given in section 4.1.5, but to no avail: the paradox remains. Meanwhile, linguistic intuition has been standing by unhappily: there can be no doubt that in this V (9a), (9b) and (9c) are simply false.

One might think of resorting to a solution involving some form of universal quantification. For example, it might be proposed that (9a) should be analysed as (10), in restricted quantification:[2]

(10) $\forall x$: dog$[(\neg$Ted owns x$) \lor (x$ is fierce$)]$

But then we run again into scope problems, just as Geach's solution to (2a) and (2b) is up against scope problems (section 4.1.1). Take

(11) Either Jack does not know that Ted has a dog, or he hopes that it is fierce.

---

[2] This proposal, as well as (12) below, would anyway be impossible in our theory. If (10) is translated into our quantificational language, we get, with minimal negation:

$\forall (\hat{\ }x(\lor(\sim(own(y: \text{"Ted"}(y), x))), fierce(x)), \hat{\ }x(dog(x)))$

But this will be refused by the grammar because, after Object Incorporation, the complex predicate "$\forall - dog(\hat{\ }x)$" must be lowered into the subject term to the position occupied by the bound variable. But there are two such positions, which means that Quantifier Lowering is blocked. Analogously for (12).

which does not allow for an interpretation whereby of all dogs either Jack does not know that (or: if) Ted owns them or he hopes that they are fierce. This appears clearly when one considers that (11) is true also if, although Jack knows of no particular dog in the world that (or: if) Ted owns it, Jack knows that Ted is a dog-owner and Jack hopes that the dog Ted owns is fierce. Truth under this interpretation would remain unaccounted for in analyses like (10).

Or one might propose universal quantification for only the second disjunct, in something like the following way:

(12) $(\neg \exists x: dog\,[Ted\ owns\ x])\ \vee\ (\forall x: dog\,[Ted\ owns\ x \supset x\ is\ fierce])$

But now we face other problems. First, it might well be asked why on earth universal quantification should apply in these cases but existential quantification in Geach-type conjunctions such as (2a) and (2b), where universal quantification would improperly establish contradiction between (2a) and (2b). By anything like the principle of "parity of form" (Russell 1905: 483) one would expect some explanatory regularity in the semantics of definite terms. But, more seriously even, this solution fails when cases are considered like

(13) Either Ted has no dog, or he has a dog and it is fierce ánd he has a
      dog and it is not fierce.

Here universal quantification along the lines of (12) would make it logically impossible for Ted to own any dog at all. So let us disregard analyses in terms of universal quantification for the disjunctions at hand.

We seem to have no choice but to regard disjunctions of the type (8a) or (8b) as genuine disjunctions, while avoiding paradoxes. We can do so with the help of the available apparatus and without damage to the logic. Let us consider the disjunctions first.

It will be remembered that the logical predicate *or* (or "∨") is defined truth-conditionally as follows ((37d) in section 3.2.4):

(14) $\sigma(\vee) = \{\langle e^*, f^* \rangle$ s.t. for all p, q, if $\rho(p) = e$ and $\rho(q) = f$, then:
      $not(\varphi(p) = \varphi(q) = 3)\ |\ not(\varphi(\neg p) = \varphi(\neg q) = 1)\}$

The satisfaction condition is formulated with respect to the negated disjuncts, not the disjuncts themselves. In general, this makes no difference at all, given the truth-functionality of the classical negation operator which is involved. But it makes just the right difference here. If truth for disjunctions were defined in terms of the disjuncts themselves, then, given (8a) or (8b) and the verification domain V as described, there would be no way to get the value "false", since "Ted has a dog and it is fierce" is true in V. Now, however, the truth for disjunctions depends on the truth-values of the negated disjuncts. In the case at hand, this means that we need to know the values of

"Ted has a dog", i.e. the negated first disjunct, and "it is not fierce" for (8a), or "it is not true that Ted has a dog and that it is fierce" for (8b), and we must make sure that the conjunction of both is false. That is, for (8a) "$A \wedge \neg B$" must be false, and for (8b) "$A \wedge \neg(A \wedge B)$" must be false. But the latter is equivalent with the former, so that for both it must be shown that "$A \wedge \neg B$" is false in V for (8a) or (8b) to be true in V. Now, in this V, "$A \wedge \neg B$" is true since Ted has two dogs, a fierce one and a meek one. Therefore, (8a) and (8b) are false, as they should be. Radical falsity is excluded since "A" is true, so that the precondition of (14) is fulfilled. What remains is minimal falsity.

As for the conditional case, i.e. (8c), essentially the same solution applies. The satisfaction condition for *if*, as given in section 4.1.5 under (52), requires that "must($\neg(A \wedge \neg B)$)" be true, where "A" stands for the antecedent clause (i.e. *Ted has a dog*) and "B" for the consequent clause (i.e. *it is fierce*). The epistemic necessity operator simply requires that "$\neg(A \wedge \neg B)$" follows from a set of known true statements **T** (see section 5.2). But with or without *must* it is required for the truth of (8c) that "$A \wedge \neg B$" be false. However, in the verification domain as specified above, with Ted owning two dogs, a fierce one and a meek one, "$A \wedge \neg B$" is true, given the meek dog. Hence (8c) is false.

We can thus conclude that with the apparatus developed so far the problem of gatecrash falsifiers for disjunctions and conditionals of the form (8a), (8b) and (8c) is solved semantically. There remains the logical problem resulting in the paradox that it is possible, given certain Vs, to say truthfully both "*A and B*" and "*A and not-B*". This is possible only if A opens up a new address d and B closes d. The problem of Geach-type conjunctions, discussed in section 4.1.1 and solved both semantically and logically for cases where both conjunctions are actually added to the D at hand (in that case the second A and the second B represent different propositions from their preceding namesakes), is thus seen to have a sequel. In order to avoid paradox we must stipulate that propositional calculus does not apply to pairs of propositions $\langle p, q \rangle$ where p opens an address d and q closes d. Semantically, sentences formed with two such propositions and the predicates *and*, *or* or *if* are real conjunctions, disjunctions and conditionals, respectively. But logically they are not, or only with special provisos. What the logic is for the unruly pairs of an address-opening and an address-closing proposition, or how the gremlin can be removed from the logical works, is a question that will be allowed to rest here, our interest being primarily in semantics and not in logic.

The curious problem of gatecrash falsifiers shows again that the logic of natural language is epiphenomenal upon the machinery of discourse domains and reference through denotation and designation. The gatecrashers problem is a direct consequence of the fact that the interpretation of utterances in natural language is heavily discourse-dependent. The complications it brings about are more interesting for an engineer of semantic interpretative systems than for a logician working in mathematical space.

6.4 Proper names

Proper names are an ancient problem in philosophical semantics because they achieve reference without any significant descriptive lexical material and without any anaphoric help. They are essentially devoid of meaning and yet manage to arrive at the proper referent without any help from adjacent context. Proper names do sometimes contain descriptive lexical material, but this is not crucial to their functioning as proper names. A name can happen to be 'significant', as when a boxer is called *Steel*, but such coincidences are nothing but anecdotal. A real semantically active description may turn into a proper name, as when the local blacksmith is henceforth Mr Smith, but this is not essential for names. Names are in principle not significant and arbitrary, just like ordinary words (or morphemes). But unlike lexical words, which have sets of entities as extensions, proper names are not predicates and take individuals (or entities) as their extension. Again, as part of the give-and-take between semantically functional descriptions and proper names, a name can become a predicate and thus a part of the lexicon, as when I say that Henry is a real Hitler (which means, of course, that he is not really Hitler), or a second Hitler, but these are processes of linguistic innovation and change. They do not explain how a proper name arrives at the proper referent: any account invoking predicate status for the proper name so that the referent is fixed through the truth-conditions associated with the predicate will be circular.

Unless the idea is given up that referents are fixed, for definite descriptions, by virtue of the meaning of the terms referring to them. The old dictum that a term refers to its reference object by means of its meaning is not beside the truth but it is incomplete. A term refers to its reference object by means of its meaning ánd the fact that rigid designation relations are established between discourse addresses and individuals in V. Now all a term has to do in order to refer properly is to denote the right address. If this address designates some individual r in V, then the term, no matter how deficient truth-conditionally, refers to r. A term can do with minimal, sometimes only pronominal, directives to find its address, and thus to refer, if the address has a designatum. The meaning inherent in a descriptive definite term may be quite insufficient by itself to determine the referent. In fact, as was pointed out by Donnellan (1966), the term may even contain incorrect descriptive material, but as long as the address at which it lands has a referent, the term will refer to that referent.

There is an interesting corollary to this concerning Kripke's theory of proper names. Kripke (1972; 1980) takes up Frege's identity problem again, but now with proper names instead of descriptive phrases. His example is *Hesperus is Phosphorus*, and he shows that the problem which struck Frege also affects this sentence: substitution of one co-extensive term for the other changes a posteriori truth into a priori truth. Kripke then proceeds to argue that Frege's solution for cases like *The Morning Star is the Evening Star* does not apply here. Frege's solution is based on the distinction between sense and reference, but Kripke argues that proper names have no sense but only a reference. Hence, Frege's solution is not valid here, and another solution must be found. His argument for saying that proper names have no sense, unlike definite descriptions of the standard lexical type, is that descriptions may have variable reference, as in one sense of the sentence *The Pope has always lived in Rome*, or in counterfactuals of the type *If Reagan had stuck to his trade, the President of the US in 1983 would have been more popular with Congress*, whereas proper names are "rigid designators": they always refer to the same individual (their reference is fixed through all possible worlds). Their connection with their reference object is of a causal nature: once the object has been 'baptized' it bears its name in eternity. Identity statements involving different but co-extensive proper names are, on the one hand, necessary truths, since the thing called "Hesperus" could not have been not that same thing; yet, on the other hand, they are a posteriori (just as Goldbach's conjecture in arithmetic, if true, is true both necessarily and a posteriori).

Kripke (1980: 68–70) criticizes Kneale (1962) for analysing the proper name *Socrates* as "the individual called *Socrates*". This, Kripke says, is circular, for "how are we supposed to know to whom [the speaker] refers? By using the description which gives the sense of it ... If this were all there was to the meaning of a proper name, then no reference would get off the ground at all." It is clear from the foregoing that Kripke's argument, though correct, is based on the incorrect premiss that descriptions get at their referents just by means of their sense, i.e. their descriptive content. If that were so, then indeed no reference would get off the ground at all with proper names defined the Kneale way. But this Fregean theory of reference is untenable since it fails to take into account the fact that definite terms very often refer in spite of the insufficiency of their descriptive content. That they can still refer is due to the mediating role of the more richly endowed discourse addresses, which stand in a primary 'rigid' designation relation to specific entities. As soon as an address has been set up for the specific individual called "Socrates", with the information that this individual has that name, the name suffices for a term to denote that address and thus to refer to the intended individual. In our theory of discourse-mediated reference, the Kneale analysis is not circular. It has the advantage of treating proper names as a subclass of the class of definite descriptions, where the descriptive content consists in the predicate "be called so-and-so".

Kripke's theory of proper names is of a highly metaphysical nature. It fails to fit the facts of language. In particular, there is no good reason why proper names should not be considered descriptive terms, though of a special kind. Their referential behaviour is not essentially different from ordinary descriptions. They do allow for variable reference, contrary to what Kripke asserts. Next to *The Pope has always lived in Rome*, we have, for example, *Quintus was not always the fifth son in a Roman family*. And next to the Reagan-sentence we have, for example, *If Wojtyla had stayed in Poland, John Paul II would have been more popular with the Left*. Proper names can be used attributively (in Donnellan's (1966) sense), such as *Jack the Ripper*, who has been named but was never found. Proper names can be given to recurrent entities whose identity has to be established on the basis of some formula, such as *Easter*. Proper names are, of course, context-bound just as ordinary descriptions – a fact too trivial to dwell upon. Proper names can, therefore, also shift from one name-bearer to another. The name *Calabria*, for example, was used in Roman times for the 'heel' of Southern Italy; nowadays that same name is used for the 'toe', the change being due to some medieval squire conquering new territory and losing his original base, but carrying the name *Calabria* with him in the process. There is, in short, no convincing reason why proper names should not be considered a special class of descriptive phrases, though they must, of course, not be treated as 'abbreviating descriptions' in the sense that *Aristotle*, for example, were to go proxy for something like "Plato's most famous pupil". Kripke's criticism of this notion is entirely to the point.

We shall be content with Kneale's analysis of proper names. It does not prevent reference from getting off the ground. On the contrary. And it has the great theoretical advantage that it is not necessary to create a highly special category of definite terms. We can, moreover, apply Frege's solution in terms of sense and reference (albeit in terms of discourse semantics) to identify statements involving descriptions as well as proper names. There is thus no need to introduce metaphysics into linguistic analysis by stipulating that *Phosphorus is Hesperus* is both necessary and a posteriori. (I have no quarrel with the metaphysics, at least not here, nor generally with metaphysical arguments, which should teach us a good deal about the architecture of the universe. But there does not seem to be any good reason to suppose that metaphysical notions play a part in the process of understanding and interpretation of utterances in natural language.)

This is the justification for the practice upheld throughout in this book to treat proper names as definite descriptions, where the identifying predicate is ""NN"", this standing for "being called 'NN'". The predicate ""NN"", given the machinery of discourse domains, is sufficient for picking out one unique address in D. If this address has a designatum in V, then the proper name refers to this designatum. At the same time, however, a proper name retains its potential for variable reference, non-specific reference, intensional reference, counterfactual reference, and whatever variety of reference is reserved for standard definite descriptions denoting their addresses by means of lexical predicate material.

6.5 Intensional entities

As has been said repeatedly in the preceding chapters, questions of reference cannot be limited to cases of reference to really existing individuals. Although in philosophical theories of reference and, generally, in philosophical semantics it has been customary to hold the view that nothing is referred to when a term (which parades as a referring term) does not have a real world entity which can count as its reference value, the facts of language rule out this view as incoherent. They press home the fact that all definite terms in natural language utterances must be about something and must, therefore, refer. One may quibble over the term "refer", and wish to stipulate that this term is applicable only when what is referred to really exists, but it is not clear what would be gained by such terminological quibbles. A term would be needed, anyway, for the relation between a definite term and the non-existing thing it is about when the term is about something particular but not part of the really existing extensional world.

We have no choice but to maintain that there are things which do not exist. This is so for a variety of reasons which can be summarized under one exemplary argument. If it were the case that whatever is there, also actually exists, then intensional terms, such as *the actual king of France*, or *the philospher's stone*, would be co-extensive, both referring to the null-class, and there would be no way of distinguishing the truth-conditions of (15) from those of (16):

(15) Louise is looking for the actual king of France.
(16) Louise is looking for the philosopher's stone.

Yet, the one may be true while the other is false. Hence, even though there is neither a king of France nor a philosopher's stone, the corresponding definite descriptions must be given different reference-values.

In his famous essay 'On what there is' (1953: 1-19), Quine declares war on all things that do not exist. Brandishing Ockham's razor, he threatens to shave off Plato's beard altogether. Yet, as we shall see, some well-ordered growth will have to be spared, out of necessity. It is no doubt true that "a plurality should never be posited without necessity" ("numquam ponenda est pluralitas sine necessitate", according to Kneale and Kneale (1962: 243) Ockham's own formulation of the razor). But it is equally true that, if necessary, a plurality must be let in. Theories that are kept on too poor an ontological diet (such as behaviourism) will fail to yield insight, and will eventually die.

The argument is quite simple. Suppose I hold up a picture of a dog, not of any specific dog that has been portrayed, but of a dog as conceived in the artist's mind and as it would appear if it were a real life animal. I now say, in truth,

(17) This represents a dog.

Now, one could say, since there is nothing in the whole world which this picture represents, it represents nothing. But pictures representing nothing are called abstract. Hence this is an abstract picture. Yet this argument must be fallacious, because the picture clearly does not qualify as abstract art (if art it is); on the contrary, it clearly is the opposite of abstract, it is representational and it represents a dog. So there *is* something which it represents: it represents a dog, but not a really existing dog. There are, therefore, dogs which do not really exist, such as dogs in pictures. And in general, there are things that do not exist.

Quine's argument against non-existent things is based on considerations of overcrowding of the universe (Plato's tangled beard). Invoking an imaginary opponent, Mr Wyman, who confers to non-existent entities the status of unactualized possibles, Quine comments (1953: 4), unleashing rare powers of rhetoric:

> Wyman's overpopulated universe is in many ways unlovely. It offends the aesthetic sense of us who have a taste for desert landscapes, but this is not the worst of it. Wyman's slum of possibles is a breeding ground for disorderly elements. Take, for instance, the possible fat man in that doorway; and, again, the possible bald man in that doorway. Are they the same possible man, or two possible men? How do we decide? How many possible men are there in that doorway? Are there more possible thin ones than fat ones? How many of them are alike? Or would their being alike make them one? Are no *two* possible things alike? Is this the same as saying that it is impossible for two things to be alike? Or, finally, is the concept of identity simply inapplicable to unactualized possibles? But what sense can be found in talking of entities which cannot meaningfully be said to be identical with themselves and distinct from one another? These elements are well-nigh incorrigible. By a Fregean therapy of individual concepts, some effort might be made at rehabilitation; but I feel we'd do better simply to clear Wyman's slum and be done with it.

Later in the book, on p. 152, he discusses the idea of Frege's senses of names, or Carnap's individual concepts, in much less thundering terms than those used on Wyman. Senses are, apparently, in Quine's eyes, less incorrigible and disorderly than Wyman's unactualized possibles. Yet, they still find no grace and Quine considers them unfit for purposes of quantification from outside intensional predicates.

There is another objection, apart from those offered by Quine, to taking refuge in the "Fregean therapy of individual concepts". In asserting (17) I say that the picture represents an animal, not a concept. Or, when I say

(18) This picture represents Pegasus.

then I am speaking of the mythical figure, the winged horse carrying Zeus' thunderbolt, and not of a concept. The confusion is obvious, and Quine even saves his worst imaginary opponent, the philosopher McX, from the ignominy of confusing the Parthenon with the Parthenon-idea (1953: 2). So we shall not say that the referent of *Pegasus* in (18) is a concept, or that what is quantified over in (17) is a concept. We need an object as the reference-value of *Pegasus* or as the value of the existentially quantified variable in (17). Nothing else will do, unless we deny altogether that (17) and (18) mean what they mean.

Is there no escape, then, from the dilemma between denying the reality of obvious meanings and Wyman's overpopulated universe? Can we not save the meanings, and populate our desert landscape with orderly settlers? Is there no way to stop possible men in doorways from coming and going and merging? All we need is *intensional objects* that stay under strict identity criteria. Quine, in his antimentalist universe, had no other choice than between Wyman's overpopulated universe and the arid world of only extensional, i.e. really existing, entities. But in a universe that includes the mental world we have more and better choices than these. Unactualized possibles are all right, as long as they are ruled by epistemic possibility, or at any rate the epistemic powers of imagination and planning. Thought-domains *create* intensional objects, which may not ever be found in the actual world, but are nevertheless legitimate objects of reference. They are defined by the conditions under which anything that does actually exist will be recognized as their implementation. It is the house that is planned but perhaps not yet built, or the solution that is being looked for but has not been found yet, if it can be found. It is even the impossible construction of the round square cupola on Berkeley College (Quine 1953: 4), which will never be found to exist.

Clearly, the positing of intensional objects is by virtue of an appeal to the intentional powers of the mind, mysterious as they still are. But the fact that no explicit theory is available to explain intentionality phenomena cannot be a valid reason for ignoring them altogether. On the contrary, we have no choice but to accept the phenomena and take them into due account, even though they are wholly or in part unexplained. This is standard procedure. We thus accept that we can suppose there to be a fat man in that doorway, to hark back to Quine's example. And we can suppose there to be a bald man in that doorway. Let Quine now ask whether they are the same man or different men. Where he was unable to answer the question for men-in-the-doorway set up under metaphysical ("strict") possibility, we are perfectly able to answer. The answer is: that depends on what the supposing subject has supposed. If he supposes them to be one man, he is one man, but if he supposes them to be different, then that is what they are. Having posited a fat man in the doorway, I can say of *him* that he is also bald. Now the question of there 'being' one or two possible men in the doorway does not arise, since I have put only one man there, who is both fat and bald. I may, of course, also posit two men in the doorway, or three, but if I go on like this you will soon protest that there is not enough room for so many men in that one doorway. Quine's argument, therefore, does not destroy unactualized possibles, but it blows a breach in the ancient parapets of metaphysical possibility.

We will, however, not speak of our intensional objects as *possible* entities, mainly because *impossible* constructions such as the round square cupola on Berkeley College must equally qualify as intensional entities, and also because the predicate "possible" loses much of its meaning since actually existing entities must inevitably also be possible entities, given the rule *ab esse ad posse*. Instead of "unactualized possibles" we shall speak of "unactualized values of reference functions". A reference function takes domain addresses (and, for each address d_n, all linguistically occurring definite descriptions denoting d_n) to reference values. Reference values are either extensional or intensional, according to the way the world is made. Reference values that are actualized in the world are extensional; if they are unactualized they are intensional. Thought processes create intensional entities by providing a set of criteria to be satisfied by any extensional entity that is to qualify as the thing designated by a given address. Addresses for which no extensional value is found will have to do with intensional entities as their values.

The assumption of intensional objects licenses a few important generalizations. We can now say that all interpretable definite descriptions and all domain addresses of any depth have an entity (or set of entities) as their reference-value (ρ-value). It is customary to say of a definite description lacking an extensional, i.e. really existing, reference value that it "fails to refer". The expression has gained currency, but it is misleading in that, besides primary extensional reference, there is the second echelon of reference to intensional entities, which is indispensable in any theory of reference. We say that a term "fails to refer" when its reference value is not defined.

Another generalization which is saved is the definition of truth employed throughout: a sentence $P^n(t_1, \ldots, t_n)$ is true just in case the n-tuple $\langle \rho(t_1), \ldots, \rho(t_n) \rangle$ is a member of the extension set of P, $\sigma(P)$. The set $\sigma(P)$ for every predicate P is determined by the way the world is. Likewise, as we have seen, whether $\rho(t)$, for any interpretable definite description t, has an extensional value or only an intensional one is also determined by the way the world happens to be. Yet we want our ability to assign truth-values to interpretably uttered sentences with respect to a given verification domain to be independent of the contingencies of reality. That is, we must be able to determine reference values also for non-extensionally referring terms, for if such values cannot be determined, there is no way of deciding if the n-tuple of term-references is a member of the extension set of the predicate. For purely extensional predicates we might say that non-extensionally referring terms have the value "∅" (the null set), and stipulate that "∅" may never occur in an n-tuple which is an element of the extension set of a purely extensional predicate. But this ploy fails to work for cases such as (15) and (16):

(15) Louise is looking for the actual king of France.
(16) Louise is looking for the philosopher's stone.

Here we cannot impose an embargo on zero-terms in object position, since *look for* is intensional with respect to its object. In fact, as we observed, the one may be true while the other is false, which shows that the assignment of "∅" as the reference value to the object-terms in (15) and (16) is insufficient for the discrimination of truth and falsity. It is here that intensional reference values are indispensable. And they can be imported without any danger of havoc being wreaked.

6.6 More on intensionality and reference

In section 3.2.4 a few things were said about the extension of set-denoting terms. The general principle was formulated there that the extension of an SD-term is the set denoted, as it is in the real world. This principle is upheld throughout.

A set-denoting term is of the general form:

(20) $\hat{x}(P_1^n(t_{1_1}, \ldots /x/ \ldots, t_{1_n}), \ldots, P_i^m(t_{i_1}, \ldots /x/ \ldots, t_{i_m}))$

where "/x/" indicates that one of the terms must be the bound variable x. Since multiterm predicates are notationally cumbersome it is convenient to reduce them to one-term predicates for purposes of calculus and definition, by means of lambda extraction. (20) is equivalent with

(21) $\hat{x}(\lambda y(P_1^n(t_{1_1}, \ldots /y/ \ldots, t_{1_n}))(x), \ldots, \lambda y(P_i^m(t_{i_1}, \ldots /y/ \ldots, t_{i_m}))(x))$

which contains only one-term predicates and where the bound variable for each of the predicates is extracted. Now the general form of set-denoting terms is

(22) $\hat{x}(P_1(x), \ldots, P_i(x))$.

The reference value (ρ-value) of a set-denoting term is the intersection of the extension sets of the predicates involved,

(23) $\rho(\hat{}x(P_1(x), \ldots, P_i(x))) = \cap\ \sigma(\mathbf{P})$

where "$\sigma(\mathbf{P})$" is defined as $\{\sigma(P_1), \ldots, \sigma(P_i)\}$. We want (23) to be applicable in all cases.

No problems arise when $P_1, \ldots, P_i$ are all extensional with respect to the term position occupied by the bound variable. For example, if the set-denoting term is as follows,

(24) $\hat{}x(car(x), \lambda y(own(z: \text{"John"}(z), y))(x))$

then its ρ-value is $\sigma(car) \cap \sigma(\lambda y(own(z: \text{"John"}(z), y)))$, i.e. the set of all cars owned by John. This set may be empty. A set-denoting term such as (24) will occur as the subject term in the SA of sentences like

(25) a. All these vehicles are cars owned by John.

   b. Some vehicles are cars owned by John.

with their SA-representations[3]

(25) a'. $\forall(\hat{}x(car(x), own(y: \text{"John"}(y), x)), x: these vehicles(x))$
   b'. $\exists(\hat{}x(car(x), own(y: \text{"John"}(y), x)), \hat{}x(vehicle(x)))$

As object term it occurs in the Semantic Analysis of sentences like

(25) c. All cars owned by John are red.

   d. Some cars owned by John were stolen.

We need, however, also terms denoting non-extensional sets, since natural language sentences can be used to quantify over non-extensional entities as well. As was shown in section 5.3.6, a predicate which is intensional with respect to the term quantified over automatically has a non-extensional extension, or at least may have one: $\sigma(popular) = \hat{}x(popular(x))$, i.e. the set all things popular, whether they have real existence or not. A predicate which is extensional with respect to the term quantified over can be intensionalized, as was shown in section 5.3.6: $\sigma(dog) = \hat{}x(dog(x))$, i.e. the set of all real dogs, but $\sigma(*dog) = \hat{}x(*dog(x))$, and is the set of all real or imagined dogs. In order to have complex non-extensional set-denoting terms it is stipulated that if in an SD-term some predicate is intensional with respect to the term quantified over, then all predicates in the term are intensional, either by nature or by intensionalization. Now not only is definition (23) generally

---

[3] The SA-representations (25a') and (25b') are grammatically in order, unlike the example in note 2 above. The multiple occurrence of the bound variable in the subject term does not block the transformational process because here, due to the operation of the cyclic rules of English, by the time the quantifier must be lowered into what is then the subject-S, only one occurrence of the bound variable has remained: "car owned by John(x)". The quantifier is then lowered into the position of this x.

applicable, but an expression like *the dogs Harry talks about* is also analysed in terms which assign it its proper extension, comprising both real and imagined dogs if V is such that those are the dogs that Harry talks about.

It was, moreover, required, in section 5.3.6, that if a term *t* is matched under a quantifier by an intensional set-denoting or definite term, then *t* must also be intensional, by nature or, if need be, by intensionalization. As a consequence, sentences like

(26) a. All dogs Harry talks about are faithful.
(27) a. All dogs Harry thinks are white are black.

are analysed as, respectively,

(26) b. $\forall$ [ˆx(*faithful(x)), ˆx(*dog(x),
$$\lambda x(\text{talk about}(y: \text{"Harry"}(y), x))(x))]$$
(27) b. $\forall$ [ˆx(*black(x)), ˆx(*dog(x),
$$\lambda x(\text{think}(y: \text{"Harry"}(y), \text{white}(x)))(x))]$$

or, respectively, "the set of dogs, real or imaginary, that Harry talks about is a subset of the set of things, real or imaginary, that are faithful", and "the set of dogs, real or imaginary, that Harry thinks are white is a subset of the set of things, real or imaginary, that are black". The object terms in (26b) and (27b) are intensional on account of the λ-predicates which are intensional 'by nature', i.e. by virtue of the lexicon. They 'infect' the remainder of the set-denoting terms in question, as well as the terms that match them under the quantifier. This result is supported by intuitive truth-value judgements: (26a) is true even if Harry never talks about any but non-existent faithful dogs, and (27a) is true even if all dogs thought by Harry to be white are imaginary dogs (in a story, a painting, or the report of someone's talk), and are imagined (said, painted) as being black. But it is, of course, not necessary that the dogs in question be imaginary animals, just as it is not necessary that they really exist.

For this to work, however, an intensional analysis must be given of sentences like:

(28) a. The dog Harry talks about is faithful.
    b. The dog Harry thinks is white is black.
    c. The girls Nigel dreams of are blonde.
    d. The unicorn Alex is looking for limps.

In this analysis these sentences must have a chance of being true even though the subject terms refer to non-existing things. This seems to run flatly counter to the theory developed in chapter 3, where radical falsity is prescribed for uttered sentences figuring an extensional predicate and a non-extensional term. The predicates *faithful, black, blonde* and *limp* are normal extensional predicates, which presuppose the existence of their subject term extensions. And there is no reason to doubt the correctness of this analysis. Yet we must also account for the fact that the sentences of (28) may well be considered true even though the dog is not literally faithful or black, the girls are not literally blonde, and the unicorn does not really limp. Harry may talk or think about a non-existent dog, Nigel may dream of imaginary girls, and Alex is most likely to be after an invented unicorn. We thus need an intensional analysis for these sentences. We need such an analysis not only because of observational requirements of factual correctness regarding the truth-conditions of these sentences, but also because, given the truth-conditional definition of the extension set of the universal quantifier as specified in (38b) in section 3.2.4, (26a) and (27a) require for truth that any sentence formed with the predicate in question and as subject a definite term t referring to any member of the set of dogs that Harry talks about, for (26a), or the set of dogs that Harry thinks are white, for (27a), must be true. This means that, for example, (28a) and (28b) must be true, and not radically false (which would make (26a) and (27a) radically false, according to (38a) in section 3.2.4).

In order to account for such cases we stipulate the following rule:

(R1)   If a term t denotes an address d_i^m and its predicate is incrementable in D^l $(l < m)$ and is t-extensional, the predication is added under d_i^m in D^m, *nullo obstante*; otherwise in any D^n $(n > m)$ also containing d_i^m.

This rule ensures that the predicates *faithful, black, blonde* and *limp* in (28a)–(28d) are attached to the proper addresses: if the increment function i finds them in D^0 there is ordinary extensional use, but if the addresses are indexed for some intensional subdomain then that is where the increment is implemented, and we have non-extensional reference and non-extensional use of the sentence, i.e. the sentence is used as a non-extensional proposition.

This, however, is only half the story. The resulting domain structures are now adequate from a truth-conditional point of view, but the sentences are not. If taken 'literally', these sentences are radically false, since the existential precondition is not satisfied. If we want the sentences of (28) to be true we must modify the truth-definitions of the predicates in question. The means for doing so has already been provided: we can intensionalize the predicates. The following rule is thus in order:

(R2)   If a proposition $P(t_1, \ldots, t_n)$ incrementable in D^l is incremented in some D^m $(m > 1)$ under some address d_j^m and P is extensional with respect to the t_i denoting d_j^m, P is changed into *P for the purpose of truth-testing.

$\sigma(^*P)$ is the set of all things, real or imagined, that have the property designated by P, or have the property of having the property designated by P assigned to them under some intensional operator. Thus, if Nigel dreams that Harry talks about a dog of Harry's own invention (but Harry is in fact innocent of inventing non-existent dogs), then the dog-address is in Nigel's dream-domain. Given this information in D, (28a) can be uttered and can be true. The intensional object referred to by *the dog Harry talks about* is at two removes from reality, but as long as it falls within σ(*faithful), the sentence can be deemed true.

We thus have different possible incrementations for a sentence like (28a), depending on what D^m it is incremented to. If D has been built up from preceding sentences like *There is a dog; Harry talks about it*, then there is normal extensional reference, and the resulting increment will be:

(29) a.

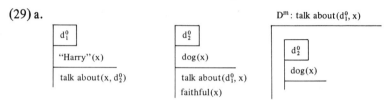

But if the preceding discourse has been something like *Harry talks about a dog*, then the resulting D will contain the increment:

(29) b.

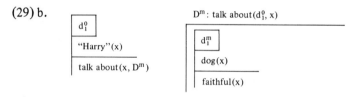

There are predicates, such as *dream up*, which have as a precondition the non-existence of some term-extension (in this case, the object term), just as some verbs are 'antifactive', such as German *wähnen* or its English translation *be under the illusion that* (see note 5 in chapter 5), or *pretend*, or *lie*. These have as a precondition the falsity of the dependent clause. *Dream up* has, furthermore, the special property that whatever is said to be dreamt up *must* be incremented in the subdomain reserved for what the subject dreams up; no other intensional subdomain will do. This means that an address characterized by a predicate like *dream up* must not only be excluded from D^0 but also from any other subdomain than the D^m associated for this verb in this D. Thus in

(30) The girls Nigel dreams up are blonde.

the subject-term must refer non-extensionally, and the girls-address must be in D^m. The predicate *blonde must now be used for truth-testing, since the increment of (30) cannot but be implemented in the subdomain of what Nigel dreams up.

The increment procedure under rule R1 is, of course, subject to the same acceptability conditions as have so far been assumed. Thus, contradiction makes any domain unacceptable. This has a filtering effect on possible readings. Consider the sentence:

(31) The dark-haired girls Nigel dreams of are blonde.

The subject term *the dark-haired girls* must denote an address outside Nigel's dream-domain, since if the increment is implemented in it, that domain will be unacceptable. After the processing of (31), D will contain the following structure, supposing that the girls-address is in D^0:

(32) a.

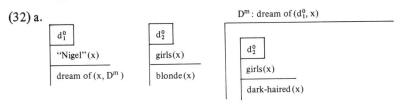

If the girls-address is indexed for D^m, (31) is unacceptable:

(32) b.

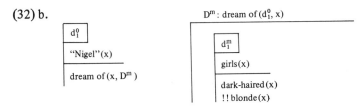

And the sentence *The dark-haired girls Nigel dreams up are blonde* is simply contradictory.

The subdomain need not be given explicitly in the sentence itself. The sentence

(33) The white dog is black.

allows for an interpretation whereby the subject-term refers extensionally, but the dog-address in D^0 is indirectly closed in some subdomain D^m where it is given the predicate *white*. This occurs, for example, when one is talking about a painting representing a really existing set of entities, and one wants to say that the dog which is painted as a white dog is in fact black (cp. Fauconnier 1979). The increment value of (33) will thus be structurally similar to (34):

(34)

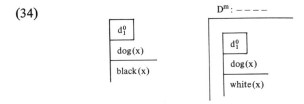

But the converse of this interpretation is also possible. Instead of reading "The white^m dog is black^0", the sentence may also be understood as "The white^0 dog is black^m", as when one is talking about a white dog and says that that dog is represented, in a painting or wherever, as being black. For this to be possible the discourse must contain a subdomain D^m for the proposition to be incremented to, e.g. a subdomain under "in the painting", and this subdomain must fulfil certain conditions of 'salience' (comparable, probably, to the salience conditions for external anaphora), so that the proposition is understood as being incrementable to D^m. If this is so, "The white^m dog is black^0" is incrementally equivalent to "The black^0 dog is white^m", except for the order in which the resulting D-structure is put together. For truth-testing, according to R2, the predicate "white" must be read as *white*.

6.7 Concluding remarks

The announcement made at the beginning of this book, that the book is essentially a report on extensive forays into the unknown territory of discourse-dependent linguistic interpretation, is now filled with intension: the reader who has found his way through the preceding pages now has an idea of what has been discovered. It is heady stuff, but there is no denying that the interpretation of utterances in natural language is inextricably bound up with discourse processes, and that this fact has, so far, not been given the attention it deserves in linguistic theorizing. Lip-service is sometimes paid, and non-committing and imprecise principles are sometimes formulated or invoked, but systematic and precise investigations are still rare. It will have become clear, by now, that discourse structures and processes harbour an immense potential for better understanding of and insight into the reality of human language. It has been the main purpose of this study to reveal a glimpse of this potential. Although the possibility cannot be discounted that the perspectives that have become visible are inadequate or incongruous, which is a risk to be reckoned with when partial views are opened, what has become visible looks definitely enticing.

APPENDIX

Presuppositional propositional calculi

A. WEIJTERS

Introduction

This appendix* is primarily a technical elaboration of the three-valued pre-suppositional propositional calculus devised by Pieter Seuren and presented in chapter 3 of this book. Many of the insights that form the basis of what is presented here are thus due to him, especially the ideas underlying sections 1, 2, 3 and 6.3.

Besides the calculi presented here, there are many other many-valued propositional calculi. Rescher (1969) gives a good survey. Yet most of these calculi are based on semantic notions that are very different from those underlying the *presuppositional* propositional calculus presented here.

An exception must be made for the three-valued calculi developed by Kleene (1959) and by Blau (1978). Kleene never developed his calculus any further, contrary to Blau. At first sight, there seem to be many similarities between the thoroughly elaborated three-valued logic designed by Blau and the propositional calculus presented here. The two negations of each system, in particular, are mutually translatable. There are also, however, important differences, especially concerning the underlying semantic motivations. In Blau's system, the third value is assigned to a proposition whenever the predicate is vague, or whenever descriptions fail to refer. Blau does not allow for other than referential presuppositions to be accounted for through the third value. Our propositional calculus, on the contrary, aims at covering all presuppositional phenomena, including the non-referential cases. Blau's system thus seems complementary to ours. A comparative evaluation of the two approaches may well be useful. Yet in this paper, the matter will be allowed to rest.

In section 1 an exposé is given of the semantic background of the three-valued presuppositional propositional calculus (=PPC(3)) presented, followed

* This study is an adapted version of an MA thesis in the Faculty of Philosophy at Nijmegen University in June 1981. The author wishes to thank Pieter Seuren, Göran Sundholm and Harrie de Swart, who read the manuscript and offered many helpful comments. Pieter Seuren made the translation from Dutch into English.

by a semantics framework for PPC(3) and PPC(n). In section 2 a set-theoretic basis is developed, which proves to be useful for the consistency proof of Gentzen-type proof theory for PPC(3). Section 3 contains a first classification of n-valued logical systems, as well as an investigation into some of their properties. A Hilbert-type proof theory for PPC(3) is given in section 4, and a Gentzen-type proof theory in section 5. The paper ends with a further elaboration of the classification started in section 3, with the proof of the presuppositional completeness of the set of connectives $\{\wedge, \vee, \sim, \simeq\}$, and with an observation about the special status of PPC(3) with respect to the classification given in sections 3 and 6.

The logically trained reader will probably find this essay too easy to read and may feel that much of the formalism as well as of the exposition could be omitted given established knowledge, practice and conventions. This reader, however, may feel a little appeased when he realizes that other readers of this book will be less familiar with these matters.

1 A framework for the semantics of presuppositional propositional calculi (PPCs)

1.1 A survey of tables

1.1.1 Tables of the logical predicates of the three-valued PPC (PPC(3))

Table 1

A	$\sim$A	$\simeq$A	$\neg$A
1	2	2	2
2	1	2	1
3	3	1	1

Table 2

A	B	A∧B	A∨B	A⊃B	A⊇B	A⊃$_L$B	A→B
1	1	1	1	1	1	1	1
1	2	2	1	2	2	2	2
1	3	3	1	2	2	2	2
2	1	2	1	1	1	1	1
2	2	2	2	1	2	1	1
2	3	3	2	1	2	1	1
3	1	3	1	1	1	3	1
3	2	3	2	2	1	3	1
3	3	3	3	3	1	3	1

$\neg A := \sim A \lor \simeq A$
$A \supset B := \sim A \lor B$
$A \supseteq B := \simeq A \lor B$
$A \supset_L B := \sim A \lor (A \triangle B)$
$A \rightarrow B := \neg A \lor B$

1.1.2 Tables of the logical predicates of the n-valued PPC (PPC(n))

Table 3

A	$\sim A$	$\simeq A$	$\ldots$	$\underset{n-1}{\sim} A$	$\neg A$
1	2	2	$\ldots$	2	2
2	1	2	$\ldots$	2	1
3	3	1	$\ldots$	2	1
4	4	2	$\ldots$	2	1
$\vdots$	$\vdots$	$\vdots$	$\vdots$	$\vdots$	$\vdots$
n	n	2	$\ldots$	1	1

Table 4

A	B	$A \land B$	$A \lor B$	$A \rightarrow B$
1	1	1	1	1
1	2	2	1	2
1	3	3	1	2
$\vdots$	$\vdots$	$\vdots$	$\vdots$	$\vdots$
1	n	n	1	2
2	1	2	1	1
2	2	2	2	1
2	3	3	2	1
$\vdots$	$\vdots$	$\vdots$	$\vdots$	$\vdots$
2	n	n	2	1
$\vdots$	$\vdots$	$\vdots$	$\vdots$	$\vdots$
n	1	n	1	1
n	2	n	2	1
n	3	n	3	1
$\vdots$	$\vdots$	$\vdots$	$\vdots$	$\vdots$
n	n	n	n	1

$\neg A := \sim A \lor \simeq A \lor \ldots \lor \underset{n-1}{\sim} A$
$A \rightarrow B := \neg A \lor B$

1.2   A framework for the semantics of a three-valued PPC (PPC(3))

We posit the functions σ_1 and σ_2. σ_1 assigns to a predicate P an extension set $\sigma_1(P)$, by which the *truth conditions* for P are fixed. Likewise, σ_2 assigns an extension set to P, $\sigma_2(P)$, by which the *presupposition conditions* for P are fixed. (Our logical language L3 contains only predicates and terms.)

1.2.1 Def Alphabet of L3 :=

    (i) $P_1^1, P_2^1, P_3^1, \ldots$ predicate symbols with one position
        $P_1^2, P_2^2, P_3^2, \ldots$ predicate symbols with two positions
        $P_1^n, P_2^n, P_3^n, \ldots$ predicate symbols with n positions
    (ii) $\sim$, $\simeq$ logical predicates (predicate constants) with one position
        $\wedge$, $\vee$ logical predicates (predicate constants) with two positions
    (iii) ', e, :, (,) auxiliary symbols

1.2.2 Def Terms of L3 :=

    (i) If $t_1, \ldots, t_{j-1}$, $t_{j+1}, \ldots, t_m$ are terms and P^m is a predicate symbol with m positions, then 'e:$P^m(t_1, \ldots, t_{j-1}, e, t_{j+1}, \ldots, t_m)$ is a term.
    (ii) If A is a *formula* of L3, then 'A' is a term.

Note that also 'e:$P^1(e)$ is a term.

1.2.3 Def Formulae of L3 :=
    If $t_1, \ldots, t_n$ are terms and P^n is a predicate symbol or a logical predicate with n positions, then $P^n(t_1, \ldots, t_n)$ is a formula of L3.

1.2.4 Def Term := the set of all terms in L3.
        Wff := the set of all formulae in L3.
        Pred := the set of all predicate symbols (including the logical predicates) in L3.
      NB: *Def* 1.2.2 and *def* 1.2.3 form a recursive pair. Furthermore, if A, B $\in$ Wff, then also $\wedge$ ('$\sim$('A')', 'B') $\in$ Wff.

1.2.5 Def $\langle$I, ρ, σ_1, σ_2, $\varphi\rangle$ is a *model* (interpretation) for L3 :=

    (i) I is a non-empty set.
    (ii) ρ : Term $\to$ I $\cup$ $\{\emptyset\}$ such that
        (a) ρ('e:$P^m(t_1, \ldots, t_{j-1}, e, t_{j+1}, \ldots, t_m)$) = the specific $i \in I$ with $\langle\rho(t_1), \ldots, \rho(t_{j-1}), i, \rho(t_{j+1}), \ldots, \rho(t_m)\rangle \in \sigma_1(P^m)$, if there is such a specific $i \in I$;
         ρ('e:$P^m(t_1, \ldots, t_{j-1}, e, t_{j+1}, \ldots, t_m)$) = $\emptyset$ otherwise.
        (b) ρ('A') = A.

(iii) (a) σ_1: Pred $\rightarrow \bigcup_{n \in \mathbb{N}} (\mathscr{P}(I^n))$ such that if P^n is a predicate symbol
with n positions, then $\sigma_1(P^n) \in \mathscr{P}(I^n)$ (the power set of I^n).

(b) σ_2: Pred $\rightarrow \bigcup_{n \in \mathbb{N}} (\mathscr{P}(I^n))$ such that if P^n is a predicate symbol
with n positions, then $\sigma_2(P^n) \in \mathscr{P}(I^n)$.

(c) For every $P \in$ Pred: $\sigma_1(P) \subseteq \sigma_2(P)$.

(iv) $\varphi(P^n(t_1, \ldots, t_n)) = 1$ iff $\langle \rho(t_1), \ldots, \rho(t_n) \rangle \in \sigma_1(P^n)$.
$\varphi(P^n(t_1, \ldots, t_n)) = 2$ iff $\langle \rho(t_1), \ldots, \rho(t_n) \rangle \notin \sigma_1(P^n)$.
and $\langle \rho(t_1), \ldots, \rho(t_n) \rangle \in \sigma_2(P^n$.
$\varphi(P^n(t_1, \ldots, t_n)) = 3$ iff $\langle \rho(t_1), \ldots, \rho(t_n) \rangle \notin \sigma_2(P^n)$.
and for all t_1 ($i \in \{1, 2, \ldots, n\}$), $\rho(t_i) \neq \emptyset$.
$\varphi(P^n(t_1, \ldots, t_n)) =$ undefined iff for some $i \in \{1, 2, \ldots, n\}$,
$\rho(t_i) = \emptyset$.

Note that the set I contains, besides individuals, also the well-formed formulae of L3. The advantages of this decision will be illustrated below when 1.2.7 is discussed.

Often, the set σ_1 must be specified by enumeration. σ_2 is always specifiable through characterization. The definition of the extension sets σ_1 and σ_2 is the task of the special sciences dealing with the predicates in question. It is thus incumbent upon us to specify the extension sets of the logical predicates.

1.2.6 Def Extension sets of the logical predicates:

(i) $\sigma_1(\sim) := \{\rho(t_1) \mid \varphi(\rho(t_1) \in \{2\}\}$
$\sigma_2(\sim) := \{\rho(t_1) \mid \varphi(\rho(t_1) \in \{1, 2\}\}$

NB: Since if $A \in$ Wff, $\rho(t_1) = A$, we can give the following more convenient definition:

$\sigma_1(\sim) := \{A \mid \varphi(A) \in \{2\}\}$
$\sigma_2(\sim) := \{A \mid \varphi(A) \in \{1, 2\}\}$

(ii) $\sigma_1(\approx) := \{A \mid \varphi(A) \in \{3\}\}$
$\sigma_2(\approx) := \{A \mid \varphi(A) \in \{1, 2, 3\}\}$

(iii) $\sigma_1(\wedge) := \{\langle A, B \rangle \mid \varphi(A), \varphi(B) \in \{1\}\}$
$\sigma_2(\wedge) := \{\langle A, B \rangle \mid \varphi(A), \varphi(B) \in \{1, 2\}\}$

(iv) $\sigma_1(\vee) := \{\langle A, B \rangle \mid \varphi(A) \in \{1\}$ or $\varphi(B) \in \{1\}\}$
$\sigma_2(\vee) := \{\langle A, B \rangle \mid \varphi(A) \in \{1, 2\}$ or $\varphi(B) \in \{1, 2\}\}$

1.2.7 Ex Analysis of the sentence:

John discovers that his car is broken, and Mary is ill.

This sentence has the following predicate-term structure: *and (discovers (John, broken (John's car), ill (Mary)).*

Predicates: P_1^1: be John's car
P_2^1: be called 'Mary'

P_3^1: be called 'John'
P_4^1: broken
P_5^1: ill
P_6^2: discover
$\wedge$: and
P_8^1: capable of perception (auxiliary predicate)

Starting from within, this gives:

(i) *Terms:*　'e:P_1^1(e)　　　　John's car
　　　　　　　'e:P_2^1(e)　　　　Mary
　　　　　　　'e:P_3^1(e)　　　　John
(ii) *Formula:* P_4^1('e:P_1^1(e))　　　broken(John's car)
(iii) *Term:*　'P_4^1('e:P_1^1(e))'
(iv) *Formula:* P_6^2('e:P_3^1(e), 'P_4^1('e:P_1^1(e))')　discovers(John, broken
　　　　　　　　　　　　　　　　　　　　　　　(John's car))
(v) *Term:*　'P_6^2('e:P_3^1(e), 'P_4^1('e:P_1^1(e))')'
(vi) *Formula:* P_5^1('e:P_2^1(e))　　　　ill(Mary)
(vii) *Term:*　'P_5^1('e:P_2^1(e))'
(viii) *Formula:* $\wedge$ ('P_6^2('e:P_3^1(e), 'P_4^1('e:P_1^1(e))')', 'P_5^1('e:P_2^1(e))')

Now take the following model $\langle I, \rho, \sigma_1, \sigma_2, \varphi \rangle$:

$I = \{$John, John's car, Mary, P_4^1('e:P_1^1(e)), P_6^2('e:P_3^1(e), 'P_4^1('e:P_1^1(e))'),
　　P_5^1('e:P_2^1(e)), $\wedge$ ('P_6^2('e:P_3^1(e), 'P_4^1('e:P_1^1(e))')', 'P_5^1('e:P_2^1(e))'), $\cdots\}$

$\sigma_1(P_1^1) := \{$John's car$\}$
$\sigma_1(P_2^1) := \{$Mary$\}$
$\sigma_1(P_3^1) := \{$John$\}$
$\sigma_1(P_4^1) := \{$John's car, $\cdots\}$ = extension set of the predicate *broken*
$\sigma_1(P_5^1) := \{$Mary, $\cdots\}$ = extension set of the predicate *ill*
$\sigma_1(P_6^2) := \{\langle$John, P_4^1('e:P_1^1(e))$\rangle$, $\cdots\}$ = extension set of *discover*
$\sigma_1(\Delta) :=$ see *Def* 1.2.6
$\sigma_1(P_8^1) := \{$John, Mary, $\cdots\}$ = extension set of the predicate *capable of perception*
$\sigma_2(P_6^2) := \{\langle\rho(t_1), \rho(t_2)\rangle \mid \rho(t_1) \in \sigma_1(P_8^1), \varphi(\rho(t_2)) = 1\}$

This definition of $\sigma_2(P_6^2)$ expresses the fact that if $\rho(t_1)$ discovers $\rho(t_2)$, then $\rho(t_1)$ must possess sensory organs and $\rho(t_2)$ must be true.

The σ_2-sets of the remaining predicates are not relevant for this example. We will now compute φ of Formula (viii).

As given in *Def* 1.2.6 (iii), $\sigma_1(\wedge) := \{\langle A, B\rangle \mid \varphi(A) = 1$ and $\varphi(B) = 1\}$. Let us inspect $\varphi(A)$ and $\varphi(B)$.

$A = P_6^2$('e:P_3^1(e), 'P_4^1('e:P_1^1(e))') $\in$ Wff.
$B = P_5^1$('e:P_2^1(e)) $\in$ Wff.

What is the value of $\varphi(A)$?

$\rho('e:P_3^1(e)) = $ John, since John is the unique element of $\sigma_I(P_3^1)$.
$\rho('P_4^1('e:P_1^1(e))') = P_4^1('e:P_1^1(e))$.

Therefore, $\varphi(A)$ is defined. Furthermore: $\langle$John, $P_4^1('e:P_1^1(e))\rangle \in \sigma_1(P_6^2)$.
So $\varphi(A) = 1$.

What is the value of $\varphi(B)$?

$\rho('e:P_2^1(e)) = $ Mary, since Mary is the unique element of $\sigma_I(P_2^1)$.

Moreover, Mary $\in \sigma_I(P_5^1)$. Hence, $\varphi(B) = 1$. Therefore, $\varphi(\wedge('A', 'B')) = 1$.

What are the presuppositions of *Ex* 1.2.7? Among the presuppositions are:
(a) *John's car is broken*, and (b) *John is capable of perception*. Since:
$\sigma_I(P_6^2) \subseteq \sigma_2(P_6^2)$, according to *Def* 1.2.5 (iiic).

Now $\langle$John, $P_4^1('e:P_1^1(e))\rangle \in \sigma_I(P_6^2)$, and therefore $\langle$John, $P_4^1('e:P_1^1(e))\rangle \in \sigma_2(P_6^2)$. Since John is $\rho(t_1)$ of $\sigma_2(P_6^2)$, it follows that John $\in \sigma_I(P_8^1)$, i.e. *John is capable of perception.* (b)

As regards (a), $\varphi(P_4^1('e:P_1^1(e)) = 1$. That is: $\rho('e:P_1^1(e)) \in \sigma_I(P_4^1)$. Now $\rho('e:P_1^1(e)) = $ John's car, since John's car is the unique element in $\sigma_I(P_1^1)$. Hence John's car $\in \sigma_I(P_4^1)$, i.e. *John's car is broken.*

Now suppose we change the preceding model in the following way: $\sigma_I(P_6^2)$ does *not* contain the pair $\langle$John, $P_4^1('e:P_1^1(e))\rangle$. All else remains the same. We then find that $\varphi(A) = 2$ and $\varphi(B) = 1$. Hence $\varphi(\wedge('A', 'B')) = 2$ (minimally false). But the sentence still presupposes (a) and (b), because $\varphi(A) = 2$, which means that $\langle\rho('e:P_3^1(e)), \rho('P_4^1('e:P_1^1(e))')\rangle \notin \sigma_I(P_6^2)$, but $\langle\rho('e:P_3^1(e)), \rho('P_4^1('e:P_1^1(e))')\rangle \in \sigma_2(P_6^2)$, according to *Def* 1.2.5 (iv). From now on, we can follow the derivation of (b) and (a) as given above.

When the σ_2 of the remaining predicates are given, we can specify the presuppositions of *Ex* 1.2.7 not dealt with so far.

The definition of "A presupposes B" $(A \geqslant B)$ is postponed, for practical reasons, till section 2 (see *Def* 2.1.8).

From the definitions of the extension sets of the logical predicates ($\wedge$, $\vee$, $\sim$, $\approx$) we can derive the truth-tables for the logical predicates in a simple manner, using *Def* 1.2.6 and *Def* 1.2.5.

$\sim$ The values of $\varphi(\sim('A'))$, where A $\in$ Wff.
$\sim('A') \in$ Wff, and $\rho('A') = A$. Therefore, $\varphi(\sim('A'))$ is defined.
Let $\varphi(A) = 1$, then $\varphi(A) \in \{1, 2\}$ and $\varphi(A) \notin \{2\}$. Hence $\varphi(\sim('A')) = 2$,
Let $\varphi(A) = 2$, then $\varphi(A) \in \{1, 2\}$ and $\varphi(A) \in \{2\}$. Hence $\varphi(\sim('A')) = 1$.
Let $\varphi(A) = 3$, then $\varphi(A) \notin \{1, 2\}$. Hence $\varphi(\sim('A')) = 3$.
$\approx$ The values of $\varphi(\approx('A'))$.
Let $\varphi(A) = 1$, then $\varphi(A) \in \{1, 2, 3\}$ and $\varphi(A) \notin \{3\}$. Hence $\varphi(\approx('A')) = 2$.
Let $\varphi(A) = 2$, then $\varphi(A) \in \{1, 2, 3\}$ and $\varphi(A) \notin \{3\}$. Hence $\varphi(\approx('A')) = 2$.
Let $\varphi(A) = 3$, then $\varphi(A) \in \{1, 2, 3\}$ and $\varphi(A) \in \{3\}$. Hence $\varphi(\approx('A')) = 1$.

∧ The values of $\varphi(\wedge(\text{'A'}, \text{'B'}))$, where A, B ∈ Wff.

Let $\varphi(A) = 1$ and $\varphi(B) = 1$, then $\varphi(A), \varphi(B) \in \{1, 2\}$ and $\varphi(A), \varphi(B) \in \{1\}$. Hence $\varphi(\wedge(\text{'A'}, \text{'B'})) = 1$.

Let $\varphi(A) = 1$ and $\varphi(B) = 2$, then $\varphi(A), \varphi(B) \in \{1, 2\}$ and $\varphi(A) \in \{1\}$, $\varphi(B) \notin \{1\}$. Hence $\varphi(\wedge(\text{'A'}, \text{'B'})) = 2$.

Let $\varphi(A) = 1$ and $\varphi(B) = 3$, then $\varphi(B) \notin \{1, 2\}$. Hence $\varphi(\wedge(\text{'A'}, \text{'B'})) = 3$.

∨ The values of $\varphi(\vee(\text{'A'}, \text{'B'}))$.

Let $\varphi(A) = 1$ and $\varphi(B) \in \{1, 2, 3\}$, then $\varphi(A) \in \{1, 2\}$ and $\varphi(A) \in \{1\}$. Hence $\varphi(\vee(\text{'A'}, \text{'B'})) = 1$.

Let $\varphi(A) = 2$ and $\varphi(B) \in \{2, 3\}$, then $\varphi(A) \in \{1, 2\}$ and $\varphi(A) \notin \{1\}$, $\varphi(B) \notin \{1\}$. Hence $\varphi(\vee(\text{'A'}, \text{'B'})) = 2$.

Let $\varphi(A) = 3$ and $\varphi(B) = 3$, then $\varphi(A) \notin \{1, 2\}$ and $\varphi(B) \notin \{1, 2\}$. Hence $\varphi(\vee(\text{'A'}, \text{'B'})) = 3$.

This yields the following table 5:

Table 5

A	B	~('A')	≃('B')	∧ ('A', 'B')	∨ ('A', 'B')
1	1	2	2	1	1
1	2	2	2	2	1
1	3	2	1	3	1
2	1	1	2	2	1
2	2	1	2	2	2
2	3	1	1	3	2
3	1	3	2	3	1
3	2	3	2	3	2
3	3	3	1	3	3

In section 2.2 we will show how the truth-tables of the logical predicates (which will then be logical connectives) can be established without an appeal to *Def* 1.2.6. The method used here is useful for an extrapolation to PPC(n) (*Def* 1.3.6).

Note that the logical predicates ~, ≃, ∧ and ∨ are *not complete*: a formula with only these logical predicates cannot be assigned the value *3* on line 1 of the truth-table. But these logical predicates are *presuppositionally complete* (see 6.2).

Instead of ~('A'), ≃('A'), ∧ ('A', 'B'), ∨ ('A', 'B') we will often write: ~A, ≃A, A ∧ B, A ∨ B, respectively.

The truth-tables given here are identical to those presented by Seuren.

The following logical predicates can be defined in terms of those already given:

1.2.8 Def If $A, B \in \text{Wff}$, then we define:

(i) *minimal implication* $\supset$ - $A \supset B$ $:= \sim A \vee B$
(ii) *radical implication* $\supseteq$ - $A \supseteq B$ $:= \approx A \vee B$
(iii) *linguistic implication* $\supset_L$ - $A \supset_L B := \sim A \vee (A \wedge B)$

For the tables associated with these newly defined logical predicates, see 1.1.1.

A number of problems to do with the relation between logical systems and natural language are still unsolved in the theory given so far. A sentence such as 'John is looking for the unicorn' still causes trouble. This appears clearly when we give the following possible definition of the extension set associated with the predicate *look for*:

$$\sigma_2(\text{look for}) := \{\langle \rho(t_1), \rho(t_2)\rangle \mid \rho(t_1) \in \sigma_1(\text{capable of perception})\}$$

(No special requirements are given for $\rho(t_2)$: one may look for anything.) However, we have stipulated that no truth-value results when $\rho(t_i) = \emptyset$ for any of the terms. In order to assign a truth-value to the sentence 'John is looking for the unicorn' we must drop this stipulation, and replace it by a presuppositional requirement. But then, the following problem presents itself. Let the sentence 'John is looking for the unicorn' be true, then $\langle \rho(\text{John}), \rho(\text{unicorn})\rangle \in \sigma_1(\text{look for})$, or, in other words, $\langle \rho(\text{John}), \emptyset\rangle \in \sigma_1(\text{look for})$. But the same truth-condition now holds for, e.g. 'John is looking for the philosopher's stone', which, likewise, if true, amounts to $\langle \rho(\text{John}), \emptyset\rangle \in \sigma_1$ (look for). Yet the former sentence may be true while the latter is false, or vice versa. The reason is (see chapter 5) that 'the unicorn' and 'the philosopher's stone' must have been defined in some subdomain attributed to and considered part of John's thinking. But this has as a consequence that the function ρ, which takes its values from the real world for extensional terms of predicates, must take its values from a realm of intensional entities defined by, in this case, John's thinking, for intensional terms that are non-sentential, such as the object-term of the predicate *look for*. We shall not go into these problems here, since they are less logical than semantic. It must be clear, however, that three-valuedness of the logical system offers no solution to problems of intensionality.

1.3 A framework for the semantics of an n-valued PPC (PPC(n))

Although our primary interest remains in PPC(3), the transition from PPC(3) to PPC(n) is important for a good insight into presuppositional propositional calculi generally.

Let us first consider an example illustrating the transition from PPC(3) to PPC(4). Take the sentence 'John discovers that his car is broken' (cp. *Ex* 1.2.7). Let

$$\sigma_1(\text{discover}) := \{\langle\text{John, 'John's car is broken'}\rangle, \cdots\}$$
$$\sigma_2(\text{discover}) := \{\langle\rho(t_1), \rho(t_2)\rangle \mid \rho(t_1) \in \sigma_1(\text{capable of perception}),$$
$$\rho(t_2) \in \text{Wff}, \varphi(\rho(t_2)) = 1\}$$

In PPC(3) the sentence 'John discovers that his car is broken' is now true. The sentence 'Harold discovers that his car is broken' is either true or minimally false, but certainly not radically false – assuming that Harold owns a car. We can, however, define a $\sigma_3(\text{discover})$, with $\sigma_2(\text{discover}) \subseteq \sigma_3(\text{discover})$:

$$\sigma_3(\text{discover}) := \{\rho(t_1), \rho(t_2)\rangle \mid \rho(t_1) \in \sigma_1(\text{alive}), \rho(t_2) \in \text{Wff}\}$$

Intuitively, we might say that $\sigma_2(\text{discover})$ gives *all* information about the reference values of the terms of the predicate *discover* that must be available before a classical value can be assigned. $\sigma_3(\text{discover})$ gives *some*, but not necessarily *all* such information. Obviously, given our primary interest in the semantics of natural language, PPC(3) is more relevant than PPC(4), since σ_2 gives all the information needed beforehand (i.e. before a classical value can be assigned).

Analogously, we can define $\sigma_4, \sigma_5, \ldots, \sigma_{n-1}$, with $\sigma_4(P) \subseteq \sigma_5(P) \subseteq \ldots \subseteq \sigma_{n-1}(P)$. Given this, we can now proceed to giving a framework for the semantics of an n-valued PPC.

1.3.1 Def Alphabet of Ln :=

(i) $P_1^1, P_2^1, P_3^1, \ldots$ one-place predicate symbols
   $P_1^2, P_2^2, P_3^2, \ldots$ two-place predicate symbols
   $P_1^m, P_2^m, P_3^m, \ldots$ m-place predicate symbols
(ii) $\Upsilon, \widetilde{\Upsilon}, \mathfrak{Z}, \ldots$ one-place logical predicates (predicate constants)
   $\wedge, \vee$ two-place logical predicates (predicate constants)
(iii) ', e, :, (,) auxiliary symbols.

1.3.2 Def Terms of Ln :=

(i) If $t_1, \ldots, t_{j-1}, t_{j+1}, \ldots, t_m$ are terms and P^m is an m-place predicate symbol, then $'e : P^m(t_1, \ldots, t_{j-1}, e, t_{j+1}, \ldots, t_m)$ is a term.
(ii) If A is a formula of Ln, then $'A'$ is a term.

1.3.3 Def Formulae of Ln :=

If $t_1, \ldots, t_m$ are terms and P^m is a predicate symbol or a logical predicate with m places, then $P^m(t_1, \ldots, t_m)$ is a formula of Ln.

1.3.4 Def Term := the set of all terms in Ln.

Wff := the set of all formulas in Ln.

Pred := the set of all predicate symbols (including the logical predicates) in Ln.

1.3.5 Def $\langle I, \rho, \sigma_1, \sigma_2, \ldots, \sigma_{n-1}, \varphi \rangle$ is a *model* (interpretation) for Ln :=

(i) I is a non-empty set.

(ii) $\rho : \text{Term} \to I \cup \{\emptyset\}$ such that

(a) $\rho('e : P^m(t_1, \ldots, t_{j-1}, e, t_{j+1}, \ldots, t_m)) =$ the specific $i \in I$ with $\langle \rho(t_1), \ldots, \rho(t_{j-1}), i, \rho(t_{j+1}), \ldots, \rho(t_m) \rangle \in \sigma_1(P^m)$ if there is such a specific $i \in I$;

$\rho('e : P^m(t_1, \ldots, t_{j-1}, e, t_{j+1}, \ldots, t_m)) = \emptyset$ otherwise.

(b) $\rho('A') = A$.

(iii) $\sigma_j : \text{Pred} \to \bigcup_{m \in \mathbb{N}} (\mathscr{P}(I^m))$, $(j \in \{1, \ldots, n-1\})$, such that if P^m is an m-place predicate symbol, then $\sigma_j(P^m) \in \mathscr{P}(I^m)$ and $\sigma_1(P^m) \subseteq \sigma_2(P^m) \subseteq - \subseteq \sigma_{n-1}(P^m)$.

(iv) $\varphi : \text{Wff} \to \{1, 2, \ldots, n\}$ such that

$\varphi(P^m(t_1, \ldots, t_m)) = 1$ iff $\langle \rho(t_1), \ldots, \rho(t_m) \rangle \in \sigma_1(P^m)$.

$\varphi(P^m(t_1, \ldots, t_m)) = 2$ iff $\langle \rho(t_1), \ldots, \rho(t_m) \rangle \notin \sigma_1(P^m)$, $\in \sigma_2(P^m)$.

$$\vdots$$

$\varphi(P^m(t_1, \ldots, t_m)) = j$ iff $\langle \rho(t_1), \ldots, \rho(t_m) \rangle \notin \sigma_{j-1}(P^m)$, $\in \sigma_j(P^m)$.

$$\vdots$$

$\varphi(P^m(t_1, \ldots, t_m)) = n$ iff $\langle \rho(t_1), \ldots, \rho(t_m) \rangle \notin \sigma_{n-1}(P^m)$, and for all $i \in \{1, 2, \ldots, m\}, \rho(t_i) \neq \emptyset$.

$\varphi(P^m(t_1, \ldots, t_m)) =$ undefined iff for some $i \in \{1, 2, \ldots, m\}$, $\rho(t_i) = \emptyset$.

1.3.6 Def $A, B \in \text{Wff}$.

(i) $\sigma_1(\curlyvee) := \{A \mid \varphi(A) \in \{2\}\}$

$\sigma_2(\curlyvee) := \{A \mid \varphi(A) \in \{1, 2\}\}$

$\sigma_j(\curlyvee) := \{A \mid \varphi(A) \in \{1, 2, \ldots, j\}\}, j \in \{3, 4, \ldots, n-1\}$

(ii) $\sigma_1(\widetilde{\curlyvee}) := \{A \mid \varphi(A) \in \{i\}\}$

$\sigma_j(\widetilde{\curlyvee}) := \{A \mid \varphi(A) \in \{1, 2, \ldots, n\}\}, i \in \{2, 3, \ldots, n-1\}$, $j \in \{2, 3, \ldots, n-1\}$

(iii) $\sigma_j(\wedge) := \{\langle A, B \rangle \mid \varphi(A), \varphi(B) \in \{1, 2, \ldots, j\}\}$, $j \in \{1, 2, \ldots, n-1\}$

(iv) $\sigma_j(\vee) := \{\langle A, B \rangle \mid \varphi(A) \in \{1, 2, \ldots, j\} \text{ or } \varphi(B) \in \{1, 2, \ldots, j\}\}$, $j \in \{1, 2, \ldots, n-1\}$

It is easily established that the tables 1.1.2 result from the preceding definitions:

Let $\varphi(A) = 1$, then $\varphi(\sim A) = 2$, $\varphi(\approx A) = 2$, $\varphi(\gamma A) = 2, \ldots, \varphi(_n\overset{\sim}{}_1 A) = 2$.
Let $\varphi(A) = 2$, then $\varphi(\sim A) = 1$, $\varphi(\approx A) = 2$, $\varphi(\gamma A) = 2, \ldots, \varphi(_n\overset{\sim}{}_1 A) = 2$.
Let $\varphi(A) = 3$, then $\varphi(\sim A) = 3$, $\varphi(\approx A) = 1$, $\varphi(\gamma A) = 2, \ldots, \varphi(_n\overset{\sim}{}_1 A) = 2$.

$\vdots$

Let $\varphi(A) = n$, then $\varphi(\sim A) = 2$, $\varphi(\approx A) = 2$, $\varphi(\gamma A) = 2, \ldots, \varphi(_n\overset{\sim}{}_1 A) = 1$.
Let $\varphi(A) = a$, $\varphi(B) = b$; $a, b \in \{1, 2, \ldots, b\}$; $a \leqslant b$. Then $\varphi(A), \varphi(B) \in \{1, 2, \ldots, b\}$. Hence $\varphi(A \wedge B) = b$, and $\varphi(A \vee B) = a$.

Note that for $n = 2$ we generate precisely the tables of the classical propositional calculus, PPC(2), and for $n = 3$ the tables of PPC(3).

2 A set-theoretic basis for PPC(n)

In this section a uniform set-theoretic basis is provided for n-valued PPCs. We aim at gaining a better insight into the logical system PPC(3) through its set-theoretic basis. This proves, moreover, very useful for proving consistency of the Gentzen-type rules for PPC(3), as in section 5.

2.1 Some basic notations

In section 1 a framework is given for the semantics of PPCs, where all propositions have a predicate-term structure. As from *Def* 1.2.7 we have concentrated on the *logical predicates*, a concern that will remain constant throughout the following section. For this reason it is practical to make a few new definitions, as in *Def* 2.1.1. These are, however, in complete agreement with what has been given in section 1.

2.1.1 Def Formal language of PPC(n)

    (i) Alphabet of PPC(n)
        (a) $P_1, P_2, P_3, \ldots$ prime formulae or propositional variables
        (b) $\wedge, \vee, \gamma, \ldots, _n\overset{\sim}{}_1$ connectives or logical predicates
        (c) $(,)$ brackets

    P, Q, R are used to indicate arbitrary prime formulas.

    (ii) Formulae of PPC(n)
        (a) Every prime formula is a formula.
        (b) If A and B are formulas, then $A \wedge B$, $A \vee B$, $\gamma A, \ldots, _n\overset{\sim}{}_1 A$ are formulas.

A *prime formula*, in this context, is a well-formed formula according to *Def* 1.3.3, not containing any logical predicates. Given A, B $\in$ Wff, *Def* 1.3.3

allows, of course, for the construction of complex formulae through the logical predicates. The simplified notation gives the complex formulas of *Def* 2.1.1 (ii).

For every prime formula P we assume that we know whether P is *true* (i.e. *1*), or *minimally false* (i.e. *2*), or *radically false to some extent* (i.e. *3*, ..., n). Thus, our designated value is *1*.

The truth-tables associated with PPC(n) are those given in 1.1.2 (and derived in section 1).

2.1.2 Def If $\Gamma \subseteq$ UVar (= the set of propositional variables of PPC(n)), and Γ is finite, we define:

$v_\Gamma^n \colon \Gamma \to \{1, 2, \ldots, n\}$ is a *valuation function* for Γ.

2.1.3 Def $V_\Gamma^n := \{v_\Gamma^n \mid v_\Gamma^n \colon \Gamma \to \{1, 2, \ldots, n\}\}$ is the set of all valuations for Γ. (We will often write 'v' and 'V' instead of 'v_Γ^n' and 'V_Γ^n' respectively.)

2.1.4 Def For all $A \in$ Wff, UVar(A) := the set of all propositional variables (prime formulae) occurring in A.

NB: If Γ has precisely m elements, and the logic is n-valued, then V_Γ^n has precisely n^m elements.

2.1.5 Def If $B \in$ Wff of PPC(n), and UVar(B) = Γ, then we define B *is valid* ($\models$ B) as: $\forall v \in V_\Gamma^n [\bar{v}(B) = 1]$.

NB: $\bar{v}(B)$ is the value for B in the valuation v.

2.1.6 Def If $A_1, \ldots, A_m$, $B \in$ Wff of PPC(n), and UVar(A_1) $\cup \ldots \cup$ UVar(A_m) $\cup$ UVar(B) = Γ, then we define B *is entailed by* $A_1, \ldots, A_m$ ($A_1, \ldots, A_m \models B$) as: $\forall v \in V_\Gamma^n$ [if $\bar{v}(A_1) = \ldots = \bar{v}(A_m) = 1$, then $\bar{v}(B) = 1$].

2.1.7 Theorem If $A_1, \ldots, A_m$, $B \in$ Wff of PPC(n), and UVar(A_1) $\cup \ldots \cup$ UVar(A_m) $\cup$ UVar(B) = Γ, then $A_1 \wedge \ldots \wedge A_m \models B$ iff $A_1, \ldots, A_m \models B$.

Proof: $A_1 \wedge \ldots \wedge A_m \models B \Longleftrightarrow \forall v \in V_\Gamma^n [\text{if } \bar{v}(A_1 \wedge \ldots \wedge A_m) = 1, \text{ then } \bar{v}(B) = 1] \Longleftrightarrow \forall v \in V_\Gamma^n [\text{if } \bar{v}(A_1) = \ldots = \bar{v}(A_m) = 1, \text{ then } \bar{v}(B) = 1] \Longleftrightarrow A_1, \ldots, A_m \models B$, q.e.d.

2.1.8 Def A *presupposes* B ($A \gg B$) := $A \vee \sim A \models B$ (we write '$\sim$' for '$\curlyvee$').

This is a purely logical definition of 'presupposition', not the logico-semantic definition given in chapter 3 of this book. According to (28) in chapter 3, if $A \gg B$, then $A \models B$ and $\sim A \models B$, but not vice versa, although, if $\neg B \models \simeq A$, then, if $A \not\gg B$, then there must be an X such that $B \models X$ and $A \gg X$. The reason why the logico-semantic definition of presupposition cannot be applied here is simply that, in this appendix, we are concerned with a purely logical, and not a logico-semantic system.

We can now prove the following theorem with respect to this definition:

2.1.9 Theorem   (i) If $A \gg B$, then $\sim A \gg B$

          (ii) If $A \gg B$, then $(A \supset_L C) \gg B$

          (iii) If $A \gg B$ and $B \gg C$, then $A \gg C$.

Proof: (i) Let $A \gg B$ (i.e. $A \vee \sim A \models B$). Suppose $\sim A \not\gg B$, i.e. $\sim A \vee \sim\sim A \not\models B$. Then, for some $v \in V$: $\bar{v}(\sim A \vee \sim\sim A) = 1$ and $\bar{v}(B) \neq 1$. But from $\bar{v}(\sim A \vee \sim\sim A) = 1$ we conclude that either $\bar{v}(\sim A) = 1$ or $\bar{v}(\sim\sim A) = \bar{v}(A) = 1$. Hence $\bar{v}(A \vee \sim A) = 1$, and, since $A \vee \sim A \models B$, also $\bar{v}(B) = 1$. The supposition that $\sim A \not\gg B$ therefore leads to contradiction.

  (ii) Let $A \gg B$ (i.e. $A \vee \sim A \models B$). We have to show that, for any C, $((A \supset_L C) \vee \sim (A \supset_L C)) \models B$, or: $(\sim A \vee (A \wedge C)) \vee \sim (\sim A \vee (A \wedge C))) \models B$. Suppose the latter is false. Then, for some $v \in V$: $\bar{v}(\sim A \vee (A \wedge C)) = 1$ or $\bar{v}(\sim (\sim A \vee (A \wedge C))) = 1$, and $\bar{v}(B) \neq 1$. But if $\bar{v}(\sim A \vee (A \wedge C)) = 1$, then $\bar{v}(\sim A) = 1$ or $\bar{v}(A \wedge C) = 1$, hence $\bar{v}(\sim A \vee A) = 1$ and, since $A \vee \sim A \models B$, as given, $\bar{v}(B) = 1$. And if $\bar{v}(\sim (\sim A \vee (A \wedge C))) = 1$, then $\bar{v}(\sim A \vee (A \wedge C)) = 1$, hence $\bar{v}(\sim A) = 1$ or $\bar{v}(A \wedge C) = 1$, i.e. either $\bar{v}(A) = 1$ or $\bar{v}(A) = 2$. Therefore, $\bar{v}(A \vee \sim A) = 1$, and $\bar{v}(B) = 1$ (since $A \vee \sim A \models B$). The supposition, therefore, leads to contradiction.

  (iii) Let $A \gg B$ and $B \gg C$ (i.e. $A \vee \sim A \models B$ and $B \vee \sim B \models C$). We must show that $A \vee \sim A \models C$. Now suppose that $A \vee \sim A \not\models C$. Then for some $v \in V$: $\bar{v}(A \vee \sim A) = 1$ and $\bar{v}(C) \neq 1$. But if $\bar{v}(A \vee \sim A) = 1$ then $\bar{v}(B) = 1$. But then also $\bar{v}(B \vee \sim B) = 1$, hence $\bar{v}(C) = 1$. The supposition is thus seen to lead to contradiction.

2.2. *A set-theoretic basis for PPC(3)*

In order to give a set-theoretic basis for PPC(3), we first give set-theoretic definitions for truth, minimal falsity and radical falsity of prime formulae. Then we will give set-theoretic definitions for these three truth-values for complex formulae constructed with the help of the connectives (which are shown to be presuppositionally complete in section 6).

We will now define the functions g_1, g_2, and g_3, with g_i (i.e. $\{1, 2, 3\}$):
Wff $\to \mathscr{P}(V)$. (We will write 'v' and 'V', instead of 'v_Γ^3' and 'V_Γ^3', respectively.)

2.2.1 Def   If $P \in \Gamma$ and $\Gamma \subseteq$ UVar, we define:

    (i) $g_1(P) := \{v \in V \mid \bar{v}(P) \in \{1\}\}$
    (ii) $g_2(P) := \{v \in V \mid \bar{v}(P) \in \{1, 2\}\}$
    (iii) $g_3(P) := \{v \in V \mid \bar{v}(P) \in \{1, 2, 3\}\}$

Note that it follows from *Def* 2.2.1 that $g_1(P) \subseteq g_2(P) \subseteq g_3(P)$.

2.2.2 Def   (i) $\bar{g}_1 = g_1$
         (ii) $\bar{g}_2 = g_2 - g_1$
         (iii) $\bar{g}_3 = g_3 - g_2$

The preceding definitions can be illustrated by Venn diagrams as follows:

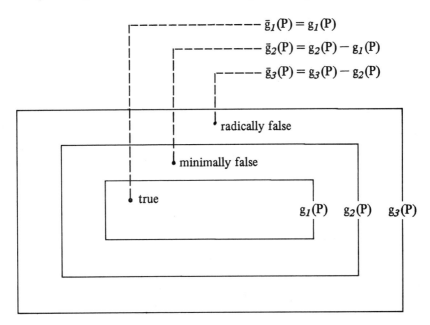

Note that it follows from *Def* 2.2.2 that $\bar{g}_1(A) \cap \bar{g}_2(A) = \emptyset$; $\bar{g}_1(A) \cap \bar{g}_3(A) = \emptyset$; $\bar{g}_2(A) \cap \bar{g}_3(A) = \emptyset$.

2.2.3 Def   If $P \in \Gamma$, we define:

    (i) P is *true* in v $:= v \in \bar{g}_1(P)$
    (ii) P is *minimally false* in v $:= v \in \bar{g}_2(P)$
    (iii) P is *radically false* in v $:= v \in \bar{g}_3(P)$.

2.2.4 Def If $\alpha \in \{g_1, g_2, g_3\}$ and A, B $\in$ Wff and UVar(A)$\cup$UVar(B)$\subseteq \Gamma$, we define:

(i) $\alpha(A \wedge B) := \alpha(A) \cap \alpha(B)$
(ii) $\alpha(A \vee B) := \alpha(A) \cup \alpha(B)$
(iii) $g_1(\sim A) := \bar{g}_2(A)$
$\quad g_2(\sim A) := g_2(A)$
$\quad g_3(\sim A) := V$
(iv) $g_1(\simeq A) := \bar{g}_3(A)$
$\quad g_2(\simeq A) := g_3(A)$
$\quad g_3(\simeq A) := V$

Note the analogy of (iii) and (iv).

2.2.5 Theorem If A $\in$ Wff and UVar(A) $\subseteq \Gamma$, then:

(i) A is *true* in v $\Longleftrightarrow$ v $\in \bar{g}_1(A)$
(ii) A is *minimally false* in v $\Longleftrightarrow$ v $\in \bar{g}_2(A)$
(iii) A is *radically false* in v $\Longleftrightarrow$ v $\in \bar{g}_3(A)$.

Proof: induction to the construction of A.

(i) *initial step:* If A = P then Theorem 2.2.5 follows trivially from *Def* 2.2.3.
(ii) *induction steps:* We must show that if Theorem 2.2.5 is correct for A_1 and A_2, it is correct for: (1) $A = A_1 \wedge A_2$
$\qquad\qquad\qquad\qquad\qquad\qquad$ (2) $A = A_1 \vee A_2$
$\qquad\qquad\qquad\qquad\qquad\qquad$ (3) $A = \sim A_1$
$\qquad\qquad\qquad\qquad\qquad\qquad$ (4) $A = \simeq A_1$.

(1) $A = A_1 \wedge A_2$

(a) To be shown: $v \in \bar{g}_1(A_1 \wedge A_2) \Longleftrightarrow A_1 \wedge A_2$ is *true* in v.
Now $v \in \bar{g}_1(A_1 \wedge A_2) \Longleftrightarrow v \in g_1(A_1 \wedge A_2) \Longleftrightarrow v \in g_1(A_1) \cap g_1(A_2) \Longleftrightarrow v \in g_1(A_1) \wedge v \in g_1(A_2)$.
And: $A_1 \wedge A_2$ is *true* in v $\Longleftrightarrow A_1$ is true in v and A_2 is true in v $\Longleftrightarrow v \in g_1(A_1) \wedge v \in g_1(A_2)$.

(b) To be shown: $v \in \bar{g}_2(A_1 \wedge A_2) \Longleftrightarrow A_1 \wedge A_2$ is *minimally false* in v.
Now $v \in \bar{g}_2(A_1 \wedge A_2) \Longleftrightarrow v \in g_2(A_1 \wedge A_2) - g_1(A_1 \wedge A_2) \Longleftrightarrow (v \in g_2(A_1) \wedge v \in g_2(A_2)) \wedge (v \notin g_1(A_1) \vee v \notin g_1(A_2))$.
And: $A_1 \wedge A_2$ is *minimally false* in v $\Longleftrightarrow A_1$ is true or minimally false in v ánd A_2 is true or minimally false in v, but A_1 and A_2 are not both true in v $\Longleftrightarrow (v \in g_2(A_1) \wedge v \in g_2(A_2)) \wedge (v \notin g_1(A_1) \vee v \notin g_1(A_2))$.

(c) To be shown: $v \in \bar{g}_3(A_1 \wedge A_2) \Longleftrightarrow A_1 \wedge A_2$ is *radically false* in v.

Now $v \in \bar{g}_3(A_1 \wedge A_2) \Longleftrightarrow v \in g_3(A_1 \wedge A_2) - g_2(A_1 \wedge A_2)$
$\Longleftrightarrow (v \in g_3(A_1) \wedge v \in g_3(A_2)) \wedge (v \notin g_2(A_1) \vee v \notin g_2(A_2))$
$\Longleftrightarrow v \notin g_2(A_1) \vee v \notin g_2(A_2)$ (since $g_3(B) = V$).

And: $A_1 \wedge A_2$ is *radically false* in $v \Longleftrightarrow A_1$ is radically false in v ór A_2 is radically false in $v \Longleftrightarrow v \in \bar{g}_3(A_1) \vee v \in \bar{g}_3(A_2) \Longleftrightarrow$
$(v \in g_3(A_1) \wedge v \notin g_2(A_1)) \vee (v \in g_3(A_2) \wedge v \notin g_2(A_2)) \Longleftrightarrow$
$v \notin g_2(A_1) \vee v \notin g_2(A_2)$ (since $g_3(B) = V$).

(2) $A = A_1 \vee A_2$

(a) To be shown: $v \in \bar{g}_1(A_1 \vee A_2) \Longleftrightarrow A_1 \vee A_2$ is *true* in v.
Now $v \in \bar{g}_1(A_1 \vee A_2) \Longleftrightarrow v \in g_1(A_1) \vee v \in g_1(A_2)$.
And: $A_1 \vee A_2$ is *true* in $v \Longleftrightarrow A_1$ is true in v ór A_2 is true in $v \Longleftrightarrow v \in g_1(A_1) \vee v \in g_1(A_2)$.

(b) To be shown: $v \in \bar{g}_2(A_1 \vee A_2) \Longleftrightarrow A_1 \vee A_2$ is *minimally false* in v.
Now $v \in \bar{g}_2(A_1 \vee A_2) \Longleftrightarrow v \in g_2(A_1 \vee A_2) - g_1(A_1 \vee A_2)$
$\Longleftrightarrow (v \in g_2(A_1) \vee v \in g_2(A_2)) \wedge v \notin g_1(A_1) \wedge v \notin g_1(A_2)$.
And: $A_1 \vee A_2$ is *minimally false* in $v \Longleftrightarrow A_1$ is minimally false in v ór A_2 is minimally false in v, and neither A_1 nor A_2 is true in $v \Longleftrightarrow (v \in g_2(A_1) \vee v \in g_2(A_2)) \wedge v \notin g_1(A_1) \wedge v \notin g_1(A_2)$.

(c) To be shown: $v \in \bar{g}_3(A_1 \vee A_2) \Longleftrightarrow A_1 \vee A_2$ is *radically false* in v.
Now $v \in \bar{g}_3(A_1 \vee A_2) \Longleftrightarrow v \in g_3(A_1 \vee A_2) - g_2(A_1 \vee A_2)$
$\Longleftrightarrow v \notin g_2(A_1 \vee A_2)$ (since $g_3(A_1 \vee A_2) = V$) $\Longleftrightarrow v \notin g_2(A_1)$
$\wedge v \notin g_2(A_2)$.
And: $A_1 \vee A_2$ is *radically false* in $v \Longleftrightarrow A_1$ is radically false in v ánd A_2 is radically false in $v \Longleftrightarrow v \in \bar{g}_3(A_1)$ and $v \in \bar{g}_3(A_2)$
$\Longleftrightarrow v \in g_3(A_1) \wedge v \notin g_2(A_1) \wedge v \in g_3(A_2) \wedge v \notin g_2(A_2) \Longleftrightarrow$
$v \notin g_2(A_1) \wedge v \notin g_2(A_2)$ (since $g_3(B) = v$).

(3) $A = \sim A_1$

(a) To be shown: $v \in \bar{g}_1(\sim A_1) \Longleftrightarrow \sim A_1$ is *true* in v.
Now $v \in \bar{g}_1(\sim A_1) \Longleftrightarrow v \in g_1(\sim A_1) \Longleftrightarrow v \in \bar{g}_2(A_1)$.
And: $\sim A_1$ is *true* in $v \Longleftrightarrow A_1$ is minimally false in $v \Longleftrightarrow v \in \bar{g}_2(A_1)$.

(b) To be shown: $v \in \bar{g}_2(\sim A_1) \Longleftrightarrow \sim A_1$ is *minimally false* in v.
Now $v \in \bar{g}_2(\sim A_1) \Longleftrightarrow v \in g_2(\sim A_1) - g_1(\sim A_1) \Longleftrightarrow v \in g_2(A_1) - \bar{g}_2(A_1) \Longleftrightarrow v \in g_1(A_1)$.
And: $\sim A_1$ is *minimally false* in $v \Longleftrightarrow A_1$ is true in $v \Longleftrightarrow v \in g_1(A_1)$.

(c) To be shown: $v \in \bar{g}_3(\sim A_1) \Longleftrightarrow \sim A_1$ is *radically false* in v.
Now $v \in \bar{g}_3(\sim A_1) \Longleftrightarrow v \in g_3(\sim A_1) - g_2(\sim A_1) \Longleftrightarrow v \in V \wedge$
$v \in V \wedge v \notin g_2(A_1) \Longleftrightarrow v \in \bar{g}_3(A_1)$.
And: $\sim A_1$ is *radically false* in v $\Longleftrightarrow A_1$ is radically false in v
$\Longleftrightarrow v \in \bar{g}_3(A_1)$.

(4) $A = \simeq A_1$

(a) To be shown: $v \in \bar{g}_1(\simeq A_1) \Longleftrightarrow \simeq A_1$ is *true* in v.
Now $v \in \bar{g}_1(\simeq A_1) \Longleftrightarrow v \in \bar{g}_3(A_1)$.
And: $\simeq A_1$ is *true* in v $\Longleftrightarrow A_1$ is radically false in v $\Longleftrightarrow v \in$
$\bar{g}_3(A_1)$.

(b) To be shown: $v \in \bar{g}_2(\simeq A_1) \Longleftrightarrow \simeq A_1$ is *minimally false* in v.
Now $v \in \bar{g}_2(\simeq A_1) \Longleftrightarrow v \in g_2(\simeq A_1) - g_1(\simeq A_1) \Longleftrightarrow v \in$
$g_3(A_1) - \bar{g}_3(A_1) \Longleftrightarrow v \in g_2(A_1)$.
And: $\simeq A_1$ is *minimally false* in v $\Longleftrightarrow A_1$ is true in v ór A_1 is
minimally false in v $\Longleftrightarrow v \in \bar{g}_1(A_1) \vee v \in \bar{g}_2(A_1) \Longleftrightarrow v \in$
$g_2(A_1)$.

(c) To be shown: $v \in \bar{g}_3(\simeq A_1) \Longleftrightarrow \simeq A_1$ is *radically false* in v.
Now $v \in \bar{g}_3(\simeq A_1) \Longleftrightarrow v \in g_3(\simeq A_1) - g_2(\simeq A_1) \Longleftrightarrow v \in V -$
$V \Longleftrightarrow v \in \emptyset$, which is a contradiction with the premiss.
And: $\simeq A_1$ is *radically false* is contradictory.

This proves Theorem 2.2.5.

2.2.6 Corollary If $B \in$ Wff and $\Gamma =$ UVar(E), then $\models B$ iff $\bar{g}_1(B) = V_\Gamma^3$.
Proof: $\models B \Longleftrightarrow \forall v \in V_\Gamma^3 [\bar{v}(B) = 1] \Longleftrightarrow \bar{g}_1(B) = V_\Gamma^3$, q.e.d.

2.3 A set-theoretic basis for PPC(n)

The set-theoretic basis for PPC(3) can be extended to a *uniform* set-theoretic basis for PPC(n). For $n = 2$ we thus get a set-theoretic basis for the classical propositional calculus, for $n = 3$ we get the basis provided in 2.2. The proof of Theorem 2.3.5 in this section is entirely analogous to that of 2.2.5 in the preceding section. For this reason it will not be written out in detail.
First we will define the functions g_s and $\bar{g}_s$ from UVar to $\mathscr{P}(V_\Gamma^n)$.

2.3.1 Def If $P \in \Gamma$ and $\Gamma \subseteq$ UVar, we define:

$$g_s(P) := \{v \in V_\Gamma^n \mid v_\Gamma^n(P) \in \{1, 2, \ldots, s\}\}, s \in \{1, 2, \ldots, n\}.$$

2.3.2 Def $\bar{g}_1 := g_1$
$\bar{g}_s := g_s - g_{s-1}$ for $s \in \{2, 3, \ldots, n\}$.

(We will often write 'V' and 'v' instead of 'V_Γ^n' and 'v_Γ^n', respectively.)

2.3.3 Def If $P \in \Gamma$, we define:

  (i) P is *true* in $v := v \in \bar{g}_1(P)$

  (ii) P is *minimally false* in $v := v \in \bar{g}_2(P)$

  (iii) P is $\underset{s}{\gamma}$ false in $v := v \in \bar{g}_{s+1}(P)$, $s \in \{2, 3, \ldots, n-1\}$

  NB: 'P is $\underset{\sim}{\gamma}$ false in v' means 'P is radically false'. For 'P is γ false in v', etc., we have no special terminology.

2.3.4 Def If $\alpha \in \{g_1, g_2, \ldots, g_n\}$ and $\beta \in \{g_3, g_4, \ldots, g_n\}$ and A, B $\in$ Wff of PPC(n), we define:

  (i) $\alpha(A \wedge B) := \alpha(A) \cap \alpha(B)$

  (ii) $\alpha(A \vee B) := \alpha(A) \cup \alpha(B)$

  (iii) $g_1(\gamma A) := \bar{g}_2(A)$

     $g_2(\gamma A) := g_2(A)$

     $\beta(\gamma A) := \beta(A)$

  (iv) $g_1(\underset{s}{\gamma} A) := \bar{g}_{s+1}(A)$, $s \in \{2, 3, \ldots, n-1\}$

     $g_2(\underset{s}{\gamma} A) := V$

     $\beta(\underset{s}{\gamma} A) := V$

2.3.5 Theorem If A $\in$ Wff of PPC(n) and UVar(A) $\subseteq \Gamma$, then:

  (i) A is *true* in $v \Longleftrightarrow v \in \bar{g}_1(A)$

  (ii) A is *minimally false* in $v \Longleftrightarrow v \in \bar{g}_2(A)$

  (iii) A is $\underset{s}{\gamma}$ *false* in $v \Longleftrightarrow v \in \bar{g}_{s+1}(A)$, $s \in \{2, 3, \ldots, n-1\}$.

Proof: by induction: if Theorem 2.3.5 is correct for A_1 and A_2, it must be correct for: (1) $A_1 \wedge A_2$

                        (2) $A_1 \vee A_2$

                        (3) γA_1

                        (4) $\underset{t}{\gamma} A_1$, $t \in \{2, 3, \ldots, n-1\}$

(1) $A_1 \wedge A_2$

  (a) As in 2.2.5.

  (b) As in 2.2.5.

  (c) To be shown: $v \in \bar{g}_{s+1}(A_1 \wedge A_2) \Longleftrightarrow A_1 \wedge A_2$ is $\underset{s}{\gamma}$ false in v, $s \in \{2, 3, \ldots, n-1\}$.

     Etc., as in 2.1.5, but read '$\underset{s}{\gamma}$ false' for 'radically false', 'g_{s+1}' for 'g_3' and 'g_s' for 'g_2'.

(2) $A_1 \vee A_2$

  The induction is entirely analogous to that of $A_1 \wedge A_2$.

(3) γA_1

  Analogous to 2.2.5.

(4) $\tilde{}_t A$, $t \in \{2, 3, \ldots, n-1\}$

(a) As is 2.2.5, but read '$\tilde{}_t$ false' for 'radically false', 'g_{t+1}' for 'g_3' and '$\tilde{}_t$' for '$\simeq$'.

(b) to be shown: $v \in \bar{g}_2(\tilde{}_t A_1) \Longleftrightarrow \tilde{}_t A_1$ is *minimally false* in v.
Now $v \in \bar{g}_2(\tilde{}_t A_1) \Longleftrightarrow v \in g_2(\tilde{}_t A_1) - g_1(\tilde{}_t A_1) \Longleftrightarrow v \in V - \bar{g}_{t+1}(A_1) \Longleftrightarrow v \notin \bar{g}_{t+1}(A_1)$.
And: $\tilde{}_t A_1$ is *minimally false* in $v \Longleftrightarrow A_1$ is not $\tilde{}_t$ false in v $\Longleftrightarrow v \notin \bar{g}_{t+1}(A_1)$.

(c) To be shown: for $s \in \{2, 3, \ldots, n-1\}$, $v \in \bar{g}_{s+1}(\tilde{}_t A_1) \Longleftrightarrow \tilde{}_t A_1$ is $\tilde{}_s$ false in v.
Now $v \in \bar{g}_{s+1}(\tilde{}_t A_1) \Longleftrightarrow v \in g_{s+1}(\tilde{}_t A_1) - g_s(\tilde{}_t A_1) \Longleftrightarrow v \in V - V \Longleftrightarrow v \in \emptyset$, i.e., contradiction.
And $\tilde{}_t A_1$ is $\tilde{}_s$ false in v is likewise contradictory.

3   A first approach towards a classification of n-valued logical systems

3.1   *Intermezzo*

This section is a first approach towards a classification of n-valued logical systems. A further elaboration is given in section 6. This first approach is given here in order to make the method and contents of the proof theory developed in the sections 4 and 5 more perspicuous.

In the proof theory, the logical predicates $\neg$ and $\rightarrow$ as defined in 1.1.2 will play an important role. They turn out to be useful also for the classification of n-valued logical systems.

The first class which we distinguish is the class of *regular logics*. Regular logics are closely connected with classical propositional calculus, as will become clear below.

We shall first make a few observations aimed at clarifying the approach and method of the following sections and chapters.

1 In section 1 a sketch was presented of a framework for the semantics of PPC(n). In PPC(3) a distinction is made between the minimal negation (symbol: $\sim$) and the radical negation (symbol: $\simeq$). We may wonder what happens to PPC(3) when we drop this distinction by defining the negation $\neg$ as: $\neg A := \sim A \vee \simeq A$. Will this bring us back to PPC(2), i.e. classical propositional calculus? Analogously, in PPC(n) we distinguish $n-1$ negations. What happens when we drop this distinction by defining the negation $\neg$ as $\neg A := \tilde{}_1 A \vee \ldots \vee {}_{n-1}A$? We may also ask the following question: suppose, in PPC(6), we define $\overset{1}{\neg} A := \tilde{}_1 A \vee \tilde{}_2 A \vee \tilde{}_3 A$, and $\overset{2}{\neg} A := \tilde{}_4 A \vee \tilde{}_5 A$. Will this take us back to PPC(3) and, if so, how

precisely? A partial answer to these and similar questions is given in the present chapter.

2 The following equivalences do not hold in PPC(3):

(1) $A \models B$ iff $\models A \supset B$
(2) $A \models B$ iff $\models A \sqsupseteq B$
(3) $A \models B$ iff $\models A \supset_L B$

Counter-examples: (1) although $P \models P \vee Q$, not $\models P \supset (P \vee Q)$
                    (2) although $P \wedge Q \models P$, not $\models P \wedge Q \sqsupseteq P$
                    (3) although $P \wedge Q \models P$, not $\models P \wedge Q \supset_L P$.

When we set up a proof theory for PPC(3), an implication that does provide this equivalence would be very useful. Theorem 3.2.8 shows that this equivalence holds not only for PPC(3) but also for PPC(n), when we define an implication $\rightarrow$.

3 The concepts of validity and logical consequence have been defined, in 2.1.5 and 2.1.6, without any use being made of the distinct forms of negation. For this reason, it is hardly surprising that the negation $\neg$ and the implication $\rightarrow$, which is closely connected with $\neg$, play an important role in the construction of a proof theory for PPC(3).

3.2 Regular logics

Before we define the concept of a regular logic, a few basic notions must be introduced. NB: L_n is always an arbitrary n-valued logic.

3.2.1 Def A *proof* of B in L_n := a finite list of formulae of L_n with B as its last member, such that each formula in the list *either* is one of the axioms of L_n, *or* can be obtained through application of the *rules* of L_n, applied to a pair of preceding formulas.

3.2.2 Def B is *provable* in L_n := there is a proof of B in L_n. (Notation: $\vdash_{L_n} B$)

3.2.3 Def A *derivation* of B from $A_1, \ldots, A_m$ in L_n := a finite list of formulas of L_n with B as its last member, such that each formula in the list *either* is one of the axioms of L_n, *or* is one of the formulae $A_1, \ldots, A_m$, *or* can be obtained through application of the *rules* of L_n, applied to a pair of preceding formulae.

3.2.4 Def B is *derivable* in L_n from $A_1, \ldots, A_m$:= there is a derivation of B from $A_1, \ldots, A_m$. (Notation: $A_1, \ldots, A_m \vdash_{L_n} B$)

3.2.5 Def If L_n is an n-valued logic, we define:

(1) The *conjunction* (symbol: $\wedge$) of L_n is *regular* iff $\bar{v}(A \wedge B) = \max(\bar{v}(A), \bar{v}(B))$.

(2) The *disjunction* (symbol: $\vee$) of L_n is *regular* iff $\bar{v}(A \vee B) = \min(\bar{v}(A), \bar{v}(B))$.

(3) The *negation* (symbol: $\neg$) of L_n is *regular* iff

$$\bar{v}(\neg A) = 2 \text{ iff } \bar{v}(A) = 1$$
$$= 1 \text{ iff } \bar{v}(A) \neq 1$$

3.2.6 Def An *n-valued logic* L_n is $(\wedge, \vee, \neg)$ *regular* iff the conjunction, the disjunction, and the negation are regular.

3.2.7 Def If $\neg$ is a regular negation, then $A \rightarrow B := \neg A \vee B$.

We can not formulate the following theorem:

3.2.8 Theorem If L_n is $(\wedge, \vee, \neg)$ regular, then:

(i) if $\models A$ and $\models A \rightarrow B$, then $\models B$

(ii) $A, A \rightarrow B \models B$

(iii) $A_1, \ldots, A_m \models B$ iff $A_1, \ldots, A_{m-1} \models A_m \rightarrow B$.

Proof: (i) Let $\models A$ and $\models A \rightarrow B$. Suppose $\not\models B$, i.e. on one row of the truth table for $A \rightarrow B$, B has a value other than 1 ($\bar{v}(B) \neq 1$). But $\models A \rightarrow B$, i.e. $\models \neg A \vee B$. Therefore, on that row $\bar{v}(\neg A \vee B) = \min(\bar{v}(\neg A), \bar{v}(B)) = 1$. Now $\bar{v}(B) \neq 1$, as supposed. Therefore $\bar{v}(\neg A) = 1$; hence $\bar{v}(A) \neq 1$. But, since $\models A$, $\bar{v}(A) = 1$. Therefore, if $\models A$ and $\models A \rightarrow B$, then $\models B$.

(ii) and (iii) follow directly from the definitions given.

Regular logics preserve the axioms of classical propositional calculus.

3.2.9 Theorem If L_n is $(\wedge, \vee, \neg)$ regular, then:

(i) $\models A \rightarrow (B \rightarrow A)$

(ii) $\models (A \rightarrow B) \rightarrow [(A \rightarrow (B \rightarrow C)) \rightarrow (A \rightarrow C)]$

(iii) $\models A \rightarrow (B \rightarrow A \wedge B)$

(iv) $\models A \wedge B \rightarrow A$
     $\models A \wedge B \rightarrow B$

(v) $\models A \rightarrow A \vee B$
    $\models B \rightarrow A \vee B$

(vi) $\models (A \rightarrow C) \rightarrow [(B \rightarrow C) \rightarrow (A \vee B \rightarrow C)]$

(vii) $\models (A \rightarrow B) \rightarrow [(A \rightarrow \neg B) \rightarrow \neg A]$

(viii) $\models \neg\neg A \rightarrow A$

Proof: (i) To be shown that $\models A \to (B \to A)$, or: $\models \neg A \lor (\neg B \lor A)$. Let $\bar{v}(\neg A \lor (\neg B \lor A)) \neq 1$, i.e. $\min(\bar{v}(\neg A), \bar{v}(\neg B), \bar{v}(A)) \neq 1$. Then $\bar{v}(\neg A) \neq 1$, hence $\bar{v}(A) = 1$ (by (3.2.5). Then, however, $\min(\bar{v}(\neg A), \bar{v}(\neg B), \bar{v}(A)) = 1$, so that there is contradiction. Hence, $\models A \to (B \to A)$.

The proofs of (ii)–(viii) are easily found along analogous lines.

3.2.10 Def Production method for the *regular logic* $L_n :=$

(a) *Axioms:* (i) $A \to (B \to A)$
          (ii) $(A \to B) \to [(A \to (B \to C)) \to (A \to C)]$
         (iii) $A \to (B \to A \land B)$
        (iv) $A \land B \to A$
             $A \land B \to B$
        (v) $A \to A \lor B$
           $B \to A \lor B$
       (vi) $(A \to C) \to [(B \to C) \to (A \lor B \to C)]$
      (vii) $(A \to B) \to [(A \to \neg B) \to \neg A]$
     (viii) $\neg\neg A \to A$

(b) *Rule:* $\dfrac{A \quad A \to B}{B}$

(c) The concepts 'proof', 'provable', 'derivation', and 'derivable' are defined as in 3.2.1-3.2.4.

It is important to note that the production method given here is both *consistent* and *complete* for classical propositional calculus (CPC). It is, furthermore, *consistent* for L_n, as shown by the following theorem.

3.2.11 Theorem (i) If $\vdash_{L_n} B$, then $\models_{L_n} B$.
             (ii) If $A_1, \ldots, A_m \vdash_{L_n} B$, then $A_1, \ldots, A_m \models_{L_n} B$.

Proof: (i) Let $\vdash_{L_n} B$. Then there is a schema as described in *Def* 3.2.1. We have:

    (a) the axioms are valid (Theorem 3.2.9);
    (b) the L_n-rule applied to two valid formulae yields a valid formula (Theorem 3.2.8 (i)).

Hence, B, which is the last formula in the schema, is valid:
$\models_{L_n} B$.

(ii) Let $A_1, \ldots, A_m \vdash_{L_n} B$. Then there is a schema as described in *Def* 3.2.3. We have:

(a) the axioms are valid, hence true for every interpretation;

(b) the L_n-rule applied to two true formulae yields a true formula (Theorem 3.1.8 (ii)).

Suppose $A_1, \ldots, A_m$ are all true in some interpretation. Then the last formula in the schema, B, is also true. Hence $A_1, \ldots, A_m \models_{L_n} B$.

3.2.12 Corollary (i) If $\models_{CPC} B$, then $\models_{L_n} B$.

(ii) If $A_1, \ldots, A_m \models_{CPC} B$, then $A_1, \ldots, A_m \models_{L_n} B$.

Proof: (i) Let $\models_{CPC} B$. Then, by the completeness theorem of CPC, also $\vdash_{CPC} B$. But proof for B in CPC is also a proof for B in L_n. Hence $\vdash_{L_n} B$. By the preceding theorem: $\models_{L_n} B$.

(ii) Let $A_1, \ldots, A_m \models_{CPC} B$. Then, by the completeness theorem of CPC, also $A_1, \ldots, A_m \vdash_{CPC} B$. But a derivation of B from $A_1, \ldots, A_m$ in CPC is also a derivation of B from $A_1, \ldots, A_m$ in L_n. Hence $A_1, \ldots, A_m \vdash_{L_n} B$. By the preceding theorem: $A_1, \ldots, A_m \models_{L_n} B$.

3.2.12 Theorem If $A_1, \ldots, A_m$, B are formulae of L_n containing no other logical predicates (connectives) than $\land$, $\lor$, $\lnot$, and $\to$, then:

(i) if $\models_{L_n} B$, then $\models_{CPC} B$;

(ii) if $A_1, A_2, \ldots, A_m \models_{L_n} B$, then $A_1, A_2, \ldots, A_m \models_{CPC} B$.

Proof: (i) Let $\models_{L_n} B$. Now consider those rows of the L_n-table for B where the propositional variables occurring in B have the value *2* or *1*. Notice that in this partial table the only values occurring are *2* and *1*. This subtable is precisely a CPC-table for B. Since on each row of the entire table for B there is the value *1*, this cannot but be the case for the CPC-subtable. Hence $\models_{CPC} B$.

(ii) The proof is entirely analogous to (i).

It follows from 3.2.12 and 3.2.13 that the following important corollary holds for all regular logics:

3.2.14 Corollary If $A_1, A_2, \ldots, A_m$, B are formulae of the regular logic L_n, containing no other than the connectives $\wedge$, $\vee$, $\neg$, and $\rightarrow$, then:

(i) $\models_{L_n} B$ iff $\models_{CPC} B$;

(ii) $A_1, A_2, \ldots, A_m \models_{L_n} B$ iff $A_1, A_2, \ldots, A_m \models_{CPC} B$.

In addition, the following theorem holds for all $(\wedge, \vee, \neg)$ regular logics L_n:

3.2.15 Theorem If L_n is $(\wedge, \vee, \neg)$ regular, then: $A_1, \ldots, A_{m-1}, A_m \vdash_{L_n} B$ iff $A_1, \ldots, A_{m-1} \vdash_{L_n} A_m \rightarrow B$.

Proof: Suppose we have $A_1, \ldots, A_m \vdash_{L_n} B$; i.e. we have a schema α according to which B is derived from $A_1, \ldots, A_m$. Since L_n is $(\wedge, \vee, \neg)$ regular, we have, by Theorem 3.1.9, the axioms of CPC. Therefore, α can be transformed in the usual way (see, e.g., Kleene 1967, I § 10) to a correct schema for $A_1, \ldots,$ $A_{m-1} \vdash_{L_n} A_m \rightarrow B$.

The preceding results for $(\wedge, \vee, \neg)$ regular logics L_n can be used for the study of logical systems PPC(n) and for the construction of a proof theory for PPC(3). This is so because, trivially, for each $n \in \{2, 3, \ldots\}$, PPC(n) is $(\wedge, \vee, \neg)$ regular (see the tables 1.1.2). Note that PPC(n) is *not* the unique regular n-valued logic. Now, since PPC(n) is $(\wedge, \vee, \neg)$ regular, all preceding results apply to PPC(n). This gives a first important start to a Hilbert-type proof theory for PPC(3). We make the *non-complete* production method of *Def* 3.2.10 *complete* for PPC(3). No other changes are made to the production method of *Def* 3.2.10. We thus have a few useful results for the construction of a proof theory for PPC(3).

4 Hilbert-type proof theory for PPC(3)

In this section we define a production method for PPC(3). This is done by adding a number of axioms to the production method of *Def* 3.2.10. In 4.1 we shall demonstrate that this production method is *consistent*. In 4.2 this production method will be shown to be *complete*.

4.1 Production method for PPC(3) and its consistency

4.1.1 Def Production method for PPC(3) :=

(a) *Axioms:* the axioms (i)–(viii) of *Def* 3.2.10;

(ix) $((A \wedge \sim B) \vee (\sim A \wedge \sim B) \vee (\sim A \wedge B)) \rightarrow \sim (A \wedge B)$

(x) $\simeq A \vee \simeq B \rightarrow \simeq (A \wedge B)$

(xi) $((\sim A \wedge \simeq B) \vee (\sim A \wedge \sim B) \vee (\simeq A \wedge \sim B)) \rightarrow \sim (A \vee B)$

(xii) $\simeq A \wedge \simeq B \rightarrow \simeq (A \vee B)$

(xiii) $A \rightarrow \sim \sim A$

(xiv) $\simeq A \rightarrow \simeq \sim A$

(xv) $(A \vee \sim A) \rightarrow \sim \simeq A$

(b) *Rule:* $\dfrac{A \quad A \rightarrow B}{B}$

(c) The concepts 'proof', 'provable', 'derivation', and 'derivable' are defined as in *Defs* 3.2.1-3.2.4.

NB   We do not claim that the axioms (i)-(xv) are mutually independent, nor that they are very elegant. The axioms (i)-(viii) of CPC have been repeated on purpose: this enables us to use the results of section 3 in this section. Notice, furthermore, the analogy between the Gentzen-rules of PPC(3) (*Def* 5.1.2) and the axioms defined here.

Before we set out to prove the consistency of the production method of 4.1.1, we must prove a few lemmas.

4.1.2 Lemma   If E is a formula of PPC(3) with the propositional variables $P_1, \ldots, P_n$, and E* is the formula resulting from E by the replacement of $P_1, \ldots, P_n$ by $A_1, \ldots, A_n$, respectively, then: if $\models_{\overline{PPC(3)}} E$, then $\models_{\overline{PPC(3)}} E*$.

Proof: (We shall often omit the specification "PPC(3)" with "$\models$" in this chapter, for practical reasons.)

Suppose $\models E$, i.e. E is true for all valuations v of $P_1, \ldots, P_n$. Let $Q_1, \ldots, Q_m$ be the propositional variables of E*. Now, for arbitrary valuation v' of $Q_1, \ldots, Q_m$, when in computing $\bar{v}'(E*)$ we compute first $\bar{v}'(A_1)$ to $\bar{v}'(A_n)$, then, depending on the result, some valuation v of $P_1, \ldots, P_n$ will generate that $\bar{v}'(E*) = 1$. This is so because the structure of E* with $A_1, \ldots, A_n$ as constituent formulae is identical with the structure of E with $P_1, \ldots, P_n$ as constituents.

4.1.3 Lemma   The axioms (i)-(xv) of *Def* 4.1.1 are valid in PPC(3).

Proof: Obvious in the light of Lemma 4.1.2 and the truth-tables of PPC(3) (see 1.2.1).

4.1.4 Lemma   *Deduction theorem for PPC(3):* $A_1, \ldots, A_m \vdash B$ iff $A_1, \ldots, A_{m-1} \vdash A_m \rightarrow B$.

Proof: Since only axioms have been added to the production method of *Def* 3.2.10, the proof follows from Theorem 3.2.15, from the observation that PPC(3) is ($\wedge$, $\vee$, $\neg$) regular, and from the definition of the production method for PPC(3).

4.1.5 Theorem Consistence theorem for PPC(3):

(i) If $\vdash$ B, then $\models$ B;

(ii) If $A_1, \ldots, A_m \vdash$ B, then $A_1, \ldots, A_m \models$ B.

Proof: (i) Let $\vdash$ B, then there is a schema of the form defined in 3.2.1. Now:

(a) the axioms are valid (Lemma 4.2.3);

(b) the L_n-rule, applied to two valid formulas, yields a valid formula (Theorem 3.2.8 (i)).

Hence, the last formula of the schema, i.e. B, is valid. Hence $\models$ B.

(ii) Follows from (i), through Theorem 2.1.7 and Lemma 4.1.4.

In the following section *completeness* will be demonstrated.

4.2 Completeness of the production method for PPC(3)

Before we set out to demonstrate the *completeness* of the production method for PPC(3), we must prove a few simple but useful lemmas.

4.2.1 Lemmas For PPC(3):

(i) $A_1, \ldots, A_m \vdash A_r$ ($r \in \{1, 2, \ldots, m\}$)

(ii) If $A_1, \ldots, A_m \vdash B_1$ and ----- $A_1, \ldots, A_m \vdash B_p$ and $B_1, \ldots, B_p \vdash C$, then $A_1, \ldots, A_m \vdash C$

(iii) $\vdash A \rightarrow A$

(iv) If $A_1 \vee \ldots \vee A_m \vdash B$, then $A_r \vdash B$ ($r \in \{1, 2, \ldots, m\}$)

(v) If $A \vdash C$, then $A, B \vdash C$

(vi) If $A, B \vdash C$, then $A \wedge B \vdash C$

(vii) If $A \wedge B \vdash C$, then $A, B \vdash C$

(viii) If $\Gamma, A \vdash C$ and $\Gamma, B \vdash C$, then $\Gamma, A \vee B \vdash C$.

Proof: The proofs of (i)–(viii) are analogous to their proofs in CPC.

Now follows the completeness-proof for PPC(3). We shall use the method developed by Kalmàr. First, four lemmas will be proved; then completeness can be harvested.

4.2.2 *Lemma I* For each row in each of the four truth-tables for $\wedge$, $\vee$, $\sim$ and $\simeq$ (see 1.1.1), a corresponding derivability relation holds:

$t(A), t(B) \vdash t(E)$, where:

$t(C) = C$ if C has a *1* on that row;
$\quad = \sim C$ if C has a *2* on that row;
$\quad = \simeq C$ if C has a *3* on that row.

$C \in \{A, B, A \wedge B, A \vee B, \sim A, \simeq A\}$
$E \in \{A \wedge B, A \vee B, \sim A, \simeq A\}$

Proof: We must show the following 24 derivability relations:

(1) $A, B \vdash A \wedge B$ (13) $\sim A, B \vdash A \vee B$

(2) $A, \sim B \vdash \sim (A \wedge B)$ (14) $\sim A, \sim B \vdash \sim (A \vee B)$

(3) $A, \simeq B \vdash \simeq (A \wedge B)$ (15) $\sim A, \simeq B \vdash \sim (A \vee B)$

(4) $\sim A, B \vdash \sim (A \wedge B)$ (16) $\simeq A, B \vdash A \vee B$

(5) $\sim A, \sim B \vdash \sim (A \wedge B)$ (17) $\simeq A, \sim B \vdash \sim (A \vee B)$

(6) $\sim A, \simeq B \vdash \simeq (A \wedge B)$ (18) $\simeq A, \simeq B \vdash \simeq (A \vee B)$

(7) $\simeq A, B \vdash \simeq (A \wedge B)$ (19) $A \vdash \sim \sim A$

(8) $\simeq A, \sim B \vdash \simeq (A \wedge B)$ (20) $\sim A \vdash \sim A$

(9) $\simeq A, \simeq B \vdash \simeq (A \wedge B)$ (21) $\simeq A \vdash \simeq \sim A$

(10) $A, B \vdash A \vee B$ (22) $A \vdash \sim \simeq A$

(11) $A, \sim B \vdash A \vee B$ (23) $\sim A \vdash \sim \simeq A$

(12) $A, \simeq B \vdash A \vee B$ (24) $\simeq A \vdash \simeq A$

By using the axioms of PPC(3) and the lemmas of 4.2.1, we can easily show these derivability relations:

(1) Ax. 3: $\vdash A \rightarrow (B \rightarrow A \wedge B)$. Apply the deduction theorem twice. This yields: $A, B \vdash A \wedge B$.

(2) Ax. 9: $\vdash ((A \wedge \sim B) \vee (\sim A \wedge \sim B) \vee (\sim A \wedge B)) \rightarrow \sim (A \wedge B)$. Apply the deduction theorem, and 4.2.1 (iv). This yields: $A \wedge \sim B \vdash \sim (A \wedge B)$. Apply 4.2.1 (vii). This yields: $A, \sim B \vdash \sim (A \wedge B)$.

(3) Ax. 10: $\vdash \simeq B \rightarrow \simeq (A \wedge B)$. Apply the deduction theorem and 4.2.1 (v). This yields: $A, \simeq B \vdash \simeq (A \wedge B)$.

(4) and (5) are proved analogously to (2).

(6), (7), (8), (9) are proved analogously to (3).

(10) Ax. 5: $\vdash A \rightarrow A \vee B$. Apply the deduction theorem and 4.2.1 (v). This yields: $A, B \vdash A \vee B$.

(11), (12), (13) are proved analogously to (10).

(14) Ax. 11: $\vdash ((\sim A \wedge \simeq B) \vee (\sim A \wedge \sim B) \vee (\simeq A \wedge \sim B)) \rightarrow \sim (A \vee B)$. Apply the deduction theorem and 4.2.1 (iv) and 4.2.1 (vii). This yields: $\sim A, \sim B \vdash \sim (A \vee B)$.

(15) is proved analogously to (14).

(16) is proved analogously to (10).

(17) is proved analogously to (14).

(18) Ax. 12: $\vdash (\simeq A \wedge \; \simeq B) \rightarrow \; \simeq (A \vee B)$. Apply the deduction theorem, and 4.2.1 (vii). This yields: $\simeq A, \; \simeq B \vdash \; \simeq (A \vee B)$.

(19) Ax. 13: $\vdash A \rightarrow \sim \sim A$; hence, according to the deduction theorem: $A \vdash \sim \sim A$.

(20) follows directly from 4.2.1 (iii).

(21) Ax. 14: $\vdash \; \simeq A \rightarrow \; \simeq \sim A$; hence, according to the deduction theorem: $\simeq A \vdash \; \simeq \sim A$.

(22) Ax. 15: $\vdash (A \vee \sim A) \rightarrow \sim \; \simeq A$; hence, according to the deduction theorem and 4.2.1 (iv): $A \vdash \sim \; \simeq A$.

(23) is proved analogously to (22).

(24) follows directly from 4.2.1 (iii).

4.2.3 Lemma II Consider the truth-table of a formula E which contains at most the propositional variables $P_1, \ldots, P_n$. For each row of the table for E the following corresponding derivability relation holds:

$t(P_1), \ldots, t(P_n) \vdash t(E)$, where:

$t(C) = C$ if C has a *1* on that row;
$= \sim C$ if C has a *2* on that row;
$= \; \simeq C$ if C has a *3* on that row.

$C \in \{P_1, \ldots, P_n, E\}$.

Proof: Induction towards the construction of E.

(i) *Basic step:* $E = P_1$; proved because $A \vdash A$ (4.2.1 (iii)).

(ii) *Induction steps:* (a) $E = A \wedge B$. Induction hypothesis:

$t(P_1), \ldots, t(P_n) \vdash t(A); t(P_1), \ldots, t(P_n) \vdash t(B)$.

Now, according to Lemma I: $t(A), t(B) \vdash t(A \wedge B)$. Hence, according to 4.2.1 (ii) also: $t(P_1), \ldots, t(P_n) \vdash t(A \wedge B)$.

(a) $E = A \vee B$
(c) $E = \sim A$ } are proved analogously.
(d) $E = \; \simeq A$

It follows from (i) and (ii) that for each row of the table for E, the derivability relation defined holds.

4.2.4 Lemma III E is a formula containing at most the propositional variables $P_1, \ldots, P_n$. If $\models E$, then also $P_1 \vee \sim P_1 \vee \simeq P_1 \vee \ldots \vee P_n \vee \sim P_n \vee \simeq P_n \vdash E$.

Proof: Consider the truth-table for E:

P_1	P_2	...	P_{n-1}	P_n	E
1	*1*		*1*	*1*	*1*
1	*1*		*1*	*2*	*1*
1	*1*		*1*	*3*	*1*
- - -	- - -	- - -	- - -	- - -	- - -
3	*3*		*3*	*3*	*1*

The first three rows give, according to Lemma II:

$$\left.\begin{array}{l} P_1,\ldots,P_{n-1}, P_n \vdash E \\ P_1,\ldots,P_{n-1}, \sim P_n \vdash E \\ P_1,\ldots,P_{n-1}, \simeq P_n \vdash E. \end{array}\right\} \Rightarrow P_1,\ldots,P_{n-1}, P_n \vee \sim P_n \vee \simeq P_n \vdash E$$

Carrying on in the same manner, we get, eventually:

$$P_1 \vee \sim P_1 \vee \simeq P_1 \vee \ldots \vee P_n \vee \sim P_n \vee \simeq P_n \vdash E. \text{ QED.}$$

4.2.5 Lemma IV $\vdash A \vee \sim A \vee \simeq A$.

Proof: In PPC(3), $\vdash A \vee \sim A \vee \simeq A$ is identical with $\vdash_{\text{PPC}(3)} A \vee \neg$
A. Now, $\vdash_{\text{CPC}} A \vee \neg A$. Hence, according to theorem 3.2.14,
also $\vdash_{\text{PPC}(3)} A \vee \neg A$.

4.2.6 Theorem: Completeness theorem for PPC(3).

If $\vDash E$, then $\vdash E$.

Proof: The proof follows directly from Lemma III, Lemma IV, and
4.2.1 (ii).

Notice that the ease of this proof is crucially due to PPC(3) being *regular*.
The results of 4.2.6 and of 4.1.5 (completeness and consistency) can be
combined:

4.2.7 Corollary For PPC(3): (i) $\vDash B$ iff $\vdash B$;
(ii) $A_1,\ldots,A_m \vDash B$ iff $A_1,\ldots,A_m \vdash B$.

Proof: (i) from left to right: 4.2.6;
from right to left: 4.1.5 (i);
(ii) from left to right: suppose $A_1,\ldots,A_m \vDash B$; then $\vDash A_1 \rightarrow$
$\rightarrow (A_2 \rightarrow (\ldots \rightarrow (A_m \rightarrow B)\ldots))$; $\vDash A_1 \rightarrow (\ldots \rightarrow (A_m \rightarrow B)\ldots)$.
Hence (4.2.7 (i)); $\vdash A_1 \rightarrow (\ldots \rightarrow (A_m \rightarrow B)\ldots)$. Hence
4.1.15) $A_1,\ldots,A_m \vdash B$; from right to left: 4.1.5 (ii).

5 Gentzen-type proof theory for PPC(3)

In this section, a Gentzen-type proof theory is presented for PPC(3). In 5.1 *consistency* is proved by making use of the set-theoretic basis of PPC(3). (This method seems not to have been practised in the existing literature.) In 5.2 we first define a *systematic* procedure for the construction of a Gentzen-proof for any given formula B of PPC(3). This procedure either gives a Gentzen-proof of B or, if the attempt fails, a countermodel for B is given by the failed attempt. Hence we shall prove *completeness*, by using the constructive proof method developed by Kripke (1963).

The simplified notation for this type of rule, as used, e.g., in Kleene 1967/VI, §54, cannot be used here, due to the three-valuedness of PPC(3).

5.1 Gentzen-type proof theory (system of natural deduction) with consistency for PPC(3)

5.1.1 Def If $A \in$ Wff (of PPC(3)), then TA, FA and RFA are *signed formulae*. A finite sequence of signed formulae we call a *sequence* (notation: S).

Read: TA: 'A is true'; FA: 'A is minimally false'; RFA: 'A is radically false'.

5.1.2 Def Gentzen-rules for PPC(3):

$$\sim \quad \frac{S, T \sim A}{S, FA} \quad \frac{S, F \sim A}{S, TA} \quad \frac{S, RF \sim A}{S, RFA}$$

$$\simeq \quad \frac{S, T \simeq A}{S, RFA} \quad \frac{S, F \simeq A}{S, TA/S, FA} \quad \frac{S, RF \simeq A}{TA, FA}$$

$$\wedge \quad \frac{S, TA \wedge B}{S, TA, TB} \quad \frac{S, FA \wedge B}{S, FA, TB/S, FA, FB/S, TA, FB} \quad \frac{S, RFA \wedge B}{S, RFA/S, RFB}$$

$$\vee \quad \frac{S, TA \vee B}{S, TA/S, TB} \quad \frac{S, FA \vee B}{S, FA, RFB/S, FA, FB/S, RFA, FB} \quad \frac{S, RFA \vee B}{S, RFA, RFB}$$

In these rules, S, $TA_1, .., TA_m$, $FB_1, \ldots, FB_n$, $RFC_1, \ldots, RFC_p$ is an abbreviation of $S \cup \{TA_1, \ldots, TA_m, FB_1, \ldots, FB_n, RFC_1, \ldots, RFC_p\}$.

5.1.3 Def A *G-proof of A* in PPC(3) is a finite schema of sequences, starting with FA/RFA, such that each sequence in the schema (except the first) is obtained by means of one of the rules of PPC(3) applied to a preceding sequence, and such that, for a certain formula B, each of the final sequences contains either TB and FB, or TB and RFB, or FB and RFB.

5.1.4 Def A is *G-provable* in PPC(3) iff there is a proof of A in PPC(3). Notation: $\vdash_{\text{PPC(3)}}$ A. Instead of this, we shall often write: $\vdash$ A (PPC(3)), or $\vdash$ A.

5.1.5 Def B is G-derivable from $A_1, \ldots, A_m$ in PPC(3) iff there is a G-proof of $A_1 \wedge A_2 \wedge \ldots \wedge A_m \to B$ in PPC(3). Notation: $A_1, \ldots, A_m$ $\vdash_{\text{PPC(3)}}$ B.

Observation: In *Def* 5.1.5 we reduce the notion 'derivable', via the implication denoted by '$\to$', to the notion 'provable'. Cp. the deduction theorem for PPC(3) (= 3.2.15).

5.1.6 Theorem *Consistency* for the G-rules.

If $\vdash$ A, then $\models$ A.

Observation: Our plan, in proving this theorem, is as follows: read a sequence in the G-proof of A (S = {$TA_1, \ldots, TA_m$, $FB_1, \ldots, FB_n, RFC_1, \ldots, RFC_p$}) as: {$\bar{g}_1(A_1) \cap \ldots \cap \bar{g}_1(A_m)$ $\cap \bar{g}_2(B_1) \cap \ldots \cap \bar{g}_2(B_n) \cap \bar{g}_3(C_1) \cap \ldots \cap \bar{g}_3(C_p)$}. We then continue:

Basic steps: The lowest sequence in a derivation (all lowest sequences are closed) yields, in the reading specified, the null set.

Induction steps: For all rules of PPC(3), when read from bottom to top, they lead from null sets to null sets – in the reading specified. For the top sequences, especially FA/RFA, the result is that $\bar{g}_2(A) = \emptyset$ and $\bar{g}_3(A) = \emptyset$. Hence $\bar{g}_1(A) =$ V, because $\bar{g}_1(A) \cup \bar{g}_2(A) \cup \bar{g}_3(A) = $ V. Hence, according to Corollary 2.2.6, $\models$ A.

In proving 5.1.6 we shall use the following lemma:

5.1.7 Lemma If V, X, Y, Z are sets, then, if $X \cap Y = V$ and $X \cap Z = V$ then $X \cap (Y \cup Z) = V$.

Proof of the consistence theorem 5.1.6:

Suppose $\vdash$ A, then:

(i) *Basic step:* For each of the final sequences in the proof of A, for some formula B, (TB $\in$ S and FB $\in$ S) or (TB $\in$ S and RFB $\in$ S) or (FB $\in$ S and RFB $\in$ S). We must thus show: X $\cap$

$\bar{g}_1(B) \cap \bar{g}_2(B) = \emptyset$ and $X \cap \bar{g}_1(B) \cap \bar{g}_3(B) = \emptyset$ and $X \cap \bar{g}_2(B) \cap \bar{g}_3(B) = \emptyset$, where X is the set constructed from the remaining signed formulae of the final sequence in question.

That this is so follows from the fact that definitions 2.2.1 and 2.2.2 make it necessary that $\bar{g}_1(B)$, $\bar{g}_2(B)$ and $\bar{g}_3(B)$ are mutually disjunct. We now need to take the $4 \times 3 = 12$ induction steps.

(ii) *Induction steps:*

(1) S, T $\sim$ A
 S, FA; hence: suppose $X \cap \bar{g}_2(A) = \emptyset$, where X is constructed from S. We need to show that $X \cap \bar{g}_1(\sim A) = \emptyset$.
 Now, $\bar{g}_1(\sim A) = g_1(\sim A) = \bar{g}_2(A)$. Hence also $X \cap \bar{g}_1(\sim A) = \emptyset$.

(2) S, F $\sim$ A (3) S, RF $\sim$ A (4) S, T $\simeq$ A are easily shown.
 S, TA   S, RFA   S, RFA

(5) S, F $\simeq$ A
 S, TA/S, FA; hence: suppose $X \cap \bar{g}_1(A) = \emptyset$ (a), ánd $X \cap \bar{g}_2(A) = \emptyset$ (b). We need to show that $X \cap \bar{g}_2(\simeq A) = \emptyset$ (c).
 Now, $\bar{g}_2(\simeq A) = g_2(\simeq A) - g_1(\simeq A) = V - \bar{g}_3(A) = \bar{g}_1(A) \cup \bar{g}_2(A)$. But it follows from (a) and (b) (using the Lemma): $X \cap (\bar{g}_1(A) \cup \bar{g}_2(A)) = X \cap \bar{g}_2(\simeq A) = \emptyset$.

(6) S, RF $\simeq$ A   (7) S, TA $\wedge$ B   are easily shown.
 S, TA, FA   S, TA, TB

(8) S, FA $\wedge$ B
 S, FA, TB/S, FA, FB/S, TA, FB; hence: suppose
 (a) $X \cap \bar{g}_2(A) \cap \bar{g}_1(B) = \emptyset$
 (b) $X \cap \bar{g}_2(A) \cap \bar{g}_2(B) = \emptyset$
 (c) $X \cap \bar{g}_1(A) \cap \bar{g}_2(B) = \emptyset$.

To be shown: $X \cap \bar{g}_2(A \wedge B) = \emptyset$.
Now, it follows from (a) and (b) (using the Lemma) that $X \cap \bar{g}_2(A) \cap (\bar{g}_1(B) \cup \bar{g}_2(B)) = \emptyset \Longleftrightarrow X \cap \bar{g}_2(A) \cap g_2(B) = \emptyset$ (I).
Using the Lemma, we see that it follows from (b) and (c) that $X \cap \bar{g}_2(B) \cap (\bar{g}_1(A) \cup \bar{g}_2(A)) = \emptyset \Longleftrightarrow X \cap \bar{g}_2(B) \cap g_2(A) = \emptyset$ (II).
Now suppose $x \in X \cap \bar{g}_2(A \wedge B) \Longleftrightarrow x \in X \cap g_2(A \wedge B) - g_1(A \wedge B) \Longleftrightarrow x \in X \wedge x \in g_2(A) \wedge x \in g_2(B) \wedge (x \notin g_1(A) \vee x \notin g_1(B)) \Longleftrightarrow (x \in X \wedge x \in g_2(A) \wedge x \in g_2(B) \wedge x \notin g_1(A)) \vee (x \in X \wedge x \in g_2(A) \wedge x \in g_2(B) \wedge x \notin$

$g_1(B)) \Longleftrightarrow (x \in X \wedge x \in g_2(B) \wedge x \in \bar{g}_2(A)) \vee (x \in X \wedge x \in g_2(A) \wedge x \in \bar{g}_2(B)) \Longleftrightarrow x \in X \cap \bar{g}_2(A) \cap g_2(B) \vee x \in X \cap \bar{g}_2(B) \cap g_2(A).$

This, however, is in contradiction with (I) and (II). Hence, $X \cap \bar{g}_2(A \wedge B) = \emptyset.$

(9) S, RFA $\wedge$ B   (10) S, TA $\vee$ B
   S, RFA/S, RFB   S, TA/S, TB
(11) S, FA $\vee$ B   (12) S, RFA $\vee$ B
   S, FA, RFB/S, FA, FB/S, RFA, FB   S, RFA, RFB

are easily shown, with the help of the Lemma.

From (i) and (ii) it follows that: if $\vdash$ A, then $\models$ A. QED.

5.1.8 Corollary If $A_1, \ldots, A_m \vdash B$, then $A_1, \ldots, A_m \models B$.

    Proof: Suppose $A_1, \ldots, A_m \vdash B$. That is, by definition, $\vdash A_1, \ldots, A_m \to B$.
    Hence, by theorem 5.1.6, also $\models A_1 \wedge \ldots \wedge A_m \to B$. Hence, by 3.1.8 (iii) and 2.0.7, also $A_1, \ldots, A_m \models B$.

5.2 Completeness of Gentzen-rules for PPC(3)

5.2.1 Def Systematic procedure for finding a G-proof in PPC(3) for A, given the formula A in PPC(3).

    (i) Start a schema of sequences with FA, and another schema with RFA.

    (ii) Now apply the appropriate rules of PPC(3) in some *fixed* order (where the order chosen is irrelevant). If, for example, we apply the rule F $\simeq$ to S, F $\simeq$ B, we make two copies of what there is, one being extended with S, TB, the other with S, FB. Likewise when the rules F $\wedge$, RF $\wedge$, T $\vee$ and F $\vee$ are applied.

5.2.2 Def The schemata of sequences obtained through the systematic procedure of *Def* 5.2.1 we call *search trees* for A.
    A search tree for A is *closed* if the search tree for a certain formula B contains TB and FB or TB and RFB or FB and RFB.
    A search tree for A is *open* if it is not closed.

5.2.3 Def If Δ is an *open search tree* for A, we define $v_\Delta : UVar(A) \to \{1, 2, 3\}$ as:

    (i) $v_\Delta(P) = 1$ iff TP occurs in Δ;
    (ii) $v_\Delta(P) = 2$ iff FP occurs in Δ;
    (iii) $v_\Delta(P) = 3$ iff RFP occurs in Δ.

Observation: This is a correct definition, since Δ is an *open search tree* for A.

5.2.4 Lemma If Δ is an open search tree for A, then for every formula B:

    (i) if TB occurs in Δ, then $\bar{v}_\Delta(B) = 1$;
    (ii) if FB occurs in Δ, then $\bar{v}_\Delta(B) = 2$;
    (iii) if RFB occurs in Δ, then $\bar{v}_\Delta(B) = 3$.

Proof: By induction to the construction of B.

Basic steps: (1) If B = P and TP occurs in Δ, then by definition $\bar{v}_\Delta(P) = 1$. (2) If B = P and FP occurs in Δ, then $\bar{v}_\Delta(P) = 2$. (3) If B = P and RFP occurs in Δ, then $\bar{v}_\Delta(P) = 3$.

Induction steps: Suppose (i), (ii) and (iii) are correct for C and D (induction hypothesis). Then it is to be proved that for (a) ∼ C, (b) ≃C, (c) C ∧ D, (d) C ∨ D, (i), (ii), (iii) are correct. Now:

  (a-i) B = ∼ C and T ∼ C occurs in Δ; then FC also occurs in Δ. Hence, by the induction hypothesis, $\bar{v}_\Delta(C) = 2$. Hence $\bar{v}_\Delta(\sim C) = 1$.

  (a-ii) B = ∼ C and F ∼ C occurs in Δ; then TC also occurs in Δ. Hence, by the induction hypothesis, $\bar{v}_\Delta(C) = 1$. Hence $\bar{v}_\Delta(\sim C) = 2$.

  (a-iii) B = ∼ C and RF ∼ C occurs in Δ; then RFC also occurs in Δ. Hence, by the induction hypothesis, $\bar{v}_\Delta(C) = 3$. Hence $\bar{v}_\Delta(\sim C) = 3$.

Analogous proofs are easily given for the cases of (b), (c) and (d).

Hence, from the basic steps and the induction steps we conclude to Lemma 5.2.4.

5.2.5 Lemma If all search trees of B are closed, then ⊢ B.

Proof: This lemma follows immediately from the definition of ⊢ B, the definition of a search tree for B, and the fact that the number of search trees for B is finite.

5.2.6 Theorem (Completeness) If ⊨ B, then ⊢ B.

Proof: Suppose ⊨ B. Now apply to B the systematic procedure of *Def* 5.2.1. If there is an open search tree Δ of B, then by Lemma 5.2.4, $\bar{v}_\Delta(B) = 2$ or $\bar{v}_\Delta(B) = 3$ (depending on whether the open tree starts with FB or with RFB). But both $\bar{v}_\Delta(B) = 2$ and $\bar{v}_\Delta(B) = 3$ are in contradiction with ⊨ B. Hence, no open search tree of B will be found. Hence, by Lemma 5.2.5, ⊢ B.

5.2.7 Corollary If $A_1, \ldots, A_m \models B$, then $A_1, \ldots, A_m \vdash B$.

    Proof: Suppose $A_1, \ldots, A_m \models B$. Then also, by the theorems 2.1.7 and 3.2.15, $\models A_1 \wedge \ldots \wedge A_m \to B$. Hence, by theorem 5.2.6, $\vdash A_1 \wedge \ldots \wedge A_m \to B$. By definition, this is equivalent to $A_1, \ldots, A_m \vdash B$.

6 A further elaboration of the classification of n-valued logical systems

In section 3 a first start was made with the classification of n-valued logical systems. Here we shall elaborate this classification somewhat further. In section 6.1 the concept of *presuppositional logic* will be defined, and some properties of presuppositional logics will be investigated. In section 6.2 we shall show that the three-valued presuppositional proposition calculus (PPC(3)) is *presuppositionally complete*. Finally in section 6.3, we shall define the concept of *efficient logic*. PPC(3) then appears to be the *uniquely determined three-valued efficient logic*.

6.1 Presuppositional logics

In this section we attempt to define the characteristic properties of pre-suppositional logics (propositional calculi). The following intuitive ideas underly the definitions 6.1.1 and 6.1.2.

(i)   If a complex proposition E is radically false, i.e. $\bar{v}_1(E) = t \geqslant 3$, then at least one of the component parts of E must be radically false to the same degree.

(ii)   If a complex proposition E is radically false $(\bar{v}_1(E) = t \geqslant 3)$, then another valuation v_2 may change this only if v_2 differs from v_1 in its $\geqslant t$ values.

These intuitive and imprecise ideas we now try to cast into a precise form, in the definitions 6.1.1 and 6.1.2. The theorems 6.1.3 and 6.1.4 will bring further clarity.

    First we define the concept of "t-successor", in order to make observation (ii) more precise.

6.1.1 Def   Let L_n be an n-valued logic; $v_1, v_2 \in V_\Gamma^n$ and $t \in \{3, 4, \ldots, n\}$. Then we define: v_2 is a *t-successor* of v_1 (notation: $v_1 >^t > v_2$) :=

$$\forall P \in \Gamma [v_1(P) \geqslant t \Rightarrow v_1(P) = v_2(P) \text{ ánd } v_1(P) < t \Rightarrow v_2(P) \leqslant t].$$

Example L_5; $\Gamma = \{P_1, P_2, P_3, P_4, P_5, P_6\}$; $t = 4 \in \{3, 4, 5\}$.

Table 6

	P_1	P_2	P_3	P_4	P_5	P_6
v_1	*1*	*4*	*3*	*4*	*5*	*2*

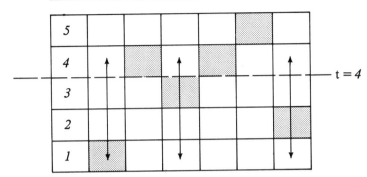

A valuation v_2 with $v_1 > ^t > v_2$ is a valuation such that $v_2(P_2) = 4$, $v_2(P_4) = 4$, $v_2(P_5) = 5$, and $v_2(P_1) \in \{1, 2, 3, 4\}$, $v_2(P_3) \in \{1, 2, 3, 4\}$, $v_2(P_6) \in \{1, 2, 3, 4\}$.

6.1.2 Def   Let L_n be an n-valued logic; $A, B \in$ Wff of L_n; $v_1, v_2 \in V^n_{\text{UVar}(A)} \cup \text{UVar}(B)$. We then define:

(i) A *unary connective* (Δ) of L_n *is presuppositional* $:=$

  (a) $\forall v_1 \forall t \in \mathbb{N}[\bar{v}_1(\Delta A) = t \geqslant 3 \Rightarrow \bar{v}_1(A) = t]$
  (b) $\forall v_1, v_2 \forall t \in \mathbb{N}[\bar{v}_1(\Delta A) = t \geqslant 3 \text{ and } v_1 > ^t > v_2 \Rightarrow \bar{v}_2(\Delta A) = t]$

(ii) A *binary connective* (Θ) of L_n *is presuppositional* $:=$

  (a) $\forall v_1 \forall t \in \mathbb{N}[\bar{v}_1(A \Theta B) = t \geqslant 3 \Rightarrow \bar{v}_1(A) = t \text{ or } \bar{v}_1(B) = t]$
  (b) $\forall v_1, v_2 \forall t \in \mathbb{N}[\bar{v}_1(A \Theta B) = t \geqslant 3 \text{ and } v_1 > ^t > v_2 \Rightarrow \bar{v}_2(A \Theta B) = t]$

(iii) L_n *is presuppositional* if all connectives of L_n are presuppositional.

6.1.3 Theorem   The logic L_n is presuppositional iff

  (i) $\forall v_1 \forall t \in \mathbb{N}[\bar{v}_1(A) = t \geqslant 3 \Rightarrow \exists P \in \text{UVar}(A)[v_1(P) = t]]$
  (ii) $\forall v_1, v_2 \forall t \in \mathbb{N}[\bar{v}_1(A) = t \geqslant 3 \text{ and } v_1 > ^t > v_2 \Rightarrow \bar{v}_2(A) = t]$;
  $v_1, v_2 \in V^n_{\text{UVar}(A)}$, $A \in$ Wff of L_n.

Proof: Suppose (i) and (ii) of the theorem hold. From (i) it follows that 6.1.2 (i-a) and 6.1.2 (ii-a). From (ii) it follows that 6.1.2 (i-b) and 6.1.2 (ii-b).

Suppose L_n is presuppositional. Now (i) and (ii) of Theorem 6.1.3 are to be proved.

(i) Induction towards the construction of A.

    (a) *Basic step:* Suppose $A = P_1$ and $v_1(P_1) = t \geqslant 3$. Then

$$\exists P \in UVar(A)[v_1(P) = t].$$

    (b) *Induction step:* Suppose the statement is correct for A_1 and A_2 (induction hypothesis). It then must be shown that the statement is correct for (i) $\Delta A_1 = A$, and (ii) $A_1 \ominus A_2 = A$. Now:

        (i) Let $\bar{v}_1(\Delta A) = t \geqslant 3$. Then, by 6.1.2 (i-a), $\bar{v}_1(A_1) = t$. Hence, by the induction hypothesis, $\exists P \in UVar(A_1)$ $[v_1(P) = t]$. But then also $\exists P \in UVar(\Delta A_1)[v_1(P) = t]$.

        (ii) Let $\bar{v}_1(A_1 \ominus A_2) = t \geqslant 3$. Then, by 6.1.2 (ii-a), $\bar{v}_1(A_1) = t$ or $\bar{v}_1(A_2) = t$. Hence, by the induction hypothesis, $\exists P \in UVar(A_1)[v_1(P) = t]$ or $\exists P \in UVar(A_2)[v_1(P) = t]$. But then also $\exists P \in UVar(A_1 \ominus A_2)[v_1(P) = t]$.

(ii) Induction towards the construction of A.

    (a) *Basic step:* Suppose $A = P_1$ and $v_1(P_1) = t \geqslant 3$. Then it follows from the definition of $v_1 >^t> v_2$ that $v_2(P_1) = t$.

    (b) *Induction step:* Suppose the statement is correct for A_1 and A_2 (induction hypothesis). It then needs to be shown that the statement is correct for (i) $\Delta A_1 = A$, and (ii) $A_1 \ominus A_2 = A$.

        (i) Let $\bar{v}_1(\Delta A_1) = t \geqslant 3$. Then, by 6.1.2 (i-b), also $\bar{v}_2(\Delta A) = t \geqslant 3$ (provided $v_1 >^t> v_2$).

        (ii) Let $\bar{v}_1(A_1 \ominus A_2) = t \geqslant 3$. Then by 6.1.2 (ii-b), also $\bar{v}_2(A_1 \ominus A_2) = t \geqslant 3$ (provided $v_1 >^t> v_2$).

6.1.4 Theorem   PPC(n) is presuppositional (for each $n \in \{2, 3, \ldots\}$).

    Proof: Follows directly from the tables 1.1.2 of PPC(n).

The definition 6.1.2 is an attempt at defining the characteristic properties of presuppositional logics. It is not, however, a matter of course that *Def* 6.1.2 is both complete and correct. Theorem 6.1.3 boosts confidence in *Def* 6.1.2. Let us now see how *Def* 6.1.2 works in what is to follow.

6.2 *Presuppositional completeness of the set of connectives* $\{\wedge, \vee, \sim, \approx\}$ *for PPC(3)*

It has been noted above that the set of connectives $\{\wedge, \vee, \sim, \approx\}$ is not complete for PPC(3). Theorem 6.1.4 states that PPC(3) is a presuppositional logic. But then each formula A, constructed from the atomic propositions P_1 and P_2 and the connectives $\wedge$, $\vee$, $\sim$, $\approx$, has a topmost row in its truthtable not containing the value *3*. This is generally so for presuppositional logics.

The set of connectives $\{\wedge, \vee, \sim, \approx\}$ proves to be presuppositionally complete. That is, each presuppositional connective (see *Def* 6.1.2) can be rewritten as a combination of the connectives given. This fact is further illustrated in the present section.

First we give the classical definition for completeness of an n-valued logic L_n.

6.2.1 Def Let L_n be an n-valued logic.

$X := \{f \mid f : \{1, 2, \ldots, n\}^m \to \{1, 2, \ldots, n\},\ m \in \{1, 2, \ldots\}\}$ is the *set of all possible connectives* (unary, binary, etc.) of L_n.

6.2.2 Def The set of connectives Y ($Y \subseteq X$) is a *complete* set of connectives for L_n iff each function $f \in X$ can be rewritten as a composition of functions from Y.

The question of the completeness of a set Y for L_n can be solved by giving the necessary and sufficient conditions. See, e.g., Martin (1954), Muzio (1970). These results, however, cannot be used for the question of presuppositional completeness of presuppositional connectives.

6.2.3 Def Let X be the set of all presuppositional connectives of the n-valued logic L_n. *The set Y* ($Y \subseteq X$) *is presuppositionally complete* for L_n iff each presuppositional connectives in X can be rewritten as a composition of connectives from Y.

We now wish to answer the following question: Is the set $\{\wedge, \vee, \sim, \approx\}$ of presuppositional connectives of PPC(3) presuppositionally complete? We shall give the answer step by step.

6.2.4 Lemma I All $2^2 \cdot 3 = 12$ unary presuppositional connectives of PPC(3) are expressible in $\wedge$, $\vee$, $\sim$, $\approx$.

Appendix

Proof:

Table 7

A	1^0	2^0	3^0	4^0	5^0	6^0	7^0	8^0	9^0	10^0	11^0	12^0
1	*1*	*1*	*1*	*1*	*1*	*1*	*2*	*2*	*2*	*2*	*2*	*2*
2	*1*	*1*	*1*	*2*	*2*	*2*	*1*	*1*	*1*	*2*	*2*	*2*
3	*1*	*2*	*3*	*1*	*2*	*3*	*1*	*2*	*3*	*1*	*2*	*3*

Now: 1^0 A $\lor \sim$ A $\lor \simeq$ A $\qquad 5^0 \sim (\sim$ A $\lor \simeq$ A$)$ $\qquad 9^0 \sim$ A

$\quad 2^0 \sim \simeq$ A $\qquad\qquad\qquad 6^0$ A $\qquad\qquad\qquad 10^0 \simeq$ A

$\quad 3^0$ A $\lor \sim$ A $\qquad\qquad 7^0 \sim$ A $\lor \simeq$ A $\qquad 11^0 \simeq \simeq$ A

$\quad 4^0$ A $\lor \simeq$ A $\qquad\qquad 8^0 \sim ($ A $\lor \simeq$ A$)$ $\qquad 12^0$ A $\land \sim$ A   QED.

We now ask the analogous question with respect to the binary connectives of PPC(3). How many are there, and which are they? Now consider table 8. On each row of the table the value *1* and *2* may occur. From *Def* 6.1.2 (ii-a) it follows that only the rows r_3, r_6, r_7, r_8 and r_9 may have the value *3*. From *Def* 6.1.2 (ii-b) it follows, moreover, that:

if r_3 has *3*, then also r_6 and r_9;
if r_6 has *3*, then also r_3 and r_9;
if r_7 has *3*, then also r_8 and r_9;
if r_8 has *3*, then also r_7 and r_9.

Table 8

A	B	$A \ominus B$
1	*1*	r_1
1	*2*	r_2
1	*3*	r_3
2	*1*	r_4
2	*2*	r_5
2	*3*	r_6
3	*1*	r_7
3	*2*	r_8
3	*3*	r_9

This can be represented schematically as follows:

Table 9

A	B	M_1	M_2	M_3	M_4	M_5
1	*1*	*1* or *2*	*1* or *2*	*1* or *2*	*1* or *2*	*1* or *2*
1	*2*	*1* or *2*	*1* or *2*	*1* or *2*	*1* or *2*	*1* or *2*
1	*3*	*1* or *2*	*1* or *2*	*1* or *2*	*3*	*3*
2	*1*	*1* or *2*	*1* or *2*	*1* or *2*	*1* or *2*	*1* or *2*
2	*2*	*1* or *2*	*1* or *2*	*1* or *2*	*1* or *2*	*1* or *2*
2	*3*	*1* or *2*	*1* or *2*	*1* or *2*	*3*	*3*
3	*1*	*1* or *2*	*1* or *2*	*3*	*1* or *2*	*3*
3	*2*	*1* or *2*	*1* or *2*	*3*	*1* or *2*	*3*
3	*3*	*1* or *2*	*3*	*3*	*3*	*3*

M_1 gives $2^9 = 512$ possibilities M_4 gives $2^6 = 64$ possibilities
M_2 gives $2^8 = 256$ possibilities M_5 gives $2^4 = 16$ possibilities
M_3 gives $2^6 = 64$ possibilities

Total 912 possibilities

We must now show that these 912 possible presuppositional connectives of PPC(3) are expressible in $\wedge$, $\vee$, $\sim$, $\simeq$. We shall demonstrate this by elaborating an example from each of the possibilities M_1 to M_5. The method applied will be seen to be always successful.

M_1: 512 possible connectives, where *1* and *2* on each row.

Example: *Table 10*

A	B	M_1	M_2
1	*1*	*1*	*1*
1	*2*	*1*	*2*
1	*3*	*2*	*1*
2	*1*	*1*	*2*
2	*2*	*1*	*2*
2	*3*	*2*	*2*
3	*1*	*2*	*2*
3	*2*	*2*	*1*
3	*3*	*2*	*3*

Consider the rows of M_1 where $A \ominus B$ has the value *1*. These are r_1, r_2, r_6.

r_1 gives $A \wedge B$, since $\bar{v}(A) = 1$ and $\bar{v}(B) = 1$.
r_2 gives $A \wedge \sim B$, since $\bar{v}(A) = 1$ and $\bar{v}(B) = 2$.
r_6 gives $\sim A \wedge \simeq B$, since $\bar{v}(A) = 2$ and $\bar{v}(B) = 3$. Now:
$A \wedge B$ has the value *1* only on r_1.
$A \wedge \sim B$ has the value *1* only on r_2.
$\sim A \wedge \simeq B$ has the value *1* only on r_6.

Hence, $(A \wedge B) \vee (A \wedge \sim B) \vee (\sim A \wedge \simeq B) = E$ has the value *1* only on r_1, r_2 and r_6; on the other rows, E has *2* or *3*. Now take $\sim (\sim E \vee \simeq E)$. 6.2.4 ($5^0$) shows that the table called for can be constructed.

It is clear that this method can be applied generally to M_1.

M_2: r_9 has *3*; the other rows have *1* or *2*. Consider the rows where $A \ominus B$ has *1*. Apply the method of M_1, so that under $\sim (\sim E \vee \simeq E)$ a table is constructed with *1* on r_1, r_3 and r_8, and with *2* on the other rows. Now consider r_9, where $A \ominus B$ has the value *3*. $A \vee B$ has the value *3* only on r_9. Now take $F = (A \vee B) \vee \sim (A \vee B)$. By 5.2.4 ($3^0$), F has *3* on r_9 only, and *1* on the other rows. But now $\sim (\sim E \vee \simeq E) \wedge F$ gives precisely the table called for.

M_3: Analogous to M_2, but with $F = (A \wedge \simeq B) \vee \sim (A \wedge \simeq B)$
M_4: Analogous to M_2, but with $F = (\simeq A \wedge B) \vee \sim (\simeq A \wedge B)$
M_5: Analogous to M_2, but with $F = (A \wedge \simeq B) \vee \sim (A \wedge \simeq B) \wedge (\simeq A \wedge B)$ $\vee \sim (\simeq A \wedge B)$.

We can now formulate the following lemma:

6.2.5 Lemma II All 912 binary presuppositional connectives of PPC(3) are expressible in $\wedge$, $\vee$, $\sim$, $\simeq$.

6.2.6 Theorem The set $\{\wedge, \vee, \sim, \simeq\}$ is presuppositionally complete for PPC(3).

Proof: The theorem follows directly from Lemma I and Lemma II.

6.3 *Efficient logics*

In section 6.1 we defined the notion of presuppositional logic. In this section we define the notion of efficient logic. (Efficiency is seen mainly in relation to the construction of a proof theory, as in the sections 4 and 5.)

6.3.1 Def   Let L_n be an n-valued presuppositional logic. $\widetilde{1}, \ldots, n\widetilde{}1$ are unary connectives of L_n. $\wedge$, $\vee$ are binary connectives of L_n. We now define:

L_n is $(\wedge, \vee, \widetilde{1}, \ldots, n\widetilde{}1)$ efficient iff:

   (i) L_n is $(\wedge, \vee, \neg)$ regular $(\neg A := \widetilde{1} A \vee \ldots \vee n\widetilde{}1 A)$;
   (ii) $\forall v \in V^n_{U\text{Var}(A)} \ \forall s, t \in \{1, 2, \ldots, n\} \ [s \neq t \Rightarrow \bar{v}(\widetilde{s} A \wedge \widetilde{t} A) \neq 1] \ (\widetilde{0} A = A)$;
   (iii) $\{\wedge, \vee, \widetilde{1}, \ldots, n\widetilde{}1\}$ is presuppositionally complete.

It will be clear that many of the results of this and preceding chapters are applicable to efficient logics. The L_3 which is $(\wedge, \vee, \sim, \approx)$ efficient has one further special property.

6.3.2 Theorem   Let L_3 be a three-valued logic which is efficient w.r.t $(\wedge, \vee, \sim, \approx)$. Then $L_3 = PPC(3)$.

   Proof: (i) From the fact that L_3 is $(\wedge, \vee, \neg)$ regular it follows that the tables for $\wedge$ and $\vee$ are precisely the tables 1.1.1.
     (ii) Consider the tables for $\sim$ and $\approx$.

Table 11

A	$\sim A$	$\approx A$
1	a_0	b_0
2	a_1	b_1
3	a_2	b_2

Since the logic is $(\wedge, \vee, \neg)$ regular, it follows that $a_1 = 1$ and $b_2 = 1$, or $b_1 = 1$ and $a_2 = 1$. Take, without loss of generality, the former alternative. 6.3.1 (ii) gives: $a_0 \neq 1$. Moreover, $a_0 \neq 3$, since the logic is presuppositional. Hence, $a_0 = 2$. Then, 6.3.1 (ii) gives: $b_0 \neq 1$ and $b_1 \neq 1$. Moreover, $b_0 \neq 3$ and $b_1 \neq 3$, since the logic is presuppositional. Hence, $b_0 = 2$ and $b_1 = 2$. This shows that L_3 has precisely the tables of $PPC(3)$.

References

Akmajian, A. and Jackendoff, R., 1970: Coreferentiality and stress. *Linguistic Inquiry* 1.1: 124–6.

Allwood, J., 1972/1977: Negation and the strength of presuppositions. Gothenburgh University, *Logical Grammar Report* 2; 1972. Republished (with revisions) in: Dahl (ed.) 1977: 11–52.

Atlas, J. D., 1975: Presupposition: a semantic-pragmatic account. *Pragmatics Microfiche* 1.4, D13-G9.

Atlas, J. D., 1977: Negation, ambiguity, and presupposition. *Linguistics and Philosophy* 1.3: 321–36.

Atlas, J. D., 1979: How linguistics matters to philosophy: presupposition, truth, and meaning. In: Oh and Dinneen: 265–81.

Baker, C. L., 1970a: Double negatives. *Linguistic Inquiry* 1.2: 196–86.

Baker, C. L., 1970b: Notes on the description of English questions: the role of an abstract question morpheme. *Foundations of Language* 6.2: 197–219. (Also in: Seuren (ed.) 1974: 123–42).

Barwick, K., 1957: *Probleme der stoischen Sprachlehre und Rhetorik.* Abhandlungen der Sächsischen Akademie der Wissenschaften zu Leipzig. Philologisch-historische Klasse, Band 49, Heft, 3. Akademie-Verlag, Berlin.

Barwise, J. and Cooper, R., 1981: Generalized quantifiers and natural language. *Linguistics and Philosophy* 4.2: 159–219.

Beesley, K. R., 1982: Evaluative adjectives as one-place predicates in Montague grammar. *Journal of Semantics* 1.3: 195–249.

Bergmann, M., 1981: Presupposition and two-dimensional logic. *Journal of Philosophical Logic* 10.1: 27–53.

Blau, U., 1978: *Die dreiwertige Logik der Sprache. Ihre Syntax, Semantik und Anwendung in der Sprachanalyse.* Walter de Gruyter, Berlin-New York.

Bloomfield, L., 1914: *An Introduction to the Study of Language.* Holt, New York.

Bloomfield, L., 1933: *Language.* Holt, New York.

Boër, S. and Lycan, W., 1976: The myth of semantic presupposition. Indiana University Linguistics Club.

Bosch, P. W., 1983: *Agreement and Anaphora. A Study of the Role of Pronouns in Syntax and Discourse.* Academic Press, London–New York.

Bresnan, J., 1978: A realistic transformational grammar. In: Halle, Bresnan and Miller (eds): 1–59.

Carnap, R., 1947: *Meaning and Necessity.* The University of Chicago Press, Chicago.

Coates, J., 1983: *The Semantics of the Modal Auxiliaries.* Croom Helm, London–Canberra.

Cole, P. (ed.), 1978: *Pragmatics* (= Syntax and Semantics 9). Academic Press, New York–San Francisco–London.

Cole, P. and Morgan, J. L. (eds), 1975: *Speech Acts* (= Syntax and Semantics 3). Academic Press, New York–San Francisco–London.

Dahl, Ö. (ed.), 1977: *Logic, Pragmatics, and Grammar.* Department of Linguistics, University of Göteborg.

Davidson, D. and Harman, G. (eds), 1972: *Semantics of Natural Language.* Reidel, Dordrecht.

Davidson, D. and Hintikka, J. (eds), 1969: *Words and Objections. Essays on the Work of W. V. Quine.* Reidel, Dordrecht.

DeCamp, D., 1971: Toward a generative analysis of a post-Creole continuum. In: Hymes (ed.): 349–70.

De Rijk, R. P. G., 1974: A note on prelexical predicate raising. In: Seuren (ed.): 43–74.

Dinsmore, J., 1981: *The Inheritance of Presupposition* (= Pragmatics and Beyond II: 1). John Benjamins, Amsterdam.

Donnellan, K., 1966: Reference and definite descriptions. *Philosophical Review* 75: 281–304.

Dowty, D. R., Wall, R. E. and Peters, S., 1981: *Introduction to Montague Semantics* (= Synthese Language Library 11). Reidel, Dordrecht.

Evans, G., 1980: Pronouns. *Linguistic Inquiry* 11.2: 337–62.

Evers, A., 1975: The Transformational Cycle in Dutch and German. Ph.D. thesis, Utrecht.

Fauconnier, G., 1975: Pragmatic scales and logical structure. *Linguistic Inquiry* 6.3: 353–75.

Fauconnier, G., 1979: Mental spaces. Unpublished paper. Université de Paris VIII, Vincennes.

Fillmore, Ch. J., 1971: Types of lexical information. In: Steinberg and Jakobovits (eds): 370–92.

Fillmore, Ch. J. and Langendoen, D. T. (eds), 1971: *Studies in Linguistic Semantics.* Holt, Rinehart and Winston, New York.

Fodor, J. A., 1970: Three reasons for not deriving "kill" from "cause to die". *Linguistic Inquiry* 1.4: 429–38.

Fodor, J.A., 1983: *The Modularity of Mind. An Essay on Faculty Psychology.* MIT Press, Cambridge, Mass.

Fodor, J. A., Bever, T. G. and Garrett, M. F., 1974: *The Psychology of Language. An Introduction to Psycholinguistics and Generative Grammar.* McGraw Hill, New York.

Fodor, J. A. and Katz, J. J. (eds), 1964: *The Structure of Language. Readings in the Philosophy of Language.* Prentice-Hall, Englewood Cliffs, NJ.

Fraser, B., 1971: An analysis of "even" in English. In: Fillmore and Langendoen (eds): 151–78.

Frege, G., 1892: Ueber Sinn und Bedeutung. *Zeitschrift für Philosophie und philosophische Kritik* 100: 25–50. (Also in: Patzig (ed.) 1969: 40–65.)

Gabbay, D. and Moravcsik, J., 1978: Negation and denial. In: Guenthner and Rohrer (eds): 251–65.

Garrod, S. C. and Sanford, A. J., 1982: The mental representation of discourse in a focused memory system: implications for the interpretation of anaphoric pronouns. *Journal of Semantics* 1.1: 21–41.

Gazdar, G., 1979: *Pragmatics, Implicature, Presupposition, and Logical Form.* Academic Press, New York–San Francisco–London.

Geach, P. T., 1962: *Reference and Generality. An Examination of Some Medieval and Modern Theories.* Cornell University Press, Ithaca, NY.

Geach, P. T., 1969: Quine's syntactical insights. In: Davidson and Hintikka (eds): 146–57. (Also in: Geach 1972: 115–27)

Geach, P. T., 1972: *Logic Matters.* Basil Blackwell, Oxford.

Geach, P. T. and Black, M. (eds), 1952: *Translations from the Philosophical Writings of Gottlob Frege.* Basil Blackwell, Oxford.

Greenberg, J. H., 1963: Some universals of grammar with particular reference to the order of meaningful elements. In: Greenberg (ed.): 73–113.

Greenberg, J. H. (ed.), 1963: *Universals of Language.* MIT Press, Cambridge, Mass.

Grevisse, M., 1969: *Le bon usage. Grammaire française avec des remarques sur la langue française d'aujourd'hui.* Duculot-Geuthner, Paris.

Grice, H. P., 1968: William James Lectures. Harvard. Unpublished.

Grice, H. P., 1975: Logic and conversation. In: Cole and Morgan (eds): 41–58.

Grice, H. P., 1978: Further notes on logic and conversation. In: Cole (ed.): 113–27.

Groenendijk, J. A. G., Janssen, T. M. V. and Stokhof, M. B. J. (eds), 1981: *Formal Methods in the Study of Language.* 2 vols. Mathematical Centre Tracts 135. Mathematisch Centrum, Amsterdam.

Guenthner, F. and Rohrer, Chr. (eds), 1978: *Studies in Formal Semantics. Intensionality, Temporality, Negation.* North-Holland Linguistic Series 35. North-Holland Publishing Company, Amsterdam.

Halle, M., Bresnan, J. and Miller, G. A. (eds), 1978: *Linguistic Theory and Psychological Reality.* MIT Press, Cambridge, Mass.

Harris, Z. S., 1951: *Methods in Structural Linguistics.* The University of Chicago Press, Chicago.

Harris, Z. S., 1957: Co-occurrence and transformations in linguistic structure. *Language* 33.3: 283–340.

Hausser, R. R., 1976: Presuppositions in Montague grammar. *Theoretical Linguistics* 3: 245–80.

Hausser, R. R., 1983: On vagueness. *Journal of Semantics* 2.3/4: 273–302.

Hawkins, J. A., 1978: *Definiteness and Indefiniteness. A Study in Reference and Grammaticality Prediction.* Croom Helm/Humanities Press, London/ Atlantic Highlands, NJ.

Heny, F. and Richards, B. (eds), 1983: *Linguistic Categories. Auxiliaries and Related Puzzles.* Vol. 2, Reidel, Dordrecht.

Herskovits, M. J. and Herskovits, F. S., 1936: *Suriname Folk-Lore.* Columbia University Press, New York.

Herzberger, H. G., 1973: Dimensions of truth. *Journal of Philosophical Logic* 2.4: 535–56.

Hinton, G. E. and Anderson, J. A. (eds), 1981: *Parallel Models of Associative Memory.* Erlbaum, Hillsdale, NJ.

Hoeksema, J., 1983: Negative polarity and the comparative. *Natural Language and Linguistic Theory* 1: 403–34.

Hoppenbrouwers, G., 1983: Polariteit. Een literatuuronderzoek. *NIS Working Papers* 2, Nijmegen.

Horn, L. R., 1969: A presuppositional analysis of "only" and "even". *Chicago Linguistic Society* 5: 98–107.

Hovdhaugen, E., 1982: *Foundations of Western Linguistics. From the Beginning to the End of the First Millennium AD* Universitetsforlaget, Oslo.

Hymes, D. (ed.), 1971: *Pidginization and Creolization of Languages.* Cambridge University Press, Cambridge.

Jacobs, R. A. and Rosenbaum, P. S. (eds), 1970: *Readings in English Transformational Grammar.* Ginn, Waltham, Mass.

Janssen, T. A. J. M., 1976: *Hebben-konstrukties en Indirekt-objektskonstrukties.* Ph.D. thesis, Nijmegen. HES Publishers, Utrecht.

Janssen, T. M. V., 1983: *Foundations and Applications of Montague Grammar.* Ph.D. thesis, Amsterdam University. Mathematisch Centrum, Amsterdam.

Kaplan, D., 1969: Quantifying in. In: Davidson and Hintikka (eds): 206–42.

Karttunen, L., 1969: Pronouns and variables. *Chicago Linguistic Society* 5: 108–16.

Karttunen, L., 1973: Presuppositions of compound sentences. *Linguistic Inquiry* 4.2: 169–93.

Karttunen, L., 1974: Presupposition and linguistic context. *Theoretical Linguistics* 1.1/2: 181–94.

Karttunen, L. and Peters, S., 1979: Conventional implicature. In: Oh and Dinneen (eds): 1–56.

Katz, J. J., 1972: *Semantic Theory.* Harper and Row, New York.

Katz, J. J. and Langendoen, D. T., 1976: Pragmatics and presupposition. *Language* 52.1: 1–17.

Katz, J. J. and Postal, P. M., 1964: *An Integrated Theory of Linguistic Descriptions.* MIT Press, Cambridge, Mass.

Keenan, E. L., 1971: Quantifier structures in English. *Foundations of Language* 7.2: 225–84.

Keenan, E. L., 1976: Remarkable subjects in Malagasy. In: Li (ed.): 247–301.

Kempson, R. M., 1975: *Presupposition and the Delimitation of Semantics.* Cambridge Studies in Linguistics 15. Cambridge University Press, Cambridge.

Kiefer, F. and Ruwet, N. (eds), 1973: *Generative Grammar in Europe.* Reidel, Dordrecht.

Kiparsky, P. and Kiparsky, C., 1971: In: Steinberg and Jakobovits (eds): 345–69.

Kleene, S. C., 1959: *Introduction to Metamathematics.* North-Holland Publishing Company, Amsterdam.

Kleene, S. C., 1967: *Mathematical Logic.* Wiley and Sons, New York–London–Sydney.

Klein, W. and Jarvella, R. T. (eds), 1982: *Speech, Place, and Action.* Wiley, Chichester.

Klima, E. S., 1964: Negation in English. In: Fodor and Katz (eds): 246–323.

Kneale, W., 1962: Modality, De Dicto and De Re. In: Nagel, Suppes, Tarski (eds): 622–33.

Kneale, W. and Kneale, M., 1962: *The Development of Logic.* Oxford University Press, Oxford.

Koster, J., 1975: Dutch as an SOV-language. *Linguistic Analysis* 1: 111–36.

Koster, J., 1978: *Locality Principles in Syntax.* Foris, Dordrecht.

Kraak, A., 1968: A search for missing agents. *Le langage et l'homme* 8: 146–56.

Kripke, S., 1963: Semantical analysis of modal logic I, normal propositional calculi. *Zeitschrift für Mathematische Logik und Grundlagen der Mathematik* 9: 67–96.

Kripke, S., 1972: Naming and necessity. In: Davidson and Harman (eds): 253–355.

Kripke, S., 1980: *Naming and Necessity.* Basil Blackwell, Oxford.

Kuno, S., 1972: Pronominalization, reflexivization, and direct discourse. *Linguistic Inquiry* 3.2: 161–95.

Kuno, S., 1978: Japanese. A characteristic OV-language. In: Lehmann (ed.): 57–138.

Kuroda, S.-Y., 1965: Causative forms in Japanese. *Foundations of Language* 1.1: 30–50.

Labov, W., 1966: *The Social Stratification of English in New York City.* Center for Applied Linguistics, Washington DC.

Labov, W., 1972a: *Sociolinguistic Patterns* (= Conduct and Communication 4). University of Pennsylvania Press, Philadelphia. Basil Blackwell, Oxford.

Labov, W., 1972b: Negation attraction and negative concord in English grammar. *Language* 48.4: 773–818.

Ladusaw, W. A., 1979: *Polarity Sensitivity as Inherent Scope Relations.* Ph.D. diss., University of Texas at Austin.

Lakoff, G., 1968/1976: Pronouns and reference. Published in: McCawley (ed.), 1976: 275–335.

Lakoff, G., 1970: A note on ambiguity and vagueness. *Linguistic Inquiry* 1.3: 357–9.

Lakoff, G., 1971a: On generative semantics. In: Steinberg and Jakobovits (eds): 232–96.

Lakoff, G., 1971b: Presupposition and relative wellformedness. In: Steinberg and Jakobovits (eds): 329–40.

Lambert, K. (ed.), 1969: *The Logical Way of Doing Things.* Yale University Press, New Haven–London.

Langacker, R. W., 1969: On pronominalization and the chain of command. In: Reibel and Schane (eds): 160–86.

Langacker, R. W., 1970: Predicate Raising: some Uto-Aztecan evidence. Unpublished paper, University of California at San Diego, La Jolla, California.

Langendoen, D. T. and Savin, H. B., 1971: The projection problem for presuppositions. In: Fillmore and Langendoen (eds): 55–60.

Leech, G. N., 1971: *Meaning and the English Verb.* Longman, London.

Lehmann, W. P. (ed.), 1978: *Syntactic Typology. Studies in the Phenomenology of Language.* Harvester Press, Hassocks, Sussex.

Lewis, C. I., 1918: *A Survey of Symbolic Logic.* University of California Press, Berkeley.

Li, Ch. N. (ed.), 1976: *Subject and Topic.* Academic Press, New York–San Francisco–London.

Lightfoot, D., 1982: *The Language Lottery.* MIT Press, Cambridge, Mass.

Lindholm, J. M., 1969: Negative-Raising and sentence pronominalization. *Chicago Linguistic Society* 5: 148–58.

Linsky, L. (ed.), 1971: *Reference and Modality.* Oxford Readings in Philosophy. Oxford University Press, Oxford.

Lyons, J., 1968: *Introduction to Theoretical Linguistics.* Cambridge University Press, Cambridge.

Manley, T., 1972: *Outline of Sre Structure.* Oceanic Linguistics, Special Publication no. 12. University of Hawaii Press, Honolulu.

Marslen-Wilson, W., Levy, E. and Tyler, L. K., 1982: Producing interpretable discourse: the establishment and maintenance of reference. In: Klein and Jarvella (eds): 339–78.

Martin, J. N., 1982: Negation, ambiguity, and the identity test. *Journal of Semantics* 1.3: 251–74.

Martin, N. M., 1954: The Sheffer functions of 3-valued logic. *Journal of Symbolic Logic* 19: 45–51.

Martinon, Ph., 1927: *Comment on parle en français.* Larousse, Paris.

May, R., 1977: The Grammar of Quantification. Ph.D. thesis, MIT.

McCawley, J. D., 1968: Lexical insertion in a transformational grammar without deep structure. *Chicago Linguistic Society* 4: 71–80.

McCawley. J. D., 1970: English as a VSO-language. *Language* 46.2: 286–99. (Also in: Seuren (ed.) 1974: 75–95.)

McCawley, J. D., 1971: Tense and time reference in English. In: Fillmore and Langendoen (eds): 96–113.

McCawley, J. D., 1972: A program for logic. In: Davidson and Harman (eds): 498–544.

McCawley, J. D., 1980: Review of Newmeyer 1980. *Linguistics* 18.9/10: 911–30.

McCawley, J. D., 1981: *Everything that Linguists Have Always Wanted to Know about Logic* *but were ashamed to ask.* Basil Blackwell, Oxford/

532 References

University of Chicago Press, Chicago.

McCawley, J. D., 1982: *Thirty Million Theories of Grammar*. The University of Chicago Press, Chicago.

McCawley, J. D. (ed.), 1976: *Notes from the Linguistic Underground* (= Syntax and Semantics 7). Academic Press, New York–San Francisco–London.

Montague, R., 1974: *Formal Philosophy. Selected Papers of Richard Montague*. Edited and with an introduction by Richmond H. Thomason. Yale University Press, New Haven–London.

Morris, Ch. W., 1946: *Signs, Language, and Behavior*. Prentice Hall, Englewood Cliffs, NJ.

Muzio, J. C., 1970: A decision process for 3-valued Sheffer functions I. *Zeitschrift für Mathematische Logik und Grundlagen der Mathematik* 16: 271–80.

Nagel, E., Suppes, P. and Tarski, A. (eds), 1962: *Logic, Methodology and the Philosophy of Science. Proceedings of the 1960 International Congress*. Stanford University Press, Stanford.

Newmeyer, F. J., 1980: *Linguistic Theory in America. The First Quarter-Century of Transformational Generative Grammar*. Academic Press, New York–San Francisco–London.

Norden, E., 1898: *Die antike Kunstprosa. Vom VI. Jahrhundert v. Chr. bis in die Zeit der Renaissance*. 2 vols. Teubner, Leipzig.

Oh, Ch.-K. and Dinneen, D. A. (eds), 1979: *Presupposition* (= Syntax and Semantics 11). Academic Press, New York–San Francisco–London.

Palmer, F. R., 1974: *The English Verb*. Longman, London.

Patzig, G. (ed.), 1969: *Gottlob Frege, Funktion, Begriff, Bedeutung. Fünf logische Studien*. Vandenhoeck and Ruprecht, Göttingen.

Perlutter, D. M., 1970: The two vergs *begin*. In: Jacobs and Rosenbaum (eds): 107–19.

Perlmutter, D. M., 1971: *Deep and Surface Structure Constraints in Syntax*. Holt, Rinehart and Winston, New York.

Postal, P. M., 1974: *On Raising. One Rule of English Grammar and its Theoretical Implications*. MIT Press, Cambridge, Mass.

Quine, W. V. O., 1953: *From a Logical Point of View*. Harvard University Press, Cambridge, Mass.

Quine, W. V. O., 1953/1971: Reference and modality. In: Quine 1953: 139–59. (Also in: Linsky (ed.) 1971: 17–34.)

Quine, W. V. O., 1960: *Word and Object*. MIT Press, Cambridge, Mass.

Quine, W. V. O., 1966: *The Ways of Paradox and Other Essays*. Random House, New York.

Reibel, D. A. and Schane, S. A. (eds), 1969: *Modern Studies in English. Readings in Transformational Grammar*. Prentice Hall, Englewood Cliffs, NJ.

Reichenbach, H., 1947: *Elements of Symbolic Logic*. Macmillan, London.

Reichgelt, H., 1979: Oordelen over de soort (on)waarheid van verschillende soorten onwelgevormde zinnen. Unpublished paper, Nijmegen University.

Reinhart, T., 1976: The Syntactic Domain of Anaphora. Ph.D. thesis, MIT.

Reinhart, T., 1983: *Anaphora and Semantic Interpretation*. Croom Helm, London–Canberra.

Rescher, N., 1969: *Many-valued Logic*. McGraw Hill, New York.

Rigter, G. H., 1980: Laying the ghost of times past. *Linguistics* 18: 849–70.

Robins, R. H., 1967: *A Short History of Linguistics*. Longmans, London.

Ross, J. R., 1967: Constraints on Variables in Syntax. Ph.D. thesis, MIT.

Russell, B., 1905: On denoting. *Mind* 14: 479–93.

Ruwet, N., 1972: *Théorie syntaxique et syntaxe du français*. Du Seuil, Paris.

Růžička, R., 1983: Remarks on control. *Linguistic Inquiry* 14.2: 309–25.

Sag, I. A., 1976: Deletion and Logical Form. Ph.D. thesis, MIT.

Sanford, A. J. and Garrod, S. C., 1981: *Understanding Written Language. Explorations in Comprehension beyond the Sentence*. Wiley and Sons, Chichester.

Seuren, P. A. M., 1967: Negation in Dutch. *Neophilologus* 51.4: 327–63.

Seuren, P. A. M., 1969: *Operators and Nucleus. A Contribution to the Theory of Grammar*. Cambridge University Press, Cambridge.

Seuren, P. A. M., 1972a: Predicate Raising and dative in French and sundry languages. Unpublished paper, Magdalen College, Oxford. (Circulated by LAUT, Trier.)

Seuren, P. A. M., 1972b: Taaluniversalia in de transformationele grammatika. *Leuvense Bijdragen* 61.4: 311–70.

Seuren, P. A. M., 1973a: The comparative. In: Kiefer and Ruwet (eds): 528–64.

Seuren, P. A. M., 1973b: Zero-output rules. *Foundations of Language* 10: 317–28.

Seuren, P. A. M., 1974: Negative's travels. In: Seuren (ed.), 1974: 183–208.

Seuren, P. A. M., 1976: Clitic pronoun clusters. *Italian Linguistics* 2: 7–35.

Seuren, P. A. M., 1977: Forme logique et forme sémantique: un argument contre M. Geach. *Logique et Analyse* 79, vol. 20: 338–47.

Seuren, P. A. M., 1978: Grammar as an underground process. In: Sinclair et al. (eds): 201–23.

Seuren, P. A. M., 1979: The logic of presuppositional semantics. Unpublished paper, Nijmegen University.

Seuren, P. A. M., 1981: Tense and aspect in Sranan. *Linguistics* 19: 1043–76.

Seuren, P. A. M., 1982: Internal variability in competence. *Linguistische Berichte* 77: 1–31.

Seuren, P. A. M., 1983: The auxiliary system in Sranan. In: Heny and Richards (eds): 219–51.

Seuren, P. A. M., 1984: The comparative revisited. *Journal of Semantics* 3.1–2: 109–41.

Seuren, P. A. M. (ed.), 1974: *Semantic Syntax*. Oxford Readings in Philosophy. Oxford University Press, Oxford.

Shadbolt, N., 1983: Processing reference. *Journal of Semantics* 2.1: 63–98.

Sinclair, A., Jarvella, R. J. and Levelt, W. J. M. (eds), 1978: *The Child's Conception of Language*. Springer, Heidelberg–New York.

Starosta, S., 1971: Lexical derivation in a Case Grammar. *Working Papers in Linguistics* 3.8. University of Hawaii, Honolulu.

Steedman, M., 1983a: On the generality of the nested dependency constraint and the reason for an exception in Dutch. *Linguistics* 21.1: 35–66.

Steedman, M., 1983b: Dependency and coordination in the grammar of Dutch and English. Draft, November 1983.

534   References

Steinberg, D. D. and Jakobovits, L. A. (eds), 1971: *Semantics. An Inter-disciplinary Reader in Philosophy, Linguistics, and Psychology.* Cambridge University Press, Cambridge.

Steinthal, H., 1890/1961: *Geschichte der Sprachwissenschaft bei den Griechen und Römern, mit besonderer Rücksicht auf die Logik.* 2 vols. Anastatic reprint of 2nd edition, Berlin 1890. G. Olms, Verlagsbuchhandlung, Hildesheim.

Stern, G., 1932: *Meaning and Change of Meaning* (= Göteborg Högskolas Årsskrift 38.1). Göteborg.

Straumann, H., 1935: *Newspaper Headlines. A Study in Linguistic Method.* Allen and Unwin, London.

Strawson, P. F., 1950: On referring. *Mind* 59: 320–44.

Strawson, P. F., 1952: *Introduction to Logical Theory.* Methuen, London.

Strawson, P. F., 1954: A reply to Mr Sellars. *Philosophical Review* 63.2: 216–31.

Strawson, P. F., 1964: Identifying reference and truth-values. *Theoria* 30.2: 96–118.

Strawson, P. F., 1974: *Subject and Predicate in Logic and Grammar.* Methuen, London.

Szabolcsi, A., 1981: The semantics of topic-focus articulation. In: Groenendijk et al. (eds): 513–40.

Tasmowski-De Ryck, L. and Verluyten, S. P., 1982: Linguistic control of pronouns. *Journal of Semantics* 1.4: 323–46.

Travis, Ch., 1981: *The True and the False: the Domain of the Pragmatic* (= Pragmatics and Beyond II: 2). John Benjamins, Amsterdam.

Tyler, L. K. and Marslen-Wilson, W., 1982: Processing utterances in discourse contexts: on-line resolution of anaphors. *Journal of Semantics* 1.4: 297–314.

Van der Sandt, R. A., 1982: *Kontekst en Presuppositie. Een studie van het projektieprobleem en de presuppositionele eigenschappen van de logische konnektieven.* Ph.D. thesis, NIS, Nijmegen.

Van Fraassen, B., 1966: Singular terms, truth-value gaps, and free logic. *Journal of Philosophy* 63: 481–95.

Van Fraassen, B., 1968: Presupposition, implication, and self-reference. *Journal of Philosophy* 65: 136–52.

Van Fraassen, B., 1969: Presuppositions, supervaluations, and free logic. In: Lambert (ed.): 67–91.

Van Fraassen, B., 1971: *Formal Semantics and Logic.* Macmillan, New York-London.

Vliegen, M., in preparation: *Auditive Wahrnehmung im niederländischen und deutschen Verbwortschatz.* Ph.D. thesis, Nijmegen.

Voorhoeve, J. and Lichtveld, U. M. (eds), 1975: *Creole Drum. An Anthology of Creole Literature in Surinam.* Yale University Press, New Haven-London.

Wilson, D., 1975: *Presuppositions and Non-Truth-Conditional Semantics.* Academic Press, London-New York-San Francisco.

Zwarts, F., 1981: Negatief polaire uitdrukkingen I. *Glot* 4.1: 35–132.

Index of names

Index of subjects

accent 274, 302, 452(n)
  contrastive 24(n), 67, 231, 296,
    297, 299(n), 302, 364, 365
acceptability 9, 10, 32, 270, 273–5,
    325, 337, 340, 402, 403,
    407(n), 443–54, 480
addresses
  V-restricting vs V-relaxing 9, 325,
    328, 329, 345
  closure of 31, 317–19, 414, 458–
    61
adoption 82, 86, 129(n), 172, 175,
    205
ambiguity
  tests of 261, 262, 435
  of *not* 260–6
analogism 3, 13, 35–51, 209
anaphora 267, 346–86
  and transformational grammar 348
  do-so 204
  in indirect relative clauses 114,
    140, 255, 256
  it vs *so* 140, 255, 256
  sentence external 16, 376
  sentence internal 189 (*see also*
    pronouns)
  sloppy 346, 458
anomalism 3, 14, 35–51
antifactive predicates 395, 480

Bach–Peters paradox 376, 378, 379
background knowledge 2, 32, 33,
    246, 275, 284–95, 410, 456

behaviourism 12, 53, 63, 473
by-phrase 162(n), 174, 187, 188,
    191, 192, 194, 196

case 180, 181
catachresis 199
categorical syncretism 70
category mistake 242, 243
causality 50, 52–4, 203
causative verbs 123, 124, 202–8
clefts and pseudoclefts 231, 271,
    295–304, 365, 367
command 358, 362
  c-command 358(n), 367, 368
comment 16, 17, 303, 373
comparatives 123(n), 346
Complex Noun Phrase Constraint 23
compositionality 26, 48, 49, 65–7,
    214, 388
conditionals 9, 337–46, 419(n),
    465–8
  and generic existentials 373
  increment value of 344
  predicate, extension of 340
  under negation 281, 332
conjunction 158, 159, 270(n), 333
  and incrementation 35, 280–4,
    460(n)
  extension of 253
  Geach-type 319–22, 413(n), 459,
    460(n), 464, 468
  reduction 96, 97, 128, 159–66,
    346, 443